HOUSE OF

European Union Committee

21st Report of Session 2007–08

The Progress of the Common Fisheries Policy

Volume II: Evidence

Ordered to be printed 15 July 2008 and published 22 July 2008

Published by the Authority of the House of Lords

London : The Stationery Office Limited
£26.00

HL Paper 146–II

CONTENTS

Written Evidence was also received from:
Avril Doyle MEP
Royal Ministry of Fisheries and Coastal Affairs, Norwegian Government
This has not been not been printed, but is available for inspection at the
House of Lords Record Office (020 7219 5314).

We would like to take the opportunity to thank all our witnesses for their
submissions to our inquiry.

NOTE:
The Report of the Committee is published in Volume I (HL Paper 146-I)

Minutes of Evidence

TAKEN BEFORE THE SELECT COMMITTEE ON THE EUROPEAN UNION (SUB-COMMITTEE D)

WEDNESDAY 5 MARCH 2008

Present	Arran, E of	Sewel, L (Chairman)
	Jones of Whitchurch, B	Sharp of Guildford, B
	Palmer, L	Ullswater, V
	Plumb, L	

Memorandum by The Centre for Environment, Fisheries and Aquaculture Science (CEFAS)

BACKGROUND TO CEFAS

The Centre for Environment, Fisheries & Aquaculture Science (Cefas) is an Executive Agency of Defra. Cefas was established over 100 years ago in response to national and international concerns about over-fishing and how the nature of the seas affected fisheries. The same pressures helped to establish the International Council for Exploration of the Seas (ICES) which is a main source of international advice on fisheries. Consequently, Cefas has a long established role in fisheries and marine environment monitoring, assessment, research and advice.

For fisheries, Cefas' scientists undertake annual monitoring and assessment of our key commercial fish stocks. This is mainly an international process undertaken through ICES. Our scientists contribute to advice for fisheries through ICES advisory committees on fisheries, ecosystems and the environment, and through the EC's Scientific, Technical and Economic Committee for Fisheries.

Underpinning research is undertaken: on the effect of the environment on fisheries; the effect of fisheries on the ecosystems; and applied fisheries management. In addition there are complementary programmes covering the marine environment and aquaculture. The Fishery Science Partnership provides additional studies and fosters improved relationships between industry and scientists.

Cefas is an important source of advice to Defra for policy development and implementation, and we support Defra Ministers at negotiations. We work in close collaboration with scientists at Fisheries Research Services, Scotland, and the Agri-Food and Biosciences Institute of Northern Ireland.

QUESTIONS

Conservation and Management

1. *Chapter II of Regulation 2371/2002 on the conservation and sustainable exploitation of fisheries resources under the Common Fisheries Policy introduced new methods of ensuring conservation and sustainability, including recovery plans, management plans and emergency measures. To what extent have these been effective?*

Recovery Plans have been introduced for various cod stocks, northern hake, southern hake and Nephrops, bluefin tuna, and eels.

Multi-annual management plans have been agreed for North Sea plaice and sole, western Channel sole and Bay of Biscay sole. Other management targets have been agreed for some jointly managed EU-Norway stocks.

These two measures require some time in operation before their effectiveness can be determined. For example, the cod recovery measures, if fully implemented would have needed a decade to achieve safe levels for cod. The cod recovery plans were formally agreed for 2003, although measures outside of the formal plans were being progressed before then. A key part of the plans was the control of effort through days-at-sea. The effort levels by country and gear have been monitored. Scientific advice in 2007 showed that fishing mortality on North Sea cod has eventually been reduced significantly (to the lowest level for 40 years), and this has been a very important step to the recovery of the stock. However, fishing mortality remains stubbornly high on other cod stocks. Even in the North Sea, effort restrictions have primarily impacted the northern fisheries, and little attention has been paid to the sub-structure of cod populations within the North Sea. So the conservation effectiveness has been mixed. The effect on some sectors of the industry has been severe, and the use of vessel determined days-at-sea has introduced economic inefficiencies. Conceptually, recovery plans are appropriate tools giving a discipline within which managers can make decisions and the industry can plan better. However a weakness has been the poor relationship of initial, and subsequent, Commission proposals for effort levels to fishing mortality targets, and this has resulted in considerable year on year uncertainty in implementation.

Emergency measures were introduced to protect cold water corals (the Darwin Mounds) and these were subsequently made permanent. A UK attempt to ban pair trawling for bass in the Channel to protect dolphins was rejected by the Commission, and the UK resorted to a unilateral measure. We have reviewed the processes involved in achieving emergency measure in the context of, for example, real time closures to protect a large in-coming year-class, and concluded that they are still too sluggish. We proposed to the Commission, a few years ago, that they might consider some advance planning for predictable "emergencies" such as sole being killed in large numbers by cold weather (or indeed a large year class being identified) but this has not been picked up.

2. *A wide range of management tools are available to fisheries managers. What are your views on the following tools:*
   — *Total Allowable Catches (TACs);*
   — *Effort limitation, including "days at sea", marine conservation areas and real-time closures;*
   — *Rights-Based Management tools; and*
   — *Technical Conservation Measures.*

There is not one management tool that will solve all fisheries management problems, and a tool-box of measures is necessary. However the plethora of current rules suggest that the tools are not being used optimally.

Probably the most important measure is to ensure that the size of the international fleets is appropriate to the size of the resource. We are committed to achieving by 2015 fisheries at "MSY" levels, and for many fisheries this implies lower fishing mortality, and effort, giving higher stock sizes, greater landings and more stability. If such a balance is achieved then more annual flexibility in catches and effort could be safely accommodated.

TACs are best suited to fisheries targeting near single species, such as many large pelagic fisheries. They are a poor tool for our mixed fisheries, as they require a reasonably accurate estimate of stock sizes and catches for all the key species. Imbalances of the TACs with the resource, or with the fishing opportunities, result in discarding. Accurate estimates of stocks and TACs sizes requires good estimates of catches and if reported landings do not reflect catches then the TAC system becomes difficult to operate.

Effort limitation seems a better tool for mixed fisheries. But experience in applying effort management in cod recovery plans shows that implementation is far from straightforward. How do you compare a days long-lining with a days beam-trawling? There are steady increases in efficiency, which will leap under a full effort regime, which would need to be continually addressed. Effort is easier to enforce. But it is more difficult to allocate amongst nations and to relate to fishing mortalities than TACs. Strategically aligning capacity and effort with the size of the resources is essential both for conservation and the economics of the industry, but tactical management of effort has unresolved difficulties.

Closed or restricted areas are a common tool in EU fisheries management. Flatfish and mackerel spawning grounds are protected, as are herring spawning grounds. Industrial fisheries are banned, in the north-western North Sea, to stop the killing of whitefish. It has proved difficult to find closed areas, or MPAs, to protect North Sea cod. They are highly migratory and cod protected in one area can be caught elsewhere. Closed areas are generally not effective conservation tools for migratory fish. However, in some instances, aggregations of fish can be sufficiently high that even if fishing effort is redistributed there is still a conservation benefit. For more static species, such as scallops, closed areas are demonstrably effective. Consequently, for fisheries management, each area and fishery needs to evaluated on a case-by-case basis. MPAs are not a magic bullet. They also have some problems. A closed area for cod was introduced in the North Sea in 2001, and displaced effort impacted upon sensitive biodiversity. For the protection of the environment and biodiversity closed areas may be essential, but it may not be necessary to prohibit all fishing to achieve a particular desired objective.

Technical conservation measures are important. Mesh size and gear configurations can reduce discarding and can be used to target some species. They are probably all that is necessary for some nationally managed shellfish species. The main technical conservation regulation is being revised at present (EC 850/98). There may be advantages in considering more "outcome oriented" regulations rather than in the specification of large numbers of detailed technical regulations.

3. *To what extent have current management tools increased the levels of discards and bycatch? What is your view on how these problems can best be tackled?*

In 2006 8,100 tonnes of cod was discarded in the North Sea. In 1986 it was 139,000 tonnes. The main reasons for discards are : legally undersized fish; unmarketable fish; over quota but marketable fish and "high grading". With the different reasons for discarding come different solutions. Gear technologies can help to reduce the capture of small fish but if the target species is small, for example the sole fisheries, then many other fish will be caught. There are recent examples of the industry seeking markets for previously discarded fish. For marketable fish, it is necessary that TACs be set in line with effort levels or vice versa. Iceland bans discards and a market has to be found for over-quota fish. However, if fishing effort and mortality achieve the lower levels anticipated the WSSD MSY targets, then mortality rates will be less, fewer fish will be caught and discarded, the fish typically will be bigger and the stock larger, so discard rates will fall dramatically.

Implementation of current cod recovery measures has resulted in higher levels of marketable cod discards. UK Ministers have argued that TAC levels on North Sea cod are out of line with effort levels and that a larger TAC should have been set in 2008. Currently the fishing industry is exploring ways of more actively avoiding cod.

4. *Do you consider that fisheries management policies may need to adapt to climate change? If so, how might this be achieved?*

Climate change will affect both the abundance of fish and the mix of species; at present there is limited predictability of what change will occur. A recent publication, which used international fisheries monitoring data, has shown large increases in the number of fish species in the North Sea.

A fisheries management system resilient to such unpredictable changes would probably be based more on effort management and on fishing mortality rate targets rather than on absolute TAC levels or target stock sizes. Current precautionary reference levels include absolute measures of stock size. Such a change would also affect the fishery science input to management, which at present is dominated by detailed analyses of large, single stocks. More generic advice on the management of a mix of stocks may be necessary.

There may also be consequences for "relative stability" and access to stocks. Current allocation is based upon historical relative catches. As fish abundances change then so will fishing opportunities.

CONTROL AND ENFORCEMENT

We have not provided evidence for the specific questions posed, but wish to stress the importance of good compliance for proper governance of fisheries and in particular for the provision of accurate catch data which underpin the setting of appropriate TACs.

Structural Policy

7. *Chapter III of Regulation 2371/2002 obliged Member States to put in place measures to adjust the capacity of their fleets in order to achieve a stable and enduring balance between such fishing capacity and their fishing opportunities. To what extent has this been successful?*

We have not provided evidence to Q7, but as the evidence to other questions demonstrates the proper balance of fishing capacity with resources is fundamental to good biological and economic management.

8. *The new fisheries structural fund, the European Fisheries Fund (EFF), has now come into force. What has been your experience thus far with the new instrument?*

As yet we have no experience of the very new EFF, however the previous fund (FIFG) was helpful in facilitating a range of Cefas-industry conservation projects.

9. *What are your views on the possible impact on EU fisheries structural policy of WTO-level discussions as regards subsidies in the fishing sector?*

No evidence presented.

GOVERNANCE

10. *As a result of Regulation 2371/2002, Regional Advisory Councils (RACs) were established to advise the Commission on matters of fisheries management in respect of certain sea areas or fishing zones. What is your assessment of the success thus far of the RACs? What is your view on their future evolution?*

As pointed out in "Net Benefits" exclusion of the fishing industry from EC decisions resulted in alienation from fisheries management and any commitment to its decisions. The RACs are a major step forward in providing an international, industry input to key policy decisions. The UK, and Cefas scientists, have given a high priority to making the RACs successful.

The RACs have delivered high quality advice to the Commission on a range of important policy issues. This has been remarkable given the modest resources available to the RACs and particularly the fishing industry. They have taken on a significant amount of work. The impression is that most impact has been made on strategic issues rather than the detail of the annual round of quota negotiations. The RACs have also been able to commission some research, supported by Defra, and have started annual meetings with the International Council for Exploration of the Seas which produces much of the advice for fisheries management.

The RACs should have a future. There are major regional variations in the character of fisheries across the EC, even across the UK. The current centralised system of management is not responsive to such real variations and dependencies. The RACs could play a more significant role in delivering strategies agreed at a higher level.

11. *How do you consider EU fisheries should ideally be governed? How appropriate and feasible do you consider a regional management model to be?*

See above for some comments on current management.

In a wider context, EC marine environment and biodiversity management is moving towards a more geographically regional approach, with management within marine regions and sub-regions. It would be appropriate for the detail of fisheries management to be more fully embedded in this wider environment management as fisheries is a significant pressure on ecosystems. Such structures would more readily facilitate an "ecosystems approach" to fisheries and environment management. We see some promising recent moves in this direction, with CFP decisions to close the Darwin Mounds to trawled gears, and to close several areas off south-western Ireland to a range of gears, as these features are designated under the Habitats Directive. However the decisions are at present *ad hoc*.

14 February 2008

Examination of Witness

Witness: DR JOE HORWOOD, CEFAS Chief Scientific Adviser and Defra Chief Fisheries Science Adviser, examined.

Q1 Chairman: Thank you very much indeed for finding the time to come and talk to us and to help us with our inquiry. I have to say a few formal things first of all: this is a formal session so there will be a record taken and you will get a transcript as soon as we can get it to you. Look through and make any changes that may be necessary. We are also webcast, whatever that might be; I usually say at this stage that there is a possibility that somebody may be listening to us. We have never had any evidence that that is the case, but given an error rate of plus or minus 40% there might be someone somewhere. Would you prefer to start off by giving a general statement or would you prefer to go straight into the questions and answers?
Dr Horwood: I am quite happy to go straight into the questions and answers; any general statement is covered by the CEFAS and the Defra submissions.

Q2 Chairman: Let me start off. It seems to me that there is a desperate need and objective to make fisheries policy science-led and more evidence-based and that seems to be a sensible way forward. Could you outline to us briefly what fisheries science is all about: how the data is collected, how it is interpreted and how it feeds into the policy process and then perhaps what the shortcomings may be and why we have what seems to be a continuing conflict between the producers and the scientists on interpreting the data and the results of the data.
Dr Horwood: Fisheries science has been established for quite a long while as a particular science in its own right. It is now much more merged with marine science as a whole but its initial inception really was because the fisheries had been so important to so many countries and it has always been a very quantitative science, you know, how much fish are

taken and how much can be taken. It has also had a strong international character because we have all caught fish together, so the nature of fisheries science is really, firstly, that it was established quite early, secondly, it has always been fairly quantitative compared with many of the other comparable sciences and, thirdly, that it is essentially international. That is the broad context of it. When we talk about fisheries science and its relationship to policy and management, more often than not we come down to the stock assessments: how many fish are there and what are the quotas; that is only a small part of the work but it tends to be the most political and the rawest part. To start off with we have a monitoring system where at the ports the number of fish that are caught are recorded. They are sampled, so that we know what the catches are by species and length and we take their ages, so that we know for instance that from the Irish Sea we caught so many thousand tonnes of cod and so many one-year olds, two-year olds, three-year olds, four-year olds. At sea our research vessels conduct surveys in a consistent way and this produces two sorts of information. The first is the number of young fish which are about to enter the fishery, because we use nets that are smaller than the commercial fleet so we pick them up often a year before the fishery will see them, so that allows us to put them into our forecast. The second is that we actually see through these surveys the trends in abundance of the fish—are our catch rates going up or are they going down for particular species. That is the basic building blocks and all the different countries, say around the North Sea, will be doing the same and we all get together and pool that key information. The stock assessment process is then to determine how many fish are there now. One of the ways we do this is mathematically complicated, but the principle is fairly simple. If we go back to fish born in 1990, say, they will have been caught as one year-old in 1991, as two years-old in 1992, three years-old in 1993 and we record all the numbers of fish that were caught at these different ages, and so after ten years we can add them all up again to say in 1991 we actually saw this many one-year-old fish. We can add a little bit on for those that died naturally and then we see what the catch rates of our research vessels or the commercial fleets were and we can actually calibrate it, so when our research vessel now is catching so many cod at age one we can compare that with what we saw there as the catch rate in 1990 and therefore infer the absolute number of one-year-old cod. It is basically a calibration method; there are quite a lot of statistics, but that is the key principle behind it. There is a second method which is less frequently used because it is much more expensive, but for instance for mackerel we will estimate the number of fish in the sea by going out and measuring the number of eggs in the plankton, so we tow plankton samplers behind the research vessels, capture the eggs and count them. We do this throughout the production cycle so over the entire area we will be sampling the eggs and over the three months that they spawn we will be sampling them to find out how many eggs have been put in the sea. We know how many eggs a single mackerel will produce, so you divide one by the other and that is another way in which we end up getting an absolute measure. From the basic data we can then do this mathematical exercise, and the output will be what is the absolute number of fish that we have now in 2007 at age one, two, three, four and five and what were the numbers in the past, so we have the history and we can see: has the stock declined significantly, has it increased or is it stable. Then if you say what is the forecast, so what can the fishermen take in the following year, we can project those numbers forward but also bring in the number of youngsters that we have seen through our surveys, the little fish, and add on to these estimates from the stock assessments the estimates of recruiting fish to give us a forecast of how many fish there are in the sea. That is the basic data and underlying principle and it is all done internationally, most of it at the International Council for the Exploration of the Sea, which brings these parties together to do the assessments. How good is it? There are, I guess, two elements of it. In terms of supporting a TAC system as a whole it is actually quite difficult to count the number of fish in the sea and we reckon that if circumstances are reasonably good, if we have a good assessment and there are not any major problems, then we will end up with what we call a co-efficient of variation of about 20%. What that means is that one year in every 20 we could be out by 40% more or 40% less, which is still quite difficult for the fishery to handle. It could mean that we actually close the fishery in the middle of September in error, when in actual fact they could safely have fished until December, but I personally think that getting the number of fish in the sea to plus or minus 20% is quite good, but even that as a good answer is still quite a strain for the TAC-based system in the best of circumstances. The shortcomings and support from the industry are really quite patchy. The question of the cod has really dominated the thinking now for the last ten years and it has been a major issue for us, but the Regional Advisory Councils held a major meeting last year on cod recovery and they concluded that there had been a decline in the cod caused by heavy fishing over a period when the recruitment of a number of youngsters had been reduced, so in some major instances we are seeing and saying the same thing as the fishermen. There was an article for *Fishing News* which I bought, produced as a letter in response to a fisherman saying last year our views are out of line with the scientists, but no, actually we are essentially seeing and saying more or less the same as you about North Sea cod last year. In some areas we are very much seeing issues the same; there are some problems which are difficult and seem to be intractable, which we have not conquered, and an example is the North Sea whiting where the quality of our assessment has been very poor for a decade. At present in our advice we are saying that the whiting is in quite a poor state and the North Sea coast fishermen are saying that they cannot avoid whiting, and I have to say that I can see both sides of the argument. It is truly not clear in these instances what is going on. I am afraid that is a rather complicated answer to your question as to how good or how flawed it is, but it is quite a rich tapestry.

Q3 *Chairman:* Let us go one stage further. The industry is heavily regulated and there is clearly a need to manage the industry and catches. Really, at the end of the day, the only way that will be successful is if there is buy-in by the fishermen, if they take ownership of the whole regime. Essential to that is for there to be confidence between the producers and the scientists and the fishermen and the scientists; what could be done to improve that confidence, what could be done to have a better dialogue?
Dr Horwood: I do absolutely and wholeheartedly agree with what you say and it was a key theme underpinning the Net Benefits report and the Government response Securing the Benefits that there was a virtual spin-off of better trust, better compliance, better management as a whole. The first thing is for everybody to believe in that view and, certainly beforehand, the fishermen were hugely excluded from a system where the advice from ICES, which is commissioned by the EU, went straight to the EU and was turned into TAC and quota advice, which did not get altered an awful lot, and the fishermen just felt that they were nowhere in the system at all. There is an absolute issue of confidence and buy-in and involvement and we have recognised that. In terms of what we are doing about it, it is a great deal, because it is so important and so fundamental. First of all, the stock assessment process which I mentioned, the business of calibration and the calibration of the research vessels, we have only started to do that fairly recently because our research vessels were used in the past to only collect the pre-recruit, the young fish, information, which they did very well, but because there had been major corruption in the quality of the catch data and that would also mean the catch rate data, how many fish per hour the commercial fleet were catching, those data are no longer used in the assessments, this being the trend worldwide. There are thousands of hours more fishing that the commercial fleet do compared with the research fleet, so one key thing would be a restoration of confidence in the accuracy

of the catch and the catch rate data. A key feature underpinning the stock assessment would be the fishermen's own commercial data. That is one example, and there are more moves in the right direction. The Fisheries Science Partnership is a Defra-funded programme of £1 million a year which specifically puts fishermen and scientists together and two-thirds of that money is spent in developing their own time series, so instead of using our research vessels we are using their vessels and working with them to inform views on the state of the stocks. Those data are now just beginning to be sent into the ICES system and used in the stock assessment. The ICES is opening itself up to observers at a range of levels and through the Regional Advisory Councils and the NFFO representatives they are having greater access to that. There are, therefore, a variety of fronts that we are proceeding on for that, but the key thing is that we do actually recognise that it is fundamental to the management of this industry that they have confidence in the basic information.

Q4 *Viscount Ullswater:* Could I just put in one other factor? It seems that your research vessels measure the juvenile fish but the landings you can assess and measure and age the fish.
Dr Horwood: Yes.

Q5 *Viscount Ullswater:* What we have read in evidence is that in the North Sea maybe up to 50% of fish caught are not landed; therefore, how much could that affect the science on the total population in the sea if actually you are not having a scientific evaluation of the by-catches, of the discards. I would have thought that if there are a whole lot of fish being caught and then being put back into the sea without any form of calibration or appreciation, whatever you like to call it, of what has been taken, it then becomes slightly anecdotal, does it not?
Dr Horwood: You are quite right, that is an additional element. Again, unfortunately, there are several parts to an answer to that. First of all, if you had a situation where there was a traditional fishery that was discarding regularly 10% of catch and we did not know about it, for technical reasons that would not matter, we would still end up advising quite appropriately on the size of the catch. What is significant is if you have significant amounts of discards and they are very variable from year to year or there is a trend, that can then confound the assessments. For the key stocks we do have programmes to monitor the discards and certainly for North Sea cod and haddock they are counted through an observer programme and included in the assessments, but for many of our stock assessments the quality of the discard data is just too poor, there are too few to actually include in the regular stock assessments.

Q6 *Baroness Jones of Whitchurch:* I understand why you have said there is a big emphasis on quantitative measurement and the counting that goes on; you said that there is a mathematical formula which is always slightly above when it comes down to that. Really what would be much more useful for policymakers is an overall assessment of what is going on in a particular area. Take the North Sea, really for policymakers to be able to make sensible judgments it is not just about counting what is caught, which may just be that commercial fish at that particular time, we need to know which fish are unpopular at the moment but we maybe could encourage people to start eating, for example, or all the different trends of fish—some are coming up, others are declining, the impact of climate change. All those things mean that it is a moveable feast and we need to be able to make projections, so how do the scientists go about helping to make some of those projections because just counting what is there now is only a very, very small part of the science.

Dr Horwood: It is only a small part of the science and I did say at the beginning that we do have quite a wide job and a wide remit, but politically the real problems and the hassles were always associated with the annual stock assessment. As you say, there are a lot more issues involved. We catch, I believe, getting on for 200 different species of fish on our surveys and we have had surveys that go back to the turn of the century, so we can actually monitor the major changes that are seen in our system. There is a recent report where people have brought together all the international North Sea surveys and have shown that over the last 20 years the diversity of North Sea fish has actually increased quite significantly. There are a range of things that we do as well though it is a bit difficult to deliver to you in this instance the entire package. The marine ecosystems are changing and the key surveys that we are doing provide the basic information to say that things are changing and provide a basis for speculating on the future.

Q7 *Baroness Jones of Whitchurch:* Would you say that those assessments are any more accurate than the quantitative surveys you are doing?

Dr Horwood: Our surveys which indicate trends are very much more robust than the need to say "and for this particular stock you have got 110,000 tonnes". The indices themselves are really quite robust and they are independent of any changes in the fisheries, they are just what we are seeing out there on the ground.

Q8 *Baroness Jones of Whitchurch:* Amongst that 200 species are there some that you think that, with a bit of encouragement, the European population could be persuaded to learn to eat instead of cod, for example?

Dr Horwood: Yes. One of the points that we mentioned in the submission was that new markets are being found and also one species that is particularly heavily discarded in the South West at the moment is the gurnard, which is a lovely fish. It is a solid fish to eat, though not very big, they only tend to grow about that big (about twelve inches) but most of it is solid fish. They are now just beginning to find markets for it down in the South West and beam trawlers from Plymouth are beginning to land a lot more of their catch than just sole. Sole has totally dominated the beam trawler fleet, that is where all the value is and they have not particularly bothered with the other species, but they are now finding that in actual fact there is quite a lot of value with these other species and, of course, the more they land them the more the markets will develop. The haddock in the South West—there was never a market in Newlyn for the amount of haddock that could be landed there, they just were not getting any decent prices, and it costs a lot to handle the fish on board the ship, so they were discarded. Now they have found that the Plymouth market will take the haddock, so they are no longer discarding they are actually landing the haddock. There are, therefore, quite a lot of natural market forces driving the fishermen to land fish if there are markets for them.

Q9 *Lord Plumb:* Cynics might say that we can take reports that have been produced previously and most of them show that there is no change. The recovery and management plans were produced in 2002; presumably they are working but how satisfactorily are they working and what should happen. Secondly, from that, should they be improved and if so how should they be improved?

Dr Horwood: There are the two different sorts of plans, the recovery plans and the management plans, and the new basic regulation, the Common Fisheries Policy, actually stipulates that the fisheries should be managed as either a recovery plan or as a management plan, and you will already have found that we are not quite there yet. Dealing with the recovery plans first of all, it took quite a while to actually get to the stage of the 2002 plans. We had problems in the early/middle 1990s before we actually got round to these formal plans and a great deal of work was done to actually look at the simulated nature of what these plans would deliver. Targets were basically set and were agreed, which seemed to be a sensible thing for any plan, and a means of achieving those targets. For cod this was that a quota should be set to allow the parent stock to increase by 30% each year. You must bear in mind that the alternative that people were talking about was the complete closure of the fisheries on cod which in itself would be virtually a complete closure of the fisheries, as you will know from Scotland. The recovery plan itself was, therefore, a very severe compromise between no fishing and a plan that would allow some fishing and some quotas but at the same time recovery. If you look at what has been achieved, there seems to have been very little evidence of progress in the Irish Sea and to the west of Scotland. In the North Sea last year we saw for the first time that we do seem eventually to have reduced the fishing rate very considerably and hopefully this is a robust result which we will find out through this year's stock assessments, but the fishing mortality has been reduced to its lowest level for 40 years, which is a massive thing to have done. It has been at a huge cost, we have cut back our northern white fish fisheries by 60 to 70% which has been a massive problem for the people involved, but before last year we were only seeing cutbacks in the amount of fishing effort at sea by about 20%. However, it looks like the cuts that have been made have actually focused on the cod-type fisheries to achieve this big reduction in fishing. Having achieved that reduction in fishing we seem to have got a lot of cod in the North Sea, which is now a problem for fishing; it is a problem because it does look like in the North Sea at least that the recovery plan is working. One of the elements of the plan that was not clear was how the element of fishing effort was to be managed. Scientists, for a very long while, have said that managing by quotas alone will be ineffective: you can still go to sea, you can still catch and kill fish, it is just that you are only allowed to land a bit, so fishing effort had to be a key element of it. From day one we did not see anything explicit from the Commission as to what the proposed effort levels were in relation to the target fishing mortality and the TAC, so they were two processes that went on in a quasi-independent way. We have not been able to reduce the fishing effort to the level which the targets implied, even though the quotas are consistent with the plans. Of course, what then appears is increased discards and it is a question of how you resolve those two. There have been and there continue to be, therefore, problems with the 2000 plan. For the individual fishermen as well this has been done on a vessel-based system so when they have so many days to go to sea, which could be half their normal days, they cannot just sell up one boat and put two half days on one vessel to increase their own efficiency because then they will lose their days entitlement, so there is an element of economic efficiency that is not addressed by the current plan. We have learned a lot about recovery plans and if we have to do more then hopefully some of these things will be addressed. The management plans are for stocks that are not in such a severe position and they are meant to give a framework for making decisions. We have one agreed for the North Sea flatfish, basically the North Sea sole and the North Sea plaice. The main people who catch those two species together are the beam

trawler fleets, mainly in the southern North Sea, so they are linked, but one of the things that we have not done is to have plans that are developed for fisheries. It is not a lot of good having a management plan for haddock if it is not really well aligned with the management plan for whiting and for cod, so there is a lot more work to be done in understanding how to develop management plans for fisheries as opposed to a nice simple management plan for a fish.

Q10 Chairman: Do you think it is the way forward though?
Dr Horwood: There certainly needs to be something like that to give a framework so that the industry understands what the medium term future is, because they are investing in boats and capital that will last for 20 years and the more that you can help the fishermen see the future, the more they will be prepared to defer taking their revenue now to avoid the risk of what goes on in the future, effectively applying a high discount rate, so I think a management plan framework of some sort is important, but underlying this as well we have a commitment to move to maximum sustainable yield levels by 2015 through the World Summit on Sustainable Development; what that means is fishing levels probably quite a lot lower than we have got at present, so again if we are developing plans one needs to keep in mind some of the things that we have already signed up to.

Q11 Lord Plumb: What about the stock management plans outside the EU? The Norwegian plan for fishing apparently is supposed to fit in with the EU policy; what effect is this having and can we work together?
Dr Horwood: I do not think there is anything at all contradictory between the plans that have been agreed for the EU/Norway shared stocks; they are consistent and they set management targets for cod and haddock, for the cod when it is fully recovered and the haddock for now. They are very simple plans, that we will fish at a particular rate and if the stock begins to fall we will reduce fishing. It is a framework which imposes some discipline on those setting the quotas.

Q12 Chairman: Can I just do a general one on the emergency conservation measures. I will give you the opportunity of really saying what you want to say on emergency measures and their effectiveness or ineffectiveness and scope for improvement.
Dr Horwood: One has to say things are an awful lot better than they were before they introduced in the new basic regulations a power to introduce measures on an emergency basis but it does seem that the system is still particularly sluggish. If you imagine the difference between how we handle some of the animal

diseases where, if you have a trigger event then things across Europe immediately go into a form of action, you would expect any business to manage itself with appropriate risk plans and risk management plans, and this just does not seem to be a culture in the management of fisheries where it would seem that there are predictable types of emergencies, shall we say, which could be a very big year class of haddock that arises. The last time we had a very big year class of haddock we actually discarded over 100,000 tonnes of North Sea haddock in one year; these things can be avoided but you would need to plan for them because they just take months and months to go through the EU. I would have thought that there needs to be a slightly different way of handling, shall we say, fishermen's business in the same way as any other business would handle itself in terms of risk management.

Q13 *Chairman:* Could you say a little bit more? What would it look like?
Dr Horwood: You would have to agree that there are various events that would arise which would have a negative effect in some sense. We could say that when we get a very big year class of haddock we are really not happy that we are going to lose 100,000 tonnes of it, so you would actually trigger if you like an emergency response plan in this instance by the scientists having identified early on that there is a very big year class of haddock.

Q14 *Chairman:* That would be an in-year assessment, would it not?
Dr Horwood: The scientists will tend to see the little haddock a year before the industry start to capture them in their net. When they are too small and they go through it is not a problem, and when they are big and above marketable size then they can land them, but they will also capture very large numbers of small fish which are not marketable and those are the ones that we want to avoid capturing. You probably have actually got six months or maybe a year's notice of this event coming through. If you have already got a plan on the shelf which says in the event of this, these are the actions that we will take and there is some way of triggering this plan so it does not come as a huge surprise to everybody, even though it has occurred every ten years for the last 100 years, it would be a lot easier to implement, so you could actually develop a plan. Experience has shown that these plans are very difficult because in the case of haddock it would affect a particular locality a lot more than others—the chances are that the Netherlands would be totally disinterested. The people around Scotland would want a huge amount of discussion on the fine detail of that and it might take two or three years to actually develop a plan where there is a significant buy-in and

it is useful, but then having got it on the shelf you could actually implement it quite quickly.

Q15 *Viscount Ullswater:* In your evidence that you have given us this morning I think you are indicating that you are critical of the effectiveness of TACs. TACs may be useful in some fisheries, in the pelagic fisheries, but in the mixed fisheries, which is most of the fisheries round our shores, they seem to be rather a blunt instrument and increase the number of discards. In evidence you have been saying that fishing effort is probably a more effective way of coping with mixed fisheries. Perhaps you would like to comment on the effectiveness of TACs. Is there a way of overcoming the discards which TACs impose on these mixed fisheries?
Dr Horwood: Certainly there is an issue about getting the TAC right for the mixed fisheries. If we have an accuracy of a plus or minus 20% for each one of these species, it is really very difficult to get a package where at least one of them is not significantly off and is not causing quite a lot of discarding. It is certainly an imperfect conservation tool. Its ability to get countries to agree to a quota, however, is extremely strong through this relative stability concept. Everybody knows what a tonne of fish is. For a long while scientists have looked to the effort system and said surely this is a better way of going about it, but they have never had the responsibility of implementing it. We have seen under the current system that implementing effort control is really hugely complicated. You have a whole range of different sorts of vessels and gear which are exerting different sorts of fishing pressures. You have actually to manage that mix. Whereas everybody understands what a tonne of fish is, do we all understand what a day of sea time is for a beam trawler, a netter and a potter? All these things that the scientists are not paying a lot of attention to become hugely important and the fishermen will focus in on them and will be able to spot where their ability to increase their effort within the current rules is extremely quickly. Conceptually effort control has an awful lot of good going for it because you can regulate the amount of effort going into a fishery and then hopefully they can land it all, but our experience with the cod recovery shows that in truth this is not a simple process. It may well be that a more reasonable answer is one where our fishing capacity, ie the basic size of the fleet is much more in line with the size of the resource, so even if they are working flat out they cannot cause a significant amount of damage to the stock over one or two years. That would allow a lot more flexibility with the TAC-based system. So if it was overshot by 10 or 20% one year maybe you would not have to discard, you could land and you could work out some system where you would pay it back over a while. I think what I am suggesting is that there needs to be

probably a combination of the two but underpinned by the basic fishing effort and capacity being much more commensurate with a size that the stocks can sustain.

Q16 *Viscount Ullswater:* If there is this large amount of discard, what happens to the dead fish? Do they just float to the bottom and get wasted or are they eaten by crabs or lobsters?
Dr Horwood: They turn into lots of fulmars. Fulmars have increased enormously over the last 100 years. That being said, I know the RSPB do not think that discarding should be maintained to maintain fulmars. There are a few instances where discarding has had a really bad effect, particularly when you talk about high grading from the big pelagic vessels because they can dump a huge net full of dead fish down in one spot and other vessels have trawled through it and it is a mess and is not doing anyone any good. Most of the other discards really are just assimilated back into the ecosystem.

Q17 *Earl of Arran:* Is it not possible with technology to be able eventually to throw more fish alive back into the sea than is currently happening?
Dr Horwood: We are working all the while on different gears to help that. Let me give two examples. We have been working on some panels to put in beam trawlers and we have been trialling them down in the south-west. There are two different panels, one on the bottom and one on the top. The one on the bottom gets rid of a lot of the shellfish and the one at the top gets rid of a lot of the fish. What we have found is that they virtually lose none of their catch but the quality is improved because the fish are not abraded by a whole load of mess in cod end, so you are getting more for it at the markets. The entire south-west is now switching over to these panels. It has really been quite remarkable. When it is shown to be in the fishermen's interests they are not slow to take these things up. The other example, which is still being trialled, is something called the eliminator trawl which we found out about through one of our environmentally friendly fishing competitions. It is a net with lots of holes around the first part of it and it catches virtually no cod. We have been trialling that off the north-east coast of Scotland. There is a Scottish interest in it. One of the things we are particularly concerned about is can we fish in a way that avoids catching cod. There is something called a separator trawl, which is a normal trawl but with a horizontal mesh panel because fish behave in a different way when they enter the net. The haddock will swim upwards and in this instance would go in the top half of the net whereas cod and plaice tend to head downwards. Years ago we developed this net where the bottom panels had holes which were a lot larger, but it is such a delicate gear. The fishing

industry could use it but it is very open to abuse. A key element is the desire of the fishermen to want to reduce discards. There are quite a few gears about which can help them do it. It is always a lot easier if your target fish is not a small fish and unfortunately for the sole fisheries, sole tend to be quite small and can get through quite small holes. Most of the sole fishermen are very reluctant to move to anything more than a 90 millimetre mesh for the sole fishery, which means a lot of other fish do tend to get caught in it.

Q18 *Viscount Ullswater:* This could make a huge difference to stocks, could it not, if more of the throwback is alive than dead?
Dr Horwood: Absolutely. If we reduced the fishing effort down to the size consistent with the World Summit targets, which could be significantly lower, then the fishing mortality rate may halve. Your discard would immediately halve. Not only that, the size of the fish would be larger and the size of the stock itself would be a lot larger, so your discard rate will plummet. Lower fishing rates are probably more important than small changes to the mesh size.

Q19 *Baroness Jones of Whitchurch:* Could you just explain the panel to me? That is something that is attached to the net, is it? It is not something that happens when they are landed; it is actually attached to the net, is it?
Dr Horwood: Yes, it is part of the net. As they trawl along, the benthos, the whelks and the starfish fall through the bottom panel as opposed to going to the cod end. If they are in the cod end they are really quite rough, so the fish go to market and they have got bits of blood and grazes on them and they will not attract such a high price as a fish that really looks quite good. There are top panels that we have that are used in the haddock fishery because the haddock do move up. Most of our mesh is a diamond shape mesh and as it contracts under pressure it will squeeze shut whereas these panels tend to be square mesh the other way so they actually stay open. Even though the diamond mesh is tightening these panels remain open more.

Q20 *Baroness Sharp of Guildford:* In your evidence to us you talked about the closed areas and their use in fisheries management. Could you tell us a little bit more about how the concept of closure has been used within the European Union and what advantages and disadvantages there have proved to be? The Scottish Government has been trialling real-time closures. Are these likely to work? What barriers are there to their application? Could you tell us a little bit more about the way in which they might work?
Dr Horwood: You might be interested to know that we have recently calculated that in our own England and Wales waters 30% of the area is under some form

of Common Fisheries Policy area-based control. If we consider other non-CFP ones then 40% of our sea areas are regulated to fishing in some way. For many years now we have attempted to protect particularly the nursery grounds of fish. The flatfish in particular live on shallow sandy areas so are really more susceptible to being protected. It has been quite natural to protect these areas. It is investing in the future of the fishery. The fish themselves are of no value and they are quite tightly constrained. The other fish, such as the orange roughy, are very, very vulnerable deep water fish, very late maturing, they tend to congregate against oceanic sea mounds and the CFP has protected those from fishing. We have had some closures to protect spawning fish. We protect the herring spawning grounds because they lay their eggs sticking to the bottom and if you have trawling through them you destroy their spawn. For many years heron spawning grounds have been protected. In terms of the cod or any largely mobile fish, it becomes much more problematic that these areas are useful because if you protect the cod in one area the chances are you will be catching that same cod 50 miles away elsewhere. The cod has proved a problem. Certainly in the Irish Sea many years ago there would be a massive spawning fishery and the catch rates of cod on spawning ground would be over ten times higher than they would be elsewhere. So you can imagine if you stopped the fishermen fishing there and they were made to fish elsewhere they would only be going to catch a tenth of the fish. That would be a sensible conservation measure, but now, unfortunately, the concentrations of cod and spawning are so small that if you force them to go elsewhere you may be pushing them on to juveniles which they may be catching in even greater number. You cannot really consider these closed areas as universally good. We have always said that they need to be considered on a case-by-case basis. In relation to the real-time closures for cod that have recently been introduced in Scotland and are now being rolled out in England with some support at least from Denmark, it has been following an initiative from the industry who believe they can avoid cod and in fact need to demonstrate that they can so do. As we have said, the measures so far off the west of Scotland and the Irish Sea have not proved fruitful. It is being rolled out this year now under a formal scheme that we can operate through the CFP, through the cod recovery whereby if we manage our effort scheme not as I previously described, on a vessel by vessel basis, but as a UK pot of so many kilowatt days we could be more efficient. Providing it has various conservation elements then we can give to our fishermen additional days at sea. So we are expecting a lot of fishermen to sign up to it. On the spawning area closures, the scheme involved is that if they are catching so many fish above a particular size they will close an area of

about seven nautical miles square. There would be a maximum of nine of these at any one time. They would be closed for three weeks. You are talking about 500 square miles, which is about 0.5% of the North Sea. For juveniles it would be a slightly larger area but again a maximum of 1% of the North Sea. We have yet to see whether these real-time closures can actually provide a significant mechanism. A key thing in this is the fishermen wanting to take the initiative themselves and at the very least it is not bad. If they feel this is positive, and we want to encourage them to take more measures like this, then it is something which should be supported.

Q21 *Baroness Sharp of Guildford:* Is there sufficient co-operation between fleets? Is there a problem? We may get the Scottish fishermen buying into this, but what about the Spanish and the French fishermen?
Dr Horwood: This particular scheme is just a UK scheme. We know that some other countries have expressed an interest in either joining it or having a similar scheme of their own. Even before it was embodied by the EU in the Council regulation last year they were talking positively about wanting to do something with us on this, but it is very much a UK scheme.

Q22 *Baroness Sharp of Guildford:* Does that mean it is within the 12-mile limit that we have control over?
Dr Horwood: No. This will be in UK territorial waters and I think it might only be the North Sea that we are operating this in. I am not certain about this. I do know it is at least the North Sea, but it is our UK scheme.

Q23 *Baroness Jones of Whitchurch:* You have already talked a little bit about mesh sizes and so on, but are there any other innovations, technical or scientific, that are going on out there that are helping conservation? Is there anything that you would like to share with us that you think might help in this whole process?
Dr Horwood: There are major things now happening in Europe with the Marine Strategy Directive which is going to encourage us to develop the good ecological status of our seas or good environmental status. The marine environment side has really been a sleeping giant and is quite clearly waking up. I see the fisheries as eventually fitting in to a much more holistic management of the marine environment and marine ecosystems as a whole.

Q24 *Baroness Jones of Whitchurch:* That could be a horrible bureaucracy, could it not? It could be one bigger bureaucracy. What makes you so keen on it?
Dr Horwood: At present OSPAR, the Oslo and Paris Convention, have a particular remit to look after the environment. They increased their remit a few years

ago to include the ecology of the seas, but there are no powers for them to do anything with fishing at all, fishing is quite independent. I can see, taking your point that this will not be without its bureaucracy, that there will have to be a more coherent link between fisheries and environmental management. We got the Darwin Mounds protected under the CFP. I believe it was a requirement through the Habitats Directive that protection was given, but the mechanisms to actually protect it from international fishing just are not there, so there are some big loopholes. The TACs and quota regulation this year protected some Irish areas from fishing, but it really is a bit ad hoc. There will clearly have to be a better integration of these two branches, the fisheries and the environmental protection.

Q25 Baroness Jones of Whitchurch: And the timetable for that merger, if it is going to be a merger?
Dr Horwood: I do not believe there is one explicitly.

Q26 Baroness Jones of Whitchurch: You mentioned in your evidence that we need more outcome orientated regulation. Do you think that this new regime you are talking about will be more outcome orientated?
Dr Horwood: I doubt it. There does not seem to be a culture to go along this particular line. The system that we have at present, particularly through technical regulation, knows that it wants to achieve particular objectives such as low discards, that they do not want you to use small mesh if you are targeting the large fish and so they have constructed a massive rule book of things that fishermen must not do in order to achieve this outcome. You really believe it would be better if there was some way that you could say what is it you want to achieve and let us see if fishermen can do that and you can monitor it and leave it much more up to them to decide how they are going to achieve such measures.

Q27 Lord Palmer: I think everybody seems to agree that the policy of discards is really an absolute international scandal and indeed perhaps it was what made us embark on yet another inquiry into the Common Fisheries Policy. To what extent do you consider a discard ban would help to address the problem of discards and how might such a ban function in reality?
Dr Horwood: I think the proposal for a discard ban is extremely helpful in that it will scare people into deciding they really must do something about the issue. There are some negative issues associated with the discard ban. I really do not feel to date that it has been taken particularly seriously and I rather suspect this is where the Commission is coming from as well. The response by the Regional Advisory Councils also suggested this was the Commission putting a shot

across the bows of the industry. One of the disadvantages is a safety issue in that you will be forcing vessels to carry back to shore large amounts of unwanted material. Having got the material to shore, then instead of having what is effectively a contaminant of some sort spread across the sea floor, you are bringing it back and presumably it will be disposed of at a point source and so it is likely to prove more of a problem. I personally would not want to see markets developed for small fish. So if people are bringing back small fish and sales develop for them, do we want to encourage people to market fish like that? There are some negative elements associated with a discard ban, but I am hoping that this will be a prompt to take a much more significant step to get fishermen cutting down on their discards in the future.

Q28 Lord Palmer: Could you see a discard ban in reality actually coming into force in the next five years in your opinion?
Dr Horwood: I would have hoped that the consequence of the Commission's proposal for a discard ban will have some end point in less than five years. We have had lots of things which seem to have stuck in the Commission. Five years is not an outrageously long time for the Commission to act, but certainly Commissioner Borg has expressed his disgust with the level of discarding that is going on. You can see that there is a personal commitment to do something. It would not have to end up as a discard ban; there are other things that can be done. In Iceland and New Zealand if they catch marketable fish they are not allowed to discard those—

Q29 Chairman: That is the key issue. It is not just a discard ban; it is a discard ban of market or marketable fish.
Dr Horwood: That would be a different issue. At present it is a discard ban of all biogenic material. There are lots of loose ends which would have to be sorted out. One assumes you do not want to bring back loads of shellfish. Equally, you do not want to be bringing back 100,000 tonnes of baby haddock in Peterhead. If it is marketable fish then that becomes a rather different matter. It is possible as well to set targets of some sort for discarding and leaving it to the fishermen. They might use different nets, fish at different times and different places. It would be very difficult to monitor and observe them, but this is the sort of outcome orientated process or legislation that I was suggesting might be more fruitful.

Q30 Chairman: You could reasonably tell that they are discarding. You cannot tell what they are discarding, can you?
Dr Horwood: If it is at night you do not know what they are doing.

5 March 2008   Dr Joe Horwood

Q31 Chairman: In Scotland it is night quite a lot of the time during winter!

Dr Horwood: Monitoring this itself will be quite difficult. You do feel an awful lot of these issues would go away if there was a commitment by the fishermen to do something and the trust by others that the fishermen would actually do it. If you have not got that you end up having a massive rule book that you ask people to follow.

Q32 Viscount Ullswater: When we are talking about bycatches and discards and when measuring the amount of discards, are we talking about bycatches of controlled fish that are subject to the CFP or are we talking about just fish biomass as a bycatch?

Dr Horwood: Most of the fish discards in the south-west for instance, where we have done a big study, are of low value, non-commercial fish, gurnards, pout whiting -- Somewhere in this pile I have a list of the species. The component which is discarded through being out-of-kilter with the quota is a relatively modest part of that. It is currently a bit of a concern because the cod quota in the North Sea has been set out of line with the size of the stock and there will be a significant discard of marketable cod in the North Sea, but in general it is of small, under-sized fish and of unmarketable fish or fish for which there are not currently markets.

Q33 Viscount Ullswater: When they talk about this figure of anything between half a million and 800,000 tonnes of discards, is that basically a lot of unmarketable fish or is that only the marketable fish which is being discarded that you would want to measure for some reason?

Dr Horwood: I know the figure that you are talking about but I do not know precisely where it comes from. Our figures that would add up to what you are talking about would be mainly under-sized fish; they would be the 100,000 tonne of under-sized haddock for instance in one year.

Q34 Viscount Ullswater: But it is not the sort of gurnards and things that you were talking about, is it?

Dr Horwood: Yes.

Q35 Viscount Ullswater: That would be discarded on top of that, would it?

Dr Horwood: No, that would be included. The large percentage of that figure would not be marketable cod, haddock and whiting.

Q36 Viscount Ullswater: How does anybody come to measure the size of that particular thing? I know it is a big range that I have given you. How do we even have an idea of the tonnage?

Dr Horwood: We have observers on the vessels. I think we have about six guys or we spend about six man-years on the boats of the vessels. So we actually record all that is caught and landed and discarded. Over the years we have a very good record of what is being caught and discarded. Scotland has had a major programme for their whitefish fishery for a very long time. The EU has something called the Data Collection Regulation and it obliges countries to collect such information. As for our sampling levels, probably only about 0.5% of the trips are sampled. It is just too expensive to contemplate otherwise. Over the years you end up with a very robust database which can tell you what is going on.

Q37 Baroness Sharp of Guildford: You state that climate change is likely to affect both the abundance of fish and the mix of species and this seems to be borne out also by other long-term surveys of plankton. What implications is this likely to have upon the procedures for the management of stocks? How are we monitoring the developments as a result of climate change and how should we be monitoring it?

Dr Horwood: We have been monitoring our fisheries now for a very long time, the commercial and the non-commercial species and it has been a wonderful database to follow and to note the changes that we have been seeing. We have certainly seen some changes and they are being attributed to climate change. We have a natural oscillation in the North Atlantic which causes ten to 20-year oscillations which are likely to be much greater than a slow trend of climate change. So probably what we are seeing is a climate change signal and the effects of the North Atlantic oscillation affecting our fisheries as well. They are all indicating that we should expect changes to occur. The predictability of those changes does seem to be quite low. You can make some general statements such as maybe the warmer water species will increase and the cold water species decrease, but it is really the entire ecology that will determine whether the fish larvae survive. We really do not know how the ecology of the seas is going to change. Also, if the seas get a bit warmer, with the North Sea sole, you might think that they would expand their range further north, but they do need these particular nursery grounds. Even if the larvae food is there and the temperature is right, if they have not got coastal sandy nursery ground, which you do not see around Norway, then there would not be an expansion of the sole stock. We have got to expect change, but we cannot rely on a lot of predictability. Future management measures and tools need to be climate change proofed against such unpredictability.

Q38 Chairman: I would like to turn to Regional Advisory Councils. Your evidence is pretty positive toward RACs. Is there anything that we can point to and say that has really been delivered, an advance has been made in that area because of Regional Advisory Councils? If their importance grows what sort of help could basically the science give them? What could you feed in to enhance their competence?

Dr Horwood: The RACs publish the advice they provide to the Commission on their website and they really are worth reading. They are extremely considered pieces of advice. I think they are very polished works and quite clearly should be taken seriously by the Commission. At the Commission level, you can see from discussions that the views that the Regional Advisory Councils are a part of the natural language of the Commissioner. He does listen to them. That does not mean that their advice is taken, but it is quite clear that they are taken quite seriously. It is difficult to point to very particular successes because it is quite a grey process in Brussels sometimes to see how exactly any one decision is made. The North Sea RAC were really very scathing about the Commission's approach to the introduction of protected areas and quite rightly. I think to some degree that had a significant part in the Commission stopping their own initiatives to impose closed areas on the system. They have also been developing their own views on management plans. In many ways they are part of a group of different players that are feeding into this system. In many ways you can see they are a partner round the table in the development of plans as opposed to just responding to it. It is a bit difficult to say yes, this is a real success, but there are lots of bits of evidence which say this is clearly going the right way and their views are being sought. In terms of the scientific and technical base to help them, we would very much like to feel that there is a common science and technical base that supports the Government, the RACs and any stakeholder that actually has a part in making a decision. The EU DG FISH has said it will help the RACs feed particular questions through to ICES if ICES is the appropriate source of information for it. This is because the DG FISH provides ICES with some monies to answer some questions, but it is also aware that there is a very small finite fisheries science community which has demands on it from the EU and then, via ICES and the EU, other technical committees, the governments and if the RACs come in as well and say we want this, there does need to be a prioritisation of some sort. That is one of the things that is happening institutionally. The Government has given a high priority to empowering the RACs as a significant voice and both ourselves as scientists and our policy colleagues are really giving them as much help as we possibly can. We support their meetings. Defra funds a series of specific projects which the RACs feel they need to help them do their business. We are doing quite a lot to make them as successful as possible. This is a major new bit of work and business that is put on a relatively small group of people. They have done an excellent job with quite meager support.

Q39 Baroness Sharp of Guildford: How many RACs are there?

Dr Horwood: I should know the answer to that but I do not because some of them are Mediterranean RACs—

Q40 Baroness Sharp of Guildford: We have got one for the North Sea. Is there an Irish Sea one?

Dr Horwood: There is the North Sea one, there is a western one which covers all our western waters of interest and then there is another one that goes down to Iberia, and there is a deep sea RAC and there is a pelagic RAC. The pelagic RAC would affect the North Sea pelagic fisheries because they are really quite a separate different industry.

Q41 Lord Plumb: Do they meet together in Brussels occasionally?

Dr Horwood: I do not know the answer to that. They certainly meet under ICES because there is an annual ICES/RAC meeting where all the RACs meet with ICES in one place.

Q42 Lord Palmer: Aquaculture also comes under your responsibility. To what extent do you see developments such as cod farming alleviating the pressure on sea fisheries? In light of some of the work that you have undertaken, what risks might these developments entail? Do you see a relatively rosy future for aquaculture in the long term or are you yourself a bit sceptical about it?

Dr Horwood: I am less of an expert on aquaculture. To me it seems a priority is to get our North Sea cod stocks back up to 150,000 tonnes, which is where they should be and the bulk of our fish be taken from places like that. It is a bit difficult to see that these huge volumes of fish can be generated through aquaculture although, conceptually, they can. It takes between two and five times the weight of a fish developed in aquaculture to produce it. Of our typical whitefish, to produce a kilogram of farmed cod will take five kilograms of food, which has got to come from somewhere and that somewhere is typically our industrial fisheries, so from the North Sea sandeel fishery or the Peruvian anchovy fishery. To some degree it is affected by your philosophy as to how bona fide those fisheries are. Global fish production does seem to have peaked and stablised. In general we are not going to produce a huge amount more fish from the sea. The aquaculture side has continued to rise, but it does have to be fed. I understand they are developing non-fish food for aquaculture. There are a few vital amino acids that seem to be absent from vegetable feeds, but they seem to be solving those problems. It is possible that some of the environmental issues might be solved. It does seem that we should be producing the bulk of our fish food from our natural fisheries.

Q43 *Chairman:* Just imagine, if you can, a sort of fantasyland where the Secretary of State comes to you one day and says, "I am feeling particularly brave and farsighted and I really do want your advice on one or two policy initiatives I can take to really set us on the road towards a sustainable fisheries policy." What would you say to him or her?

Dr Horwood: I guess two things after saying that clearly the Secretary of State's view is a lot wiser than mine on these matters. A key thing is to get the capacity in line with the resource and if that happen a lot of the temporal pressures disappear from the system; people's livelihoods are much more secure. I guess the other one is to develop a greater understanding of the role of the local inshore fisheries to the local community, how that interaction is working and do we need to support it and sustain it. This is quite different from our big commercial offshore systems. There are lots of areas where you feel that small fishing is integral to the wellbeing of the community and does one secure a future for that and, if so, how.

Q44 *Viscount Ullswater:* Does that mean you are going to reduce the amount of over ten-metre boats? Is that the sort of area where the biggest modernity comes from, the ten-metre boats plus?

Dr Horwood: Yes, it does.

Q45 *Lord Palmer:* It is not the under ten-metre boats that are causing the environmental or the fish stock problems?

Dr Horwood: The vast bulk of the catch is by the offshore over ten-metre vessels. One can say that 95% of the fishing is by these larger vessels, so that is where

the big capacity issues arise. The inshore fisheries are a hugely complex network of different things. They have problems of safety, they cannot move very far and if there is some vulnerable species there they cannot necessarily avoid them. It may be a target species, for example, some species of ray which are being caught throughout the North Sea and we want to stop people fishing them if we can. This may be a massive problem for a small local less than ten-metre vessel where for two months of the year that is what they catch. They will still be catching a minute amount compared with the other vessels. They do have a different character to them.

Q46 *Chairman:* There is a bit of all that that is pretty depressing. The last time I was at all involved in fisheries policy was ten years ago and even then they were saying things like the TAC-driven system is inadequate, there is a need to reduce fishing effort, there was the hope that technical innovation would ride to the rescue, there was the horror of discards and there was a gap between the scientists and the fishermen. They all seem to be still there!

Dr Horwood: One of the things that I have found really since Net Benefits is that there has been much, much greater co-operation between the fishermen and the scientists. That does not mean at all that you have to agree on all occasions, but I have to say that the dialogue itself is much, much healthier than it was five or ten years ago. It is possible to disagree in a much more normal way. This is quite difficult because it is their livelihoods. We are saying you should cut back by 50% and they are saying, "This is my mortgage you are talking about." That element has improved. We are really working at that; it is really quite a significant priority. Unfortunately so much has been dominated by cod recovery and the issues associated with that that it colours our perception of just about everything else.

Chairman: Thank you very much indeed. I think we are going to have to refer continually to what you have said as we proceed with this inquiry, but it has been enormously helpful. Thank you.

WEDNESDAY 12 MARCH 2008

Present   Arran, E   Jones of Whitchurch, B
               Brookeborough, V   Palmer, L
               Cameron of Dillington, L   Sewel, L (Chairman)
               Dundee, E   Ullswater, V

Examination of Witness

Witness: MR AARON HATCHER, Senior Research Fellow, Centre for the Economics and Management of Aquatic Resources (CEMARE), University of Portsmouth, examined.

Q47 Chairman: Thank you very much indeed for coming along and talking to us and helping us with our inquiry. We are still in the relatively early stages of our inquiry into the reform of the Common Fisheries Policy, and so (let me put this as kindly as I can to my fellow members of the Committee) you should not assume too much knowledge.
Mr Hatcher: Okay.

Q48 Chairman: We are trying to get to grips with what the key issues are in terms of fisheries management and how that can then feed through to possible reform of the Common Fisheries Policy. A couple of formal things. This is a formal evidence-taking session, and so there will be a transcript taken. We will send you that and you will have the opportunity to correct any slips or dangers there, and it is being webcast. We have never actually found anybody who has listened to the webcast, but there is just the possibility that somebody might. The normal procedure is to invite you, if you can, or if you think it is valuable, to give an overview of the main issues, if you want to, and then to go into a question and answer session. I understand that you have seen copies of the brief and the type of questions we are going to ask.
Mr Hatcher: Yes.

Q49 Chairman: Would you like to say anything by way of introduction?
Mr Hatcher: I think it is probably best just to go straight into questions and answers. I will, obviously, briefly introduce myself. My name is Aaron Hatcher; I am a Research Fellow in the Economics Department at the University of Portsmouth. I have been interested in fisheries management for some years now and I am a member of the European Union Scientific, Technical and Economic Committee for Fisheries.
Chairman: I am going to ask the Earl of Arran to come in with, I suppose, the quick Yorker!
Earl of Arran: It is a very erudite and closely worded paper you have put before us. I find it really terribly difficult to understand. Can you explain simply what you are trying to get at, firstly. Are the suggestions that you make actually working anywhere at the

moment? I am not quite sure where we are on all your extremely interesting ideas and which governments across the world have actually paid attention and are putting them into effect, but, first of all, very simply, what are you trying to get at?

Q50 Chairman: In other words what is the big challenge and how do you get there?
Mr Hatcher: The challenge for fisheries management in general?

Q51 Chairman: Yes.
Mr Hatcher: I suppose managing fisheries has two objectives. The first one is perhaps an obvious one, which is to limit the scale of exploitation of fish stocks in such a way that we do get a yield of fish but that this yield is sustainable into the future, which implies that we do not reduce fish stocks down to levels which are not going to give a yield. From an economic perspective, the other objective of managing fisheries is to avoid economic waste, which is to try and get as much economic value as we can from fish stocks without wasting resources in the process of catching fish. Economic waste can be a result of no management, but it can also be a result of bad management or inappropriate management.

Q52 Earl of Arran: Are the economic ideas that are contained in your paper actually working?
Mr Hatcher: I am sorry; I do not know which paper you are referring to.

Q53 Chairman: Our internal specialist adviser, Mr Dillon, has produced a briefing for us which I think draws upon certain contributions that you have made from time to time.
Mr Hatcher: Are you referring to the report that we prepared for Defra?

Q54 Chairman: Yes.
Mr Hatcher: Which was primarily concerned with quota management. Broadly, economists tend to favour quota management over effort management and tend to favour as much flexibility and tradeability in quotas as possible in order that fisheries are as economically efficient as possible. The

most well-known form of the economic approach to quota management is what are referred as to ITQ systems (individual transferable quota systems), which are used with apparent great success in a number of countries, including Australia, New Zealand, Canada, Iceland, the Netherlands and a few other countries as well.

Q55 *Earl of Arran:* So your recommended solutions are working in some parts of the world?
Mr Hatcher: It seems so, yes.

Q56 *Chairman:* So why did we not adopt them? Why have they not been universally picked up?
Mr Hatcher: One would have to say that ITQ systems are not appropriate for every case, for various reasons. I think there is often political resistance to the idea of being able to trade in access to a natural resource in the same way that somebody people object to the idea of trading rights to emit pollution, for example. There is no economic argument against having tradeability in quotas—the economic arguments are all in favour rather than against—so I think resistance, where it occurs, is often political.

Q57 *Viscount Brookeborough:* Is not the success of virtually any of these quota systems -at least in the paper we have got from New Zealand—the enforcement?
Mr Hatcher: Enforcement is a big problem for, and a key to, success in any fisheries management system. If you try to apply regulations and you cannot enforce them, then clearly they are not going to work. The other key to a successful ITQ system is that trade is easy, that quota is readily divisible and readily tradable. I think one of the problems we have in this country is that quota can be traded but it is rather difficult and costly and cumbersome to do so. What is interesting in this country is that the quota management system was never set up as a tradeable quota system, but the fishermen, if you like, have voted with their feet, or their wallets, and tradeability has developed despite the design of the system, rather than as a consequence.

Q58 *Chairman:* You said you preferred quota management to effort management.
Mr Hatcher: I would observe that economists in general would prefer to control output rather than try to control inputs, which is what we mean by effort management.

Q59 *Chairman:* Why?
Mr Hatcher: Because it gives the maximum amount of operational flexibility to the industry. At the end of the day, we are always trying to restrict output. It is catches that impact upon the fish stock, and so, whatever measures we try to put in place, the ultimate

aim is to have some leverage, some control, over what has been taken out of the fish stock, and it is generally preferable to try to do that directly rather than indirectly. If we try to do it indirectly by placing controls on engine power, the size of nets, days at sea, the size of vessels, et cetera, et cetera, we have to try and second-guess the relationship between those different types of input and catches, which is very difficult to do, and it imposes a lot of unwelcome regulation on the industry. Even if we can estimate the relationships between inputs and catches, these are likely to change over time, particularly with technological advances, and so we are continually having to try and revise these guesses of what is actually going on.

Q60 *Chairman:* If you are putting it all on one, if the emphasis is on quota measurement, that inevitably leads to the issue of discards, does it not?
Mr Hatcher: Discards are an issue, but then discards will occur in fisheries even in the absence of management or even where we are trying to manage effort rather than catch. Fishermen will always discard a portion of the catch, because once you have got something in your net, you have a choice: you handle it, you sort it and gut it, (if it is finfish) and, most importantly, you have to ice it and store it, and this is costly, and so every time a fisherman catches anything he is always weighing up the likely gain from retaining it and landing it as set against the costs of keeping it on board and handling it. So, discarding is not only a problem of quota management systems, it is an inherent problem of any fishery's management system and even in the absence of management; but that being said, yes, the problem of discarding is an issue that a quota management system has to face up to and try to deal with, and countries like New Zealand and Iceland, which have fairly sophisticated quota management systems, do employ a variety of measures to try and minimise discarding.

Q61 *Chairman:* Can you give us some examples?
Mr Hatcher: Basically, trying to create incentives for fishermen to land catch rather than discard it. The systems have a variety of mechanisms that enable or that help fishermen to balance what they want to catch and land with the amount of quota they have available. The more flexible the system is to help the fishermen balance their catches and quotas, the less incentive there is for fishermen to throw fish overboard because they do not have quota for it, which is one of the biggest causes of discarding in a quota management system. The more flexible a system is, the less incentive there will be to discard. Discards are actually not allowed in New Zealand and Iceland. They are allowed in Australia. They are, of course, allowed in the European Union.

Q62 *Viscount Ullswater:* Is that because the fisheries are single-species fisheries or mixed fisheries?

Mr Hatcher: I think most of the New Zealand fisheries, or at least a lot of them, are mixed fisheries. There is a huge number of species in New Zealand that are subject to quotas and, hence, an ITQ system, so new Zealand seems to have dealt with the problem of mixed fisheries. Discard bans are all very well, but, obviously, they can be extremely difficult to enforce. It is hard enough to enforce controls on what is actually landed in port. To enforce controls on what fishermen do at sea is extremely difficult. If you have a very small number of large boats, you could maybe put an observer or an enforcement officer on every boat, but for the most part this is just too expensive to do. There are ways of encouraging fishermen to change their behaviour as well—encourage them to use more selective gear, to avoid certain areas at the times of year when they are likely to catch small, juvenile fish, for example—but, as far as I can tell from the literature, the discard rates in New Zealand and Iceland are relatively low, although, apparently, in Australia discarding is more of a problem in some of the fisheries there. Whether that is because there is no discard ban or whether the relationship is the other way round, I am not entirely sure.

Q63 *Baroness Jones of Whitchurch:* We have been touching on this anyway, but I just wanted to perhaps allow you to reinforce the point you are making on quota management and the advantages of tradeable rather than fixed quotas, which you have argued in favour of. For the record, it would be helpful if you could tell us specifically what you think are the advantages and disadvantages of tradeable quotas. What is so good about them?

Mr Hatcher: You can look at this is in various ways. One thing I would say in a general sense is that, if you have tradeable quotas, then the individual fishermen decide what quotas they need and should have for their fishing operation. If you have a system of fixed quotas or any other system that is decided by administrators sitting in Whitehall or wherever, somebody else is telling each vessel how much quota it should have. If it is based on some sort of historical catch history, then it may at one point in time approximate what the vessel actually needs, but it is likely to change over time very quickly, and fisheries are very stochastic and unpredictable, and so the likelihood that a fixed quota or a set of fixed quotas is going to match exactly what a vessel needs in order to operate profitably and efficiently is very small; but by making quotas tradeable, the fishermen themselves can decide how much quota they need in order to operate in the way they want to operate. Once again, it is interesting that the UK industry has chosen to trade in quota.

Q64 *Baroness Jones of Whitchurch:* Can I come back to the point that was made earlier about enforcement, if we are talking about the potential downsides of that sort of scheme. We heard last week from scientific advisers to Defra that in fact there is an awful lot of fishing rights trading going on out there—different countries buying and selling the rights to fish in our grounds and so on—and so already we have got quite a complex picture of who is out there and who is fishing for what. If you started trading in quotas as well, is not the enforcement going to just become unmanageable: nobody would really know who is fishing for what, who is legitimate and who is not?

Mr Hatcher: Enforcement apparently works very well in countries like New Zealand and in Iceland. There are a number of issues you have raised in your question. There is no provision in the Common Fisheries Policy for international trade in quota. There are bilateral agreements between Member States to exchange quota following the annual quota setting round, but there is no international trade in quota. The whole idea of relative stability is that Member States are given quota allocations and that is for the Member State to do what they see fit with. If you are thinking about quota hopping, that is really a different issue. That is the issue of whether a United Kingdom based business can be bought by someone from another EU Member State, and there is nothing we can do under EU law to prevent that. That is the same for any business, whether it is fishing or not.

Q65 *Baroness Jones of Whitchurch:* I think the point about all of that was how do you track it and enforce it, when potentially that is already happening, and if you allow trading of quotas as well, who is going to manage that effectively?

Mr Hatcher: What generally happens is that the administration, whether it is the Government Fisheries Ministry or an agency employed by the Ministry, basically keeps a real-time record of what quota vessels have, which in turn dictates what they are allow to catch. I think in Iceland the catch records are transmitted to the Ministry twice daily, electronically, from the ports of landing, so there is a completely up-to-date, real-time record of what individual vessels have caught and how much quota they have, and so it is just a case of enforcing that, which is probably a bit easier than the task that Defra have at the moment where we have this rather complex system involving the producer organisations and a lot of so-called "quota swaps" that are actually mostly reflecting quota leasing that is going on between individual fishermen. The only way quota can, in reality, be moved around is via these quota swaps between producer organisations that Defra has to try and keep track of but nobody really knows what any particular vessel is allowed to catch at any one time because all the producer organisations have completely different ways of allocating quota to their membership. Some just use monthly limits from a pool, some have individual quota systems for some species and it is all very complicated. A fully-fledged ITQ system would, I think, if anything, be easier to enforce than what happens at the moment. The international dimension of the CFP inevitably makes everything a bit messier than it is for countries that are in the happy situation of having their own EEZ to control, which, of course, applies to Iceland and New Zealand. We still have to rely on records coming back from ports in northern Spain for some UK registered vessels, but that is a problem that we have to deal with under any management system. I am sorry; does that answer your question?

Q66 Baroness Jones of Whitchurch: Yes. Are there any other disadvantages to the tradeable system?
Mr Hatcher: From an economic perspective, I can see no disadvantages. People may dislike the idea of trading in quota for ethical or political reasons, but from an economic perspective there is no disadvantage to trading in quota. Generally economic inefficiency follows from the inability to trade rather than the ability to trade.
Chairman: I think we are going into more detail on this area.

Q67 Lord Palmer: I have to say, I am getting slightly confused about this whole quota system; I do not know if I am the only one around the table. Can you try and explain in very simple terms how a tradeable system of quotas might actually work in reality and whether it would be best to operate it at individual vessel level or at another level, such as that of the producer organisations? You have mentioned Iceland and New Zealand several times. Have we a lot to learn from the way their fisheries are managed, do you think?
Mr Hatcher: Yes, I think so, as I referred to before, given the extra dimension of having to operate within the CFP. I cannot go into huge amounts of detail about the day-to-day operation of, say, the Iceland or the New Zealand system, but they appear to be fairly sophisticated and, in each case, there are a number of mechanisms in operation other than just the ability to trade in quota that assist fishermen to balance their catches and their quotas. Basically, the idea is that a tradeable quota system operates at the level of individual vessels, so that each vessel or each company buys and sells quota so that it has the right amount of quota that it needs for the catches that it wants to achieve.

Q68 Lord Palmer: Does this happen on a very regular basis?

Mr Hatcher: Essentially there are two types of trading. There is trade in permanent quota, which is not actually tonnage of fish, it is usually a percentage of the annual total allowable catch. In our case it would be the annual quotas that we get from Brussels. Vessels have their permanent quota holdings, which they hold in perpetuity, if you like, but most of the trade on a day-to-day basis is within year leases, so it is trade in actual tonnage of fish just for the current year so that fish that is leased will go back to its original ownership after the end of that year.

Q69 Chairman: Is there any way of making it simple? This is the nonsense question, I am afraid. Is there any way of getting instantaneous tradeability. I put my net in the sea and it comes up with haddock that I do not have cover for, and I get on the phone and say, "Look, I want some haddock quota." Is there a market I can go to and there and then get quota cover for the haddock I have got in my net?
Mr Hatcher: To some extent that happens already, but, yes, that is the way it operates. Big companies will have quota managers. Other smaller companies, or the single vessels, will rely on buying and selling quota via brokers. Essentially, the broker just puts buyers and sellers in touch with each other, and it works in a similar way to a stock market. Some countries have set up central quota exchanges, but I do not think these have been particularly successful because the institutions that have arisen spontaneously, if you like, seem to be perfectly efficient and capable of dealing with trading on a real-time basis. Particularly with the Internet, it is very easy having systems whereby buyers and sellers instantaneously are in touch with each other. Also, the Internet facilitates communication so well that fishermen know what the price of quota is at any moment in time and can make a decision about whether they want to buy more quota or stop fishing.

Q70 Lord Palmer: As we are sitting here, quota will actually be being traded at the moment?
Mr Hatcher: At this moment in this country?

Q71 Lord Palmer: Yes.
Mr Hatcher: It is, yes. This has already happened to some extent in this country, but, as I said, what economists tend to refer to as transaction costs, which are the tangible and the intangible costs of trading quota, appear to be rather burdensome at the moment. They could be made a lot less so if the system were actually designed for quota trading rather than accommodating quota trading, which is what happens at the moment. Quota trading is going on in this country but it goes on under the guise of swaps of quota between producers' organisations.

Q72 *Lord Palmer:* Going back to the Chairman's point, if he suddenly found he had an awful lot of haddock and he could not trade the quota, then presumably they would just get discarded?

Mr Hatcher: Yes, if for some reason he was unable to buy any more haddock quota, then he would either have to discard it or there may well be some system in place for him to land the fish without quota. I am not talking about what is going on at the moment, I am talking about the sort of thing that happens in other countries. There are various mechanisms that could enable him to deal with that problem after he has landed and sold the fish. He might be given a few days, a week, or a month to try and find enough quota retrospectively to cover those landings, he may be able to borrow against his quota allocation for the following year, he may be able to land the fish and sell it and pay a tax to the Government, some notional amount roughly equivalent to what he would have paid if he had been able to buy quota. Countries like New Zealand have a variety of mechanisms that they have fine-tuned over the years to try and minimise the problem of people not having quota, but there is something more fundamental that managers can do, which is, in a multi-species fishery, to try, within reason, to set quotas in more or less the proportion in which the fish are going to appear in the fisherman's net to avoid the situation that we have historically had in the North Sea where the saithe quota is just out of all proportion to the quotas for other species in the white fish fisheries. There are a number of ways in which these sorts of problems can be dealt with, but do not for a moment think that any of these problems disappear if you have a system of fixed (non-tradeable) quotas. If anything, the problems are likely to be worse.

Q73 *Baroness Jones of Whitchurch:* As an economist, surely the tendency will be for all the really big fisheries, the big companies, to absorb all the quotas and squeeze out the little guys. Is that not what is going to happen?

Mr Hatcher: That is the fear that is often raised. It does not seem to be what has happened in practice. If you introduce an ITQ system and it is very well enforced, you may then have some contraction in industry capacity, but if that happens that probably should have happened anyway because that implies that your previous level of capacity was too high—that is one thing—but the idea that all the quota will be bought up by a small number of big companies is rather unlikely and certainly does not seem to have happened in other countries to the extent that some people might have feared. There are a number of reasons why small fishing vessels may, for some stocks, be more profitable than large vessels, because they can target larger fish and land them in a better condition and serve higher value markets, and so it is

not necessarily the case that very large companies are going to be able to outbid small fishermen for quota. This does not seem to have been a concern that has been realised in practice. Interestingly, I was looking at a paper the other day by somebody writing in Norway where they have opted to have fixed-vessel quotas, which are not tradeable—they are tradeable, but you can only buy and sell the whole quota, you cannot buy and sell a part of the quota—and they are becoming more concerned about the loss of smaller vessels in Norway because it is only the bigger companies that can afford to buy and sell quota in such big lumps, if you like. Interestingly, for political reasons they have tried to avoid structural adjustments in the industry, and yet it seems to be having the opposite consequences to what they intended by not having tradeable quotas.

Q74 *Viscount Ullswater:* Before we move away from quotas, I suppose the quota is divided between the boats under ten metres and boats over ten metres. In your system of ITQs, are you suggesting that quota can be tradeable across any divide, whether it is a large boat, a small boat or in between small boats or anywhere across the whole application of quotas?

Mr Hatcher: Ideally, yes. I think in Iceland all the small boats are now part of the quota management system, and I think in New Zealand as well.

Viscount Brookeborough: The rights-based management that exists here: what is your view on how it actually works? Are you committed to a change in our system here?

Q75 *Chairman:* And is the present system making it efficient?

Mr Hatcher: I would just like to say, this is not my system or my commitment; I am speaking as an economist.

Q76 *Viscount Brookeborough:* In your view?

Mr Hatcher: In my view, I can see no reason why the UK should not move towards an ITQ system.

Q77 *Viscount Brookeborough:* And not a fixed quota allocation, although I notice that at times you said "a fixed quota allocation that is not tradeable", so there are fixed quota allocations that can be tradeable. You said it earlier.

Mr Hatcher: By a tradeable quota system I mean that, whatever quota you have, you can trade in units of a tonne, or 500 kilos, or five kilos—I do not know what the lower limit would be—but that whatever quota you have is perfectly divisible. You can buy and sell parts of it; that is what I mean.

Q78 *Viscount Brookeborough:* I notice in the paper that we have got from you that the great the majority of the sector (and this is talking about the fishermen) appeared to be happy with their POs quota management. Are you disappointed that you are failing to bring the fishermen round to your point of view? A short while ago you were suggesting that the producer organisations are not the most efficient way of managing.

Mr Hatcher: They may be able to play an extremely efficient role in a quota management system, whether it is tradeable or not. I am not saying that they are a cause of inefficiency, I am saying that the present system—

Q79 *Viscount Brookeborough:* But they are part of our system which you say could be much more efficient?

Mr Hatcher: In a tradeable quota system, the producer organisations could assist the efficiency of the system by providing a quota brokerage service for their members, by holding amounts of quota for troublesome bycatch species that members could then lease on a short term basis, by generally providing an administrative service to their members in much the same way that they do now, except now they have to work within this swap system. Some years ago the producer organisations were given quota allocations on behalf of their membership, which they tended to just hold as a pool of quota and would say to their members, "You can catch five tonnes a month of this, " or whatever. Increasingly the POs have moved towards managing individual quota systems internally, so large parts of the industry are already operating under individual quota systems, but the trading that fishermen need to do is made, I think, more difficult than it needs to be. The finding that you refer to, I think, came from a survey that we did at the time, and this was a few years ago now. I think that survey also found that a large part of the industry wanted more flexibility in their ability to trade quota, as I recall.

Q80 *Viscount Ullswater:* I can see that producer organisations, which are dealing with relatively large amounts of quota because they are dealing with the over ten-metre boats, if I am right in thinking that.

Mr Hatcher: At the moment I think there are some POs that have under ten-metre members but, because of their involvement in the quota management system, they basically represent over ten-metre boats. There is nothing to stop under ten-metre boats becoming a member.

Q81 *Viscount Ullswater:* Because they are dealing with relatively large amounts of quota, I can see a simple exchange being set up in order to deal will that—that is not beyond the wit of man, especially now with technology—but with the smaller vessels, is that more complicated? I know they do not catch the

volume of fish, but is that more complicated to trade in ITQs?

Mr Hatcher: I suppose the smaller your operation is, the more burdensome quota trading is likely to be, but I think quota brokers and POs and any organisation could help small inshore fishermen to trade in quota. I cannot see a reason why that should not happen.

Q82 *Viscount Ullswater:* The reason I am asking this is because it seems so ridiculous to catch good, saleable fish and tip them over the side because you happen to be over the quota for that particular species at that particular moment when you are landing your catch?

Mr Hatcher: Yes, but that is what happens with fixed quotas as well.

Q83 *Viscount Ullswater:* I can see that. It seems worse.

Mr Hatcher: The only way that is not going to happen is if you have no control over catches; so you are slightly between a rock and a hard place, I guess. If you have a quota management system which requires fishermen to have quota for what they catch and that is enforced, providing you can achieve some stability in the system and keep up the enforcement, then over time the catching capacity of your fleet should come more or less into line with the quotas. Under any sort of quota management system, if there are vessels that are only profitable because they have to land fish without quota, that is a sure sign that your management is not working, I would say.

Q84 *Lord Cameron of Dillington:* I can see that the ITQ system within the TAC regime is probably the most efficient way of managing it, not least because if you have actually paid for a quota then you are going to have to self-police it.

Mr Hatcher: That is also used as an argument in favour of ITQs.

Q85 *Lord Cameron of Dillington:* That is what I am saying, not least because it invokes a self-policing regime. I just want to question the effectiveness of the whole TAC regime itself. Bearing in mind that over 80% of the stocks evaluated by ICs are over exploited, the EU fleet capacity is 40% too large—possibly more than 50% in some species of the TAC is discarded or illegally marketed and the TAC itself is often set at over 50% of what the scientists actually recommend—are we not just fiddling with our roe and bones here? You mentioned various alternatives, such as the limitation on effort, and I can see that that is probably correct because people reorganise their time at sea in order to make it more effective and you have got technology creep as well in that respect. You mentioned more selective gear—I think that definitely comes under the heading of fiddling—but you did not mention, for instance, marine conservation areas where, with modern technology, you know instantly whether a boat is in or outside a conservation area and you can rigidly enforce that much more effectively than probably any other system. I was just wondering, as an alternative, whether there is any mechanism of quota'ing the actual fishing capacity in a fleet, because of this business of the fact that they are 40% too big in capacity. I am wondering whether you would like to comment on either of those two alternative methods to the whole TAC regime, which to my mind is not working.

Mr Hatcher: First of all, I would not want to defend any TAC setting approach that exceeds the levels that scientists recommend. That is for politicians to resolve.

Q86 *Lord Cameron of Dillington:* Quite.

Mr Hatcher: I think the problems that we have of over exploitation of stocks is partly due to that. I would not want to expand too much on this, but I think it is partly a problem of enforcement which is exacerbated by the international nature of the regime that we are working with. I have often heard the view expressed from fishermen: "Why should we comply with regulations when fishermen from X country are fishing in the same grounds for the same stocks and are not complying with their regulations or, indeed, are not subject to the sort of the regulations that we are?" I have heard the same arguments from fishery managers. Again, I would not want to expand too much on this, but fishery managers saying, "Why should we make extra efforts to enforce regulations when X country is not doing anything about their fishermen?" We have an international dimension that is difficult. On capacity: I think over-capacity is really a symptom of the problem rather than a cause. It is ineffective management that allows capacity to get too big. We had years and years of so-called Multi-Annual Guidance Programmes under the Common Fisheries Policy up until 2002, and now we have the same sort of thing by another name, but the sort of structural policy objectives for reducing capacity are so small in relation to the size of the fleets that technological progress would compensate easily for any changes in capacity. At the moment the EU is very concerned with new ways in which to measure capacity and to assess whether capacity is in line with fishing opportunities or TACs, if you like. It is very difficult to see how that is going to produce anything very worthwhile because of this problem of measuring capacity and measuring the relationship between nominal measures of capacity and trying to achieve sustainable exploitation. What really matters, as I said before, is the level of exploitation, is the catches. If we can measure capacity according

to output, which is what we mean by capacity, if we can really measure and control that, we can enforce a TAC, in which case there is no need to measure and enforce the capacity. If the only way we can measure capacity is by measuring inputs, like the size of vessels, the engine power, how many days they spend at sea, then, as I said before, we are trying to assess some proxy for the relationship between inputs and output.

Q87 *Lord Cameron of Dillington:* What about marine conservation areas, no-go areas?

Mr Hatcher: To some extent this is probably a question better directed at biologists. All the analyses that I have looked at suggest that if you relied on marine protected areas as your major management measure, you would have to close off something like three-quarters of the North Sea, or more, in order to achieve the sort of objectives that you would be looking at. I think my appreciation is that closed areas, or marine protected areas, have a role to play, perhaps, in avoiding sensitive habitats, nursery grounds, spawning grounds at various times of year but will never be a major plank in the management of fisheries, unless you just do not want to have fisheries, in which case, you just make the whole of the North Sea a protected area.

Q88 *Chairman:* Can I raise one issue? It seems to me that there is an underlying problem of the structure of the industry, and that is that it is structurally over capitalised: there is too much capital in fishing boats.

Mr Hatcher: I think that is generally the case for fisheries that are in trouble, yes.

Q89 *Chairman:* The question then has to be: what is the explanation as to why there is that level of over-capitalisation: because it leads, obviously, to inefficiencies on return? Why is the persistent level of over-capitalisation in fishing there? What could be done to get rid of it?

Mr Hatcher: Essentially, it is there because management is relatively ineffective. It is effective management that will bring capacity into line. We should not really need to worry about capacity. That is a problem for the industry to determine. If you can control the level of outputs, then market forces will decide on the right level of capacity.

Q90 *Chairman:* That must mean, then, that there is something going on with the outputs that we are not aware of to justify the continued level of investment?

Mr Hatcher: It implies that the level of output is greater than we would like it to be.

Q91 *Chairman:* Or that it formerly was.
Mr Hatcher: Or that it formerly was.

Q92 *Viscount Ullswater:* Do you think there is a big problem with illegally landed fish, illegally traded fish? Ben Bradshaw thinks there is a big problem.
Mr Hatcher: In general, yes.

Q93 *Viscount Ullswater:* With the Common Fisheries Policy.
Mr Hatcher: Yes.

Q94 *Viscount Ullswater:* You obviously cannot quantify what you do not know, but can you make a stab at the amount of fish that is traded in percentage terms? Is it 2%, is it 15%?
Mr Hatcher: It would vary a lot from one fishery to another, from one country to another, but if you looked at the reports of the ICES Working Groups, I think they make estimates of the level of illegal catch and I think for some fisheries it is very large. I could not give you a figure but I think you could easily find figures through ICES.

Q95 *Viscount Brookeborough:* I was definitely quite impressed by the New Zealand submission, and you have mentioned them as having perhaps a better system than our own for running their fishery. However, you placed very little emphasis on ways of avoiding discards, and the New Zealanders state quite clearly that the only way that they are able to operate the remainder of their system is by having discards illegal. I think earlier you said you would not like to see them being made illegal?
Mr Hatcher: No, I do not think I said that.

Q96 *Viscount Brookeborough:* I thought you said you would much prefer to persuade people to come in with their catch than actually making discards illegal?
Mr Hatcher: No, I was simply observing that discards were illegal in some countries and legal in others.

Q97 *Viscount Brookeborough:* Do you think making them illegal and monitoring it and, therefore, having more control over the trading would be the right answer?
Mr Hatcher: Yes, if it is possible to enforce, then make discards illegal.

Q98 *Viscount Brookeborough:* Thank you.
Mr Hatcher: The enforcement problem still remains, but to explicitly say that you must discard over quota fish is perhaps inviting fishermen to discard where perhaps it might be better not to invite them to discard, so, yes, I would agree.

Q99 *Chairman:* Turning to discard, they are uneconomic fish, are they not: fish in which there is no market value?
Mr Hatcher: Yes, to take it to the extreme, they are going to discard stones and rocks and seaweed, they are going to discard starfish and sea urchins, so they just work their way up until they are looking at small cod and haddock and whatever else. If there is no-one to stop them, then there is an incentive to throw those fish overboard if there is no market for them.

Q100 *Viscount Ullswater:* In its communication on rights-based management, the European Commission highlights one or two difficulties: relative stability, concentration of rights (in terms of both ownership and geography), initial allocation and duration of rights, discard problems (including highgrading) and the need for efficient control and enforcement. How do you evaluate those? Do you see those as barriers to the management of fisheries?
Mr Hatcher: I think we have touched on all these issues, and I think they are issues, but I do not see them as barriers to having rights-based management, if that is the expression you want to use. I do not like "rights-based management" as a term, because all management is rights-based. You have a right to fish at all if you have a licence; you have a right to a fixed amount of fish if you have a fixed quota. As soon as you start managing fisheries, you are introducing rights, and the flip-side of that is that you are denying rights to others, otherwise you just have a free-for-all, but they are all issues to be considered. Relative stability and the issue of so-called quota hopping is one that is peculiar to the CFP, but otherwise they are all issues that have had to be confronted in other countries as well and I am sure there are lots of lessons that we could learn from other countries.

Q101 *Viscount Ullswater:* You seem to almost have this sort of silver bullet approach of saying that, if we really got to grips with ITQs, if we really managed it, if we really had a communicable system which was flexible and could be retrospective, could just deal with the problems as we face them on a day-to-day basis, we would not over exploit the resource, we would not have so many discards. Am I being just too naive about it?
Mr Hatcher: I think we would probably be moving in the right direction. Where success has been attributed to ITQ systems there is sometimes a suspicion that it is the increased focus on enforcement perhaps almost as much as the change in the system that has been helpful in improving the health of fisheries, but, yes, I would feel generally positive about moves in that direction.

Q102 *Chairman:* We have talked about tradeable quotas. What else is tradeable: tradeable effort, tradeable rights to fish in particular areas. Are there examples of trades in effort and trades in right to fish elsewhere in the fishing regime?

Mr Hatcher: We have had trade in licences almost since licensing began in this country, which also involves access to areas. We have a large and complex licensing system, perhaps less complex than it used to be, but it has always been more or less tradeable.

Q103 *Chairman:* Is that a good thing or a bad thing?

Mr Hatcher: I think generally it is a good thing. There are lots of issues, but there are other issues to do with introducing tradeability which are perhaps worth thinking about. Rights to fish, essentially, give you a right to a stream of profits, because fishing is, potentially at least, very profitable, and so where quotas, for example, acquire value, that value represents the stream of profits, economic profits, that can be derived from those rights to fish. In most countries that have introduced ITQ systems, and this includes the UK even though it does not have an ITQ system proper, the way in which the initial distribution of rights to fish has been made is basically to give the rights to those to already in the industry in proportion to some indicator of their involvement in the fishery, usually their track record or catch history, or whatever you want to call it. Once those rights have been given away in that way, then the economic value of the fishery has been parcelled up and handed from the public to the fishing industry. That is what economists refer to as "resource rent". That profit that can be earned from the fishery has been given away into private hands. That is more or less the same for every country that has introduced an ITQ system, but that is usually a decision that has been taken for political reasons, not for economic reasons. That is not the way we approach things with other natural resources, oil or gas, for example, where exploitation rights are generally either leased off or subject to royalties, or whatever. Usually the state, on behalf of the public, tries to capture some of that resource rent for the public good, if you like. That is a normative issue that is not on the EU list of things to be thought about.

Q104 *Viscount Ullswater:* That could be dealt with by permits or licences, could it not, by charging for them.

Mr Hatcher: It could be dealt with by some sort of what are referred to as "rent capture mechanisms". There are ways in which some of this rent could be captured, yes, as a first step, to cover some of the costs of management and policing. There are a whole lot of design issues.

Q105 *Chairman:* You have tried these arguments with the fishermen, have you?

Mr Hatcher: The fishermen are aware of arguments for cost recovery, I think. They have a cost recovery scheme in New Zealand. One problem with rent capture is that, once you have given out the rights, effectively—the quota rights were given to the industry some years ago in this country—once you have first-round owners of fishing rights that have sold up and moved on or retired, they have taken that wealth with them; so the poor chap who has bought second-hand the fishing rights, if you start taxing him to try and extract some of the rent, then he is paying twice. That sort of thing would have to be introduced probably gradually rather than as any sort of windfall tax, but that is another issue, yes.

Q106 *Lord Cameron of Dillington:* I would like to touch on some of the socio-economic effects involved here. First of all, do I surmise from your answer to my earlier question that you probably would prefer to see the TAC, for instance, which currently is set higher than the scientific recommendations in many cases because of socio-economic politico influences, you would prefer to see the socio-economic problems perhaps caused by a reduction in capacity, for instance, to be dealt with by other methods rather than watering down what is a conservation and efficiency allowable catch? That is the first part of the question. The second part is that I was just wondering where ITQs fit into this in terms of their effect on overall employment in relation to the existing system?

Mr Hatcher: I do think that for too long fisheries policy has been used, perhaps by other countries more than the UK, as an instrument of social policy in order to maintain levels of fishing employment, which has perhaps not helped achieve conservation objectives. Yes, I think that effective and efficient management should come first and socio-economic concerns should be dealt with in working with the system rather than using the system to try and achieve employment objectives, for example. You probably cannot have an efficient and sustainable fishery and keep high levels of employment in coastal regions in the way that maybe we have to some extent so far, but most ITQ systems do constrain tradeability to some extent. There are usually limits on how much quota of any particular stock can be owned by one company, there may be restrictions on tradeability within certain geographical zones, and there are various ways that social concerns have been built into quota management systems.

Q107 *Earl of Dundee:* Lord Brookeborough mentioned the discard methods of New Zealand. What kind of practical adjustments would we have to make here if we were to adopt quite a number of details within the New Zealand Government's quota-based management model?

Mr Hatcher: If I understand what you are saying, we would have to have the flexibility in quota catch balancing that they have in countries like New Zealand, where you have a certain time period after you have landed fish in order to retrospectively, for example, balance the amount of quota you have with your catches.

Q108 *Earl of Dundee:* Would you recommend that here or not?

Mr Hatcher: Broadly, I suppose, yes, but you cannot really look at these individual mechanisms in isolation. They are part of a system that is designed for having quota tradeability.

Q109 *Lord Cameron of Dillington:* Of course the advantage New Zealand has is that it is a single country managing a fishery that really, apart from possibly Australia, nobody else does. Within your whole system would you envisage a European-wide ITQ system or a regionally-based ITQ system, either at national level or even lower?

Mr Hatcher: I am really thinking of the approach towards quota management at a national level.

Q110 *Lord Cameron of Dillington:* At a national level?

Mr Hatcher: Yes. I have not really thought long and hard about international trading in quotas.

Q111 *Lord Cameron of Dillington:* Even within a region such as the North Sea, for instance. You do not think you could manage? What about Norway?

Mr Hatcher: As things stand at the moment, it would seem to just make everything more complicated than it needs to be. To some extent there is international trading in quotas *de facto* because of Dutch interests buying up UK fishing licences, and quota allocations. The beam trawler fleet that used to operate out of Lowestoft now operates out of Ijmuiden or wherever else, but it is still UK quota.

Q112 *Viscount Brookeborough:* When you say "national", do you mean UK or EU, because, after all, this is a common fisheries policy.

Mr Hatcher: The UK is still—

Q113 *Viscount Brookeborough:* You were considering national.

Mr Hatcher: No.

Q114 *Viscount Brookeborough:* We cannot operate in isolation; therefore you are talking about EU?

Mr Hatcher: No, the UK has complete competence to manage its quotas. The Common Fisheries Policy is not really a management system; it is an allocation system. It does impose a number of common technical conservation measures, closed areas and things, and it has a terrible structural policy and it has a marketing policy, but it is not a fisheries management system. The CFP allocates national quotas from the TACs. It is completely up to the Member States to do what it wants to do with the national quotas. The Netherlands has had an ITQ system for some time now.

Q115 *Chairman:* Have you got any final words of wisdom for us?

Mr Hatcher: None at all, no!

Q116 *Chairman:* Is there a secret to getting fishermen to buy in? One of the problems, of course, is that there is a tension between the scientists or the biologists on the one side and the fishermen on the other side. There are tensions between, obviously, the fish processors as well. Is there any means by which the fishermen can buy in and have confidence in the system and, therefore, see this working in their interests rather than against their interests?

Mr Hatcher: I do not see why not. The experience in New Zealand, for example, is that there are a number of quota management companies, which are not really companies, they are more co-operatives, which are just basically quota owners coming together, and they work with the scientists to have input into stock assessments, they work with managers and they contribute towards the costs of management. It seems that there is buy-in, if you like, in the New Zealand system. I see no reason why there could not be a similar culture change here.

Q117 *Chairman:* That is interesting. I think that might be one of the keys. Thank you very much indeed. I have to say, I was extremely worried by your continual reference to New Zealand, because I fear that some of my colleagues will now argue we need to visit, whereas the best they are going to get is a trip to Peterhead!

Mr Hatcher: The focus on New Zealand was partly because it is one of the best documented systems; there is more literature available on it. Also I was specifically pointed towards New Zealand by your advisor, I believe.

Chairman: Thank you very much indeed for your time.

WEDNESDAY 19 MARCH 2008

Present   Arran, E   Palmer, L
               Brookeborough, V   Plumb, L
               Cameron of Dillington, L   Sewel, L (Chairman)
               Dundee, E of   Ullswater, V
               Jones of Whitchurch, B

Memorandum by the Scottish Fishermen's Federation

Formed in 1973 and comprising eight fishermen's Associations from all round the coast of Scotland and the Northern Isles, the Scottish Fishermen's Federation is the primary voice of Scotland's catching industry. It does not represent the aquaculture industry. Thank you for the opportunity to respond to the call for evidence for the Inquiry to review the progress, since it was reformed in 2002, of the Common Fisheries Policy.

In any discussion or inspection of the CFP, there is a tendency for the debate to focus on the past, in particular, on the shape of the arrangements at inception. The great UK distant water fleets had by that time already almost met their effective end at the hands of National limits declared by coastal states outside the European Treaty. The CFP arrangements "relative stability" subsequently created on historical track record within the European limits (in the UK's case that of the "inshore" fleets) began with a fishing industry much reduced overall from its then recent past. This has made it superficially easy to ascribe the reduction and all subsequent ills of the UK fishing industry to the CFP; this is not particularly helpful at the present stage of CFP development. Whilst the CFP has certainly not met its overall objective of sustainable development and must not be falsely defended as having done so, it must be clearly understood that international arrangements to govern effectively the common participants in an industry using common resource are vital.

It is noted that this Inquiry is into the progress of the CFP *since it was reformed in 2002* and this will govern the comments submitted.

CONSERVATION/MANAGEMENT

1. The new methods introduced in 2002 of ensuring conservation and sustainability of fish stocks have had mixed success.

Recovery Plans. The Cod Recovery Plan is perhaps the most reported on and visible example. Whilst there is recent scientific evidence of recovery, the plan has failed to meet its own main criterion of success—a dramatic year on year increase in the biomass of spawning fish. This has resulted in the automatic application of severe Total Allowable Catch (TAC) and effort restrictions, which have not in turn delivered the envisaged recovery. That a recovery plan was and is required is axiomatic, however, practical experience has demonstrated that the present arrangement contains targets which are unachievable in the time allowed.

Other recovery plans have borne more fruit, with the North Sea haddock stock now returned to a long term management plan after a period of recovery and Northern hake about to achieve a similar result.

It can therefore be concluded that the concept of recovery plans is sound and there is evidence of success as well as failure. The following can be postulated as required elements:

—   Sound scientific evidence as to the state of the stock and its progress over time.

—   Setting of realistic criteria of success. Experience suggests that targets stated in terms of biomass limits may not be the best choice; movement downwards of fishing mortality may be better where this can be realistically assessed. If targets are too rigid, as in the case of North Sea cod, the conditions for automatic failure of the plan are created. Even modest recovery will be so regarded, because it does not meet the target.

—   If the stock under recovery is caught as part of a mixed fishery, there will be difficulties in avoiding "regulatory" discarding, where the sustainable harvesting of one stock results in catching over quota of another under recovery.

Management Plans. This is accepted as a workable concept, provided again that it is realistically applied. Similar elements will be required as for Recovery Plans: sound scientific information; realistic criteria of success and in this case change triggering rules; recognition of the effects of other management plans if the stock is in a mixed fishery. Two other concepts will impinge on the success of single stock Management Plans:

— The ecosystem approach to fisheries management. This is less than completely defined, but suggests that interdependence of species should be considered. The present approach is single species.

— Maximum Sustainable Yield. There is an instinctively attractive if subjective logic to the theory that light fishing pressure on large stocks will lead to the happy result of larger catches of bigger fish for the expenditure of a given amount of effort. The objective application of this—the achievement of mutually large stocks of species which within an ecosystem eat each other or depend on the same food stocks—may constrain MSY to remain as theory. Care will be required in its application.

2. *Management Tools.* It is easier to point up the drawbacks of individual tools than to suggest viable alternatives; however the main problem in their application may be the overlaying of these tools one upon the other, making it difficult to determine relative value. Regarding for instance TACs and effort limitation, instinct suggests that one or the other should be sufficient alone to regulate fishing pressure. A few words on the following tools are offered:

— *Total Allowable Catch.* This tool works reasonably well in single species fisheries, for example North East Atlantic mackerel. When the TAC, divided into individual quotas, is reached, fishing stops. However in those fisheries where a species is a bycatch, when the quota is in one species is reached the natural reaction is "regulatory discarding" as described above.

— *Effort Limitation.* This exists in different forms: as global effort to place a ceiling on overall fishing effort; as constraints for specific purposes on individual vessels, for example within the Cod Recovery Plan.

— *Rights Based Management Tools.* The administration of the right to fish a quota is a very powerful tool in shaping Europe's fishing industry in all its components. This is delegated to Member States within the ceiling of their National quota allocations and the administrative tools utilized vary radically across the fishing Member States. A Commission comparative study is under way. Depending on what is found, it is unlikely that a centrally imposed model will contribute to sustainable fishing in an even handed way. This will require careful consideration.

— *Technical Conservation Measures.* This wide term covers a great swath of regulation and endeavour. In essence, the adaptation of fishing gear to achieve a conservation aim is an area where Scotland has participated seriously. Measures of greater effect than that required by the Commission have been introduced, for example in mesh sizes and net twine thickness; innovation and experiment is encouraged and trialled under the Scottish Industry Science Partnership. TCMs provide at least some capability to avoid regulatory discarding and should be more productive with time. "Real Time Closures" have recently been introduced as a voluntary measure to avoid juvenile and spawning cod and this

3. *Discards and bycatch.* This has been addressed to some extent above, but it should be noted that conservation measures will have as their objective the avoidance or release of fish which should not be caught. Most measures will therefore contribute to the reduction of discarding. The subject has gained some prominence by the use, including by Commissioner Borg of emotive language. It is suggested that discarding is viewed not only as a stand-alone issue but in conjunction with conservation measures. For example, the application of very restrictive TACs, with the best intentions, may simply contribute to discarding rather than enhance conservation.

4. *Climate change.* There seems to be no doubt that climate change will have an effect over time on the distribution and quantity of fish in European waters. It is important to know which influences are having what effect, for the avoidance of inappropriate management measures. For example, the biomasses of the *Gadoid* species in the North Sea during a phenomenon of the 1960–1980s known as the *Gadoid outburst* may be unattainable at any time in the foreseeable future, perhaps due in part to climate change. For the avoidance of unrealistic targets, knowledge of the effects of all influences is required.

CONTROL AND ENFORCEMENT

5. The recent report of the Court of Auditors as regards the control and enforcement of the rules of the CFP makes disappointing reading. The introduction in late 2005 across UK of the Registration of Buyers and Sellers (RBS) and in the case of Scotland the widespread decommissioning schemes of the early 2000s served the purpose of "right-sizing" the Scottish fleet and providing an effective regulatory framework for the elimination of the practice of landing "black" fish. The Court of Auditor's report considers a period before RBS and the situation in Scotland today has improved to the point of full compliance in landings. This is auditable with the Scottish Fishery Protection Agency.

6. The main request therefore from the Scottish Industry is in achievement of a "flat playing Field" across the Member States. Inequitable treatment exists not only in the field of regulation and compliance but also in very different treatment of past transgressions. This is one area where one size must be seen to fit all.

STRUCTURAL POLICY

7. The capacity of the Scottish fleet is in general terms now balanced with catching opportunity. This is an important state to be achieved across the European industry, for avoidance of commercial pressure on individual businesses to circumvent rules and apply pressure in turn to their governments to adjust regulation and compliance for them.

8. The EFF has yet to make any impact; the administrative delay in its introduction is most unhelpful.

9. There is some apparent misalignment between the WTO-level discussions and the EU structural policy.

GOVERNANCE

10. The RACs performance so far has been in overall terms successful in raising stakeholder involvement, but the process has yet to mature fully. Different RACs are at different stages of their development and each is unique in its circumstance. A few examples of this are: the North Sea RAC had an assisted start given the experience of the North Sea Commission; the Pelagic RAC has the apparently simpler task of dealing with single-species fisheries, but the greater complication of dealing with Coastal States outside the EU in almost every component pelagic fishery; the NWWRAC has the greatest cultural diversity. This will result in development proceeding at different speeds.

11. A general statement may be made with some justification that the best level of delegation of fisheries management is that closest to the stakeholders, recognising, to repeat the phrase used above, that the arrangements must govern effectively the common participants in an industry using common resource. Overly centralised control will inevitably find itself dealing in compromise and unable to deal with every detail, some of which may have fundamental importance to regional fisheries. There may be something of a temptation for governments or even industries to resist delegation, in order to retain the luxury of blame transfer. This should be resisted as for example, in the acceptance by UK Ministers at the 2007 December Council of delegated control of fisheries effort in the Cod Recovery Zone accepts in turn the responsibility to do better than the Commission in organising effort with the objective of reducing cod mortality.

3 March 2008

Examination of Witness

Witness: MR BERTIE ARMSTRONG, Chief Executive, Scottish Fisherman's Federation, gave evidence.

Q118 Chairman: Welcome. Thank you for finding the time both to prepare your written evidence and to come and see us today. We are very grateful.
Mr Armstrong: Thank you very much, my Lord Chairman. I am pleased to be here.

Q119 Chairman: We proceed on these things, if you wish—and it will be often quite helpful—to have a general statement from yourself and then we go through a question and answer session—and I hope you have an indication of the subjects that we are likely to cover. Would you like to say something in general?
Mr Armstrong: Yes, please. Although it is not necessarily wholly apposite to the questions you have asked, it is worth me making our position clear on the CFP in general, because it always becomes part of the debate. I have stated in my written evidence that if the CFP did not exist, a similar framework, an international framework, in order to properly manage a mobile resource accessed from several

different places and in several different places, would have to exist. That can be interpreted as support for the CFP *per se*. That is not the case. I would not like to be seen as an apologist for the CFP. I would like to be seen as a reforming zealot for the CFP. That is not the same as, "Armstrong agrees with the CFP in its present form". That sets the scene.

Q120 Chairman: Having said that the first question is going to be which are the key areas that you want to see reformed.
Mr Armstrong: Certainly, the CFP in the opinion of the Scottish Fishermen's Federation is badly over-centralised and top-down (to use that phrase). That presents an almost impossible job to the Commission and it manifests itself in difficulties and problems for a number of fisheries, from the northernmost latitude to the southernmost latitude. To be covered in some respects by elements of the same regulation will create unacceptable compromise. The sort of form

19 March 2008   Mr Bertie Armstrong

we would like to see is a regionalisation of decision-making, with the strategic decisions being taken centrally, and to move the decision-making process, as far as that is sensibly possible, to the stakeholder level where a regional solution—for instance, there are many examples in the Scottish fishing industry, as you know—makes it appropriate for local decision-making to be better than central. I have in mind what has happened about decentralising or devolving the control of effort, days at sea, for the Cod Recovery Zone, for those vessels so affected, to the UK as opposed to holding it all centrally in Brussels. That is one step, I think, in the right direction.

Q121 *Chairman:* You have hit on one of the key issues that we have identified so far on the basis of the evidence we have already received. I do not expect you to do it just now, but is there anything around which gives us a clearer idea of what a devolved management administrative scheme would be? That idea that you keep strategic issues central but you get the implementation of how to achieve the strategic targets at a more local, regional level. Is there anything written which shows you how you can operationalise that concept?
Mr Armstrong: Regrettably not. It has been done in a piecemeal fashion. You will know of course that quota is decentralised, in a way that is managed by each of the Member States in accordance with their own regime for that, and effort control will follow it. The only Member State to pick it up, to go through the door in the legislation this year has been the UK and we are being watched very closely. There is no central document that describes the absolutely crucial bit of this: how do we make that happen in regulatory terms? It is all a rather vague concept at the minute. It is almost an experiment or a pilot scheme to see how the UK does with effort control. We have been handed a length of rope and we can either hang ourselves or make something of it.
Chairman: Let us go on to one of the key issues: the whole basis of the scientific evidence and the relationship between the scientists and the fishermen.

Q122 *Viscount Brookeborough:* Mr Armstrong, you make a number of interesting comments about both recovery plans and management plans. The key to the success of each of these would appear to be the evidence on which they are based and the targets that are set. What is your assessment of the quality of fisheries scientific advice and to what extent do you consider there to be adequate dialogue and confidence between the fishing industry and scientists? We have noticed in the press that, basically, the scientists and fishermen seem to disagree. Would like to comment on that?

Mr Armstrong: Yes, thank you. There are two questions really. On the assessment of the quality of fisheries scientific advice: because of the size of the problem or the volume of information that would be required, that will always remain a work in progress. We hope that progress is marked by advance rather than by decline and we will probably never get to the end because fisheries science is expensive and you get to the point where you might threaten to spend more on the science than you make from the industry. The problem, if there is one, with the annual round, which looks at relevant fish stocks stock-by-stock and makes an estimate of how healthy they are and therefore how much can be withdrawn from them by fishing, is that at this point, by necessity, it works a little in the past. You are always a year or a year-and-a-half behind and you therefore make management decisions on information which is, *de facto,* a little out of date. That can be very unhelpful, particularly in a recovering stock, where you might set the TAC too low and result in regulatory or institutional discarding. The other question is rather more exciting and that is the quality of dialogue and the confidence in fisheries. When I joined the industry three years ago I found we were just emerging from an area of deep mistrust, where the fishermen would evince the argument, "I'm at sea all day every day. You do your trips. You really do not know what is happening out there." That was the general feeling: rather dismissive. For reasons of our own good, the industry and science are drawing together. If we want a more rapid assessment of fisheries than the present set-piece round can manage then we need to talk a bit more, and that has been recognized within the industry. I think there is an increasing confidence. We have moved away from the position of deep mistrust into a position now of increasing confidence. It is helped by such matters as science-industry partnerships, which are happening around the UK in several guises—certainly there is a Scottish one—which means that we, by necessity, in order to move the project forward, talk to scientists on an almost daily basis.

Q123 *Viscount Brookeborough:* Are you getting closer to, if you like, monitoring the equivalent areas within the sea? Scientists do not monitor the same area from which you are necessarily getting reports from the fishermen.
Mr Armstrong: Yes.

Q124 *Viscount Brookeborough:* And the fishermen are inevitably in real-time.
Mr Armstrong: Exactly.

Q125 *Viscount Brookeborough:* But the scientists are monitoring all age groups; therefore, why do you think their forecasting is not correct, when they are the people who analyse the age of the fish and therefore the juveniles that will therefore come into the fishery later on? Why are you sceptical about that?

Mr Armstrong: The fishermen themselves will always say the same thing. The scientists will also. The scientists say, "If I am to create a time series"—and to make a piece of science robust, it must have a time series—"I must not do this now and say, 'I found that much there, therefore I extrapolate it,' I must have a time series," and so the fisheries surveys will fish—and this is a great generalisation—in the same place, with the same gear, year after year after year. The fishermen will continuously complain, " I use different gear. I catch different fish." There are two trials going on, one north and one south of the border right now, to test that hypothesis. There will be a commercial vessel fishing alongside one of the research trawlers under Defra's auspices and a similar trial but slightly different will be happening north. That is the criticism that is levelled by the fishermen: "You always do the same thing, in the same place, and you are missing stuff" is what they say.

Q126 *Lord Cameron of Dillington:* Does that explain why the TAC is often set at 50% more than what the scientists recommend? Is that right, that it should be set like that?

Mr Armstrong: It will certainly influence the representatives in the Council of Ministers if they have strong evidence—sometimes anecdotal evidence but strong evidence—from their own fishery that what is being seen by way of abundance on the ground is very different from what the science is saying. The science, in fairness to the scientists, is often precautionary and has no real conclusion.

Q127 *Viscount Brookeborough:* You would agree to setting TACs at 50% higher than what the scientists recommend.

Mr Armstrong: No, I do not think anyone could agree with that. That would be the wrong thing to do.

Q128 *Chairman:* Good try, Alan!

Mr Armstrong: The straight answer to your question as to how that happens is that it happens in the background of a political process.

Lord Cameron of Dillington: I agree.

Q129 *Viscount Brookeborough:* Recently there were reports from fishermen that the cod stocks were recovering. But the other side of that was that they were recovering, but these were juvenile fish. Therefore, surely one cannot go along with increased catches purely on the basis of juveniles increasing because they are four or six years away from being the fish we want to catch.

Mr Armstrong: Yes. Neither the industry nor the scientists would wish to over-egg the pudding. That is a very imprecise phrase—by that I mean to set the TACs too high. There is a disparity between the opinion of the men at sea with regard to abundance of cod and where it is and present scientific evidence. That can be explained to at least some degree by the fact that the science is slightly older—it is going to be a year or so delayed—but no-one is suggesting from the industry that TACs are set artificially high. There is a point in setting TACs where, if they are set artificially low, then if they are caught—as cod is for instance in the Scots industry—as largely a bycatch in an industry chasing another species—haddock, mostly—you get institutional discard (to use that phrase again). If you cannot avoid catching them because of their abundance, they are going over the side because the TAC is artificially low. I recognize the obvious logical difficulties that that presents. It is quite a hard problem. We are trying to address that, at least to some degree, by selectivity, being more clever with the gear to let fish that you do not wish to catch go or not catch in the first place.

Q130 *Viscount Ullswater:* You talk about setting some things at a strategic level, because when you are dealing with a number of Member States and only a limited resource it has to be divided up somehow. Would you consider that the setting of TACs is still a strategic concept of the CFP?

Mr Armstrong: I would say so.

Q131 *Viscount Ullswater:* Because it is involved with politics perhaps.

Mr Armstrong: It is rather easier to describe defects in the system than to create schemes to fix them, but, yes, it is a defect in the system. The fact that the whole of the fishing opportunity for the following year is set at the December Council of Ministers is a very complicated thing. It is a big ask (to use that awful phrase) of the Council of Ministers and is inescapably going to be governed by the politics of each participant in that process. He or she may be near an election; they may have the best interests of their industry at heart and are prepared to abandon or at least pay less attention than required to the overriding principle of sustainable fishing. A way forward conceivably might be the breaking up of the process—and that has already begun to a certain extent—where all the decision-making is not taken all at once, because, if you do that, then you abandon the process to the politics if the detail is inescapably too large. Talking of strategic decisions, the setting of long-term management plans, which do not depend on an annual change but which are rigidly stuck to trends and expected adjustments in accordance with trends rather than a wholesale reset, would be the way to go.

Q132 *Viscount Ullswater:* Could I change tack a little bit? We have some evidence from Mr Horwood that as a result of EU Marine legislation there is likely to be a push towards more holistic marine management, which includes fisheries obviously. You have touched on it in your evidence with the ecosystem of the sea. Do you think that is the way forward? Is that the way we should be guided for the future, to preserve the marine environment in that holistic way?

Mr Armstrong: I think, inescapably, this is the way we must do it. There are interdependencies between all elements of the ecosystem, including, of course, counting man as part of the ecosystem—since medieval times he has been involving himself in it. Much would depend on which structure was adopted. What often happens is an arm-wrestle for primacy: are you talking about maximisation of economic benefit, or are you talking about protecting the marine environment in the long-term? The answer is that we must do both. Often we fall to arguing from the red corner and the blue corner, if you like, for primacy of one or the other. I think an element of an ecosystem approach is balance and proportionality. There are lots of examples as to how that can happen. In terrestrial terms you would not dream of having a protected area in the middle of a Sainsbury's car park: it is tarmac'd over and it is used for that. But it is entirely appropriate to have protected areas for flora and fauna where that is reasonable: in the national parks, for instance. The same could apply in the maritime area. If an area has been trawled for tens of years, then it is by no means necessarily wrecked, like a ploughed field, it is just a little different, and there is very little point in doing much with that other than continuing to use it for sustainable harvesting. But there are other areas that you may wish to protect. Proportionality and balance, with the ecosystem approach encompassing that, rather than the primacy of one or the other, which is where we tend to fall to arguing, I am afraid.

Q133 *Viscount Ullswater:* Do you add into that things like sand dredging or sea dredging and perhaps even the establishment of wind farms, which is set to go on around our coast and rather picking up.

Mr Armstrong: Yes.

Q134 *Viscount Ullswater:* Is that all part of the ecosystem as you see it?

Mr Armstrong: Inescapably, it is going to have to be taken into account. I now you know that is the stuff of the Marine Bill and two pieces of legislation coming from Brussels. The word "joined-up" management has been used and marine spatial planning has now turned into marine planning and I think marine planning is heading our way. For reasons of balancing and being proportional in the uses that you have described for all those things, I think we need to get the framework right and make the legislation that governs it good legislation (to use that term generally) which will not obstruct any of the individual endeavours or give undue primacy to any of the endeavours, either, for instance, fishing or marine nature conservation. You could get a bit purist about either.

Q135 *Chairman:* It would mean, for example, in some circumstances saying, "Okay, you have been trawling, but you cannot do it in X, Y and Z because if you did you would wreck the seabed."

Mr Armstrong: Yes, absolutely. We have noticed in very carefully inspecting, for instance, the JNCC proposals for UK offshore special areas of conservation that often these things are mutually exclusive. For instance, if you look at Stanton Bank, which happens to be to the west and south of the outer Hebrides, there are some rock formations there which are very much worth preserving. If you overlay the fishing patterns from the Scottish Fishing Protection Agency's output from vessel monitoring systems you find that the fishing happens in a small channel of muddy seabed where prawns are trawled for and the rock is largely avoided—not necessarily because the fishermen are avid conservationists but because it would wreck their gear if they were to pull it over the top of the rocks. The same thing applies to a certain extent to coldwater coral, although you can do some damage there. So there are solutions if proportionality and balance prevail.

Q136 *Chairman:* Perhaps we could switch back for a moment to the science. Is not one of the difficulties with the whole problem of the role of science in helping to set the TACs and also in the relationship of confidence between fishermen and scientists that it is a science that has a very high margin of error?

Mr Armstrong: Yes.

Q137 *Chairman:* Because of that high margin of error—some of the stuff we have read indicates it is possibly plus or minus 40%, which is huge—you are bound to get really difficult problems, like you will be setting TACs that are inaccurate or that do not live up to the reality that the fishermen experience in terms of the stocks that are being brought out of the sea.

Mr Armstrong: Yes, I must agree with that and can quote several examples in both directions where the imprecise nature of the science—

Q138 *Chairman:* Is there any mechanism of adjusting the TAC in-year, in the light of experience?

Mr Armstrong: Yes. That occasionally happens but, because of the cumbersome nature of a top-down process, as we have described the CFP as being, there will be received in the Commission from a plethora of Member States such requests, so that makes it a bit difficult. It is also difficult to drum up hard scientific proof quickly. The scientists will, quite correctly, in my view, resist that in order to produce robust science. The answer will never be reached but progress in the right direction lies in the increased dialogue which is hopefully being encouraged between fishermen and scientists. If the fishermen are saying, "Look, we've got this wrong, this is not as you are describing it," then such hard science as extra observer schemes—which are expensive but possible—total logging, a special look at that fishery, can be produced in a relatively short time in order to do that. We are going to have to do that this year to a certain degree, in offering to the Commission proof of the pudding for our control of effort rather than central control of the said effort from Brussels. The normal scientific round will not produce answers quickly enough and so we have asked for and are implementing extra observer schemes, extra reporting from sea, to see if we can—

Q139 *Lord Cameron of Dillington:* How do you play that with your demand earlier for long-term management plans that are "rigidly stuck to"?
Mr Armstrong: By "rigidly stuck to" I meant to allude to taking the sting out of the political process. If you know that the rule states that if *x* happens, if the spawning stock of biomass rises above level *y,* then there will be a maximum of a 15% increase in the TAC or likewise a match of 15% down, it sort of de-stings the political process. Anything we can do to stop widespread decisions which are not based wholly on science, happening all at once in December, will be a helpful thing.

Q140 *Viscount Brookeborough:* Currently do you know what the cost is of the scientifically gathered evidence as a proportion of the fishery industry?
Mr Armstrong: I can quote the Scots figures. The Fisheries Research Service budget is in the order of £25–£27 million, I believe, and the overall turnover of the industry in Scotland is in the order of £350 million.

Q141 *Viscount Brookeborough:* Who is paying for it?
Mr Armstrong: That is a government-funded affair.
Chairman: Could we move on to the key issue of simplification.
Lord Plumb: We like the word "simplification".
Chairman: We are a very simple lot!

Q142 *Lord Plumb:* As a reforming zealot, how would you like to simplify the management? What would you regard as the prospects of an "outcome orientated system"? That was proposed by one witness who has written to us and would involve setting objectives at European level while devolving decisions on management tools to national, regional or even individual vessel level. You partly touched on this in your opening remarks but I think it is crucial, because we do not want to be seen as a committee who have taken the last report off the shelf, dusted it and sent it back again, and so you could regard perhaps all of us as reforming zealots in this respect.
Mr Armstrong: Simplification is, indeed, very important. When I was at a meeting the other day a fisherman said, "The reason we're all sitting here is because none of us came top of the class," so simplification is a wonderful thing for all of us. I did go into a layer of detail that perhaps I should not have, in that I said that simplification was not helped by layering one measure on top of another, making it very difficult then to see which one is working, and that is the truth. The outcome-oriented system, whoever said that in written evidence—and if it was my good friend Barry Deas, we see eye-to-eye on this—as we do on most things, I hasten to add—that would indeed be the direction in which we would wish to go and the setting of objectives and the taking of the decision-maker as close to the stakeholder as you can get because then the proper dialogue can take place. The big bit about the outcome-oriented devolution of effort control, which says, "Take this bucket of kilowatt days, you sort it out within that scheme (ie, a strategic decision), but incentivise and penalise your industry as best you can to achieve the aim of a reduction of cod mortality"—and that is almost a classic pilot study in this—is that it allows something that is difficult from central control, in that you can incentivise good behaviour and penalise bad behaviour if you have the tools at your mercy, and what is being wrestled with now at administration levels is getting this right. Everybody is a bit nervous, reasonably so, and we want to get this right. The administrations would be afraid of being seen, in the end, as succoured into pandering to the industry and simply giving more effort to the industry where that is inappropriate. The industry, likewise, are carefully watching to see whether or not this is just the transfer of one less than perfect system to a lower level of less than perfect system. There is all to play for here, but I think the central principle of central goal-setting and allowing incentivisation and penalisation with a decision-maker who has a straight dialogue with the relevant fishery is helpful. Also, what might apply, even within the UK, to a Scots white fish boat, fishing for haddock half in the Norwegian sector and half at home, will be very different from a boat out of Yorkshire looking for

whiting. The point of that being that the moving of the decision-making to the decision-maker, closer to the stakeholder, is helpful.

Q143 *Lord Plumb:* Would fishermen in other European countries agree with that, do you think? Is it subject to debate in your fisheries group in Brussels?

Mr Armstrong: Yes. The Regional Advisory Councils are exactly the forum where that debate can take place. It is a difficulty. You have put your finger right upon a difficulty. Perhaps I might give you a good example: it was decided in Scotland—it has been adopted around the whole of the North Sea now—that there would be real-time closures. We do not want to catch these fish, either aggregations of juveniles or, in the spawning period at the start of the year, spawning fish, the cod stock. Therefore, when we fall upon abundances of these, we will work out a system of working out where abundances are, first of all by asking the industry and putting squares on the map and saying, "This is where we are likely to find them," and then inspecting vessels when they are in those areas during the relevant season and shutting down small areas. That had to be voluntary because you cannot put it into legislation, unless you do it at the December Council and that would never get through. We did it voluntarily and we talked to the Danes who said, "The logic is obvious. We would sign up to that." Now that system has not been abused by other nations. The obvious interpretation would be, "If they are telling me where it all is, I think I will go straight there". That has not happened—well, not with foreign vessels.

Q144 *Lord Plumb:* Would it affect the licence or the quota?

Mr Armstrong: The way the scheme has been set up now, it will affect your days at sea. The carrot and stick approach is the carrot of an inducement by way of effort to obey these rules and the penalty of losing that inducement if you break the rules. But that only applies to UK vessels. Unless the legislation has changed, it cannot apply to the other vessels of Europe.

Q145 *Chairman:* Given my background, I am in favour of devolution. If you push implementation down to regional level or something like that, at some stage somewhere along the line there needs to be the ability of the centre to impose a sanction. In this case, it would obviously have to be on the Member State eventually. What would that sanction be and how would it be applied?

Mr Armstrong: I can only speak from the experience we have had thus far—and it is very early days in the scheme—but the sanction that would be applied is withdrawal of your privileges with regard to effort

control. For instance, for people in this scheme—north of the border it has been called the Scottish Conservation Credit Scheme—if you agree to staying out of real-time closures, you will be awarded your 2007 level of days and you will be given the ability to manage your days in kilowatt hours rather than kilowatt days—the advantage of that being that there was always the rather perverse rule which meant that, if you were going to be back at five minutes after midnight, never mind the weather or fuel consumption, that used another day, so people would battle through in order to get through for 23.59 instead of 00.01.

Q146 *Chairman:* Say a Member State government was pretty lax in ensuring that the rules were being obeyed and was turning a blind-eye to various bits and pieces, what sanction would be available to impose on the Member State?

Mr Armstrong: I cannot sensibly answer that. All I can say, certainly from the industry's point of view is that such a sanction should exist. The level playing field—the old cliché—is used nearly every day in one form or another about the perceived compliance of other Member States versus us, and our own perception is that we do everything in general terms and that often this is not quite the case elsewhere. There is certainly some hard evidence of that with regard to, for instance, the penalties for past misdemeanours in the pelagic world, in the mackerel and herring catching: a disparity in the way Member States have pursued their miscreants and in the differential treatment in that respect of, for instance, Scotland. If it is *bona fide* law breaking, there is no truck with that, but it is very galling when you see that happening elsewhere and that industry is given the commercial advantage of not being penalised so much. It is a problem. I have just described the problem. I have answered your question by agreeing with it rather than saying what can be done. I would say that some action really must be available centrally, otherwise the system will fall apart, because there is a differential approach—and you know this personally very well—from Member State to Member State in the way they approach their fishing industry.

Chairman: Let us move on to discards.

Q147 *Baroness Jones of Whitchurch:* Do you think discards are an inherent part of the fishing industry? To what extent has it always been like that? I know there have been some recent scandals and pictures of wholesale throwing back into the water but is it a feature that fishermen will always keep their high value stock and chuck the rest over the side?

Mr Armstrong: I hope not. I actually did not answer the question properly that was put originally, which was: Why do discards happen? I think everyone is familiar with the answer that if they are illegal, if they are undersized, then it is not illegal to catch them but it is certainly illegal to land them and so there is nothing you can do but put them over the side. If a species has no commercial value, then if it comes in in the net it will be discarded because there is nothing you can do with it otherwise. Then there is what we could perhaps call "high grading", where a fisherman may or may not choose to keep the primest of fish and throw the rest away. All of those are undesirable things. It is fair to say that the fishing industry does not like discarding. Fishermen do not. When you see those awful pictures on television, that is a rather misguided attempt by the fishermen to say, "Look, couldn't we change the fishing regulations because look what it is making me do" rather than in any shape or form glorying in it. Apart from anything else, if you are limited in your days at sea you do not want to spend half a day catching stuff that you are going to have to sort out and throw back. How do we address it, however, is the rather more important question. It is a slightly dangerous statement to make, with regard to it being reported back, but some level of discarding is probably inevitable. In its very mildest form, you have a tow in an area and you decide that there are fish that should not be caught here, so you have to move away, then those fish themselves will get discarded. A small amount of discarding is almost inevitable but it needs to be small. It is also arguably better to put it back into the ecosystem, where it becomes an easy meal for a natural predator in the ecosystem—an undersized haddock will be eaten avidly by a juvenile cod from the recovering cod stock—rather than take it ashore and make fishmeal out of it or do something else that really has no commercial basis. A small amount of discarding is probably an element of the industry but what must be done and what is being done is a sequential move in the direction of reducing this dramatically. There are things that can be done to help. The real-time closures, avoiding fish altogether that ought not to be caught, if you can work out where they are going to be or if you determine where they are going to be—which is roughly what the Norwegians do—can help. Also, gear selectivity where that is possible—and it is very much possible in some fisheries—is very helpful: bigger meshes to let juveniles go; separator panels which take advantage of the different behaviour of different species if you want to catch one and not the other or less of one and not the other. There is a pretty widespread programme of trials going on around the UK to help with this. The actions for the recovery of the cod stock and the reduction of discards almost go hand-in-hand. They are mutually helpful. If you avoid catching cod in order to let the stock recover you will automatically avoid discarding those cod you would otherwise have caught and the other white fish that swim with them.

Q148 *Baroness Jones of Whitchurch:* If you discard the bits that you say you always have—there will always be an element in the nets of things that have no value and seaweed and bits of rock and a few misshapen fish that you really do not want—do you think the bigger problem is because the scientists are getting it wrong? In other words, they are saying, "If you go and fish here you should be able to catch the right proportion of cod" and then they put their nets down and it is completely different, so they are getting caught out by the wrong scientific advice. Do you think that is at the heart of the problem?
Mr Armstrong: The scientific advice generally helps, where it can, with where fish will be and often the science has as the basis of its evidence reports from sea. Certainly it has the landing data and the reports of catching from sea. The science can be helped by the fishermen and vice versa. I would not wish to defend discarding at all or be quoted as defending discarding and saying it is all right. It is not all right but I think the reality is that there will always be a small amount of it. I do not think the scientists are particularly getting it wrong; it is just a question of moving in the right direction with increasing dialogue all the time about discards. It is a relatively recent topic.

Q149 *Baroness Jones of Whitchurch:* In relation to the throwing back of juveniles, for example, I know it could well be argued that you should change your gear so that you do not catch smaller fish.
Mr Armstrong: I agree with that.

Q150 *Baroness Jones of Whitchurch:* But would it not be better to land them, even though it is causing problems in future years, and give them some use, rather than throw them back as fishfood for other predators?
Mr Armstrong: I do not think we should underestimate the value of them as fishfood for other predators. It may be the other fish stocks that benefit from it.

Q151 *Baroness Jones of Whitchurch:* Some have said it is all the sea birds that benefit.
Mr Armstrong: Certainly there are clouds of sea birds—there is much visual evidence in every picture that RSPB produces of sea birds round fishing boats. One of the major problems—indeed, the major problem, I think—is that of discards in mixed fisheries. It is quite easy in, for instance, the pelagic to be chasing herring and mackerel, blue whiting or horse mackerel: fishing in the mid-water for shoals of similar fish is a pretty clean process. And that is fine. Mixed fisheries in the white fish industry are a different matter together. That is where selectivity has a part to play and selective closures, be they temporal or spatial or permanent. If you know this is always an area of juvenile nursery then, indeed, that

should be shut. A combination of measures to move in the right direction will help. The word "discard-ban" is often used, but an immediate ban early would be difficult. It is interesting to note the Norwegian experience in this respect. They have, indeed, a discard ban but a very interesting fact is that very little of the amount of money and facilities they laid aside to processing all these discards that were not going to happen now and were going to be brought ashore has been spent. The Norwegian administration would argue that that is because of behaviour change at sea: people have really put their mind to avoiding these fish with a combination of the fact that they know that is a good idea anyway and there is a legislative framework which is for heavily penalising.

Q152 Chairman: We have heard the Norwegian ban being described as a "pragmatic ban".
Mr Armstrong: Yes. Hence the lack of fishmeal factories supplied with thousands of tonnes of small fish.

Q153 Chairman: We are going to have to move on but, having said that, I am going to abuse my position as Chairman and ask one question on discards. The type of discard that people find most difficult to understand is when a fisherman brings up the net and in it are fish that, because of the TAC, because of quota, he does not have quota for and he is throwing back fish dead that are—
Mr Armstrong: Saleable fish.

Q154 Chairman: Saleable fish, high quality. How can that be avoided? In particular, is it possible to get a system where, if you bring up the net and in the net are fish for which a TAC exists, quota exists, and you do not have that particular quota cover, some sort of mechanism and requirement could be put in place where the fishermen would have to buy the quota cover to cover what is in the net?
Mr Armstrong: That exists to a certain extent already. You cannot do it on the hoof at sea.

Q155 Chairman: That is the problem, is it not?
Mr Armstrong: Yes. You could certainly do it if you prepare for that and say, "I'm going to try to catch that amount this year and I therefore am going to go to my producer organisation and buy the quota that is available."

Q156 Viscount Ullswater: Could you do it retrospectively?
Mr Armstrong: That would lead to difficulty in individual producer organisations. It is very easy to describe several ways where this might be tackled. One might be an effort only system, where you take a great leap of faith and say, "If I only let them fish for

that amount of time, then they bring back everything that is commercially available and we see what happens." Actually, it can be a little more scientific than that: you can guesstimate what would happen. But that would be a radical and revolutionary departure and one that might have some risk in it. Adjustment of quota on the hoof at sea would seem to make sense as well, but it would fall into the problem of how the producer organisations then work because they have no control. Their job is: "I have this amount of fish to distribute and I am supposed to prevent anyone else catching any more of that" and it would make their job more difficult. It is hard to see at this point exactly which of those schemes would work best. All of them would have merit for investigation. There are a couple of places where effort only schemes are being tried. Or you might try quota only. In fact we have tried quota only and effort control was the result of that not working.
Chairman: All right, let us press on. Real-time closures.

Q157 Earl of Dundee: You have already said that you think the Scottish system of real-time closures is working well. If so, how then do you see that developing and extending?
Mr Armstrong: If it would become mandatory for all and not voluntary for all—and mandatory for the Scots fleet or the UK fleet if you wish to stay within that system—then it would have to be applied in legislation at the end of each year. It would have to be in the TAC and quota regulations for each year. That would be perhaps the direction we need to go. Everyone is watching this now. The Commission declared about last September time that delegation of effort control to Member States was coming. We were the only ones who picked it up in the UK, so everybody is watching us now to see if we do hang ourselves with this piece of rope or not. Once it becomes universal, assuming that we make it work and the Commission decides so, then it can be embedded in the annual TAC and quota regulations and be mandatorily applied to all.

Q158 Earl of Dundee: If you say that everybody is watching it, is the first stage of what they look at to see how we make it within UK law mandatory?
Mr Armstrong: No, I think they are waiting rather more to see the practical effect of it: Does this do anything for the fish stocks and can the industry live with it or can the industry and the administration between the pair of them make it work?

Q159 Earl of Dundee: How long will that process of assessment probably take?
Mr Armstrong: It is going to be done in year, this year. We started voluntarily ourselves, without any form of legislative underpinning, last September. It will

run all this year, underpinned by the TAC and quota regulations that presently exist, and we will see what happens next. Our problem—and I think we have touched on this—is producing robust scientific evidence that it is doing anything for the fish stocks.
Chairman: Let us go on to a hobby-horse of mine: "black" fish.

Q160 *Lord Palmer:* You mentioned that the practice of landing "black" fish has virtually now been eliminated. To what do you ascribe this success? What do you consider to be the key pillars of any revised EU control and enforcement regime?
Mr Armstrong: I would ascribe it to two things. There are two pillars supporting this table top. One is legislation that applies or regulation that applies to all, and that was the introduction of registration of buyers and sellers which made it a criminal act not only to sell the fish but also to buy it and the records have to match. Almost at a stroke, everyone breathed a sigh of relief and said, "I can now abandon the Tragedy of the Commons. If he is doing it, I have to do it, otherwise I am commercially disadvantaged. We are all going to get caught; therefore none of us will do it." That is the common explanation of what happened. That made the playing field flat in the UK for everybody. You can supply fish into a market only if they are legal. The first thing that happened was that the price of fish went up, so people immediately had a commercial impetus to carry on doing this. That is the first pillar, the regulatory pillar that bites or that works. The second, talking of the heaving of a sigh of relief, is the recognition of the industry that this makes absolute logical sense. There is no point in "black" fish if it is widespread: it distorts the market; it distorts the science, because scientists have to make some sort of guess as to what you are doing; and it is absolutely no good for fish stocks. It is a happy story and it is auditable, I am now delighted to say, with the Scottish fishing industry, God bless them, boastfully producing charts that show their intelligence (what we think you are doing) and the prosecutions (what we caught you doing), with the curves coinciding down at the *x* axis, which is wonderful.
Chairman: My own little story on "black" fish is that many, many, many years ago I made a speech attacking the practice of "black" fish and a senior and distinguished member of the industry came up to me afterwards and said to me that he totally agreed with me as long as we made sure the Scottish fishermen got their fair share of the "black" fish! Let us go on.

Q161 *Lord Cameron of Dillington:* You have already spoken about a level playing field in terms of effort control and I suspect there was an innuendo of a level playing field in terms of "black" fish in some of your answers there, but I want to talk about capacity

because, ultimately, that is really what it is all about. You claim that the capacity in the Scottish fleet is now balanced with catching opportunity. I would be quite interested to know what you base this on but, more importantly, how can we achieve the decommissioning or the right-sizing of capacity across Europe? It may be the same answer you gave to the Chairman on effort control, that you do not really know how to answer it, but does the European Fisheries Fund help? Could that be reorganised or restructured in a way that might make it more relevant?
Mr Armstrong: I think we are where we are with the European Fisheries Fund and it does not help overmuch. There is not an enormously significant amount of money in it. The basis of evidence of right-sizing of the Scottish fleet—which is the one I can talk about on the statistics—is that two rounds of decommissioning took out about 65% of the capacity of white fish. There was a really swingeing pair of rounds of decommissioning. We are now seeing—and this I offer as evidence of right-sizing—a degree of optimism in the fleet: people are now making enough money to consider fleet renewal. That is by no means fleet expansion—we cannot do that under the rules—but fleet renewal. People now have the confidence to go and buy another boat or have another one built. I would say that is the best evidence of right-sizing because people are turning a profit, making enough money to make it viable. There will always be ups and downs in an ecosystem where everything eats everything else, but we are seeing fish stocks which you might describe as relatively stable and relatively hopeful. There is work to be done in all directions but we are not on a downward spiral of a decline in fish stocks. That, combined with commercial viability, would seem to indicate about right-sizing of the fleet. How you get this spread across Europe is, indeed, a similar answer to the one I gave to my Lord Chairman where I described the problem in more detail: I have no real sensible answers to how we do that, except to note that it is an extremely desirable thing for it to happen.
Chairman: Let us finish off with RACs.

Q162 *Earl of Arran:* We have touched on this so far but, as you say in your evidence, some RACs are further advanced than others due to a complex remix of different RACs, et cetera, and they are pretty much in their early stages, but do you think they do have the potential for more power being given to them?
Mr Armstrong: It is a very interesting question as to whether more power is the central question. I would stick my neck out and say, and I have no mandate to say this—not because it is outrageous; we have not discussed it—that they are not in a condition yet where they can make rules. Unanimous recommendations can be made. I would shy away

from saying they are at the level of development where that ought to be mandatory, taken as the rule-making. Where they can certainly give of their best, I believe, is in the formulation of longer-term management plans because that is the form in which the industries and stakeholders are set up, the NGOs. There is a degree of balance there. If you get a unanimous decision from a RAC, then probably it is due to two things. One is that it is the correct decision—and we hope that will be the case in most cases—or it is very local and nobody else cares. We have to guard for that, that the small species in one corner of the Bay of Biscay gets a unanimous decision from a RAC because nobody cares. I would not wish to be disparaging but a unanimous decision is good. Delegation of power? Yet? It is a bit early but we hope that—

Q163 *Earl of Arran:* How about responsibility rather than power?

Mr Armstrong: I think we could turn that around to say that the RACs probably will not survive unless they demonstrate responsibility. We will all lose faith, both as Member States and no doubt the Commission also, if there is continuous lobbying in an unreasonable fashion for matters which do not properly deal with matters conservation or are excessively local.

Q164 *Lord Palmer:* You mentioned about some of your members reinvesting in boats. Can you remind us very roughly what the lifespan of a boat is?

Mr Armstrong: It can be almost anything you care to make it if you cannot afford a new one. There are boats on the Clyde which are 30 or 40 years old. On the other hand, at this point in time—

Q165 *Chairman:* I think you have just made a few enemies.

Mr Armstrong: The commercial viability of, for instance, the pelagic sector means that these boats get replaced: five/seven years is their lifespan. It is wholly dependent on the individual.

Q166 *Chairman:* The other underlying thing here is that one of the problems with the industry is that it is overcapitalised in any case.

Mr Armstrong: Yes. Would it be all right, my Lord Chairman, just to have a mention on rights-based management?

Q167 *Chairman:* Yes.

Mr Armstrong: The most important thing, the blood in the veins of the fisheries body, is quota. How that is organised or allowed to flow is the biggest lever that can be pulled to create a change in direction or an alteration in the industry. If you glance around the European industries, how they organise their quotas

is at least significant in how they are organised. There is a general move towards considering that a market-based solution to fisheries is the best thing: If you had individual tradeable quotas (ITQs) then that would fix it, would it not, because the market could then decide and it would have to be profitable and it would not be profitable if it was not sustainable? It is interesting to note that the way the UK industry but most especially the Scots industry is set at present is a large collection of small- and medium-sized enterprises mostly. A lot of it is family owned. A change to ITQs would internationalise the whole thing very quickly and you might take a global view, an economist's snapshot perhaps, of the European fishing industry and say, "After that happened, things got better," but you might wonder whether you had done the best thing for UK plc by doing that. A glance at the map of the UK industry and particularly the Scots industry is that we have got what everybody else wants. We have in that swathe of water a world-class resource. If you look at the size of the continental shelf of, for instance, Spain and then the size of their industry you get a surprise and say, "How on earth did it grow that big and why?" which leads to a daily attack on relative stability. The first thing that would change the character of the European fishing industry and transfer ownership into an international sphere but, actually, dare I say it, straight to identifiable other Member States and beyond the EU at a stroke, would be the creation of ITQs, so great care is needed here. This is the biggest lever that can be pulled. If it is to go in the direction of ITQs we will change things mightily.

Q168 *Lord Cameron of Dillington:* But no-one is forcing anyone to sell.

Mr Armstrong: No, but if you create the conditions where, if it suits an Icelander to wait for a downturn in the price of mackerel and come along and say, "Would you like to be in the Caribbean tomorrow? I have a forklift or money here," the unstated sentence is—and this is a completely fictitious example—

Q169 *Chairman:* We do not stop foreigners buying farms.

Mr Armstrong: Whether you support globalisation or internationalisation is not at the heart of the argument; at the heart of the argument is what will be the effect of creating this and the economist view probably is that it will be for the betterment of the whole European industry if it is allowed to be subject to market conditions, because that will automatically fix things. We need to be careful because I am not arguing for a backward look here but you need to be absolutely aware of what will happen if that occurs. It may be that the transfer of the pelagic fleet of the United Kingdom into Icelandic/Dutch hands is not a problem or you may find that the only fishing vessels in the North Sea are the very efficient and nice new Spanish vessels which are coming from Vigo because they bought everything. That may well make for a percentage price reduction on Waitrose's shelves, but it is whether that is a desirable matter altogether for UK Plc. I am not arguing for trade protection, I am just arguing for wide-open eyes as to the effects of these changes and as to whether or not the most efficient market in European terms is the best solution in United Kingdom fishing terms.

Chairman: Thank you very much; it is always nice to end on an uncontroversial note. It has been really interesting and very helpful for us; thank you.

WEDNESDAY 19 MARCH 2008

Present	Arran, E	Palmer, L
	Brookeborough, V	Plumb, L
	Cameron of Dillington, L	Sewel, L (Chairman)
	Dundee, E of	Ullswater, V
	Jones of Whitchurch, B	

Memorandum by the National Federation of Fishermen's Organisations

INTRODUCTION

The NFFO is the representative body for fishermen in England, Wales and Northern Ireland. Our member vessels range from 40 metre stern trawlers operating at North Norway and Greenland to small, under 10metre vessels, beach launched and with limited range. The Federation holds seats on the EC Advisory Committee for Fisheries and Aquaculture, and the North Sea, North West Waters, Pelagic and Long Distance regional advisory councils. The NFFO is also a member of Europeche, the European trade federation for the fishing industry.

THE ISSUE

The reformed Common Fisheries Policy had as its objective the sustainable exploitation of aquatic resources. Whilst some progress has been made in this direction over the past five years, there are important institutional and policy obstacles to a fully effective CFP.

GOVERNANCE

A senior Commission official remarked recently that 95% of what is wrong with the CFP is poor governance; although the precise percentage might be open for debate, we would not disagree with the central thrust of that remark. An impossible role has been imposed on the Directorate for Fisheries and Marine Affairs and the attempt to control (some would say micro-manage) a wide range of fisheries, in a broad spectrum of circumstances, through 40 degrees of latitude, has led to the use of blunt and often ineffective measures.

A further phase of reform is required. Managing commercial fish stocks is an environmentally, economically and socially sustainable way requires that the Commission's role evolves from micro-management to an auditing, overseeing, and refereeing role. Day to day management should be devolved to the fishing industry, regional advisory councils and the member states within a coordinating framework. The need to move in this direction is recognised by the Commission. Its Communication on discards published in 2007, contains the elements of such an approach: Discard reduction initiatives would be advanced by the fishing industry, and supported by the member state. The member state authorities would ensure that the arrangements in place are valid and verifiable. Economic incentives in the management system would be aligned with the objectives of that system, rather than as is often the case at present in contradiction to them. These are the components of a successful fisheries management system that could deliver its objectives, and would have a high degree of buy-in from the people it affects.

The present CFP relies on too much on setting targets and producing legislation rather than managing for outcomes. The result is a cycle in which failure is built in from the outset. Even where there are signs of progress, for example in the recovery of Northern Hake or North Sea Cod, it is not at all clear that the stocks are responding *directly* to the management measures in place.

TOTAL ALLOWABLE CATCH, TACs

It is widely recognised that from a conservation perspective, TACs and quotas are a blunt instrument. In fact their primary function has been as a convenient mechanism to share fisheries resources between member states and, within the member states, between groups of fishermen. Any alternative would have to offer a similar distributive mechanism.

TACs aim to adjust the fishing mortality rate to a level which is consistent with the desired replacement rate. As such, the system depends upon scientific advice, currently provided by ICES. One of the weaknesses of the system is that for a variety of reasons there can be a high degree of uncertainty surrounding stock assessments; for around 50% of the stocks there is insufficient data for a full analytical assessment. Nonetheless, it should be noted that there are a number of joint initiatives between fishermen and scientists aimed at improving the quality of assessments and that there are moves to long term management that would not be so dependent on the annual cycle of assessments. Annual volatility in the level of TAC is a cause of inefficiency within the industry. Dramatic cuts in quota are difficult to plan for and cause uncertainty and significant economic hardship. All this supports the need to move to more stable stocks through Long-term Management Plans. TACs can be successful where they are accepted as legitimate, or fair, and are effectively enforced. It should be emphasised, however, that applying TACs in a multi-species fishery, with major by-catches, poses its own challenges.

Historically, the TAC system and the fish stock assessment process on which it is based was seriously undermined by over-quota, and unreported, landings. In the UK the introduction of Buyers and Sellers Registration, in 2005, along with a range of other controls has meant that any "black fish" in the system have been pushed to the margin. As a result the price of fish and quota has risen significantly.

The use of TACs in mixed fisheries poses particular challenges, not least in the area of discards. For this reason TACs have been supplemented by other measures. These include rules to require more selective fishing gear, restrictions on time at sea (effort control) and more innovative approaches such as cod avoidance plans.

EFFORT CONTROL

Effort Control, or the limitation of Days-at-Sea, was introduced by the EU in 2003 to deal with the fact that, due to endemic unreported landings, TACs were ineffectual in controlling fishing mortality. Effort Control has the advantage that it can be applied easily at a distance but it remains a crude and economically perverse instrument. In addition, its effects are not always those that are anticipated.

Experience in the Pacific, Norway and Iceland indicates that the effect of Effort Control is to intensify fishing during the available period. At its worst an effort regime is capable of causing a spiralling decrease in fishing stocks. In addition, there are negative consequences for prices and costs.

In European Fisheries effort control generates the same kind of response—an intensification of fishing pressure during the time that vessels can go to sea. Examples include reducing steaming time in a variety of ways, "capital stuffing" and technological creep as well as high-grading of stocks to maximise the return on capital.[1]

Effort Control is best understood as a policy response to excess capacity. The real solution is a reduction in capacity through a voluntary, publicly funded decommissioning scheme.

The NFFO has consistently argued against the imposition of effort restrictions for the reasons given above.

DISCARDS

The Commission has announced and already begun to move in the direction of a total ban on discards.[2] The NFFO believes that a total ban is unworkable in our mixed fisheries but it does support the Commission's philosophy involving pilot schemes, incentives, the involvement of stakeholders and an incremental approach. The gradual introduction of measures to reduce discards on a fishery by fishery basis, focusing on the outcome to be achieved, rather than being simply prescriptive, is welcomed.

It is, however, important to recognise the varying reasons that underlie discarding. Some discarding is caused by prescriptive regulations (minimum landing size, catch composition rules, quotas, effort control, etc), some by the difficulty of species selectivity in a multi-species fishery (by-catches, unmarketable fish), yet others are due to biological factors in a wild environment (fish spawn and are immature juveniles, catch densities are not uniform)

A simple ban will not, of itself, remove all the reasons for discarding fish. The NFFO believes that Avoidance Plans, Real Time Closures, RTC, and MLS, properly enforced and coupled with gear selectivity offer the best way forward so long as TACs exist, provided the proper incentive structures exist.

---

[1] There has been extensive academic criticism of Effort Control. One of the most prominent critics is Professor Lee G. Anderson. A brief introduction to his position may be found in *The Microeconomics of Vessel Behaviour: A Detailed Short-Run Analysis of the Effects of Regulation*, Marine Resource Economics, Volume 14, pp 129—150.

[2] Communication from the Commission to the Council and the European Parliament A policy to reduce unwanted by-catches and eliminate discards in European fisheries, COM(2007)136 final.

One of the principle concerns with moving to a total ban—so that everything caught is landed—is that it may encourage the targeting of small fish. The experience of other countries, particularly Norway, has been studied and has relevance but could not safely be slavishly applied to our fisheries.

COD AVOIDANCE

Drawing on its own experience, the industry has suggested Cod Avoidance Plans as a way of reducing discards whilst moving towards sustainable fisheries. The main features of such plans are:

Use of fishermen's knowledge—The Cod Avoidance plans draw on the fishermen's knowledge of the target species and their habits, thus increasing their commitment as stakeholders in the process.

Bottom up management—The initiative comes from the bottom up with the industry taking responsibility for its own activities at the grass roots level. Cod Avoidance Plans are drawn up for individual vessels, or a fleet of similar vessels. They provide precise details of the target fishery (or fisheries), the gear that will be used, the precise location of the activity and the period of time over which activity will take place. Provision is made for inspection and verification.

Incentives aligned with management objectives—The plans seek to optimise the fishing activities of the vessel by changing fishery, gear, place and period in order to avoid catching cod, thus contributing towards the Cod Recovery Plan. In exchange, the vessel, or vessels, will obtain a degree of freedom with respect to effort control.

Discard reduction/elimination—With such Cod Avoidance Plans, vessels will significantly reduce their by-catch of cod (it should not be forgotten that 60% of cod is caught as a by-catch). In addition, such plans encourage greater gear selectivity with a view to decreasing, if not totally eliminating, discards.

Need for safeguards—Verification is obviously key to any successful scheme. The Cod Avoidance Plan makes provision for verification through on board observers, random inspections, prior notification of landings and certification of sales.

The Cod Avoidance Plan is supported in principle by the North Sea and North West Water RACs, and they are currently working on the detail.

The NFFO strongly supports the Cod Avoidance Plans and believes that they provide a valuable guide for future action.

REGIONAL ADVISORY COUNCILS, RACs

The RACs in which the UK participates have made a promising start, and their growing maturity has enabled them to start the process of moving from confrontation among the stakeholders to cooperation.

Much has been expected of the RACs, since the reform of the CFP which envisaged the RACs as providing a means for stakeholders to influence policy. The NFFO is committed to this development since it believes that the future of European fisheries lies in a more devolved structure of governance, as opposed to the top/down control approach that characterised the earlier years of the CFP. Although RACs have already made a substantial contribution, the RACs will demonstrate their worth mainly though the development of long-term management plans.

It is a matter of concern, therefore, that the funding of the RACs has not kept pace with the role that is expected of them. Without such support it will be difficult to continue the development of Long-term Management Plans. The NFFO strongly believes that more funding should be made available for the RACs.

LONG-TERM MANAGEMENT PLANS

At the *Johannesburg World Summit on Sustainable Development* in 2002 the EU underlined its commitment to sustainable development, first made with the Rio Declaration of 1992. *The Johannesburg Implementation Plan* committed the EU[3] to:

> *Maintain or restore stocks to levels that can produce the maximum sustainable yield with the aim of achieving these goals for depleted stocks on an urgent basis and where possible not later than 2015;*

These objectives effectively meant that the CFP became concerned with the need to elaborate Long-term Management Plans for those fisheries deemed to be under threat. Plans were to be introduced on a fishery by fishery basis.

---

[3] Article 31.

The NFFO agrees in principle to the introduction of Long-term Management Plans which offer the benefit of stability to the industry. Such plans can not, however, be implemented without reference to the industry capacity or they will create economic and social hardship. The NFFO believes that the key requirements for the success of such Long-term Management Plans are sound science and buy-in from stakeholders. The RACs have played a critical role both in assisting with the science and also in securing the buy-in of stakeholders. In addition they have provided a forum in which negotiations can take place. Developing Long-term Management Plans is an intensive process requiring funding for both the science and the stakeholders meetings.

Progress has been slow. Whilst the CFP stresses the importance of Recovery Plans and Long-term Management Plans, in fact only six have been adopted over the past five years (Cod, Northern Hake, Biscay Sole, Nephrops off the Iberian Coast, Southern Hake and North Sea Flatfish). At the present time, Northern Hake is moving from a Recovery Plan to a Long-term Management Plan. Haddock, mackerel and saithe are considered to be at around MSY but should be able to sustain a Long-term Management plan.

SUMMARY

The reform of the CFP has not so far delivered the benefits in terms of sustainability of fish stocks that was its primary objective.

The NFFO believes that a major reason for this shortfall is poor governance and lack of clarity in decision-making in a multi-species environment. The move away from a top-down control structure to a more devolved, stakeholder driven, form of organisation has only just begun to take place and risks being stifled. It accepts TACs as an allocatory mechanism and as the least worst solution in an MSY world. It continues to view them as a very blunt instrument. In the recent past illegal fishing has been a problem, but the NFFO believes that, the evidence shows that, since 2005 this is no longer the case. The NFFO has never viewed effort control as a solution because it intensifies pressure on resources.

In so far as the future is concerned, the NFFO believes that the development of Avoidance Plans offers positive benefits. In addition, there should be more Long-term Management Plans, drawn up by stakeholders through the RACs whose role should be expanded.

3 March 2008

Examination of Witness

Witness: MR BARRIE DEAS, Chief Executive, National Federation of Fishermen's Organisations, examined.

Q170 *Chairman:* Welcome and thank you first of all for the written evidence but also for finding time to come and talk to us and help us with our inquiry. I have to go through two formal things. First of all this is a formal evidence session so a transcript will be taken; you will get a copy of that and have an opportunity to make any corrections and iron out any issues. The other thing is that these hearings are all webcast so what we are saying here is going into stellar space and somebody might pick it up somewhere, most likely on the lost planet. Let us proceed, would you like to start by making a general statement and then we can go into a question and answer session, or do you want to go straight into the Q&A?
Mr Deas: Only to introduce myself as Barrie Deas, Chief Executive of the National Federation of Fishermen's Organisations, which is the representative body for fishermen in England, Wales and Northern Ireland. That is my day job—that is who pays my salary; I am also Vice-President of Europeche, the European association of fishermen's organisations, and the Chairman of the demersal working group of the North Sea RAC and I am on the executive committee of the North West Waters RAC and the External Waters RAC.

Q171 *Chairman:* That is pretty impressive; thank you very much. I wonder if I could start by really asking you what you see as the objectives or should be the objectives of the Common Fisheries Policy, how successful is it in achieving those objectives and what are the reforms that you would like to see—fairly simple?
Mr Deas: The objectives—I have to start with sustainability of stocks because without that you do not have anything else. There are certain realities that are imposed on our fisheries, by their nature; these are some of the most complex fisheries in the world: multi-gear, multi-species, multi-jurisdiction and so the reality is that we have shared stocks and we therefore need institutional arrangements to manage those shared stocks. Sustainability and a living for fishermen and those who depend on fish landings in my view, (perhaps a simplistic view) should be the objectives. The reforms in 2002 were very much a mixed bag; there were some advantages and some movements forward, particularly in relation to the establishment of regional advisory councils, and there were other items, particularly the road which the Commission have gone down in terms of stock recovery plans that have not been quite so palatable. The central failing of the Common Fisheries Policy

was diagnosed some time ago: it is over-centralised, it is almost an Eastern European (pre-the Wall) set of institutions.

Q172 *Chairman:* A bit like the CAP then really.

Mr Deas: That is right. It is over-centralised and the DG Fisheries does a good job in extremely difficult circumstances, it is not a huge number of people and yet, as somebody has pointed out, they have got responsibility for fisheries over 40 degrees of latitude and very different kinds of fisheries. That has influenced their choice of instrument, particularly for example effort control—TAC's and quotas and effort control. TACs and quotas are difficult to get away from because you need to share the cake somehow in this complicated set-up, so they are a given unless you can identify some alternative way of sharing the cake. Effort control has been chosen because it is a way in which Brussels can reach out and theoretically control what happens at sea by limiting the amount of time. I happen to have fairly strong views that that is not what happens but those are some opening and very broad remarks that I would like to make about the CFP.

Q173 *Chairman:* Can we just press you on what you said about effort control, saying that that is not what happens. What do you mean by that?

Mr Deas: Effort control is a restriction on the time that a vessel can go to sea, it does not influence what the vessel does when it is at sea. There are a number of responses that vessels can make in order to maintain their earnings when they are pushed for time at sea. They can obtain additional days, buy days, and that is what happens, so that increases the cost to the industry, but an alternative might be to high-grade— in other words the fish that you do catch you keep the highest value ones so it is an encouragement to discard—or you could limit the geographical range of where you fish. In other words you could be fishing in juvenile inshore stocks rather than going a bit further afield, so there are 101 ways in which fishermen can and will react to restrictions on time at sea if they really bite, in order to make their fishing operations more efficient. That could be technical gear, discarding, where they fish, crewing, a whole range, so my argument is that effort control provides an incentive to increase the intensity of fishing when you are at sea and I think that is entirely counter-productive. Iceland had an effort control system for its small boat fleet and they got down to allocations of 80 days a year before abandoning it because they could see that the vessels were, what they call "capital stuffing"—putting in bigger engines so that their steaming time to the grounds was reduced etc but they abandoned it. The Norwegians scoff at effort control because they see it as a substitute for a structural regime that addresses the issue of capacity

and, as I say, the European Commission have chosen effort control because from their point of view it exerts control at a distance.

Q174 *Lord Cameron of Dillington:* You have already stated that it is too big and the European Commission cannot control it all; therefore you suggest that governance should be moved down the line a bit to the fish industry, to the regional advisory councils and to Member States. We are a bit dubious about the efficacy of this and all those levels of governance at a lower level; will they actually impose what is needed for conservation of the fishing stocks? I was wondering whether you could explain really how you see it actually working in practice.

Mr Deas: The Commission itself is thinking along these lines; it is struggling and there is a debate within the Commission about how far to go down these routes. I attended a meeting organised by ICES in Copenhagen a few weeks ago; its title was "Reversing the burden of proof in fisheries" and as I understand it the idea would be that the Commission and Member States would set principles and standards and the RACs would be involved at that level as well to find what would be appropriate principles and standards for fisheries, but after that it would be down to industry. There would be a transfer of responsibility to the industry, so instead of having this whole panoply of highly prescriptive rules that are difficult to enforce, difficult to understand—and that is not just the industry, the enforcement side as well find it difficult and highly complex (and leaving aside just for a second what we mean by the industry, at what sort of level) industry groups would submit plans for, say, three to five years, a three to five-year operational plan in which it would specify how it would fish sustainably in line with these principles and standards that have been set. That process would be audited, so the Commission's role would change from setting the standards, to auditing the process, auditing the paperwork and ensuring that the plans, which might include technical measures or any other include the instruments that were chosen, how they would meet environmental standards and the whole panoply. And the scientists would audit those plans. To me, from an industry point of view, there are threats and opportunities in all of that, and the idea of responsibility and a less prescriptive system is very attractive, but the big question is who goes to jail when it all goes wrong.

Q175 *Lord Cameron of Dillington:* That is what I was going to ask you about enforcement; how do you enforce this and how do you ensure that the fishermen do not take advantage of the fact, because presumably the fishermen have a majority on the regional advisory councils. Who is to say that in every area they are going to behave responsibly?

Mr Deas: I did park the issue of what we are talking about when we say industry. The RACs certainly have a role in helping to define the standards and principles, but it may be that industry groups and voluntary groups of owners—that might be national, it might be international, it may be down to individual vessel level, that is all for discussion, but the principle of moving in that direction is a sound one. We certainly have a lot of work to do on the practicalities but we are not dealing with ideals here, we are talking about looking at a system that we have now that has had a considerable amount of time to work, and whether we continue with highly prescriptive rules imposed from above or whether we move to something that has a lot more flexibility but transfers a considerable amount of responsibility and authority to the industry.

Q176 *Lord Cameron of Dillington:* Can the RACs fulfil this role as they develop?
Mr Deas: I do not know the answer to that question. RACs have a role, for example, in developing long-term management plans which would really feed into the standards rather than the lower level; the lower level is really about demonstrating a group of owners' commitment to a particular plan and following through that plan. It has to be at a lower level than the RACs because the RACs' strong points are the involvement of the industry but also the involvement of other stakeholders, and they provide a forum, but if you are going to have a system in which the industry is taking responsibility then you could not have other stakeholders involved in that.

Q177 *Lord Cameron of Dillington:* In your plans scientists and conservationists would have no say, it would entirely be the local fishermen who say what they should catch. I do not think that sounds a very good idea.
Mr Deas: I do not think that is what I am saying and bear in mind that scientists are not formally members of RACs anyway; they are invited along and play a big role and we would have liked to have had them as full members but that was not the way it worked out. The scientists have a role in auditing the process and in writing the plans before that and there needs to be a realignment of the role. Whilst touching on scientists, at the moment their role is largely restricted to pointing and saying "You are getting too close to the cliff edge, you are getting too close to the cliff edge." A much more constructive role would be for scientists to provide options and say if you want to get to something like maximum sustainable yield, or maximum economic yield, here are some ways of getting there for discussion, that is a much more productive role. That is what the scientists that are currently involved in the RACs want. To answer your questions more directly, the scientists are

involved in helping to define the plans and the auditing process and the Commission and the various control authorities in the Member States, the European Fisheries Control Agency, their central role would be the auditing process.
Chairman: Let us move on to the economics of fisheries management; Viscount Ullswater.

Q178 *Viscount Ullswater:* In your evidence you have labelled TAC's as being a very blunt instrument, and yet you have also said that any alternative system would need to offer a similar distributive mechanism. You have just said to My Lord Chairman that the effort control is one that has proved to be non-viable and you gave evidence from Iceland and from Norway, so if you are looking at more of an outcome system to deliver sustainability and to maximise economic returns, how do you see that being controlled and are there some management tools which need to be devised or relaxed in order to make that happen?
Mr Deas: We are stuck with TACs and quotas because I cannot see an alternative way of sharing the cake out. We can dispense quite happily with effort control, particularly as across Europe we are moving towards a situation where there is a much higher degree of compliance. Effort control was introduced to underpin TACs and quotas because there was large-scale black fish; that era seems to have come to an end and therefore the fundamental rationale for effort control is not there. The instruments are long term management plans that would define where we want to get to, but the more detailed instruments and measures under the scenario that I described earlier would be for the industry to define the detail, so that instead of saying what size holes should be in your net you would say, as part of your plan, "I will be using these kinds of gears that will deliver this level of selectivity." If a group of fishermen want to use effort control restrictions on their time at sea voluntarily, who am I to say no to that; my problem with that is using it as a broad, long-distance restriction. If we are thinking about 2012 and the reform of the Common Fisheries Policy and what might replace the current arrangements, those are the kinds of ideas that we need to explore.

Q179 *Viscount Ullswater:* You have to accept that TACs are there, the quota is there.
Mr Deas: Yes.

Q180 *Viscount Ullswater:* Yet what you are saying is that it should be much more flexible in the long-term management plan; you have a basis of quota allocation and yet you can operate within a more flexible arrangement of quota, or does quota have to be absolutely distinct for each Member States, each fishery or whatever it is?

Mr Deas: There are different levels of question there. I was making the assumption that we would continue with the principle of relative stability and the level of TAC would continue to be set on a broader level, but in terms of how you take that quota and the instrument you use—we are talking here about the technical conservation regulation, effort control, how you meet environmental objects, that is the kind of item that could be included in annual or bi-annual or tri-annual operational plans.

Q181 *Viscount Ullswater:* Can I just continue with this a little bit? Are you suggesting that there will be no need for an annual Council meeting in December to decide on TACs year after year, that somehow TACs will evolve in a sustainable way that does not need this precise decision-taking? Do your long-term management plans include the flexible quota system according to the science and according to the monitoring of the fish caught, according to the selectivity of the fisheries and how competent the fishermen are at delivering the sort of fishery management that you are talking about?

Mr Deas: With the exception of a few short-lived species the fact that we have annual quotas and the science cycle works on an annual basis is entirely superfluous. There is a huge amount of effort involved in turning the wheel every year to churn out these figures, and bear in mind that 50% of the stocks that we are talking about here ICES consider the level of data insufficient to call them analytical TACs. That is a large number and of even those that are analytical, there are quite a number of those that we would have concerns about, and we can perhaps talk about the science a little later. It would be much more preferable to just concentrate on a particular stock or group of stocks in mixed fisheries: where are we now, where do we want to be and how do we get there in an incremental, phased, way, and then the plans would be matched to that. There are different levels that we are talking about here but apart from a few stocks I do not see the need to have annual TACs. With the nephrops stocks, for example, we are already on a two-year cycle and that principle could be developed.

Q182 *Baroness Jones of Whitchurch:* What proportion of the fish that are caught come from mixed stocks roughly—is it 20% or 80%?

Mr Deas: With white fish stocks you would have to say the majority, the vast majority, there are very few pure white fish fisheries. With the pelagic species of herring and mackerel, which in tonnage terms is very large, that is much more of a single species. As you move up to the North, North Norway Barents Sea cod, that becomes a much cleaner fishery, but down where we are the demersal stocks are highly mixed. Nearly all the time when we are talking about demersal stocks we are talking about very mixed fisheries to some degree or other.

Q183 *Viscount Ullswater:* Perhaps I should just round off the economics side and ask you whether you feel that there is a role for the rights-based approach to fisheries management?

Mr Deas: Yes. In the UK we have gone quite far down that road already with fixed quota allocations and if a fisherman wants to buy quota he can buy quota. There is an issue about legal title and whether ultimately ownership resides with the Government as a public resource, so there is a debate to be had about that but actually we have gone quite far down the road of quota trading, not in a particularly planned way, I think it developed inadvertently; there were a number of changes to the management system and we realised we had tradable quotas without anybody specifically arguing that that is the direction we should go in. It is there, it plays an important part and on the whole the industry, with the exception of the under-ten sector, is content with the arrangements that are there. There is certainly some need for fine-tuning, but after the introduction of FQAs (fixed quota allocations) the amount of grumbling about quotas and allocations evaporated because if a fisherman wanted quota and he could afford it, he could buy it.

Q184 *Viscount Brookeborough:* Just before I turn to the scientific question you and other witnesses have spoken about net technology if you like and the developments in avoiding catching certain species. That has been spoken about for years; has this technology advanced or why do we not have better results when the actual fish species have not changed? On a previous inquiry we were shown lots of new technology like windows, different compartments where different fish might be found and the net could open and let them out. What has been the improvement (if any) over the last 15 years or why are we still talking about letting the same species out of the net as we were then?

Mr Deas: There has been development and I am sure there will continue to be great improvements in selectivity. The problem has been in providing the right kind of incentives to encourage the uptake, and here there is a link between the last question and this question which is why we have advocated cod avoidance plans that would provide an exemption from the days at sea regime. If you put forward a plan how you were going to operate in the coming year that might include selective gear, amongst other things. For example, there is a new net that has been designed in the United States called "the Eliminator"—pause for laughter—which eliminates cod in your catch. In the past it has been relatively easy to release whiting and haddock because when they go into a net they swim upwards and you have a square mesh panel at the top and they escape. Cod is more awkward because of their size, they have big bodies, and they react in a net on the whole by swimming downwards. This net addresses that particular behavioural pattern, so there are technical developments there but in my opinion the full advantages of selective gear have not been fulfilled to their optimum which is why I am very keen to explore how you can put arrangements in place that encourage their adoption and use. It is more of an economics and incentives issue than a technical issue, the technical development will continue.

Q185 *Viscount Brookeborough:* Thank you very much. We will now move on to scientific analysis and you have already spoken just a little bit about it and we understand that there is a great deal of uncertainty in the scientific analysis. What is your opinion of the methodology and do you think they can improve it without putting so much more money into it that it is counterproductive on the fishery industry. Would you also comment on the success or the progress of joint initiatives between fishermen and scientists when we are led to believe that definitely in years past they were streets apart and could not possibly agree or get together; is there some progress on this?

Mr Deas: On the question of uncertainty there is a joint recognition by the industry and the scientists that there are large areas of uncertainty and there is a new commitment to do something about that. Later this year we are to meet and establish what are called data workshops that will begin to introduce knowledge that is held by fishermen about the stocks in a systematic way. Fishermen have always had opinions about the stocks, but they have tended to be dismissed as anecdotal if not self-serving sometimes, and the challenge is to find ways in which that information can be captured and fed into the system to supplement the more conventional methods based on official landing statistics and surveys. Landing statistics as a pillar of the stock assessments were corrupted to a very high degree by black fish and a very destructive cycle evolved in which black fish led to poor information, led to more stringent TACs, which led to economic pressures, more black fish and more poor information and the whole cycle went round. That should be improving now—the scientists tell us that it is improving—but even granted that and also taking into account that the science tends to be retrospective, tends to be a couple of years out of date. Fishermen are experiencing in real time what is happening to the stocks, all of that can be fed in in a collaborative way if we can find the ways to do it. A lot of this is about trust and confidence, so at the RAC level both the North Sea RAC and the North West Waters RAC are heavily involved in efforts to improve the quality of the assessments of the stocks

that they are involved in. One idea that has been put forward and seems to be finding favour with ICES is a traffic light system so that when ICES is fully confident with its assessment then it gets a green light, if there are real problems there is a red light and then something in between. That will help direct us and our efforts to the stocks that really need to be addressed. On the second part of your question about collaboration, there was a big breakthrough just after 2002 when the Government agreed with our suggestion that fisheries science partnerships should be established where CEFAS and the industry jointly define a particular problem, jointly gather the data and do the respective analysis. That has been so successful that we now have a time series in particular fisheries that are now being taken into account by ICES. As a model it has been adopted elsewhere in the UK and in Europe and it has transformed the relationships between fishermen and scientists which had previously been restricted to an annual very controversial meeting in the autumn when the scientists said these are the results of our work over the year and your quotas are going down. You can imagine the kind of reaction that that gave, but this brings fishermen and scientists into collaboration aboard the commercial fishing vessels; it is shared work and shared results and there is a sense of ownership of those results throughout. That is a model for many areas or fisheries where sworn enemies can work together.

Q186 *Viscount Brookeborough:* Is that one area where either side doubts the other's credibility because they are simply not monitoring the same areas at any one time because the scientists include not necessarily one fishery but it could include one and a half other fisheries. We were told by a witness earlier that the area the scientists operate in is not the same as a single fishery and therefore when they do not agree with each other they say well of course the statistics do not really come out of the area that we are in?

Mr Deas: I can see the argument, which is that ICES squares are at too broad a level and you need a lower level resolution, and that is where fisheries science partnerships can contribute, providing seasonal data and lower level resolution data and feed that in to the process. Indeed, that is what some of the time series impose and the fisheries science partnerships do.

Q187 *Chairman:* Can we move on to discards, and let us say that on discards there is recognition that a total ban is never going to effectively happen and there will always be a degree of discarding, that the Norwegian ban is a pragmatic ban and most likely could not be applied in the context of the United Kingdom. Taking the large margin of error associated with fish stock prediction that the science comes up with, there is at the moment a real problem of the fishermen putting his net in, pulling out fish for which a TAC exists but he does not have quota for and so that is discarded. That seems to be the most offensive element of discard.

Mr Deas: Yes.

Q188 *Chairman:* How can we remove that problem?

Mr Deas: I agree with your opening remarks and the solution has to be fishery by fishery, but again I come back to the idea—and this is an idea that has been advanced by our Federation—of cod avoidance plans. Really what you are talking about there is avoiding catching cod over and above your legitimate quota because at present, as I explained earlier, the incentive can be to go out, catch what you catch and then throw overboard the lower grades in order to maximise your income. A cod avoidance plan would be incentivised through an exemption to days at sea, and that means money, because if you are a white fish boat you can only be viable if you buy extra days so there is a direct financial incentive. That could be in a variety of ways, it could be using the Eliminator net that I described, for example, more selective gear, or it could be through spatial avoidance, in other words fishing in grounds where you know there is a high probability that there is low cod, or it could be a whole mixture throughout the year, it could be a mixture of those reasons. We prepared a draft pilot cod avoidance plan for a particular vessel out of Whitby. Over the year that vessel was involved in five separate fisheries: it started fishing for whiting, it then moved to the Norwegian sector targeting saithe and pollock, it then moved to a nephrops fishery that had some cod by-catch and then to a relatively clean nephrops fishery and finished the year targeting haddock. It had about 100 tonnes of cod, partly pooled, partly purchased, and the plan defined how that vessel would operate to ensure that it did not catch more than its legitimate quota. If, for example, when it was in the Norwegian sector it caught more than the expected 11% of cod, then it would move to the next fishery in its portfolio of catching opportunities earlier. Temporal, spatial, gear adaptations were all part of that, and that is probably quite a complicated one, you could have a fishery that was just following the same kind of pattern throughout the year or maybe a couple of fisheries winter and summer, but that gets the general idea across. Probably the question that you are going to ask is okay he has a plan but how do we know he is following his own plan? There has to be an element of observer programme in that and the vessel operators would be willing to accept that. An alternative may be something like CCTV attached to the winch which is used in some NFFO fisheries at the moment. CCTV applied by the state smacks of big brother, but as a cheap alternative to having an observer on board might be a bit more of an attractive option.

Q189 *Chairman:* It might close down at critical periods though, might it not?

Mr Deas: We have to take all of these things into account, but the same thing can be said about VMS, there is nothing that is foolproof, you have to look at the balance of these things.

Q190 *Chairman:* Is there a way though if I bring up haddock and I have not got a quota for haddock but there is haddock quota being held by either my PO or somebody else's PO, is there a mechanism that means that either there or then or once I have landed I buy quota to cover my catch?

Mr Deas: That happens.

Q191 *Chairman:* Is that happening routinely?

Mr Deas: Yes. What you have got to remember is that what you are talking about there are the quota rules but then the catch composition rules, the technical conservation rules, require you to have your catch composition in terms of the species aboard right after 24 hours. If you have gone out and caught too much whiting or too much cod or whatever in your first 24 hours, you are then supposed to discard that and then go fishing for it again later in the trip, there is an inherent madness about that.

Chairman: We are all speechless.

Q192 *Baroness Jones of Whitchurch:* Why do you not do what the Chairman was just talking about where you agree what happens in those circumstances; why do they not get on the phone or get on the radio and start trading?

Mr Deas: That is okay when you land, but if you are boarded at sea and you have your catch composition wrong you are prosecuted.

Q193 *Baroness Jones of Whitchurch:* You can only do that trading when you land.

Mr Deas: Yes. If we were allowed to have our catch compositions right just as we landed that would not be a problem, but at the moment after 24 hours—the Navy can board you and say your catch composition is wrong for the mesh size that you are using. It is interesting that earlier this year in Dublin there was a meeting on technical conservation and the Commission's presentation was very illuminating because it was highly critical of the current regulation and how we could have got in the position where we are discarding to meet catch composition rules when Commissioner Borg has got this initiative to reduce discarding. It is why, I think, I have come around to the view that the idea of moving away from highly prescriptive rules like that that create perverse results as I have just described has to be one of our objectives.

Q194 *Chairman:* What is the rationale for the 24-hour catch composition requirement?
Mr Deas: Instead of having legal and illegal mesh sizes you could use any mesh size but then you would have to have your catch composition to justify using that. That was the rationale which we argued against at the time, but unsuccessfully.

Q195 *Viscount Ullswater:* In your evidence you say "it should not be forgotten that 60% of cod is caught as a by-catch". To us that is a terrible waste of a very marketable fish, but is it a waste, is that what you are saying?
Mr Deas: It is by-catch but it is not discarded. You might be targeting haddock or saithe and small amounts are caught across a whole range of fisheries; you just need to be careful how you interpret that, it is not being discarded. Nevertheless, the industry certainly talked about 40,000 tonnes of cod in the North Sea being discarded; I do not know if that is the correct figure but certainly that is what was being discussed last year and that seems to be entirely counter-productive to a recovery plan.

Q196 *Lord Palmer:* Would you be able to give us the accurate figure?
Mr Deas: No.

Q197 *Lord Palmer:* Because you do not know what has been discarded.
Mr Deas: It is hearsay.
Chairman: We weigh it before we discard it. Let us go on to control and enforcement; Lord Palmer.

Q198 *Lord Palmer:* You were in the audience when I asked Mr Armstrong this same question. "Black fish" in the system seem to have been pushed right into the margin and illegal fishing does not seem to have been a problem since the year 2005. To what do you really ascribe this success and what do you consider to be the key pillars of any revised EU control and enforcement regime?
Mr Deas: I agree with Bertie Armstrong that the buyers and sellers registration has produced a remarkable turnaround and that is reflected in not only the rising price of fish but the rising price of quota. The fact that the black fish has been extinguished and therefore to cover legal landings a vessel requires more quota and so that pushed the price up, which is a very good indicator I think as well as the official statistics. What should be the pillars of an EU control policy? It is worth recalling the *Net Benefits* report—I do not agree with everything in it but I thought on the whole it was a quality document. The part of that document that I thought was most

illuminating was something called the fisheries management jigsaw—it is a jigsaw because all the pieces interlink—and it said that for a successful management policy you need capacity broadly in line with resources, you need the fleet to be profitable, the management needs to be based on good information, and that includes fish stock assessments, and there needs to be a high level of compliance because if there is not a high level of compliance the system is broken. The *Net Benefits* report was talking about the UK but you could equally apply those to the EU: you are not going to get good compliance if you do not have capacity broadly in line with resources, which is almost the same as saying profitability. If there is a huge gulf in perceptions about the stock you have compliance problems as well—if the fishermen disagree profoundly with what the science is saying—and all of those things come together and develop in a culture of compliance where fishermen take responsibility for the resource that they depend on. Again, it is a jigsaw because you cannot have one of those in isolation, they all feed into each other and are linked to each other.

Q199 *Chairman:* Let us just summarise the business on structural policy. You say no to efforts and you prefer capacity reduction; the question I suppose is, what is the most effective way of managing capacity reduction? Straightforward decommissioning is not a one-for-one relationship.
Mr Deas: No, it is not but then again neither is effort control; you think you are doing one thing and the result is something else. Decommissioning does work. It is not one-to-one but the reduction in the English fleet from 1993 onwards and in the Scottish fleet from 2001, when there was a substantial reduction in capacity and effort—a 67% reduction in effort—in the North Sea has been a major contributor to the reduction of fishing mortality on cod and therefore a contribution to the recovery of cod at sea. I do not think decommissioning is perfect, but none of the instruments that we are talking about here are. I would also add that to my knowledge the Irish have a white fish decommissioning scheme in the pipeline; the Dutch have taken out a significant number of their large beam trawlers through decommissioning; there is a decommissioning scheme proposed in France as part of this financial package; the Spanish have reduced the size of their fleet through a fleet modernisation scheme—they have taken a lot of capacity out but put new capacity in, which is a way of doing it—the Danes were actually the first to undertake major decommissioning, going well back before 1993, so it would be entirely false to think that decommissioning has only taken place in the UK, there have been substantial decommissioning schemes elsewhere and I think that needs to be taken into account.

Q200 *Chairman:* There is a hard question lurking there, is there not, which is really why should the taxpayer be expected to fund a scheme that makes the industry more economically efficient and effective but improves the returns for those who remain in the industry?

Mr Deas: The public increasingly has an interest in the marine environment and fisheries are an important part of that, and the right size of fisheries is not just therefore something that should be laid at the fisherman's door; there is a public interest in getting it right. Also, had Government intervened early enough to put the proper licensing arrangements in we would not have seen the over-capacity during the Gadoid outburst outburst during the 1970s and 1980s, along with subsidies, that fuelled the expansion of the white fish fleet that really underpins the problem with the stocks that we have been dealing with over the last few years.

Q201 *Baroness Jones of Whitchurch:* Following on from the decommissioning issue what has been the socio-economic impact of that? I can remember seeing on television in the seventies and eighties people saying "You are going to wreck our communities if you cut the quotas" et cetera et cetera, but what has actually happened to those, particularly the very isolated communities where they have had decommissioning. Have they found other jobs or have they been neglected?

Mr Deas: The short answer is that I do not know. Socio-economic is that kind of word that is bandied around, but we do not really know, I do not think there is anybody collecting information on where crew from decommissioned vessels have gone. Socio-economic is a word that the Commission reads in one way which is that whenever they see the word they think "Here is an argument for us not to take the kind of measures that we need to take to put things on a proper footing", it is an excuse kind of argument. I see the economic dimension as an integral part of whether management measures work or not, whether they provide the right kind of incentives, so we are really talking there about understanding it in terms of a result-based approach. There is pitiful little socio-economic data gathered and it is one of the reasons why the North Sea RAC has established a working group to at least begin to gather that kind of information, and it is one of the responsibilities that the Commission certainly expects RACs to perform, to feed in these kinds of socio-economic dimensions.

Q202 *Chairman:* Let us finish where Mr Armstrong finished. You have talked about rights-based managed and you heard Mr Armstrong's concern that ITQs would lead basically to an international market and he used the phrase "would not necessarily be in the interests of Great Britain Plc". What is your view?

Mr Deas: My view is that there is a contradiction between national quotas and the treaty obligations on freedom of movement of labour and capital and the right of establishment, which is why this country got into deep water with the European Court in the *Factortame* case. Post *Factortame* it is clear that if fishermen from another Member State wish to buy quota in this country they can, as long as they comply with the economic links. We already have a pretty open system and it is interesting that the Anglo-Dutch and Anglo-Spanish, which are the main fishermen from other Member States that have bought quota, have bought quota on the stocks that they are interested in, so for the Spanish it was hake, megrim and monkfish and for the Dutch there was a big surplus in the UK at one time of North Sea plaice. Beyond that you do not see either the Dutch or the Anglo-Spanish pushing further and further. That is not to say that other interests might not come in in the future; if you have an open market that is what you have to accept. The fear is that as time goes on you would see an erosion of quotas held by the traditional UK fleet, but I think in the NFFO we were undoubtedly one of the strongest arguing for measures to restrict quota-hoppers. Post *Factortame* we have taken an entirely different view and say it is an open market, and in fact we have Anglo-Spanish and Anglo-Dutch members of our organisation now because we took the view that some of our members were trading quota or leasing quota with these interests and it is entirely hypocritical therefore not to have them in membership of a national organisation where we can talk about the issues and share perspectives. We found them to be very responsible, serious people and so I have a rather different view from Bertie Armstrong, reflecting our different experiences. Ultimately what it boils down to is the judgment in the European Court and the subsequent exchange of letters between Tony Blair and Jacques Santer that defined the limits of what a Member State can do in terms of requiring economic links.

Chairman: Thank you very much indeed. I do apologise that as we have ended we are down to a relatively sparsely-attended meeting, but from my point of view it is quite nice because where I sit the whole right wing has disappeared. Thank you very much.

Supplementary Memorandum by the National Federation of Fishermen's Organisations

COD AVOIDANCE PLANS: FROM CONCEPT TO IMPLEMENTATION

Background

1. Annex 1 to this paper is the NFFO concept note which outlines the general concept of cod avoidance plans.

2. Cod avoidance plans are designed to address the problem of fishing for economically important non-recovery species whilst limiting the impact on the recovery stock, in this case cod. An individual vessel plan will demonstrate how a vessel will keep its catches to its allocated quota, with minimal discards of cod. In aggregate terms, cod avoidance plans are a way of providing some assurance that increasing the TAC will not be accompanied by the increased targeting of cod or high grading. They are also a way of incentivising fishing patterns that are aligned with, rather than in conflict with management objectives. In this way, cod avoidance plans can contribute to a further reduction in fishing mortality.

3. The North Sea RAC and the North West Waters RAC have both supported the idea of cod avoidance plans and committed themselves to developing verifiable and practical arrangements that would allow for their introduction

4. The Commission's non-paper *A New Approach to Effort Management Under Annex II of the TAC Regulation* suggests that the Commission is actively considering the approach outlined in the NFFO concept paper:

> *"Given that a past history does not necessarily determine future behaviour, what is being proposed now is a result-oriented approach: the special treatment (not counting effort against the KW-days allocation) is given only if the low-catch condition is met and verified by observers."*

> *"To benefit from these exemptions,(from days at sea restrictions) vessels have to be involved into a specific plan aiming at the avoidance of species subject to recovery, properly designed and documented and including on-board observers and special landing checks."*

5. The Commission suggested, at its meeting with the RACs and ACFA on 13 November, that what it meant by observer coverage is a commitment by the vessel operator to accept an observer rather than 100% coverage of every vessel.

6. During the recent EU/Norway negotiations, which concluded on 26 November 2007:

The Community delegation informed the Norwegian delegation of its intention of reducing the discard rate (ie the proportion of the catch that is discarded) of cod to 10%. This is to be implemented by three measures:

— *Incentives to change the behaviour of fishermen, such as through cod avoidance measures to be developed at the industry's initiative and monitored with observer coverage: or*

— *Introduction of technical measures, to be tested in 2008 on a commercial scale with scientifically qualified observers during the test phase and introduced on a wide scale in 2009: and*

— *Where the two foregoing measures cannot be applied, a further reduction in fishing effort for vessels catching significant amounts of cod.*

Cod avoidance plans: implementation

7. Although, for the purposes of illustration, the NFFO concept note explains cod avoidance plans in terms of an individual vessel, it may be desirable and would be perfectly possible, to submit aggregate plans at fleet level covering 10, 20 or 200 vessels, so long as their characteristics and patterns of operation are homogeneous enough to make the plans meaningful.

8. Annex II to this paper is a draft individual vessel plan for the Whitby based whitefish/nephrops twin-rig trawler Our Lass II. Its inclusion provides a basis for further discussion and development, as well as a template that can be customised for other types of fishing vessel.

9. Cod avoidance plans will only be acceptable if they are transparent, robust and above all verifiable. To this end, the following safeguards could be considered by each vessel owner for inclusion in their plan. This should be regarded as a menu because the circumstances of each vessel, or fleet, may vary. However, the plan may include:

— Observer Coverage;

— CC TV coverage of deck area (linked to winch activity);

— Prior Notification of landings;

— Full monitoring of landings (subject to Authorities' resources);

— All cod sold through the auction; and

— Agreement to increased inspection at sea.

10. Sanctions: As cod avoidance plans will offer a very substantial incentive (exemption from the effort control regime) it is important that they are not abused. We would suggest that a vessel found guilty of flouting the provisions of its own cod avoidance plan should be obliged to revert to the effort regime for the remainder of that year with appropriate pro-rata reductions), and be disallowed from submitting a cod avoidance plan in the following year.

11. Cod avoidance plans would be prepared by the vessel or his agent (fish-selling agent, producer organisation etc) in discussion with the local representative of the fisheries management and control authorities.

12. Pilot: In order to test the practical operation of cod avoidance plans, we propose a pilot exercise in 2008 covering:

— two Whitefish vessels from Grimsby;

— two Whitefish/nephrops vessels from the Yorkshire coast;

— two Saithe vessels from Hull;

— two Nephrops trawlers from North Shields;

— two North Sea beam trawlers; and

— two Irish Sea nephrops/whitefish trawlers.

13. Each vessel in the pilot will submit a cod avoidance plan that states the vessel's fishing intentions for the coming year, the means to be employed to ensure that the vessel fishes its quota allocation with minimal cod discards and the safeguards/conditions to apply.

14. It should be possible to modify the plan during the year in two respects:

— the management periods, where the vessel might change its mode of fishing in year and or target species with different conditions applying; and

— the vessel's quota allocations of cod where these have been adjusted by quota sale, swap or transfer.

15. If at the end of six months, the pilot demonstrates the cod avoidance plans can be implemented successfully, applications could be invited from the rest of the fleet subject to effort restrictions. At an aggregate level this would address some of the concerns that:

— the increased "catchability" of cod as a result of the 2005 year-class will lead to increased targeting of cod;

— that effort control is too blunt an instrument to effectively reduce discards; and

— further reductions in fishing mortality are required to ensure the continuing rebuilding of the cod stocks.

Discard reduction

16. Discards/High Grading: Cod avoidance plans are designed to address the issue highlighted in ICES advice for 2008 that the focus of management measures should be on the total out-take of cod from the stock, not just on landings. Leaving aside possible changes in natural mortality, during 2007 in the North Sea a dramatic increase in discarding has been the consequence of a low TAC for cod, along with a significant increase in the abundance of cod and fleets which take cod mainly as a by-catch to other economically important fisheries. Higher value grades of cod have been retained on board whilst cod of marketable size but lower value have been discarded. It is primarily this type of discarding that cod avoidance plans will reduce.

17. Discarding undersized cod: Cod avoidance plans will also discourage discarding of juvenile cod below the minimum landing size. Measures to minimise this type of discarding are most effectively addressed through:

— more selective fishing gear; and

— real time closures of the type being piloted in Scotland.

However vessels submitting cod avoidance plans for approval would signal their intention to observe any voluntary real time closures in place as a contribution to reducing discards of undersized fish. In any event cod avoidance plans will discourage targeting of cod aggregations

November 2007

COD AVOIDANCE PLANS: A CONCEPT PAPER FOR DISCUSSION

BACKGROUND

The Commission's non-paper on the future of the EU cod recovery plan poses two mutually unpalatable alternatives. In order to bring about a rapid recovery of cod stocks in European waters the Commission argues that it is necessary to reduce fishing mortality on cod much further than the measures in place appear to have done so. This, it argued, can be done by suppressing effort on cod by reducing TACs and effort allocations across all those fleets which catch cod. Alternatively, fleets which catch only small amounts of cod could be *decoupled* from cod fisheries with separate, less restrictive effort ceilings. Although such fisheries would face less severe restrictions, it is acknowledged that decoupling would involve much more bureaucratic arrangements than have applied hitherto, with sub-area and gear effort ceilings and a much more restrictive regime on transfers of vessels and effort across fleet boundaries.

COD AVOIDANCE PLANS

As an alternative to these two approaches we propose *individual vessel cod avoidance plans*. We envisage that Cod Avoidance Plans would operate in the following way:

(i)   The vessel operator would <u>volunteer</u> to prepare a Cod Avoidance Plan;

(ii)   Those vessel operators opting to prepare a plan would discuss the matter with member state authorities who could provide advice on the content of the plans. (Such guidance would be the subject of a prior consultative exercise);

(iii)   The vessel operator (with assistance, if requested) would prepare a specific cod avoidance plan for that vessel for the coming 12 months;

(iv)   The vessel's Cod Avoidance Plan would specify ways in which the vessel would operate in the coming year to avoid catching cod above that covered by the vessels' legitimate quota. This could be through:

— spatial avoidance,

— temporal/seasonal avoidance,

— selective gear, or

— or any other method devised by the vessel operator.

(v)   The vessel operator would undertake, through these means, to keep cod catches within the vessel's quota allocations and in any event, below 5% by weight over the course of the year;

(vi)   The Cod Avoidance Plan would be submitted to the member state authorities for approval;

(vii)   If the vessel's Cod Avoidance Plan is approved the vessel would be exempt from effort control measures for the coming year;

(viii) Conditions: vessels participating in the cod avoidance plan scheme would undertake to provide enhanced data on fishing activities, including estimates of discards;

(ix)   Vessels breaching their conditions would be required to operate for the rest of the year and the subsequent fishing year, within the effort control regime;

(x)   Safeguards: in order to provide confidence that the cod avoidance plans would not be abused, a number of safeguards would apply:

— An observer programme on a number of vessels in the fleet,

— enhanced data reporting, including self-sampling, and

— cross-checking of cod catches with other similar vessels operating in the same area.

NOTES

1. Technical advances in the ability to make fishing gear more selective have not been matched by an institutional structure which incentivises the application of such gear. By specifying and agreeing the outcome (low catches of cod) the ingenuity and knowledge of fishermen will be directed to finding ways to reduce catches of cod. At present no such incentive structure exists.

2. Catches—Inclusive of landings and discards. Acceptable bycatch limits to be agreed but probably about a 5% maximum.

3. An approach based on Cod Avoidance Plans would be consistent with:

— the objectives of the cod recovery programme;

— the Commission's initiative on discards; and

— improved selectivity—the objective of the new revised technical conservation regulation.

WEDNESDAY 26 MARCH 2008

Present:	Arran, E of	Palmer, L
	Cameron of Dillington, L	Plumb, L
	Dundee, E of	Sewel, L (Chairman)
	Jones of Whitchurch, B	Ullswater, V

Memorandum by The Royal Society for the Protection of Birds

INTRODUCTION

1. The RSPB advocates fisheries management which maintains the balance between fishing effort and living marine resources, thus ensuring the long-term sustainability of fish stocks and their supporting ecosystems. As UK partner of BirdLife International, the RSPB plays a key role in delivering science-based advocacy to the fishing industry and its managers in Europe and beyond.

2. The Common Fisheries Policy was reviewed in 2002, and is due for its next review in 2012. Sometimes there is a mid-term review which, in this cycle, would naturally have fallen in 2007, but so far there has been no such openly public review this year. The CFP review in 2002, while not a radical overhaul, achieved some significant changes in direction, notably:

— a halt to public aid for building and modernising fishing vessels;

— commitment to develop an ecosystem-based approach to fisheries management; and

— first steps towards regionalising the CFP by creating Regional Advisory Councils.

3. Despite the 2002 review, while it can be argued that the reforms need time to work, the CFP is manifestly failing to deliver sustainable fisheries across a wide range of indicators.

4. *Fish stocks are still highly degraded:* About four-fifths of stocks remain *'outside safe biological limits'*. The number of fish stocks at risk in Community Waters appears to be neither decreasing nor increasing (DG Fisheries 2007).

5. *Excessive discarding:* Total discards in the North Sea are estimated at 500,000 to 880,000 tonnes annually, representing about half the weight of fish actually landed. A major cause is insufficient emphasis on preventing the capture of undersized fish and non-target species in the first place. The RSPB supports the introduction of a discard ban in trial fisheries.

6. *Excess capacity:* While some progress has been made to reduce excess capacity across Community fleets (notably in the Scottish whitefish fleet), the rate is too slow and reductions are nullified by increases in the technical efficiency of fishing.

7. *Recovery plans and long-term management plans:* These need to be extended, strengthened and speeded up.

8. *Illegal fishing:* Too much is still going on, undermining stocks and the credibility of management. The Commission is developing strong proposals for action, which we support.

9. *Ecosystem Approach:* The EC still has no overall strategy for implementing this, despite progress in some areas. The strength of the Commission's forthcoming Communication on implementation of the ecosystem approach will be an acid test.

10. *Governance:* The top-down governance of the CFP increasingly fails to deliver sustainable fisheries. Regionalisation of the CFP, begun with the inauguration of Regional Advisory Councils (RACs), needs to be developed further. The decision-making role of the Council, so often an obstacle to sustainable fisheries, should be changed and options for new institutional structures and devolution of powers explored in a wide-ranging public debate.

CONSERVATION/MANAGEMENT

Methods of ensuring conservation and sustainability

1. According to the Commission (COM(2007)295),[4] long-term management arrangements for northern hake, Biscay sole, North Sea haddock, mackerel and saithe have benefited stocks, and improved fishing opportunities for the sector. Northern hake appears to have recovered and returned within safe biological limits. However, the recovery plan for cod has not resulted in improvement at the rate anticipated and the stock remains well below safe biological limits.

2. Looking at all Community stocks in the round, however, there has been no change since the 2002 reforms. In the Commission's analysis of assessments by the International Council for the Exploration of the Sea (ICES), the number of stocks at risk appears to be neither decreasing nor increasing, with around four-fifths (35 out of 43 = 81%) remaining outside safe biological limits. These appalling figures would be even worse if they included deepwater fisheries which are not formally assessed although ICES considers that most are fished beyond safe biological limits.

3. Only three stocks subject to Total Allowable Catches (TACs), namely North Sea haddock, North Sea saithe and megrims in the Bay of Biscay, are being exploited at their Maximum Sustainable Yield (MSY) as aspired to by the UN World Summit on Sustainable Development in Johannesburg, 2002.

4. On the basis of such statistics, Sissenwine and Symes (2007)[5] conclude that the *"fisheries of the CFP suffer a much higher rate overfishing than occurs on average worldwide and in a comparable developed country"*. Analysis of global fisheries performance by the UN Food and Agriculture Organisation (FAO) supports this bleak conclusion, with the North-East Atlantic (including the Mediterranean and Black Seas) identified as *"the areas with stocks having the greatest need for recovery."*

5. This reinforces the need for long-term management plans, which are progressively being introduced. Integral to these is the definition of a target rate of fishing mortality, and a means to reach that target incrementally, rather than seeking to manage stock biomass levels. Such built-in harvesting rules should also militate against political manipulation of catch limits in the Fisheries Council.

6. The increasing role of environmental pressures on certain fish stocks, over which man has little short-term control, underlines further the need for a precautionary approach and a tight rein on fishing mortality. Eg the North Sea herring recovery plan, established in 1997, was initially successful but—for reasons not fully understood but suspected to be related to sea warming—all the year classes since 2001 are among the weakest since the late 1970s. This culminated in a 41% reduction on the 2008 catch limit at the December 2007 Fisheries Council. So even a recovery plan does not guarantee good returns; however, it does safeguard against even worse performance.

7. Art 2 of Council Regulation 2371/2002 mandated the progressive development of an ecosystem-based approach to fisheries management. To date, however, the EU's response to this has been too piecemeal, reactive and does not amount to a coherent strategy. This failure has allowed damage to marine ecosystems to go unchecked. The Commission will produce a Communication this year on implementing an ecosystem-based approach which may go some way towards remedying this. However, the Communication should be scrutinised to determine the extent to which it offers just further guidance, as distinct from a much-needed strategic plan for implementation.

8. The RSPB's view is that there is a need to implement the ecosystem approach on a regional seas basis (ie for the North Sea, Irish Sea, Baltic etc) by developing Fisheries Ecosystem Plans (FEPs) for each. The methodology for this is well understood, and would, in the RSPB's view, embed an ecosystem approach in the management of fisheries in UK and other Community waters. Defra is launching a pilot to trial an ecosystem-based approach to SW England fisheries—this could help to serve as a model for developing FEPs elsewhere.

9. In this context, however, DG Fisheries has lamentably little capacity for addressing the environmental dimension of the CFP. This calls for two things: (a) closer institutional liaison between DG Fish and DG Environment; (b) the need for MEPs to lobby in the European Parliament for greater resources to build environmental capacity in DG Fish.

---

[4] Fishing opportunities for 2008—policy statement from the European Commission. Communication from the Commission to Council. COM(2007)295.

[5] Sissenwine, M and Symes, D (2007) Reflections on the Common Fisheries Policy: report to the General Directorate for Fisheries and Maritime Affairs of the European Commission.

Management tools are available to fisheries managers

It is important to appreciate at the outset that, inasmuch as different tools suit different fisheries, it is not possible to address these tools in a prescriptive "one-size-fits-all" basis.

Total Allowable Catches (TACs)

10. These serve pelagic fisheries rather well but have proved to be a blunt instrument for managing mixed whitefish stocks of the sort found in the North Sea. Apart from the fact that Ministers routinely set TACs at levels higher than scientific advice, TACs tend to generate misreporting and discarding. TACs, since they are effectively Total Allowable *Landings*, suffer in these ways largely because they represent control by *output* rather than *input*. In this respect, there is merit in shifting the onus more towards controlling effort (see below) than catches/landings.

11. For the most degraded stocks, like cod, we argue for allocating only a 'bycatch quota' whereby there is no directed fishery for the species, and all cod taken would be as a component of an associated fishery (eg Nephrops) with the bycatch quota used to limit the mortality of the bycatch species (cod). There would then be huge incentive to fishermen to use their knowledge to limit catching excess (ie over-quota) cod.

Effort limitation, including "days at sea", marine conservation areas and real-time closures

12. The RSPB welcomes that the emphasis of managing Community fisheries is shifting more towards effort limitation (management of inputs) and away from management by catch limits (management of outputs), although the process in the Fisheries Council is generally to begin with a catch limit and translate it into an effort limit. All things being equal, it is more sensitive control to regulate how many vessels put to sea for how many days (ie fishing effort), than to try and regulate exclusively what they catch and land.

13. *Marine Conservation Areas* and *real-time closures* have a valuable role to play in supplementing effort control. Although closed areas (boxes) have been a routine part of UK fisheries management for many years (classed as Technical Conservation Measures), the proven benefits—in the right circumstances—of marine conservation areas (if this means "No-Take Zones") and real-time closures have been overlooked for far too long by the UK Government. *Real-time closures* have only just been recently introduced on a voluntary basis by the Scottish whitefish fishermen to avoid areas of spawning and juvenile cod. They have been a successful part of Norwegian fisheries management for years and deserve much stronger societal support.

14. *Marine Conservation Areas* are always claimed by UK scientists and the sector to be beneficial only for relatively sedentary species (like scallops) but there has been no political will to trial them for more mobile species (as has been done in the Georges Bank, NE United States). A setback was the 10-week closure for cod in the North imposed by the European Commission in 2001—this did not assist cod but merely displaced damaging fishing effort onto adjacent grounds, discrediting the whole approach so that the baby was effectively thrown out with the bathwater. What has been lacking has been a well-designed systematic pilot closure, with the objectives well defined and the effort displacement anticipated and adjusted for. This is in no small part down to a strong lobby by the sector to resist such closures whether they might be beneficial to long-term recovery or not.

Rights-Based Management tools (RBM)

15. It is not widely understood that various sorts of RBM already operate in a number of EU Member States, with the UK no exception: through the Producer Organisations' (POs) share-out and trading, the UK already has a *de facto* system of Individual Transferable Quotas (ITQs), even if it is not as explicit as, eg, that operating in the Dutch beam-trawler fleet.

16. One of the main criticisms of ITQs is that, over time, they can result in an unhealthy centralisation of fishing power, to the detriment of small-scale, fisheries-dependent communities, a trend apparent in Iceland. At the other extreme, RBM is sometimes over-sold as a "silver bullet", on the grounds that if you give a fisherman exclusive ownership rights of a resource, he will look after it better.

17. On balance, the RSPB can agree with Sissenwine and Symes (2007) that *"the Commission's initiative on RBM [ie its 2007 Communication] is important and worthwhile. The Commission should not push too hard, but it should keep the dialog[sic] alive, and it should not undermine formal and informal arrangements that facilitate a quasi market in rights between Member States".*

Technical Conservation Measures

18. Technical Conservation Measures (TCMs) are, and increasingly need to be, vital tools in the CFP's armoury. Much more effort needs to be put into the development of separator grids, separator trials, and other devices which improve gear selectivity in trawl nets. TCMs can reduce and even totally eliminate the bycatch not just of non-target *fish* species, however, but also of marine birds, turtles, cetaceans, etc. Where appropriate, successful and widespread uptake of TCMs needs to incentivised, however, so that fishermen reap some reward for "smarter" fishing; this can be mediated through allocating extra days at sea, differential access to sensitive fishing grounds, etc. For example, preferential access to fish in a Marine Protected Area could be conditional on a vessel adapting its gear such that it did not pose a risk to the nature conservation value of the site. The new European Fisheries Fund recognises the potential for this direction much more than did its predecessor and should revitalise gear modification for stock recovery and for more environmentally-friendly fishing. While there is a role for incentives, the introduction of more-selective fishing gear should, in other cases, be mandatory, with sticks rather than carrots for galvanising compliance (see below).

Discards and bycatch

19. A recent (2007) Government study of the amount of fish discarded (because it is too small or the wrong species) in UK waters found that almost two-thirds of fish caught were discarded. In the study, between 2002 and 2005, an estimated 186 million fish weighing 72,000t was caught by English and Welsh vessels operating in the English Channel, Western Approaches, Celtic and Irish Seas, of which 24,500t (63%) was discarded. In addition, the FAO estimates that discards in the North Sea amount to 500,000 to 880,000 tonnes.

20. Currently it is a Commission priority to reduce discards, and to this end, they produced a Communication[6] last year. On 31 January 2008, the European Parliament adopted a resolution[7] responding to that Communication.

21. The RSPB considers that a policy on bycatch and discards should be complementary to, and not replace, other necessary management measures, such as capacity reduction, technical measures and Marine Protected Areas. The key issue is to avoid, insofar as possible, unwanted catches in the first place. By requiring, for example, Best Available Technology for gear and real-time closures, we are likely to see changes in fishing behaviour and technology.

22. The RSPB is highly supportive of the Commission's approach to tackle the issue on a fishery by fishery basis, and to require a range of measures tailored to specific fisheries ("métiers"). The Commission also suggests real-time closures and the obligation to switch fishing grounds (if you exceed a bycatch limit) as two of the key ways of avoiding bycatch (as is key to the Norwegian system of bycatch/discard reduction).

23. These and other tried-and-tested technical measures for improved gear selectivity, such as a separator grid for Nephrops (langoustine) trawl nets or a separator panel for whitefish nets (in both cases to facilitate especially the escape of juvenile cod), should be made *mandatory* across all Community fleets, and the UK Government should push for this. At the moment, some proven measures are subject only to voluntary uptake, and fishermen are reluctant to use more selective gear and thus forfeit bycatch if they see that their competitors are shunning those measures and retaining that bycatch.

24. The RSPB supports the key element of the Commission's strategy which is to set a *maximum acceptable bycatch* of "non-target" fish for a given fishery, and to require that bycatch to be retained and landed. This is what a *"discard ban"* means in practice, ie non-target fish are no longer discarded at sea but rather retained on board and subsequently landed.

25. In the Commission's approach, this maximum bycatch level for each fishery will be progressively reduced over time to encourage the technologies capable of avoiding this level of bycatch in the first place. In this approach, instead of introducing a particular set of discard reduction measures ("micro-management"), as has been the traditional approach hitherto, the Commission is putting the onus on the sector to come up with its own solutions to reach the reduction target by whatever means they can think of.

26. The European Parliament's resolution differs from the Commission in wanting to put off the discard ban (ie landing bycatch) until such time as it can be shown that the other measures (to avoid bycatch) have failed, with a maximum of five years until the discard ban enters force. The RSPB rejects the European Parliament's five-year stay of execution before a discard ban kicks in. Instead we support the Commission's approach to make a discard ban integral from the outset to discard reduction in selected trial fisheries. We have concerns

---

6 A policy to reduce unwanted by-catches and eliminate discards in European fisheries. Communication from the Commission to the Council and the European Parliament. COM(2007)136 final.
7 European Parliament resolution of 31 January 2008 on a policy to reduce unwanted by-catches and eliminate discards in European fisheries (2007/2112(INI).

that unless a ban is applied from the start, we will not force the solutions (to avoid catching unwanted fish) quickly enough.

27. The efficacy of a discard ban depends on (a) being able to enforce it, which will require an on-board observer scheme (b) provision of incentives to the fishermen to retain bycatch.

28. The latter includes importantly the sensitive issue of what compensation fishermen should receive for landing discards (which may then assist the production of fish-meal/oil and help relieve the need to target sandeels). It is important to avoid the scenario in which the market value of landed discards is not so great as to create an incentive to target fish which the vessel should be trying to avoid catching in the first place. To avoid this perverse outcome, the fishermen could receive as compensation a small percentage of the value of the unmarketable landed catch, as is currently the case in Norway and New Zealand.

29. Lastly, in the Commission's Communication, it is suggested that only finfish and crustaceans caught will have to be landed. We urge the UK Government to support widening this to the entire catch, creating the same incentive to avoid bycatch of other sorts of invertebrates, corals, marine mammals, seabirds and turtles.

Adapting to climate change

30. It is clear that sea warming and other shifts driven by climate change will take generations to stabilise and reverse, even if we act now. These changes can be perceived as having both positive and negative impacts on fisheries. On the positive side, the movement of traditionally warm-water species into our latitudes is creating some new fishing opportunities, such as the new squid fisheries in the North Sea. Fisheries management needs to be flexible enough to be responsive to these changes.

31. On the negative side, it appears that cold-water species such as cod and sandeel may be less resilient to rapid sea warming, with recruitment adversely affected by changes in the timing and productivity of the greatly altered plankton community on which newly hatched fish larvae depend. These are changes over which man has limited control in the short term, so it behoves fisheries management to be more *precautionary* and reduce fishing effort as necessary.

32. The harvesting rules for sandeel, for example, had to be radically altered to take account of a chronic downturn in the stock, and we support this kind of *adaptive management*. By the same token, cod (another species affected by sea warming) has not been recovering as rapidly as anticipated from the recovery plan, calling for innovative measures, some of which the sector is starting to implement proactively (eg cod avoidance plans and real-time closures).

CONTROL AND ENFORCEMENT

The control and enforcement of the rules of the Common Fisheries Policy

33. The European Court of Auditors Special Report (December 4, 2007) exposes the failure by Member States to effectively control fishing activities by their fleets, demonstrating the urgent need to seriously strengthen EU control and inspection systems. Despite claims that existing rules are sufficient to prevent or seriously limit Illegal, Unreported and Unregulated (IUU) fishing by EU fleets, the Court of Auditors report states that *"If the political authorities want the CFP to achieve its objective of sustainable exploitation of the fisheries resources, the present control, inspection and sanction mechanisms must be strengthened considerably."*

34. The Court of Auditors' report characterises current sanctions as merely *"the cost of doing business"*. It is vital to give urgent support to strengthening controls from "net to plate". In practical terms, many Member States are not doing enough because, for many fisheries, the cost of controls outstrips the value of the actual fish caught.

35. In view of this, the RSPB strongly supports the Commission's proposal for a Council Regulation establishing a system to prevent, deter and eliminate IUU fishing. The review and revision of the Control Regulation in 2008 will provide the opportunity to adopt further corrective action.

36. According to a Commission report in 2007, areas in which Member States need to improve control include hiring more skilled personnel, dedicating more resources to checking vessels which fish in international waters, better training for inspectors, closer cooperation between Member States, and stronger penalties for flouting the rules.

37. These developments set the agenda for the Community Fisheries Control Agency (CFCA), established in 2005. Apart from combating IUU fishing, current priorities for the CFCA include the monitoring of the recovery and management of cod stocks, protection of bluefin tuna, and the reduction of destructive fishing

practices and discards. With cod stocks still below safe biological limits and Mediterranean bluefin tuna close to collapse (and subject to rife IUU fishing), the CFCA faces a huge challenge. With the Agency still in its infancy, however, progress over the next two years will be a yardstick of its ability to deliver.

Serious infringements of the CFP

38. In October 2007, the Commission produced a Communication and a proposal for a Council Regulation to address the issue of IUU fishing. The RSPB strongly endorses the intent behind this proposal to address *inter alia* the issue of inequity across Member States in sanctions against illegal fishing. We look to the UK Government to support the adoption of a robust Regulation in this regard when it is comes before the Fisheries Council.

39. The proposed Regulation would: (a) strengthen the responsibility of Member States to impose sanctions on their nationals who engage in or support IUU fishing, inside or outside Community Waters; (b) set measures to harmonise across Member States the maximum levels of sanctions (such as fines and confiscation of catches).

40. This harmonisation process is vital in the fight against IUU fishing. Firstly, it is necessary to counter the industry-held view in several Member States that, on the subsidiarity principle, sanctions should be the prerogative of individual Member States, and therefore that there is no need for harmonisation. Secondly, a major cause of rule-breaking, even by vessels in Member States who give high priority to control and enforcement, is the perception that vessels flagged to other States are subject to weak national controls. This lack of a level playing field tends to engender a culture of non-compliance across all fleets; harmonisation of penalties would go a long way to remedying this.

STRUCTURAL POLICY

Measures to adjust the capacity of fleets

41. Since 2002, all Member States have reported a gradual reduction in fleet capacity, mainly as a result of vessel decommissioning. The overall reduction in tonnage and horsepower for the EU-15 Member States for 2003–05 was 6.27% and 7.28%, respectively. In contrast, the reduction in both these capacity measures for the new Member States was 18%. Most of this reduction was funded by public aid, especially for the EU-15 Member States.

42. Over the same period, most Member States also reported a steady decrease in fishing effort, probably reflecting more a reduction in fishing opportunities (eg effort limits and lower TACs) than in fleet capacity. Increasing fuel prices have also probably also helped to put a brake on fishing effort. Against this background, reduction in fleet capacity is probably not the main driver of less fishing, although the problem might have been worse if capacity had not been reduced.

43. Another key reason why the capacity reductions achieved have not *per se* been hugely influential is the phenomenon of the increasing fishing efficiency, year on year, of those vessels *not* decommissioned, so-called "technical creep". The International Council for the Exploration of the Sea (ICES) indicates that the introduction of new fishing technology increases fishing power by 1-3% annually (some studies suggest up to 4%), such that reductions in fleet capacity may have little or no ability to curb overfishing.

44. Despite this, it is notable that, in recent years, Scottish whitefish fleet capacity has almost certainly declined in real terms, decommissioning resulting in the number of vessels over 10 metres declining by 46% between 1996 and 2006 (Scottish Government statistics).

The European Fisheries Fund (EFF)

45. The RSPB welcomes the new EFF 2007-13, with its overarching commitment to sustainable development, to an ecosystem-based approach to fisheries management, its emphasis on the promotion of small-scale coastal fishing and the inshore sector, and capacity to foster the protection of biodiversity and nature conservation. The latter is important, given that the EFF also includes measures to allocate funding to vessel modernisation and installation of new engines, both of which have the potential to increase pressure on already depleted fish stocks.

46. However, the fund is relatively small, and barely commensurate with the aspirations of its new framework, so it will take considerable effort, imagination and external scrutiny to avoid a "business as usual" re-run of the deployment of the Financial Instrument for Fisheries Guidance (FIFG) which it replaces.

47. Member States are mainly responsible for selecting projects and implementing their share of the EFF according to their national and regional priorities. As such, the UK was required to draft a National Strategic Plan and an Operational Programme.

48. In February 2006, the RSPB responded to Defra's consultation on the UK's draft National Strategic Plan which needed to address the sustainable development of the sector in a balanced way that took due account of environmental considerations. While the UK's stated Objectives and Priorities for 2007–13 achieved that balance, the underlying analysis tended to prioritise the short-term, economic profitability of the sector (catching, processing and aquaculture), to the detriment of wider sustainability issues and stakeholder breadth.

49. Whereas the Scottish Executive consulted in November 2006 on its proposals for how the EFF should be delivered in Scotland, they acknowledged that full public consultation on their plans would need to be part of the UK-wide consultation on the UK Operational Programme. However, development of the latter has been subject to undue delay, due to the challenge of agreeing the split in convergence between the four Fisheries Administrations. Grants cannot be administered until this has been reconciled, consulted upon, and a final text agreed. This represents a frustrating loss of the EFF's momentum but is symptomatic, as is the painfully slow development of the Marine Bill, of the quagmire that engulfs the development of coherent and equitable policy in a devolved UK.

Impact of WTO-level discussions

50. The Doha Round has long been pronounced dead in circles beyond government trade ministries and WTO headquarters. Hopefully, a mini-ministerial meeting to resurrect it may be held in April 2008. However, prospects for an agreement this year remain unclear, not least because of the US elections.

51. In November 2007, a draft fisheries text was tabled which, if agreed (a big "if"), would impose tough limits on subsidies, which the RSPB welcomes if we are to seriously address global overfishing, including in EU waters. The proposals on 'rules' do not propose a blanket ban on all subsidies but they list a large number of subsidies that would be banned, including those for the construction of new vessels, and for operating costs of fisheries, including fuel. This could have a major impact on the EU which subsidises fuel for fishing vessels. The RSPB sees no justification for subsidising fuel costs as this, in turn, fuels overfishing.

52. The Doha Round negotiating group held their first formal meeting in January 2008 to discuss the November 2007 draft fisheries text. The meeting highlighted the usual strong divisions between Member States, from countries supporting an abolition of all fishing subsidies to others looking to retain them.

53. Among numerous contentious issues was whether an exception should be made for subsidising small-scale fishermen, eg because they contribute less to overfishing than big offshore vessels. The EU, whose small scale fleets make up 80% of overall fleet capacity, urged that all small-scale fishermen should be eligible for subsidies in ways currently permitted only for developing countries. They argued that such fishermen were among the most vulnerable communities in developed countries as well as poor ones.

54. The RSPB would be very concerned if small-scale fishermen in the EU were singled out for subsidy, not least because small-scale fishing in developed countries like those of the EU is just as capable of overfishing and inflicting environmental damage as are offshore fleets. We would certainly not support any loosening the criteria for EFF spend, given that the EFF already allows grants for engine replacement which could indirectly increase fishing capacity.

GOVERNANCE

Regional Advisory Councils (RACs)

55. The RSPB is represented on two of the RACs (North Sea RAC and North Western Waters RAC) and has some insight into their performance to date. The advent of the RACs has led to more constructive dialogue among stakeholders, not least between the fishing sector and environmental NGOs. It is early days but some useful advice is being delivered to the Commission. Key constraints, however, are:

  (i) The fishing sector has two-thirds majority so clearly dominates the agenda and outcomes.

  (ii) There is a tendency of the sector to default to short-term issues (such as TACs and quotas), rather than focussing on the long-term sustainability issues of much greater interest to NGOs, eg the sector has no appetite for developing an ecosystem-based approach to fisheries management so it is an uphill struggle to get this on the agenda.

(iii) The proliferation of RACs (there will be seven in all), each with its structure of General Assembly, Executive Committee, working groups and focus groups, is imposing a great strain on the capacity of all stakeholders to service the RACs adequately. It is important to retain the balance of stakeholder participation at all levels in each RAC in order to deliver equitable outcomes. The challenge of the NGOs to meet their existing obligations to the RACs makes them wary, however, of arguing for stronger representation (relative to the sector's majority).

(iv) By being classed as bodies of public interest, the RACs have recently been afforded greater funding security by the Commission but are still challenged in the areas of communication, research and development. Defra is very supportive of the North Sea RAC but is alone among Member States in providing facilities for meetings etc.

56. In pursuit of more decentralised governance, the RACs should better funded to enable them, for example, to commission their own research. For the time being, their remit should certainly be restricted to an advisory role, and any putative transition to executive-decision making powers should be seen as part of an evolutionary process which will require many checks and balances.

How should EU fisheries ideally be governed

57. The CFP's 'command and control' approach to fisheries management from Brussels is becoming unsustainable with Community expansion, indeed has been for many years, and has alienated many of those it seeks to manage. In *'Reflections on the Common Fisheries Policy'* (2007), David Symes characterises the situation as:

'Today . . . there is something faintly ludicrous about DG Fish—a bureaucracy probably no bigger than the planning department of an average local sized authority—attempting to regulate the fisheries of an area that stretches through 40° of latitude from the Gulf of Bothnia to the Canary Islands and 60° of longitude from the Azores to the eastern Mediterranean. Even Napoleon might have baulked at an empire of these dimensions!"

58. Where is the system broken? For too long, UK and other EU Ministers in the Fisheries Council have traded short-term socio-economic benefits against long term stock conservation and prosperity for the fishing sector. In recent years, according to the Commission's own analysis (COM(2007)295), the Fisheries Council has routinely set catch limits 40–50% higher than those advised by the scientists, contributing to the demise of fish stocks such as North Sea cod. The justification for this inflation is the invoking of socio-economic considerations but is more realistically an appeasement to fishing constituencies.

59. The EU has to find a way of eliminating the horse-trading in the December Council which subordinates scientific advice and sustainability too much to socio-economic considerations. To this end, the Council should be allotted a lesser role in annual (short-term) decision-making, and needs to attend more to long term strategic issues. Short-term political manipulation will also be reduced if the exploitation limits of fisheries are increasingly "locked in" by Harvest Control Rules' which cannot be gainsaid by socio-economic overlay.

60. If there is to be less dependancy on the Council for annual decision-making, then there is a need for a rebalance of current roles and responsibilities. The European Parliament is already guaranteed co-decision on strategic fisheries issues if the Lisbon Treaty is ratified (see Annex, below). Other options include:

(i) Some form of regionalisation such as giving the Regional Advisory Councils (RACs) a more formal role to develop plans which the Commission can implement without having to defer to annual decisions by the Council.

(ii) Making more use of Commission working groups to more fully negotiate proposals before they reach the Council for adoption.

61. The RSPB supports the need to develop a more regionalised approach to the delivery of the CFP, not least as this fits with the model of Integrated Marine Management propounded by the EC's new *Marine Strategy Directive and Maritime Policy* (see Annex). The CFP is already regionalised to an extent but a truly regionalised structure calls for radical reappraisal of roles, responsibilities and institutional structures. Just how this should happen should be the subject of a wide-ranging debate initiated by the Commission. This needs to start well in advance of the next CFP review in 2012 if we are to have any hope of achieving Maximum Sustainable Yield (MSY) of Community fisheries by 2015, as required by the UN World Summit on Sustainable Development (Johannesburg 2002).

February 2007

Annex

RELATIONSHIP OF THE CFP TO THE LISBON TREATY

If the Treaty is ratified, co-decision will apply to all parts of the CFP, except *"measures on fixing process, levies, aid and quantitative limitations and on the fixing and allocation of fishing opportunities"* (ie the European Parliament will not have co-decision on setting annual Total Allowable Catches (TACs) and quotas).

RELATIONSHIP OF THE CFP TO THE EC MARINE STRATEGY DIRECTIVE

The Marine Strategy Directive has been agreed between the Council and European Parliament but not yet adopted—this should happen early in 2008. At the heart of the Directive is the need to achieve (well-defined) *"Good Environmental Status"* (GES) by 2020. The Directive for the first time makes firm links between environmental legislation and the CFP such that, if fisheries present a problem for achieving GES, the Commission and Member States are required to act within the framework of the CFP to address the problem.

Examination of Witness

Witness: DR EUAN DUNN, Head of Marine Policy, Royal Society for the Protection of Birds, examined.

Q203 *Chairman:* Good morning. Welcome. Thank you for finding the time both to prepare your written evidence that has been submitted but also to come along this morning and help us with our inquiry. How would you like to proceed? Would you like to make an opening statement and then go on to the specific questions we have or do you want to go straight on to questions and answers?

Dr Dunn: I think we could go straight into questions and answers really. Perhaps I might just introduce myself. I am Euan Dunn, I am Head of Marine Policy at the RSPB. I have worked mainly on the Common Fisheries Policy and the environmental integration of that. I am also, in other capacities, on the board of the Marine Stewardship Council, so I have a linkage into the sustainability of the food chain and sustainable use in that way. I very much welcome this review. I thought the questions were spot on: the sorts of questions that elicit the sorts of responses you want to hear, I think. We were very engaged to get your set of questions and I look forward to elaborating on any issues that they throw up and answering any new ones.

Q204 *Chairman:* Why is the RSPB interested in the Common Fisheries Policy?

Dr Dunn: For a number of reasons. First of all, fishing is probably the most pervasive influence on the whole of the marine environment, with the possible exception of climate change which is beginning to kick in as a major driver of change. That has fundamentally changed the ecosystem over the last 100 years. We have shifted, for example, the assemblage of seabirds into a much more scavenging role as a result of the mass production of discards and we have fundamentally changed habitats, not just for seabirds but for all marine wildlife. There are also much more specific issues, like the control of industrial fishing, which is at the base of the food chain and therefore a fundamentally important prey species for not just seabirds but for cetaceans and for other marine wildlife. If we are looking at the array of human activities in the oceans and we are looking at the environmental impacts, fishing is right up at the top, and therefore the governance and the institutional framework and the structures and measures that are put in place by the Common Fisheries Policy are absolutely central to conservation of seabird populations and the ecosystem at large.

Q205 *Chairman:* Thank you. Perhaps I could kick off with the first question. As you know, article 2 of the Common Fisheries Policy Framework Regulation mandated the progressive development of an ecosystem-based approach to fisheries management. What do you think that should mean? How has it developed in practice? How would it be best delivered?

Dr Dunn: Of course that was a fundamentally important shift in the reforms in 2002 as were a number of others, so it has been a very important benchmark. Up until now and even since 2002 the implementation of an ecosystem approach has been very piecemeal, ad hoc, reactive. We have been fire-fighting. We have been lacking a coherent strategy by the European Commission to embed the ecosystem-based approach to fisheries management in the operational aspect of the Common Fisheries Policy. That is about to change. We imminently expect a communication from the European Commission, from DG Fisheries and Maritime Affairs this spring, on how they will implement an ecosystem-based approach. We await that with interest. We will be looking for a fairly robust approach. What is an ecosystem approach? There is a lot of obfuscation around this and fishermen often say they hear so many definitions and even decision-makers say they hear so many definitions. It is rather like one of these fuzzy balls. Sustainable development is often put in the same box. How can you get hold of it? To me, it is very simple. As someone once put it: "Fishing needs to try to adapt to the marine environment, not the other way around," and so it is simply how you manage fisheries to take account of its undoubted environmental impacts. There are direct impacts and there are indirect impacts. Often the indirect impacts are the important ones. These are the ones where fishing changes the food chain, which has knock-on effects for other elements of the system. The single biggest thing the eco-system approach could do if you were to implement it would be to reduce fishing pressure. That would relieve pressure on the ecosystem across a whole raft of elements, and that is sometimes overlooked. Secondly, if we are looking to do it strategically, we need to develop what have been pioneered in the United States and are known as the fisheries ecosystem plans for regional seas. Defra is in the process of embarking on developing an ecosystem-based approach to South West Waters and so that will be a very important initiative. It will build on the Invest in Fish project which is already taking place there. You assess the most important aspects of the fishery, you develop some objectives and some indicators, and then you adapt the fishing activity through a variety of means to address the gulf between current practice and sustainability. You monitor the situation, you assess it, you adapt your management as you go along. There are two other things we need to say about this. It needs to be a bottom-up stakeholder-led approach. That has been very much a hallmark of the reformed CFP and I am sure Defra will do it that way. Lastly, if we are looking to get an ecosystem approach embedded in the Common Fisheries Policy, we have a real problem with the Commission. The Commission has precious little environmental capacity in DG Fisheries and it has very little dialogue with DG Environment, and the institutional framework is just not, in my view, geared up to delivering an ecosystem approach effectively. That has to change. I do not want to sound too gloomy. International Council for the Exploration of the Seas (ICES) has set down some very, very good frameworks for developing and implementing an ecosystem-based approach. So it is all to do, but I think we can make a lot more progress from the spring onwards.

Q206 *Chairman:* How would an ecosystem approach impact on the individual fishermen? What would they see as being different?
Dr Dunn: The problem with the Common Fisheries Policy, if I can preface it like this, is that up until probably 2002 there was a divorcing of the whole sustainability of the fish stock situation from the ecosystem element. Seas were seen as a production unit for fish and it was divorced from the wider ecosystem impacts. An ecosystem approach needs to

look at all those things in the round. If you like, the fish themselves are part of the ecosystem and part of the elements that need to be protected. The fishermen will have to take on board things like the need to protect juvenile fish, protecting critical areas for spawning and recruitment. Things like minimum landing size will need to be looked at to make sure that fish have enough time to breed before they get caught, and we also need to look at reducing bycatch of sensitive species like sharks and rays and any other seabirds and whatever. This will not just be some environmental add-on, it will become root and branch, embedded in the way that the fisheries are managed and regulated.

Q207 *Viscount Ullswater:* Perhaps I could return to the present. In your excellent memorandum you note that about four-fifths of stocks remain outside safe biological limits. Could you give your view on the initial application of recovery and management plans under the reformed CFP. What measures could be taken to improve their effectiveness and to facilitate their adoption?
Dr Dunn: It has to be said that, in the first place, the introduction of two changes of direction in the Common Fisheries Policy was fundamentally important. The first was the introduction of long-term management plans for species which are not in deep trouble but to maintain them above safe biological limits; that is, those species which are already above the line, if you like, but to keep them there. The importance of that long-term management approach was to break the vicious cycle of the annual horse trading that goes on in the Fisheries Council. The fishermen that I speak to are planning long-term strategies for their businesses, they like the idea of stability from year to year. They do not like the horse trading, if you really get down to the nitty-gritty of it. Therefore, for those sorts of fish, long-term management plans, and, for fish that are below safe biological limits—like cod, which is still well below safe biological limits—the recovery plans. So far, precious few of the European fish stocks have been subjected to either of these—I think about 16% in total. It is too early to say, I think, in most cases whether these long-term management plans or recovery plans are working. The jury is out. We have to give the Commission a little bit of slack to see. They are trying to ratchet down the fishing mortality, the number of fish that are killed on an annual basis, along agreed targets—to ratchet it down year by year, and pull these fish stocks back into a safe situation. In most cases we have only had two or three years of that. Already, though, it is contentious. The cod recovery plan has already been opened up to revision after really being in place for quite a short time. To answer your question on what we need to do to improve them: the first thing, clearly, is that we

need a much closer adherence by ministers to scientific advice. We need to lock as much of the December Council as we can into fixed harvesting rules, so that the ministers cannot play politics with these recovery plans. We need to have a much greater scrutiny of what is happening on the decks of fishing boats. That means we need to have representative observer programmes—which are routine in fisheries in many of the well-managed fisheries in other parts of the world and which have not been properly addressed, no doubt for resourcing reasons, in the European Union. There are now tried and tested technical measures which work, and most of these at the moment are voluntary. In my view, separator grids in nephrops (langoustine) trawls which allow whitefish to escape should be made mandatory, once they are shown to be more useful than not, and the same for panels that allow the whitefish to escape in bottom trawls. Therefore, there is a need for observer programmes; a need for much greater mandatory requirements for technical measures to create a level playing field across the EU fleets; and a greater need for scientific advice. I think the recovery plans themselves probably need to be tightened up in a number of places. For example, they allow a latitude—some of them are plus or minus 15%—in the total allowable catch that can be set every year. For some species that is not enough: you need a greater reduction than that. I believe they are going to bring improvements, and they are already doing so for a number of species like Northern Hake and Biscay Sole and a number of others. I think we are on the right track and the Commission should stick to its guns and strengthen where necessary.

Q208 *Viscount Ullswater:* Would the sort of things you are suggesting be implemented through a licence requirement?
Dr Dunn: Yes.

Q209 *Viscount Ullswater:* So that you would not get a licence unless you took an observer with you or whatever?
Dr Dunn: The observer schemes are most needed in the demersal fisheries, for cod and haddock and whiting and the like. The pelagic fisheries are in fairly good health, although herring has taken a big knock. It is really the demersal, the bottom trawl fisheries which desperately need some onboard scrutiny and monitoring and assessment, particularly when the Commission's discard policy begins to bite. That would be, as you say, written into the criteria for gaining a licence; for example, in the southern ocean, in the CCAMLR waters (Convention for the Conservation of Antarctic Marine Living Resources), there is 100% observer coverage on all its vessels paid for by the industry, and you cannot get a licence to fish unless you carry an independent

observer on board. We regard that system in many ways as best practice. I do not think we are looking for 100% in the EU but we need to have sufficient for it to act as an enforcing stick.

Q210 *Lord Palmer:* Would you recommend that that be industry funded again?
Dr Dunn: I think that would need to be looked at. It could be a combination of things. To me that could be something that could have some linkage to the European Fisheries Fund and there could also be an industry element in paying for it. It is something that needs to be explored. I would not want to be prescriptive about it at this point.

Q211 *Baroness Jones of Whitchurch:* Are you suggesting an observer on every vessel on every trip, or that, randomly, you will turn up one day and suddenly find there is somebody going out with you? Are you talking about them doing it all the time? Because that would be fantastically expensive, would it not?
Dr Dunn: Forgive me, I tried to say that my thinking is on this that we should have observers on a representative proportion of the fleet. There is quite good practice from around the world which suggests, for different kinds of fisheries, what would be an appropriate percentage of vessels on which to carry an observer if you are going to get (a) the data scrutiny and (b) the sort of interaction between the fishermen that has almost sufficient critical mass to have an enforcing effect on the fleet as a whole. Clearly, if you only have an observer on, say, one in 20 vessels, that is a fairly soft, low-key intervention. On other fisheries around the world we are looking at 20 or 30%, something of that nature. It would have to be tailored to individual fisheries. There is no one-size-fits-all on these things. It would be a fishery-led thing and it would probably start on a trial basis to see how it works and to iron out the teething problems.

Q212 *Chairman:* One is tempted to ask if there is any data on the mortality rates of these observers!
Dr Dunn: They have to sleep and that is often when—

Q213 *Chairman:* That is when it all happens!
Dr Dunn: They cannot stay awake all night, these guys.
Chairman: Let us move on.

Q214 *Lord Cameron of Dillington:* On that last point, I have heard it put forward that possibly having cameras on mast tops might be a way of continually checking.
Dr Dunn: If I may say, that is a serious point. CCTV, if you like, onboard fishing vessels is proving very effective in some parts of the world and the fishermen

are taking it seriously. If you have a camera based on the aft deck, where all the landing and the discarding is going on, it really is like an additional surveillance tool to the satellite vessel monitoring which tells you where the vessel is at any point in time. There is real mileage in what you suggest there.

Q215 *Lord Cameron of Dillington:* I would like to move on to other methods of promoting sustainable fisheries outside the quota system. You and other NGOs seem to think that particularly marine conservation areas or effort limitation programmes would be successful. On the marine conservation area, in your evidence you talk about the failed ten-week closure for cod in 2001. I would be quite interested to know about that in detail, why it failed and how it failed and the rationale that has been deduced from its failure.

Dr Dunn: It was a disastrous thing in many ways because it was the first attempt by the Commission to try to deal with the advice that was coming from ICES—which gives its advice on stock assessment on an annual basis. It was the Commission's attempt to address their advice in that year and in a number of years since, that the fishing for cod in the North Sea and other parts of the UK waters west of Scotland should be closed, that there should be no fishing for cod. The Commission was struggling to try to find something that was tractable and workable and they came up with a ten-week closure in 2001. It was something like February to the end of March or middle of April.

Q216 *Lord Cameron of Dillington:* Over the whole of the North Sea?

Dr Dunn: No, it was an area of the North Sea. It was not the whole of the North Sea. It had one fundamental effect: it displaced the fishing that had hitherto taken place in that area into the surrounding areas where the fleet had not frequently fished in the past, and it damaged those areas. It damaged haddock grounds. It was counterproductive. The fundamental lesson to be learned from that was that, if you are going to implement an area of closure, you first of all have to have very, very clear objectives about what you hope to achieve by that closure and you need to do a bit of modelling to see what are the likely "unintended" consequences—which I think is the buzz word these days in fisheries—but, secondly, as part of that first thing you need to take account of the fact that you cannot just shift fishing effort about and expect nothing to happen. The fishermen were fishing around the edge of that closed area. They were putting very intense pressure on the margins—fishing the "line" I think is the word that was used—and you have to reduce the effort across the board to make sure that you do not intensify the effort in the places that are neighbouring the closed area. That was never

thought through properly. It set the whole thing back, because it put the fishing industry in the frame of mind that closures were fundamentally wrong and they would not achieve conservation objectives, especially for highly mobile fish like cod and mackerel. There have been trials and pilots in the North East United States, in Georges Bank, which are admittedly quite difficult to interpret because a lot of changes in management were going on at the same time, but there is some *prima facie* evidence that the closures did assist a number of stocks quite considerably: flounder and haddock and so on. I feel that the baby has been thrown out with the bathwater a bit with the area closures of that kind, and they have not been properly considered in the round. We are now seeing, of course, a different kind of closure. The fishermen themselves are becoming more confident and taking more control of their own activity. In Scotland we now have the fishermen voluntarily having so-called cod avoidance schemes, where they choose not to fish in areas where there are concentrations of spawning cod or concentrations of juvenile fish. After many years, you have to say, where this has been said, this is finally taking on board some of the best practices in the Norwegian model. The fishermen themselves are beginning to take on board the idea of area closures but in a more sensitive, less of a blunt instrument sort of way, where the area is closed as long as is necessary—whereas here we had a rather arbitrary ten-week closure of an area where the consequences of doing so had not been really figured out.

Q217 *Lord Cameron of Dillington:* How about "days at sea"? Is that effective?

Dr Dunn: I think it is here to stay. My own view is that we are always going to have TACs and quotas around as a fundamental building block of the regulations and measures. I looked at the original question that was sent and the advice the Committee had had from an economist. Is it better to control fishing by outputs than inputs? You will get as many answers as you ask people, but there is a case to be said that TACs and quotas have been a pretty blunt instrument—like that closure I mentioned—and, in principle, it is a more sensitive approach to control how many vessels are fishing in an area for how much time than to try to control what comes out at the end of the pipe. Of course, total allowable catches are not really even that: they are total allowable landings, when it comes to inspection and control. I welcome the fact that the emphasis is shifting to a significant degree in the execution of long-term management plans and control recovery plans towards effort control, although TACs and quotas are still behind those, and I think it is important that that continues.

Q218 Lord Cameron of Dillington: Going back to the marine conservation areas for a moment: if you were trying to control the fishing of cod, for example—which is obviously one of the more critical areas—in the North Sea using marine conservation areas, would there be any other regime or system you would use apart from the voluntary system being implemented by the Scots which you mentioned earlier?

Dr Dunn: Absolutely. The key to the cod fishery is the control of bycatch. It is a sad state of affairs but something like 95% of cod are caught before they have a chance to breed even once, which is why, interestingly, in the Scots fishermen's criteria for avoiding these areas of juvenile fish, the trigger for closure is when the cod reach 50 cm. The minimum landing size is about 35 cm and it was originally 35 cm in the criteria, but it was expanded to 50 cm because that means that those fish are a bit older and are likely to be approaching breeding age. You have cut yourself a bit of slack, if you like, so far as the sustainability of the cod population is concerned. To me, the discarding policy is absolutely crucial. An awful lot of the cod are being lost through bycatch in other fisheries, like the nephrops (langoustine) fisheries. I think the European Commission estimated that something like two-thirds of the juvenile cod were being lost in fisheries other than the directed cod fishery. I support the Commission's proposal for a total allowable bycatch, if you like.

Q219 Lord Cameron of Dillington: My question is on marine conservation areas. Could only the voluntary system work? Could the Commission implement any form of marine conservation area that would work effectively in the North Sea?

Dr Dunn: My view at the moment is that there is a lot to be said for going with the bottom-up approach: the fishermen coming forward with their own ideas, their own proposals. Working in the Regional Advisory Council, as I do, for the North Sea, that is where your compliance comes from. We have to get away from the more top-down approach, where fishermen will find a reason to resist the command and control. I think it is good the way it is going. The cod avoidance plans I think need to be very well observed, monitored, assessed, to see if they work. We are not just going to give them a tick and let them rip.

Q220 Chairman: Could you say a little bit more on marine conservation areas or protection areas. If you were to imagine a map, could you identify where they would be and how big they would be? Are they temporary or permanent? Are they one year, one month, five years? I just want to get a feel for what they would look like.

Dr Dunn: You have a two sorts of critical areas: spawning areas—and we are just talking about cod for the purposes of argument—and nursery areas. Some of these are fairly predictable from year to year, so they are not moving around in a random way. These are areas that are used for very particular environmental reasons by that species. The conditions suit the purpose for which they are chosen. It is not a totally random process. You can do quite a lot of marine spatial planning on this. The fishermen know where the cod are spawning and they can predict from year to year where it is likely to be. There is flexibility in that. We are not necessarily talking about massive areas. These can be quite circumscribed areas, so in that sense they are quite tractable for applying a cod avoidance approach.

Q221 Chairman: What length of time would they be in place?

Dr Dunn: Until such time as the spawning period is over or the nursery period is over and the fish disperse into other areas. John Pope knows a great deal about this. We have a good handle on the dynamics of how the fish behave through the months of the year.

Chairman: Perhaps we could go on to follow up on bycatch and discards.

Q222 Baroness Jones of Whitchurch: You have already touched on this and you quote this really shocking figure in your evidence that almost two-thirds of the fish caught in UK waters are discarded, so it is clearly a very, very serious problem. Some of the submissions we have received are arguing for a complete discard ban. Do you think that is feasible, operational, desirable?

Dr Dunn: Yes, I think it is. It is something Norway has practised for a while. They have simpler fisheries than us. The fisheries are not so mixed, so the fish swim more in unispecies shoals. Also, the age structure is generally better, because they have conserved their fish better over the years, so there are not so many juveniles. The fact that so many of our fish stocks have an age structure which has too few old, mature fish and too many of the younger ones creates the problem, because these are fish which are often below the minimum landing size and legally cannot be retained on board. My view is that the Commission's proposals and its communication on discards is a good way to go. I would like to see a trial—maybe two or three fisheries could be used as trials—on a fishery-by-fishery basis of a discard ban. A discard ban effectively means that you retain the fish on board instead of dumping it over the side and you land that retained fish as well as your marketable catch. This is how it has proved in Norway: everybody knows in Norway that the discard ban is not cast iron—as somebody said to me, "The nights are long and the waters are deep"—I am sure there is all sorts of malpractice, but, together with these real-time closures which we spoke about a moment ago, when you close an area for such time as juvenile fish are occupying it, it creates a mindset in the fishermen that these are good things to do for the sustainability of the stock. We are not looking for 100% perfection here. I would like to see a discard ban attempted on a trial basis based on this idea of the Commission's of a total allowable, maximum acceptable bycatch, so you set a bycatch limit for the fishery. The fishermen are incredibly inventive and creative. They will come up with ways which they probably know about already, in many ways, but have not had to operate in any sort of way, in vengeance and anger, if you like. They know about these ways of reducing their bycatch, and having a maximum acceptable bycatch will bring all these things out of the woodwork and the fishermen will find ways of reducing their bycatch. I am absolutely certain of that. The European Parliament's view is not to have—

Q223 Baroness Jones of Whitchurch: I am sorry to interrupt, but why do they not do that now? Why do they not reduce their bycatch now?

Dr Dunn: Because it comes down to—the other well-worn phrase you hear in fisheries a lot now—a "level playing field": if I am fishing and I have a separator grid in my fishing net which will allow things to escape but I know that the chap over there, who might even be from another Member State or another member of my own fleet, is not using that and he is catching those fish—and they are often fish that you want to keep because they may be of marketable value. For example, on the West Coast of Scotland the voluntary use of separator grids for nephrops trawls are not working as well as they should because the fishermen really want to keep some of the things that are escaping through those grids because they have market value. That is why you need to create a level playing field across all the vessels and all the Member States, so that everybody is working to the same set of rules. It is this disparity between one fleet and another, one Member State and another, which allows for individual vessels to steal a march on their competitors. That is why it does not work as well as it might.

Q224 Baroness Jones of Whitchurch: You are saying—and you were alluding to this in the Norwegian waters—that there will always be some discards. It is human nature that people will try to keep the higher value stock. If it is something they do not think has a saleable value, they will ditch it, will they not?

Dr Dunn: Indeed. Also, of course, they do not want to fill up their holds or any other part of their vessel with fish which are not of high market value. That is a real problem. I think you need two things. You need

a degree of enforcement. The main critics of discard bans say, "How will you ever enforce it?" You do need a degree of enforcement and that comes back to the observer programmes that I spoke about earlier. They may not be permanent but, hopefully, they will inculcate some kind of change in behaviour. Secondly, you need to give the fishermen some incentive for landing the fish which they do not regard, as you say, as of high marketable value. That is going to be a very sensitive issue, because you must not create such market value for those fish as to create an incentive to catch fish which you would otherwise have sought to avoid catching. In New Zealand there is a small amount of compensation and in Norway there is some compensation for the commercially important fish which you land as bycatch. It probably goes into offset the fish-meal and oil processing industry, which is a good thing. It might take some pressure of the sandeel fishery. I think it needs to be explored. It is a difficult one, but if you do not try it you will never find out if it works or not.

Q225 Chairman: I do not see immediately the justification for requiring a fisherman to land or not discard catch which comes from a species which is not subject to attack and which has zero commercial value. Why would we require fisherman to land that particular catch?

Dr Dunn: I think you are right to a degree. There is a sort of hierarchy here. Clearly the most important thing to do is to land the undersized fish from the stocks that you are targeting, so landing undersized cod, haddock, or whatever. But I think there is merit in landing fish for which there is no TAC. Incidentally, experience of the Common Fisheries Policy over the last ten years is that more and more fish stocks are becoming quota species. Even shellfish are quite likely to become quota species in the coming years because the shellfish industry is hugely commercially important now as a sector. Apart from anything else, you get a lot of information if you are bringing fish ashore. There is a lot of scientific information to be gleaned from that, and that in itself is a bonus although it is not going to be the primary driver.

Q226 Chairman: There is the possibility that a fisherman may set out on his boat—it is an expensive business to take the boat out fishing—the only catch he gets is the stuff that has no marketable value, and he has to bring that back in. That is an expensive waste of time and effort for him is it not?

Dr Dunn: I would imagine, in the event where you have a discard ban, there will be laid down the particular fish which you need to retain. In Norway it is commercially important fish and nobody is saying that you should bring back every starfish and sea urchin.

Q227 *Chairman:* I have that clarification. I think that is quite important. Two little clarifications. On the trial ban that you are advocating on discards, would the landed bycatch count against the TAC?

Dr Dunn: That is a very good question. I think that it probably should: they are all dead fish, they are all lost from the population. But that is going to be one of the most contentious issues and I think there will be a huge amount of resistance to it. In the North Sea, at the moment, I think there should be no directed cod fishery as such. I think there should be a bycatch TAC, if you like. All the cod taken in fisheries should be regarded as bycatch.

Q228 *Chairman:* Finally, if there were to be a ban on discards, that would affect bird populations, would it not?

Dr Dunn: Yes, it would. There are a few things to say on that. We have done quite an elaborate study of this over the last few years. We did a report on it about three years ago. The first thing to say is that it is not widely recognised that, although you have these very high discard burdens in the North Sea and elsewhere, the total tonnage of discarding has been going down quite dramatically over the last ten/15 years, especially of small haddock and whiting and so on. That is basically because the source populations themselves have been declining, so they have not been generating discards at the same level they used to. That is to disabuse any idea that discarding is rocketing up decade by decade. It is not so. But over the last century or so we have seen that discarding has probably fundamentally shifted the balance of the ecosystem, particularly for scavenging seabirds, so that you now have a different mixed assemblage than you used to have. That is ecosystem disruption. It is not something that I would defend. In many ways discarding is a symptom of unsustainable fishing. I would never ever argue for the promotion of the maintenance of discarding to sustain seabird populations.

Q229 *Earl of Arran:* Out of interest, for how long can a fish survive on board before it is dead?

Dr Dunn: It depends which sort of fish you are talking about. If you read *Fishing News* this week, trials have been done in the South West on the survivability of some of the fish in the South West or the Channel. Fish that have a swim bladder, like the whitefish, when you bring them to the surface the swim bladder, I think, pops—I am not too hot on my physiology there, but they are effectively goners. Deep sea fish, of course, have no chance whatsoever of surviving at the surface. But certain fish do survive quite well. Skates and rays can be returned alive. Some flatfish can

survive. There is the possibility to put a fish back which you do not want, but, obviously, the more handling it has on deck and the longer it stays in the net and so on, the less chance it has. But it is a good point, I think. It is an important point for the idea of including in that bycatch the whole concept of catching things like turtles and seabirds and sharks—things that are important, vulnerable species for which there is global concern. The idea of returning those to the wild, so to speak, after capture is very important indeed and should be, to my view, part of an integrated discard policy of the Commission.

Chairman: Thank you. Lord Plumb on climate change.

Q230 *Lord Plumb:* You say in your report that climate change has positive and negative implications for fisheries in creating some opportunities for some and the reverse for others. You have referred several times to the importance of a level playing field. How can you bring about or adapt a policy that is acceptable and suitable to meet these needs?

Dr Dunn: To a large degree down to work done in the UK by the Sir Alister Hardy Foundation. Through a wonderful device, the Continuous Plankton Recorder, which we have been using now continuously for certainly most of this century, we have a wonderful record of the plankton assemblage in our waters and in other parts of the world. Since the 1980s there has been a fundamental change in the plankton assemblage of the North Sea and western waters. Scientists do not use this word lightly, but it is a "regime" shift: the cold water plankton have been replaced by a warmer water plankton—and I am speaking now about the zoo plankton, the little tiny crustaceans—and that has fundamentally changed the ecology of our seas. It is the biggest change that has happened in decades and even, possibly, the biggest change that has happened in the North Sea since it formed after the Ice Age—who knows. We are seeing a fundamentally different set of environmental conditions. These are favouring some fish and not others. The coldwater species, cod—although there has been a lot of new evidence lately to countermand some of the more serious fears earlier on that they are finding these changed conditions totally to their disliking—seem to be disadvantaged by the warmer waters and the change in the plankton mix. Sandeels certainly seem to be, for the same reason. With sandeels, when the larvae hatch out from the eggs in the late winter they have to find the right plankton they need to survive and grow, and they are not finding the right plankton they need to survive and grow. It is a very narrow window of opportunity for them to break into the recruitment age group. They are not doing that and sandeel populations are massively reduced compared to what they were just five/ten years ago. To answer your question more directly, I think fishing has to go with the grain of this. This is not something that we will reverse in our lifetimes or even our grandchildren's lifetimes, but we can do short-term things about fishing. Fishing has to go with the grain of this and, in my view, has to be more precautionary and take these changes into account as part of the equation. For sandeel fishing, cod fishing, herring fishing—herring has had a succession of very poor recruitment years since 2000, probably due to sea warming again—you simply have to ratchet back your effort to take account of these changes which you cannot possibly control in the short-term. On the other hand, you have species moving into our waters from the south: mullet, bream, horse mackerel, squid. There is a thriving squid fishery in the Moray Firth now which was not there years ago. We can be alert to these new fishing opportunities, and it will be particularly useful, I think, for the beleaguered inshore fisheries to cash in on some of these smaller species. There are fishing opportunities there but, on balance, I think it is negative. I think these new opportunities are likely to be outweighed by the disruption of our traditional coldwater stocks.

Q231 *Lord Plumb:* Whilst this is obviously the long-term change, would you see much development in the next decade?

Dr Dunn: I think so. Nothing that I have read disabuses the thought that sea warming is continuing and will continue to get worse. This will have some predictable effects and it will have lots of unpredictable effects. An unpredictable effect—and the jury is out on the implication now of the involvement of sea warming—is that our seas are awash from here to the Barents Sea, right up into the North, with pipefish. They are little, leathery fish, with bony scales on the outside like an exoskeleton. They are highly inedible. Seabirds are bringing them ashore in vast quantities, maybe mistaking them for sandeel. They have no nutritional value. They choke seabird chicks. They are probably choking lots of other things as well that are trying to eat them. Nobody even knows what they are doing to fish populations that prey on them. There are a lot of unexpected changes happening in our seas and we are not quite sure where it is all going to end, I suppose.

Q232 *Lord Plumb:* Do you think sufficient research is being done in that whole field?

Dr Dunn: I think Defra and the institutes, organisations like SAHFOS (Sir Alister Hardy Foundation for Ocean Science) and Plymouth University and others, are alive to this. There is a lot of effort going in. It is a big worry. If we cannot understand how the ecosystem is changing, we cannot properly introduce an ecosystem-based approach. We have to keep our finger on the pulse of these things and the pulse is racing.

Chairman: Lord Palmer on control and enforcement.

Q233 *Lord Palmer:* You have really answered the question about the enforcement but how big a problem do you think illegal fishing is within the EU waters? Perhaps you could expand a little bit on how to control the enforcement regulations to solve the problem, so to speak.

Dr Dunn: IUU, so-called—illegal, unreported, unregulated fishing—has a very high profile now. You probably know the High Seas Task Force, which was headed up by a UK minister over the last five years, reported last year. It has a very high profile. It is a global problem. In the EU, illegal fishing is patchy in its distribution. I think there is probably a lot of illegal fishing going on in the inshore fleet in England and Wales, which is in desperate straits at the moment, and this was reported in *The Guardian* yesterday. It was a very useful and well-researched article, I felt. The Scottish fleet had a very, very bad record of "black fish" landings up until a few years ago and I am fairly convinced, having spoken to a number of the markets, the processors and the practitioners, that they have cleaned up their act. They have very, very good registration of landings, they have very, very good monitoring of fish from net to plate, if you like, and the Scottish fleet is doing an exemplary job after a pretty muddy time in the 1980s and 1990s. With the inshore fleet in England and Wales, I think there are issues there. Not in Scotland. There is certainly a lot of illegal fishing going on in other parts of the European Union. I think it is still, to a large extent, being driven by overcapacity in a number of fleets. We like to think that the CFP has kicked into that problem pretty hard with the abolition of public aid for vessel building and so on, but there is still overcapacity. I would say there is overcapacity in the beam trawl fleet, particularly the Dutch beam trawl fleet. There is overcapacity in the UK and Welsh inshore fleet, I believe, and that will be slimmed down just by market forces in the coming years. A lot of illegal fishing is driven by fishermen finding themselves in straitened circumstances and feeling compelled to cheat. If you reduce capacity to match the stock resources then you certainly have to relieve that and balance that equation.

Q234 *Chairman:* This is it, is it not? Is not overcapacity the nub of the whole problem of the Common Fisheries Policy?

Dr Dunn: Overcapacity is a combination of the size of the fleet and the amount of effort it expends—if you like, deployed capacity. I believe that is absolutely the case. We still have overcapacity and there are a number of reasons for that, not least of which is the whole issue of technical creep or technological creep. The rate at which the vessels which are not decommissioned are capable equally of fulfilling the capacity of what was lost and surpassing that is quite profound. ICES reckons that technical creep is of the order of 1 to 3% per annum, but I have seen studies which have shown higher percentages, 4%. It is a very, very difficult thing to measure but it is a combination of new and more efficient gear; more efficient fish catching methods; the high-tech: all the GPS and the sonar and the fish-finding equipment; the power of the engines. Some of the inshore vessels now are little power-packs. They may only be ten metres but they have the fishing power of an older, larger, offshore fishing vessel. That really is a problem. To me, the Commission have never successfully managed to factor technical creep into their capacity reduction targets over the years I have been doing this. Part of the reason for that is that Member States have been so unforthcoming about what is happening in their fleets. That is not entirely their fault; it is partly because it is so hard to measure but it is a problem.

Q235 Earl of Arran: Surely, any new boat with technical creep on it can be policed and disallowed.
Dr Dunn: You would think so, but the one of the loopholes in the European Fisheries Fund—or, at least, it was a very highly contested point and not everybody was happy with the outcome—is that the European Fisheries Fund can be used to replace engines on fishing vessels. There are all sorts of ways of using that as a smokescreen to introduce a more efficient engine. It may not be more powerful in strict kilowatts or horsepower but you can introduce an engine which enables your vessel to fish much better. That is very, very hard to police, and it is often not adequately policed in some of the southern European Member States particularly. There are ways around it. My grandfather was a fishermen and I spent a long time talking to him when he was alive and fishermen are incredibly inventive and clever at finding ways around all sorts of restrictions. It is in their blood.
Lord Cameron of Dillington: A bit like farmers really!
Chairman: You mentioned the European Fisheries Fund and Earl of Dundee has some questions on that.

Q236 Earl of Dundee: If we look at three connected aspects: firstly, the European Fisheries Fund; secondly, current guidelines on state aid to the fisheries sector; and, thirdly, the objectives of the Common Fisheries Policy, do you believe these considerations are sufficiently aligned?
Dr Dunn: I think there has been a really good attempt to align the European Fisheries Fund to the reformed Common Fisheries Policy. I think the spirit and the intent and the substance of the EFF its objectives, the criteria for deployment of funds, it is really in harness

pretty well with the aspirations of the reformed CFP. Certainly it is a huge step forward compared to the Financial Instrument on Fisheries Guidance (FIFG) which it replaces. There is one health warning about the EFF which is sometimes overlooked: the European Fisheries Fund is €3.8 billion. The Financial Instrument on Fisheries Guidance which it will progressively replace was €3.7 billion across 15 Member States, so now we have virtually the same pot of money but across a hugely enlarged European Union and, moreover, the FIFG gave an extra €270 million for the 10 new Member States between 2004 and 2006 as a sort of precursor to the EFF, so it had already tried to bridge that gap. We finish up with a European Fisheries Fund which is a cake which is going to have to be sliced much more thinly than its predecessor and that literally means we are going to be able to do an awful lot less with it than we could have done with the FIFG, albeit that the money will be, in my view, deployed in a much more constructive way in terms of sustaining fishing and fishing communities and the wider ecosystem.

Q237 Earl of Dundee: If that then, as you say, is the downside and the anomaly, what can we do about it?
Dr Dunn: There is no likelihood in the short term of changing the budget. I think that is pretty carved in stone and it is probably something that I assume we will come back to in 2012/2013, because, after all, the EFF is set to run from 2007 for the next five years. But I do think that it is going to be very much down to Member States to use this money in a judicious way and that is the fundamental difference between the FIFG and the EFF. The EFF is not a structural fund, as such, in the old mould. It gives much more subsidiarity to Member States on how they deploy the money. What then becomes crucial is the so-called Operational Programme of the Member State on how it deploys its money. The UK has taken a long time to develop its Operational Programme. It is a bit in the slow lane. A number of Member States have already had their Operational Programmes signed off by the Commission and are up and running with the EFF. I will not go into detail but the reason we have struggled is because we have had to deal with the whole issue of getting an Operational Pprogramme agreed across four devolved countries: Scotland, England, Northern Ireland and Wales. That has created its own problems. There has been a lot of negotiating—you can just imagine it—but we now have an Operational Programme under consultation by Defra. The consultation is going on right now to a fairly tight deadline because they know they have to speed up. I think it is very important to scrutinise that official programme to see that it does support the central pillars of the European Fisheries Fund; that it generally supports small-scale fishing; that it incentivises the development of more selective,

less environmentally damaging fishing gear; that it is thereby and in other ways more consistent with the implementation of an ecosystem approach on a progressive basis. What can you do about it was your question. At this stage now I think you can make sure that Member States are doing the right thing by the criteria that are set down in the funds, sort of terms of reference.

Q238 Earl of Dundee: Bearing in mind what you have said about overcapacity and overcapacity plus effort, as it were, any form of funding from the fishery industry is a negative, is it not, really? It is a downside. I am just wondering whether the WTO is going to have any effect on this. Do you hold out any hope?
Dr Dunn: You probably read my evidence on this.

Q239 Earl of Dundee: I did, yes.
Dr Dunn: It has been a very depressing experience, the whole process of the fishing subsidies going through the WTO. They are now trying to kick it into life. There is a draft resolution or a draft document on the table which says all the right things. If, hypothetically, the WTO states can agree this draft and the European Union as a contracting party was then bound to follow its edicts, that would put further pressure on the EU to row back even more on existing subsidies. For example, through a rather odd outlier of European funding called de minimis aid, it is a *de facto* subsidy for fuel costs in the fishing industry. If you are funding fuel, you are fuelling over-fishing. The RSPB, through our European offices of Birdlife International, in conjunction with other NGOs, fought quite hard against the changes in the de minimis criteria and funding levels. Also, you will see from my evidence that one of the hot issues in the WTO draft at the moment is looking at the extent to which small-scale fishing around the world should be seen as a special case. You can understand why that is there, because in most of the world small-scale fishing is artisanal fishing which supports the livelihoods of highly dependent fishing communities. The European Commission, I think, have been arguing in WTO talks that the European Union's fleets are made up of something like 75–80% small vessels, so they have been arguing to have the same rules applied to them as to developing countries. I think this is a nonsense really. I do not think there should be any special pleading in that way for inshore fisheries. Inshore fisheries, as I have said, because of a point I made a moment ago, can be just as destructive of fish stocks as their offshore counterparts. I think we need to get into a situation where fishing is driven mostly by market forces and the fleet is slimmed down to what the fish stocks and the market can dictate. I do not think we should be giving any special featherbedding to any particular

sector of the fleet. I think the inshore fleet has had a pretty rough deal in this country and there are other things that can be done to assist it, but not that.
Chairman: Earl of Arran on governance.

Q240 Earl of Arran: Before getting on to the important point on governance and getting back to basics for a moment, in your opinion are seabirds at risk or suffering as a result of CFP?
Dr Dunn: We have spoken about discards and I suppose that is the other side of the coin. It has been a benefit but not one that we applaud or welcome. Some seabirds are undoubtedly disadvantaged by the way the CFP has managed its fisheries. The most obvious example of that has been the sandeel fishery. For seabirds that are dependent on sandeels as a stable prey, something like 90–95% of their diet in the summer is sandeels. I am speaking about surface feeding birds like the kittiwake, a small, dainty gull, and some of the tern species that nest in places like Orkney and Shetland. These populations have been in relentless decline. The studies that have been done in Scotland in the Firth of Forth have shown that the impact of climate change, sea warming—and I described its impact on sandeels a few moments ago—and the industrial fishing for sandeels by the Danish fleet just offshore from the Firth of Forth have been a double-whammy for those seabirds. You can show incontestably that those factors have been implicated in the decline of those seabird populations. I am happy to say that as a result of a lot of advocacy and changes in thinking, the sandeel fishery is now much better managed, but I have to say that has probably come about largely because the fishing industry itself has been so undermined by climate change that they have had to pull in their horns and rein in their fisheries. Yes, some seabirds are; others are not.

Q241 Earl of Arran: Thank you. That is helpful. Moving on to governance and, in particular, the Regional Advisory Councils—of which I think you are on two at the moment, are you not?
Dr Dunn: Yes.

Q242 Earl of Arran: These have fairly recently been set up.
Dr Dunn: Yes.

Q243 Earl of Arran: In your paper you mention constraints and obstacles as regards their success. How do you think this can be overcome and improved?
Dr Dunn: First of all, I am a supporter of the Regional Advisory Councils (RACs) as a governance tool. I think that is a very, very important issue. Really what we have now is regional advice to the European Commission from different regional seas,

the North Sea, the North Western Waters and the South Western Waters and so on. I will come to your question in a moment, and I hope you will bear with me while I do this little preamble. The Commission are fundamentally changing their structure as we speak. It will be announced formally, probably in the next few days or weeks, but the Commission has been restructuring itself. DG Fisheries has been restructuring itself to reflect the regional needs of its management outreach. At a meeting only a couple of weeks ago in the Edinburgh Parliament, the chap from DG Fisheries who is responsible now for the North East Atlantic and relations with Norway was there in his new role, as overseeing the part of the European Union Community waters which are most important to us. This whole regionalisation of the Common Fisheries Policy has legs and it is not just being reflected in the creation of the RACs but is going to change the institutional structure of DG Fisheries. In fact, I think they are even going to change the name. I think they are going to be called DG MARE or something instead DG Fisheries and Maritime Affairs. What needs to be done to make the RACs work better? A few things. In my view, there is still too much focus on the short-term issues, like TACs and quotas. I think the RACs agenda needs to preoccupy itself with the long-term management issues. That is where they will give added value, because the fishing organisations like the Scottish Fishermen's Federation and the National Federation of Fishermen's Organisations are already piling into the TACs and quotas every year and you wonder if the RACs can add much to what is already being done at national level. What, after all, are the RACs? They are an international forum. They can deal with boundary issues and trans-boundary issues and they should be looking at the big picture, the long-term management plans. I also think they need to focus more on that. I think they need to be able to do their own research. They are far too dependent on hand-outs and the goodwill of a few Member States. I have to say that the North Sea RAC and the North Western Waters RAC benefit hugely from the support of Defra. Defra have piled in and given a good account of themselves. They are almost unique in the amount of support they have given—with the possible exception of Denmark to the Baltic RAC—so I applaud that. They can provide facilities for meetings, they can provide expertise and know-how, but I think the RACs need to be able to commission their own research and they have such a huge agenda and such a lot of work to do and they need to be better informed than they are. My own view is that some of the RACs are too big. I know that they were probably divided up in a fairly pragmatic sort of way but the North Sea RAC is pretty good. It has a tight little nexus of eight Member States, functions well, there is very good dialogue, there is a lot of

momentum. The North Western Waters RAC covers a huge area and a huge number of different languages: English, Portuguese, French, Spanish. There are hugely difficult problems of trying to work out what the most important issues are. The southern Member States have a different agenda from west coast Scottish fishermen, for example, and trying to find something that holds all that together is difficult. The South Western Waters RAC, to a degree, as well. At some point the size and boundaries of the RACs may have to be looked at again but for the time being those are the main things I would observe.

Q244 Earl of Arran: At the moment they are advisory, are they not? Do you think there is a danger in them becoming executive?
Dr Dunn: I do not think there is a danger in the sense of them sliding imperceptibly from an advisory to an executive decision-making role. Really the RACs are, if you like, on trial. The Commission are observing them extremely closely. The Commission feel they are getting good advice, on the large, and it is improving advice from the RACs. The Commission will also—I have sensed this at times—be looking at their own backs a little bit: they do not want to cede power to bodies like the RACs on anything other than a highly systematic stakeholder debate basis. I think we are in for a long haul really there. If the RACs prove themselves, I can see them playing a bigger role than they have, but, at the moment, I would not recommend that they have anything other than the role they have, partly because I think there is still a lot of business as usual. The issues are very traditional, the ones the fishermen focus on, the short-term issues, not a lot of interest in the ecosystem approach and so on. You are going to get the two-thirds fishing majority view on those things, with the likes of myself struggling to get a view in that consensus. Perhaps that is institutionally something that is going to be hard to ever break out of, but, however it plays out, I would not go further than the role they have at the moment. But it is working. I think it is very good and the dialogue is improving between stakeholders. It was unimaginable ten years ago for me to sit down with the national fishermen's organisations and have the sensible, measured discussion that we have nowadays. It has taken a lot heat out of the "greens" versus the fishermen. It is a more grown-up debate and I think that is very, very healthy.
Earl of Arran: My other question you have already answered. It was about the future and short-termism against long-termism. You have expanded on that, so that has been helpful. Thank you.

Q245 Viscount Ullswater: In part of your answer you say that you feel TACs and quotas are going to be with us for some time to come.

26 March 2008   Dr Euan Dunn

Dr Dunn: Yes.

Q246 *Viscount Ullswater:* As basic building structures. Are we going to have to have the annual Council with the sort of horse trading that goes on every December in order to get those settled or can the RACs somehow take the place or give the advice that would obviate the need for that sort of Council?
Dr Dunn: I think the RACs will play a stronger role. Things are changing already. One of the reasons for the lunacy of the December Council, where fishing ministers are dead on their feet at four in the morning and making decisions that affect us all, is that the scientific advice is now going to be coming much earlier. In fact this year for the first time ICES will begin to give its advice in June. That period of reflection and negotiation and consultation is invaluable because it will cut out a lot of the frenetic approach. Just as an NGO, I know that the December Council is the worst time of the year for me and it probably is for everybody. Nobody looks forward to that period between October and December. I think the frontloading, as it is called, will greatly improve it. I would like to see us move to a situation where, with long-term management plans, you have the fisheries ministers more locked into what they can and cannot agree. I would like to see them be less able to put a socio-economic spin on the scientific advice and I would like to see them more constrained in that way. I would like to see them more adopting proposals that have already been almost signed off before they get to them. The evolutionary process to me suggests that that may be the way that we are beginning to go. I also think that the lack of integration between DG Fisheries and DG Environment has been lamentable and hugely damaging to the timely implementation of an ecosystem approach. They simply do not work together and they still do not work together. DG Fisheries has, as I said right at the beginning, scarcely any capacity for environmental issues. They have one or two people in DG Fisheries who deal with environmental issues as a bespoke part of their work programme. That is deeply worrying. I am not sure I would go this far, but some people even would like to see the whole fisheries regulatory process under the aegis of DG Environment rather than DG Fisheries. That would be a long haul but at the very least I think we need to see much better institutional integration between the two if we are going to have an ecosystem approach worthy of the name. There is no point blaming the Commission; it is down to the Parliament. If we want DG Fisheries or DG MARE or whatever it is called to have better capacity, the European Parliament needs to make that case. In relation to that, the fact that under the new Treaty the European Parliament will have co-decision on all fisheries issues except for TACs and quotas could

make quite a big difference. They will have to be taken more seriously. It should theoretically or hopefully increase the democratisation of the process, so that will be helpful.

Q247 *Chairman:* You have mentioned the problem of DG Fisheries and DG Environment. Do you have any views on the relationship between the Common Fisheries Policy and things like the Marine Directive, the Habitats Directive and the Birds Directive and the way in which those environment-driven legislative frameworks are relating to this Common Fisheries Policy?
Dr Dunn: Perhaps I could take the Directives first. The meeting that the joint RACs held in Edinburgh on 5 and 6 March, just a few weeks ago, was to explore how the fishing sector engages with the emerging network of offshore marine protected areas. Member States have to submit their initial tranche of proposals for offshore sites by September of this year. These are the so-called Special Areas of Conservation under the Habitats Directive. This has been a huge thing coming. The industry have not really attended to it. I think they always thought it was something that was away in the distance, but now it is here. We had a very good meeting. DG Fisheries was there and DG Environment, and they both gave presentations. We were exploring how we designate those sites, how we make sure that different Member States manage them in an equitable way—this level playing field thing again—how we adapt the fishing activity to ensure that these sites are adequately protected to meet the conservation goals. It was a very constructive meeting and the fishing sector I think dealt with it very well and I was very heartened by it. It was a meeting that was organised by the Spatial Planning Working Group of the North Sea RAC. The synergy, if you like, between the Habitats and the Birds Directives and the CFP in operational terms is now being worked out, and the Commission have some ideas and are in the thick of it. And, I think, so far, so good. On the bigger maritime policy, the Marine Strategy Directive is going to be something that is going to slowly creep up on us all and affect issues like the Common Fisheries Policy, although it is hard to know at the moment quite how deeply. The Marine Strategy Directive which was adopted at the end of last year requires Member States to achieve something called "good environmental status" by the year 2020. That Marine Strategy Directive is the environmental strand across all European policies. It is not just the Common Fisheries Policy; it is anything else that affects the seas, like the CAP, through fertiliser run-off or whatever. For the first time, it makes firm links between environmental legislation and the Common Fisheries Policy, so that, if fisheries present a problem for achieving that good environmental status, the

Commission and the Member States are required to act within the framework of the CFP to resolve that problem. It is going to bind in the CFP more strongly than it is capable of doing of itself through its ecosystem-based approach. It is going to bind it into a bigger regulatory structure. We wait and see. There is some quite strong language in the Marine Strategy Directive that reflects directly on the Common Fisheries Policy. Perhaps I might just read one. Recommendation 39: "To achieve good environmental status, measures can be taken within the context of the CFP based on scientific evidence, including the full closure of certain areas to safeguard *inter alia* spawning and nursery grounds as well as to enable ecosystem integrity, structure and function to be maintained or restored." That is quite clear, powerful language and it gives a direct lightening rod from the Marine Strategy Directive to the CFP to say: fishery closures are something that will be expected to be part of your arsenal of tools to achieve good environmental status if that is what the objectives require. There are a number of others which make similar strong linkages to the CFP. It is difficult to see quite how powerful it is going to be, particularly in the context of maritime policy. The Marine Strategy Directive is also the environmental strand for the maritime policy which is a real catch-all for all human activities at sea: shipping, oil and gas and all the rest. But I would say one more thing. To

come back to my role as chair of the Spatial Planning Working Group in the North Sea RAC, the reason we started with marine spatial planning in the North Sea RAC is that fishing is hedged in on all sides now by a proliferation of human activity in the North Sea and elsewhere, whether it be wind farms, oil and gas exploration, aggregate extraction, and fishing has not put its mark on the map. It is in danger of being buffeted about and forced into compromising positions by these powerful industries which are very well versed in how to get a foothold. I think the Marine Strategy Directive is very important in putting marine spatial planning at the heart of its intent. It is to try to work out how the fishing sector, along with these other sectors, can be managed in a conflict-free way to the extent possible in Community waters. That is going to be perhaps one of its most important impacts as a policy because we are going to have to attend to this increasingly. We may say we were already long overdue to attend to it but it is something that we are going to have to deal with very, very firmly and systematically in the next years running up to the next CFP review.

Q248 *Chairman:* Thank you very much indeed. That was an absolutely first-class, comprehensive, thorough evidence session. We are very much in your debt. Thank you.
Dr Dunn: Thank you for the opportunity. I really appreciate it.

WEDNESDAY 2 APRIL 2008

Present: Arran, E   Palmer, L
           Brookeborough, V   Plumb, L
           Cameron of Dillington, L   Sharp of Guildford, B
           Dundee, E of   Ullswater, V (Chairman)

Memorandum by the Joint Nature Conservation Committee, Countryside Council for Wales, Scottish Natural Heritage and Natural England

Introduction

1. JNCC is the statutory advisor to Government on UK and international nature conservation, on behalf of the Council for Nature Conservation and the Countryside, the Countryside Council for Wales (CCW), Natural England (NE) and Scottish Natural Heritage (SNH). This evidence is a coordinated response from JNCC, CCW. SNH and NE ("the Agencies").

General Principles

2. There are some general objectives which we are striving to achieve in fishery policy and management. These are:

— implementing an ecosystem approach to management of marine resources;

— reducing negative impacts on biodiversity from fishing operations;

— integrating environmental/biodiversity considerations into fishery management;

— integrating fishery management with the management of wider marine resources;

— maintaining or making permanent the 6 and 12 mile limits;

— supporting the work of the RACs; and

— improving the scientific basis for informing management decisions.

Responses to Individual Questions

1. *Chapter II Regulation 2371/2002 on the conservation and sustainable exploitation of fisheries resources under the Common Fisheries Policy introduced new methods of ensuring conservation and sustainability, including recovery plans, management plans and emergency measures. To what extent have these been effective?*

3. The overall effectiveness of the CFP in conserving fisheries resources may be judged by examining the European Commission's Fishing Opportunities 2008 Policy Paper, which considered the status of 106-117 stocks over the period 2003–07. There is no evidence of an overall improvement in the status of stocks. During the period 2003–07, the number of stocks which were considered to be outside safe biological limits was estimated to be between 73 and 82%. It is worth noting that the information upon which the status of stocks can be assessed has deteriorated over time also, partly because smaller stocks are more difficult to assess, and partly because data sufficient to determine the status of only approximately half of all stocks is currently collected.

4. In relation to the new tools (including recovery plans, management plans and emergency measures) available to manage fisheries, the Agencies feel that these have not been in use long enough to reliably assess their effectiveness. In principle, the Agencies consider them to be a good way forward, and some successes have been observed (eg northern hake). In practice, however, all of them have proved more difficult to put into operation than was hoped, mostly due to (1) the need to achieve support of sufficient Member States, (2) lack of legal requirement to identify a strict deadline by which measures have to be established and (3) no specific additional resources available for their development.

5. We have twice experienced the (attempted) use of emergency measures in relation to biodiversity conservation. The UK applied for and was granted emergency measures in relation to the Darwin Mounds in 2002, prior to their permanent closure to protect cold water corals. The UK also applied in 2004 for a closure

of certain fisheries in the South-west Approaches to protect common dolphins from by-catch. This application was turned down. In both cases, the advice of ICES was sought by the Commission and was followed—for the Darwin Mounds there was clear evidence of long-term, possibly irreversible damage, while in the case of common dolphins in the South-west Approaches, ICES concluded that there was not sufficient evidence of an unsustainable (in population terms) bycatch, In both these cases, the emergency measure provisions appear to have worked well.

2. *A wide range of management tools are available to fisheries manager., What are your views on the following tools:*

    — *Total Allowable Catches;*

    — *Effort limitation, including "days at sea ", marine conservation areas and real-time closures;*

    — *Rights-Based Management tools;*

    — *Technical Conservation Measures.*

6. We agree that fisheries managers do have a wide range of tools, but within the context of the current Common Fisheries Policy, the full use of these tools is severely constrained by the political decision-making process, Political 'horse-trading' in the tactical decision-taking process can effectively undermine the best advice of scientists and intentions of managers. The Agencies consider that political input and balancing of objectives is best achieved at a strategic goal-setting level rather than at the tactical negotiation of the size of the TAC and quotas. All of these tools have slightly differing effects on fishing activity, but all depend on the contexts in which they are placed

7. Total allowable catches have the effect of limiting landings (thus really are a slight misnomer as they are effectively TALs) but have the unfortunate effect of permitting high levels of discarding to occur in mixed species fisheries either through limitations on quota for an individual species or through 'high-grading' (the practice of only retaining the highest value fish of a particular quota-limited species). However, it is difficult to imagine an alternative given the current excessive levels of capacity and expended effort in EU fisheries,

8. Effort limitation comes in many forms, but is usually associated with some sort of limits in time at sea. We have not yet analysed whether the recent proposal to distribute national "kilowatt-days" as national effort caps will be effective in limiting effort and would give biodiversity benefits. Limiting "days at sea" has an effect on the profitability of vessels and effectively produces a fleet that underperforms economically, although the Commission noted that Member States reported that only 72% of fishing effort was deployed in 2006, which they said indicated the regime did not, on average, constrain the fleet. In addition, improvements in fishing technology mean that fishing capacity effectively increases continuously. We are unaware of any recent studies of the rate of such "technical creep" but see no evidence to see any change from the 4%–8% per annum rates estimated in the late 1990s.

9. Spatial management measures are a vital component of fishery management and are used in a wide variety of contexts. Areas established for fishery management reasons can have positive biodiversity benefits and vice versa, but marine protected areas are not necessarily the answer to all management issues, and other approaches may be more effective in some circumstances. The Agencies believe that their use is valuable for target species that are sedentary or have specific location or habitat requirements at key points in their life-cycles (a good example being scallop fisheries). We also believe that any closure needs to be carefully designed to meet its specific objectives, and then needs to be monitored and managed carefully to ensure that it is achieving those objectives.

10. Real-time closures may be of particular use in mixed fisheries where there is a need to avoid particular concentrations of a species (eg cod) under particular pressure.

11. The current quota system is in practice rights-based management. Given the failure of the current system for many wide-ranging stocks, the Agencies remain to be convinced that this is a suitable way forward for mobile fisheries, In inshore areas, where fisheries measures are devolved back to Member States, Regulating Orders may be of considerable use in managing fisheries, in particular molluscan and crustacean fisheries. For this reason, and others, the Agencies continue to support subsidiarity and the management of territorial waters by Member States.

12. Technical conservation measures can be very helpful if properly researched and developed prior to their introduction and particularly if they are widely accepted by the fishing industry. We have recent experience of the introduction of technical conservation measures to limit the bycatch of harbour porpoises in certain fisheries. This attempted measure, made for thoroughly laudable purposes, is failing at present for many reasons. Other technical measures, such as square-mesh panels and separator grids that work to release non-target species from trawl nets appear to work well and have been taken up in some relevant fisheries. The issues

around these measures can be generalised to indicate that any technical conservation measure should address effectively each of the following related points:

— technical reliability and effectiveness of the measure;

— negative ecological impacts;

— economic impacts on stakeholders;

— poor compliance by fishermen with regulations;

— poor monitoring; and

— poor acceptance by stakeholders.

3. *To what extent have current management tools increased the levels of discards and bycatch? What is your view on how these problems can best be tackled?*

13. The Agencies are unaware of any evidence that current management tools have recently exacerbated the levels of discards and bycatch. The apparent high levels of cod discarding in the North Sea are probably due to management decisions not keeping pace with an increasing, but still relatively small, stock.

14. Some bycatch is an unavoidable part of nearly all fishing because gears and practices can never be entirely selective for the species being targeted. Target species themselves can become bycatch when they are not of the "correct" size in market value terms or following management regulations. Non-target bycatch species can be of considerable and marketable value and will therefore be landed or can be of no value at all and will be discarded.

15. The Agencies support any measures that reduce bycatch, but we are particularly keen to see reductions in the bycatch of species whose removal has a direct negative impact on the survival of that species or can directly harm the ecosystem. In all cases we consider that problems can largely be addressed by well designed technical measures that deal with the issues listed at the end of our answer to Question 2. We are very keen that the processes put in place by FAO on the conservation of sharks, seabirds and deep-sea species be turned into effective CFP regulations as soon as possible.

16. More specific to discards reduction, the Agencies have seen no evidence that a discard ban either is effective (it is very difficult to monitor and therefore be sure of compliance) or ecologically sound (food items returned to the sea are more likely to cycle in and maintain the marine ecosystem than are such items returned to land for use in agriculture or aquaculture).

17. Closure of areas for fishing may be appropriate in some circumstances, but there is a danger of perverse effects caused by displacement of fishing effort when closures are not considered fully prior to implementation. The process adopted in Norwegian waters of closing an area to fishing if bycatch exceeds a certain level is said to be beneficial to their fisheries. However, this does require a high level of (self-) monitoring and trust between fishers that all stop fishing at the same time and move to areas where bycatch is lower. We are not aware of an independent scientific study of the effects of these measures.

18. The Agencies consider it essential that measures to reduce discards should be assessed on an individual fishery basis and that the involvement of stakeholders in this assessment is essential. We are pleased in this respect with the Commission Consultation on Fisheries Discards and the resonance that this has had among the RACs.

4. *Do you consider that fisheries management policies may need to adapt to climate change? If so, how might this be achieved?*

19. Fisheries policies need to adapt to all drivers affecting the whole fishing system and in this climate change is no different from other causes of change or variability. Climate change has added a greater degree of uncertainty to fisheries management than was present previously. There is some evidence that hydrographic change has already caused some effects, especially in exacerbating problems brought about by over-fishing and consequent low levels of certain fish stocks. In general, a higher degree of uncertainty should lead to a higher degree of precaution in management; thus stocks need to be rebuilt to higher levels to make them more resilient than would be the case without climate change. In light of this increased uncertainty, we believe that it is important to carry out a well designed study of the effect of climate change on marine habitats and some commercially targeted species. This would require some areas to be closed to some human activities in order to understand change in the absence of confounding impacts, including fishing.

5. *Chapter V of Regulation 2371/2002 lays down the responsibilities of the Member States and the Commission as regards the control and enforcement of the rules of the Common Fisheries Policy. The recent Court of Auditors Report on the control, inspection and sanctions systems relating to the rules on conservation of Community fisheries resources was very sceptical of the systems currently in place. What is your view of the efficacy of the systems in place? To what extent has the Community Fisheries Control Agency already assisted in improving matters?*

20. The Agencies consider that the best control and enforcement systems are those that maximise the chances of infringements being detected. During the review of the CFP leading up to 2002, the country nature conservation agencies supported strongly the introduction of regulations that allowed for the tracking of fish sales (so called forensic accounting) as a method to reduce illegal landings of fish. While such landings have not ceased completely, the "buyers and sellers" regulations have proved effective in dealing with this illegal behaviour. The introduction of satellite vessel monitoring systems has helped in further detection of illegal behaviour (fishing in the wrong place) but crosschecks using direct satellite and aerial observation have shown that ways of avoiding detection (eg tampering with VMS transmitters) persist. We are not aware of any improvements brought about by the Community Fisheries Control Agency, but it may be that the Agency is still too young to judge its performance.

21. The benefits of electronic data collection and vessel position monitoring are considerable and as a general principle we are keen to see these continue to develop. We believe that it is a reasonable medium to long term aspiration to see these systems develop for use on vessels smaller than those to which regulations currently apply but that in the meantime there is considerable merit in encouraging the development and use of voluntary electronic data systems, as have been applied in a number of research and local management scenarios.

6. *The European Commission has regularly highlighted how serious infringements of the CFP are penalised differently across the Community. This was a matter that was also raised by the Court of Auditors and sanctions were included in the recent Commission Proposal in IUU fishing. What is your view on the issue?*

22. We agree that a general principle of enforcement should be to establish a level playing field across Europe. The extent to which perceived unfairness across Member States can undermine the effectiveness of management measures should not be underestimated.

7. *Chapter III of Regulation 2371/2002 obliged Member States to put in place measures to adjust the capacity of their fleets in order to achieve a stable and enduring balance between such fishing capacity and their fishing opportunities. To what extent has this been successful?*

23. AB noted in the answer to Question 2 above, it is apparent that such a balance has not been achieved. There is no doubt though that without the reductions in fleet capacity that have occurred, the situation would be much worse. A good example of the inadequate attempts to reduce capacity and also the effects of technical creep has been provided recently by the crisis in the under 10m fleet where the scale of fishing (landings) by the under 10m fleet and the rate of increase in the fishing effectiveness of these smaller vessels appears to have gone unnoticed until recently. It is plain that much further work is required to reduce the level of fishing capacity in UK and EU fleets.

24. The Agencies are concerned that some capacity reduction measures may have resulted in the diversion of fishing effort into other parts of the world less able to police their fisheries and sometimes onto stocks already being fished at full capacity. The concerns around this issue need further study.

8. *The new fisheries structural fund, the European Fisheries Fund (EFF), has now come into force. What has been your experience thus far with the new instrument?*

25. The Agencies have not yet gained any experience with this fund, but note that the administrations in the UK have to provide a National Operational Programme (and a strategic environmental assessment, SEA) for this fund before it can be used. We have only just received this SEA.

26. Structural funding should support good environmental practice in fishery management and operations, including the introduction of an ecosystem approach to management. A wider range of measures could be supported by EFF—including the further development of accreditation schemes, the further use of spatial management regimes and related codes of (environmental) practice.

9. *What are your views on the possible impact on EU fisheries structural policy of WTO level discussions as regards subsidies in the fishing sector?*

27. At present the European fleet is over-capacity and in many cases, if all subsidies were removed, would be unprofitable. This overcapacity lies close to the root of many problems facing the Common Fisheries Policy. The proposals for reform of the CFP in 2002 and for the establishment of the European Fisheries Fund were very progressive in reducing subsidies, both direct and hidden. These proposals were softened and in some cases negated as they went through the European process such that many subsidies are hidden in allowable costs such as replacement engines. We note that such allowable costs do not apply for other industries such as shipping or road transport. Fuel costs may also not be taxed—an effective subsidy to all fishers. We also note that fishermen pay little towards the cost of enforcing or managing inshore fisheries. The Agencies would welcome reduction in any subsidies that can lead directly or indirectly to environmental damage.

10. *As a result of Regulation 2371/2002, Regional Advisory Councils (RACs) were established to advise the Commission on matters of fisheries management in respect of certain sea areas or fishing zones. What is your assessment of the success thus far of the RACs? What is your view on their future evolution?*

28. In the run-up to the 2002 reform of the CFP, the country nature conservation agencies were enthusiastic supporters of the concept of regional management and of the opportunity for all stakeholders to better own the fisheries management process. This support was based primarily on the belief that legislation that is "owned" by users is more likely to be adhered to and that greater stakeholder involvement would help reduce the "tragedy of the commons" through which excessive pressure is placed on a common resource. We feel that in general the longer-established RACs (notably the North Sea and the NWW RACs) have made good progress in bringing together the various nations and diverse cultures fishing in their regional sea. Progress has not been perfect though, and it is very apparent that in the more newly-established RACs the culture is likely to be heavily dominated by fishing interests with very little input from other stakeholders such as environmental NGOs. However, it might be argued that it is too early to judge these RACs and that more time is needed for them to become mature.

29. We note that the original concept was for RACs to become self-funding after about five years in existence, but even this requirement has now been dropped in favour of central funding of a majority of activities from the Commission. We feel that such funding should be dependent on meeting certain performance criteria (such as ensuring a fully representative attendance at meetings) otherwise there is a risk of the RACs becoming yet another industry lobby group, but this time funded by the European tax-payer.

30. There has been little evidence of the RACs attempting to proactively adopt an ecosystem-based approach. We are pleased that a workshop on marine protected areas is to be held in March 2008, and the cod recovery symposium was organised in 2007 among the RACs. We are pleased that the UK has started to encourage an examination of management of fisheries in each of the four areas of the NWWRAC. We believe that RACs should remain primarily as advisory bodies.

11. *How do you consider EU fisheries should ideally be governed? How appropriate and feasible do you consider a regional management model to be?*

31. Fisheries are but one activity occurring in European seas and their management at the moment is still highly centralised and subject to considerable short-term political interference that we believe is not helping to achieve long-term sustainability. As outlined earlier, we believe that politicians should be encouraged to take strategic decisions in order to balance competing demands on the marine environment. This will mean that fisheries governance needs to be much more closely integrated with the governance of other marine activities. This will demand the establishment of new frameworks and the introduction of mechanisms such as impact assessments to put fisheries on the same footing as most other marine activities. We would hope that any strategic decision-taking mechanism would also take account of international agreements, including relevant FAO guidelines. Mechanisms to ensure that the views of all stakeholders can be heard are also essential.

32. Such a large-scale integrated marine management system would not work if management needs to be attuned to regional circumstances. Decisions taken for the Black and Mediterranean Seas are biologically, socially and economically likely to be very different to those for the North Sea. We thus think some sort of regional management system is essential. We think it feasible to devise appropriate regional management systems.

February 2008

Examination of Witnesses

Witnesses: DR CLARE ENO, Senior Fisheries Policy Officer, Countryside Council for Wales, PROFESSOR COLIN GALBRAITH, Director of Policy and Advice, Scottish Natural Heritage, MR MARK TASKER, Head of Marine Advice, Joint Nature Conservation Committee, and DR TOM TEW, Chief Scientist, Natural England, examined.

Q249 Chairman: Could I start by welcoming you to this morning's session and mention one or two preliminaries? This session will be webcast; it means there is a possibility that somebody might hear this session, but what that really means is that it is in the public domain. A note of what is being said is being recorded, you will be provided with a transcript and there will be a possibility of looking through it and if there is anything that you feel has not been properly taken down and reported then there is an opportunity of correcting the transcript. Mr Tasker, you are leading the delegation, are you not?

Mr Tasker: I have been co-ordinating the delegation but I would like to pass over to my good friend and colleague, Professor Colin Galbraith, to actually lead us today.

Q250 Chairman: What I would suggest is that if you wish to make an opening statement we would be very pleased to hear it, otherwise I believe you have a list of pre-prepared questions which will be asked. Perhaps between you you could decide who is going to lead on the answer to each question as that will save me from going down the line and saying are there any more comments to be made. Professor Galbraith, would you like to start?

Professor Galbraith: My Lord Chairman, thank you very much indeed for the invitation, we are delighted to be here, and I should probably briefly introduce my colleagues to you. On my right is Dr Tom Tew, who is Chief Scientist at Natural England, then Mark Tasker who is the Head of Marine Advice in JNCC and Dr Clare Eno from CCW who is involved in marine and fishery matters for them. Very briefly, just by way of introduction, it is important that we say from the statutory agencies that our aim is to manage the natural heritage and biodiversity around us in a manner that ensures its conservation but also that ensures its sustainability where that is appropriate, and that encompasses the fishing interest and the fish interest in the seas around the UK. It is important also that I say we recognise the great economic and cultural importance of fishing to the UK and that its future management is really at a critical stage now; we are aiming to develop the sustainable management of the sea collectively with others. The food from the marine environment is indeed a key service that we get from that ecosystem. We will hopefully return to the ecosystem word a little later on, but that food is a key service provided by a healthy ecosystem, and that is a service that requires careful management and planning. We note, just in passing, that many of the global fisheries are actually in decline or have declined over recent years and indeed we see this as a critical time, and a real opportunity, to try to address some of the management issues that are inherent in fishery management within the UK, within Europe and globally. We should say also that we are keen to continue to work with the fishing industry, with government and with others to develop the way forward for this important industry that we have around our shores. That is really all we need to say by way of introduction, but it might help if I explained a little bit briefly about our role in the agencies. We are, as you know, Government-funded bodies, we are advisers to the Government on the natural environment and its conservation, and that positions us to advise on fish matters and fishing is part of that; so we advise on land-based issues, on agriculture, and on sea-based issues in relation to fish and fisheries. We advise at the UK level to the UK Government, co-ordinated through JNCC, and Mark Tasker is co-ordinating today, but we also advise the devolved administrations in their own right on these matters, and again we do that in a variety of manners. I should mention also that we do have some international roles and, again, my colleague Mark Tasker has an international advisory function in relation to marine and fisheries management, so hopefully that positions us, with our remit on biodiversity, our role in developing marine protected areas through the Habitats Directive in particular, to have a dialogue today and indeed beyond today. We are interested in how the Common Fisheries Policy, for example, relates to other directives—to the Habitats Directive, the Birds Directive—and to other interests that are coming to the fore in the marine environment. I hope that background gives you the position as to where we are coming from.

Chairman: Thank you very much.

Q251 Viscount Brookeborough: You said you were UK-wide, can I ask you why, perhaps, there is no representation from Northern Ireland?

Professor Galbraith: Northern Ireland is part of the Joint Committee. The Environment Department in Northern Ireland is an agency of government, slightly separate from ourselves, so it is closer to government than we are. Mark, you may want to tackle the JNCC level.

Mr Tasker: That more or less answers the question in that the Environment and Heritage Service, which we work with most closely, is part of the Northern Ireland Government as compared with our slightly offset roles as agencies, so we can give our advice but they are actually part of the receivers as well as the givers of the advice in Northern Ireland. We do involve them in most of our discussions on fisheries.

Q252 *Chairman:* They are not excluded it sounds then.
Mr Tasker: Not at all, they are very, very welcome.

Q253 *Viscount Brookeborough:* Poachers and gamekeepers.
Professor Galbraith: Yes.

Q254 *Chairman:* You have really answered the first question which is to outline the role of the agencies with respect to the CFP. Perhaps I could move on to the ecosystem-based approach to fisheries management. One of the general objectives that you are striving to achieve in fisheries policy and management is the implementation of this ecosystem-based approach to fisheries management which was introduced in the 2002 CFP reform regulation. We heard last week from the RSPB that the concept is rather loosely defined, this ecosystem approach, and we would as a Committee be grateful to hear how you interpret it and also how you feel that something of that nature can be delivered.
Professor Galbraith: I personally have a background in ecosystem management and in ecosystem thinking. By way of introduction, for me ecosystem management really means five things: one is about scale, so it has to be a large enough scale to be meaningful and an ecosystem could encompass that; secondly, it has to be holistic, so it has to take on board not just one species or two, not just one habitat or two, but as much as we can together, in a way of thinking; thirdly, it has to be long term, and that is an important part in today's discussion, it is about planning for the long term, for sustainability; fourthly, it has to involve people and behind that are the economics and the services that they get from the ecosystem, so the people dimension, getting them involved in the planning, is absolutely crucial to the ecosystem approach; and then, fifthly, it is the environmental processes behind it. It is not just about looking at numbers of animals, of fish or anything, it is looking at how they interact. Getting that understanding on all five categories may appear complex, but we can hopefully simplify that in the years ahead. The key point for me though is leading all that to an agreed outcome; we have to get an agreed outcome on how to manage any ecosystem, and when you apply that to the marine environment you can see the difficulties in terms of the scale and in terms of the complexity, but taking that together is the way that we would like to see things progress. You could then say "what does that actually mean"? Take any one of the words, take long term, there are issues that we could develop in terms of long term

planning: we could look to see how the people, communities and others are built into that planning system, so the ecosystem approach is fairly well worked through. Applying it to the marine system in particular is tricky, it is difficult, but it is a sensible way to progress and I do think that much of what has happened in the past ten years or so takes us towards an ecosystem style of management and the marine environment should be able to cope with that.

Q255 *Chairman:* How far do you think we have got down the road on that?
Professor Galbraith: There is a long, long way to go. There is an information base that we have got to address to get an understanding of what is happening in the marine environment; to understand people's involvement and people's perception is important as well, and what they think is happening in the environment, so there is a long way to go but it is possible to take that approach forward. If you are looking to develop a sustainable and healthy ecosystem you have to adopt the wider approach, the longer term approach, and one that does look at the processes as well as the individual populations. It sounds complex, but there are bits in there that can be adopted in years to come. My colleagues may want to add to that.
Dr Tew: I would just add some context around why it is difficult in the marine ecosystem and compare it with terrestrial habitats, because on land we tend to manage the big primary producers called trees and therefore you end up managing the habitat, in effect, and how the herbivores and carnivores fit into that is intuitive to us because we manage habitat, whereas at sea we are effectively always trying to manage the top of the food chain, the predators, the single species of fish. It is not intuitive for us to understand that their production depends on the healthy marine ecosystem, and that is why I think we have a long way to go. There is an increasing body of evidence from around the world that healthy ecosystems, indeed straight measures of biodiversity, are actually well correlated with a range of other services such as the amount of fish or other ecosystem services, so that evidence is growing but I do not think it is intuitive to us as humans as to why that is important.
Mr Tasker: My Lord Chairman, if I could come in too, recognising that Professor Pope is here, and who has written several good papers on ecosystem approach, the question relates particularly to an ecosystem-based approach to fisheries management, and the fisheries management bit is perhaps the bit that we need to drill down into in relation to the CFP. I have always felt that we are trying to run, we are trying to get too complex too early. One of the fundamental things that we are still not doing very well is taking account of what effect the ecosystem has on fish stocks and then taking account of what

effect fishing is having on the ecosystem. Both of those things are getting more tractable in terms of scientific understanding, but building those into the science system and building them into the advice system still is proving quite challenging. If I can give an example, if you have a very cold winter many young sole are killed; we do not have a system by which shortly after a very cold winter you actually decrease the amount of fishing going on in the sole fishery, so there are some fairly simple mechanisms, in my view, that can be brought in. I should actually say on the positive side that there are some approaches where this is working—and I again refer to Professor Pope who used to be a professor at Tromsø University in north Norway—there they are responding in fisheries management with a rather simple system to temperature changes. Changes in sea temperature change what they decide to do. That could be applied much more widely, but the drive has not really been there to do it and it is partly because we may have over-elaborated this view of what the ecosystem approach is and, rather than taking it step by step by step, we have gone a bit too complex too early. That is an answer to how we would like to implement, or how can we deliver, the interpretation that was given by my colleagues.

Q256 Lord Cameron of Dillington: Just to follow up on that for a moment, do you think it is challenging and very difficult because we are not funding the research enough? Is it a matter of putting more money into more complex research and do you think that it is possible to bring the scientific research perhaps closer in agreement to the fishermen?
Mr Tasker: There are two good questions there. Are we funding science enough? It is difficult to judge. If you ask any scientist they will always say no and it also depends on what you spend it on. We are doing a lot of almost knee-jerk tracking of things that we have been doing for many years, which maybe we could simplify a bit and divert that money into some of these other interfaces of how the ecosystem might be changing that may not have gone through the system. I have now forgotten your second question.
Professor Galbraith: We would welcome a trial of the ecosystem approach; there is work on land, if you like, and it would be very good to have a parallel in the marine environment to take what we might now hear as a way forward, to perhaps put it into practice and then monitor that very carefully, so in that regard, yes, it would be appropriate to fund this.

Q257 Chairman: Perhaps we need Richard Attenborough to do a television programme.
Professor Galbraith: That would be very helpful.

Q258 Lord Cameron of Dillington: My Lord Chairman, my other question was do you think that the scientists can be brought perhaps closer to the fishermen in terms of understanding each other's business?
Professor Galbraith: I have a particular view on that, I believe they can, and when you look at many of the issues that we have dealt with over the past ten or 15 years you start at opposite ends of the spectrum, on the poles as it were, and the only way forward is to bring people towards the middle, so I certainly have a very clear hope and optimism that we have to come together. Again, whether that is a land-based problem or whether, in this case, it is the marine fisheries then it is, in a way, the only way forward.
Dr Tew: Can I just add a comment which partly addresses both questions. To me a large part of the answer is to do with scale, because work on doing research in the marine environment is complicated and expensive and difficult so you end up doing small-scale experiments, and the fishermen can see that you cannot extrapolate. So the science needs to be done on a bigger scale and that will bring the scientists closer together with the fishermen's understanding because the fishermen understand how the marine ecosystem works. When you do a small-scale experiment over a seabed perhaps the size of this room, then you will get colonisation from species simply walking in, you will not replicate the real damage to the ecosystems or the real ecosystem processes that are working, so for me scale is an issue. The second issue really is the mix of science between near shore and inshore research and offshore research, and we do need to be careful how we balance those two because there are a lot of large sums of money being spent on very sexy and innovative deep sea research and we are all in favour of that, but we are sometimes at risk of ignoring some of the things which are literally closer to home, about which we do not have much information—I do not want to paint a picture that we are ignorant of what is happening out there, but we could do a lot more.
Chairman: Thank you very much for that; that is really a look at the future and we ought to seek your views on the current issues and the current management. Lord Plumb.

Q259 Lord Plumb: It is encouraging, My Lord Chairman, to hear that there is a possibility of science and practice working more closely together, and one hopes soon, and it is also encouraging to hear comments moving towards simplification. It all sounds complicated and if you had been with us yesterday, listening to the debate on the Lisbon Treaty, you would have heard several times the importance of working alone rather than the reverse and the word subsidiarity was continually arising and so on; nevertheless, we are dealing with a European policy and, reading your five points under "Management tools", they are quite interesting but you do seem to be a little cautious over management tools and we would like you to expand perhaps on these, as to how you see the future. The RSPB was strongly in favour of capacity and effort limitation, arguing that TACs are too blunt a tool, and then a witness we had from CEMARE insisted that efficient management should be via outputs and not inputs. Everything surely depends on the management tools and the acceptability of those management tools, both by the scientists and by the operator, so it is important from our point of view that you give us factually the benefits of your advice on how this can be done.

Professor Galbraith: I will ask my colleague Dr Tew to lead on that.

Dr Tew: My Lord Chairman, if this does get too complicated please stop me and I will try to explain it in a better way.

Q260 *Lord Plumb:* If I do not understand it I will.

Dr Tew: I will try and make the point clearly. The single point I wish to make is that in terms of comparing output and input controls there is no single answer; if there was a single answer we would surely have adopted it by now because some of the best brains on the planet have been addressing the problem, and the fishermen themselves indeed want to see the problem solved, so our key message—which I am sure is not new to you—is that there is no simple answer. It is a box of tools that you need and you need to pull out those tools in appropriate circumstances. I would like to compare and contrast the situation of a single species, pelagic deep sea fishery such as mackerel or herring with a mixed demersal species fishery such as cod, haddock and plaice and I want to illustrate why no single solution is going to work. For single species perhaps we have relatively few, relatively large, relatively modern boats, modern equipment able to target, the fish they are after and highly skilled at doing so, and then we would agree with the economists that output measures, TACs or total allowable landings can work efficiently. Indeed, one struggles to come up with better alternatives in those circumstances. Of course, when you transpose that to more complex mixed demersal fisheries then those exact same tools are not going to work; in fact they are going to be counterproductive because, as you know, once fishermen have met the quota of one species they will continue to fish after other species to fill those quotas, or they will continue to pursue non-quota species, or even they will continue to look for the most commercially valuable individuals of the particular species of quotas; I am sure you are familiar with all this. It leads to excess catch and discarding and we feel strongly that such effects are going to be exacerbated when you have over-capacity because where you have got ten boats all doing that in a mixed demersal fishery, all after that most commercially valuable one tonne, then they will be all discarding non-target species. In short, in perhaps the majority of those circumstances, output controls are not going to deal with over fishing and you are going to get excess catch and discards, and the causal problem of course is the financial incentive systems that encourage them to go on fishing after they have caught the quota. We may come back to this under discards. The question you asked then is how should we manage demersal fisheries if you are saying that that is not going to work, and the principles that we set out are fairly clear: management based on science at all times, capacity and effort matched to the resource and spatial and temporal flexibility of management out at sea. The management measures that we think therefore should be included in that toolbox would encompass real-time closures, which again we might be coming to later, closures for limited periods over limited areas—to protect spawning grounds for instance—and essentially a range of other input controls that complement output controls, the 18-day at sea rule out in the North Sea for instance. As we may come on to perhaps in the next question, and we note it in our written evidence, there is a range of technical conservation measures which we believe can work if properly applied. I will finish by giving you a good example of where the toolbox can work well and it is the mussel and cockle fisheries at The Wash. I know this is not an international pelagic example but nevertheless it is a very good example that demonstrates how measures can work well because, as you may know, on The Wash there is limited entry, there is shared ownership of the rights and responsibilities between those with rights of access. The fishery is managed so that it is effectively matched to resource availability, there are spatial and temporal controls to prevent damage to certain parts of The Wash at certain times of the year, there is not much by catch and discard; it is all based on science and the fishermen are on board, the fishermen are part of the solution. What we have seen there is moving from a situation in the 1990s when the stocks and indeed the fishing industry was on its knees with a zero total allowable catch to the situation we had last year where we landed 5,000 tonnes, a third of the standing stock of both mussels and cockles, we had a vibrant stock and a vibrant fishing industry in that part of the world, so there are examples where the toolbox can work well.

Chairman: What you have not mentioned in all of this is whether licensing has a part to play.

Q261 *Lord Plumb:* Could we have the quota too?

Mr Tasker: Thank you, My Lord Chairman, licensing certainly does have a part to play and in the example just given by Dr Tew they are licensed to fish in The Wash, so it is one way of limiting capacity as you limit the licences.

Q262 Chairman: That was done by restricting licences or increasing licences at the right time.
Mr Tasker: Yes, in other words working out approximately how many fishing vessels would be needed to take the catch that they thought could be taken and then only licensing that many.

Q263 Chairman: What happens to the ones that previously were fishing but lose their licences; is there a decommissioning system?
Mr Tasker: The licence includes very often the number of days you can actually go and fish, so it is not the absolute numbers of fishing vessels, it is the amount of fishing you can exert. In terms of the quota, as asked by Lord Plumb, in The Wash there is a quota per vessel. In wider fisheries, obviously, total allowable catch is another means and the quota is a division of that catch; that will always apply.

Q264 Lord Plumb: Can I just ask one further extension of what you have been saying—and I did understand what you were saying—how do you see technology developing? One's impression, not as a fisherman but as a son of the soil, the impression you get is that they are out there hoovering the sea, that it is now simple to gather the fish compared with how it used to be. This has to fit into the management tools somewhere in order to try to control the fisheries; the Commissioner responsible for fisheries once said to me in Brussels, "Henry, if you can keep the fish still we will decide the problem" and of course that is surely the difficulty, is it not, that the shoals move around the seas?
Mr Tasker: Indeed. Most of what we are talking about is an improvement in the ability to find and be able to catch fish, which is an improvement in efficiency of fishing. This is known by the rather fine jargon term as "technological creep", in other words things get progressively more efficient in catching fish. There was a study done in the 1990s which I do not think has been repeated since, which indicated that technological creep was working at the rate of about 4 to 8% cent a year, and it does not take a great mathematician to work out that that means that you get over-fishing quite rapidly because of those improvements in efficiency and improvements in the way of finding fish. These can be simple things, like when I first went to sea 25 years ago we were not exactly shooting the sun but we were using a rather antiquated electronic machine telling you where you were. Now with GPS you can go precisely back to exactly where you want to be, and that actually makes quite a big difference in some fisheries, you are not searching around within 100 metres, you can go precisely there. Little things, therefore, which do not

actually initially strike you as being important in terms of fishing—and it is not just an increase in engine power or better nets or anything else—are actually adding to efficiency the whole time. The toolbox then essentially has to allow for that, when you choose your tools you have to actually build in some method of decreasing fishing capacity and there are a number of ways of doing that.
Dr Tew: I would agree fully with the point that technology presents opportunities as well as challenges and, for instance, if we who care about conservation of habitats on the seabed can be clear about where they are and how vulnerable they are, then we can give clear guidance to fishers on the areas that they should avoid, or how frequently they should or should not go there. If you have some ecosystems which recover relatively rapidly, then you are going to have a different set of sensitivities than those that are vulnerable to, for instance, the hoovering of the seabed and take 100 years to recover. It is the technological advancement of understanding what is happening on the seabed and knowing exactly where it is, as Mark describes, which actually provides opportunities for conservation and for conservationists to work closer with fishermen.
Chairman: Would you like to move on to technical measures, Henry?

Q265 Lord Plumb: It naturally follows, does it not? You say you welcome the technical conservation measures but you say they are not always successful, and that of course we understand, but can you give us an example of why they are not successful and how we could make them successful?
Professor Galbraith: We could certainly try and I will ask Dr Eno to take us through the answer.
Dr Eno: We welcome technical conservation measures because actually they should improve the sustainability of fisheries. One example that may be drawn upon in relation to successes—and really as long as fishing has been going on there have been measures in relation to mesh size to select different fish—is that more recently there has been the development of square mesh panels. The trouble with cod-ends at the closed end of the trawl is that when the trawl gets full it will pull tight and so it does not allow the fish out as the mesh becomes more like a flattened diamond that becomes of increasingly less and less diameter, so if you have measures which allow square mesh panels at the top of the trawl, where the fish automatically want to swim out, this allows the escape of juvenile and undersize fish and therefore reduces the need for discards et cetera. Another success is separator grids and again there has been quite a lot of research recently, particularly in relation to nephrops and shrimps, where the grids would divert and allow the fish to escape. As I come from the Countryside Council for Wales I should

mention the Shrimp Fishing Nets (Wales) Order 2003 which essentially stops British vessels from carrying shrimp trawls unless they are fitted with grid and escape routes for fish. Those are certainly some successes. We have not seen many successes which apply to a lot of the species that we are concerned about, of nature conservation interest, but fortunately one example so far has been in relation to, the harbour porpoise. There was a by-catch regulation 812, released in 2004, and essentially that deals with the by-catch of harbour porpoises in gillnet fisheries. What was suggested within the regulation was the attachment of a noise-making device, a pinger, which would deter the harbour porpoises and so they would be scared away. There was a lot of pressure to move forward very quickly on this, particularly coming from the NGOs, and it was accepted that this should be going forward because the by-catch was really not sustainable. The scientists said that the devices worked experimentally and they advised that there should be fleet-wide tests of them; it probably moved forward too fast and what happened was that the pingers failed, partly for technical reasons, but a lot of it was through a lack of acceptance by the industry—they had some concerns about safety and there were difficulties in enforcement. The thing that is important about this is that there are real lessons to be learnt. The regulation was probably over-prescriptive at the time it was produced. You need to ensure that there is the necessary investment in research and development to really ensure that the technology is right and, where possible, bring the fishermen into the development of the technical conservation measure. In Wales, we are working with fishermen in relation to a couple of technical conservation measures that will hopefully improve the sustainability of inshore crustacean fisheries and that is the way to do it, to work with the fishermen. You asked how to make them effective. We wondered about whether or not they should be voluntary or compulsory and the trouble is that while you get more buy-in if they are voluntary and if all the industry agree to it, the trouble is that very often in industry there might be sectors of the industry that do not agree for various reasons and that is really where you have to bring in compulsory measures in order to ensure a level playing field. Again, how to make it effective, really it is horses for courses: if you have an issue which is European-wide then you are going to have to have a TCM brought in by the Commission but there might be more specific local issues which, again, would be down to, for instance, individual Sea Fisheries Committees or fisheries advisory bodies. What is important to recognise in relation to ensuring that these technical conservation measures are effective is that they are technically reliable, preferably before they are put out for wider use, they actually do the job intended. We certainly promote

any moves to environmentally-friendly fishing methods—we think there should be a lot of encouragement in that respect—and we think there should be consideration of the economic impacts on stakeholders so that you get buy-in and address the potential for poor compliance and poor acceptance by the stakeholders. Once you bring them in you have to monitor how effective they are. Overall the jury is still out as to whether or not they are effective or on how many successes there have been compared to failures, but we have not seen very many successes as yet in relation to benefits to the environment and the ecosystem more widely. On that basis we maybe prefer targets as opposed to micro-legislation because if you give fishermen targets they are very resourceful, they will help achieve that and they will gain ownership of that TCM themselves. We feel there should be more emphasis on actually carrying through the research to the implementation stage; for instance, with regard to these pingers, the work needs to be continued so that ultimately it will need to form an effective measure. Nowadays there is far more environmental legislation and as we are advisers to the Government on that, we do feel that we should be brought in increasingly in terms of advising on the development of TCMs. Certainly, there is some work going on at the moment looking at extracting razor fish—which are the long razor shells that you have probably seen on the beach. The fishermen want to fish them in an environmentally-friendly way using electricity, which is quite an interesting area. It is important that we are there as advisers so that when they do finally come up with a method and there is a technical conservation method brought in, with derogations from various aspects of the European legislation, it will go through and it will be acceptable.

Q266 Lord Plumb: You are really saying that you would not press for compulsory measures at the moment until you have more information on the voluntary action that is being taken in different areas, but if it is workable you would eventually make it European-wide.
Dr Eno: If everybody agrees that it is a good idea there is no need to make it compulsory but the fishing industry is a very large group of sectors and while you might get some of the sectors agreeing and some of the fishermen's associations agreeing, not all fishermen are members of associations so you might find that some do not buy into it, in which case to ensure there is a level playing field, you then have to have compulsory measures.

Q267 Lord Cameron of Dillington: In your written evidence you indicate that you think spatial management can be successful. We have heard a whole lot of divergent views on that, and particularly there are doubts looking at cod, as a well-travelled species and the problems there. I am just wondering whether you want to comment a bit further and also what your view is of the voluntary system of real-time closure that has been happening in Scotland recently.

Professor Galbraith: If I could answer the second question that you asked there and perhaps come to Mark on the issues around cod, in relation to the real-time closure we welcome that, we think it is a novel and innovative measure and we are actually very pleased that it has come forward and been put in place by the industry—that shows a willingness on their side to actually manage the stock in a new and different way, so we do welcome that. We think it is very early days yet and we need to learn from the experience as we go along, and part of that has to be effective monitoring of the actions, where has it taken place, how often, and how effective has it been, recognising the difficulties in that monitoring programme. We welcome it, and in principle it should be effective if you limit or close a fishery where you are picking up areas of juvenile fish, that is to me a commonsense thing to do, that you are protecting the next generation of your own fishery, of your own industry. In due course we will hopefully get the report on how effective the industry feels it has been, but we would very much welcome further dialogue with the industry on that particular point, we do see it as a step forward. On the issue of cod, perhaps I could turn to Mark.

Mr Tasker: There are some principles here, My Lord Chairman, and you are quite right in referring to a wide-ranging species and the difficulty of getting spatial closures on those things. There are some principles underlying it in that the more static your organism or whatever it is you want to protect, the easier it is to have a spatial protection, and that is static over longer timescales. There are closures already for coral, for instance, that is not going to move very far, and therefore is a good thing to have a closure on. There are some organisms which we harvest—scallops for instance—which do not move hugely, but move a bit, and closures are probably pretty good measures, and then you have things which move a lot and move on different spatial timescales too, so one year the cod may be particularly good in one particular area and it might be a difficult thing to close it then, but the next year it might be somewhere completely different, so you then need some sort of way, if you want to use spatial closures, of having a responsive spatial closure. The principles basically are how much does the organism move, how much can your fishery move too; in other words if you close an area for cod and people still want to catch that cod, will they just go and spend more effort catching it somewhere else, in which case the end result on the cod stock will be effectively the same. One way of dealing with that would be to make

it a very, very big closure, but what is the acceptability among the stakeholders, be they fishers or anyone else, of closing a very big area, so there is a spatial scale of how much you can close related to what biologically and economically will work. It is a tool again, going back to our earlier question, that you would apply in particular ways to achieve a particular purpose, and you do need to do some analysis on that, you would not just say we want a protected area to do something, you need to do the analysis first and figure out the best tools to use; if it is a protected area then fine.

Professor Galbraith: Quickly picking up the real-time closure point finally, we could see that being more widely applied around the United Kingdom if it works in the Scottish situation, and in principle there would be no reason not to try it elsewhere but it is a very helpful sign that the industry are moving in that direction.

Q268 *Chairman:* What about enforcement? Are you satisfied that GPS monitoring of where the boats are is sufficient for you to recognise that that actual area is not being fished?

Professor Galbraith: This is where technology can help as the years roll by and the more specific we can be about where the boats are then the better for everybody and, in a sense, the better for the fishing stock and for the industry itself. Technology, as Mark Tasker said, has moved hugely in the past five to ten years and that is likely to continue, as the more specific we can be the better it becomes for all.

Q269 *Lord Cameron of Dillington:* The real problem of course will be getting multi-state fishermen buy-in. Scotland has obviously been quite successful, but what about others?

Professor Galbraith: Absolutely.

Mr Tasker: In the case of the voluntary real-time closure in Scotland that actually some other Member States' fishers have started agreeing they will do that too—Denmark has done that. That maybe another function—and we will come to it a bit later on—of the Regional Advisory Councils where you have different States' fishing communities talking to each other and gaining trust with each other and you may find the voluntary works better internationally because of that sort of mechanism.

Q270 *Earl of Dundee:* Could you tell us a little bit about your experience with the emergency measures provisions?

Professor Galbraith: Yes, and again I will ask Mark to lead on this.

Mr Tasker: There are two experiences, but I am a little unsure as to how much detail you would like me to go into because I could not give you all the dates and so on, but it might actually be easier to give you it in writing.

Q271 *Chairman:* Certainly that would be helpful.

Mr Tasker: If you would like that sort of data in writing I can then talk more generally about the principles. The first emergency measure that was bid for related to the Darwin Mounds, an area of coral in about 1000 metres water depth, about 150 miles north-west of Scotland where there is a coldwater coral reef. Not many people know that you can get corals in cold waters, but they are there and in that area they are growing on the top of some several metres high mounds of sand. These were discovered during a survey in 1998 and when we went back to have another look at them the following year and in 2000 we found that they were being trawled quite heavily, such that one could see where a coral was before and now there was just a smear of seabed and no coral. That became a cause celebre and various questions were asked through ICES—I should perhaps declare an interest here in that I am a quarter employed by the International Council for the Exploration of the Sea—which are the main advisers on scientific fishery management issues inside the CFP. They came back with the answers, yes, this appears to be long-lasting damage to biodiversity and then after a while they closed the area. When I say "after a while" that glosses over about three years, so an emergency was noticed but the response was a little bit slow. Nevertheless, the closure is there, that has been accepted by the fishermen, it went through various fishermen and stakeholder consultations and everything else and it went from emergency to permanent, and there is a general presumption that if there is an emergency, the mechanism under the CFP in fact only lasts for three months, extendable to six months, and then you have to go to the more permanent measure. As I said, it worked but it was slow. The other experience we had related to by-catch of common dolphins off the south-west of England where increasing numbers of dolphins were turning up dead on the beach, that had evidently been in contact with a net of some sort—sometimes they had a net wrapped around them which made it quite easy, but other times you would just see the mark. That was creating understandable public concern and although there was evidence that that was going on from the 1980s it was not until 2000, the early part of this decade, that there were really very large numbers coming in, and again one might expect that you would get these changes over time in the way that things are distributed. At almost the same time a fishery that was not going on before had grown up, and this was a pair trawl fishery for bass. Quite a lot of people will put two and two together and say obviously it is the pair trawl fishery causing these dead dolphins on our beach, and the

Government reacted by saying we would like a closure of that fishery, and they took the evidence they had to the European Commission and asked for an emergency measure to do that. The Commission, again, asked ICES "Can you give us all the scientific background to this?" and the scientific background revealed that, yes, that was occurring but probably the by-catch was sustainable in population terms. That is not to say it is a good thing for any individual dolphin but it is not doing dramatic and unsustainable damage to the dolphin population, so the Commission did not allow an emergency measure in that case. To an extent that was quite a good example in that one should take a step back and say, is this really affecting something in a non-sustainable way for the long term or not, so in that case we did not get the emergency measure but it was an experience of trying to use the mechanism. As I said before, I can give you all of that as a potted history in writing which may help.

Q272 *Earl of Dundee:* Thinking of emergency measures in a more general way or as part of the strategy of dealing with things, do you believe that emergency measures in themselves constitute a very necessary management tool? Obviously in one sense by definition it is that, but in another way do you anticipate an increase of emergency measures and do you think that the deployment of them is right?

Professor Galbraith: The one thing we can learn from history, not just in fisheries but generally, is that things happen in a very unexpected way and you can have a very healthy state in a fishery and suddenly a collapse. To have some provision built in for emergency measures and to react timeously or really quite quickly is eminently sensible as a principle. Mark may know more in terms of the detail of the marine fisheries, but as a principle, absolutely, yes.

Mr Tasker: The difficulty is that the CFP at the moment has only got a number of timescales that one can take measures over: there is either the annual scale or the emergency scale. There is a good argument to be had for saying we should have something else as well. An example I might come up with is if we have a new Natura site, a new offshore protected area for nature conservation, it would be very good to have some sort of mechanism by which measures can be brought in automatically. At the moment we either choose emergency—which is effectively what happened with the Darwin Mounds—or you choose something that is much longer term, in which case quite a lot of damage could happen before that long term one comes in. Another version would be coming back to the point I made a little bit earlier about if you have had a bad winter and you know that the sole stock is going to be in a bad shape, again, another measure that came in automatically would be useful, so tuning the tools or finding another tool that does those things and is not called an emergency would be helpful, and one would rather hope that actually you could get away from emergencies. You should not have emergencies, you should be able to look forward, recognising of course that some unexpected things always happen and the sea is quite good at generating unexpected things.

Q273 *Chairman*: From the simplicity point of view would it be sensible to call those emergency measures—you were talking about the sole fishery and if the temperature drops you can bring in an emergency measure. I am just trying not to complicate things with a lot of different measures all running maybe in parallel or maybe not in parallel.
Mr Tasker: I do not think it should be called emergency; I would rather see that built into a long term management plan as part of the ecosystem approach. There are quite a lot of things out there that are more predictable now and management plans should allow for anything that is more predictable.

Q274 *Chairman*: And to be able to react.
Mr Tasker: To bring those in automatically, so that there are automatic measures or something like that. The word "emergency" tends to bring in some other connotations.
Dr Tew: My Lord Chairman, I agree with Professor Galbraith's point that things happen at sea faster than the legislative timetable can allow so you do need the tool in the box to be able to introduce things rapidly. The proposals under the Marine Bill will allow Sea Fisheries Committees to bring in emergency by-laws which we are very much in favour of as another tool in the box.
Chairman: Lord Palmer, perhaps we can turn to discards.

Q275 *Lord Palmer*: As we all know this is a very controversial subject and I cannot remember which one of you mentioned public disquiet about dolphins, but there is obviously a great deal of public unease about the principle of discards. You have actually mentioned that they are difficult to enforce and ecologically unsound, whereas the other day the RSPB said that discards do indeed go back into the ecosystem but they fundamentally distorted it. I would be most interested if you could all quickly chip in on the subject and tell us what your views really are.
Professor Galbraith: Peehaps I could ask Dr Tew to lead us through that.
Dr Tew: Thank you. I am going to answer your question directly in a minute, My Lord Chairman, but indirectly to start with if you will forgive me, I would like to make the point that actually dealing with the symptom is not really the main issue, the

main issue is the cause and it is the amount of extra and unwanted fish that are killed. That ranges across vulnerable commercial species, young cod that are caught by prawn fishers, vulnerable non-commercial species like deep sea fish which are caught, brought up and killed and the huge amount of non-fish biodiversity that is dredged up from the sea and discarded, so the issue really is to find ways to reduce that unwanted catch, but the question is on the discard themselves. Certainly we recognise that discards do distort the ecosystem and the evidence that is now increasingly persuasive about things like fulmars where we are seeing whole populations of rising numbers because fulmars are starting to follow the ships at sea, and indeed scavenging species on the seabed: the crabs, the invertebrates and the small fish. I think there is good evidence that ecosystems are being disrupted so we would not disagree with RSPB on those points. However, it is not clear to us, it is not categorically one way or the other as to whether the bad effects, the disruption to the ecosystems, are so much markedly worse than some of the good effects of returning that biomass, returning those nutrients, back to the marine ecosystem rather than taking them on shore and disposing of them there. For us, therefore, there is a balance in that argument. Further, we know that some of the species which are caught and are discarded actually survive that process—skates in particular—so by allowing discard at sea you are actually promoting the survival or at least mitigating the damage done to some of the species.

Q276 *Lord Palmer*: But the percentage of survival must be very small in reality.
Dr Tew: The evidence is not clear on that but actually we think there is increasing evidence that there is quite a high survival for some species. If it only works for some species but they are vulnerable, such as the largest skates, longest-lived then that might be important. A final point I would like to make is if you had a discard ban—and we do believe anecdotal evidence from elsewhere shows that it is terribly difficult to enforce—you have a discard ban but people ignore it, they discard then they leave it at sea and effectively you are losing that information, that data on catch is lost to the system. That makes it very hard, in what is already a difficult system to analyse scientifically, because you are losing that information. We are not against a discard ban but we are probably going to sit on the fence a wee bit over this—we do not completely disagree with the RSPB, we think that discard bans could work in the right place at the right time and again we go back to our punch line which is a toolbox—but neither are we in unanimous support of a complete discard ban across the piece. I conclude by going back to my main point which is that it is not dealing with the symptom of the

problem that is the important thing, it is dealing with the causal issue, which is the huge number of unwanted fish which are caught.

Chairman: Lady Sharp, could we go on to access restrictions.

Q277 *Baroness Sharp of Guildford:* Under the Common Fisheries Policy decision-making on territorial matters is devolved to Member States. One of your objectives to be achieved in the fisheries policy and management is to maintain or make permanent the six and the twelve mile limits. Could you tell us a little bit more about what you want to do here and what your aims and objectives are?

Professor Galbraith: We can indeed and I will ask Dr Eno to lead our response.

Dr Eno: Thank you, Lady Sharp. Initially the six and twelve mile limits were set up as a derogation to the Treaty of Rome in relation to the principle of access and indeed the last Common Fisheries Policy review maintained that derogation. We would like to really push for that derogation to be made permanent as opposed to being reviewed every time the fisheries policy is assessed. A lot of the rationale for making it permanent is that it would allow the Member States to manage their inshore resources and their inshore activities in really a more integrated way, which is the basis for marine spatial planning. You will be aware that on the whole the number and complexities of activities that are going on get less as you go further away from the coast, so it makes it particularly important that you have this derogation, particularly in the nought to six miles and then the six to twelve because at the moment in that nought to six only the Member State vessels have access and they are managed primarily by inshore fisheries managers. If you opened it up and allowed open access it would make the job of inshore fisheries managers much harder and it would threaten the fish stocks, the biodiversity in terms of the habitats and species and the management itself. Currently you will be aware that the Marine Bill is going through and my colleague Dr Tew referred to the potential for emergency bylaw-making powers which are included; certainly, the management ability of inshore fisheries regulators will be improved by those powers coming through the Marine Bill and it would be unfortunate if that was thrown away by allowing open access. It is very difficult already in relation to inshore management of Natura 2000 sites to legislate for the activity of roaming UK vessels and this might make it even harder. You will be aware that currently the UK, in common with other Member States, is about to embark upon the implementation of marine spatial planning and to just come back to that point it would really be helpful if there was stability in the question of fisheries management jurisdiction in that respect. We do not see why you cannot do it; there is

no political impediment to keeping the six and twelve mile limits and none of the other Member States have objected to it and certainly in the last CFP review they did not object.

Q278 *Baroness Sharp of Guildford:* Forgive my ignorance; you have talked about the six mile limit but what is the precise relationship between the six mile and the twelve mile limits?

Dr Eno: As I said, nought to six miles is the exclusive access to the host Member State, between the six and twelve mile limits there is access dependent upon historic rights, which were set up when the Common Fisheries Policy was initially introduced, and so you have quite a complicated system allowing certain countries access to fish certain stocks in certain areas. Those arrangements have continued but they add complexity and make it difficult for inshore fishing managers to cope or to establish stable management regimes.

Q279 *Baroness Sharp of Guildford:* In relation to emergency measures, these can be introduced within the six mile limits at the discretion of Member States, is that correct?

Dr Eno: Yes, they have the powers to do that.

Q280 *Baroness Sharp of Guildford:* Whereas within the 12 mile limit this would require what?

Dr Eno: Between six and twelve if there are other Member States who have access it has to be negotiated and most of those negotiations are still under way.

Q281 *Chairman:* What you are saying is there is no pressure from any Member State to reduce the six mile limit, is that correct?

Dr Eno: I do not think there is any pressure to remove either the six or twelve.

Q282 *Chairman:* Why does it have to be negotiated, you cannot think of any reason why it is still a derogation?

Dr Eno: It is just that it is a derogation from open access. The single market and open access seem to be the driving forces behind that.

Mr Tasker: If I might add, My Lord Chairman, the only reason why the CFP has to be reviewed every ten or twenty years is because of that derogation, so it is a testable way of doing something.

Q283 *Chairman:* I see, it is a trigger.

Mr Tasker: Yes.

Q284 *Baroness Sharp of Guildford:* Are there not Member States which have relatively little in the way of continental shelf who are anxious to see it reduced?

Mr Tasker: The history last time around is that everyone was afraid that the Spanish wanted to come and fish all the way up to beaches, but when it came to the negotiation there was no bid for it.

Chairman: Good. Lord Arran, perhaps we could tackle control and enforcement.

Q285 *Earl of Arran:* Thank you, My Lord Chairman. Obviously, one of the key management tools is control and enforcement and, from the point of view of protection at sea, illegal fishing. Do you consider that the control regulation should be compulsory on all vessels, which it is not at the moment—it is voluntary on some smaller ones at the moment—thereby achieving a level playing field? Would it work, or what is the situation at the moment and what is the aspiration.

Professor Galbraith: This is an area that I know Mark Tasker has some detailed knowledge on so I will let Mark lead for us on this.

Mr Tasker: Thank you. You are probably referring to the so-called VMS, the satellite monitoring system.

Q286 *Earl of Arran:* Correct.

Mr Tasker: But I would just point out that there are other electronic control systems which we would also be interested in as well, but in terms of the satellite data, yes, at the moment there is a limit to vessels over 15 metres and we would be very keen to see the limit at least brought down to over ten metres length. As you come down in size of course there are problems in the opposite direction of too much data flowing in, too much to handle, so we would certainly say more than ten metres should have VMS on in the near future. For smaller vessels we really would be quite interested in areas where there is a particular feature we are interested in controlling and where we think there may be problems. Our experience with that is that in some near shore areas, as you mentioned yourself, there is voluntary use of VMS. Examples would be that the Northern Irish have a mussel dredge fishery in an area which has VMS on the vessels there, the Isle of Man scallop fishery has similar and there is some research on the Firth of Clyde nephrops fishery which had VMS. Where VMS is voluntary, there is not really a problem, in other words vessels will take VMS units; where VMS is not voluntary there is an argument who pays for all of these things, particularly for the small vessels that have a comparatively small income because you are actually paying rather a lot to gain maybe not as much as would be ideal. At the moment we say certainly more than ten where there is a reasonable profitability and they can pay for that system, but below that in areas where there is particular concern over enforcement we would be keen on having it.

Q287 *Earl of Arran:* You are not going to get a proper readout at the moment if some have got systems on board and others have not.

Mr Tasker: That is true, but on the other hand where do you draw your line on fishing, do you go all the way down to recreational fleets, do you stop at boats that only go out at the weekend and are only five metres in length? You still need some sort of cut-off and the cut-off we would suggest would be one where we think a significant impact is possible if you are infringing a regulation.

Q288 *Chairman:* Are you suggesting an area based approach rather than a size based approach for that particular thing that you talked about?

Mr Tasker: We are suggesting both, My Lord Chairman; in other words it is another tool that can be used in particular circumstances.

Q289 *Chairman:* Would that be part of a licence for the boats or how would that work?

Mr Tasker: That would be a possible way of doing it.

Q290 *Earl of Arran:* You also suggest in your evidence that some of the monitoring systems are being tampered with. Is there real evidence of that, or what is actually happening, how serious is it?

Mr Tasker: Yes, there is evidence of tampering, to answer the question straight. If one goes onto the internet and you actually type in and look at VMS systems there are kits available that can adjust many of the current commercially available systems. There is a rather good paper that was presented at the ICES annual science meeting two years ago comparing satellite over- flight data—in other words photographs of the earth and of vessels location—and where the VMS was saying they were meant to be. There was quite a big difference. Those vessels were, admittedly, some way offshore because they were looking mostly at the high seas to avoid implicating any particular Member State—it was done by part of the European Commission—but VMS can be tampered with and yes VMS are being tampered with, but we are not sure of the level at which that is happening.

Q291 *Earl of Arran:* It is very difficult to police this tampering, I imagine, as well.

Mr Tasker: I am not certain about that because the difficulty of policing is actually the amount of time you have available to look at the records. If you have suddenly got a vessel that speeds up that cannot do more than 12 knots and is suddenly doing 20 knots, that would indicate there is something going on there, but actually the number of vessels out there and the number of people who are available to look at those automatic reports coming in is that the two do not work together very well. I am fairly certain that some

2 April 2008   Dr Clare Eno, Professor Colin Galbraith, Mr Mark Tasker and Dr Tom Tew

vessels have been detected doing that and have been given warnings on it, but I do not think we could do it systematically without a substantial increase in the enforcement capability in the system.

Q292 Chairman: What about CCTV to deal with discards or high grading or whatever it is that could be going on?

Mr Tasker: That is why I mentioned we are interested in the other electronic data collection systems, so electronic logbooks—which are one thing which have been talked for many years, and those are the fishermen filling in what they have caught where more or less in real time—would be very useful indeed. The negotiation on that has gone on for more than ten years and we are still not there, but that would be an extremely useful tool. You mentioned CCTV, yes, certainly, and those systems are being used elsewhere in the world. One of my other areas of knowledge is in relation to by-catch of albatrosses on long-lines and they found on some vessels that pointing a television camera at the long-line being hauled is actually quite a good way of recording the number of birds that were also on that line. It does work and it is another tool for a specific circumstance.

Q293 Lord Cameron of Dillington: We are really agreed that the nub of the problem is the over-capacity in the EU fleet really, and if we could solve that we would certainly solve some of the fishery problems although maybe not some of the ecosystem problems. Some Member States seem to be pushing the bands of Member State subsidies to the very limits in order to keep their fleet's capacity up or even increasing it; I am just wondering whether you have any ideas for how we might achieve a reduction in capacity of the EU fishing fleet.

Professor Galbraith: We are back to the earlier discussion around the ecosystem. You can see that long term sustainability really will only be achieved if we do get continual reduction in the fleet, and that has to be balanced against the technical efficiency of those boats that remain—and again we had an earlier discussion. Historically there have been two main methods: the market can decide or there can be subsidised capacity, reduction overall, but again Mark Tasker has been involved in this for a number of years and perhaps Mark could give some more details.

Mr Tasker: That essentially has put it in a nutshell, but there are advantages and disadvantages of both. Using the market has certainly been attempted in the UK in the past but that does not work across the European Union with differing ways of addressing subsidies. Certainly previous administrations inside the UK have tried to take out all subsidies, but when you have a subsidised fleet somewhere across the

Channel it does not really work in terms of a level playing field. The difficulty with the subsidised capacity reduction is that there is quite a lot of vessels sitting around not doing a great deal, waiting for the subsidised capacity reduction to come along—in other words the available capacity is much bigger than the used capacity and as soon as you get a subsidised capacity reduction you get a reduction in the available capacity rather than the used one. One way of dealing with that might be to remove the fishing licence at the same time, but actually that is one of the main investments that the fishermen have got and that is quite difficult to do. Yes, we think we do need to reduce and, going back to the point we were making earlier about the continual technological creep, it is a continuous process because of improving efficiency all the time and you need to choose the correct tool at the right time for various fleets.

Q294 Earl of Arran: On the subject of governance some of the RACs have been delivered more quickly and more effectively than others—the others probably for the reasons that they have very complicated and different remits et cetera, but if those RACs had not existed how do you think the industry might be worse off than it is now? My real question is what are the benefits really of the RACs and do you think they have a future?

Professor Galbraith: We mentioned earlier again in the ecosystem discussion about getting people to be involved in decision-taking, and they are part of that structure in terms of getting as local a buy-in as we can even on a large scale. Again, Dr Eno has been involved in some of the discussions on this.

Dr Eno: Thank you, Professor. I was certainly involved with my colleagues in relation to advising the select committee that previously reviewed the Common Fisheries Policy and at that stage we were strongly supporting the establishment of Regional Advisory Councils. Now most of them are established, we have been able to see are some positives, but there are still some negatives as they are going through teething problems. It would be useful in terms of responding to your question to illustrate some of the positives and negatives. One of the positives has been in the convening of some extremely good workshops. There was one a few years ago on marine spatial planning, then one looking at cod recovery—that was a joint RAC meeting—and then last month there was one specifically on marine protected areas which was very progressive, and that was held within the Scottish Parliament. For the first time ever there were representatives from all seven RACs, including ones that are not even established yet. The environmental groups were all represented and the Commission was there in force, which was tremendous because it brought all these different decision-makers and stakeholders together to talk about marine protected areas. It was a tremendous opportunity to debate the implications of Directives such as the Habitats Directive and the Birds Directive and how they would apply and certainly for the Commission officials to clarify the interpretation of these. What the workshops allowed was discussion between fishers and others to assess the scientific findings and best practice and also concepts for some potential collaborative ways forward before we actually reaching a crisis point. Another thing that came out of the marine spatial planning workshop was that a spatial planning sub-group was set up and that has been chaired by Euan Dunn, who I believe gave evidence to you last week. That led to some excellent work mapping fishing activity in important fishing areas in the North Sea itself. I have been aware of a tremendous exchange of emails around the various Regional Advisory Councils and certainly the North Western Waters and North Sea RACs have had a large amount of input to debates about maximum sustainable yield and capacity in this last year and in relation to the deep sea. They also make a detailed input when they are talking about specific technical conservation measures that come up. This has been very positive because the views are bounced backwards and forwards between fishers and other stakeholders all around Europe, and what happens is that this allows the thinking to mature. This is something which did not really happen very much prior to the RACs being in existence and that is very useful to Commission officials when they are developing new regulations. It also, as far as we are concerned, provided a mechanism for non-fishing interests to communicate with the fishing industry at a wider European level in relation, for instance, in relation to the offshore Special Areas of Conservation consultation and related regulations but in terms of that particular point we have got some reservations. In a sense they start with the fact that fishing interests dominate the Regional Advisory Councils and they tend to be more interested in immediate concerns rather than horizon scanning. Thinking back to the Natura 2000 sites, we gave a paper to the RACs essentially outlining the situation about Natura 2000 sites and offshore Natura 2000 site regulations but there was no interest. We gave that paper in the summer of 2006 and there was no interest until the following spring when the Irish started announcing their offshore Natura 2000 sites and at that stage, thankfully, we had the status of observers and so we were present and we were able to reiterate that offer of help that we made previously and so they started dealing particularly with JNCC and my colleague Mark Tasker here. We were able to really bring them on board from the UK perspective because what happened in Ireland really did not go down well, so as far as progressing the UK offshore

Natura 2000 sites it has worked better because of that. The consequence of not listening to our earlier advice was essentially that they missed the opportunity to make input to the offshore habitat regulations when they were being drafted, so it was done and dusted by the time they finally woke up to it. There is still a limited extent of engagement and involvement in the RACs by the environmental groups and while that is not a criticism of those NGOs who are currently involved and it is probably more down to the manpower resources that they have, it does mean that the environmental input is somewhat marginalised still. We are very concerned about that because a lot of our reasons for supporting and promoting Regional Advisory Councils previously were because they are a mechanism for encouraging an ecosystem-based approach to fisheries management and there has really been very little uptake of that. There is a great opportunity for them, they are sitting around the table and they have stakeholders there who they could talk to about this but basically there is little willingness to embrace it, and partly that is because they are not looking to the longer term. Not looking to the longer term also relates to management strategies. When you now have a new method of managing the geographic region, which essentially is what these Regional Advisory Councils are, the first thing you could do is go in and say "Right, let us look at that region and let us come up with a management strategy for that region." There has been a lot of resistance to doing that and while Defra has actually pushed it forward enormously it has been viewed with suspicion by other Member States and other countries' fishers. I hope the RACs will be able to overcome that and build more trust and a more common vision of the future. I would say in relation to the successes and how they work that a lot of it is down to the sterling work that is done by the secretariats of some of the RACs in essentially organising a somewhat unlikely group of individuals, and then there have been individuals as well who have done really good work and I would particularly emphasise the work that has been done by many from the UK in this respect.

Q295 *Earl of Arran:* On balance in your opinion they are beneficial, although you may have criticisms.
Dr Eno: Yes.

Q296 *Earl of Arran:* Suppose they had an executive role rather than an advisory role, what would you think about that?
Dr Eno: It would need to be looked at very carefully; I do not think they are ready to go there yet. Some of the Regional Advisory Councils are more advanced—the North Sea RAC and the North Western Waters RAC are more established and

maybe they are starting to move to that stage where they are working in a responsible manner.

Mr Tasker: Can I just add one thing on that last question? There is a subsidiarity principle that might apply here and I do not see any reason—going back to our earlier comment on the goal-setting approach from Professor Galbraith—why some of those goals cannot be handed over to the RACs on the subsidiarity principle. That would give them a bit of an executive role, if you see what I mean, rather than a whole executive.

Q297 *Earl of Arran:* A dangerous compromise.

Mr Tasker: That is what subsidiarity is about after all, is it not? There are some things which already they might be best at—here is your goal, go away and do it.

Q298 *Baroness Sharp of Guildford:* And there is the buy-in that you get from that.

Mr Tasker: Exactly.

Q299 *Lord Cameron of Dillington:* We all agree with you that we need to look at the whole ecosystem approach really, but I guess my question can be summed up in the words are we willing? Dr Eno's report on the RACs was slightly more depressing than I thought it was going to be because some of them, particularly the North Sea and the North Western ones, seem as if there is light at the end of the tunnel and that might be the right approach. I am just wondering whether, as well as answering the question are we willing, do you think the marine initiatives such as the Marine Bill, the Habitats Directive, the Marine Strategy Directive are going to make a difference to whether we win or not?

Professor Galbraith: They will make a difference in two ways, one way will I hope be effective on the ground or in the water as it were, but I believe they will change people's perception as well and what you are seeing happening in the marine environment now you could say happened on the land ten years back in terms of the approaches that people take, the ecosystem approach, the buy-in from people, so we will change the perception and will change the level of activity if you like. That will be a big challenge for many people there; for the conservation side it is certainly a big challenge and it will equally be for the fisheries side in terms of managing their work, perhaps in a different way, but managing alongside other people who have come into that area and who have an interest suddenly, and who, under directives, have a statutory role to be there; that will change the situation quite considerably. Again, this is Mark Tasker's territory and he has been there for quite a number of years; perhaps Mark would like to comment.

Mr Tasker: I have been interested in this area for a very long time and, to answer your first question are we winning, I think we are in that we have at least stopped the decline and, certainly looking back to the last review, a lot of the things that came through that last review were positive, and the RACs are one of those, even though they have not bedded in as fast as we really would like on that particular issue. You asked about the other initiatives and perhaps we could split those between the EU ones and the UK ones. The Marine Strategy Framework Directive has regionalisation right at its core and, coming back to a question you were asking as well which is how would regionalisation work, I think that will help a great deal. To me it has always seemed ludicrous that a minister from the UK can decide on what is going on in the fisheries off Romania and vice versa; we need some form of regionalisation at that level at the top. We know that in fact DG MARE—that used to be called DG Fisheries and Marine Affairs—is now regionalising inside its sub-structures, so in other words I assume those units will be bringing forward proposals on a regional basis. That chimes quite well with the Framework Directive that is also coming through, although there are a lot of challenges left, as Colin has mentioned. In terms of the other initiatives, you have mentioned the Habitats Directive and I would remind you that there is also a Birds Directive. We have got the Strategic Environment Assessment, we have got the EIA, the Environmental Impact Assessment, and then underneath the Habitats Directive there are Appropriate Assessments. All of those assessment processes apply to most other marine industries except fisheries and one of the things we would be very keen on doing, and one of the things that would bring these other initiatives together, would be making sure that all industries, regardless of whether it is fishing or not, are on a level playing field in regard to their environmental performance. To translate that, if the oil industry wants to go out and drill a hole it has to do an EIA in advance of that, it has to be accepted before it is allowed to do it. There are challenges in doing that inside the fishing sector and we are taking up some of those challenges: we have a pilot project on Strategic Environmental Assessment running off the north-east coast at the moment with the North East Sea Fisheries Committee. An SEA is also being done on the European Fisheries Fund proposals so those tools could be applied to produce a lot more and would help integration. Coming back to the UK I would say Marine Bbills—I live in Aberdeen, Colin comes from Scotland; there is going to be a Scottish Marine Bill as well as the English/UK one. The English/UK one seems to have got rather long and gangly; I believe it is going to be published tomorrow so we have not actually seen the full details but there are a lot of extra bits and pieces being added into that and, broadly, we are slightly worried that that is not going to do all the implementation necessary for the Marine Strategy Framework Directive. The Scottish, on the other hand, are taking a slightly longer approach to this and are saying that they want the Scottish Bill to actually implement the Directive in Scottish waters. The danger you can see in England is that we are going to have one lot of marine legislation and then a little while later another lot of marine legislation, so we are advising that we would like to try and see those brought together, although understanding that the UK/English Marine Bill has taken a long, long time in gestation and there is a political necessity to perhaps get something out there sooner. In relation to fisheries both Bills indicate a better management of the nearshore in different ways—the nearshore area being the six to twelve miles and inside six miles, Sea Fisheries Committees having enhanced powers south of the border and some form of similar system north of the border but different from Sea Fisheries Committees. We would also note that the UK/English Marine Bill does allow for the development of marine conservation zones beyond 12 miles but coming back the other way on integration, unless those are agreed at a European level you are not going to get any fisheries measures for these and one of our opening statements is that the thing that affects the marine environment most is fisheries. If you cannot manage the main thing that might affect your protected area you have a problem. That is why it is important that we make sure that the marine bills do implement something European in relation to Marine Conservation Zones otherwise we are going to have paper parks and not ones that have been managed properly.

Dr Tew: I would be foolish to disagree with my colleague of course but I am nervous about the "we are winning" message, I think that needs to be held carefully and lightly because the European Commission's fishing paper this year looked at 110 stocks and there is no evidence of an overall improvement in the status of any of those stocks, and between 2003 and 2007, 80% of these stocks were considered to be outside the safe biological limits. There was a paper in *Science* last year looking at the impacts of biodiversity loss and it concluded: "Marine biodiversity loss is increasingly impairing the oceans' capacity to provide food, maintain water quality and recover from perturbations, yet available data suggests at this point that these trends are still reversible", so I am much happier with a picture that shows it is not over yet, there is still much we can do and we are making significant progress. I am not sure I would conclude we are winning at this stage.

Q300 *Chairman:* Certainly in your memorandum in paragraph 3 you note those things and you also say that the information is deteriorating, which is quite a

concern. Could I perhaps ask you this question: it seems that TACs and quotas are very political in that they are discussed and agreed at the Fisheries Council in December every year; is that the right place for those decisions to be taken? You advise Government and you therefore advise ministers; should ministers sit much more with a strategic view as to what the future should be and some other mechanism to deal with the detail which otherwise looks as if there is this huge body of work that has to be done between September and December and then a huge volume of work that has to be done before 1 January; is that really the way that we should be dealing with it?

Professor Galbraith: When you have a subject like this which is a mix of ecology, of scientific disciplines, politics, economics and local communities I suspect it is inevitable that you will have something of a less than perfect decision-making system around that. I suppose you could draw back and say, yes, theoretically you can design different systems and that would be advantageous; it is difficult to suggest that we should change radically because what are the possibilities of that, recognising all that complexity. I will come to my colleagues but I think in theory probably yes, in practice it may be somewhat harder to achieve.

Dr Tew: Leave it all to the scientists.

Mr Tasker: Colin is very close to the answer there but I do think we have mentioned a few other things in our evidence today. Long term management plans are essentially things decided on by politicians. What politicians should be looking at is the balance of how much risk do you want to place your fish stock at, how much damage would you allow the environment to take. That is a thing that politicians should do, it is taking an overall broad view, but once you have got that broad view then the expression of that in technical and in management terms, I do not really see the need for politicians. The last CFP reform actually pointed heavily in the direction of multi-annual recovery plans and multi-annual management plans. They are taking a very long time to put in place; some have been put there but not very many and they have taken a fair bit of effort. Those should be more or less automatic: we get the signal from this particular indicator saying the environment or the fish stock is in such a state, that should feed through that and then there is an almost automatic output. We would very much like to see that on a regional scale, and I think that is achievable still. The other point I made was about the decision process in December. That is changing a bit in that a lot of that was driven by the timing of when the science advice arrived. ICES has reformed—I have personally been quite a large part of that—the timing of when advice will be available, so advice is going to be available much earlier in the year but with a degree more uncertainty attached to it, so most of it will be out in

June for the main stocks that are of interest the UK. That means that you should not have to end up in December with so much of an intense pressure at that time. The science has done its bit, can the political system do its bit? The jury is out on that.

Chairman: It remains for me to thank all of you—Dr Eno, Mr Tasker, Professor Galbraith and Dr Tew—very much indeed for the evidence that you have given to us. It has been very helpful to our inquiry and we have learnt a great deal; again, we are just very grateful to you for having come and given evidence.

Supplementary Memorandum by the Joint Nature Conservation Committee

INTRODUCTION

At the evidence session of the Sub-Committee on 2 April, we were invited to answer a question detailing our experience of "emergency" measures under the Common Fisheries Policy. Mark Tasker responded to this question and offered to provide detail on dates etc in writing subsequently. This note provides that detail.

JNCC has had twice experienced the use of these measures, on both occasions in our role as governmental advisors on UK nature conservation.

The first such experience relates to the Darwin Mounds.

— The Darwin Mounds were discovered 150 km off NW Scotland in May 1998 in water 1000m deep. They consist of sandy mounds with cold-water coral growing on top, therefore peculiarly vulnerable to permanent damage from fishing gears (particularly trawls) that touch the seabed.

— Further surveys in 1999 and 2000 showed increasing damage from trawling, believed to be mostly French in origin.

— European Commission asked the International Council for the Exploration of the Sea (ICES) for "urgent advice" in July 2000. This was requested to help fulfil the Commission's mandate to protect sensitive marine habitats.

— ICES answered this request in spring 2002 (the delay was caused by the letter from the Commission becoming accidentally lost in ICES).

— More detailed advice was requested of ICES and supplied in spring 2003; all supported the scientific case for closure.

— UK applied for an emergency closure in August 2003, indicating that it would put the site forward as a Special Area of Conservation under the Habitats Directive as soon as it had the powers to do so. A 3-month emergency closure was granted and later extended to six months.

— European Commission put forward proposals and Council agreed to a permanent closure in April 2004.

— The UK has treated the site as if it was an SAC from this point, and has not licensed any non-fishery activities in the area.

There was some initial resentment from industry (particularly in France) and from some regulators, but there is now reasonable acceptance of the closure (as indicated by the lack of adverse comment on the sites proposed designation in recent consultations by JNCC on the SAC proposal for the site. Evidence from VMS indicates occasional minor transgressions of the site closure. There has been no independent science survey of the site since 2000.

The second attempted use of emergency measures relates to the bycatch of common dolphins off south-west England.

— Understandable concern at rising numbers of common dolphins washing up dead on beaches in south west England in late winter started in late 1990s. There is evidence that these strandings had been occurring, albeit to a lesser extent, since at least the mid 1980s. At the same time, some pelagic pair-trawl operators asked for help in solving a bycatch of common dolphins in their fishery.

— Following an NGO campaign, UK government to apply for an emergency closure of pair trawl fishery on grounds of excessive catch of common dolphins in July 2004.

— Following non-agreement to this closure by other nations fishing in the area, the European Commission asked ICES for advice in early 2005 on status of common dolphin population (size etc), bycatch and any mitigation measures that might be suitable.

— ICES advised the Commission in May 2005 that there were in the order of 500,000 dolphins in one genetic population, with unknown bycatch, but unlikely to exceed unsustainable levels.

— Based on this ICES advice, Commission chose not grant emergency closure.

— Bycatch has continued, but increasing evidence that substantial proportion of the bycatch is not caused by pair-trawls.

April 2008

WEDNESDAY 23 APRIL 2008

Present:

Brookeborough, V		Plumb, L	
Cameron of Dillington, L		Sewel, L (Chairman)	
Jones of Whitchurch, B		Sharp of Guildford, B	
Palmer, L		Ullswater, V	

Examination of Witnesses

Witnesses: MR SAM LAMBOURN, Chairman, North Western Waters Regional Advisory Council, MS ANN BELL, Executive Secretary, North Sea Regional Advisory Council and MR HUGO ANDERSON, Chair of the North Sea Regional Advisory Council, gave evidence.

Q301 Chairman: Good morning. Welcome and thank you all very much for coming to see us and helping us with our inquiry. We are actually quite enthused and inspired by RACs so I hope you can enlighten us even further. There are a couple of housekeeping points to deal with before we start. Firstly, this is a formal evidence session so a transcript will be taken and made available to you within a few days so you can look through it and if there have been any slips or errors that have crept in then it is an opportunity to correct them. Secondly—this is the embarrassing bit—these proceedings are actually web cast so there is a possibility that somewhere in the outer reaches of the galaxy someone may be listening to what is being said. I do have to say that we have had no convincing evidence that that is the case. Would you like to start by making an opening statement or would you like to proceed to the question and answer session straight away?
Ms Bell: Just proceed.

Q302 Chairman: In which case I will start off with a general opener. Can you give us a brief history of your individual RACs and how they came into existence? What was the impetus behind setting them up?
Mr Anderson: First of all I will introduce myself. I am Hugo Anderson, chairing the North Sea RAC since it started three and a half years ago, actually four years ago on an interim basis in June 2004. I come from Sweden and my background is in politics, working for the government in Sweden, and after that working in industry in Sweden. Since 2004 I have been chairing the North Sea RAC. As you will be aware, the Council took a decision regarding the Common Fisheries Policy at the end of 2002 and one of the new things in that provision was that regional advisory councils should be established. At that time we had an organisation in the North Sea which we called the Partnership for Fisheries and the Partnership consisted of representatives from industry and from the scientific world (biologists mainly, working for ICES). The aim for the

Partnership was to get those two groups together to speak to each other—not to speak about each other—and we had worked for several years very successfully. When this decision was taken in the Council that there should be a RAC for the North Sea we discussed whether we should convert to be the RAC or not. We came to the conclusion that we should not convert but we should stay as the Partnership but we were prepared to be helpful in establishing the RAC. We set up a working group to start to deal with possible rules and procedures dealing with everything for a RAC because at that time there were no official documents from the Commission stating how it should be working and so on. We had a proposal which we delivered to the Commission in July 2003 and they were very grateful for our contribution. Later on in 2003—I think it was in November—the first proposal from the Commission showed up with the details of how a RAC should be organised and so on. That proposal was very much in line with what we had presented to them earlier that same year. After this there was the process in Brussels. There was a Council decision in May 2004. In June 2004 we decided to establish on an interim basis the North Sea RAC and had a meeting in Aberdeen. In November of the same year we were recognised by the Commission and we had our first General Assembly on 3 November in Edinburgh. That is the background and also the reason why we were over year before the RAC was established. We had this structure with the Partnership which helped a lot.

Q303 Chairman: When was the partnership established?
Mr Anderson: I think it was 1999 or 2000.
Ms Bell: Your Lordship may remember that you chaired that meeting in 1998. We had a conference in Aberdeenshire and the theme of that conference was *Scientists and fishermen working together to manage the North Sea*. Lord Sewel chaired that first meeting so I always say he was responsible and it is all his fault! The conclusion of that meeting was that there should be a standing committee assembly to work to

manage the North Sea. That was the very beginning of this process way back in 1998.

Mr Lambourn: My name is Sam Lambourn. I chair the North Western Waters RAC. I also chair the Cornish Fish Producers Organisation. My day job is an active fisherman; I still fish. It is sometimes—and very often—my night time job as well. I operate a boat out of Newlyn and I have a very patient crew. As far as establishing our RAC we started the process somewhere in the mid-1990s. We had a series of trans-national meetings with the Spanish, the French, the Dutch, the Belgians and the Irish talking about No-Take Zones. Our PO was particularly interested in No-Take Zones at that time, however the agenda very quickly moved on to some sort of form of regional management in all the different Member States. We spent all our time talking about how we might manage if ever we had the opportunity so that when these things were set up as a result of the CFP review in 2002 it was quite a natural move and I knew practically all of the players by that time and of course we all knew each other to some extent. It was a natural move and very much welcomed. Our PO and I think certainly the other people involved in these talks on No-Take Zones were all very active in suggesting that fisheries policy should move in this direction. That is how we came to be.

Q304 *Lord Plumb:* I wonder why it took so long. I had the privilege of chairing COPA for some years. COPA was set up about 50 years ago. You are talking about setting this up five years ago. Farmers and fishermen have been pretty close over many years and I was always surprised in COPA days that there was not a gathering of fishermen. We used to ask the question regularly at that time and quite obviously you are making progress now, but with all the difficulties we have had—although we are not here to talk about history we can learn from history—I wonder why it took so long. You have given a very good account of the procedures that have taken place since. There is only one difference in what you said. You said that the Commission advised you on how you might proceed; in my COPA days we were advising the Commission on how they might proceed. It does surprise me a little that it has not been going for a longer time.

Mr Anderson: There is and has been cooperation on a European level among industry for many years. The news now is that we are on a regional base and I think that was obvious in the Common Fisheries Policy that there needs to be some kind of regionalisation in the process of improving the Common Fisheries Policy. There are differences in different regions and you cannot have exactly the same rules all over European waters because it does not fit in. There is still cooperation on a European level between organisations but also on the decision of the

Commission there are advisory councils also on the European level. AGFA is the one for dealing with fisheries and there are also sub groups under AGFA. There is now cooperation both on the European horizontal level and the regional level.

Ms Bell: When we first set in place the partnership it was to get scientists and fishermen into one room to talk to one another. I am sure Sam will agree that for fishermen to talk to one another when they are not actually out in Brussels negotiating work quotas was difficult. It was a case of proving that this partnership worked to the cynics both nationally and in Brussels and to the scientists within ICES. It took us almost a year before we were in ICES with the fishermen there and they were given access to the assessments so they could actually give comment on the assessments and review them. That was a huge step in the right direction. It was maybe five years but actually, in the grand scheme of things, I think for industry and for science it was relatively quick.

Mr Lambourn: I would agree with that. It always struck me as a fisherman that I spent all day fishing amongst the Spanish and the French yet we seemed to have no contact with them at all; they may as well have been Martians. I have no idea why it took so long, but all I can say is that it was long overdue. The difference from my perspective about these regional advisory councils is that they are grass roots organisations; they are driven from the fishermen, the fishermen have the ownership. As chairman of my RAC I am continually re-enforcing that: this is their organisation, they drive it. Some things are seen as rather abstract and remote by the grass roots fishermen, and they have no influence; these RACs are supposed to be different.

Ms Bell: One of the differences of the RACs as well, especially in the North Western and the North Sea, we made a conscious decision that we would not have all our meetings in Brussels otherwise we would just be seen as another Brussels bureaucratic organisation. We decided to move round ports so in the North Sea we move right the way round and Sam does the same. Sometimes it is not practical and we have to have meetings in Brussels, but that was so that we were seen to be nearer the coal face than we would have been in Brussels.

Q305 *Viscount Ullswater:* Can you bring us up to date with how the RACs are working? Perhaps you could describe the hierarchy between the Assembly, the Executive Committee and the working groups. What sort of scientific advice do you seek? Also how easy or how difficult is it to reach a common decision, and where does that power lie? Does it lie in the Executive Committee? Do you have to refer it to the General Assembly? I am really asking how the RAC works.

Mr Lambourn: I will speak for the North Western Waters. We are made up of an Executive Committee and a series of working groups which are geographically based. That is where the work is done; they are the engines that drive the RAC. The Executive has the decision process using the advice from the working groups or the recommendations. It is for the Executive members then to adopt them or not. It is not debated at Executive level. If it is not accepted then it is returned to the working group. The working group is where the grass roots have their input. Any fisherman or any member can go there and make their point or insist on an agenda item. That is how that works. I chair the Executive but I also sit in on the working groups but I have no part in them. It is apparent and has been from day one that neither the working groups nor the Executive function satisfactorily without scientists being present. The first question generally, when any topic is raised, is: what can science tell us? That is the starting position. It seems to be, for one reason or another, essential that they set the base line from where the discussion can go. The benefit of that is that it does ground the discussion and it does not wander too far away from where the evidence is. For my money the single most important aspect of a RAC is that any advice we give has to be evidence based. We are not lobbyists. For any particular Member State or representative of the RAC to take up a position it has to be evidence based. No amount of arm twisting is worth anything. From my position as Chair that is such a relief because everything is judged on evidence and it does do away with an awful lot of what otherwise would be posturing. That is how it works with us.

Mr Anderson: I agree very much with what Sam has said. The basic structure is regulated in the Council decision that we should have an Assembly and we should have an Executive Committee. Then we have a number of working groups which differ between the different RACs. We have a working group which deals with all fish related issues in all waters except part of the North Sea which has a special management unit, mainly business for Sweden and Denmark. That is a separate working group. Then we have a working group for spatial planning which is a little bit unusual if you compare it with other RACs. We have worked out that there are a lot of demands from other interests on the water, on the sea bed and the area as such. We thought it would be interesting to have a look at that, to make some kind of mapping and to see what the other interests are, how much impact do they have on fisheries but also in the long term out in the spawning areas which are developed for windfarms or harbours or whatever it is. That is quite an interesting work. We have dealt especially with windfarms and also with the MPA which is the subject for discussion today. We have the Nature 2000 which is also in that part. The management of the Nature 2000 area is now in progress. Those are our main working groups and then we have smaller working groups which deal with long term management, maximum sustainable yield (MSY); there are five for that subject. That is the basic structure. How do we reach consensus? When I started in this position as Chairman I thought it would be quite difficult to reach consensus but I have been positively surprised that we have reached consensus in most of the important decisions. Of course there are parts where it is quite difficult to reach consensus but I think all representatives from organisations who have started to work in the RACs have found that they should try to reach consensus with all these different groups because that is the way we can be strong from a political point of view in Brussels, if we can show unanimous opinion from the RACs in certain issues.

Q306 *Viscount Brookeborough:* Can I just ask you about transparency? I only mention it because in the notes we have on the North Sea RACs it says: "The meetings o f the General Assembly are open to the public". How open are the Executive Committee meetings?

Ms Bell: Anybody can walk in off the streets and come in.

Q307 *Viscount Brookeborough:* The impression I would have normally is that our fishermen do not get on with the fishermen of other nations and therefore the PR side is not as good as it might be.

Mr Anderson: Openness and transparency are key words for the RACs. People can take part in meetings. As Ann said, we move around with the meetings to make sure that local people can take part. We have a website where we give information about our opinions and activities.

Q308 *Lord Plumb:* Do the media show a lot of interest?

Ms Bell: It depends on the topic being discussed. If there is something controversial then sometimes they come but otherwise no. We even have Norway sitting in with most of our meetings; the Norwegian ministry attends and fishermen attend. Most of the North Sea RAC attends. This can cause problems, especially at the end of the year when Norway is sitting and listening. We also have a social and economic focus group which looks at the impacts. There is a signed protocol for the North Sea RAC and we have to take account of the social and economic consequences of any advice that we give so that we are protecting our communities. The chair of that working group is the chair of the North Sea Women's Network and that was quite deliberate.

Q309 *Baroness Sharp of Guildford:* Do you hold your meetings in English or do you have translations?

Ms Bell: Translations.

Baroness Jones of Whitchurch: I was interested to hear what you said about evidence based and scientists. How competent is the advice is that you are given on this? We have heard that the scientific advice is quite often retrospective, it is not current, so there is always that gap between what your experience is out in the ocean and what the scientists are telling you is the case.

Q310 *Chairman:* It has been put to us that what the scientists come up with is subject to an error margin of plus or minus 40%.

Mr Lambourn: The scientific advice we are given is the best that there is. The scientists have been extremely open and really thrived in the regional advisory councils. I think the percentage of uncertainty in what they are saying is probably greatly in excess of 40%—it may well be 400%—but it is still the best we have and we have to work from somewhere otherwise it has no base. I did not answer the previous question about reaching consensus. In my experience it is quite difficult if it is a topic that is current. We are much better as a RAC at dealing with longer and medium term issues. Something that is happening today gets much more difficult. The irony of that is that we need to be relevant to our grass roots and it is the short-term issues that are uppermost in the grass roots minds and not what may happen in 12 or 15 years' time. We have a balance to do there. We are much better at the long term issues but our grass roots want us to deal with the issues that they are confronted with today and tomorrow and the quotas and so on at the end of the year. Part of the reason we have difficulty in reaching consensus with the environmental NGOs and so on is that they have policy positions on various topics such as, for example, deep water species, and it is very difficult for them to compromise without undermining their stated policy position. They have a real and genuine problem there and I think they are struggling on how to enter into the sort of debate that goes on at a RAC without undermining their organisations' policy position. The industry is used to this and we take care to avoid making too many decisions that tie our hands and feet, but that is not the case for the E-NGOs. Quite often we have reached a consensus—I do not want to give the impression that we have not—but it requires hard work in my experience and it has not been particularly easy on some of them. I quite agree that giving the Commission non-consensual advice is almost worthless; the Commission does not know what to do with it either. I think that is the power of the RACs and all members need to appreciate this is a very powerful advisory tool here,

but the discipline is that you must reach consensus on your advice.

Q311 *Chairman:* Can I just take up this business about the NGOs, the point that the NGOs have these clear policies of what they are in favour of and what they are against. They almost get themselves into a bit of a box that they cannot get out of. The other way round that to get the environmental input is not just to have representatives from NGOs but to have free-standing environmental scientists. Do you have those people on the RACs?

Mr Lambourn: Not as members because scientists are not members of the RAC. The seats we have for the environmental organisations are not fully taken up which I think is a weakness. There are eight seats available and only three or perhaps four are taken up, and even those that are taken up maybe do not have a very strong European element; they may be one particular Member State.

Ms Bell: It is exactly the opposite with us; we do not have enough seats. All our NGO seats are completely taken up and we have people joining the General Assembly so that they are General Assembly members. Although they do not have any voting they can still come to meetings and have access to all the papers, which anybody has.

Mr Anderson: There is a process in order to get these different groups to understand each other and to understand each other's positions. It takes time. Maybe they have to go back also to their organisations and continue that discussion that they have had in the RACs and see that maybe it is not as simply as to just stop fishery or whatever it is; there are a lot of things you have to consider. You have to give it some time to learn to work in this new forum because it is quite new. In some parts of Europe it has just started; one has not even started yet. I think it is important to realise that this is a process which takes some time.

Q312 *Lord Palmer:* Last year the financing arrangement changed and you are now given a status allowing you to be financed from the Community budget on a long term basis. Could you explain exactly how the financing works? Is it, for example, index linked? Do you think in reality you do have enough funding to achieve your objectives?

Ms Bell: That is where I come in. I did not introduce myself earlier; I am the Director and Executive Secretary for the North Sea RAC and I was the manager of the North Sea Commission Partnership of Scientists and Fishermen. That is my background. As to the finance, we got an amendment through and that amendment came because we also have an InterRAC committee of all the administrators and chairs and they came with a consensus opinion to the Commission that the budget had to change. We got an amendment last year to give us 250,000 per annum right through without the five year plan they had originally. Originally we got 250,000 digressively towards the five year, but now we are a permanent part of the process. Each RAC is a legal entity, so in other words we are companies. Not only do we have to have audits for the Commission, but in the North Sea RAC we are a company under Scottish law so we have to provide audits to Companies House. That goes against what the Commission does because we are paid for projects. We get some money up front and the rest we do not get until maybe four or five months after the work is finished.

Q313 *Lord Palmer:* Do you have to indent for this?
Ms Bell: Yes. For the North Sea RAC Aberdeenshire Council is our underwriter and they actually pay the bills for us. They then invoice us and get the money back. Other RACs are not as fortunate as we are because it is a difficulty. The amount of money we have—the 250,000—we can survive on because all the secretariats are very prudent and careful with our budgets; we do not pay unless we have to. Because of the new status we can actually access funding for projects as long as we do not double-fund. The inflexibility of the budget is the problem that we have. We have a budget which we have to guesstimate every year and then by the end of the year we will find that our travel budget is higher than other bits of the budget and rather than be flexible like a company where you transfer funds from one part of the company to another to make sure your bottom line is correct, the Commission says, "No, you are not allowed to do that yet; each line has to be exactly as you said" and that is impossible. That is our fight with the Commission right now, not for more money but to be allowed more flexibility within our budget so that we can operate. We know that everything we spend has to be eligible; if it is not eligible our auditors will soon tell us. So long as our costs are eligible, to make all our lives easier, we are looking for flexibility in the budget. The amount of work we do with that 250,000 per year include a lot of meetings, a lot of advice given. We are very fortunate with some Member States who help us pay for research carried out and also Defra and the Scottish Executive.

Q314 *Lord Palmer:* Can you explain how the Scottish Executive and Defra and all the other agencies actually provide the money?
Ms Bell: Two years ago we had a joint project between the North Western Waters RAC and the North Sea RAC and we held a conference on cod: *Is cod recoverable?* The Scottish Executive funded that seminar—they paid for the room, for the travel, for everything else—and it was funded between the two RACs. We match funded getting scientists there.

That is how they help us, by providing funding for conferences. We had another one in Peterhead on control with Commissioner Borg. Again the Scottish Government helped to pay for that. Defra has paid for the project on special planning; they paid for the project on the social and economic gathering of data. They also help us by providing scientists. SEAFAST does an amazing amount of work for both the North Sea and the North Western Waters RACs. We do not get actual cash but by providing scientists, by providing rooms for our meetings—we are having a meeting in London on 6 May and Defra will provide rooms for us—that is the sort of money; we get help in kind. Each Member State, when we move round, will provide a room for our General Assembly or our Executive Committee and will provide dinner. That all helps our budgets, so that means that part of the budget we do not have to use. This is where I come back to flexibility: we do not spend it on that so we want maybe to spend it on something else. It is very complex as most of our InterRAC meetings would tell you.

Q315 *Viscount Brookeborough:* Originally how was it thought that you would be funded before the EU changed the status of it?
Ms Bell: We got 250,000 for the first year which was 90% of the budget. Each Member State provides the RACs with 240,000 euros per annum and that is their match funding. The North Sea has nine Member States and that provides the match funding for the Commission's budget. Every year the original status went down so we had 90% then 75%, 65% right down until we were going to be self-funding. However, because the RACs have done such a good job and have been recognised for their contribution and because all the RACs came to a consensus opinion they looked at it and the Council amended it. We are now bodies pursuing a European interest, or something like that. It means that we have financial stability and there is not going to be somebody at the end of five years saying, "That's it guys, you've had enough".

Q316 *Viscount Brookeborough:* You have already mentioned your cooperation in organising conferences, one of which was in Edinburgh. Would you like to say anything more about the cooperation between RACs? Several of the RACs are fairly new. Are you cooperating with them at the moment? What are the issues which you can achieve most on by your cooperation?
Ms Bell: We have an InterRAC committee; we were very clear at the beginning that we needed to talk to one another. All the executive secretaries formed an InterRAC committee and the aim of that committee was to ensure the effective financial management of the RACs and to avoid duplication because if we are

doing something and Sam's RAC is doing something else and the South Western Waters RAC is doing the same thing, then when it comes to science there is a finite amount of fisheries scientists in Europe so we have to make sure that we do not duplicate. That InterRAC committee works very closely. We always meet before the coordination meetings with the Commission so that we get our act together before we go into them and if there are any issues that we need to deal with we try to deal with them collectively so that when we go we go with one voice. That makes administrative sense. Sometimes this InterRAC is asked to coordinate meetings of different working groups. As RACs we do cooperate and talk to one another on a very regular basis.

Mr Lambourn: I would certainly agree with that. The sorts of issues that we approach jointly would be things like how to reach MSY (maximum sustainable yield) and data collection. The data that fishermen hold can be fed into the ICES process and improve this business of uncertainty in the science. We generally work together in these cross-cutting issues. If there is something related to a species that occurs within the jurisdiction of one or each of the RACs then of course we have to deal with it on our own, but there are many issues that cut right across and we are very conscious of trying to work together, not just with the North Sea but with the South Western Waters as well. If we can reach a common position there again it is that much more meaningful in terms of whether the Commission will accept it. That is where go from there.

Q317 *Viscount Brookeborough:* We have a map here in the notes which shows that the North Sea area goes right up to the coast of Norway. The Norwegians fish within that area but they only sometimes attend your RAC. Are they part of it or not? If not, are you part of some similar organisation that they have?

Mr Anderson: They are observers in the North Sea RAC because they are not allowed to be members according to European legislation. As Ann said before, they take part in most of our activities on a very high level so they show a big interest in what is going on in the RAC.

Q318 *Viscount Brookeborough:* They fish by different rules and have different regulations on discarding and so on.

Mr Anderson: Yes, they have of course, but we meet on this subject where there is negotiation between Europe and Norway. It has been quite interesting to see their big interest for the work going on in the North Sea RAC. Also, to add to what Sam said, the cooperation is also a question of being more and more efficient but also to be stronger vis-à-vis the Commission. Ann mentioned the conference we had on cod and cod recovery a year ago in Edinburgh.

Two hundred participants from different groups who have an interest in this both in Europe and also international representatives attended. Of course that has had a big impact on the revision of the cod recovery plan. That is a way of working in a way that we can show that we are strong and can have an impact on the Common Fisheries Policy. If the issues and problems are similar we should work together and that is what we are doing.

Ms Bell: We also work with other agencies. We work very closely with ICES on different issues and are now also working very closely with the new control agency. The RACs have observership on the control agency and Hugo sits on the Management Committee representing all the RACs and we work very closely with them. In fact our next Executive Committee meeting of the North Sea is in Vigo at their headquarters. We all try working with the different agencies to avoid conflict.

Mr Anderson: We have formal annual meetings with ICES where we discuss the cooperation between the scientists and the RACs where all RACs are represented. ICES also say that we are an important player in the Common Fisheries Policy so they want to have close cooperation. We started with a partnership when we kicked open the door to ICES because ICES had been a very secret organisation; no-one was allowed to enter the building even. We managed to open the door and have access to their meetings, take part and discuss. That is the way they are now proceeding; they have become a much more transparent organisation over the past five or six years.

Q319 *Lord Cameron of Dillington:* Both of your RACs are obviously more advanced than others. I was just wondering whether you had any comments on the way some of the other RACs work, what is different, what is the same; what is better, what is worse? Do you have any insight into why the Mediterranean RAC has not even started?

Mr Anderson: Of course there are differences in the way the RACs work because there are regional differences in the sector. One RAC which is very special is the Pelagic RAC which deals with four species in the whole area except the Mediterranean and the Baltic. They are working in a very special way, so there are differences. There has never been any cooperation in the Mediterranean area and it would be very strange if they were to start now establishing a RAC. There are of course historic reasons. There is no history of cooperation and a great number of Member States fish in the Mediterranean and there is also some international fishery going on in the Mediterranean. I think it will be very difficult to establish a RAC in the Mediterranean, especially if they work in the same

way as we do. Maybe there could be some solution to establish something, but I think it is a long way away.
Ms Bell: They are trying very hard to get it up and running but I think it is a bit like the North Western Waters, it is a big area to cover. As an administrator we all try to help them and offer help. The other RACs—for example the Baltic—are all members of InterRAC. We do try to support all the RACs wherever possible, but they are all different.

Q320 *Lord Cameron of Dillington:* We are obviously looking at the Common Fisheries Policy as a whole and it is very interesting listening to the history and details of your RACs. Do you have any insight into any particular problems?
Ms Bell: Maybe the Baltic RAC. The new accession countries maybe do not have the budgets for meetings. The Baltic is one that does not have any organisation behind it financially so they cannot pay upfront unlike us who have finance behind us to pay travel and subsistence.

Q321 *Chairman:* Does Sweden have an interest in the Baltic RAC?
Mr Anderson: Yes.

Q322 *Chairman:* What is the difference between the North Sea and the Baltic RAC?
Ms Bell: The Baltic is quite special as an area; it is semi closed area with all the environmental problems showing up in that sea. As Ann mentioned there are a number of new members in the European Union. In the Baltic we had a big problem with Poland until their election in November last year when there was a new government. The previous government did not care about the Fisheries Policy; they just fished and have been over-fishing by 50% or 100%. No-one knows exactly but now there are different signals from the government and they have decided to follow the Common Fisheries Policy and the quotas and so on. They have been punished for the last years and will pay back over the next years. That is a problem for the Baltic, that there are different levels on the experience in cooperation. The history for the Baltic is that there was a structure, the International Baltic Sea Fisheries Commission, which was managing the Baltic until three or four years ago when interested Member States in the Baltic became members of the European Union. It is only European Union members and Russia who have an interest in the Baltic today, so there is bilateral negotiation between the Commission and Russia. Russia has a small interest in the Baltic. There is long experience of cooperation but at that time when the Soviet Union existed Moscow took place in the meetings, so the experience from Estonia, Latvia, Lithuania and Poland to cooperate in that manner is not so long.

Q323 *Viscount Brookeborough:* You say the Baltic is semi-closed; is there much migration of fish between the North Sea and the Baltic?
Mr Anderson: Some herring stocks are migrating, but not cod or salmon. There are only four species which are regulated in the Baltic.

Q324 *Baroness Sharp of Guildford:* You have given us some indication that one of your main functions is to reach consensus on particular issues and then you issue opinions on those issues. Could you give us some idea of how those opinions have been developed and adopted and how they have been received by the European Commission? I think there have been a number of different opinions that you have issued over the course of the last couple of years, two that come to mind are on the North West Waters RAC, the opinion on the hake fisheries position where you rejected the recovery plan and went instead for a management plan, and in relation to the discards on the North Sea where again you rejected the discard ban and went instead for a fishery by fishery long term management plan. Could you give us a little bit of an idea as to what happened then?
Mr Lambourn: The hake recovery plan becoming the hake management plan is really quite an interesting one because that is happening right now. I think there has been quite a bit of disappointment from members of the RAC in that we have been two years in a recovery plan and if anything it seems to have worked; the hake stock is now in considerably better shape than it was and we satisfied the criteria to move towards a management plan. You would have thought that for a stock in relatively good state the management plan might offer some encouragement in terms of being less restrictive, but the non-paper that the Commission has issued is draconian. The members are now wishing they had stayed with the recovery plan and not pressed to move to a management plan, so this one is going to be very interesting to see how it plays out. At the outset the Spanish, for example, are outraged that the management plan should be so negative and so restrictive and they are wondering how they are going to manage. They were looking forward to a slightly more relaxed regime moving towards some sort of stability, but it appears that the mortality of the hake stock has got to be very much more reduced which means there will have to be less fishing capacity one way or the other and they are up in arms about it. We shall see how it pans out.

Q325 *Baroness Sharp of Guildford:* Have your other opinions been better received?
Mr Lambourn: We have given advice on certain specific issues—mainly technical—that have been accepted by the Commission. That has been very satisfactory. More often the advice we give is to move

in a particular direction or to emphasise something rather than something else, rather than being the complete solution. That is how it generally works. As a RAC we find we are being asked to advise the Commission on a number of issues and those numbers are increasing. We are finding that we are having to run harder to keep up. One of my hopes was for our particular RAC to have a number of initiatives coming from the grass roots, but we are so taken up with responding to demands from the Commission that we are going to have to prioritise and make strategic decisions as to whether we are going to cover a lot of subjects in a shallow fashion or whether we are going to say that we cannot give advice on this, this and this, but we are really going to work hard on this. We have reached the point now where we are going to have to do something because the members are complaining that they have meeting overload and they are swamped by e-mails.

Q326 *Baroness Sharp of Guildford:* Being driven too much by the Commission.
Mr Lambourn: Yes. We have come to quite an interesting stage in the development of the RACs and we have to decide where we are going to go from here.

Q327 *Baroness Sharp of Guildford:* Mr Anderson and Ms Bell, is it the same experience in the North Sea?
Mr Anderson: Yes, it is the same experience. I can add also that it is not only the formal advice we have given to the Commission that has had an impact on the policy. I mentioned before this cod seminar, that was not a formal decision making meeting, it was a conference with a report written from the conference and there were some conclusions made in the report but they were mainly the rapporteurs' conclusions. That report has had a big impact on the cod policy in the North Sea. I do not have a number of the formal advice we give to the Commission but it is more than ten annually, big or small, but there are also these other activities which also have an impact on the development of the Fisheries Policy.

Q328 *Baroness Sharp of Guildford:* On the whole you have had a fairly positive response from the Commission.
Mr Anderson: Yes.

Q329 *Baroness Sharp of Guildford:* The danger with your hake decision could be if you are seen just as a talking shop and the Commission do not pay any attention to it.
Mr Lambourn: You are quite right. I think the Pelagic RAC rather felt that last year. They gave some advice on herring in the North Sea which the Commission did not take and there were immediate questions as to what is the point of the Pelagic RAC if nobody is

listening to us? Generally speaking I have to say that the Commission have been very supportive of the RACs; they continue to be very supportive. In terms of giving the grass roots access to the Commission and putting a human face to the Commission I think that has worked well, it is working well and it is very welcome.
Mr Anderson: I would agree with that and say also that there is also a commitment in a special Commission report that they should really consider the consensus advice given by each RAC before they take a decision and if they do not then they should come back and argue why they do not follow our advice. It is positive; I agree with Sam about that. There is the question of discard where we have had an opinion and given advice to the Commission. There are many reasons for us to come to that conclusion, but a discard ban sounds quite easy and efficient but it is not. Discard depends on many reasons. We have one kind which I think would be easy to get away from, that is the discard that is the result of management decisions. You have a mixed fishery with a number of stocks and suddenly one of the stocks runs out of quota. You have still caught them but you have to discard them. That is what I call a management based discard which you must find ways round so you can catch, land and sell the catch you have. The problem shows up in the relative stability when you start to find the solutions to that problem. If you really want to solve the discard problem you have to find ways around that. You have a problem with a fixed fishery that the minimal landing size is different for different fish and you can be forced to discard fish because they are under-sized. The mesh is often set for the smallest minimal landing size species. There is high grading which is a discard where the fishermen want to keep the fish of the highest value and discard the rest. I think we would have to look quite deeply into the backgrounds for discard, look at each reason and look at each stock; type of fishing and type of gear also has some bearing on discard. It is quite complicated. There will be a hearing in Brussels next month discussing discard because that is a priority from the Commission's side.

Q330 *Viscount Ullswater:* Mr Lambourn, can I ask you for a bit more detail about this movement from the hake recovery plan to the management plan and the status of the non paper which Brussels has issued. When we are looking at the advisory councils we see that maybe as a way for the future for the management of the fishing grounds round the UK. It would be very disappointing, therefore, if the Commission did not pay great attention to what you are saying about it. I was slightly perturbed when you indicated that the terms of the management plan looked very severe and it was not quite the way you wanted to move. Could you give any indication as to whether you think that the Commission will listen to the representations that you are making and that other consultees might be making?

Mr Lambourn: It is a non paper so this is at the discussion stage. I would certainly agree that we should manage our stocks on the basis of management plans and whether they are mixes of stock, but we certainly want to get away from this annual negotiation which is so wasteful in all sorts of respects and move to long term plans where we know where we are going and how we are going to get there. In that sense I think that as hake is the first management plan it is of crucial importance that we get this right. There is no question that it did come as a shock to those who have a majority interest in this stock; I am talking about the French and the Spanish here. They made some comments to the Executive that whoever had drawn this up must have been having a mental breakdown. They were taken completely by surprise. It may be that the final proposal for the management plan is going to be very much different from what we have seen thus far. I think the fundamental difference between the industry that has an interest in this fishery and the Commission is that we all want to reach the same point but it is how quickly do we want to get to it because that has all sorts of socio-economic consequences in terms of jobs and so on. The Spanish and the French very much look at these issues from a socio-economic angle and in that respect, as an aside, it is interesting to sit on the RAC and see how different Member States view the same problem. That is one of the differences that is very striking to me. It is very much jobs and socio-economic considerations from certainly Spain and France whereas perhaps the UK would be looking at the biological and environmental consequences first and foremost. As far as the hake management plan is concerned, I do not know how it is going to end because, as I say, the thing is happening as we speak. I said that we have geographic working groups; there are also a number of focus groups, as we call them, and there is a hake focus group which is going to meet in Madrid and thrash out a response to this problem. I hope it is not negative because this is the direction we are going and there will be management plans for a number of other stocks, ultimately cod as well, and it is very important that we get the ground rules right. For my money—I am aware of the Johannesburg Declaration that says we must have these stocks at MSY by 2015—my advice would be that it is much more important to get to them at MSY, but whether that is 2015 or 2020, let us see what we can do without there being too many adverse consequences. Basically it is just that the mortality rates in this hake management plan that the Commission is looking for have taken the fisheries by surprise, when this is stock which is supposed to be at a relatively good level,

moving in the right direction, it is a good news story, and all of a sudden there has been a bit of a reality shock. I cannot say how it will turn out. Perhaps it will be different and there is a bit of posturing going on as well. It will be interesting to see.

Q331 *Viscount Brookeborough:* You said it was a two to three years recovery plan. Presumably hake mature at six to seven years old, so how has this happened? I do not disbelieve you but this would appear to be the fisherman's angle as opposed to the scientific one. How can they have recovered in such a short length of time? What you are talking about is getting a large quantity of mature fish which take a far longer time frame.

Mr Lambourn: I do not know and nor does anybody else, because of things such as global warming, whether everything is down to fishing. I suspect fishing is an element in a number of factors and maybe they have all come together in a fortuitous way with respect to hake. There is no doubt between the fishermen and the scientists that the size of the mature stock is increasing and has increased year on year for a number of years, and has moved above what was regarded as a critical level.

Q332 *Viscount Brookeborough:* The scientists and the fishermen are agreeing, are they?

Mr Lambourn: Yes, absolutely; there is no doubt about that.

Ms Bell: In the recovery plans or anything else that we do, if we do not have the science supporting us then it is very difficult to make a case. When you get science and industry agreeing then it is very difficult to swallow when the Commission then come in and say the opposite.

Q333 *Baroness Jones of Whitchurch:* Both of your websites emphasise that your organisations are there to represent the stakeholders, but how can that be? How can you claim that you cover that broad range of stakeholders when your bodies are so dominated by the fishing interests? Is there not something wrong with your constitutions, the way that your bodies are established?

Ms Bell: We are constituted by the Council. It was a Council decision that we should have 24 members, two thirds would be from the industry side and one third from others, and the two thirds would have to have fishing representatives from each country represented, at least one. In the one third we have the NGOs, the Women's Network and other outside bodies. The one third is merely represented by a European body rather than the Scottish Fisherman's Federation or the NNFO or the Swedish Fishermen's Federation. The NGO level you have at European level and that makes them more than able to deal with their side of it.

Q334 *Baroness Jones of Whitchurch:* They are in the minority, the poor old NGOs.

Mr Anderson: In the way they work I do not see this is a problem. Normally the green NGOs are at European level and I sometimes get the feeling that they have a problem in taking the time needed to cover all activities and so on. I think it is important that we have some activity or are invited to something that the green organisations should be represented. It is quite difficult to find someone who has the time to take part. In the decision making process we seek consensus and then there is no real problem with that because you have to find the consensus.

Q335 *Baroness Jones of Whitchurch:* How do you represent the consumer interest in your stakeholder plan?

Ms Bell: With great difficulty because we cannot find a consumer organisation.

Mr Anderson: We have had one that has asked for membership. The consumers are not so well organised in Europe so it is quite difficult. I know there is one in the Baltic RAC which represents a Swedish consumer organisation and there are some at a European level. I think that is the only RAC to have it so far.

Q336 *Chairman:* There are the cynics who maintain the whole European structure is a conspiracy against the consumer. I would not dream of saying that, of course!

Ms Bell: In both our RACs we have a chair and we have vice chairs. One of the vice chairs represents the two thirds and one vice chair represents the one third. We have always been very strong on that, that there is a balance. In the North Sea RAC we have a board of directors because we are company; we have one from the NGO side and one from the other. In all things we try to keep a balance.

Q337 *Chairman:* Are there any changes in your composition that you would improve the information and the perspectives coming into the process and secondly improve your credibility?

Ms Bell: We have been asked by industry and NGO for this, we would like to have more of a working group so we could have the scientists and the fishermen once again having the opportunity to sit down together. That is something that both our RACs feel is lacking. We have scientists always there and they do as much as they can, but to get industry and the scientists together, especially to discuss issues in an open forum, is very difficult. That is where the partnership works. We work at Chatham House so that both the scientists and the fishermen could discuss anything knowing that it would never go outside the door, and it never did. We need

something like that where science and industry can really get down to the nitty-gritty. I personally think that would help all the RACs if that were possible.

Q338 *Baroness Jones of Whitchurch:* A suggestion was made earlier about some sort of free standing environmental scientist, do you think there is scope for that? Are you satisfied that the current scientists are sufficiently concerned about the environmental aspects of fishing?

Mr Lambourn: I think I am, yes. They are of a good calibre and they are not particularly sympathetic to the fishing at all; they are scientists and should be ruled by science. To go back to your previous question, I think that if I were a fisherman and had a one third seat on a group that was two thirds E-NGO I might feel a little bit marginalised as well. Perhaps some years down the road it might be better to be more balanced, but I would like to refer back to the point I made earlier. I want the E-NGOs to be able to negotiate and compromise on stated policy positions, otherwise it is very difficult to have a constructive dialogue. We both agree where we want to be, but it is the getting there that is the problem. They want to do it in one leap; I want to do it in ten steps, maybe two of which are backwards from their point of view, but I will get there in the end. I do hear comments from NGOs that they feel marginalised and what is the point anyway. I think there is a huge point. I think it has been a real education for some Member States' representatives to sit down and talk to E-NGOs who, I am sure, would not even know what they look like, and to hear in many cases good sense and some well argued positions coming out from them has been really very good for those representatives. I would encourage the E-NGOs to persist. I just wish there was a bigger take up of the seats available on our RAC. I think also the NGOs have said they simply do not have the resources to attend all the meetings in all the venues; they have run out of carbon miles and things like that. They are simply not big enough to do it, but I think the industry needs to be aware of the influence that, for example, DG Environment has within the whole management of fisheries. That was very evident at last year's Council and perhaps the previous one. We need to work much more closely with the environmentalists than we have in the past and really treat them as equal partners. I think you have a point, but we are not there yet.

Q339 *Baroness Jones of Whitchurch:* We had evidence a couple of weeks ago from the Royal Society for the Protection of Birds and they seemed to talk immensely good sense. They are not all being outrageous or making ridiculous demands; they do have quite a lot of scientific knowledge themselves.

Ms Bell: Euan Dunn from BirdLife International chairs our spatial planning working group; we have a number of NGOs who chair the different focus groups. We make sure it is not just industry chairing groups.

Q340 *Viscount Ullswater:* Could I just investigate the point about the consumer? In some of the papers we have read a few years ago there was no market for monkfish; now it seems to be one of the most valuable fish you can catch because, I suppose, of the reduction in the cod. Who drives that? Is it the consumer that drives that? Now there is another species I think called gurnard(?) which is now being actively fished for because there is a market for it. Is that not consumer driven? Could that not be consumer driven so that some of the fish that you now say there is no market for could be developed into a market? If there are no consumers or supermarkets saying "We can sell this, that or the other" the change in the pattern from the producers' side is perhaps not complete
Mr Lambourn: I agree. I would like to see the consumers represented and the retailers, representatives from supermarkets because that is where fish is sold in this country. One of the drivers for these other species coming forward has been these celebrity chefs, for want of a better word. When I was young certainly people used to look at the fish we were catching and ask, "Is it a cod?" Now they will tell you what the species is, what the relative value is, how to cook it and whether it is good or bad; they really are quite knowledgeable and I suppose that has come about by many of these people such as Rick Stein.

Q341 *Chairman:* You have been able to bring the catchers and the scientists together; you have not done it with the consumers. Have you been able to bring the catchers and the processors together?
Mr Lambourn: That is much closer than might appear. It is a necessity really.

Q342 *Chairman:* It used to be quite a strange thing really, that the catchers had no idea what the processors wanted.
Mr Lambourn: I think all of these barriers are breaking down.
Ms Bell: It is getting much better.

Q343 *Lord Plumb:* You have proved to us without doubt that you are as concerned about long term issues as short term issues. If you refer particularly to global warming, climate change, pollution and so on, fishermen have a responsibility as well as the rest of the industry in dealing with these problems. Are they discussed and at what level?

Mr Anderson: Our agenda is very much driven by the Commission's agenda, with all the proposals they send out that they want recommendations on. That is what we are dealing with most. We have our own initiatives but also issues affecting the medium term and long term we have not really had time for so far. However, I agree. We are not organised to give advice on the immediate issues; we are organised to work mid-term and long-term. That is the structure of the RAC. Also I believe if we should have a successful Fisheries Policies we need to work more on mid-term and long-term issues because I think that is where the solution is. We still have the focus on annual decisions, especially at the December Council where all the taxes and quotas for next year and the management decisions will be taken. That is not relevant if you look at the environment where we are fishing and working; fish do not care about the New Year. We need to be looking at long-term management. That is where we could play a key role also, we are well suited for that.
Ms Bell: Within the long-term management plans we do have to be aware of climate change; it is something we have had scientific presentations from environmental scientists on trying to address the issue of climate change. We are aware of it and we do discuss it. Although we are not dealing with it, it is very much part of everything we do.

Q344 *Lord Plumb:* You are advised by the Commission on the sorts of things you should be discussing, but should you not go to the Commission and say, "We can't hide this away; it is something we are part of and have to be concerned with"? Is this not the sort of approach you ought to be taking?
Ms Bell: We do that. We have many initiatives where we actually go to the Commission, like the control, like the cod, looking at MPAs and spatial planning and the social and economic side. There is a social economic unit with DG and that was because we were pushing for it. We certainly do push; we have not pushed the climate change issue yet, but that is not to say that we are not progressing. The scientists are looking at it much more than they did before.

Q345 *Baroness Sharp of Guildford:* Do you feel that the Commission are requiring you to be too reactive? They are posing the agenda to you and you are not actually having enough opportunity to create the agenda to be proactive on your own part?
Ms Bell: We do. We are asked constantly for advice and because we do cooperate we can come up with our own initiatives and we do stretch our budgets. Member States also help us. We have come up with quite a lot of our own initiatives and ideas that we have driven forward and have made a difference. Even the regionalisation of the Commission very much came out of the conference where we were

looking at regional management. We were very pleased to see that the Commission has now been divided into regional directorates. There are things that we are dealing with, but we are very new, young organisations. We are driving as hard as we can.

Mr Anderson: It also comes back to the resources available to us. We are restricted by both the rules we have but also by resources, the funding. If we had more resources we could work with more things; we could have our initiatives and projects and work much deeper, engage scientists to help us and so on. They help us today but that is a contribution from Member States actually because ICES scientists are Member States scientists and they make a contribution. It would be increased if we could have the resources to engage scientists to do specific projects in order to take forward our own initiatives.

Ms Bell: By that we do not mean that we trying to supersede ICES. Whenever you mention having your own scientists immediately people think you want to take over from ICES but that is not what we mean at all. We are working with ICES scientists and we meet with them regularly as all RACs do, and we do actually look at different projects that we can do with ICES, but there is more that can be done.

Mr Lambourn: I am a little more independent minded. I keep referring back to the fishermen's industries being grass roots. We should remember that that is the way it is and it is for the RAC to inform the Commission to some extent as to what they are going to do. We should not necessarily jump when the Commission says we should or asks us to. I have issues about that. I always encourage the independent line. I would like, for example, to be able as a RAC to commission independent scientific work directly with ICES but we have to work through the Commission according to the Memorandum of Understanding which means that it has to have the rubber stamp from the Commission. I am not suggesting I am going to go out and do something extraordinary or wasteful, but I think there is just the principle there that I am a bit jealous in protecting. This is not a Commission driven organisation; this is driven by the grass roots, which is the industry in this case, plus the other stakeholders and I would like to see an even balance on it. We have to be quite mindful of our independence and be strong enough to say on some occasions that we cannot give advice in eight weeks, it is too short a time and they will have to proceed without us.

Ms Bell: We do do that; that is why we are not very popular.

Q346 *Chairman:* You have indicated, quite rightly, that you are relatively young organisations. I would like to ask you to look to the future and how you see the role of RACs developing? Where do you see

the role of RACs developing? Where do you see yourselves in, say, five year's time or so? Will the role have developed? If so, in which directions?

Mr Lambourn: I think it is going to be very much a matter of resources. Essentially the RACs are run now on people's free time. Everybody who is a member of a RAC has other jobs; this is fitted in by taking days from whatever your day time job is and I do not think ultimately that you can run a fisheries advisory or management on that basis. This will have to be decided at some stage. The Commission will have to decide what it wants from these RACs. Does the Commission want good quality advice on an increasing number of subjects? If it does then it cannot be run on a free time, spare time basis by willing volunteers. I do not think that is satisfactory. These are not easy questions. They require a lot of effort, a lot of work and a lot of research. You cannot do it in five minutes. Where will we be in five years? I do not know. Some people are very concerned that we should have more management power rather than just advisory. I think that is something perhaps we ought to earn. If it is good quality advice it is awfully close to decision. That is my feeling. Good quality, consensual advice requires a discipline and we need to be better at it. I am not sounding as if I am very satisfied or very content; I think we are doing well but we have a long way to go.

Mr Anderson: If one should come to the conclusion in the revision of the Common Fisheries Policy that there should also be regional management for the Fisheries Policy, I think there is a willingness at least from part of Europe from Member States to take on that responsibility. I agree with Sam that the RACs today do not have the structure to be a management unit but there could be changes so that we could be a management unit. Sam and I went to the States together with some other people a couple of years ago and looked at their regional management boards. Of course they basically have a structure which is more or less the same as we have, different groups together, but they also have the task to manage fisheries in their area. That could be a way forward if the Ministry of Fisheries in the Council were to see that change in the Common Fisheries Policy.

Q347 *Chairman:* It seems to be that the Common Fisheries Policy is a very top down approach to managing an industry and it is layer upon layer of regulation. As soon as a regulation is imposed there are ways round any regulation so what you do is put another layer of regulation on top. The nature of the industry must be that the only way to overcome it is to get a buy-in from the grass roots upwards. RACs are the only organisations that exist that give you that opportunity to do it. I really am asking whether you see RACs changing their role from being one of advising the Commission to actually managing the fisheries?

Mr Lambourn: Not for me. Not in the near future but perhaps a little further away. You just made a comment there about the industry having to buy into this. It has to have grass roots buy-in. The Commission issued a proposal for control and compliance. This is very much an issue at the moment. I notice they have nine objectives within this and to get the industry to agree and to have buy-in was only objective number six out of the nine. From where I am coming from that is by far and away the most important one because unless everybody really agrees that we have to abide by the rules then it does not matter how big a stick you have, it will never in the end be satisfactory. It is certainly very much the philosophy of the Commission and it continues to be, that what you need is a bigger stick, you need more power and cultivating a culture of compliance is something that will come naturally and does not need to be encouraged by explicit initiatives. I absolutely disagree with that because I think they have it completely round the wrong way.

Ms Bell: As I said to you, there was a conference at Peterhead on control. The name of the conference was *Developing a Culture of Compliance*. We had Commissioner Borg there and we had the Assistant Director General of FEO, but we only had a very junior member of the Commission staff. The reason they gave was because they were very busy developing the control and compliance regulations. This is what we were having the conference about. The industry was there; we had stakeholders; many NGOs attended (more than come to the meetings). I said that is why we were having the conference for everyone to discuss the matter. It was a very good conference, a lot of good debate. The Commission representative was a technician and could not feed back. That is why, on our own initiative, we pushed them because we were going to do it. They did not think we should have that conference. They thought we should have it much later after they had made their decision, but we moved very quickly. I would like to see the RACs move forward. We are moving towards looking at long-term management plans and I think that is the way the RACs will be able to have a major influence on the future of fisheries management, by developing these plans. These plans are coming from the grass roots, but from all levels including the NGOs. Unless they agree with what we are doing we have no consensus so we have no strength. I think if we keep on that route then we will eventually become quasi management. I totally agree with Sam that if we can provide good, scientifically based, evidence based advice to the Commission that has been agreed by consensus, it is very difficult for the Commission of any Member State to actually disagree with us. It is not just the Commission, we have to speak to the politicians. It is the Council of Ministers that makes the decisions and the politicians

need to look at the work the RACs are doing and become involved in our work, and then they make the decisions and tell the Commission, not the other way round.

Q348 *Chairman:* If you do go down this route, are you confident that you can keep your stakeholders on board with this long-term thinking?
Ms Bell: I think we have to make sure that all the people who are in the RACs believe that the advice they are giving—and giving up a lot of time and effort to create that advice—is being listened to. It is up to us within the RACs as well to feed back the good bits that come back from the Commission down to the grass roots. I am not sure that all the organisations are very good at doing that. We have to keep the people at the very lowest level aware of what is happening.
Mr Lambourn: If it was to move to management E-NGOs would insist on a 50/50 split in the composition of the RACs. It could not be dominated by one group of stakeholders or another three or four groups of stakeholders.
Mr Anderson: One initiative taken by the members of Scotland, a real time closure system, has to be managed and that could be one part of management of a policy which, I guess, is best suited to be handled on a regional level. The crucial question is that there has to be a willingness from the Member States to see a development towards a regional management system in the Common Fisheries Policy. If so, I think we are prepared to find the forms for handling it. Some sort of regional management body must be established and take its part from the RACs.

Q349 *Lord Cameron of Dillington:* Thank you very much for those last few remarks; we will certainly be taking them to the Commission in a couple of weeks' time. I would like to have a conversation with Mr Lambourn about his producer organisation, the Cornish Fish Producers Organisation. I wonder if you could perhaps explain how you see its role, how you manage the quotas and perhaps elaborate a bit about how the quota transfer could or might take place either within or even outside the organisation?
Mr Lambourn: There are quite a number of questions there. The role of the PO in one sentence is to look after the interests of its members. Traditionally we have done all sorts and everything in that respect. We have largely stayed away from marketing. I think maybe we are being asked to do one or two things in that direction, for example with hand line caught tuna: can we develop a market for that? We have taken the initiative and talked to processors and retailers and so on to try to get a premium for that product because you cannot compete with the nets unless there is. I think we are getting rather more into marketing issues. Up until this stage it has been very

much representative with both the national government and the Commission on any issues that affect them in any way at all. There is a very broad spectrum. We are there as the first point of call for any fisherman who has some sort of grievance. The quota is of course one of the very important aspects that the PO manages. Each PO handles this slightly differently. Traditionally our PO managed all our quota on a pool basis; we all pooled the quota and then it was up to the chief executive of the PO to manage our monthly uptakes so that globally we did not exceed what all the members had pooled. That had the advantage of keeping as much flexibility within our membership in terms of the methods they employ, provided we did not all go and do one thing. It meant that you could go and catch prawns one day and maybe go and do something else the next day without having to make sure that you had the necessary quota to do it. That worked very well for a number of years until fish quota allocations were introduced whereby you were given a track record associated with what your vessel had caught; that was your share although the ownership of that legally is still wide open. The next step was that there was a trade introduced in these quota shares so that one fisherman can buy another fisherman's quota shares in order that he can fish harder. Now we run a mix of a pool which is not as big as the pool used to be and also members have what they call a ring fenced quota which is this quota shares business. We run a sort of mixture. The PO still issues monthly bulletins to all our members, which is what they may catch if they do not already or have not acquired quota shares for some reason. Those that have can then catch the pool and they have also got so many tons of whatever it is—cod or hake or whatever—that they can catch as well and they can decide how they uptake those bits. We are at a halfway stage.

Q350 *Lord Cameron of Dillington:* On the personal bit, as it were, can they sell that to another member of the organisation?
Mr Lambourn: Yes, but it has to be done through the PO. Yes with strings, that is the answer to your question. I think your written question was: Am I content with it moving to rights based management? No, I am not content but I am rather resigned because I think that is ultimately where it will end up. I hope that perhaps there is a division and the national government retains a certain amount of quota for the under-tens and that remains there in order that there should be some inshore fishery around the country just for the reasons of tradition, heritage and tourism. I come from Cornwall and people go to these little harbours, they want to see fishing boats and they want to see fish. I think we would lose something very important if there were no fish left. If you go to rights-based management you

could end up with no fish landed in Cornwall at all, it could all be owned elsewhere.

Q351 *Lord Cameron of Dillington:* Is that not up to the Cornish fishermen rather than the Government?
Mr Lambourn: Yes, and we are doing various things about it. There is what is called the "Dutch Fish Quota Company" which is owned by the fishermen and we buy up as much quota as we can and lease it back to ourselves. There are these sorts of initiatives but there are very strict rules on how far you can go down this road. Of course there is never enough money to buy the quota as it becomes available, and then you are competing with other interests that are very much more wealthy. We are trying but it is not enough. If I lived in Utopia I guess I would like no individual to own any quota at all and all to be owned by the community to which it was originally allocated and then somehow leased back. The fact is that we have gone down this road, there has never been a policy but we have tip-toed down this road to ITQs (individual transferable quotas) little bit by little bit. We have not taken the last few steps yet but it is hard to see how we could avoid it. I would imagine that that is where it will eventually end up. It does have advantages, I quite agree, from the management perspective. You get this ownership asset built up and it is much easier for the ministry to manage this sort of thing. There are pluses but there are also, I think, disadvantages in that that quota, as anybody knows, can migrate out of the area to which it was originally allocated and I am not sure how to get around that. I do not think you can.

Q352 *Lord Palmer:* I have been mulling over the answer you gave to my question over an hour ago about your community budget of 250,000. That is presumably euros.
Ms Bell: Yes.

Q353 *Lord Palmer:* Can I ask, you have both come from Scotland, did you get a little help with your expenses coming down today from the Scottish Executive, let alone your overnight accommodation?
Ms Bell: No. I have come from Scotland, Hugo has come from Sweden and Sam has come from Cornwall and that is part of our budget. All our travel is paid for by the RAC; it comes from the 250,000 euros. Most of the budgets of all the RACs go to pay for travel, accommodation and meetings. Anything we do otherwise as secretariats we have to be very creative and find it from somewhere.

Q354 *Lord Palmer:* Your salary as Chief Executive, where does that come from?
Ms Bell: Part of it is paid for by Aberdeenshire. I am only part time. I do about a 100% RAC work but officially 100 days of my time is paid for the RAC, but

Aberdeenshire Council is very generous. My assistant, Joyce, is paid for; she does 20 hours a week. There is only myself and her and another colleague of mine that Aberdeenshire provide. Sixty thousand euros of our budget is on salaries and the rest of it is on meetings, travel and subsistence, which is why we need to be flexible and be able to move it around. This inflexibility is what is crippling us. We go to the Commission with our funding and they say that we have moved this from there to there; we are only allowed to move 10,000 so we have lost 20,000 euros. Twenty thousand euros to us is a fortune; to the Commission it is a pittance, as I continually remind them.

Q355 Lord Palmer: So flexibility is your great message to take away.

Ms Bell: Yes, flexibility within the budget. Do not let us do anything that is illegal or non-eligible and we do not want more money, just let us do what we want to do with it and do not cripple us.

Mr Lambourn: I would also underline that we would not function as a RAC were it not for the Member States making various facilities available for us to hold our meetings free of charge and translations; translation is a very big issue in our RAC and, for example, the Spanish administration have given us a secretarial assistant for three years at their expense which has proved enormously invaluable. Different Member States all help. In the Spanish administration case, for example, he is trilingual so it

helps with the translation as well. Translation is a real big issue with our RAC because in many instances the Spanish and the French are at a disadvantage in debates because they have not had the papers in the right language soon enough.

Ms Bell: In the North Sea RAC we always have to have French and we have agreed that whichever Member State we are in, if we are in Sweden we have Swedish interpretation. We are very fortunate; most of the Scandinavian countries speak English so we do not spend nearly as much in translation as others do.

Q356 Lord Plumb: I was interested in the flexibility on the sale of quotas. I was on a quay in Mevagissey not very long ago and I talked to a lot of fishermen who were well satisfied, I understood from them, with the Fisheries Policy and then complained bitterly about the Spanish fishermen pinching their fish. I did ask how they got hold of the quotas and I did not really get an answer. Is this a major problem in certain areas?

Mr Lambourn: I am not sure I can describe it as a problem, but it is a fact that it is the Cornish fishermen who have sold their quotas to Spanish fishermen.

Lord Plumb: They were complaining to the passers-by that the Spanish were pinching their fish but they did not tell them that they could sit on the quay and watch them do it.

Chairman: I think that is it. Thank you very much indeed; that was a very worthwhile session.

WEDNESDAY 30 APRIL 2008

Present:	Arran, E	Palmer, L
	Brookeborough, V	Plumb, L
	Cameron of Dillington, L	Sewel, L (Chairman)
	Dundee, E	Sharp of Guildford, B
	Jones of Whitchurch, B	Ullswater, V

Examination of Witness

Witness: MR CLIFF MORRISON, Chair, Food and Drink Federation Seafood Group and Technical Adviser to Foodvest, examined.

Q357 Chairman: First of all, thank you very much for coming along to help us and finding the time to do so, we are very indebted to you.
Mr Morrison: It is my pleasure.

Q358 Chairman: A couple of formal things. This is a formal evidence-taking session so there will be a transcript that will be made available to you as soon as it is ready so you can have a look and see if there are any little errors or slips that have crept in and revise them. Secondly, we are technically webcast, so there is a possibility that somewhere someone might be listening.
Mr Morrison: Yes, I have just heard that they will be listening at FDF.

Q359 Chairman: There we are. Hello there! On our best behaviour now. How would you like to proceed? Would you like to make a brief opening statement and then go on to questions and answers.
Mr Morrison: I was just going to say I was slightly surprised that a lot of the emphasis in the questions was directed towards Young's Foodvest. I had assumed that I was being asked on behalf of the industry as a whole rather than Foodvest in particular. Just to give some of my background. I took early retirement from UB Frozen and Chilled Foods, when Young's was part of United Biscuits. When the changes happened, Young's and Bluecrest came together in a capitalist organisation, I decided to take early retirement at that time. For the last six years or so I have been working part-time as Technical Adviser to Young's, and it is now called Foodvest. I am not directly involved in day-to-day business or strategy, but I will answer those questions. If you want more detail I might suggest that Mike Parker, who is the Deputy CEO and is responsible for purchasing and technical strategy, has expressed a willingness to come and give evidence if you want more detail than I am possibly able to give you on the Young's questions.

Q360 Chairman: I think that is a very valid point that you have made. I think it would be helpful to us if you could answer the questions on an industry basis rather than a specifically Young's basis.
Mr Morrison: There were about four questions specifically directed to Young's Foodvest and whilst I was going to give you a specific answer on them I was also going to broaden it out to an industry perspective.

Q361 Chairman: For example, there is a question on discards and that could be very much an industry-wide type question rather than specific to Young's, if that is okay. Are you happy to go straight into questions?
Mr Morrison: Yes.

Q362 Chairman: Just to set the scene if you could for us, could you give us an outline of the number, range and scope of companies that are involved in the organisation that you are a part of. What is their share of the EU market fisheries?
Mr Morrison: I was going to express it in terms of the UK market, but I can provide you with further information. I have done written responses, so if I read these and then I can answer questions if that is okay.

Q363 Chairman: Surely.
Mr Morrison: As you will be aware, the FDF is the principal voice of the food processing industry in the UK with links to our European sister organisations via the CIAA in Brussels. The CIAA represents FDF equivalents across Europe. The Seafood Group is a specific sector within the Food and Drink Federation and has links directly with an organisation called AIPCE-CEP, which is the European Seafood Processors and Traders' Association. That is also based in Brussels. AIPCE has 13 Member State organisations, the equivalent of the FDF Seafood Group if you like, and as associates we have Norway and Morocco. They can only be associates because we are members of ACFA as well, the Advisory Committee on Fisheries and Agriculture and, therefore, we receive some subsistence from the EC.

There are 13 Member State organisations. We are able to represent our industry both at the national level with DEFRA, DFID, the Food Standards Agency and the devolved administrations. We do a lot of work with the Scottish Government. At the EU level, we work with DG Mare, as they are now called, and DG SANCO. As I have just said, as AIPCE we have seats at the ACFA, Advisory Committee on Fisheries and Agriculture. Our Seafood Group membership comprises of 30 companies, including the major secondary added-value processors and brand owners, many of which co-produce for the retailers and the food service companies. We also have some primary processing interests, particularly in Nephrops, the langoustine, although other white fish sectors have tended to close or redirect their businesses over the past few years. In fact, I think we have probably lost four or five members in the primary processing sector over the last five years as they have either gone bankrupt or just closed. As you will be aware, Nephrops is the largest UK fishery and our members represent something like 85% of the UK processing industry, so we have a long-established sector dealing with this with its own chairman. More recently, we have also created the tuna, salmon and aquaculture sub-groups, all of which are chaired by our members. Our members include the largest fish canner in the UK, that is IFC International, which packs mainly pelagic fish for most major brands. We also are very much involved with frozen and chilled foods. Some of our largest members, in alphabetical order, include Alfresca, Birdseye-Igloo, Dawnfresh, Foodvest, which is Young's and Findus, and the Icelandic Group. So we are represented across all key processing sectors. You will recognise the brands, such as Lyons, Dawnfresh, Birdseye and Young's in particular but, as stated, our members also pack for all of the retailers and food service companies. We estimate that our members are responsible for about £2 billion of seafood products in the UK. Depending on how you estimate the value of the industry as a whole, that is certainly 50, 55% or more of the total market in the UK. However, a number of our members do have wider European interests as well. For example, Alfresca, which is an Icelandic company, is represented here by Lyons and Farne Salmon, in the north-east, and in France they have Labeyrie also majoring in salmon. Birdseye, of course, is well-represented on the continent via the Igloo brand and the Icelandic Group as well, which is Seachill here, has a number of interests in France and Germany, in Germany as Pickenpack which is a very large secondary processor. Foodvest, who I work for, of course, on a part-time basis, has a total turnover of £1.1 billion and approximately £600 million of that is in the UK with the Young's brand and what they pack as well for the retailers. Then they have £500 million in Scandinavia and France, and

that is with the Findus brand. Whilst the UK, the Young's brand, is 100% seafood, the Findus brand on the continent is 75% seafood and there are some other frozen interests as well. Of that £500 million, £400 million is in the EU and the Findus brand in Norway is £100 million. It is £1 billion of turnover in the EU and then £100 million in Norway. It is a big company. Total seafood purchases by Foodvest are approximately £360 million, of which 32% originates from within the EU and that is £71 million from wild capture and £42.5 million from aquaculture. Globally, we have estimated that 45% of fish consumption is represented by aquaculture products. You will be aware of the importance of carp and tilapia in Asia, for instance. Carp dominates aquaculture in the world as a whole, although it is not important in Europe any more and certainly not in the UK. However, in Europe the proportion of aquaculture is significantly less than this 45% but is growing quickly and we would estimate at the moment that it is somewhere between 35% and 45% of all seafood. Obviously this will vary from company to company. If you take Lyons, for example, they are major producers of shrimps and a high proportion of what they do is from aquaculture. Seachill, which is part of the Icelandic Group in Grimsby, are major packers for the retailers and are heavily into salmon, all of which is aquaculture, of course. Overall, 38.5% of Foodvest's seafood purchases are from aquaculture and that is predominantly salmon and shrimps, although they do have interests, as other companies do, in sea bass and sea bream from the Mediterranean. I think it is worth mentioning at the moment a species called Pangasius, which is a catfish species that is principally grown via aquaculture in Vietnam. That is currently undergoing exponential growth. It has gone from just a few thousand tonnes to last year I believe it was 1.1 million tonnes. It is literally going up like that. Although it is catfish, when it is filleted the skinless fillets look very much like a sole and it is becoming a very, very popular species because it is quite bland, very white, and is now seen as a potential substitute for a number of the maritime white fish species. I think you will see a lot more of that over the coming years.

Q364 Baroness Sharp of Guildford: Sorry, could you say the name of the fish again?
Mr Morrison: Pangasius, P-a-n-g-a-s-i-u-s. It is sold here as Basa. A number of companies are currently selling it as Basa in the UK. Just as a slight aside, under the marketing regulations of 2004 each Member State is required to officially register the names of species and if new species come along they have to establish a species name. The Food Standards Agency has an expert committee, and I sit on that along with scientists and people from the industry as well, and there was a big debate on what

we should call Pangasius, because that is the Latin name. It is known locally as Basa in Vietnam and it is called that in Australia as well, so after a big debate we decided that is what the name should be here. That has now been drawn up into UK legislation. Just as another slight digression, all of this gets rather complicated because if you think of Nephrops, norvegicus langoustine, the official legal name in the UK is scampi, and langoustine is a small lobster, of course, but if you go on to the Continent, Greece, Germany and various other countries, the name scampi is used for large shrimps. We do not have uniformity across the EU and it can be complicated.

Q365 *Lord Plumb:* Is there any danger of Basa being sold under another name?
Mr Morrison: Somebody created the name "Vietnamese sole" and I got very concerned about this, so as part of the steering group I actually had that name taken off the UK food labelling legislation. I had that taken off because, one, it is not a sole and, two, when it is filleted it looks rather like a sole and there was a very good chance of substitution. I would suggest, particularly when you are in Brussels, if you have sole and the price does not seem right you look carefully.
Lord Plumb: That is exactly what I was thinking.

Q366 *Chairman:* My impression is that the variety of fish that is coming onto the market now is much greater, it has grown enormously from even a few years ago.
Mr Morrison: Absolutely. One of the reasons for this, of course, is the British public fly all over the world. When I started in the industry it was cod, haddock and plaice and they would not divert from that. Now they go to the Mediterranean, they see the snappers and the langoustine there, most of which has come from Scotland, and they are becoming very much more adventurous. Companies like Seachill, as I have mentioned, and Young's that supply into the chilled market, if you look in Sainsbury's, Tesco or Marks & Spencer, they can pack 62 different species over the course of a week and because they have relatively short runs they can do as many as 30 species in a day of chilled product. The chilled market is huge in the UK compared to the rest of Europe and it is very much based on fresh products, well-prepared products of a whole range of species, and many of these are flown in. The snappers, for instance, will be flown in. Tuna loins, which I will mention later, are flown in on a daily basis as well.

Q367 *Lord Cameron of Dillington:* When you say that 35–40% of the EU is aquaculture, your definition of aquaculture is both ranched fish and farmed fish, is it?

Mr Morrison: Yes. Salmon obviously dominates here. It will include some mariculture as well. Just to finish on this question. In terms of wild caught fish, the white whitefish species, such as cod, haddock and Alaska Pollock, dominate here in the UK and flatfish species are also very important. Herring and mackerel used to be very important here in the UK but as those stocks declined popularity never came back, in particular as the herring came back. I was just going to mention the exotic species, but we have dealt with that. That was my response to question one.

Q368 *Chairman:* Thank you very much. What aspects of the Common Fisheries Policy are most relevant to your interests?
Mr Morrison: The most important aspect of the CFP is the implementation of effort and stock management to ourselves and regimes to ensure conservation and sustainable harvesting of commercial fish stocks that should be managed within safe biological limits. Of course, part and parcel of all of that is good control. You see all of the headlines in the papers about fish stocks declining and over-fishing, illegal fishing, et cetera, and the first point of contact on matters like that would be the retailers or the major brand owners. Interestingly, in these days when many of the companies are owned by venture capitalist and banks, it is very often the investors coming on the phone asking, "What is the state of stocks? Are they in a perilous condition and what does this mean for our companies?" Not only do we have the consumer concerns but we have the financial investor concerns as well. It is sustainability and making sure that the fish is legal.

Q369 *Chairman:* Pressure from your venture capitalists is actually to say, "Make sure that we have sustainability of stocks"?
Mr Morrison: Absolutely, sustainability, making sure it is legal, and is the fish here tomorrow as well. A company like Young's, or any of our major companies, has got a long-term investment in seafood and we need to make sure that it is here for tomorrow as well as today, which is why we put so much effort into trying to promote sustainability and legal catch.

Q370 *Chairman:* What is your judgment on where we are in terms of controlling illegal landings?
Mr Morrison: I think it has got very, very much better. I know that the first-time buyers and sellers controls should have come in in 1992, the Directive, and as the UK we did not bring them in until 2005. At the time we were heavily in favour of bringing them in as quickly as possible even though a number of interests wanted to put it back. There were all sorts of things being said, such as "It'll be the death of the

industry", et cetera, but now everybody is saying what a great success it has been. Prices have gone up as well. There is less fish being landed, but the fish that is being landed is getting a much better return. I think everybody now feels much more confident. I think that the UK is pretty okay now. Not all Member States have yet put this legislation in place. Some have, Germany and the Netherlands, where it has been in operation for some time, but not all others have put it in place or are policing it as effectively as we are now.

Q371 Chairman: Would you care to identify them?
Mr Morrison: It is probably to best not.

Q372 Viscount Ullswater: In some of the figures that you gave us, I think you said that only 32% of the processed fish came from the EU and about 68% was imported, therefore the catching and the processing are interlinked to that extent. Is the volume of processing increasing and where will the increase in volume come from? Will it come from imported fish or more aquaculture, or do you see the EU catch increasing? Perhaps you could help us with employment numbers and that sort of thing as well.
Mr Morrison: Okay. I can go into some detail on that as well. If I read what I have here and if you want to put specific questions I can come back. An interesting general statement that can be made is that we export what the UK fleet catches, and perhaps this is not always understood, and we import what we eat. For example, 90% of all the mackerel and the herring that we land goes eastwards as far as Japan and much of the whitefish that is landed in the north-east of Scotland, for example, you can see in the Madrid market. I was at the Madrid Seafood Market last year and it was like being in Scotland. So much of the product is exported and certainly an awful lot of the shellfish from the South Coast goes straight into vehicles and is exported to France and Spain. I mention the Nephrops as well. Even though Nephrops is the major species for us as processors in the UK, we only process about a third of it and the rest goes to the Continent, to France, Spain and Italy. It either goes fresh or frozen or as vivier—live—shipped straight down to Spain in particular. That is why I was saying earlier that when holidaymakers go to the Mediterranean they eat the nephrops and they think it is great, but it was landed in Scotland or Ireland. It is perverse, really.

Q373 Viscount Ullswater: Can you just go into the economics of that? I am not quite sure how I understand the economics of it. You must be able to import fish cheaper than it is landed in Peterhead.
Mr Morrison: Yes, but one of the issues that we have—and we had a lot of debate about this in Brussels at ACFA and with DG Fish a few years

ago—was that they were saying, "Everything we're doing with respect to cod, and the price is going down. Why is this?" Nobody could understand it. The answer, effectively, is that there is not enough cod landed now—it started in the UK or in northern ports—to make it worth our while to process it economically. It is small volumes and it is landed on a regular basis. This has changed massively. When I first started in the industry, we had block producers. You are aware that fish fingers are cut from fish blocks by highly specialised, mechanical processes. You therefore have to make a fish block that weighs something like $7\frac{1}{2}$ kg. It is made by layering the fillets in a frame; that is plate-frozen under pressure so that you get a very regular block; and then you can cut it. Virtually all of the cod that went into the processing industry used to be made into blocks. There were several block production facilities in Hull, Grimsby and also across Scotland. There were lots in Norway, lots in Denmark in particular, and in Germany. All those have now gone because there is not the cod available, landed locally, to be able to use. The last one in the UK I think went three years ago. I was doing a study with the Food Standards Agency, looking at fish content of fish—analytical methods—and we started off in one factory, which went bankrupt. We had to move to another and another, and the last one that went bankrupt was the last one; so we could never finish the study. It was terrible! The only block production company left now is in Poland. I think that there are just two in Poland, and the rest have gone. It has all gone to China. I have completely gone away from my script now, but never mind.
Chairman: It is absolutely fascinating!

Q374 Baroness Jones of Whitchurch: Is China using cod? Is China doing blocks of cod or different sorts of fish?
Mr Morrison: There was never that much cod actually landed from the North Sea that went into processing. There was an awful lot from the Baltic, because the Baltic at one time was a huge fishery at 350,000 tonnes; but that has gone down dramatically over the years, just as the North Sea has, and the Baltic was a major source of cod for cod blocks. What has happened with the fish that is left is, because there is not enough for us and it was not worth our while buying it, the Scottish Government and Defra had strategy meetings and a whole programme to look at how we could best utilise UK fish. Our position was, "There is not the volume here. We can't buy it to go into bulk processing as we used to do. What we should do as an industry is land high-quality product at a lower volume, move that into niche markets and let us market it. If we want to put it into the chill chain, into the retail chain, and there is sufficient of, say, Scottish cod or whatever, if you can supply it on

a regular basis we can develop a specific line for a specific retailer and market it that way".

Q375 Chairman: Is that happening?
Mr Morrison: That happens, yes. Certainly the attitude of the UK catchers has changed dramatically. It is now all about, "Yes, let's maximise the value that we can get from our product"; but, of course, it is not good for secondary processors, who need the volume.

Q376 Chairman: Could I follow this up a little? When I had any contact with the industry at all, which is over ten years ago now, one of the problems seemed to be that there was very little dialogue between the catchers and the processors.
Mr Morrison: It has changed dramatically. We work hard on that, from both sides.

Q377 Chairman: The catchers were going out and their emphasis was on quantity, and the processors were saying, "It's all right having that, but the quality is so poor that we don't want it".
Mr Morrison: Exactly. That has changed dramatically.

Q378 Chairman: That is very important.
Mr Morrison: Of course, we do not take much of it now, as I say, because there is not the volume there; but they recognise the need for quality. Seafood Scotland plays an important part in that and Seafood Cornwall also plays an important part. Seafood Cornwall has developed this Cornish mackerel and they are also working very closely with retailers to develop markets for their pelagic fish. Yes, it is a massive change. I never thought that I would see it, but it is very encouraging.

Q379 Baroness Sharp of Guildford: Does that also mean that all the fish fingers we have in Britain today come from China?
Mr Morrison: Yes, indirectly.
Baroness Jones of Whitchurch: People do not eat fish fingers any more, do they?
Baroness Sharp of Guildford: No. Now that my kids have grown up, I do not!

Q380 Viscount Brookeborough: As wages rise in eastern Europe, will the Polish blockers have a problem too?
Mr Morrison: Probably, yes. At one time everything was moving east into Poland, but now the bulk of it has gone further.

Q381 Viscount Brookeborough: So Mr Bird's Eye is going further and further away with his fish finger manufacture?
Mr Morrison: Yes.

Q382 Viscount Ullswater: Is the volume of fish processing in this country going up or down?
Mr Morrison: Obviously primary fish has gone right down. Secondary volumes are going up. We went through a period where there was a slight decline in the proportion of frozen fish products but, to counteract that, chill fish products have captured a huge part of the market. Consumers now recognise the nutritional value of fish and they recognise the quality of chill products. That sector of the market has therefore seen a huge growth. I do not have the figures with me but if you wanted that kind of information, I could provide it to the Committee.

Q383 Lord Palmer: Could I ask a question for clarification? When you talk about "secondary", do you mean readymade meals, such as fish pie or whatever?
Mr Morrison: Yes. The primary processing is essentially taking the fish, creating fillets out of it and selling that as a basic product. The secondary processing, at its most basic level, would be to take that fillet and to produce portion-controlled pieces out of it—loins or tail pieces—which could be sold into the chill market, nicely packaged. That is how the consumer wants it these days. They do not want anything to do with preparation. We can command a very good price for that, providing the quality is there as well, of course. That would be secondary processing, but at its most basic level. Most of seafood production now is added value products, such as the fish fingers—again at their most basic—crispy coated products, battered products, or the fish pies. The biggest single meal in the UK is the fisherman's pie. It outstrips any of the meat products or any of the vegetable products.

Q384 Chairman: Tell us where it is coming from. Where is the fisherman's pie coming from?
Mr Morrison: That is produced by Young's, by Foodvest.

Q385 Chairman: And the fish that goes into the fisherman's pie is coming from . . . ?
Mr Morrison: There are two sources of the fish. One is cod, which would come from blocks that would be diced. This is whole fillet blocks. Essentially, those blocks would be from the Barents Sea or Icelandic cod. People become very concerned about the amount of cod that is available, but there is 800,000 tonnes of cod up in those northern waters. It is a local problem that we have; it is an EU problem that we have in terms of cod. There is a lot in the north. That cod would be frozen as what is called "H and G"—headed and gutted. These days, it tends to be frozen on board vessels; it is palletised and then that fish would be delivered into, say, Rotterdam, as a major exporting port. It would then go on to a container

ship. It would go to the processing factories in China, where it would be processed. It would then come back as blocks or it could come back as fillet portions, but not as finished products. As you will be aware—and I will just concentrate on cod for the moment—most of our cod comes from Norway, Barents Sea, Iceland, and they used to make blocks out of it: cheap and cheerful blocks. They would do that by mechanical means; so the fish would go through what is known as a Baader filleting machine. The whole fish would first of all be gutted; it would then go on to a machine and two blades come along and cut the fillets off; then those fillets would be trimmed up by hand. As you are probably aware, there are pin bones down the centre of a fillet. What they would then do for speed is what is called a "V-cut". When I first joined the industry a V-cut would be 14% of the fillet. As the price of fish has gone up and availability has gone down, then they cut very much less out. That prime fillet that is now cut out as V-cut goes for mincing and bone extraction; so you end up with a fillet which maybe goes into a block and mince that goes into a block. You have the two: a mince block and a fillet block. The yield on that? 35%, something of that sort. However, if you take that same fish, headed and gutted, and send it to China, the Chinese are able to cut that fish manually—as we used to do many years ago. They do it slowly and they produce no mince at all, because they cut a very fine line down where the pin bones are; they extract those pin bones; they close the fillet up so that you no longer know that it has been cut; there is no mince, which of course has a low value; and their actual yield can be 10% higher than we can get here.

Q386 Chairman: The attraction of China is obviously partly the low costs, therefore, but it is also increased yield.

Mr Morrison: Yes, and because to put the fish through these mechanical Baaders it has to be fully defrosted; but the Chinese will handle it from almost frozen, just slightly defrosted. You end up with a consistently better quality, a better colour and this massive yield improvement. There is a huge advantage. I know that there are a lot of questions about food miles, but there is this plus-10% of yield and that is a natural 10%, not 10% of the yield. There is a lot of misunderstanding about bulk shipments, but these modern vessels are very efficient. About 18 months ago the first of the large container vessels came on-stream for handling frozen containerised fish, and other containers obviously—14,000 container units. That is the kind of single unit you see on the back of a vehicle—about 20 tonnes. They can handle 14,000 containers. This was a great revolution. I was in Felixstowe last October or thereabouts. I asked, "Have you had this new vessel in often?" and they said, "There are three of them

now". We have therefore gone from one at the beginning of last year to three, and they just keep growing in numbers. The UK Fisheries Director, Rodney Anderson, and one of his colleagues were going to China to discuss some projects, I am not sure what, in Beijing last year. Since we talk a lot about this—and when Rodney first came into the industry four years ago or so, Stephen and I took him all round the processing industry in the UK and into Scotland, with David Wilson who was then the Scottish Government director—I suggested to him, "This will be an opportunity for you to see exactly what happens in China". I was not the least bit concerned about taking him, because the factories over there are absolutely state of the art. They are all new. All of the operatives are extremely well cared for. Most of them tend to be migrant workers from the north of China. They have extremely good facilities and dormitories. I therefore had no qualms at all about taking him. He never actually said, but I think it was a complete eye-opener; I think he changed his mind totally on what he saw. The difference between there and here is that if we say, "We want this in the factory. You will do this, that or the other", they will do it to the letter. That is very good.

Q387 Viscount Brookeborough: You have partly answered my question, but when we did a previous inquiry into fishing we were told that the freshest fish you could have on your plate was that which was frozen quickest from catching, and that actually fish that may have been brought some distance that was not frozen was not necessarily as fresh as you thought. First, you seem to be saying that the consumer actually disregards that and likes chilled fish rather than frozen necessarily. The second thing is to do with the Chinese factories. I was rather worried that frozen fish was going all the way to China, then being defrosted, then cut up, then filleted, then chilled and then frozen again. I was always told that you must never defrost and re-freeze fish without doing something to it in between, like cooking it.

Mr Morrison: It is interesting that retailers now, when they sell chill products, do say that you can freeze it. One of the differences, of course, is that modern domestic freezers freeze quickly. The issue with freezing fish is that if you freeze it slowly you destroy the structure. Then, when it is defrosted, you get all the liquor moving away just as drip; so you end up with a rather dry product. In the industry, however, we have produced double-frozen blocks for many years now; because if you are catching at sea and it is H and G—headed and gutted and frozen—it comes back and has to be defrosted to make the blocks, and we have always done that.

Q388 *Viscount Brookeborough:* Then it is re-frozen again?

Mr Morrison: Re-frozen, yes. There used to be an exception to that, where there were fresh boats landing after a six-day trip, and it is okay to process that as fresh. That is known as a single-frozen block. The single-frozen block always used to be a higher quality, because it had better texture, than the double-frozen block. Certainly, with the way these Chinese are producing product in air-conditioned factories, you would be hard-pressed to tell the difference now.

Q389 *Viscount Brookeborough:* A home freezer would not do that properly?

Mr Morrison: No, because it is freezing too slowly.

Q390 *Viscount Brookeborough:* Because this is blast-freezing.

Mr Morrison: Fresh products—yes, if you can get fish that is up to eight days old, then it is extremely good quality.

Q391 *Lord Palmer:* What roughly would the timescale be from a piece of cod leaving the North Sea to returning to a supermarket shelf in this country?

Mr Morrison: Typically, a chill product would have a five-day shelf life. The fish could be five or six days old; so 11 or 12 days, perhaps—something of that sort.

Q392 *Earl of Arran:* As regards the legality of harvesting the supply chain, or illegality, in your opinion what effect will this new proposed EU regulation, under what I think is called IUU, have on the industry? Will it be effective? Will it have teeth or is it just a bland statement, in your opinion?

Mr Morrison: It should be very effective. As both FDF and as AIPCE we have supported the whole concept from the very beginning when it was first proposed. We have contributed through consultation right from the beginning and we have been very, very positive; but we are now having concerns. The particular section of the IUU regulation is Article 15, specifically 15.2, which requires the fish to be certified as legal. That is okay in itself, but the actual process that is being described is that, at every point in the movement of that fish, you have to have a paper document confirming that it is the fish that was originally certified, right through the whole chain, right to us and onwards. Taking the simplest case, without all of the other requirements—and I have mentioned tuna already—a number of our members buy tuna from the Indian Ocean. That tuna is flown into Heathrow on a weekly basis and more regularly, and then it goes to their factories for processing. It comes as tuna loins. A typical consignment could be

50 tuna loins, originating from 50 fish. I had not realised, until we had a discussion in Brussels with a supplier last week, that they could come from 50 vessels, because it is literally almost one vessel, one fish landed. We will therefore need 50 certificates, but the origin of the vessels could be from Sri Lanka, from India, from Indonesia, or Thailand even. If those vessels are landing into Sri Lanka, say, how will the flag state give a meaningful certificate to say that that fish was caught legally? I therefore have a question mark over the certificate as it will be presented. The logistics of bringing those 50 certificates together on one plane and then keeping track of this paper certificate all the way through will be a nightmare. Of course, if you read the legislation it says that if there is any doubt they can hold product for 14 days—so it might be a bit complicated! If you take the example of product going to China—and I have mentioned the size of these containers—what we would have would be frozen fish from a whole series of vessels, brought together at a port, a border inspection port maybe in the Netherlands, and we would need certificates for every one of those batches from each of the trawlers. If it is the Netherlands, the Dutch authorities will communicate with the Russians. This system is beginning to work quite well under NEAFC Port State Controls—the North-East Atlantic Fisheries—RFMO, Regional Fisheries Management Organisation. This part would work quite well. The Dutch would confirm that that trawler was allowed to catch that fish and that it still had quota. You therefore get a certificate there. However, the way the system is proposed to work is that it has to be a paper system. The chap in charge in Brussels said that he did not trust electronic systems because they could be manipulated, but I am sure that paper can be manipulated too!

Q393 *Chairman:* Just put a couple of noughts on!

Mr Morrison: We have this certificate, therefore, and we could have a whole series of certificates going into containers going to China; but when the fish is landed it will have to go into a cold store to begin with, until they can assemble all of the product; so you will need a traceability signature to say that it went in, that the same volume came out and it has not changed. It then goes on the vessel; it goes to China. That fish could go to three different companies, say—this is just me making it up, but it could easily happen—and so the Chinese authorities are going to have to look at those certificates and say, "Yes, this fish has come in". They are then going to have to trace and sign off at each point where this has gone. If it goes to three factories, the fish will be in different size grades; so what we could find is that if Young's or Birds Eye want a specific portion size, they will have to take from several consignments. We then need traceability, linking the certificates from the several consignments together, to make up an order; then the Chinese have to countersign that again. It then comes all the way back, and there will be quite a number of batches in the containers coming back. We will have a great wodge of paper. The EU is serious about doing this; we are serious about wanting it; Defra is very serious about wanting it; but we see the whole thing collapsing under a great wodge of paper. As AIPCE, we have therefore been saying, "This is over-complicated". We went to see the Director General, Mr Fotiadis, with his people and they were adamant that they wanted to stick to this system. If you look at what was introduced under the health regulations, you have certified vessels, a certified chain, and certified factories; all of these factories in China have been inspected. Our proposal, therefore, is to link the health process that we have in place with this certification—this system that they want. We do not have all the paper coming back; that is all kept to the factories and it is there for inspection if DG Sanco, the veterinary inspectors, want to look at it. Then they can do a complete paper chase. We can do the same. I do not see why DG Fish, or DG Mare as they are now called, want to introduce such a complex system. Why do they not try to merge the two? When we suggested this, they said "Oh, well, that's DG Sanco and we're DG Fish". This is absolutely crazy!

Chairman: We will be asking that question when we see them.

Q394 Earl of Arran: Is the illegality such that it requires this kind of offensive?

Mr Morrison: The Commonwealth Office is looking at a new fisheries initiative and, last night, we attended; and the DfID minister, the Defra minister and Elliot Morley were there doing presentations. Somebody in the audience said, "You shouldn't be looking at the illegal fishing that is going on". That was originally estimated by MRAG here, on behalf of Defra, as worth £9 billion worldwide, but they are now saying that it is something between £10 and £22 billion, so it is a huge problem. Somebody asked a question of the ministers last night, suggesting that it is the processors who are in league with the fishers to launder this illegal fish. It is quite likely that some companies are; but, overall, I do not think that our UK or most of the European companies are looking at this, because it is international crime. There will be examples, but my concern—and this is what we said in the original consultations—is let us target the known fisheries and let us put in legislation to target those, on a risk-based approach. That was totally dismissed by DG Fish. They said, "No, we've got to have blanket legislation and a blanket approach. Otherwise, this fish will be laundered through". That seems wrong to us; but they are now talking about maybe, when this blanket legislation comes in, targeting vessels without nationality or what they

would call "rogue flag states"—which is fine, but they could do that without having such a draconian approach. We have had discussions with Defra, and certainly minister Shaw last night said that he would prefer an approach of preferred economic operators and go for a risk-based approach. He is clearly thinking in the same way that we are. I wrote to the minister recently on behalf of our members and I heard from one of his staff last night that he is going to respond sympathetically. We want the legislation. I would hope that we can have a practical working solution.

Chairman: Let us go to Lord Plumb on the assessment process. This is a Young's-phrased question.

Q395 Lord Plumb: I assumed that the "Ten Principles" that are set out in the statement would be approved by all, but then I started to have doubts when you were answering the last point on whether all would respond to the ten points that are set out there. Under the "objective assessment", there is reference to the fact that the status of aquatic eco-systems is dynamic but that it is often poorly understood. We have been taking evidence from the scientists and this seems to be a major problem between the scientific evidence that is taken and the fishermen themselves, who are at the surface collecting the fish. How do you see this? Is there a sufficient response to take account of the evolving scientific assessment of the different fisheries?

Mr Morrison: You will be aware that ICES say that we should have zero catch, and politically that would not be possible in a number of instances; so Young's now do not take cod from the North Sea. In the Baltic we have had this huge problem of known IUU cod, that is estimated at 40% of the catch. There has therefore been a huge debate, not only by Young's but by other major companies, as to whether they should stay in the Baltic or whether they should pull away totally from an EU fishery—which is making a huge statement. Young's have therefore worked very hard and have talked with ICES on the issues about management control in the Baltic, and they have also addressed the Baltic and the North Sea RACs and have tried to persuade them to be more effective in reducing the level of IUU. As AIPCE we have an annual general assembly, which last year was in October and, coincidentally, it was in Poland. This was at a time when the Polish elections were going on and there was this 40% of over-catch. The European fisheries associations were also complaining through ACFA that DG Fish was not taking effective action on this over-catch. Our organisation was going to Poland and we decided that we must address this issue directly with the Polish processors. We were expecting reluctance; instead of that, they were with us and saying, "This is terrible, because we cannot sell our processed fish into major processors in Europe. They don't want it, because they are concerned about the level of over-fishing". We ended up from a position of expecting a problem to producing a joint statement with the Polish processors—not fishers, although some of them are linked directly with the catching sector through an integrated business system. We actually produced a statement condemning the over-fishing and condemning the Polish Government for not being effective, which I thought was a great success. It is now coming down. When you have a situation like that where the major companies, Foodvest included—and one big company actually pulled out totally—will make the necessary arrangements to withdraw from a fishery, and to do that with an EU fishery, is terrible really. However, looking wider, globally, Young's have developed a system, which I suppose is a little bit like the MSC system, where you look at the stock sustainability; you look at the eco-effects of fishing; you look at the management controls; and you make a decision from there. They do it on a risk-based assessment. They do not do traffic lights, but another way would be the red, amber and green. If it is green then it is okay—and any fishery that is MSC they would say is green. They would therefore say, "Yes, we can go there". If it is red, because it is over-fished or the stocks are in a state of collapse, then they would say, "No, we can't go there". If it is amber, then there would be a decision made as to whether to take from that fishery, or whether to take from it and try to exert political pressure to improve its status. How do they do this? They have employed fishery experts on a consultancy basis; they go and discuss fishery management with ICES on a regular basis several times a year; they do the same with other scientific experts; and they will also speak to the trade associations in the relevant countries. From all the data that they collect, they then decide whether they are going to take from those fisheries. That is how it is done. It is based on science. It is also particularly important for data-deficient fisheries. It has meant that they have pulled out from a number of fisheries. I know that others of our members—Birds Eye, for instance—have adopted a similar system. It was certainly in place in the Unilever days of Birds Eye and their more global approach. I know that it is in McDonald's; I know that Iceland have a similar kind of system. The difference is that Young's have decided to come upfront and they have to stand by it, whereas others do not have to make such a deliberate statement. However, all of the companies do work towards this kind of approach and, as I say, part of the reason has been that there has been this big divide between science and politics. That is the basis of it, therefore.

Q396 *Chairman:* It is very good that the responsible processors are behaving like this but, at the end of the day, the real test is do the stocks improve as a result

of your coming out or do other, let us say, less—I am trying to seek a word—less responsible processors move in and say, "We can make a killing now because our rivals have quit"?
Mr Morrison: This will be a concern for the Baltic, for instance, because there is easy access right across Europe. It is therefore essential that we have effective management control to stop IUU. It is always a concern. Of course, if they come out of a fishery— which is why companies will not come out quickly from even something like the Baltic: they would prefer to get it right—if they do come out and that fish then goes into the market by other means, it will be there at a cheaper price, which means that they have created an non-level playing field. It is a very difficult balance, and I know that companies have considered that in some depth in the past. I know that when Unilever, prior to Birds Eye, was in existence in a fishery business capacity they fought long and hard about Alaska pollock from eastern Russia, where they thought it was probably better to be staying in that fishery and trying to influence it rather than just pulling away. That is the second-biggest fishery in the world. The Alaska pollock fishery in the US is now MSC-certified, and so that is the main supply route for Alaska pollock—which, next to cod, is the biggest whitefish fishery that we have for processed products. However, Russia, by continuing to be influenced, is now looking at MSC certification as well. They are sorting out the IUU problems that they have and they have recently gone through pre-assessment. We could therefore see that second-biggest fishery being very well managed in the future. There is also a good argument to stay in the fishery, therefore, and to try to influence it.
Chairman: Let us move on to discards.

Q397 *Viscount Brookeborough:* Just on the last subject for one second, on the traffic-lighting of sustainable imported fish and Sainsbury's saying "red", meaning that there were major concerns— "We will not sell it"—are any western European processors selling it, or is that a statement that everybody abides by?
Mr Morrison: I suspect that some would, yes. If Sainsbury's say no, then, as we were saying, that would have a huge influence in trying to manage it more effectively.

Q398 *Viscount Brookeborough:* Young's have a very clear policy on discards. In the first paragraph of their submission to us, they believe that there should be a complete ban. Without a doubt, every sane person would agree that there should be no discarding, but is it practical and what is the FDF opinion on it being something which can be put into practice?
Mr Morrison: This is a difficult one.

Q399 Viscount Brookeborough: It is an aspiration. It is a lovely aspiration.

Mr Morrison: In fact, that is what I have written here. I have put, "The Foodvest policy statement on discards is aspirational". It is designed to establish a point of principle that discarding is fundamentally bad and, coincidentally, was introduced at a time when Commissioner Borg was also making the same kind of statement. I discussed it with Foodvest and they said, "If we don't make that kind of statement, we will all be down in the quagmire all of the time, trying to work our way through it. We would like to rise above that. Let's make a clear statement". I think that is a good approach. As FDF, with all our membership, we have actively engaged; we have responded on the consultations; we are backing reduced discards and backing technical measures to reduce discards wherever we can. That would be our position, therefore. I think that what they have done in north-east Scotland in terms of their credit system, of not fishing in areas where there is juvenile fish et cetera, is very creditable. We would very much favour actions like that. We would also support any efforts to reduce discards. However, it is difficult in a mixed fishery. There is another problem that I have, and this is a personal view. If we bring all of the discards back and we try to create markets for them, are we creating a future problem for ourselves? Many years ago when I used to work with United Biscuits we had crumb, and we created biscuit for the crumb. That then became bigger than we could get crumb for. Could something similar happen if we started to land all this discard fish? It is therefore much better to stop catching it—which I think is where the EU wants to be. They do not want to land it: they want to prevent it being caught in the first place. I think that is where we should be.

Q400 Viscount Brookeborough: On that score, I understand that with line-caught cod and haddock you do get far less of a discard problem.

Mr Morrison: Yes.

Q401 Viscount Brookeborough: I was unaware that so much line-caught haddock were available. First of all, where are they available from? Secondly, if it comes from further away, that will be much more expensive. How on earth do they compete, if they have 100% of this expensive, line-caught haddock?

Mr Morrison: You can catch large volumes of fish with line—

Q402 Viscount Brookeborough: But where are these fish caught?

Mr Morrison: Iceland produce an awful lot of line-caught fish; Norway also produce a lot of line-caught fish, as does Russia.

Q403 Viscount Brookeborough: Why do we not, when we are so close to Norway? In fact, our fisheries actually merge on each other. Why do we not in Scotland?

Mr Morrison: There is a difference. In the North Sea we have mixed fisheries, and so it is quite different to large sections of the Barents Sea or the Norwegian Sea or Iceland, where they tend to be single-species fisheries. It really is quite different between the North Sea and only a few hundred miles further north. That is not often appreciated. These longlines go for miles. It is quite extraordinary to see them being baited up and run off the back of the vessels. It is a volume process, therefore.

Q404 Viscount Brookeborough: It is not that much more expensive therefore?

Mr Morrison: It is more expensive. I do not know to what extent it is more expensive. I can find that out if you want me to put a written submission in to you.

Q405 Viscount Ullswater: On discards, in developing the niche market approach for the landed fish, say, from the UK—and obviously the quality and the size of fish are very important in that—are you encouraging a form of high-grading, which would then end up with discarding?

Mr Morrison: I would hope not. I know that high-grading used to go on but, if that were ever suspected, I think that we would try to take action to stop it. High-grading is appalling really, particularly with cod. As a slight aside, a number of years ago I was on a Norwegian fishing vessel and I needed to get off and to go back, because they were out for longer than I was anticipating. They were boarded by the inspection service. They did all the net checks and things. I therefore hitched a ride back with them and, on the way back, we would follow vessels just over the horizon and follow in their wake. They were looking for discards. If it was evident that a vessel was discarding, they would come up very fast and try and take action. I was very impressed with that approach by the Norwegians.

Lord Palmer: We have something in common, in that I used to make biscuits as well, albeit for the opposition—United Biscuits.

Chairman: Notice the name!

Q406 Lord Palmer: In your opening remarks you mentioned that a lot of your members pack for the retailers. Do you mean own-brand by that?

Mr Morrison: Yes.

Q407 Lord Palmer: Own-brand, particularly in the frozen fish market, is presumably tiny, is it not?

Mr Morrison: No.

Q408 *Lord Palmer:* It is not?

Mr Morrison: No. I guess it will be at least 30 or 40%.

Q409 *Lord Palmer:* My main question, though—and you did touch on this when answering My Lord Chairman's supplementary—is what level of engagement is there now between the processors, retailers and the actual catch sector? You alluded to the fact that it is very much better than it used to be.

Mr Morrison: Looking first at the EU level, ACFA, the advisory committee, has representation of all stakeholders, including the NGOs, the banks, all sectors of the fishing industry, the process workers and also AIPCE. We therefore have regular contact with all of our European counterparts through ACFA. We also need to get together outside of normal sessions. For instance, with the IUU regulations that we have just been talking about, we will get together to produce position statements; so we are working together from that point of view. If you look at the RACs where the fishermen are the principal people involved, there are also other stakeholders there, including ourselves; so there is regular contact with the fisher people from that perspective. Over the last four years we have had an initiative in the Clyde, where all stakeholders have been working to look at responsible fishing in the Clyde with three fishermen's organisations from Northern Ireland, the trawlers and the potters, WWF and the Scottish environmental group—I forget what they are called—the equivalent of Natural England.

Q410 *Chairman:* Scottish Natural Heritage.

Mr Morrison: Yes. We therefore have a wide stakeholder group there and we develop responsible fishing initiatives. That cross-fertilisation has been very good. It is now leading to MSC certification of the nephrops fishery and looking at discards and all sorts of issues. We have therefore been working on that. In turn, that has led to other fisheries looking at MSC certification. In north-east Scotland our members are helping to fund the Scottish fishermen in terms of the haddock and the nephrops fisheries. I mentioned Seafood Scotland and also Seafood Cornwall. There are these very good working relationships. Another area that has developed well, through Seafish initially, is something called the Common Language Group, where we wanted to understand each other's concerns. That has proved incredibly successful, and we have Defra and DfID on that as well. They are coming from a completely different perspective when they are in our meetings, as opposed to us being in theirs. We also have the NGOs and the fishers. You will be aware of all the issues on skates and rays last year or the year before. That group came together and devised a policy. We have therefore been working together hugely in those areas. Young's/Foodvest helped to fund the Fisheries Science Partnership with the fishermen in the North Sea. I recently went to Murmansk with WWF to talk to the fishermen's associations there about MSC and our responsible fishing initiatives through AIPCE, which I have not actually mentioned yet. Yes, there is very good interaction now. I have mentioned Seafish as well. The Seafish committees have all the stakeholders on them. It has changed so much.

Chairman: Regional Advisory Councils—we were particularly interested in Regional Advisory Councils. Earl of Dundee?

Q411 *Earl of Dundee:* How useful do you find them to be?

Mr Morrison: We were not sure when they first started. The way that we have access to the RACs is via AIPCE, via our European association; so we are allowed to be on all the committees via that route. We attend the North West RAC, as we are the official AIPCE representative on the North West Waters RAC. Our Dutch counterparts are on the North Sea; our Danish counterparts are on the Baltic; and I think the Spanish are on the Distant Waters—which you would naturally expect. Our view is that, from a dubious start, we believe they are now becoming very effective. They are able, on a regional basis, to look at the issues affecting them by bringing in scientists and study.

Q412 *Earl of Dundee:* What have they achieved, though? What has happened which is worthwhile, through them?

Mr Morrison: It is early days, is it not? In the North Sea, I have mentioned these credit systems, and a lot of that has gone through the RACs. All of those initiatives have therefore come about via that North Sea RAC. I have mentioned all these issues in the Baltic on over-fishing. Certainly the RACs are taking steps towards trying to curb that as well. They are doing extra science, looking at the difference in stocks between the eastern and the western cod stocks there. We are therefore getting far more scientific data than we ever used to. In the North West RAC we have also been looking at introducing observer schemes and getting agreement on those. That is why I said that it is early days. There was always this question about how they were going to be financed longer-term, but that has now been resolved. Our view is that they will become evermore important and we very much welcome the whole concept of managing fisheries on a regional basis. This, of course, has been the problem with DG Fish up until now. However, the restructuring of DG Fish and Maritime Affairs to DG Mare, where other divisions are also being created—that, working in conjunction with the RACs, I think will be very effective in the years to come.

Q413 Chairman: Can we push you? Where do you see them developing? Not geographically, but how far can they develop in terms of managing?

Mr Morrison: I do not actually sit on them, but I believe that they can become self-sufficient—and this may again be aspirational—in their regions, and do the management, the stock assessment, and also quota management. I would like to think that that would be the ultimate goal.

Q414 Lord Plumb: When we took evidence from the RACs last week, they said that they worked under the guidance of a Commission. I thought that was the wrong way round.

Mr Morrison: Of course, the Commission have been dictatorial over the years. There has been huge frustration in the regions, because they have said, "You don't know what you're talking about". Bear in mind here that I am a processor; I am not a fisherman. I think that this has now been recognised by Brussels. As I say, the very fact that they are now following a similar regionalisation approach within the new DG Mare is testament to that—which is why I have confidence that, going forward, they will manage their own affairs.

Q415 Lord Palmer: Albeit with very limited resources. We were all amazed at how they managed on the budget that they had.

Mr Morrison: Yes, but we pay fees and do not always claim our expenses as well, which might help.

Q416 Baroness Sharp of Guildford: This was another Young's question, but can we pose it more generally and ask what scope do you see for the development and application of new technologies? And could you give us some examples?

Mr Morrison: The initial intent behind the implementation of these new technologies has really been to gather data about the status of fish stocks, which comes back to what we were talking about earlier, and the traceability of our products. Amongst the halo effects that Foodvest have seen are a better understanding and developing of the structures of the fisheries and, consequently, we have seen improved handling of fish on board the vessels that we buy from. In almost every circumstance we have seen either an improvement in the quality, resulting in better returns to the catchers and hence consumer offerings, or a reduction in waste, which has benefited the resource and cost. It is difficult for Foodvest to influence what happens at sea, because they do not own fishing vessels, but we have taken huge steps on land to improve processing and to maximise quality, quantity and the whole food chain. We have therefore taken positive steps all the way along. Some examples of the technology include work that they are currently doing on what is called the coverless

trawl trials in the nephrops fisheries in the west of Scotland. The concept behind this coverless trawl that Young's/Foodvest are investing in is to reduce by-catch of whiting and of haddock, and they are doing this work in conjunction with Glasgow University—the fishing part of the university there. In the Western Isles we have developed a catch registration system, known as Young's Trace. This has been implemented not only in the west of Scotland but also in Sri Lanka. This is a data-recording system that is on vessels. None of these vessels, of course, are owned by Young's; they are all in the hands of private fishers, but there is a contract with them that we will bag their catch. As soon as the vessel goes out of port this is automatically triggered; so we know where the vessel is, how much it has caught and when it is coming back. Nobody every thought that we would be able to get this kind of system onto vessels and that the skippers would allow that information to go up into the sky and back down to a processor. It is incredible, and it has been quite a breakthrough. There is a similar system on land at quaysides, so that those vessels that do not have this system in place can record all of their data as well. I know that has resulted in an improved return for those fishers that have put that information on board, because it helps Young's to determine the best place to go for the best sizes and quality of fish, of nephrops. It has therefore been a unique experience. The systems are in place in large vessels around the world, but they are owned by the fishing vessel. I think that is a unique concept. You can actually see on the screen in certain restaurants where the fish came from.

Q417 Lord Cameron of Dillington: What is the difference in price between MSC-certified fish and non-certified fish?

Mr Morrison: The seafood industry is highly competitive; so whether you can command a price differential in the marketplace is questionable. It is difficult to say, but there are examples of fisheries where, by being MSC-certified, those fisheries get a much better return. I know that happened with the Thames herring and I know it happens with the mackerel, but they are small fisheries. This question always comes up and my argument is that you are guaranteeing a good market. You will always be able to feed into companies that are prepared to pay for an MSC product; so you are not just putting it in the market and getting the best price at the time. It is very difficult to put a value on it.

Q418 Lord Cameron of Dillington: Is the public generally aware of MSC certification and could it be made more aware? Let me ask this. Could it be made more aware and therefore does it work? Could you get more help from the EU, for instance? Let us face it, if all the fish sold was MSC-certified it would considerably help the Common Fisheries Policy and what they are trying to achieve by another means: by consumer preference. Is the public aware? That is probably the first question.

Mr Morrison: Yes, and it is a bit like chicken-and-egg. You have to build up sufficient certified fisheries before you can go ahead and effectively promote. It is getting there in the first place.

Q419 *Baroness Sharp of Guildford:* I take it that the registration scheme that you were talking about actually feeds into this, does it?

Mr Morrison: It will do, yes. The fishery up in north-west Scotland, Young's are paying for that to be certified at this time—in the Hebrides area. I mentioned the Clyde, which Young's have helped to finance but we have had money from the Scottish Government and FIFG to do that. I know that certification scheme will help with the MSC certification and certainly chain of custody: there is no doubt about that. Overall, I think 7 or 8% of the world's fisheries are MSC-certified at this time. That is beginning to increase quite rapidly now and there are an awful lot of fisheries in the certification loop at this moment. I can see that growing quite significantly. As we get more companies involved, I can certainly see that there will be greater demand and the public awareness will also go up. However, I do know that MSC are looking at a new initiative to promote the MSC certification label and awareness of it.

Q420 *Lord Cameron of Dillington:* Are DG Fish/Mare interested? If they really support it and put some money behind it, it would alleviate them more.

Mr Morrison: Yes. The work that the Americans have done up in the North West has been absolutely great. We have got the salmon certified; we have got the Alaska pollock; we have got Pacific cod, and a couple of other local species as well. There is a huge amount of fish available there. I have been a great advocate of the MSC back from 1996. I have been on various of their committees and, at the moment, I am on the technical advisory board and also chair their chain of custody group within that. However, there was a great reluctance in the European fisheries to begin with, and certainly there was massive reluctance in Scotland. Some of my fishing colleagues used to say, "How could you ever be involved in something like this?" Now they have changed totally and they are very much looking towards certification. There has therefore been a whole culture change, which is very encouraging. If we go back a little while, however, there was a lobby group of the Norway and Iceland governments who were opposed to the whole concept. They were saying, "Who are the MSC to come in and tell us how to manage our fisheries?"—

and to some extent that also applied here. The MSC, of course, are not trying to manage fisheries; what the MSC is doing is looking at the process. With any certification system you cannot actually tell a company or the fishery how to manage. If a fishery, or for that matter an ISO 9000 process that is in application, is found to be wanting, all you can do is say, "These are the areas that need attention" and then it is up to the organisation to decide whether they want to progress with it or not. Iceland and Norway talked about developing their own eco-label and then they tried to influence Brussels to develop an eco-label. I recall going to Iceland a few years ago with the then chief executive of Young's and the chief executive of Birds Eye. The fisheries minister at the time, Arni Mathieson, said "We want our own government label" and the response from my CEO was, "If you think I'm ever going to put a government label onto one of my private patch, you've got to be kidding!"—which I think was a bit of a surprise to him. However, I think that in Iceland they are still interested in developing their own label. In Norway, that position has now changed, because there are a number of certifications ongoing in Norway at this moment.

Q421 *Lord Cameron of Dillington:* In terms of the EU—bear in mind that we are an EU committee—it sounds to me as though the answer is no, they are not interested.

Mr Morrison: I am sorry, I am rambling a bit! Was it two years ago that the European Parliament accused the Commission of not moving fast enough on eco-labelling? The Commission therefore came up with three proposals for consultation. One was to do nothing on certification. The second was to develop an EU eco-label, following the Icelandic position. The third was to develop a standard to which certifying bodies would comply. As the processing industry, we went very much in favour of the latter, *i.e.* develop a standard to which others comply. The parallel to this, of course, is the organic approach, where there is an organic directive that certifiers have to comply with. This is where I would hope that the EU will eventually come to. What the Commission did do was to set up a working party to look at how to go forward, a technical group, and I was on that. It proved to be very difficult in this group, because the fisher interests on the group wanted not only to include sustainability but also the ILO—the international labour laws—as well. They wanted to include ethical aspects, which would have gone all the way into secondary processing. They said that our factories in China should also be included, and I objected totally to this. We agreed the international labour laws should be taken into account on board vessels, but I drew the line at that. They said that I was appalling, that I was terrible—which is quite interesting! However, in terms of secondary processors in China, as far as I am aware all the companies, all our members, have ethical audits—in China, Vietnam or wherever—so all of those aspects are covered. My concern about drawing these aspects into an eco-label would be that we would dilute the sustainability aspects of it. I therefore opposed that. The EU had representation at the FAO when the FAO developed their eco-labelling guidelines. My view is that we already have an established set of guidelines in place, approved by the FAO, so the EU should simply adopt those and get cracking with it. What we are now finding is that there are a number of certification bodies coming forward who are claiming to be able to certify fisheries. There is one organisation that simply does a desktop analysis and says, "Yes, that fishery is okay". If you look at that against the requirements of the FAO standard, which are very detailed and require a huge amount of research and follow-through—and the MSC is the only organisation that complies with the FAO at this time—in my opinion, the sooner the EU does something (and only on Option 3, because we would not want the other options) so that we do not get a proliferation of lower-level certifications, the better.

Q422 *Baroness Jones of Whitchurch:* My question follows on from that. You talked a bit about the industry wanting long-term sustainability, but to what extent are consumers demanding sustainability? Is it just industry-led or is there a genuine demand from consumers? I suppose that you have half-answered this. How do they know what they should buy and what they should not buy, given the different, complex messages they are getting?
Mr Morrison: It is incredibly complex. My view is that the consumer is confused about the issues. I was looking at some surveys and, in the autumn of 2007, Seafish undertook a survey quantifying consumer attitudes towards sustainability. The results of that were that 19% of the general population would look for information about sustainable seafood and then change their buying habits and behaviour; 38% were worried by the "no fish in 2048" campaign. You will probably recall that there was a scientific paper, I think it was about 18 months ago, saying that if we continued fishing the way we are there would be no fish left in 2048, and people were very concerned about that. Then 57% sought reassurance from the pack that the fish was not at risk. That is what came out of the Seafish study. Young's have recently undertaken consumer research and, in a survey of 1,100 consumers, 95% of them expressed concern about fish sustainability; 52% were saying that it was a very important issue; and 31% were claiming to have changed their eating habits over fears of fish sustainability. There is definitely a growing awareness now and that is good, because it is no longer just the corporates and it is no longer the investors: it is the consumers that are taking an interest as well.

Q423 *Baroness Jones of Whitchurch:* The only independent indication that anybody has in their shopping at the moment that something is sustainable is the Marine Stewardship Council; that is all they have.
Mr Morrison: Yes.

Q424 *Baroness Jones of Whitchurch:* Young's could write what they like on the pack but it is not independently verified, is it?
Mr Morrison: Some of what they would do would certainly be third-party certified; but I agree that that is the only way at the moment. Of course, it does come down to brand integrity as well. Consumers do have confidence particularly in the retailers and they assume, because it is a complex issue, that the retailers or the bigger brands will take this issue responsibly. I think that, if ever they found that a brand was not taking it responsibly, that is when they would take action about not buying. That would be my view on it.

Q425 *Chairman:* Thank you very much indeed. That was an aspect of the industry that was absolutely fascinating.
Mr Morrison: There was one part that I did not cover. Do you have five minutes?

Q426 *Chairman:* Yes, we will give you five minutes.
Mr Morrison: You asked about, and we went slightly away from it, how we ensured legality. I have mentioned the issues about IUU in the Barents Sea and, at the time, that was estimated to be 160,000 tonnes of IUU cod. We clearly had to do something about that. All of our members have buying policies that look for preferred suppliers; that audit the chain, et cetera. However, as AIPCE, we felt that we had to devise a common approach. We therefore developed what we called our "poachers' control document" for the Barents Sea. We brought all our key buyers together from across Europe and looked at the key aspects, to ensure that we would be able to buy responsibly and we put this into a control document. We consulted with DG Fish and with Defra on this, and also with WWF Europe, which gave it their tick—which was very good. We instituted this, not as a stand-alone but to be drawn into all of our members' purchasing systems. We also included letters of warranty. Many of the aspects that are now in the NEAFC Port State Control system that came in on 1 May last year were actually in our document. We have therefore considered that to be a huge success. Last week, at the Brussels Seafood Show,

WWF International had a gathering at which we had the Russian ministry, the Norwegian deputy fisheries minister, Mr Fotiadis, DG at DG Mare, together with our own AIPCE president, and WWF congratulated us all for the work that we had done in trying to control the Barents Sea. The estimate for last year was that the IUU cod was down to 40,000 tonnes. I believe that it is less than that, much less, but that is the Norwegian estimate. We believe that with our control document we have played a very important part. We then moved on last year and produced a control document for the Baltic Sea. Although that is for cod as well and all around this 40% IUU, the Baltic is really quite different. The Baltic is a fresh fishery; the Barents Sea is a frozen

fishery. We therefore had to produce a quite different risk-assessed document. We believe that is being successful as well. We now need to look at the other areas that we will progress with. I mentioned the tuna. As FDF, we are now in the process of developing a similar risk document for flown-in tuna. We are also working with Seafish to develop an audit protocol, to look at the whole system—again risk-based. We hope to get something out on that over this coming year. It was interesting that both the DfID and Defra ministers also mentioned this last night. This links back into the legislation that I was talking about. It is much better to do it on a fishery-by-fishery, risk-based system.

Chairman: Thank you very much again.

THURSDAY 1 MAY 2008

Present:	Arran, E	Jones of Whitchurch, B
	Brookeborough, V	Plumb, L
	Cameron of Dillington, L	Sharp of Guildford, B
	Dundee, E	Ullswater, V

Memorandum by the Marine Directorate, Scottish Government

INTRODUCTION

(i) The Scottish Government welcomes the House of Lords EU Committee Review of the Common Fisheries Policy (CFP). This response provides an overview of some of the key issues of the CFP as seen from the Scottish Government's perspective.

CONTEXT

(ii) Scotland is the major fishing nation within the UK and one of the most significant fishing nations within the EU.

— Scotland's fisheries zone comprises 60.1% (470,063 km^2) of the UK total area and represents the biggest share of EU waters (excluding overseas territories). These waters are some of the most productive fishing grounds in the world.

— 69% of key UK quotas are held by Scottish Producer Organisations.

— Scotland lands around 66% of the UK quota stocks by value, (England and Wales 28%, and Northern Ireland 6%).

(iii) The Scottish Fishing industry (sea fishing and processing sector) is the lifeblood of a large number of coastal communities. In overall terms, it accounts for 1% of Scottish GDP compared to 0.1% for the UK as a whole. Thus fishing is 10 times more important to Scotland in pure economic terms than it is to the UK.

(iv) The Scottish industry is beginning to emerge from a period of decline. Since 2001 the over 10 metre whitefish fleet has reduced by 25% with knock on impacts on fishing communities across Scotland.

(v) The Scottish industry has been at the forefront of efforts to ensure sustainable fisheries. Fishermen in Scotland use larger mesh sizes and have additional gear measures which go beyond those of their EU counterparts. Around half of all Scottish fisheries are engaged in the process of Marine Stewardship Council certification. Most recently, Scotland has implemented a ground-breaking series of Real-Time Closures (RTCs) in EU waters to protect young cod. These closures are being voluntarily adhered to by fishermen. Statutory closures are not feasible through the CFP within a timescale which would provide meaningful protection to young cod. This is an example of how the CFP fails to protect stocks, while national action backed by stakeholders can provide effective conservation.

THE CFP AND SCOTLAND

(vi) The CFP has to deal with the most complex fisheries in the world. This complexity is both technical (managing over 50 commercially significant stocks and many other minor stocks) and political (with 27 Member States involved in decision making, around a dozen of whom have an interest in commercial sea fishing).

(vii) Given this context, it is unsurprising that the CFP often fails to meet its objectives. In Scotland's case, **the CFP's disbenefits have outweighed its benefits**. Most tellingly over the course of the CFP's existence both the Scottish fishing industry and the majority of stocks have declined.

(viii) The political arrangements for the CFP leave Scotland, as a major EU fishing nation, disenfranchised. Although fisheries management is fully devolved to Scotland, EU negotiations remain a function reserved to the UK Government. In principle, landlocked countries such as Austria can have a greater influence on fishing matters than can Scotland. This situation is both nonsensical and unjust. The Scottish Government remains committed to seeking to lead for the UK on fisheries matters in Europe to help address this in the short term.

(ix) From Scotland's perspective, the CFP has often appeared a distant, centralised, unresponsive and discredited policy. It has been marked by the Commission's attempt to micro-mange every aspect of fisheries (TACs, net sizes, where to fish, catch composition, vessel power, days at sea etc) from Brussels. This approach has led to a top down, control heavy regime which has done little to win the support of individual fishermen. As a result the CFP has become increasingly complex and much harder for even well informed stakeholders to follow. The resulting mutual suspicion from fishermen and the Commission has impeded mutual respect and trust leading to a corresponding decrease in effective policy making

(x) The Commission may have recognised that this version of the CFP can no longer work and appears to be considering moves towards greater regionalisation and self management. In this context it would be for the Council of Ministers to set broad policy goals (to reduce cod mortality to a set level for example) and for Member States to decide how to achieve that: in effect a move towards a more "directive" based approach rather than a 'regulation' based approach. In this sense the Commission's decision to allow Scotland to pilot its Conservation Credits scheme is revolutionary and very welcome.

Scotland's approach to the CFP Review

(xi) **The Scottish Government does not believe that membership of the CFP serves Scotland's interests and is committed to seeking withdrawal. While working towards this it is recognised that the current constitutional set-up and UK Government policy would have to change before such a course of action became feasible. This will not prevent the Scottish Government from developing alternative models of fisheries management drawing on experience from outside the European Union.**

(xii) In December 2007 the First Minister Alex Salmond announced the Scottish Government's intention to establish an expert panel to consider and develop fisheries management models which better serve the needs of Scotland's fishermen. There are examples of fisheries management practices outwith the EU which show greater success in supporting fishing communities and protecting fish stocks. For example, the Faroese regulate fishing through effort and gear controls rather than quotas. With no minimum landing size all fish can be legally landed so discarding of non-quota or undersize fish does not occur. Iceland, on the hand, has adopted as system of Individual Transferable Quotas (ITQs). While not necessarily an appropriate system for Scottish vessels, it has increased the profitability of many of the Icelandic fishing companies.

(xiii) We will also seek ways to improve the CFP in the context of the 2012 CFP reform process. Given the substantial shortcomings of the CFP, even taking account of the 2002 reform, we will argue that the European Commission should be ambitious and radical in seeking to reshape EU fisheries policies if unwilling to abolish the CFP in its entirety.

(xiv) The remainder of this document responds to the Committee's specific questions. The Scottish Government is also aware of the response provided by Fisheries Research Services in Aberdeen, the Scottish Government's statutory scientific advisors on fisheries management, and concurs with their points.

CONSERVATION AND MANAGEMENT

Q1. *Recovery plans, management plans and emergency measures*

Recovery plans

1.1 There have been two distinct periods of EU recovery measures. The first period, from 1998, relied on increasingly restrictive catch and quota limits supported by complex technical conservation measures. By the end of 2002 it had become clear that these measures alone had not had adequate impact on the prospects of some stocks, which remained in decline. Further measures were added for 2003. These included fishing effort management ('days at sea') and improved landings controls arrangements, complemented by national decommissioning schemes in several Member States.

1.2 It has become clear that the second period of attempted recovery has been more successful than the first, although still not ideal. At the very least, for example, in the North Sea it can be demonstrated that fishing mortality rates have declined across most stocks. However, scientific assessments indicate that some stocks have not yet recovered to within safe biological limits, and that there is a risk of their not doing so without further reductions in fishing mortality rates. The Scottish Government's views on the cod recovery plan were set out in its paper of October 2007.

Management plans

1.3 We welcome the improved stability offered by long term management plans. Developing and adhering to such plans, on the basis of moderate fishing pressure, should be a priority. In doing this explicit account needs to be taken of socio-economic factors: there is little point in seeking to ensure long-term stability of stocks at commercial levels if, in the meantime, the fishing industry and communities exploiting the resource have disappeared. Greater involvement of stakeholders in the development of long term plans would help address this.

1.4 The development of management plans needs to take into account the overall health of both the stock and the industry. A weak fishing industry is not able to sign up to challenging long term plans if the projected benefit is in the distant future. As an example, both the haddock and the saithe stocks are healthy. It was possible to agree a long term management plan based on moderate fishing pressure which was acceptable to all sides. This was possible as it "locked in" current levels of effort only allowing fishing effort to increase or decrease in line with the size of the stock.

1.5 The greater stability this brings to both the stock and the industry is welcome, but it would not be possible at this stage for a stock like cod where cuts in effort (and therefore boat income) would be sharp and remain so for a number of years before the increased stock could be fished. In the interim a number of boats would undoubtedly go bankrupt. Therefore, there should be a clear distinction between recovery plans and management plans and an understanding that management plans can only be put in place once a stock is healthy.

Emergency measures

1.6 Emergency measures have been used in Scottish waters previously, for example to close the area known as the Darwin Mounds to bottom trawl fisheries to protect deep sea corals. However, the process, although speedy by EU standards, is still too time-consuming to provide real-time management of fisheries. For example, real-time closures, such as those voluntarily agreed to by Scottish fishermen, are not practicable through emergency measures.

Q2. *TACs, Effort limitation, rights based management, technical conservation*

TACs and effort limitation

2.1 We agree with the emerging consensus in support of adopting management targets based on fishing mortality rates (F), which we are easier to control, instead of biomass (SSB) targets. But TAC constraints alone are a far from perfect tool for controlling fishing, and especially fishing mortality rates in the mixed fisheries which characterise the North Sea. Unrecorded landings, grading of the catch and the prevalence of discards have all contributed to undermine the effect of quota limitations, and an over-reliance or excessive emphasis on this single management tool would be a failure to learn from our experience so far.

2.2 Instead the revised harvest control rules should be treated as a firm template for recovery, but a greater emphasis should be placed on the full suite of measures adopted and developed for the different stocks, region-by-region. This approach would enable Member States and national fleets, co-operating as necessary, to develop the solutions which they agree are most able to deliver agreed targets effectively. Agreed harvest rules should set the desired framework for sustainability but not the full prescription for delivery mechanisms.

2.3 We disagree with the continued reliance on the blunt instrument of further general cuts in effort or quota. **We believe it should be for individual Member States to draw on the full range of measures which might make a contribution to further reductions in mortality, constructing packages that are appropriately balanced to meet the specific needs of distinctive fisheries interacting with different stocks.** In appropriate places that might include further fishing gear developments, new spatial or seasonal management measures such as closed areas or further changes to fleet capacity or fishing entitlements. In devising measures we must go with the grain of behaviour on the fishing grounds, taking full account both of fishermen's expertise and their legitimate associated interests.

2.4 We endorse adoption of the approach described by the Commission as "decoupling". The starting point for decoupling fisheries is to manage all fisheries in the best possible way for themselves. This measure has already been adopted in the haddock and saithe fisheries, with agreement reached on long term management plans based on moderate fishing pressure consistent with maximum sustainable yield. A commitment has also been made to move towards managing the plaice and sole fisheries this way. Adopting the MSY-derived approach has been beneficial for health of the target stocks, for the long term commercial interests of fishing-dependant businesses built around them and for the protection of the marine environment from any damaging impacts of fishing behaviours.

Rights based management

2.5 It should be noted that under the current system of "Relative Stability" each Member State's share of a stock is guaranteed. Therefore it is for each Member State to decide how national quota is distributed to individual fishermen. Within the UK this is a devolved matter.

2.6 Under plans for a Scottish Quota Management and Licensing system, we are looking to resolve the uncertainty that exists on the current definition to harvest this important resource, and look to provide more stability to quota holders, while maintaining the Scottish Government's interest in this national asset. We plan, therefore, to consult Scottish stakeholders on proposals to establish "stewardship rights". Subject to the outcome of consultation, these (user) rights would be granted on a long-term basis but not in perpetuity.

2.7 We will not strengthen property rights on fishing quotas, and move towards a "pure" rights based management system. In order to encourage sustainable economic growth and support prosperous fishing communities, a shared approach between quota holders and the Scottish Government is required. This will help facilitate industry stability, and encourage fishing rights to remain in fishing communities for the benefit of future generations.

Technical conservation measures

2.8 Technical conservation measures have a major role to play in managing fisheries, particularly in mixed fisheries. They also have a role in reducing adverse environmental impacts. Previously technical measures have been effective in principle, but less successful in practice. This is often because fishermen wish to avoid the unwanted effect of technical measures (the loss of some marketable fish) and have proved adept at circumventing these measures. Experience therefore suggests that, in order to ensure technical conservation measures do provide real benefits to sustainable fishing, measures must be appropriate and accepted by the industry and designed and implemented in close liaison with not only scientists but also enforcement experts. Implementing measures through incentives is likely to be more effective in practice than compulsory measures. **Provided these conditions are met, technical measures can make an important contribution.**

2.9 The most effective technical recovery measures will be developed regionally, drawing fully on the expertise of active fishermen. It is clear that fishing conditions differ in different areas and solutions developed for one area may not work, or have unintended consequences, in another area. Attempts to impose technical measures across the whole of Europe without sufficient consultation or buy-in from the fishing industry are likely to be circumvented.

Q3. *Discards and bycatch*

3.1 Discards and bycatches occur for a range of reasons, some of which are aggravated by CFP policies. It is very important that steps are taken to tackle this issue. The Scottish Government and Scottish industry have undertaken measures which go beyond those required by the CFP to reduce discards and bycatches and will continue to seek new means of further reductions, including under the Conservation Credits Scheme. However, we are sceptical of the merits of a discard ban. In the absence of root and branch reform of the CFP such a ban would have serious practical implications, in particular for enforcement.

Q4. *Climate change*

4.1 In the face of environmental change the CFP is a cumbersome and inflexible policy. Whilst quota shares established regionally and based on historic catch records give important reassurance to national fishing industries, they will obviously be inadequate in the face of rapid change. Thus there is an inherent difficulty in accounting for changes in fish stock population and distribution in terms of allowing fleets to follow fish stocks.

4.2 There is evidence of certain species extending their range northwards. These may, in time, provide new fishing opportunities available to fishermen, while other fishing opportunities decline. Establishing a "relative stability" key for such new stocks may disadvantage northern countries with southern countries having benefited from a longer track record in exploiting these species. However, as yet we have little evidence of any major migration of stocks from their current recognised grounds.

4.3 A major concern is the impact of climate change on food webs. Changes in planktonic species in the North Sea have been noted, which in turn affects food availability of primary and secondary consumers with the potential to impact on commercial populations.

Control and Enforcement

Q5. *Court of Auditors report*

5.1 We welcome opportunities to compare levels of controls and enforcement. However, the position described on control, inspection and sanction systems by the recent Court of Auditors Report is in many ways a historic perspective with many of the deficiencies identified already addressed. As the assessment of UK systems only referred to England and Wales, the Scottish Government would not wish to offer specific comments on the detail of the Report. Having said that, the Scottish Government recognises the importance of ensuring continuing compliance with the Common Fisheries Policy To that end we have been working extensively with the European Commission and key stakeholders to promote responsible and sustainable fishing practices, and to protect vulnerable fish stocks. National measures operating in Scotland to protect juvenile and spawning cod are two recently established examples. The very significant progress we have made in this area has been widely recognised. **A key priority both for the current CFP and for whatever arrangements apply after 2012 must be to ensure equity throughout the EU in terms of the standards of control and enforcement.**

5.2 The Community Fisheries Control Agency ("CFCA") exists primarily to promote and coordinate co-operation between Member States in work, primarily through inspections at sea, related to stock recovery programmes. Much of that work took over from bilateral arrangements that already existed between Member States. The Scottish Government works closely with counterparts in Norway, Russia and key EU Member States on fisheries control issues and continues to play a lead role in initial CFCA operations in the North Sea.

Q6. *Harmonisation of penalties*

6.1 We recognise that this is a sensitive issue with associated questions of Commission competence. The emphasis should be on equivalence in terms of the rigour and severity of monitoring, controls and deterrence, rather than on imposing uniform approaches which do not correspond to the systems applying in the different jurisdictions.

Structural Policy

Q7. *Capacity reduction*

7.1 Since 1993, Scotland has decommissioned 361 Scottish vessels. As a result of this considerable sacrifice by our industry and our fishing communities, we believe capacity in the demersal fleet is now in much better balance with the available resource. We do not believe other Member States have reduced their effort to a corresponding degree (see Fig 1). The principle of equity to which we refer in paragraph 5.1 should also apply here.

Q8. *European Fisheries Fund*

8.1 The Scottish Government welcomes the European Fisheries Fund as the successor to the Financial Instrument for Fisheries Guidance. We will seek to maximise the value of European Fisheries Fund (EFF) resources to support the sustainable and strategic development of the Scottish fisheries, processing and aquaculture sectors and their dependent communities.

8.2 EFF funding will make an important contribution to the Scottish Government's commitment to promoting and supporting national and community strategies for the sustainable exploitation of fishery resources. It will build on the existing competitiveness of the Scottish fisheries industry and sustainably developing new markets for the export of product and expertise and the development of fisheries activities outside community waters, as well as the longer term sustainable development of Scotland's fisheries communities.

Figure 1. Effort (KW days) in the CRZ using CRG for selected nations 2001–06

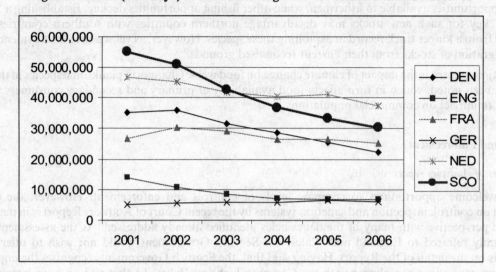

Governance

Q10. *Regional Advisory Councils*

10.1 The Scottish Government believe that the establishment of RACs represented a positive step in EU fisheries policies in terms of greater stakeholder involvement and a more regional approach to fisheries management. We have provided significant support to the RACs to help them establish themselves and Scottish stakeholders have been particularly active in these forums. Certain RACs have been more successful than others in influencing and cooperating with the Commission. The role of the North Sea RAC on cod recovery has been a good example of what can be achieved. Crucial to the success of RACs will be their ability to provide credible, responsible and timely advice and the Commission's willingness to engage in genuine dialogue. We would like to see the role of RACs enhanced in the future in terms of genuine participation in fisheries management, such as the development of long term management plans and wider marine environmental policy issues.

Q11. *Future governance*

11.1 This is a crucial issue to which there is no quick answer. This is precisely the issue which we intend the expert panel, alluded to earlier, to address. It is expected that the panel will wish to cast its net widely to review and analysis alternative fishing regimes from across the globe and which have had notably more success than the CFP.

Conclusion

(i)   The Scottish Government believes a radical approach is needed in addressing the future of the CFP. We would welcome further opportunities to help the Committee with its work on this important issue.

Marine Directorate, the Scottish Government

February 2008

Examination of Witnesses

Witnesses: MR FRANK STRANG, Deputy Director, Sea Fisheries Conservation, Marine Directorate, MR STEPHEN NOON, Senior Policy Adviser, and MR PAUL MCCARTHY, Policy Manager, Stock Conservation and Negotiation Team, Scottish Executive, examined.

Q427 Chairman: Can I start by thanking you all very much for coming. It is enormously helpful to us, as we get to the second half of our inquiry on the Common Fisheries Policy, to hear the voice of the Scottish Executive. This is a formal evidence session so a transcript will be taken. You will get the opportunity to correct any slips and errors that have crept in. Normally at this stage I have to say that the session is being webcast and that somewhere out there there may be some poor soul who is listening. We have never had any evidence that that is the case but today we are not even making the pretence that there is the possibility that somebody will be listening out there because we are not being webcast. Would you prefer to make a general opening statement and then we will get on to Qs and As?
Mr Strang: Very briefly, Chairman. Thank you very much for the opportunity to give evidence. We are very glad that you have come to Peterhead. The first thing I should do is apologise on behalf of the Cabinet Secretary, Richard Lochhead. There will be some statistics today but the important statistic to start with is that, at just under nine pounds and at 11.58 on Monday morning, Fraser Lochhead was born, so you will understand why he is not here.

Q428 Chairman: I hope you will convey our congratulations and best wishes.
Mr Strang: I am Frank Strang, Head of Sea Fisheries Conservation in the Marine Directorate of the Scottish Government.
Mr Noon: I am Stephen Noon. I am Senior Policy Adviser to the First Minister.
Mr McCarthy: I am Paul McCarthy, Policy Executive at the Scottish Government for Stock Conservation and Negotiations.
Mr Strang: The reason we are glad you have come to Scotland, and we will not go into all the statistics; some of them are in our paper, is the importance of fishing to Scotland. It is important in terms of our culture and heritage, obviously, but, as I hope you will have seen today from your visit to the market and the harbour, also in terms of our future. It is an important industry, an important sector, and because fishing is important the CFP is therefore important. You will have seen the Scottish Government's view that the CFP has not served Scotland's interests and that we would rather be out of it, and we will be exploring alternatives to the CFP. We are aware that under the current constitutional position withdrawing from the CFP is not an option and so we are very happy to be involved in your work and other work to achieve radical reform of the CFP in the meantime.

Q429 Chairman: I suppose we ought to start with that and explore that policy statement that you have made, that you would rather be "out of it", recognising, as you say, that under the present constitutional arrangements that is not possible. Let us put the constitutional arrangements aside for one moment. Let us assume there is not a constitutional impediment. How would you get out of it?
Mr Noon: Europe has certain realities. Denmark and the UK are not members of the euro. Ireland is voting on the EU Treaty and if the Irish people do not support the EU Treaty it will not be ratified across the Union, so Member States have the ability to influence wider policy across Europe in their own national interest, so part of the mechanism of how the EU works is how we would negotiate our way out of the CFP.

Q430 Chairman: But it is part of the *acquis*.
Mr Noon: What I would say to you is that it is perfectly within the ability of governments to negotiate in their national interest. That is demonstrated by the UK not being part of Schengen, it is demonstrated by Denmark not being part of the euro and it is demonstrated by Ireland, a small country of similar size to Scotland, having an influence in the people of Ireland in their referendum being able to decide whether or not to accept the European Treaty and if they do not accept it the Treaty does not go ahead. Member States have got influence, the ability to work in their national interest.
Mr Strang: The words "look at alternatives to the CFP" are quite important. In other words, it is not about us taking our ball away and playing with it elsewhere. It is about the fact that we believe the CFP has not been in Scotland's interests, and actually we believe the CFP is not particularly in Europe's interests, and so we are exploring alternatives to the CFP, I guess, conscious (as you are) that it is due to expire in 2011. We believe it is in the interests of Europe to have alternatives to the CFP.

Q431 Lord Cameron of Dillington: So you would what, have private waters? How do you share your waters under those circumstances?
Mr Strang: We are about to set up an expert panel to explore these alternatives. The honest answer to you is that we believe it is not serving our interests. We believe there are problems with the policy (as you do too, of course), and we believe there are good examples out there in the international sphere. We are very conscious that international stocks do not respect boundaries and it has to be an international

solution, but there are good examples out there—Norway, the Faroe Islands, Iceland and other places—and we want to learn from them and see what alternative models there are for international fisheries management. We do not have the answers; that is the point, but the timescale that you have, the timescale for the expiry of the current CFP, is the timescale that we have in mind.

Q432 *Chairman:* Can I just check this point? There is an enormous difference between working towards a reform of the CFP or something to replace it with the agreement of other Member States and saying that you will withdraw from something called a Common Fisheries Policy. If you say that the policy is to withdraw unilaterally from the Common Fisheries Policy, not trying to reform it, which I understand is your position, is that correct?
Mr Noon: We have to work within the reality of where we are at the moment, so we cannot withdraw from the Common Fisheries Policy today, but what we can do is suggest improvements to the Common Fisheries Policy.

Q433 *Chairman:* So it is not a policy of withdrawal?
Mr Noon: It is a reality of where we are today.

Q434 *Chairman:* What is that?
Mr Noon: That we do not have the ability in Scotland to decide on that sort of issue.

Q435 *Chairman:* I understand that the First Minister wishes to have a referendum fairly quickly on independence. If, say, that was successful, and I make no value judgments on the basis of whether that is a good thing or a bad thing; I just want to get the practicalities and the technicalities right, Scotland would be in the position—and this is not clear—of either applying for membership of the EU or continuing in membership of the EU. It does not matter which, does it?
Mr Noon: It is pretty clear that we would continue to be members of it.

Q436 *Chairman:* Again, that is not my point, but if we accept the position of continuing in membership of the EU, that must bring with it acceptance of the *acquis* and there is no example of a state seeking membership of the Union that has negotiated a permanent change to the *acquis*.
Mr Noon: As I said to you at the start, there are political realities within the EU, and Member States have got—

Q437 *Chairman:* I do not understand that. You are saying it as a formula. There is something called the Common Fisheries Policy. That is embedded in the Treaty. The only way you get treaty changes is through unanimity. Do you agree with that?
Mr Noon: That is the point I was making in relation to Ireland. The people of Ireland have the ability in a referendum to say yes or no to a treaty that affects the whole of Europe. Scotland would have that same ability.

Q438 *Chairman:* But the boot is on the other foot.
Mr Noon: I would disagree with you, with respect. If the Scottish people wanted withdrawal from the Common Fisheries Policy and had the ability to decide on a European treaty in a referendum and rejected that treaty, that would block that treaty for the whole of Europe. Scotland is a Member State and, as you said, there has to be unanimity in treaty changes. That gives Scotland huge influence in terms of negotiating policy positions that are in our national interest. There are the examples I gave to you about Schengen and the euro. The euro is an important common policy for Europe but Member States are not part of it. In the news a few months ago there was discussion and thought that perhaps some Member States might have to pull out of the euro, so, just in terms of the political reality, Scotland negotiating a withdrawal from the CFP is within that mainstream of what happens in Europe.

Q439 *Chairman:* The political reality is that Scotland would require the unanimous agreement of all other Member States to change the Common Fisheries Policy and get some form of exclusion from it. Do you honestly believe that all other Member States, if Scotland was a separate member of the EU, would turn round and say, "Yes, Scotland can leave the Common Fisheries Policy"?
Mr Noon: An example I would refer you back to is Denmark and the Maastricht Treaty. When the Danish rejected the Maastricht treaty in a referendum Europe had to go back and make an accommodation that suited the Danish national interest.

Q440 *Chairman:* No; that is a new treaty. There would not be a new treaty, would there?
Mr Noon: You are saying there is never going to be a new treaty ever again in the European Union? There is going to be a point where we are going to be discussing the next treaty and Scotland is an independent country. Scotland as a Member State will have a huge influence on—

Q441 *Chairman:* So you would wait until a normal treaty revision, if there were to be one?
Mr Noon: The Scottish Government has said that we will have a referendum on independence in 2010, so the earliest that Scotland would be independent would be after 2010, and if you look at the timescale

of when European treaties have been negotiated we are talking about that sort of timescale. We cannot pretend that Scotland tomorrow will be independent, much as I would love Scotland to be independent tomorrow. The reality is that this is not going to happen tomorrow.

Q442 *Chairman:* I think we ought to bring this to an end but I just want to get something absolutely clear. Do you accept that Scottish withdrawal from the Common Fisheries Policy would mean a change to the treaty and that treaty change can only be done through unanimity?
Mr Noon: Which gives Scotland—

Q443 *Chairman:* No; I just want to know whether you believe that my formulation is correct.
Mr Noon: I am not a lawyer so I accept, without having a lawyer sitting beside me, that that is the exact position.

Q444 *Chairman:* But I would have thought you would have checked on this. It is such a central part of your policy position, is it not? You mean you do not know the legality of the process?
Mr Noon: I have just told you what I think is the reality of the process, the fact that unanimity has to be part of this and Scotland has huge influence, so that is the point. Can I just make one additional point? In terms of what we want from a future fisheries policy, it is not creating a tartan boundary around Scottish waters. It is about engagement with the rest of Europe but doing it in a way that recognises that we have a distinct interest and a desire to make this fishery flourish, and we think that can be done through a different sort of partnership with the EU which is not a common policy. I just want to refer you to a report that was done recently for the European Commission which described the CFP as a "top-down, command and control fisheries management instrument". We do not want that. We want something that gives the nations around the North Sea, the nations with an interest in the West of Scotland fishery, primacy in terms of deciding the right policy for that area. The Common Fisheries Policy does not deliver that and that is why we want to withdraw and why we have made that a priority of our European policy when we have the ability to do so.

Q445 *Chairman:* Okay. I think we might get on to more shared ground if we look at the details of the policy. You have just mentioned that one of your criticisms is that it is a very heavy, top-down regime and you want to build upon moves which I think started with the establishment of the fishing partnerships in what happened to be round about 1997 to 1999 and the growth of the Regional

Advisory Councils. To what extent do you think it is possible to build upon that and have much greater self-management of the fisheries by the direct stakeholders?
Mr Strang: Reflecting on why is it we do not like the CFP, why are we taking this position and what is it that we are saying does not serve Scotland's interest, it is partly to do with outcomes, it is to do with what has happened to stocks over a period, what has happened to fishing communities, what has happened to the sector. It is partly about the fact that the CFP seems to be discredited. I would be interested to see your conclusions from what stakeholders have said to you. It is not just us saying it. It is the Court of Auditors. It is a discredited policy. Why these two things? I guess one of the key reasons is this top-down, prescriptive thing, one-size-fits-all, whether it is Shetland or the Bay of Biscay, and in great detail. That matters to us because you get bad decisions because the Commission does not have the capacity to get it right in each of these places and it does not have the capacity to focus on different seas, and it matters because you often get no decision because it does not have the capacity to look at the different areas or to change decisions which were taken a long time ago. It is about the quality of decisions but also about stakeholder acceptance of them in that often stakeholders are not on side, either because they do not understand because of the complexity which comes from all that or because they do not want to be on side because they have not been involved in the discussion because it is all happening in the centre. Therefore, the great ingenuity of the sector is used to get round it rather than go with it, so regionalisation is really important and matters to us, and that very question will be one of the things that the expert panel we talked about will look at—how we could regionalise policy. In terms of the answer, I think there is something for us in the lessons we are learning this year in Scotland in what we are implementing here right now (and I will come back later to the detail) in terms of our conservation credits and real-time closure schemes. This has allowed us to focus on particular seas, particular fleets, working with the sector to develop solutions which apply in those areas, and then implement those decisions without having to go through STECF, the Commission, Council, and we can adjust them if we find they are not working. It is about focusing on a particular area, local ability to work things out with stakeholders, the ability to adjust in-year and, importantly, a focus on what the outcomes are that we are trying to deliver. The Commission and other Member States are interested in the outcomes; they are not interested in the detail of how we do it. I am not coming at this from a theoretical point of view but learning lessons from what we are doing now. On the RACs and whether the RACs are part of the

answer, we are very positive about the Regional Advisory Councils. From the outset they have involved stakeholders well and they look at things in a regional way, as the name suggests. We have been supportive from the beginning, from the launch of the North Sea RAC at Edinburgh Castle all the way through to the big event here in Peterhead a month and a bit ago on compliance, so we have done lots and lots of support, and the sector is very supportive of various RACs. I guess the performance of RACs has been mixed but where it has been most effective has been when their advice was timely and relevant and so therefore we had open ears from the Commission. It is very important that the Commission are listening, so part of our support is encouraging the Commission to listen. It is about timely and relevant advice and when it is .credible because it is holistic and it has consensus amongst the whole RACs, including the NGOs. A good example would be the Cod Symposium in Edinburgh in March last year. It may well be that RACs are part of the answer to this more regionalised approach and it may well be that, for example, they could be involved in devising regional fisheries plans, but if they continue building the capacity they would need to perform well and it depends a bit on the overarching framework we end up with.

Mr Noon: May I just add that when thinking about regionalisation I think it is important to remember that in the regions we deal with a lot of the fishing interest is coming from non-members of the EU and non-members of the Common Fisheries Policy, so there is an engagement with Norway, Iceland and the Faroes which is important to consider in this.

Mr Strang: I think that is a good general point in terms of your inquiry generally. Over 50% of our stocks are governed in the external talks, not the Common Fisheries Policy, so when we are thinking about a different CFP it is about what is the impact on Norway, et cetera, and what does "regional" mean here?

Q446 *Chairman:* Can I just follow the RAC thing for a moment? I detect that you are not quite sure whether the RACs are a vehicle for regional management in the way you see it developing. Is that right?

Mr Strang: I think they are important because they identify the need to move down a level. They are still quite big. The North Western Waters RAC covers a huge area and there is a thing about the North Sea RAC, for example, having been established first and having proven itself in the quality of its advice and others are still working to develop quality-wise. We just have to clarify where fisheries managers fit in this, where administrations fit in, so there is a question about not just the scale at which we are deciding but

who is deciding, so some of that stuff has to be teased out, I guess.

Mr McCarthy: As things stand RACs are a creature of the Common Fisheries Policy which limits the usefulness of certain RACs, for example, the Pelagic RAC. The pelagic industry includes Norway, the Faroes and Iceland as well as various EU MS. They are all very important in dealing with the pelagic species and they are not represented in RACs and they will not be represented in RAC form because it is a creature of the Common Fisheries Policy, so when you are looking at regionalisation it is another reason to think about thinking outside the CFP.

Q447 *Baroness Jones of Whitchurch:* Can I follow up on the composition of the RACs because in the dialogue we have had with them even they have accepted that they are not truly representative of stakeholders and they are very much dominated by the industry, if you like, and it is quite hard for environmental and consumer interests to get a foothold and to feel that their voice is being heard in that. You have not mentioned that but I would have thought that that was one of the criticisms of the RACs in the way they are currently composed.

Mr Strang: I take that point. I did say that when they are most effective is when there is a holistic consensus point of view, including the NGOs. The Commission are very clear that when advice comes forward in unanimity from RACs the standard position will be that it will be listened to and followed. In other words, that gives quite a lot of power to the other 20% that is not from the industrial side. I take your point. I particularly take your point that there is a capacity thing for some of these organisations, an ability to service these different RACs, and, incidentally, the more we regionalise the more there is a capacity issue across the board and sometimes it is in the small number of people, but it does institutionalise the fact that advice which has a consensus behind it is much more powerful than advice which just comes from one particular section. There are examples, and I will not quote them, where the advice has not necessarily reflected that. That brings the RACs into disrepute, so it is very important to us to build up the capacity of the RACs.

Mr Noon: It is also important to remember that RACs only have an advisory role. Certainly, where we are coming from, the interests in the fisheries, the decisions should be taken by nations and stakeholders with an interest in the fisheries, so that is one weakness of the RACs.

Mr Strang: One reflection I had was a parallel between the RACs and the in-shore fishery groups we are developing in Scotland, a bit like the English Sea Fisheries Committees, but where we are getting local groups together to take decisions about a management plan for their local area, a dozen around the coast, and the key message there is that it does not have to be the same solution all the way round the Scottish coast. You can have different solutions in different places, so the IFGs and the RACs can learn from each other.

Chairman: The devil is in the detail. In all this regional management things there is bound to be an element of top-down and it is how the bottom-up meets the top-down, is it not? That is always the problem.

Q448 Lord Plumb: Having talked to a lot of the fishermen this morning and those who are concerned in the market, and we were not all together to listen to individual fishermen but I got a lot of very positive vibes from the fishermen, and I think if I had said to them, "We are going to recommend as a group to pull out of it", I think it would have been shock, horror. That is my opinion and what we have heard this morning does not reflect what I heard in the marketplace earlier. Neither does what you have said reflect what it says in your report. You say in the report regarding management, "The Scottish Government welcomes the improved stability that it may offer through the importance of involving stakeholders", and that you have just said and that is a major point, "which is emphasised in order that socio-economic factors can be fully taken into account". Your concern nevertheless, quite rightly, is about the recovery plan and therefore let us assume that we are in the market and let us assume we are going to stay in the market because it is the first I have heard that we are going to consider the CFP expiring in 2011. As I understand it, at that stage we shall be looking at the possible recovery, or at least we shall be looking at improvements to the CFP, which are not overdue, and so in that context I think if we can be positive we might ask you what changes you would make in the two policy tools, that is, in present management and in the recovery plans and how content you are at this stage with the European Commission's proposals for a revised cod recovery plan which was published on 2 April.

Mr Strang: It is good to hear what the skippers are saying to you and in some ways that is encouraging, the tone of what they are saying. There are two things I would say about that. One is that we are not saying that everything about the CFP is bad.

Q449 Lord Plumb: But you did. You wanted to pull out.

Mr Strang: Not everything about the CFP is bad, maybe in what it implied, but we will come to that. Who knows why people say what they are saying, but the sense of confidence at the moment here is partly about a sense of more control that we are developing our own Conservation Credits, et cetera, if you see what I mean, so I think there is a bit of that. We are

positive about the management plans, for example. They give a bit of stability into the medium term; it is not just year by year. It is about finding a medium term outcome and being less detailed about how you get there and an outcome of moderate fishing pressure which is in everyone's interest. Haddock is a good example where we have managed to fish longer on the stock. It is famous for the vicissitudes of the recruitment and the management plan has allowed us to go on longer, so that is great. I suppose one comment would be that sometimes the socio-economic aspect is tagged on at the end, it is all biology anyway, so it is working through from the outset the rules of the management plan and how we take account of the impact, and it is quite difficult to do but it is about doing it explicitly from early on. Recovery plans, of course, are much more about how you get to the state where you can have a management plan. There are two problems. One is the kinds of targets which are set in recovery plans. Sometimes it is about the wrong thing; it is about biomass, over which we have very little control, it is nature rather than fisheries management decisions, and sometimes the pace of change is unrealistic. Also, sometimes the recovery plans are prescriptive. In other words, there are lots of detailed things you have to do rather than it being about the outcome. We want the future recovery plans to be about realistic targets, about things we have control over and at a decent pace, and to be a bit more about the outcome and devising ways of getting there. When it comes to the Commission's proposals, which came out in time for the last Council, they measure up not too badly on those principles but the devil, of course, will be in the detail and we are all digesting the detail. We are having discussions with the sector. There are still concerns about the pace of change. A 25% cut every year is quite radical. I am particularly concerned about the effort pot given to Member States. One concern for me is that it allows Member States to incentivise people to do the right thing but it does not give a Member State a reward for doing the right thing. In other words, no matter what you do in your Member State or your region or whatever, you will get the same effort allocation as another Member State. You have to incentivise fishermen within the Member State but you also have to say to the Member State, "If you do the right thing you will have a bigger effort pot than you had last year". At the moment it still looks like a regional approach, giving Member States effort pots, but all the effort pots go down or up in the same way depending on how the stock is doing. There is no reflection of what you have done as a Member State.

Q450 Viscount Ullswater: Perhaps I could turn to something which looks like a success, and that is the agreements that you have been able to reach with your Scottish fishermen about real-time closures. Although I know that very briefly you touched on the adequacy of emergency procedures in getting these sorts of closures, how do you think it could be implemented in a reformed CFP if there were to be one? Should it be something that the RACs could do and agree amongst themselves if they had unanimity on it, and is that something which then could be implemented to ensure that the benefit of real-time closures was sustained?

Mr Strang: Thank you for that question because we are really excited about real-time closures. They are going well. It is a new measure and it has got the prospect of success. It is very much a first in EU terms and we have had a lot of interest from Member States that really want to know what is going on, and in fact at the conference I alluded to here in Peterhead there was a lot of interest from Member States. Shall I describe how it works? Basically, they stem from industry enthusiasm to take action where there are genuine aggregations of cod. They see aggregations of cod but they do not want to have to take action just themselves; they want others to do so too, and the key thing is that as long as they are real time so they reflect the reality now, not what was in the ICES advice 18 months ago, and as long as they are time limited so they do not stay in place for ever, like the famous wind sock closure off the west coast of Scotland which has a permanent nature about it. These are temporary and they are real time and they reflect reality. As long as that is the case the industry is very much up for these measures and last year in the autumn we developed voluntary measures based on juvenile cod. It is slightly more formal this year. The first thing is that it is not all about closures and restrictions. There is an exhortation part of this in that the industry have identified, "These are where we think spawning is happening". We publicise that and say, "Please avoid those areas", and if everybody is up for the sustainability of cod, which we believe they are, that is something they can do; they can contribute to it. Just as an aside, it is really encouraging that the industry identified those areas, not us. Ten years ago, if you had asked the industry to identify spawning areas they would not have done so because of fear we would have closed them permanently. We have a responsibility to trust them. They have to trust us with the information and we have to have integrity as to how we use the information because it is tempting for us to say, "That must be where it is spawning so therefore we will close", and therefore we would never get the information again. It is a long-term trust thing. There is exhortation. In terms of closures, vessels are boarded anywhere on the sea but particularly focusing around those spawning areas by our agency, and I think you are seeing a colleague from the agency later on, the Scottish Fisheries Protection

Agency. Samples are taken and if the quantity of cod over a particular period is above a certain threshold per hour, and those thresholds for the first part of the year are about adult cod for spawning and in the second half of the year about juvenile, so we change round about now to a different threshold, the Marine Directorate informs us, we decide to close and there is an automaticity about. If it is above a certain number we close an area which is 15 miles by 15 miles for 21 days. Everyone knows exactly what the rules are and we inform all our vessels. We also inform other Member States, crucially, as to where the closures are. This is partly, I suppose you could say, a contract with the industry. There are safeguards around it. In terms of our own capacity, there are only nine closed at any one time, we probably could not cope with many more than that, and we have a commercial impact zone within a 45-mile radius, only three at any one time, so that economically in one particular port you do not have everything closed. It is a combination of what science tells us and what is pragmatic. We have had nine closures so far this year, and there is a map here if you want to see. It is important to say that compliance has been excellent. Part of what we want to look at at the end of the year from our VMS data is, are people changing their behaviour? Are they moving away from where they were before because of these measures, and compliance both by Scottish vessels but by other vessels too. In terms of taking it to EU level, that is a very good question. First of all, I am encouraged that the Scottish industry were prepared to do that even without us having done that. Does that make sense? In the past the idea that we closed our seas and that our fishermen could not go there but a Danish vessel could was not popular, but that is very encouraging, that it is no longer, "We will wait for everybody before we do it". However, it would be much better if it was respected by everybody. You are quite right that the CFP is slow-moving. Twenty-eight days is the fastest you could ever do an emergency measure and by then we are saying in 21 days it disperses. You can imagine in due course a provision where Member States are allowed, subject to certain criteria, to introduce real-time closures which others respect. Because of the mutual suspicion in the Council, I have to say, that is quite hard work, in the same way as I can tell you that in some of the RAC discussions people immediately assume that our real-time closures are a protectionist measure, and if we saw some other Member States instituting some closures we would think, "Is that because of ours?". there is a suspicion there but you could imagine getting there. I have not thought this through but the RACs could have a role in that. At the moment, because there is still that suspicion, it is still early days, we are much more pursuing a bilateral arrangement. For example, the Danish administration and the Danish Fishing

Association have said to their industry, "Please respect the Scottish closures. Here are the details and we would like you to respect those closures."

Q451 Viscount Ullswater: I just want to get this clear. If it was a shared fishing ground, although it may be a Scottish initiative, is it respected by other Member States?
Mr Strang: Up to now in practice—

Q452 Chairman: On a voluntary basis?
Mr Strang: Yes, on a voluntary basis, correct.

Q453 Viscount Ullswater: And up to now it is?
Mr Strang: Exactly, yes.

Q454 Viscount Ullswater: But, for all the reasons why you say you will continue doing so, there are suspicions that it is protectionism?
Mr Strang: Yes, that is right.
Mr McCarthy: It is possible to envisage that a future management plan for cod or other species would have a system of RTCs built into it which would provide that automaticity, whereby, if anyone who signed up to that management plan detected undersized cod or any undersized fish that a described area would be automatically closed. Again, that management plan would need to be beyond the EU level because I note that one third of the current closures have impacted on outside regional waters, so again there is a need to bring in members outside the EU in order to make this really effective.
Mr Strang: One point that has been made before to me is how powerful this is with the consumers and the media. It is good for the stock, that is for sure, but it is also something people can understand, the fishing sector can understand that we are doing something constructive to rebuild stocks and they are proud of it. It is something they have come up with and have worked with us on.

Q455 Chairman: Almost the reverse problem, the opposite problem, is where, at the time the TAC is set, fisheries science being an inexact science, it is set too low and that becomes obvious a few months into the year. That leads to quota running out and excessive discarding. Have you thought how to get round that particular problem?
Mr Strang: Part of that, and it will be very acute this year again as it was last year and I know it is in certain parts around the UK, is the speed of reaction within the Commission, and it is very frustrating. We have had it in the past with monkfish abundance. The Commission have promised in-year reviews. Commission officials are dealing with all the stocks. They cannot cope, so therefore you do not get the adjustment, the whole thing gets discredited and people do not respect the rules for that very reason.

It was interesting last year that on North Sea cod advice was early. It was in June rather than October and there were surveys over the summer which were brought to bear in October, so they updated the science in-year, but I think that is going to be rare. I do not think we can rely on that very often. All I am saying is that you have put your finger on a key problem and that is to do with the capacity of the Commission. To be very honest, it can go both ways, of course. It could be that the stock is much worse than we had thought and so there can be in-year adjustments the other way.

Q456 Lord Cameron of Dillington: Would it be helpful if there were three-year quotas, longer term quotas, and you managed the longevity of the quota system by using the real-time closures? Is that another way forward?
Mr Strang: Yes. I think the more we can have a medium term approach the more stability there will be; it is a good thing. I have to say that it would depend on the stock because with some stock there is such a variance between one year and the next. An example would be North Sea herring where last year the RAC advised that we try and go for a three-year approach, but the *caveats* you would have to have around that, say, if biomass did X or Y, would have to be so strong so it is not really worth having in that sense. However, there are other stocks where it would be possible to do such a thing.
Mr Noon: In terms of the capacity of the Commission, one of the things we have been trying to do in the Scottish Government is have the sector develop a more strategic responsibility for setting outcomes and trusting local areas, local government, and fishing partners, to deliver on outcomes, and, in terms of reform for the Committee to consider, perhaps we are looking at a common approach across Europe rather than a common policy and we are seeking strategic direction, in other words, a series of outcomes which they trust nation states to get on and deliver because it is in our interest to have flourishing fishing.

Q457 Chairman: I think that is a very attractive approach. The trouble then is that you need to have some sanction lurking around to land on the Member State that plays ducks and drakes.
Mr Strang: You could always try an incentive. You are right. The mind says always "sanction" and sanction is part of it, but what I was saying about the cod recovery plan was that if you say to people, "If you do the right thing you will have slightly more to play with next time". It is both.
Mr Noon: The sanction is perhaps a local one. If fishery stocks fall there is an economic price, a social price, to be paid in the country, and ultimately we have to be responsible for what is happening in our

country, so perhaps having a big stick in the centre is just governments being responsible in their own nations.

Q458 Viscount Brookeborough: And this is very much the approach from the fishermen's point of view. What do the scientists feel about real-time closures because quite clearly all their evidence is history based and not in any way current?
Mr Strang: The FRS scientists, are very involved in devising the scheme. In other words, they are working out what the thresholds should be and what the impact would be and when they were dispersed, and they are very encouraged at the idea of trying something different. There is a bit of a sense that we have had the effort regime for a long time and the North Sea is in a bit of recovery but elsewhere there is not much happening, so anything which takes the sector with us and is doing the right kind of thing they are up for. What they do say, quite rightly, is that this is not the be-all and end-all, and if it were to be the be-all and end-all real-time closures would have to be very big. We need other things and we need selectivity measures which we are also introducing. We need to keep an eye on efforts generally. There is a whole range of things you have to do. Real-time closures are not everything, that is for sure. I suppose they would press us to make sure that real-time closures really do bite, that the thresholds are sufficiently low to make an impact.

Q459 Earl of Dundee: Why do you believe that technical conservation measures will necessarily be a better advance for acceptance than coercion?
Mr Strang: Scotland has been very active in technical conservation measures for a long time, as you probably know. There are various places where we have been ahead of Europe in terms of single twine, in terms of the mesh size, et cetera. Of course, that is for a fishery a logical thing to do, and it is encouraging, by the way, that technical measures are part of the range of tools which the Commission are contemplating; it is not just days and TACs. Our past experience is that if the industry does not like a technical measure it will find a way round it. It is impossible to police every boat and they are clever guys and they will find ways round it if they do not want to implement it, so they must want to. Therefore, they have to share the objective that we are trying to achieve, so dialogue is very important. You have to make sure that the technical measures you are talking about go with the grain of the industry and can work in practice, so trialling is really important so that the scientists are happy that it will give the outcome you want and the industry thinks it works. We have tried one without the other and it does not work. In terms of incentive, I suppose it is the same point about the industry being much more

likely to want it to work if it is not seen as a penalty coming from somewhere else but there is an incentive to do it. I guess it is the same point. It is not only incentives. There are some things which must be done.

Q460 Earl of Dundee: So you would mix the stick with the carrot?
Mr Strang: Yes, I think that is right.

Q461 Earl of Dundee: How would you do so?
Mr Strang: The point is there are already plenty of sticks there. You can only catch X stock with X size of mesh, this kind of thing. Our point is that it has always been sticks so far and you can use incentives in the form of EFF money to incentivise people. I think MSC accreditation is a kind of incentive, but in our case it is days at sea, the kilowatt day scheme and so on, where we are saying to people that, following the trials we are doing right now, we hope to be able to introduce a scheme whereby, if a nephrops vessel includes a 120-millimetre square mesh panel at a certain point, they will get more days. Because they are involved in developing it, they were involved in the trials, they are more receptive to it. In fact, even choosing the trials is a very tricky thing—what horsepower, which part of the sea. We are very particular about this. We have had dialogue all round the country about that. We have got a limited number of trials we can do but because they know they were involved they believe these things will make a difference and so it is all part of that. This is partly optimism about the sea. A really important thing I am going to say is that we are going to be measuring outcomes. We are not just doing wishful thinking but we actually have a sense that this is a new start and we are doing things differently and incentive is a part of that, I guess.
Mr Noon: It is getting people engaged in a joint purpose which is making the fishery more profitable. I suppose the biggest incentive is giving people a sense that they have a real influence on decisions that affect their livelihood, and that is certainly the approach that we are trying to come from as a government.

Q462 Viscount Ullswater: Will you control that through licensing the individual boats if they apply the technical measures in order to get that extra?
Mr Strang: There are two aspects to it. At the moment under the Conservation Credits Scheme the whole fleet is receiving in 2008 the same days at sea it received in 2007 and as a requirement of that the nephrops fleet will have to carry a square mesh panel of 110 millimetres from 1 July and we will be controlling it.

Q463 *Viscount Ullswater:* That is the whole fleet?

Mr Strang: The whole nephrops fleet, and those that do not comply will have a cut in their days at sea available. It is as simple as that. That is the simplest way we can do it.

Chairman: Just as an aside on this, as you may suspect, devolution is done in favour of getting decision-making down as far as possible. This morning there was a remarkable conversation a number of colleagues and I had with fishermen actually exploring this route and there was almost a cry of, "There is a need to save us from ourselves", which we were not expecting.

Lord Cameron of Dillington: Particularly the nephrops fleet—"There are too many boats being built. Give it a couple of years and it will be completely over-fished. Why don't you do something?".

Q464 *Chairman:* "The Government has to come in and tell people to stop this". It is not something that I was expecting.

Mr Strang: As an aside, the development of the Conservation Credits Scheme has been a very interesting point in our relationship with the sector. It has changed our relationship because we can no longer say it is the European Commission's fault. We have to have a discussion with the sector and we are saying to them, "This is a fantastic opportunity to design our own scheme but we have to be responsible and responsibility is obviously about the state of the stocks but if we want this model to work in the future we have to use our powers responsibly now". We have a steering group involving the main fisheries, involving WWF, involving scientists, but there have been occasions where we have had to say, "We, Government, assume our responsibility and we think X". It means that we cannot cosy up together and say it is all London or Brussels or somewhere else who is at fault.

Mr Noon: It is a leadership role from both Government and the industry ultimately. It cannot just come from us.

Q465 *Earl of Arran:* You mentioned stewardship rights. What exactly are they and what would be the benefits of them if they came about?

Mr Strang: On that I am afraid I am not going to be terribly helpful to the Committee. In terms of our review of the quota management system, Mr Lochhead will be issuing later this month a consultation document on the arrangements which we think should apply for managing quota in Scotland and I do not particularly want to pre-empt that if you will forgive me. What we are saying though is that access to fishing is one of the key ingredients for a fishing community and we have to preserve that for future generations. We have to take

that seriously and so we have arrangements which are not necessarily radically different from the ones now but they suit Scottish circumstances, so there will be consultation on that, and I guess it is about balancing and combining and safeguarding what is a national asset for future generations but it is also allowing individual businesses to grow and thrive. I think probably the best thing I can do is undertake to provide the Committee with the document later in the month when it is out.

Q466 *Earl of Arran:* How do you expect these proposals to be taken by the fishermen?

Mr Strang: I think they will on the whole welcome the fact that we are taking seriously the future of the sector in Scotland fishing communities and the fact that this is an important national asset and we want to make sure it is available for future generations. Individuals will look carefully at their own financial situation and what it means, what the impact is for them, and I think the majority will say what I have just said but it will not be a unanimous reaction, as you would expect in any consultation.

Q467 *Earl of Arran:* It sounds to me as though it could be quite controversial.

Mr Strang: We will see. I think you will have heard that this is very important to people. I suppose what I am really saying is that it is the kind of thing you have to see as a package, not just to do one little bit and not the others because that would mislead. You have to look at it in the round.

Q468 *Chairman:* Can you say anything on geographical restrictions of trading rights?

Mr Strang: I do not think I should. I think I will leave that.

Chairman: That is all right. Let us get straight into discards.

Q469 *Baroness Jones of Whitchurch:* Discards are one of the issues on which we can all unite and say we find abhorrent. Fishermen say it, the consumers say it, the politicians say it. We can all agree that we do not think discards are a welcome side of the fishing industry. You have mentioned the Conservation Credits Scheme and that you think that is a helpful way of dealing with them. Can you tell us a little bit more about that but also give us a practical analysis? Are discards always going to be with us? Are they an inevitable by-product of the fishing industry?

Mr Strang: I will tell you a bit about the Conservation Credits Scheme. I have probably covered quite a lot of that already but I am happy to add to it. The context of the conservation credits is cod recovery and our overall position set out in a Scottish Government document last October about cod recovery was that we were about a reduction in mortality; that is what we are trying to achieve, but doing it in ways other than blanket cuts at sea. Doing it through innovative ways, doing it locally and doing it with the sector were the big themes. The Council decision last December ticked all those boxes, the kilowatt days provision, for example, so that Member States can devise a scheme which is about reducing mortality, local solutions, et cetera. We are excited about it. The overall principle is rewarding people for doing the right thing, credit for your conservation measures. We have worked in very close collaboration with the sector and in practice there will be a basic scheme from 1 February which rewards people. It gives people their 2007 days back so they are not getting a cut in return for real-time closures and selectivity measures. In due course we hope to give more days to people which have more selective gear. What impact will the scheme have? We want to give a carrot for outcomes. This is partly what we are saying. We are not just happily sailing away. It is difficult to measure the impact on stock first thing because the Scottish industry is only part of those who have an impact on the cod stocks because there is a delay in the scientific advice—you will not know for a year what the outcome is. Another important thing, and this applies to discards too, is that there is a trend already. What we know about the 2005 cod year class in the North Sea, for example, and the TAC as set, as you alluded to, Chairman, is that discards are going to increase before they get less, so the impact of this scheme will be about what is the difference from the trend that we were expecting? With all those *caveats* I guess we would expect real-time closures, which are about avoiding aggregations, to reduce discards because you will not catch such a by-catch in getting your quota because there is not such an aggregation, and obviously selectivity. Selectivity measures are particularly good for discards of haddock and whiting which these measures we are talking will have more of an impact on, so we are interested in other white fish because the levels of discard are pretty unacceptable in some places on those stocks. Incidentally, we will be increasing our observer programme. We are employing some more observers to increase by 500 days a year the amount of observing at sea we are doing. That will give us a better sense of it. Probably the biggest measure is going to be the discard rate because we can observe that and the trick will be to see what the trend would have been and what is the difference. We do not know that yet so we will have to work that through. That is the conservation credits side of it and what it might do for discards.

Q470 *Baroness Jones of Whitchurch:* Do you think a discard ban would be practical?

Mr Strang: You could conceive of situations where it might be just about feasible if there were a clean fishery and a single jurisdiction, but in a mixed fishery with a multiple jurisdiction it does throw up a lot of issues. I should say as an aside that reducing discards is absolutely the right thing to do but a discard ban has implications for quota allocations. What do you do about quota for individuals? What about relative stability? There are implications for minimum landing sizes and I think a very important implication for enforcement in that fishermen have no incentive to obey this discard ban. It will have to be policed and enforced. That means boarding boats. It happens on the sea, and the one thing, and you may have heard this from the market this morning, is that the big change in enforcement has been moving to on land. There is a big investment in the registration of buyers and sellers, et cetera, and you would have to reverse all that, so there is a big enforcement issue there. I guess we would say that the Commission's communication on discards is a good thing because it talks about an outcome we are trying to achieve. It talks about reductions in discards rather than all the detail but going to a discards ban without dealing with all these other issues is problematic.

Mr Noon: It is also important to reflect in the context in which these decisions are being taken that the Council of Ministers itself has had the pleasure of being the first one in December, and, to be frank, it is shambolic. It is a sort of lowest common denominator approach when you have a 24-hour period where you are negotiating the commercial interest of a fishery and so my concern is that these important bigger picture issues do not get dealt with in the structures which exist around the Council of Ministers, which is a challenge.

Q471 *Baroness Jones of Whitchurch:* If you have never had a discard ban, the way the current quota system works it would have to be something radically beyond that, would it not, which would allow people to bring back mixed catches and so on? In the longer term does it not make sense to have something flexible in terms of what you allow people to catch and therefore saying it is illegal, for example, just because you do not think it has much value so you chuck it over the side rather than land it?

Mr Strang: That must be right, to try and find ways of doing that. This illustrates a problem with the CFP which is the accumulation of layer upon layer of different policies without standing back and saying how these inter-relate. There is a lack of credibility and coherence. We have quotas, we have technical conservation measures, we have days at sea, we have capacity measures, and to come along and say, "On top of all that we have got a discards ban", no-one is standing back and saying, "How does that all fit together?". Regardless of the discussion we had earlier about the politics of the CFP, we want an expert to look with a blank sheet of paper at what would be standing back and taking elements from other places and saying what would be the right kind of fisheries management regime for these waters? We need to do that rather than CFP reform being about the margins of more stakeholder involvement.

Mr Noon: We have done it on the basis of two agreed national outcomes, one of which is increasing the number of sustainable fish stocks and the other is biodiversity, or buying into those outcomes rather than arguing about specific details.

Lord Cameron of Dillington: Can you explain the logic in your cod recovery paper of October last year about increasing the cod quota in order to reduce discarding? My impression from fishermen is that they will go up to the limit and you will still have the same amount of discarding.

Q472 *Chairman:* The TAC was wrong. The science produced the wrong TAC.

Mr Strang: The abundance was such that, even with a reduction in effort, people were still going to be taking a bigger TAC, and so it was not serving any purpose to have a restrictive TAC that would just be discarded.

Q473 *Viscount Brookeborough:* I was speaking to one fisherman this morning and he said, "I avoid these areas where I would run into the cod because I would have to discard them. However, there are others around here who do not know as much as I do and they go into those areas by misadventure and they then have to discard". I said, "Why do you not tell them about those areas?". "Oh, no. There are people here who do that and that is not my affair to stop them". He said, "This is doing the damage to the stocks in the long term", so I said, "What would you do?", and he said, "I would increase the quota", but, of course discarding is the wrong thing and we all agree with that. However, it actually has the same result whether you discard them or whether you eat them, so it makes no difference in the end result.

Mr McCarthy: That example illustrates that there is a difference between discarding and catching. The main thing for us, as the first fishermen said, would be to avoid catching them, the fish, in the first place and if there are ways we can incentivise fishermen to avoid catching the fish, which will be discarded, in the first place then there may be ways that we could deal with discards which might not be quite as complex.

Q474 *Viscount Brookeborough:* But if fishermen are against discarding but they will not talk to each other is it worth going down that route?

Mr McCarthy: They are in competition with each other to land as well.

Q475 *Chairman:* That is the fundamental problem.

Mr Strang: That is a very interesting point and I am sure anything I say here will be secret and the fishing industry will not hear about it. There is an issue for us about information provision and the way we have approached conservation credits is getting the whole fleet involved. In order to target our real-time closures we would love to know where the cod aggregations are right now so we can board, and some of that is okay because we have got the spawning areas that they have already told us about and they are turning out to be reasonably accurate on that, but we do have a provision in the Conservation Credits Scheme which is that fishermen will make reasonable efforts to inform us of cod aggregations, and what we are learning is that they do not want to do that personally but they might anonymously through their fishing associations give us the information, so there is a cultural behavioural change that we are working on. We give them as simple templates as we can for the information so that we can use that information. I suppose it is all about a collective effort. Where we want to get to is that the whole sector is up for this and therefore there is peer control going on here, that the consensus, as has been the case with black fish and compliance, is, "We have changed that behaviour and if people are out of line we will let other people know". We cannot police everybody.

Q476 *Chairman:* Just on discards, my old friend and opponent, John McKay, used to have an approach which was, "Look: go back to that December Fisheries Council and there you get quota swapping on the basis of extra cod equivalence", so why not require fishermen to land all their marketable fish and have an overall cod equivalent quota, one cod equals three whiting, that sort of approach? You have to land everything that is of marketable value and you work out a formula.

Mr Strang: I have not heard that before. I do not know whether there would be relative stability issues because there would be a big issue about whether the cod equivalence was still up to date and all that, because it is all very well if it is traded. That is different from the impact on relative stability, and I guess the important issue would still be there. We do not think a discard ban has been thought through to a model that works but we are not saying it could not be thought through and find a model that works. One important thing to say is that we are very chummy with our Norwegian partners across the water and we work closely with them; they are very important to us, but a discard ban, if you go and look at the Norwegian discards ban, is not quite a discard ban. The whole system, including real-time closures, is based on the premise that there will not be discards, so they can structure it around there not being discards. That is a slightly different thing from saying that whenever we find someone who is discarding they are breaking the law. They would have to answer for themselves exactly how it works but we should not assume that because people use the language we are talking about the same thing.

Q477 Chairman: But you might want to look at something like a cod equivalent quota.
Mr Strang: Yes.

Q478 Viscount Ullswater: Another comment that was made to me in the market when I was going round with a fishermen was, "Look: you see all these relatively small cod but none is below the minimum size. If you see all these it usually means that they have been high graded because here is marketable fish but a lot of them are small fish and therefore probably a lot of smaller fish have been discarded". Do you have any solution to that?
Mr Strang: I do not have a solution. It is a feature of the fishery, particularly last year. That was people's reaction to the fact that the TAC was out of line with what they were seeing in reality and I guess that is about the responsiveness of the TAC. It is also about if we have a common cause to recover cod then we are requiring of fishermen a behavioural change to move away from places where this is more likely. We are saying to them, "You cannot help catching your cod quota this year, no matter where you go, so with these real-time closures and other things please avoid places which will mean that in taking your quota you take an awful lot more of other stuff".

Q479 Baroness Sharp of Guildford: Can I pick up on this discard issue and put one further point to you, which again arose from our discussions this morning? This is the idea that the quotas might run from April to April rather than from January to January, the essence of this being that you run out of quota at the end of the year, and if you ran out in the January through to March period, which is the time when the fish are spawning, it would be advantageous because the fish could then spawn and so forth, whereas you would be picking up the larger fish in the November/December period when frequently they would run out of quota now. Do you feel this might be a feasible way forward?
Mr Strang: I think that and the previous idea are interesting ideas to look at. It is, I guess, similar to an answer to Lord Cameron, that different stocks have different characteristics biologically. My immediate reaction is that what you would find in an April-to-April quota year is that fishermen would be telling us that the science, which is delivered in June, is awfully out of date by April. This brings us to the December bunfight, or whatever the right noun is, that the problem is that in December the Commission are

creating a package that everybody can physically accept so they have to decide all the stocks together, so even if some are biologically such that you could decide on an April start, dealing with them in isolation you are much more unlikely to get a deal. However, I still think it is worth looking at.

Q480 Baroness Sharp of Guildford: Can I move on to control and enforcement where the Commission are preparing a revised Regulation on Control and Enforcement? Would you like to see that regulation? You note that you do not wish to see sanctions harmonised but could you tell us whether you would support a harmonised level of minimum sanctions?
Mr Strang: Like lots of these questions, it is a really important issue. If you ask people about the CFP in Scotland controls are one of the things people talk about a lot, a level playing field, this kind of thing, and poor and unequal controls are a key factor in the perception of the CFP. The Court of Auditors report conclusion was that the controls are not capable of ensuring rules are effectively applied, so from the Court of Auditors, which is the highest level within the EU, that is a serious indictment. It particularly grieves us because of the efforts taken in Scotland and the UK in recent years, and I do not know if the Committee has heard this but the sense of cultural compliance, a sense of what the figures looked like five or six years ago and negligible levels of black fish now, and probably that has been the case for well over 18 months. It is a big deal for us and therefore we want to see that kind of thing everywhere. It is partly a legislative issue so the control regulation is important. As an aside, we are concerned about the lack of time we will have had to input into it. It seems to be happening last minute and I know you are going to Brussels. I will not go into details but in terms of headlines what we want out of the control regulation I guess is the same point about outcomes in that it talks about what it is we are trying to achieve, the high level things Member States have to do but not going into all the detail of what Member States should do to deploy their resources in a risk-based way and what is most appropriate for them. We would like (and this is linked to the comment about land-based controls) the focus to continue to be on land-based controls, having seen that here. We would like to continue progress using technology, electronic reporting, and to make that standard practice. There are areas where the famous expression "level playing field" comes up. An example for us would be how you deal with historic over-fishing so you have the same principles applying everywhere. Legislation is partly the answer, obviously, but the biggest answer is the will to make this happen. It is the will not just of Member States to do it but of the Council and the Commission to hold Member States to account. That brings me to the last part of your question about

minimum sanctions and all that. For wider reasons of Member State competence we do not want the Commission and the Council saying this is what your sanction should be in a criminal court across the board but there are ways in which administrative penalties could be developed not in the criminal courts. They could be a serious deterrent—people are tied up for a certain number of days or weeks. That hits people in a way which sometimes financial penalties do not if they factor them into their running costs, and there is scope to develop those, I guess. In any event, whilst the Court of Auditors report was uncomfortable reading in some ways, the idea of transparency about standards in different Member States, transparency about what the controls are like, like holding each other to account, must be a good thing.

Q481 *Chairman:* Given the success of the registration of buyers and sellers, one of the big things must be to try and make sure that errant Member States implement it.
Mr Strang: Yes.

Q482 *Viscount Brookeborough:* You believe in your report that the capacity for the demersal fleet is now "in much better balance with the available resource". To what extent do you consider that there may be a need for a further reduction in order to bring it more fully into balance or with your future predictions?
Mr Strang: I guess what is important is that hidden in our comment there is what we have been through in the last ten years. It is always important, especially in Peterhead and around the coast of the north east, to remember what happened in 2001/2003, 165 white fish vessels going out at £56 million cost to the taxpayer and a serious impact on fishing communities. In the cod recovery we are making sure that we get credit for the things we have done in the past. I guess because of that we think that in broad terms most fleets are in balance with stocks. There might be some fine-tuning in some places. We have not identified those, but we believe they are mostly in line with the requirement. I guess there is an issue there with a level playing field (you always have to say the phrase "level playing field" many times in these things) to do with others taking capacity out and, to be fair, there are more and more stories around the Council table in Brussels on other Member States taking capacity out but it is all very un-transparent. If there was more information available about what other Member States are doing to ensure that we are all responding as required to reduce capacity that is what we would see as the priority.

Q483 *Viscount Brookeborough:* I wonder if you would like to comment on areas outside Peterhead. What has surprised me by coming here is that there is

apparently only one per cent unemployment and that there is a large migrant workforce, and I was told this morning that if it disappeared the fishing industry would collapse. Here, quite obviously, you have got the newish oil industry which has taken up not only a lot of the employment but many fishermen's hours doing similar type jobs right around the oil rigs. What is the effect on the west coast compared with here employment-wise?
Mr Strang: Obviously, you will be able to talk to the Council representative shortly about that question. In terms of the west coast, there are different aspects to this. There is a sense of people believing in the sector again in terms of, if you look at the Banff and Buchan College and other places that used to have hardly any skippers, we have now got more people coming through to be skippers. There is a sense that this is a sector worth being in. There is more enthusiasm for the sector. There is certainly no doubt that workers from other places, such as eastern Europe (as was) are very important to the economy, processing in particular. I myself was talking to a processor this weekend, saying, "This is really good, really important, it is working very well, but we have to also develop our own workforce too in that, as these economies grow, people might not stay". It is always important to remember that there are more people employed in the processing than in the catching and for me part of the story is about processing being part of the food industry, Scotland being a place of good food and drink, and we have a government priority to make it a niche quality product, which is part of what we are about, and so to get people to say that this is part of the future of the sector.

Q484 *Viscount Brookeborough:* But the fact is that on the east coast, as far as we have seen, the reduction in the fishing fleet over the last ten years has not meant a destruction of the social community because there has been significant other employment.
Mr Strang: I cannot comment on that. If you went to some other places, some of the villages around the Moray Firth, for instance, you might get a different story.

Q485 *Chairman:* Talking about fish processing, what we heard yesterday from the processors' representative was that increasingly second-level processing is going off to China, so fish caught in Scotland may be headed and gutted in Scotland and frozen, go out to China for filleting, be blocked and then come back, and apparently there is not any blocking facility in the UK now.
Mr Strang: You are into world economy issues and market forces here to a certain extent. I personally think that carbon footprints and all that may be more and more of an issue and I think there will be more

and more about provenance and more and more about local British goods. As an aside, 50% or so of the Scottish production is now going for MSC certification, so there is a big issue around sustainability but that particular one does not necessarily capture carbon footprint and food miles, so food miles and provenance will certainly be more important.

Mr Noon: There is a parallel policy process going on where we are currently engaged in trying to develop a national food policy for Scotland and part of that is issues around labelling and promotion of local food and engaging with the supermarkets on these sorts of issues. It is part of a wider economic assessment.

Q486 *Lord Cameron of Dillington:* Just on that last one, I suspect the provenance of that cod is probably "Norwegian sea cod". The fact that it has been to China and back does not get mentioned. Fisheries are only one cog in the overall marine management and here, as has already been mentioned, you have got oil, you have probably got wind power, you have got bird life, marine habitats and so on. I am just wondering to what extent your fisheries policy, either in or out of the Common Fisheries Policy, is totally predominant in your marine management. Can you imagine a scenario in which, say, fisheries take second place to bird life?

Mr Strang: You are quite right: at every level, European, Scottish, UK, we are looking at things in the wider marine context and the marine environment in its widest sense, and actually I suppose we are realising in Scotland more and more that, just as food and drink are a really important asset for us, our seas are a fantastic asset too in lots of different ways. We are responsible in fisheries management terms for the biggest area of the EU fishing waters at least of the continental area, so it is a huge area and is hugely important, and not just in fishing terms. In defining our marine objectives for the seas we have talked about them being safe and clean, being healthy and biologically diverse and being productive, all those things. Obviously, within that we are saying socio-economic matters and fishing are part of that cog. It is not the only thing. There are lots of energy ideas, et cetera, in devising our own marine planning ideas, our own marine bill, our input to the EU. Obviously, fishing will shape some of what we say, but there are two things I would say about that. One is that the more we look at the seas as a whole the more regionalisation matters. If we can get a holistic approach then we are looking at particular seas and the Marine Strategy Directive is about regional seas. It is the same kind of theme as our fisheries management. The other point for me is that in dealing with the fishing sector this subject is a two-way street. It is partly about influencing marine

policy so that they take account of legitimate fishing interests, but it is also about what is the fishing sector doing for the marine environment? It is about to what extent can they help identify the coral bank off Rockall, which is now closed. There are various things they can do. They can contribute. I guess it is the same old point, that the more they are involved in devising the marine policies, the more at a local understandable level which they are stewarding, the more likely they are to contribute to the outcomes.

Mr Noon: The Scottish Government's approach is that we have set ourselves a national purpose, which is to increase sustainable economic growth. We have five strategic objectives which take into account environmental and economic factors and we have a series of outcomes and indicators, and so in terms of the balance between a thriving fishing industry and thriving bird stocks they are part of the creation of a sustainable successful Scotland. It is about awareness in the Government's mind. We are trying to adopt a holistic approach, and I think what is important in the context of where we are policy-wise is that one of the big discussions at the moment is over marine legislation. There is marine legislation about to go through Westminster and about to come through in the Scottish Parliament as well. One of the things we think is important in terms of fisheries is being able to have co-ordination here in Scotland over the range of policy inputs in Scottish waters. We are very ambitious for offshore energy developments. There are planning issues, there are energy consent issues, there are conservation issues, there are fisheries issues, and the majority in the Scottish Parliament would agree that it is better to have these decisions within the responsibility of the Scottish Parliament rather than having some taken by the UK Government and some taken by the Scottish Government because that is when you risk clashing policies or policies that do not quite meld with each other. We just think in terms of the policy environment the more responsibility that Scotland has the more likely it is to co-ordinate it.

Mr McCarthy: Just to round off on this point, I can think of measures we have introduced in Shetland and on the west coast, and indeed in the North Sea. I would avoid saying that one species is more important than another, but in order to go and prevent competition between seabirds and fishermen for sand eels at times when seabirds need them for feeding their young chicks.

Q487 *Chairman:* I think that is it. Can I thank you very much for coming and talking to us. Can I just check one thing with you, going back to the first discussion we had, and I do not want to re-open it? I just want to make sure that we understand the procedural framework. You have mentioned the expiry of the Common Fisheries Policy. My memory,

and it may be at fault here, is that that is renewed through regulation and that it is on qualified majority, co-decision. Is that your understanding?
Mr Strang: That is my understanding of it too. The co-decision is an interesting point, incidentally, in that everything we do from January is likely to be co-decision.

Q488 *Chairman:* So the idea of using the need for renewal and trying to operate a veto in that context is not possible?
Mr Noon: That was not the context we were talking about, a veto. The context was the political reality of Member States having the ability to try to forward

their specific national interests and the various mechanisms within the European Union which allow that to happen.

Q489 *Chairman:* There are various mechanisms that prevent you from doing it as well. Okay. Thank you all very much indeed.
Mr Strang: I understand you are reporting quite soon. Richard Lochhead has asked me to say that if, when he is back in the office, he is down in London some time and he can help he would be very happy to do so.
Chairman: And, as I said at the beginning, please convey to him our congratulations and best wishes.

Examination of Witnesses

Witnesses: MR CHRIS WHITE, Buchan Area Manager, and MR MALCOLM MORRISON, Fishing Co-ordinator, Economic Development, Aberdeenshire Council, examined.

Q490 *Chairman:* Chris and Malcolm, hello and welcome, and thank you for everything you have done in making this visit so smooth this morning.
Mr White: Thank you, Chairman. I hope you have a productive session as a result of that.

Q491 *Chairman:* Would you like to kick off with an opening statement?
Mr White: I would like to make an opening few comments. I have been asked to keep this as brief as possible because your fish and chips are waiting for you at half past 12. Can I reiterate the welcome that I am sure you have received from the Peterhead Port Authority and welcome you to the town of Peterhead. My name is Chris White and for the last eight years I have been acting as Buchan's Area Manager for Aberdeenshire Council. Just to explain that role, Aberdeenshire decentralises its decision-making to a large degree. We are a unitary authority, one of 32 in Scotland, as I am sure you know. We turn over something like £500 million per year non-housing on council housing activity, so by any estimation we are a substantial player in terms of the local economy, both in terms of employment and in terms of the impact of what we do. Most of that budget does not come my way so I have relatively slim pickings from the table in terms of allocating financially what we do, but we do meet here every three weeks. As an Area Committee we look primarily at things like planning issues, consenting issues, increasingly at policy development issues as well, so we are starting to have a greater input into where we are going in terms of in terms of housing management; we will be looking at evidence from various scrutiny and audit investigations, so that just gives you a very quick flavour of the decentralised role of Aberdeenshire. I should also say I lead the Area Management Team which consists of the heads

of property, heads of planning, heads of housing, heads of social work, so I have a fair grasp of what goes on at community level in this town. That has some input from economic development but not a huge one, so if you are going to ask me technical questions regarding mesh size and its implications you will meet a very blank stare. Malcolm Morrison, my colleague, and Ann Bell, who has given evidence to you already, deal with that job for the council and I rely upon them for information. One of the joys of having an information service in Aberdeen is producing some pretty good statistics which I hope the Committee will find helpful, showing the changes in total allowable catches over the years, the employment and fleet size in the north east of Scotland and some of the value and fish landing statistics. It may be that you are fully up to speed with these and it may be that you are not, but it will, I think, give a good picture of what has really been happening in the fishing industry in the north east of Scotland over the last ten years or so, particularly since 2002, which is the bit that you are most concerned with. I will just explain a bit more of the detail of my remit. I cover the town of Peterhead with something like 18,000 in this community and 2,000 people in Boddam just two miles to the south. Peterhead is a 16th century port which has grown and changed radically as the fortunes of whaling, herring and other fish-catching issues have emerged. The seventies saw Peterhead take off to a very large degree and I heard one of the submitters of evidence recently talking about oil and gas. It is probably as important to the future of this town as fishing. The same could not be said of Fraserburgh. Oil and gas have been a major logistics issue in terms of Peterhead, access to the North Sea being its key advantage, so the unique selling point of Peterhead is very much its access to the North Sea and the issues which relate to that. It has been a strength and a strength which has been played on increasingly recently. My remit also covers 20,000 agricultural people just ten miles to the west and north and south of here, so we have a balance between town issues and country issues, and the combination and inter-relation of those is always an interesting challenge in that the issues facing rural Buchan are quite different from those facing Peterhead. I want to digress a little bit onto statistics. I have a couple of other roles for the council. One is leading on external funding effort and the other is leading on a Scottish Government initiative called the regeneration outcome agreement. That is targeted around some useful figures—and I can get some more figures to the clerk perhaps afterwards—in terms of Scottish indicators of multiple deprivation. It looks at health and employment skills, housing and income issues and charts those. It is quite interesting in providing a balance between Peterhead and rural Buchan issues. Rural Buchan, is uniformly in the second top 20%, so four out of five in terms of ticks in the box in terms of affluence. When you come to Peterhead things get much more interesting. In three data zones immediately out of sight of this window we have three zones of only six in Aberdeenshire in the bottom 20%. We also have seven in the top 20%, so the picture I am trying to paint for you is of quite a polarised community in terms of affluence and issues of welfare between newer, bigger, modern housing on the edge of the community and some definite pockets of urban deprivation, not at a scale which is going to even flicker on the Scottish register but nevertheless very much a concern in terms of where we are going. I give you that as a bit of background. I should also state that I have no responsibility directly for Fraserburgh but I do look at the regeneration outcome agreement for Fraserburgh. The figures almost exactly mirror Peterhead in a slightly different shape in that immediately around the ports you have got three data zones in the bottom 20%, so that is an interesting view perhaps of slightly polarised community effects. I am sure you will be well aware that Peterhead and Fraserburgh are two of the most fishery dependent communities in the UK and two of the most significant players in terms of landing and processing of fish, and you will have heard, I am sure, in great depth about all of that inter-relation. If there is a key challenge facing both of the communities it would be peripherality in the European context, peripherality in the UK context and even peripherality in the Aberdeenshire context. When you look at the road transport, which you will have used to get from the airport last night up here, it is far from perfect, although there are plans to dual the Balmedie-Tipperty road at the moment. This is not just in terms of road transport but also in terms of IT infrastructure, the companies in this area can feel

very remote from not just Scotland and the UK but also decision takers in various places and I want to just develop that a bit further. 2002, when you are looking at the Common Fisheries Policy, was very definitely seen by the skippers in this town as being a far distant imposition of some regulation that they could not really grasp and there was a lot of angst and meetings at the Waterside Hotel, which Malcolm might well have been at. I remember the Provost of Aberdeenshire Council, who was trying to lead on fighting their issues, being pilloried by the fishermen saying, "You are not doing enough. You are doing this to us", a real feeling of distance from the decision taker to the various sectors of the fishing industry, and also I grasped at that time some real divisions within the community where you had pelagic against demersal, you had catcher against processor. Everything was somebody else's fault. It was the French, the Spanish. There was really no consensus about where the remediation might come from other than that it was becoming increasingly apparent that it was not going to be a case of *laissez-faire*. Something had to be done and some management had to be put in place and that was going to come through the Common Fisheries Policy. At the same time two very crucial decisions were going on at UK level and at Scottish Government level. The economy at this time was very much supported by 514 airmen based at RAF Buchan just five miles to the south. I was talking to one of you from Norfolk a minute ago. The decision was made to pull out of Buchan and concentrate on RAF Neatishead. That immediately removed £10 million from the local economy and I think it was very much viewed as Westminster as well as Europe being bad to Buchan. At the same time the Scottish Prison Service announced the closure of HMP Peterhead with the loss of 300 jobs associated with it, again resulting in something like £10 million of annual turnover taken out of the local economy. That decision became overturned after a local community campaign, which I was certainly part of, as were several other people in this town, quite a rare thing, I think, fighting for retention of a prison just because, if nothing else, that shows you the fragility and feelings of suspicion at the time. Faced with those challenges, the council, along with the local enterprise company, Scottish Enterprise Grampian, and the local affordable housing provider on behalf of the Government, Communities Scotland, as they then were, formed a tripartite agreement called Building Buchan. That was to take a holistic look at this, and I do appreciate you are looking at a somewhat sectoral issue, but with all these various community threats coming up contemporaneously there was a real feeling that the media might grasp onto, "The world is full of doom and gloom, the world stops at Ellon. Nothing ever happens north of there", and there would be a real drift of folk and community apathy as a result of that. We therefore took a very holistic look at where the towns were at through a mechanism called the Aberdeenshire Towns Partnership and started to produce some broad-range strategies, looking at as many different aspects of community regeneration as we possibly could, and I am very willing to be questioned on the detail of that later. Most significantly, in terms of headline indicators, unemployment hit a record in November 2007. It was a record low, 1.2 per cent. I do not know your own conceptions of this, and I know some of you are Scots based but, certainly when I was going through university, 1.2 per cent was well above what the rate of full employment would have been regarded as, well below the UK and Scots national averages as well, and so the overall impression as a straightforward headline indicator is that we have traded through those three big impact hits all contemporaneously in 2002, and community confidence at the moment is about as strong as it has ever been, certainly in my time in Peterhead, which goes back 20 years. I am not saying for a moment that everything is a basketful of roses and that things cannot go wrong again. We have some fairly fragile economies which are very sectorally driven and it does not take much to bring the threats back to the table. We are by no means complacent and a lot of the effort of Building Buchan was about starting to look at other activities that could happen. I will go into the depth of it a bit more but a major factor has been the energy industry. The St Fergus gas terminal is five miles to the north. The North Sea oil industry has been going through some restructuring with all the people who arrived in the late sixties, early seventies reaching the time of life when they need replacing with incoming folk, so to a large degree, I think, some of the actions outwith the fishing community have been the saviour of some of the pain that has had to be borne since 2002. I do not know if that is evidence that you are getting from others. I did hear a comment along those lines as I walked into the room, so the buoyancy of the north east economy generally in construction, in oil and gas, in terms of offshore employment has been very positive, and we have just missed out on what would have been a very significant contribution to climate change in terms of carbon capture, as some of you may well know, at Peterhead Power Station which would have been a world first. We got pretty close with BP and Scottish and Southern to making that happen and the consent was on the verge of being given but the finances in the end have just got a bit too messy. Rolling forward, clearly employment has become more of a concern. I said 1.2 per cent unemployment, but there are also cited figures, the most recent ones being provided by Grampian Racial Equality Council, in terms of migrant workers. I know that is one of the things you are probably concerned with. The most recent

estimate is of 1,000 in Peterhead and 1,000 in Fraserburgh who are currently working coming to live in the north east and partly forming new communities here. I was talking to Malcolm briefly and there is some counter evidence to suggest that, with the strength of the euro and with wage levels rising in Poland, there are early indications of a reversal of that trend. What we are picking up is a bit of a change in that we have had east Europeans, young, single male workers coming into the town probably five years ago and now a second wave of more family orientated people, children certainly coming to the local secondary and primary schools. There are six primary schools in Peterhead. Peterhead Central now has 26 different nationalities in the primary school, just to give you a feel for the level of challenge it presents to teachers, but secondly the width of nationalities coming and being represented in the community, by and large, I have to say, very happily. We have run literacy and other developments in very close contact with Grampian Police and the Chief Inspector up the road. We are not picking up on major problems. We have had to explain one or two simple practicalities, things like, "Please don't take your gun to the pub. That's really not acceptable behaviour in Scotland", "Please don't leave your seven-year old in the house overnight by himself", and, "You can call the Fire Brigade without expecting a large bill. They will put your fire out", very simple things which the Scots probably take for granted but have been fairly major social integration issues for the council and its partners. Can I pause there? I have been provided with a set list of things that you might want answered in a bit more depth but if there are general points about my role and about what I perceive as happening in Peterhead since 2002 I would be very pleased to answer them.

Q492 *Chairman:* Can I say two things, and they are not general points, I am afraid; they are specific points? One of my indicators for community affluence is the number of charity shops in a high street. You have a lot of charity shops in the high street.
Mr White: That is undoubtedly true. I could try and explain that away by saying that we have a lot of voluntary sector activity—never underestimate the role of religion in both Peterhead and Fraserburgh—and a lot of activity by fishers' wives in terms of wanting to volunteer and be involved. Obviously, exemption from various rates and taxes also plays a big factor, and across Scotland we have definitely been facing issues of town centres contracting, concentrating less on direct retail and more on service trades. That is very common across the north east, as you all know well. Peterhead has yet to lift its boot straps on this. My contention would be that supermarkets eat more and more of the general

market and trying to compete with supermarkets on quantity never works. You have to compete on quality. There are towns in the north east of Scotland that have done that extremely well and Inverurie is the best example which has probably done better than most. Clearly these have been about personal services and about trading on quality. Peterhead has semblances of that but it is really not showing well. I am more concerned for Fraserburgh. When you are in Fraserburgh at the moment there are a lot of vacant shops, let alone charity shops, and the overall impact of the town centre in Fraserburgh at the moment, and Malcolm knows better than I, is not great.

Q493 *Chairman:* Would you also like to say something about drugs?

Mr White: You can take several viewpoints on drugs. First, the fishing industry itself has an implication in it. Heroin in particular had a reputation in Fraserburgh for some time and banner headlines were trotted out as soon as even minor seizures were made of anything or there was yet another incident of fatalities and health related issues. There was almost a denial in Fraserburgh or a lack of willingness to address the issue and I think that still exists to a fair degree. I am not saying for a moment that it does not exist in Peterhead. However, when you talk to the Police Service locally, the superintendent here has returned fairly recently. He said he could not believe how low the level of crime in Peterhead was generally. I hope I am not being hopelessly naïve here but there is an understanding of who the dealers are, that it is a local market, and the view of the NHS locally and Grampian Police is that it is contained. I am not saying for a moment that for the families involved it is not devastating and that as a parent it is very hard to contain your emotions in terms of what that might mean. However, the level of significance, as I understand it from the NHS, is that it is not rising, it is contained and a large degree of it probably comes down to the level of affluence that exists in young fishermen coming back on shore with too much money immediately available, who would traditionally have gone out and bought the biggest, fastest car they possibly could before the tax bill arrived but who now have another opportunity for spending that money on something which clearly is not going to do them any good in the long term, although neither would driving an Opel Manta GTE far too fast.

Q494 *Chairman:* When our predecessor committee looked at the current fisheries policy in 2003 it made the point that the economic return to fishing communities was pretty low, profitability levels were low and there was declining employment. It is difficult to get the mix because you have the oil as

well. What is your view on employment levels and wealth coming in through fishing?

Mr White: I can give you my perception and it is a slightly different one in Peterhead from Fraserburgh. The Peterhead issue would be that it is pretty much right sized, to use a horribly trite phrase, but nevertheless those boats which were coming to the end of their shelf life anyway and those skippers who were coming to the point of life when they would have benefited financially from simply coming out of the fleet took the opportunity to do so and by and large the view within the community was good luck to them for doing so. Some of those folk will be living in the bright blue top 20% areas in the town now, or possibly in Spain. That is fair and good to a degree. I suspect also we have seen a lot of investment into the pelagic fleet and Malcolm knows about that far better than I do. The tradition has been that you look at the fishing fleet as a whole but it is very definitely two different sectors in my humble estimation. I think the biggest impacts have been in white fish where boats were smaller, generally more ageing. The profits and proceeds in pelagic have been rising, certainly up until recently. I know there are real threats, which I am sure you have been hearing about from others, about oil prices and what that might mean in terms of future proceeds. It would be simplistic to say that the overall view is that things are now right sized, and you might hear differently down at the Dolphin Café very shortly, but actually they are doing okay is the perception that is reaching me, and that there still are plenty of fish out in the sea, which they will no doubt be lobbying you about, saying, "We need to ease off our quotas", or whatever. The technical evidence perhaps is not quite that now but nevertheless the overriding impression is of an industry which had to go through turmoil, did go through turmoil and has probably come out more healthy as a result of doing so.

Q495 *Chairman:* Looking at the fishing industry and the difference between the catching side and the processing side, where is the processing side now?

Mr White: I am sure you will have heard the phrase "vertical integration". Going back to what I said about 2002, definitely fingers are being pointed in all directions. The people I feel sorriest for are the white fish processing sector who have been subject to fewer fish and much higher prices. The knock-on effect of that industry-wise has meant contraction. They have faced major rises in water charges, difficulties in keeping retained labour with any great skills and several of the local white fish processors have gone to the wall over the last few years, particularly the smaller ones who did not have the economies of scale and the breadth and tradition of knowing the markets well enough. There have been some job losses in the white fish processing sector generally.

The overview on the pelagics has been quite the opposite. As you leave the town you will see Lunar. They are investing in a major new fish processing facility there, but the general overriding concern is that we are bit too quick to bang a lid on the box and send the fish away. We are not adding enough value to the fish before it leaves the port to head to Boulogne and other places across Europe. One of the other points I wish to make is that we have not looked after the supply chain well enough in terms of the overall look of the fishing industry, the guys that make the ice boxes in the past that have been reliant on marine engineering and the supply trades that have provided the paint and the food to go offshore. A lot of these guys have struggled pretty manfully and if you are looking around the inner harbour, for instance, the marine engineering side has definitely struggled.

Q496 *Viscount Brookeborough:* I think you have almost completely addressed the two questions on employment and nationality that I had. However, you do point out that Peterhead is perhaps one of the exceptions in being able to take the downturn since the year 2001 and 2005 and to and taking up other industries. Where you do have problems with alternative employment have you been able to access such funds as the European Fisheries Fund?
Mr White: Malcolm may have to add a bit of extra detail but I would have to say that I do not think it has been huge. I mentioned Building Buchan. One of the key things that did was look at diversification. I talked about ice boxes, which is about making polystyrene. There are other things you can do with polystyrene other than provide fish boxes, so we did work with quite a few of the local companies, 15 of them, to say, "This market is not going to stay static. We need to diversify and bring in new training opportunities and look at what your company does which is going to allow you to thrive". That was run through Objective 2 of the European Union's policy which provided 50% of the funding to put that scheme to hand for them and work with local business development advocates in terms of taking a good look at business plans. Far too many of the companies we dealt with had virtually no business plans so there is a certain amount of maturing needed in terms of the commercial sector as well, looking at how things are developing and where the new markets would be in a world which was not terribly reliant on fish, so, unless Malcolm is going to kick me under the table and contradict me, I do not think the grants coming from the EFF have been seen as being particularly helpful.
Mr Morrison: The previous Financial Instrument for Fisheries Guidance did not have the same social aspect to it as the European Fisheries Fund will have and Aberdeenshire Council will be looking to work

with the Government and try and get some of the social funding aspects into the north east. They already use funds on the agricultural side from the Regional Development Fund, but they are debarred from the towns of Peterhead and Fraserburgh so there will be a different kind of mechanism used for that. In terms of the Financial Instrument for Fisheries Guidance, a lot of the money did come to the processing side in the north east. There was a lot put into fishermen's training and the improvement of facilities around here but not specifically into the social aspects of it. It is a different thing.

Q497 *Viscount Brookeborough:* You have a high level of immigrant workers at the moment, as you said. Does society here mirror agricultural in some areas in that the children of current fishermen are getting a better education and leaving, and, if so, what is the future effect in the long term as to the following on generation?
Mr White: I will provide a few anecdotes here in terms of answering that question. The Director of Peterhead Academy said he had a 14-year old come to see him five years ago who said, "What do you earn?". I will not share with you what the Director of the Academy earns but it is a reasonably substantial salary, and the young guy going into the fishing industry said, "I will be making within two years more than you". The world simply did not mean anything other than fish, but he said that that has now completely changed, that whole attitude of wanting to spend life out at sea, and the desirability suddenly of jobs in the processing sector. Those of you who have been in fish factories and smelt the vinegar and put on the hat know it is not the nicest place to work in life. I am not saying there are not other jobs which can be equally bad but it is not something which I suspect the young up-and-coming Dux of the Academy immediately thinks is the very thing they would like to do for the rest of their days. It has become much more difficult, I suspect, to sell life as a fisherman and to sell life as a processor. I heard the words "Banff and Buchan College" being raised earlier when I walked into the room. There has been quite an effort which it has been leading in terms of trying to encourage marine navigation skills and the development of ship-related activities in the widest sense. I think several of the skippers probably literally jumped ship to become oil supply experts, so again the skills transferred relatively easily, I suspect, into other things which were still making money.

Q498 *Viscount Brookeborough:* And do you ever look into the crystal ball or do you dare look at what life might be like after oil?
Mr White: We have to. I remember arriving from Pimlico in 1985 to be told that oil was drying up in the north east and that within five years we would be

turning off the flues and shutting down the power stations. Quite palpably that has not been the case 20 years on. Oil and gas is still a major player in the north east economy. Expertise exists in this area. For instance, Westhill has become the world base for subsea technology and Peterhead is one of the places you can exemplify for training of new subsea vehicles. That is going to be transferable knowledge, that critical mass of expertise and skills worldwide. I certainly have neighbours and colleagues that are increasingly spending their time in Azerbaijan. The world has become a smaller place and the skills which have existed in the north east economy in the oil and gas sector, I suspect, are going to stay here to a very large degree. My concern will be for the next generation who have no immediate need to stay in the north east of Scotland but we very much want to encourage them to do so, and particularly to exert their acumen and business experience that the generation before them exerted through the major corporates, so that as the world has increasingly become less corporate in that particular sphere we make sure those skills are developed and continue to develop in the north east. My overall conception is that energy will always stay important to this part of the world. Oil and gas is going to be a major player in this part of the world for at least the next 20 years and as the price of oil rises by the day it means that previously marginal fields are no longer quite as marginal as they were and as demand for oil continues to rise along with demand for associated technologies. I mentioned briefly carbon capture. Carbon capture is probably more relevant to coal-fired power stations and the transfer of that technology. There is no reason why some of the skills that have been developed around oil and gas cannot transfer to other technologies which will become the future of worldwide concerns.

Mr Morrison: The local industries were aware of the fact that there was a problem with recruitment and they are working with the Banff and Buchan College to try and make sure that there are discrete educational results given to young guys to come into the industry and work their way through and prove that if you have been a fisherman you are not just stuck there; you can do anything you want in the world. You can go and become a Merchant Navy officer, you can go into port operations, you can do anything, but this has always been sadly lacking in the past. There was not always this discrete path through education. It is recognised that even if it does take 20 years fishing will be sustainable in that it will be here after oil and gas and the industry is trying to address these things now.

Q499 *Baroness Jones of Whitchurch:* You were talking about training and retraining, and obviously fishing is going to be a key part for a very long time

to come, but are you also trying to encourage people to stay for other reasons? Do you have another couple of sectors you are trying to grow here, that you are trying to diversify into, or is it fishing and energy or nothing?

Mr White: Not quite energy or nothing. Rather analogous to the pelagic/demersals, energy is far from one sector. Decommissioning is potentially extremely large money, not necessarily very labour intensive but definitely is a market which Peterhead is looking at very seriously at the moment, not in terms of wanting great hulking rigs sitting in the bay for a long period of time but there is a company called Score on the south edge of town which has individual valves worth £5 million sitting in boxes inside its sheds, just to give you a flavour of the extent of the value of some of the reworking of oil and gas. Renewables is another one which we are definitely targeting and increasing activity on. Transportation links are probably the principal barrier to the development of renewable technology. You cannot land a wind turbine in Peterhead. If you move it anywhere it gets stuck, so very simplistic things like that prevent some of those technologies being applied more but the skills definitely exist. Also, the quality end of food and drink still exists as a possibility for Grampian. That is something we have traded on for a very long time and there still will be opportunities, as the world becomes increasingly hooked on biofuels and the use of land for other reasons, to look at some of the key potentials which might link well to fishing, some of the analogous trades, but again it is back to the value added thing, that we are far too quick at getting rid of our product once we have made it and do not do enough with it to add value before it goes.

Q500 *Chairman:* Is not one of your basic problems that any incoming potential developer would look at 1.2% unemployment and say, "There is a problem for labour supply and there is a problem for labour costs"?

Mr White: Absolutely. That said, I would settle for a problem of 1.2% unemployment.

Q501 *Lord Plumb:* I think you have adequately answered the next question on fishing capacity and I was very interested in your comments. Through the difficult period of the fisheries policy it does not seem to me that there has been a lot of loss of employment and when we talk about capacity, of course, having seen what we have seen and talked to a lot of people this morning, it seems that technology is taking over, as it is in all industries and new ships are being built and new ships will come in but probably some of the older ships will be going out. Do you see the need for change in that capacity building? I was also interested in your comment about development policies.

Development policies, of course, overall have undoubtedly helped the economy tremendously in Scotland, and I remember it being said at the time these were fixed on a regional basis of areas that were eligible for or in need of assistance to encourage growth in employment and so on in these various areas. It was said that the inspectors who were looking at those various areas walked the length of England and they were so tired when they got up to the border that they looked over and said, "Include the rest". That was always the standing joke because a major part of Scotland was included and there were many parts in England that were left out that they thought should be included, that I thought should be included, but that is another matter. On the question, therefore, of employment overall I think your story has been not only most interesting but quite encouraging to hear. Oil procurement on the processing and the development on that side is a point you make very strongly. We are now in the business surely of taking big advantage of the export market in a way that we have not been for a very long time because of the narrowing of the gap between the value of sterling and the value of the euro and that presumably will develop still further. I know from experience that the export trade is now determining the price of food goods throughout the whole of the United Kingdom. It is leading the market; it is not the supermarkets necessarily leading the price. Do you see that same sort of thing happening in fish and could we not make a very clear statement that it does seem daft in the interests of food miles to be sending these products off far and wide and ten days later, or five days later I think we were told yesterday, bring them back from the processing that has gone on there to the market here?

Mr White: I concur with what is behind a lot of what you are saying. It strikes me as bizarre that we are sending prawns from Dumfries and Galloway to Thailand to get processed to bring back to sell in Scotland. However you view sustainable development, that is not it in my humble estimation. You could parallel that with long debates we have had about simple things like play areas. Should we be bringing coir matting from Sri Lanka to put down on the bases of play areas or should we be using local recycled tyres? I know which is cheaper but also which is the more sustainable in terms of ongoing development and fuel impacts on climate change. I think right across society we have some big questions to ask. Your point about the pound and the euro is also very apposite. We are picking up early stories of the Poles starting to be paid more in Poland than potentially they were. If the whole processing sector in Peterhead is underpinned by migrant labour, and they have been very well received by the processors, I have to say, because these are people who put in a full day's work for a full day's pay, and that is now under

threat, and the gentleman on my right may know more about than I do, that certainly gives me concerns. It is an industry which has really struggled to mechanise and so it may well be that the capacity issues and the desirability of employment in the industry needs to be re-focused and re-looked at from a UK stance as well as a European one. There is a straightforward assumption, I think, that everybody that works in fish processing is from the Baltic States. It has definitely not been the case in the past. Quite sizeable numbers of Portuguese and south east Asian migrant workers have been active in Peterhead and it may well be that if there is to be a reverse in the Baltic movement we have to look again at what that means in terms of permitting folk to come in from other parts of the European Union as wage levels start to harmonise across Europe.

Q502 *Lord Plumb:* What about the property market in Peterhead?

Mr White: That is a very interesting point. Not very long ago you could have bought a four-bedroom flat close to here for £50,000. Things would stay on the market for a couple of years without shifting. Two things have been happening. In terms of the residential market the fish companies I am sure have been very active players in terms of buying up a lot of that surplus demand and have done pretty well out of it. Peterhead, I think, was third in terms of the Scottish rises in property last year, above 30%. Fraserburgh was top at 45%, so there have been some very significant rises in real property prices. That is not just down to houses already on the market suddenly being snapped up. A lot of it is based on, going back to the blue areas on the western edges, some fairly big and reasonably comfortable high £200,000's, low £300,000's houses being built, four and five bedrooms. I would love to do an analysis to find out who is moving into these houses because they are being built at a rate faster than at any time in the eight years I have been Area Manager here. The overall mood is buoyant in the residential sector. Part of it, I am certain, will be overspill from Aberdeen where there has been a fairly constrained residential market just in terms of the supply of housing coming up quickly enough and you will get a bigger house for your money in Peterhead than you ever would in Aberdeen, so that is certainly an issue and has been an opportunity which has been seized on. It is also mirrored in the commercial sector. We have B&Q, we have Tesco looking round the town, we have Asda wanting to double, we have Morrisons wanting to double, all at the same time, so there clearly has been an uplift in terms of the general conception of the money available and the economy and the threats that we were facing in 2002. It gives me further evidence that we have traded through that. We have not got an industrial premise I could let you at the moment. They are all fully taken up and so we are now looking at rationalising some of the industrial land and trying to bring that forward, so overall I hate to be complacent but things are looking reasonably bullish.

Q503 Lord Plumb: You do not see a recession on the horizon?

Mr White: Never say never. Clearly UK-wide things are constraining. A large part of that is down to the American dollar and sub-prime mortgages, I suspect. There is no evidence yet of any of that reaching the north east of Scotland. I was talking to an Aberdeen solicitor who was saying she had been marketing property at £600,000 that sold at £750,000 only a couple of weeks ago, so that gives you a fair indication that there is still plenty of money going round the local economy in the north east. Not every house in Peterhead sells for those kinds of numbers. What I think is starting to flatten off, and we are getting evidence of this in Inverurie where there have been a lot of houses come on to the market at the same time, is the new house market. There are starting to be incentives given by some of the mainstream builders to get folk in a bit quicker. It tends to be the case in the north east that things slowly gravitate that way rather than immediately impact. It does have its own internal momentum. There are just starting to be one or two signs that things are perhaps not going quite as fast as they were, but we also have a new structure plan on the horizon which, whether or not Mr Trump gets his golf application approved or not, will lead to a sizeable number of new houses coming this way.

Q504 Earl of Dundee: To what extent do you think that transitional aid will assist fish stock recovery?

Mr Morrison: What we are looking at here would be to keep people afloat if there were temporary closures but transition aid, as far as we are concerned in the north east, should not be needed now for permanent cessation of fishing because the fleet is in balance with the resource, which is generally agreed, and there are figures coming from the Sea Fish Industry Authority. In the future they may be needed as an incentive for the further measures, the real-time closures, but not as a mainstay of the industry.

Q505 Earl of Dundee: And within a parallel yet slightly different measurement how far do you think exit payments will cause a reduction in fishing capacity?

Mr Morrison: I do not think that is relevant in the north east any more. I think the people that are in the industry now are there for the long term. It is a sustainable industry. They want to be in it, they want to have a future here. I do not think we want exit measures here. I think that is a thing of the past.

There may be other parts of the UK where they are looking for it but certainly not here.

Q506 Chairman: Why do we continually get this story through the media that the poor old fisherman is having a rough time and life is grim and awful and there is no money to be made out of fishing these days? That is still the popular picture, is it not? Why is that so rather than saying, "It is a great success and we are off to Spain next week for nine months because we do not have to work for another nine months"?

Mr Morrison: It is something that we fight against. You will never find a happy fisherman and a happy farmer. In terms of the media, no news is good news, so it is a battle that we are having to fight in the fishing industry here all the time and we need to portray it as a good industry. We need to have a perception in the media that it is a worthwhile industry, just to make sure it carries on.

Q507 Chairman: Is it that Peterhead is different from the industry elsewhere and the rest of the UK does live up to that negative stereotype?

Mr Morrison: I honestly do not think so. I think the industry throughout the UK is something to be looked up to. It is a different model in the north east. It is still primarily family owned and to me that is a great incentive for you to keep your business going if your family is involved. It is a different way of looking at it.

Mr White: I would like to make one other point which I have not got over yet. I was talking about 2002 and the fractured nature of the industry and almost the denial of the fact that there were issues to be faced. I think there has been a complete reversal, and I would be interested to hear what you hear from the skippers, in terms of attitude in working consensually towards taking matters forward, a recognition that the safeguarding of their industry is based on good information, working alongside fishery protection, working alongside the scientific community in terms of assessing fish stock, making sure that where there are increases in supply that is known about and is authenticated and validated. I am sensing a very definite change in attitude from people who would have simply said, "No, this is not an issue. We are going to land as many fish as we can as fast we can", to a recognition that landing quality fish means higher values, which leads to longer employment, which leads to a sustainable future. I hope that is the message you will get from Peterhead as a whole but it is certainly one that is related here recently.

Q508 Baroness Sharp of Guildford: We have talked already a bit about structural funds and in some of the earlier work this Committee has done on the Common Fisheries Policy we noted that the

Financial Instrument for Fisheries Guidance, the FIFG funds, had not been taken up in a big way, partly because of the way in which the UK rebate system worked. Is there still room or are you still eligible for structural funds and is there room for use of structural funds if the national authorities here in Scotland or the UK authorities were to take a slightly more helpful attitude? Can I add to that another issue that I think again came up from the discussions this morning where your Harbourmaster was very anxious that we should recognise the potential of the port here for expansion. You were saying that you have seen an increase in the landings of quality fish over the last two or three years and he feels that if the facilities in the harbour were improved there would be greater potential for expanding the capacity of Peterhead as a fishing port or as a landing port potentially for processing but certainly for passing on. That needs infrastructure funds. Do the structural funds provide a possible source of funds here?

Mr White: They do and they do not. I will answer this by saying that, if you were to take a rational approach, when you look at what the Scottish Government is doing with Scottish local authorities at the moment, forming single outcome agreements which say, "These are the things we want to achieve and this is the amount of money that we are prepared to give you to allow you to then go and develop it", you can then parallel that to European funding which works very much more sectorally in complete silos for different types of activity which do not always combine and do not always relate very well. There is real frustration there that when you look at the individual schemes which exist, some of which have their own separate and almost conflicting eligibility requirements and a huge amount of administration with government issues that relate to them as well, it is not all that easy to draw down funding for the right purpose despite very often the business case being right, despite very often the need for widespread impacts in the community having been quite easily recognisable and the opportunities very deliverable. I find that very frustrating from a personal point of view, that I can see where we want to get to but we cannot use the existing tools that we have, instead conflicting house of cards type funding packages, to allow each of those strands to support each other to deliver.

Q509 Baroness Sharp of Guildford: But these constraints are community constraints?
Mr White: Yes.

Q510 Baroness Sharp of Guildford: Neither the Scottish Government nor the UK Government can do a great deal to help you on this.

Mr White: Certainly to date. I would love to see that change.

Q511 Baroness Sharp of Guildford: Obviously, it is open to the UK Government or to either Government to put pressure on the EU authorities to change the rules.
Mr White: Yes, and certainly I would cite the concentration on outcome as being the most important thing. Clearly the money is there for a purpose and if they put the purpose before the money I think that is perhaps a way forward.
Mr Morrison: Aberdeenshire Council has lobbied, with the introduction of the European Fisheries Fund, to make sure that the intervention rates do not stay too low. If the funds are not being taken up then raise the rates so that people find it more attractive to go for something and they are all getting the funds, but we will see how that happens.

Q512 Viscount Ullswater: We have had evidence from Regional Advisory Councils and they are very complimentary about the assistance that you have given them, both financially and in the provision of meeting rooms, probably this one.
Mr White: They have been here, yes.

Q513 Viscount Ullswater: The concept is still in its infancy but what we have been hearing is that perhaps they may develop to becoming more management type councils rather than purely advisory. Do you think the composition is about right to reflect the catching sector, the processing sector, the socio-economic sector, which I would put you in? Do you sit on it? Does Buchan sit on it and how do you see it? Is it too dominated by the catching sector?
Mr White: To answer the direct question, no, I do not sit on it. I do have very good links with Ann Bell, which is the reason why I am talking to you today, I suspect. Across the council we clearly have a series of corporate roles and we play those in different ways. My colleague, Jim Knowles, the Head of Economic Development, is very influential in terms of the North Sea Regional Advisory Council. To answer your question about the catching, processing and onshore, ongoing industries, you could argue that it is, of course, catching dominated because that is certainly where the majority of issues begin. Whether that is quite balanced off with as much capacity as it should be in terms of the other sectors I am sure Malcolm will have a view about. I would certainly make a case for a widespread discussion being far more useful than a very narrowly focused one.
Mr Morrison: The Regional Advisory Councils themselves are very aware of the shortcomings on the socio-economic side particularly and they are making moves to try and address those. It has been very

difficult to get anybody from the consumer groupings to attend these things. It is an ongoing work strand trying to get consumers and even indeed to keep the NGOs engaged with it because they need to be there but they do not always see it as being quite as important as they should do.

Q514 *Viscount Ullswater:* What we have heard as a result of meetings is that if they come out with a unified voice coming from different sides then the Commission does really listen to it, so that is obviously a step in the right direction.
Mr Morrison: That is my understanding from the top of the Commission at the level of Mr Borg, that that is how he sees it. If it is a unanimous voice it has to be listened to.

Q515 *Lord Cameron of Dillington:* Judging from conversations that I have had this morning, leasing of quota, and leasing indeed of days at sea, seems to be alive and well in Peterhead. I am just wondering what you think about the idea of more permanent individual transferable quotas. We are talking, obviously, from the point of view of the local community. Would the big guys all buy out the small guys, which might not be quite such a good thing? There are several boats from Inverness I see in the harbour. Would they go further afield? What is your view? On the other hand it would give quite a lot of permanent flexibility because there is no doubt that the annual leasing charge is a real bane of a lot of people's lives?
Mr White: I hate to sound overly parochial but I am going to be a little bit here, I think. What I have written down is that to a large degree fishery operations are classic, small family businesses and that is the point we have made. I think long term sustainability is based around the continuation of traditional family-based concerns with clear buy-in from family members to their future, and certainly in terms of buying out large elements of that local control that is possibly not something which I would want to encourage. I could potentially see major threats and Inverness is one thing but you do not need to go too much further before you start thinking that it is a world economy and things are much more subject to control, back to 2002 a little bit, a feeling of alienation, of decisions being taken in far-off ports which are affecting Peterhead too closely, so my overall view would be against that.

Q516 *Earl of Arran:* Would this come under the heading of stewardship rights? The previous speaker this morning was very loathe to comment.
Mr White: I am only unwilling to comment from ignorance rather than anything else.
Mr Morrison: The Scottish Government is about to have a consultation on it.

Q517 *Earl of Arran:* That is right, the same kind of idea as you have told us.
Mr Morrison: They will be wanting to examine how this can be resolved because at the moment north of the border it is mainly family owned businesses that are fishing. South of the border you have quite a development of company businesses and with the introduction of tradable rights and these scenarios a lot of these companies are now owned by Dutch and Spanish interests. Within a given time that could disappear, so ideally in a scenario like the north east of Scotland where you have Fraserburgh and Peterhead you have MacDuff, Burghie, you have all these communities which are hugely reliant on fishing. They need to have the resource there available to them in order to continue fishing, so if you take the resource away that is the end of the industry.

Q518 *Earl of Arran:* I suggest that it could be very controversial.
Mr Morrison: Yes, so it is going to be a very important consultation.

Q519 *Chairman:* The trouble is that we did a report on the European wine industry and we went to parts of Europe where wine is produced of very poor quality not intended to be drunk at all but is grown for the distillation subsidy, and the argument there was, "If we do not do this we do not have any employment, we do not have any money and we have to do it". I am afraid that argument received pretty short shrift from us, but here it is very different in that the fish is a high quality product.
Mr Morrison: They are not looking for subsidy. They just want the right to make a living.

Q520 *Earl of Arran:* Fish and chips beckon and the final question we have is about employment, but I think I am right in saying that in the past some of the Member States did regard the CFP as an employment tool, as a welfare state almost rather than a business. My feeling is that it is very much the opposite now. Would I be right or are there still some aspects where that has to be justified?
Mr White: I want to use this question to draw two conclusions which we have discussed so far. First, the CFP began by being seen as a very distant imposition and not as something which was going to lead to where I think we are today, which is a much more consensual approach to how fishery is beginning to be managed. All the indications I have seen over the last six years have been much more about what you are referring to, about right sizing businesses, about leading to a positive future for fishing in the north east of Scotland, which I do not think people were predicting at the turn of the century looking forward. The growth of consensus across the industry sectors

has been absolutely consequential on that and to a large degree I think we are moving in the right direction at the moment through the Regional Advisory Councils and others. People are not beating a path to my door in the way that they were in 2002 with a whole host of problems. The only one I am really picking up at the moment is the fuel price being an overriding industry concern, and for that read farmers, read every other business that operates in the north east of Scotland relative to the peripheral economy. My overriding conclusion is that it has been used as a way, by hook or by crook, to get to where we needed to get to. I now think we can be positive and look forward and I think the industry is starting to feel that as well.

Q521 Earl of Arran: Did I hear you aright when you said that very few of the owners would have, for instance, a three-year business plan?
Mr White: Banff and Buchan College did some work on our behalf in terms of looking at attitudes to training and development. They interviewed a whole series of companies in Peterhead and Fraserburgh. They struggled to get through all the doors first of all, which was in itself a little concerning, bearing in mind they were bringing a chequebook with them at the time. The figure I remember was that only 30% of them had a business plan which looked more than 12 months ahead. That is maybe symptomatic of the industry and the turbulence that it was going through. It is probably more to do with, put very bluntly, some outdated attitudes towards business management.

Q522 Earl of Arran: Yes, I am sure that is right.
Mr White: They had been family concerns. If you do not mind my being colloquial, it has been the back of a fag packet stuff and that clearly had to change.

Q523 Viscount Brookeborough: On the whole would you say that you were happy with the CFP and that with some of reforms it will continue to do as good a job as you say it has done here?
Mr White: That is a dirty question. The gentleman on my right will have a much more technical background. In my view it would be yes, but he may disagree with me.
Mr Morrison: On a personal basis I would disagree with Chris on this one, that the CFP has started completely in the wrong direction. In one way that has been beneficial because it has been so wrong that everybody has struggled to find the right answer. Where the people that are affected by the decisions are involved in the decisions to a degree that can only be better for the industry in the long term.

Q524 Lord Cameron of Dillington: Looking at some of the figures we have here, I notice that Fraserburgh, for instance, has had a huge increase in the value of fish landings, which seems to be largely related to the nephrops catch. Is there is a big increase in the nephrops catch and is that a concern to you in terms of over-fishing?
Mr White: I remember a Fraserburgh skipper saying to me, "They are walking off the beach at the moment, Chris". There has been specialisation increasing over recent times. More and more of the pelagic has been based in Peterhead and more and more of the prawns based in Fraserburgh. Malcolm again will know the technical background much more than I but certainly there have been gluts in nephrops in recent times.

Q525 Lord Cameron of Dillington: Is it a concern that the nephrops catch is getting too big?
Mr Morrison: The scientific evidence says that the nephrops stock is in good standing and the level of catching is fine.

Q526 Lord Cameron of Dillington: We heard a slightly different story from a traditional nephrops fisherman this morning, but he was probably trying to lobby us.
Mr White: Perhaps he is one of those fishermen who have not had a good year.

Q527 Baroness Sharp of Guildford: Can I just raise one other thing which you mentioned? I was quite interested in the degree to which you saw the RAC as having been one of the instruments that had turned round feelings in the industry. For the question that you were asked about the RACs you rather played them down as being one of the things that was changing the industry and yet, certainly when we took evidence from them, we did get this feeling that they had helped to create a sense amongst players in the industry that they were players and also to increase trust between different players, particularly getting people together from different countries and getting the scientists talking with the fishermen themselves. On the whole your attitude is positive, not negative, towards them, is it?
Mr Morrison: I have to declare a vested interested in that I sit in the office that hosts the North Sea Regional Advisory Council. In Aberdeenshire it has long been the way that we work that the council works along with the catching side of the industry, the processing side of the industry, the scientists and the ancillary trades to try and work together and make a clear picture, and that has moved on from having the North East Scotland Fisheries Development Partnership and that moved on to the North Sea Commission and Aberdeenshire has been very strongly involved in that. Then there was a

fisheries partnership there which brought scientists and fishermen together from around the North Sea and then eventually that led on to the North Sea Regional Advisory Council, I guess. It has always been part of the way we have worked together and

hopefully the Regional Advisory Council will be something that will be remembered from here.
Chairman: Thank you very much, Malcolm, Chris. It is a nice context in which to place what we are hearing about the industry.

Examination of Witness

Witness: MR CEPHAS RALPH, Director of Operations, Scottish Fisheries Protection Agency, examined.

Q528 Chairman: Good afternoon. Thanks very much for coming along and helping us. This is a formal evidence session so a note will be taken. The transcript will be sent to you for you to look through and see if there are any slips that have come in. The other thing is that I normally have to say at this point is that it is being webcast and there might be somebody listening, but as it is not being webcast there is no chance of anybody listening. I wonder if we could fire straight in if that is all right. I do have to say I have many happy memories of the SFPA, particularly a certain ship that took me on a rather nice trip on one occasion. Could you outline the role and objectives of the organisation?
Mr Ralph: The Scottish Fisheries Protection Agency's role is to monitor compliance with fisheries legislation and regulations in the Scottish zone which extends out 200 miles and in all the ports around Scotland like Peterhead. We are present in 17 ports, all the main ports. We have nominally four ships at sea and we have two aircraft. The Agency is unique. I have quite a lot of experience of similar operations throughout the world. The Agency is self-contained. We are totally civilian. We do not rely on any military assets which would be the norm in other countries, naval ships or military aircraft, and our officers ashore are dedicated to the fisheries role. They are not harbour employees or customs officers, which is often the case in other places in the world, so it is essentially a one-stop shop for fishery protection and as such unique.

Q529 Lord Cameron of Dillington: I wanted to ask you a general question about your successes, what you see as your successes and what you see as your obstacles in working with the real-time closures system and illegal landings but also in terms of the new buyers and sellers rules and whether they have been helpful, and do you get support from the courts and adequate support in terms of fines and sentences and so on?
Mr Ralph: Where would you like me to start?

Q530 Lord Cameron of Dillington: We will leave it to you. Talk us through your successes and how it works.

Mr Ralph: As most of you will probably know, we have had a very significant historic problem with black fish, which relatively recently we have been able to overcome. That success has been due to quite a large number of factors coming together all at the same time or at similar times. A decommissioning scheme removed the over-capacity in the fleet, so that removed the financial imperative on many of the operators to land illegal fish. The registration of buyers and sellers scheme was vital because trade, of course, is a supply and demand equation. One cannot work without the other. For the first time the buyers and sellers legislation put an onus and the responsibility on the person buying fish to account for it in a way that we could come in and audit, so people who had been in the trade of buying illegal fish, essentially with impunity because once it was ashore there was very little we could do about it, were no longer able to do that.

Q531 Lord Cameron of Dillington: It is your organisation that monitors that?
Mr Ralph: Indeed, yes. Those people suddenly found themselves in the position of being unable to claim ignorance of the source. They moved into a position where they became co-conspirators if they were involved, so the vast majority of buyers did not want to be in that situation and that pretty much removed the demand side completely for black fish. That was a tremendous success. As the level of illegal activity came down we were able to adopt targeting techniques. Obviously, if the vast majority of a population are breaking the law then targeting does not really work because essentially everyone is at it, but when you come down to a more normal situation where the majority of people are sticking to the law then you can begin to introduce tried and tested police targeting techniques—the use of intelligence, the use of data analysis, to try and pinpoint those whose activities are not within the normal range, and we focused our efforts on them to further reduce the levels of illegal activity.

Q532 Lord Cameron of Dillington: What is the level of normal activity going on at the moment?
Mr Ralph: In terms of illegal landings into Scotland, our best intelligence would suggest that the levels are minimal, I would suspect less than one per cent,

probably much less. We have detected minor pockets of resurgence. The good thing from my point of view is that in many of the cases where we have detected illegal activity it has been fishermen themselves who have come to us and told us that they have suspicions about some operators in particular, and that is an extremely healthy sign.

Q533 Lord Cameron of Dillington: What about the real-time closures?
Mr Ralph: The real-time closures scheme is obviously aimed at protecting cod stocks and allowing the cod stocks to regenerate. We are integral in real-time closures in that we do inspections at sea to determine whether cod catches have reached a trigger level. If they have we propose to the Marine Directorate that a closure is put in place. If that is accepted we will then play our part in publicising the closure and monitoring compliance with it. It is not a legal requirement to comply with the closure so we do not prosecute anybody for not complying with it, but the theory is that if you comply with the closure you receive certain benefits in terms of flexibilities in the rules that govern your operation, but if you do not comply these flexibilities are removed.

Q534 Lord Cameron of Dillington: So in your view as overseer it is working, is it?
Mr Ralph: Yes.

Q535 Lord Cameron of Dillington: Have you had anybody not obeying the rules?
Mr Ralph: Yes. We have had one who claimed that he did not know. I think his claim was marginal but it was accepted. One of the problems that we had initially in the scheme was that the trigger for the closure is a large abundance of cod in the catch and cod are a fairly expensive fish. The scheme only applied to Scottish boats so in the fishery in the central North Sea where you have many nationalities one claim was that Scotland announcing a cod closure was the equivalent of putting up a big flag to other nations and saying, "It might be a bloody good idea to come and fish here because there are lots of cod about". We had specific problems in the first few weeks with some Danish vessels but that kind of faded away. Denmark are very keen to go down a similar route to us. I think they put some considerable pressure on their fleet to try and co-operate. Norway co-operates quite closely with us as well. Some of the closures that we have introduced have been on the Norwegian side of the North Sea. We can only monitor UK boats in the Norwegian zone. We rely on our Norwegian colleagues to use their technology and assets to monitor other nations and they co-operate really well with us.

Q536 Lord Plumb: Could I just ask whether you have much contact with your counterparts in other countries? Do you have regular meetings with them or do you compare notes?
Mr Ralph: Yes. I cannot explain why, but the bit of the North Sea between Scotland and England tends to be very lightly fished so there is very little cross-border interaction between the industries of Scotland and England. There is some, of course, but it is not huge, so our main day-to-day contact is not with our colleagues in London; it is with our colleagues in Bergen and in the Irish Republic and Northern Ireland, the Faroe Islands and Denmark and we have regular meetings particularly with Ireland and Norway. In fact, in two weeks' time we have an annual bilateral meeting with our counterparts in Norway and that will be hosted in Scotland. Next year it will be hosted in Norway and we had a bilateral with Southern Ireland last week in Glasgow.

Q537 Lord Plumb: And are they as strict as you?
Mr Ralph: Norwegian courts are extremely strict on fishery offences. It is not for me to say why but if you look at Norway it only has two major natural resources and one of them is fish. The court penalties in Norway are legendary. If you ask a fishermen in the street here if he would rather be prosecuted in a Scottish court or a Norwegian court his answer would always be a Scottish court. In Ireland they suffer a bit, like us, from the courts perhaps sympathising with the industry rather than viewing the impact of illegal activity. Ireland, however, have set up an enforcement agency. I attended the official opening of it last month. It was largely designed around the Scottish model. In fact, they called it the SFPA. That was an accident. The title of the organisation in Irish Gaelic is UCIM but nobody could speak Irish Gaelic so they translated it and it came out as SFPA. I would say that, certainly between ourselves and Ireland, there is a growing level of enforcement that perhaps was not present in the past. Certainly the new agency in Ireland is in my opinion a very professional organisation.

Q538 Viscount Ullswater: Can we deal with discards and discarding? You note in your 2006-2007 report that, maybe because of the registration of buyers and sellers or you may say that this is the right way forward, you have been able to divert some of your attention from the point of landing to the point of catch. I would like to hear what were the reasons that gave you that sort of feeling. Also, would that put you in a position to monitor more openly the discarding policy of the various boats and how would you feel if you were given the task of policing a discard ban?

Mr Ralph: They commented on that in our annual report and, when I went back to read it, it could be read out of context. The context in which it was written, I suppose, was the historical one where, when the Agency was formed, it had five of its own ships and two contract minesweepers from the Royal Navy. Pretty soon we realised that we were spending the vast majority of our money at sea whereas the vast majority of our problems existed ashore essentially, and we shifted the balance. We dropped the Royal Navy contract, we reduced the number of ships, we invested in new and more efficient ships to reduce the running costs and used that money to build up our resources ashore. Peterhead, for instance, is the main landing port in the UK. It is our main presence in Scotland and we have, I think, five or six officers on duty 24 hours a day seven days a week, so that is a significant number of people. We have a similar type of presence at a few other places as well and we cover the vast majority of landing opportunities by vessels landing into Scotland. What we have found in the last few years, given the high levels of compliance, is that we are essentially standing by watching people obey the law and there is a limit to how long you can do that when you have manned your organisation to deter and detect illegal activity, so we have just undergone an organisational review of our coastal officers and we have reduced manning at quite a few places. We are not reducing our overall coverage but we are, we hope, adjusting our manning to more appropriate levels given the high level of compliance. The amount of money that one extra ship would cost could never be covered by a reduction in manning ashore so it seems highly unlikely that we would be able to fund one more vessel. We might, however, be able to put additional people on the vessels, perhaps fisheries experts from shore stationed in the summer time, in the busy times, on our vessels. That is the kind of shift in emphasis that we are speaking about. It is not a wholesale move.

Q539 *Viscount Ullswater:* I am sorry; I need to just clear this up: do you put your own people onto fishing vessels or your own protection vessels?
Mr Ralph: Our own protection vessels. Obviously, they go on to fishing vessels to inspect them.

Q540 *Viscount Ullswater:* But you do not put anybody to sail out on fishing vessels?
Mr Ralph: No, we do not.

Q541 *Viscount Ullswater:* You do not do that sort of inspection?
Mr Ralph: That kind of activity is normally called observer programmes. There are provisions for observer programmes across the EU for specific instances but we are not involved in the provision of observers. The issue of discards was the other part of your question. The fishermen that I speak to, their attitude to discards is quite sensible and I really do not think we have the huge scale of discards that we might have had in the past, but the nets that are in use nowadays are generally 125 millimetres or above, which is significantly larger than anything that was in use previously and I think that is having a pretty good effect.

Q542 *Viscount Ullswater:* Just one final question. Do you think that the reduced fishing intensity in the North Sea haddock fishery has changed the discarding and the fishermen's attitude to discarding?
Mr Ralph: Yes. I think in general the fleet has reduced hugely. The white fish demersal fleet in Scotland has been reduced. I cannot remember the exact figure but it is somewhere between 50 and 60%, I think, in capacity. Those that are left really are demonstrating that they are aware that they have a huge stake in this industry and they are being responsible. Would I like to be in charge of policing a discard ban, to pre-empt the question you have not asked yet? Probably not, but I think it is likely that anyone who was involved in high levels of discards and tried to hide it, their fellow fishermen would probably tell us about it. We would never have the resources to be able to go on all the boats to police a discard ban but I think the level of buy-in that is now evident in the fleet would be the only possible way of effectively policing it.

Q543 *Viscount Ullswater:* When you are out at sea are you aware of what ships discard?
Mr Ralph: Our officers will generally board a vessel towards the end of a haul, so they are present when the nets come up and they will record and report back to headquarters what the quantities are in that haul and they will also report back the discards, so we are aware but it is not illegal.

Q544 *Chairman:* Do you think there is any benefit in putting observers on boats?
Mr Ralph: Yes, potentially it does have benefits. There are many observer schemes throughout the world. Some are discredited due to the quality of observers that are put on. A lot of observers in the oceanic fisheries find themselves at some risk to their personal safety.

Q545 *Chairman:* So limited life expectancy?
Mr Ralph: I have heard some very disturbing stories, and I do not want to say in which parts of the world, about people whose flights home were cancelled when they turned up at the airport and essentially they could not get out of the country; they could not get back to their home country. I have heard of officers who have been denied use of the communications equipment for days or weeks on end

and who have been offered bribes. Observers have a place but it is not a panacea.

Q546 Baroness Sharp of Guildford: Given your own experience and also the report from the Court of Auditors about the enforcement of the Common Fisheries Policy, what would you like to see in the revised Control and Enforcement Regulation that is currently being prepared by the European Commission, and, more generally, what changes would you like to see in the Common Fisheries Policy?
Mr Ralph: Are you asking the questions from my experience?

Q547 Baroness Sharp of Guildford: There are two parts to the question. One is, given your experience and the Court of Auditors' report on the enforcement of the CFP, the Commission are currently revising the Control and Enforcement Regulation. What would you like to see in that revision and are there any general revisions of the CFP that you would like to see?
Mr Ralph: The consultation paper produced by the Commission I thought had a few good things in it. I think the CFP is something that pretty much everyone involved can tell you what is wrong with it. I am not so sure that everyone involved can you tell you how to fix it. In my view one of the things that I hope will make it better is the move towards regionalisation. I have personal experience of very good measures being voted down in Brussels by Mediterranean or landlocked countries because of the political process that exists within the EU and connected with fisheries. If measures were proposed, implemented and evaluated on a regional basis then I think things should become more logical, and if it is more logical and the industry buy into it then they will stick to it. The job of catching fish generally takes place on a fishing vessel out at sea unobserved by anybody and, like most types of human activity, if it is unobserved by anybody then rules are theoretical rather than practical, but if the rules are believed and if people understand and accept that the rules are legitimate then we can have a good chance of people sticking to them. It is when people do not believe that the rules are legitimate and they have an economic imperative to break them that the thing has no chance. I think the original CFP was devised from a naïve scientific view of how quotas on fish stocks could be managed. It did not really give any thought to how the rules could be enforced and over time, when faced with wholesale breaking of the rules, the CFP has responded with more technical and complex rules. Most lawyers are pretty good at getting round technical and complex rules and that has been the sort of leapfrogging situation that has prevailed. If the capacity of the European fleet matched the fishing

opportunities within Europe then the rules could be relatively simple. Some of the proposals put forward by the Commission are essentially a ramping up and an introduction of greater complexity to that which is already there and my view is that that will not succeed. Simplifying the rules and matching the capacity will in my view succeed.

Q548 Baroness Sharp of Guildford: Some of the people who have given us evidence have suggested that the development of the Regional Advisory Councils has been a big step forward here, that it has brought the scientists and the fishermen together and it has also increased the mutual understanding amongst fishermen of different nations. Would you agree with that?
Mr Ralph: Yes. The Regional Advisory Councils, certainly the ones that I have experience of, which are the North Sea RAC, the Pelagic RAC and the North Western Waters RAC, are obviously not full of homogeneous views. There are many different views about the way forward and they do not have a veto on legislation.

Q549 Baroness Sharp of Guildford: No, we realise that.
Mr Ralph: But they do have the ear of those who are pulling the levers. I think for the first time people feel that they have an influence through the RACs. We have tended to keep our distance from them, certainly at the overt level, in that we take the view that we are the enforcers of the rules, we will advise on any proposals that come forward and we will tell you if something can or cannot be enforced or in our opinion if it will or will not work, but it is not really for us to become involved in what is essentially a political process.

Q550 Earl of Dundee: To achieve better results in the UK and the European Union should the Common Fisheries Policy be employed more regionally?
Mr Ralph: That would certainly be my view. I was involved with the feasibility study for the Community Fisheries Control Agency when the feasibility of such a body was being looked at, and I put forward the view very strongly that the CFCA could only operate effectively on a regional basis. There was no point, for instance, much though I am sure my officers would like it, in Scotland sending a fishery protection vessel to Sicily or Greece sending one of their vessels to the west of Scotland. There are those in Europe who think that that is what co-operation is but in my view co-operation has to be those round each pond helping each other first. The Common Fisheries Policy rules for our pond, or our two ponds; we have a North Sea pond and a North East Atlantic pond, need not be the same and they need not be influenced

by people who do not have a stake in those ponds. That is my personal view.

Q551 *Earl of Dundee:* And with an improved Common Fisheries Policy do you also believe that RACs should become managers rather than just advisers?
Mr Ralph: That is certainly something that could be looked at. I suspect that we have a way to go before that would be a possibility given the national politics that play in the management of fisheries across the EU. I do not think nation states would be willing— and this is my personal view, not an Agency or Scottish Government view—to give up that kind of control.

Q552 *Earl of Dundee:* So that might be difficult to win agreement over, that switch in role for the RACs, but, going back to your first answer, if matters can improve where the CFP becomes more regionally deployed, which expedients would you use to win agreement for that?
Mr Ralph: Across the EU, you mean, or with national governments?

Q553 *Earl of Dundee:* I think you would believe that it would be of benefit across the EU.
Mr Ralph: Yes.

Q554 *Earl of Dundee:* And you also, not least, would advise us that it would be a good thing within the UK, but to start it at all how would you proceed?
Mr Ralph: It is a concept that I had not thought of, I must admit. I suppose that if it were down to me I would start with the concept that essentially those involved in the RAC are the ones who will benefit or fall from the success of the management of the fishery, so they have everything to gain and everything to lose by its failure. I suppose the lever would be saying that the UK Government will survive if the North Sea is a barren pond but those in the Irish Sea will be out of business. They are closer to the problem so they should manage it. It is possible. Whether it would work I do not know.
Earl of Dundee: It might be some time before it was agreed to.

Q555 *Chairman:* Can I ask about the Community Fisheries Control Agency? To what extent has it played a role in assisting the co-operation between Member States at the moment and how do you see it developing in the future? Has it been a success?
Mr Ralph: The Community Fisheries Control Agency was proposed without any real thought as to how it might do its job, so the leader of the feasibility study I know had great difficulty in coming up with a precise role and remit for it or any kind of idea as to how it would go about its work. Actually, where the

regional idea came from was that he and I thrashed out this concept that it would operate on a regional basis and it would facilitate co-operation and the spread of best practice throughout that region and then, obviously, spread best practice more widely. Has it been a success? We were the co-ordinating centre for the first joint deployment programme in Scotland. We certainly tried very hard to make it a success. We essentially devised the planning techniques for joint deployment, the research that would go in, the targeting methods, the analysis of fisheries data to have the assets ashore, afloat and in the air in the right place. I suppose what I am saying is that if we cannot make it work I do not believe anybody else can make it work. The impact is difficult to gauge. I also serve on the administrative board of the Community Fisheries Control Agency. I believe you are going to take evidence next week from Harm Koster, the Executive Director. I think it is going in the right direction. I do not think the impact on fish stocks can be measured yet and I suppose that is the only measure which matters. Politically I would say it has had a big impact in that a lot of countries have been pushed together and made to work together for the first time. Those who were willingly working together before are doing more than they did before. It has limitations. It can only set up a joint deployment programme for stocks which are designated recovery stocks for which a specific recovery programme has been implemented by the EU. Essentially for Scotland that means cod and most of the cod in the North Sea is caught in two particular places, east of Shetland and to the north west of Denmark, and we were working together with Denmark and Norway anyway, so I think it would be very hard to measure any additional benefit for us. There are great things being done in the Channel under the auspices of the CFCA where England, Germany, France, the Netherlands, Belgium and Denmark are working together, but there are not many cod caught there. There are lots of sole and plaice caught there and it is having a big impact but the headline of the joint deployment programme speaks about cod.

Q556 *Chairman:* What you are saying is that where you have got the cod recovery programme the co-operation was already there so it did not make a big deal of difference.
Mr Ralph: Yes. It formalised that which was there before.

Q557 *Chairman:* The test would be if there was a species where all the Member States had not had a degree of co-operation and this provided a framework which was sufficiently strong to get them to co-operate.

Mr Ralph: Yes. I think what we have demonstrated in the Channel is that the current limitations on the CFCA are too restrictive and it should be allowed to set up joint deployment programmes across any species. It should not be limited to recovery stocks.

Q558 *Viscount Brookeborough:* I would like to ask you about satellite and airport technology. For a long time there has been talk about how satellite in particular could help and I would like you to tell us how far it has progressed and whether it is in fact a useful substitute. I notice that you have two aircraft. Have you got good technology on those? In Northern Ireland, okay, there are the Security Forces, but even watching boats and ships the technology was there from aircraft to read newspapers at three or four miles. I simply do not understand, or perhaps I am misinformed (it does happen), why we are not able to cope with a lot of this from the air. It is quite a valuable industry and even if Scotland could not do it alone could not Europe as a whole?
Mr Ralph: I will start with satellite and then come to air. We have a satellite monitoring system in the UK. It exists essentially as two mirror systems, one in London and one in Edinburgh, and they are connected. Externally it appears as if the UK has one system, so our incoming and outgoing satellite information is UK addressed, and we monitor the movements of UK vessels anywhere in the world and we monitor any non-UK vessels in the UK zone if we have reciprocal arrangements with their home state. For instance, we do not have any reciprocal arrangements with Russia, so if a Russian vessel was fishing in the UK zone we would not see him on our satellite system. Bizarrely, if he is fishing just outside the UK zone in the North East Atlantic, because we are responsible for policing the area to the west of Rockall in association with NEAFC, the North East Atlantic Fisheries Commission, we can see him there but when he crosses over into Scottish waters he becomes invisible to us on the satellite monitoring system. The satellite monitoring system works extremely well. What it does is that it tells you where boats are and how fast they are going and what they have done and you can do lots of clever things with analysis and see what they are and it is terrific for targeting your other resources. It does not really replace your other resources but it makes your other resources so much more effective, basically ships and aircraft. We have two aircraft. You have seen the pictures in our annual report. I was across in France last weekend picking up one of our new replacements. I came home with that on Saturday. It is a very similar aircraft but the technology inside is essentially 13 years newer than the technology in the old one. We do have not military grade optics but it is the grade below military. It is not for sale to the public. For instance, we bought it under an export

licence from the United States and one of the restrictions on that licence was that we do not sell it. I do not know exactly what its designation is. We cannot read newspapers at three miles but we do have extremely good day and night vision capability and we can identify boats and what they are doing.

Q559 *Viscount Brookeborough:* And can you use that as evidence?
Mr Ralph: Absolutely, yes. The satellite tells you where boats are and how fast they are going. The aircraft or a ship will tell you pretty much what they are doing and it is what they are doing that makes them illegal normally. You still have to get on board to find out who is in charge of that vessel because it is only the person in charge of the vessel that is committing an offence. The vessel itself, of course, does not commit an offence, so you need all three.

Q560 *Viscount Brookeborough:* The crew are not accessories?
Mr Ralph: Of course they are but legally what they are doing they could be doing anywhere. What they are doing is not specific to the crime as such, I suppose. That has never been an avenue we have gone down. Ultimately we do have to get on board but most of our activity is not about taking people to court. Most of our activity is about deterring illegal activity and disrupting it where we find it and we do that by our presence and advertising our presence. The technology that we have is pretty good. Satellite technology relies on a signal being sent from the fishing boat and arriving back at our HQ. In the first systems that were installed the signal was capable of being tampered with, ie, they could inject false positions, speeds, courses, and we had vessels in places where the aircraft said that we might be 500 miles apart. We developed a new tamper-proof technology. That standard was put forward and accepted as a European standard so we now, as far as I am aware, have the most secure satellite system in the world. Obviously, in the field I am in there are quite a small number of practitioners worldwide and no-one has ever been able to convince me that they have a better system than ours. The next big thing in technology will be electronic logbooks. The CFP is predicated on the theory that fishermen enter into their logbooks what they do and that is amalgamated into the scientific record of what the fleet or the nation or the whole of Europe has done. The problem with that, as I said, is that fishing is a largely unobserved activity so historically fishermen would perhaps not complete their logbooks unless they were inspected or until the very last minute and then what they put in might or might not have been historically true. The great thing about an electronic logbook is that it will automatically transmit at midnight or some similar time what has been entered in it, so the

evidence has already gone, so fill it in or do not fill it in, we will know immediately. The great strength for us is that we will be able to analyse the information coming in real time from the electronic logbook and know in real time essentially who is telling the truth and who is not. Fifteen boats all fishing in the same area might catch different amounts and different types of fish but overall, depending on their power and capacity, their catches will be broadly similar. If someone is putting wrong figures in their logbook it will jump out immediately and that is how we analyse paper logbooks to see who is cheating and we do that historically. With electronic logbooks it can be done in real time. The great thing about technology is that the satellite communications are becoming ever cheaper, computer power is becoming ever cheaper. We find that with the vast majority of illegal activity that we disrupt or detect we know it is there before we arrive. We very rarely come across things by accident any more. Most of our activity is directed by the back-room boys who do the number crunching and the statistical analysis.

Q561 *Chairman:* I am just wondering about this need to board. I have no personal knowledge of it, of course, but I understand with speed cameras on roads that if they get you it is the registered keeper who is liable unless he can demonstrate that it was somebody else who was driving the car. Does a similar thing apply to boats?

Mr Ralph: There are some instances where you can ask to see the photograph, I believe, from speed cameras and say, "That is not me", and then the case would not proceed. There are some instances where the vessel's speed alone determines its legality. There is an area to the west of Ireland where a species called orange ruffey are caught and that is in particular biological difficulties so even slowing down through that area is a criminal offence. We have not successfully prosecuted anyone for that yet. People are generally sticking to it. We have had a few occasions where people have had engine difficulties and have phoned us in and said, "Look. I am going to have to slow down but I am not fishing for orange ruffey. You can come and have a look". The automatic designation of an accused is a difficult

thing and it would have to be done in each jurisdiction. For instance, we may or may not be able to do it for a Scottish accused. I think if it was a Danish or a French or a Spanish accused it might be even more problematic. It is not my field of expertise. **Earl of Arran:** What kind of additional technology would you like to have but you just ain't got that would really help your cause? Give us your dream.

Q562 *Chairman:* "Beam me down, Scotty"!

Mr Ralph: Instant travel would, of course, be extremely useful. I suppose the next piece of dream technology that is already being used in some countries is real-time cameras where the larger units have the area of the ship where the nets are coming on board covered by CCTV. You do have to be careful with technology because you do not want to impose an undue burden on those who are sticking to the rules, and someone who does not want a CCTV camera to work on his vessel I am sure could find a few ways of making it not work. Black spray paint is pretty good if you spray the lens cover. One of the things that we have found with satellite technology for the monitoring system was that it had a button on the back marked "Off" and "On" and that was a great temptation for some, so when we designed the tamper-proof system we essentially put a small motorcycle battery in the box. If you cut the power to it it ran for three weeks but it immediately sent us a signal to say, "My power has been cut". What you have to do with technology is allow the default position to be the fail/safe, and failures are automatically communicated back to a centre. You cannot rely on technology having power all the time and you cannot rely on technology not being interfered with. You have to design it quite cleverly. Video cameras are great and those who want to prove that they are obeying the rules I am sure will keep power going to the video camera and keep the lens nice and polished and all the rest of it, but those who do not, I suspect, will interfere with it. It is not difficult to prove that something happened but on a fishing boat 400 miles out in the ocean it is very difficult to prove who did it because you are not going to have any witnesses.

Chairman: Thank you very much indeed.

Examination of Witness

Witness: MR MARK DOUGAL, Chief Executive, North East Scotland Fishermen's Organisation (a Producers' Organisation) and Board Member of Seafood Scotland, examined.

Q528 Chairman: Good afternoon. Thank you for coming to help us with our inquiry. This is a formal evidence session so a note will be taken. You will get a copy of the transcript when it is available so you can go through it and correct anything that has not come out right. The other thing is that I usually have to say at this stage that it is being webcast so there is a possibility that someone might hear it, but as we are not being webcast there is no possibility that anybody will hear it, so do not worry. You are Chief Executive of the North East Scotland Fishermen's Organisation and you are on the Board of Seafood Scotland.
Mr Dougal: Yes.

Q529 Chairman: What do those two organisations do? What is their role?
Mr Dougal: If I can start by giving you a little bit of background, my knowledge of the industry, I was brought up in a fishing family on the Scottish borders in the town of Eyemouth. My father was a fishermen. Both grandfathers were fishermen. I left school at 16/17 and I went fishing with my father for a couple of years. He asked me to leave politely. He felt as though the future was not great, it was inshore fisheries that we were working on, so I ended up coming up to Peterhead in 1989, and that is nearly 20 years I have been in Peterhead. I started off in the Fishery Office and I have noticed that one of the relevant questions is with regard to enforcement. I was a fishery officer for 12 years, solely based in Peterhead, so you can imagine the changes I have seen there. I left the Fishery Office, not under a cloud or anything. My wife was pregnant so the thought of working a shift system and young children in the house kind of forced me out, so I worked for the Sea Fish Industry Authority for a couple of years and I have now been in my present position for five years as the Chief Executive of the North East Scotland Fishermen's Organisation. That is my background, so I have kind of been gamekeeper turned poacher because I have been involved with all sectors of the industry. My current position is Chief Executive of NESFO, as it is abbreviated. As you are aware, we are a producer organisation. We are approved by the Government and the EU. Annually we submit an operational plan and an activity report through the Scottish Government to the EU Commission and it is approved. At the moment we are in the region of 45 fishing vessels. When I started five years ago there were 60 but it was just at the first stage of the decommissioning in 2003, I think it was, so just as I started we lost in the region of 15 vessels, maybe 12, but through natural wastage we now operate 45 vessels. The vessels range in size from a ten-metre vessel working in the Firth of Forth catching only prawns, just working six or seven hours in a day, to a 35-metre trawler working mainly Scottish waters into the Norwegian sector and occasionally Faroese waters, so it is a variety. We have no pelagic vessels. It is mainly white fish and nephrops vessels that we have. The 45 vessels grossed in the region of £35 million last year, so that makes us probably the second biggest producer organisation for white fish within the UK. That is a bit of background about what we are in NESFO. You are aware that we are approved by the EU, so my main role within NESFO is the administration of quotas. I do not want to go into all the intricacies of how the quotas were set up and everything like that but my main aim at the beginning of the year is to try and maintain a 12-month fishery for all my vessels. Whether that means finding additional quotas, swapping in quota, or vessels going to different methods to utilise all their quota, my main aim is that come Christmastime this year we are still fishing up to the last fish market in Peterhead. As you correctly say, I am on the Board of Seafood Scotland. I do not have that much dealing with Seafood Scotland. We only meet quarterly as a board but I think it is a unique position that Seafood Scotland has, that all the sectors of the industry are there, from the catching sector represented by the POs, occasionally there are fishermen there, you have all the processing sectors, you have the councils, you have the Government. It is unique because I do not know any other organisation within the UK that has that broad spectrum of the industry. We sit on the board. My main aim on the board is to listen to what the Chief Executive, Libby Woodhatch, is saying, but from my point of view my day-to-day dealings with the fishermen involve looking at different markets which Seafood Scotland is doing to try and improve the quality, which they have certainly done over the last three or four years. There are massive differences in the market with regard to the presentation of fish, and just looking at all this issue now that we have, with even Marks and Spencer, in that they are going green and sustainability and so on, this is where Seafood Scotland I think are going to be in the future. That is just a quick rundown of where I am with NESFO and where I am with Seafood Scotland.

Q530 Chairman: Can you very briefly talk about quota management for a little while because the quotas that individual boats have are aggregated and you manage the whole lot, do you?
Mr Dougal: Yes, that is correct.

Q531 Chairman: And if you saw, say, that you did not have a haddock quota there you would go out and look elsewhere for a haddock quota and buy it in, would you?

Mr Dougal: Yes, that is correct. One of the questions that I got from the Committee is pertinent to ITQs but in this we work a solely ITQ system. It is an internal ITQ system. Each vessel has different quotas from the gentleman sitting next to him at the table. This is all derived from FQA units that were split up from the Government in 1998 and it was all done on historical performance from 1994, 1995, 1996, 1997; I cannot remember. With regard to quota management, each vessel obviously has different quotas of cod, haddock, whiting, saithe, nephrops and monkfish as the main species that we catch. Generally, if a vessel was running short he would contact me and ideally I would swap this within the UK but, as you are well aware, there is a leasing process. Masters of the vessels lease quota to go to sea so that they can catch the extra fish that they have leased. This is in addition to the original quota that they have been allocated through myself, but as it is a producer organisation we manage it on behalf of the 45 vessels and if we do not need quota then we will hopefully swap it for something that we do need. We tend to work with about 20 POs within the UK, but where we are unique on this is that generally we do a lot of the trade outwith the UK with other Member States. This is all something that I started about five years ago just as I came into the position as the quotas were tight but then when you looked at other Member States there were huge opportunities to access additional quota. I do quite a lot of travelling abroad with contacts in different Member States to supplement the quota that we have.

Q532 *Chairman:* We had a conversation with fishermen this morning and it went something like this, "I will go out and I have quota for stock X but from next month I have not got quota for stocks A, B, C and D, so if I catch any of those I am going to have to discard them". What you are saying is that the system you operate should prevent that from occurring?
Mr Dougal: If you can get access to the fish internationally, yes, or within the UK. We are in a unique situation this year in that we are only four months into the year and there are some producer organisations already shut for the main stocks, one of which is whiting. It only closed last night so about 20 vessels that operate out of Peterhead will not be allowed to catch any more whiting for the rest of the year, and so if those 20 vessels catch any they will have to discard them. The main reason for that is that I have probably taken on a role that was not really meant to be with regard to quota management when I took over the position, but I have expanded the position a wee bit because it is not really in my remit to go out there and access quota just to give to the boats. I have done this off my own back and we are a wee bit unique within the UK in that we are the one

that started it and there are quite a few other producer organisations following on, but because I have built up contacts internationally, mainly Denmark and Holland, the Low Countries, we can access fish from there. If they have no fish then obviously we cannot do anything about it.

Q533 *Viscount Brookeborough:* Just to clarify, the quota that you go after in another country has to be quota that is applicable to the area that these boats wish to fish in?
Mr Dougal: Yes, that is correct.

Q534 *Viscount Brookeborough:* And that is a difficult thing in finding the quota for the North Sea if it is a Peterhead boat?
Mr Dougal: Yes, that is right. I just did a swap with the Netherlands last week and I brought in North Sea cod and I brought in North Sea whiting, but unfortunately we are not allowed to pay for that to other countries, so what I have to find is the swap currency. The Netherlands wanted plaice. I did not have the plaice, so I went and leased the plaice within the UK and then did the swap with the Netherlands to access the cod and the whiting that we need.

Q535 *Chairman:* You are a broker, are you not?
Mr Dougal: Basically.

Q536 *Viscount Brookeborough:* And you cannot pay across international boundaries?
Mr Dougal: No. I believe if you really pushed it with the Government there is a facility there to pay it, but most of the time it is just done with swapping. There is not much point in me paying money when they know that I can access plaice and they need the plaice. The way that I look at it is if it is not within my PO I will try and access it somewhere else but we are fully utilising every quota species that we have.

Q537 *Baroness Jones of Whitchurch:* In that example you gave of this organisation that closed last night or whatever, why are all those people not part of your producer organisation?
Mr Dougal: I do not know. You should ask them yourself.

Q538 *Baroness Jones of Whitchurch:* Do they have a choice?
Mr Dougal: Yes. There are 20 different POs. Who is to say that I may or may not have quota problems next year? I do not know.

Q539 *Chairman:* Let us move on. When our previous committee looked at the fishing industry five years ago they said economic returns were low, employment was going to go low. What is your view of the economic health of the industry at the moment?

Mr Dougal: As you say, five years ago when it was done that was when the last stage of the decommissioning came in which made a great big difference in my opinion. Do not forget I have only got five years' experience of this. In my view for the past four years it has steadily increased. This is the profitability of the vessels, the mood of the fishermen. Obviously, there are lots of fish in the sea, so they are seeing the benefits of long term recovery plans or management plans. Personally, I think it is nature. I am a great believer in nature taking its course, but of course if you take out 160-odd great big vessels that were catching cod and haddock and whiting and saithe out of the equation and they are not fishing now because there has been decommissioning, it is bound to make a difference to the stocks. You do not have to be a scientific genius to work that out. I do not have access to the vessels' accounts or anything like that. I have no idea what their profits are. I just speak to them on a regular basis, whether it is fishermen coming into my office or at my board table, because out of the 45 members 12 are board members, so that is about a quarter of them that we meet every month. They are quite optimistic about the future. This year it is totally different because of escalating fuel costs, but that is the same for everybody, not just the fishing industry.

Q540 *Lord Plumb:* You have just spoken of the growth, since 2002 presumably, and you have 45 vessels at the moment. Is that the right sort of capacity looking to the future or do you think there will be growth on that? We heard this morning that there are one or two coming in. Secondly, looking to the future, stick or carrot, in or out? If someone wants to get out what sort of facilities are there? A form of decommissioning, grants or payments or whatever? Are they operating at the moment? Are they available if people want to get out? Can they do that and do they get a bit of help in so doing? I think you might add to that what changes you see are necessary or what are acceptable in reform of the fisheries policy as we see it at the moment?

Mr Dougal: With regard to fishing capacity, the most important aspect is that it is available marine resource. How do you define available marine resource? The only way that I can do that is what the scientific evidence produces with regard to the TACs that are set. With regard to the available marine resource, I think at the moment within the Scottish industry we have the optimum level of fishing vessels. We have regular landings in Peterhead all through the week. The fishermen are becoming more responsible. Instead of everybody coming in at the same time we are trying to spread out the landings a wee bit. That, of course, helps the process inside as

well. There is not much point in getting 12,000 boxes in one day when you can get 3,000 boxes a day for four days. With regard to the resource, I feel as though we have the perfect amount of fishing vessels. It was desperately needed, the decommissioning scheme, when we had it four or five years ago, but as far as I am concerned in my organisation with 45 vessels we can generally find enough fish for them to ensure a 12-month fishery. Then you go into effort limitations, which you are probably all aware of, the time that the vessels can spend at sea. Is there enough effort, because we now have vessels who have so much quota that they are not given enough time to catch it? In my opinion that is wrong, but this all goes down to—and I am sorry I am going off the beaten track a little bit—the fact that historically when a vessel at the end of the year maybe made a profit of, for example, £200,000, the skipper may have put that in his back pocket. Some of them went out and accessed more quota, they bought more quota. These guys that spent the money to buy more quota in the past now have not got the opportunity to catch it because of effort limitation, so they have surplus quota. It is very strange but with regard to your point on decommissioning, at the time, yes, it was needed. I do not think it is needed now because, as I said in my opening remarks, I have been here for 20 years. I can honestly say that there are more fish coming in to Peterhead per vessel per catching day at sea than I have seen in those 20 years, so I do not think decommissioning is required, certainly within the Scottish industry.

Q541 *Lord Plumb:* What about the scientific evidence?

Mr Dougal: As I have already alluded to, I am a great believer in nature taking its course, but, of course, you have to work with the scientists and this is where the fishermen come in through the North Sea RAC and the stakeholders. You have to involve them. I have my doubts that the scientific evidence is always correct because, especially this year, we have got an increase in the cod quota which was needed. It is not big enough but we have a management plan so we are restricted, but, if you listen to the fishermen, the fishermen have been saying for two years that there was more and more cod available. The result is that we are now working on a TAC so that we are discarding already this year good, marketable quality fish. Fish are going back into the water dead. It is not doing anybody any good, but that is through the size. The other one is whiting. I have already alluded to some of the POs being already closed for whiting. You ask any fisherman. I am sure if you asked any of them this morning they would say, "Yes, there is lots of whiting in the sea", but we have got a dramatic cut in the whiting, in the region of 30%, which is totally unjustified, and the result now is that we are now going to have at least one PO discarding whiting for eight months and other POs are just going to follow suit.

Q542 Lord Plumb: But you do talk to the scientists?
Mr Dougal: Yes, of course. From a PO perspective we do not have a lot of discussion with the scientists. We meet maybe once or twice at the marine lab in Aberdeen. It is more from the fishermen's associations, which are the Scottish Whitefish Association or the Fishermen's Association Ltd where we meet regularly with the scientists. We are a wee bit unique in Scotland and in England through the UK in that every other PO within the Member States represents the fishermen through government level, through scientific level, but it is different in the UK because we have separate branches. Scottish Whitefish is one and Faroe is another, so they meet with the scientists. Really, the fishermen have joint representation, whether it is through the PO or the associations that they are associated with. Most of the vessels within Scotland are a member of one or the other.

Q543 Baroness Jones of Whitchurch: Are you satisfied that the stakeholders are sufficiently engaged in the policy process, in particular I would say are consumers, environmental concerns and so on, sufficiently involved in the whole process, and, if not, have you any ideas about how they could be involved more?
Mr Dougal: Historically they were not, but obviously with the formation of all the RACs it has been an effort to try and get everybody together, especially the NGOs. They are an important aspect of all the consultations that we do now. It is very early stages. I have only personally been involved with the RAC for about a year now, the North Sea RAC, so it is very early. I would not say I am really in the perfect position to give you a thorough answer to the question; I am very sorry. As I alluded to just now, you have to involve the stakeholders, but then if you have the stakeholders on one side and the science on another, 99 times out of 100 they have different assessments of the stocks.

Q544 Baroness Jones of Whitchurch: Different scientists?
Mr Dougal: Yes, different scientists, and I have always said that if you have ten fishermen in a room you will get 11 different answers to your question because they cannot agree on anything. Yes, it is imperative that we have stakeholder input into this. Mike Park is an ex-fisherman. He is still a trawler owner and he is the Scottish representative on the RAC, and he is the Chairman of the Scottish Whitefish Producers' Organisation, so he is the representative there. Round the table there are a

number of fishermen's representatives. The RACs are the only forum at the moment that the stakeholders are well represented on.

Q545 Baroness Jones of Whitchurch: What about me as a consumer? Where is my voice in all this? You are all busy setting the quotas and determining what you are going to fish and lobbying Europe. What about my voice?
Mr Dougal: That is through the NGOs. I know in the North Sea RAC it is split up. There are 24 round the table, 16 from the catch. Inside there are eight from an NGO side, so the consumer will be under the NGOs. At the moment I do not think there is any representation at all. I see Ann[1] has just come in and maybe she will correct me if I am wrong, but I do not think there is anybody, for instance, representing Marks and Spencer or Sainsburys or anything like that, and, of course, that goes down to the consumer side, but if you give your name to Ann you are very welcome to appear at the next one in June.

Q546 Chairman: Should Seafood Scotland be there?
Mr Dougal: They probably should but who do you put them with? They work with the catching sector and they work with the other side. They are split because they are doing a lot of work in the market inside. The market inside is to benefit the processors. The market inside is to benefit fishermen. I do not think it would do any harm to be there even from a consumer angle.

Q547 Lord Cameron of Dillington: I apologise for merging some of these questions but we have a plane to catch.
Mr Dougal: I am glad to hear it!

Q548 Lord Cameron of Dillington: They are on management plans and recovery plans. You have commented to some extent on them. What works, what does not work? Would you like to see longer term TACs, for instance, maybe involving catch/biomass ratios? Which of the existing management tools work or have bad outcomes and what management tools or rules would you like to see introduced?
Mr Dougal: Again, personally, I do not really have much input into this but from a fishermen's perspective some consistency with regard to the TACs that are set would be helpful. Last year we had an increase in something and then come the December council that increase would be taken away. All these fishermen have to put in business plans to their banks, so we need some kind of stability. Do management plans work? We have had a management plan for cod. The cod has come back. Is it because of the management plan or is it because

---
[1] Ann Bell, North Sea RAC

of nature? As I have already said, we have decommissioned a great amount of cod catchers, so who knows what works? I am sorry; I am not answering your question very thoroughly.

Q549 Lord Cameron of Dillington: What about having longer term quotas instead of having yearly quotas? Maybe you would not like to see that because brokering is probably quite a good income for you.
Mr Dougal: No; it is stability.

Q550 Lord Cameron of Dillington: But if you had long term stability, like a three-year quota, would that be possible?
Mr Dougal: Yes. The societies would disagree with you but from a fisherman's angle that would be beneficial because you know where you are, you can plan ahead. The fishermen are not given credit with regard to their business sense. A lot of them go out at certain times of the year and catch the stocks that they have quota for. For example, at the moment they catch quite a lot of cod and then after the cod moves away from the grounds they catch a lot of haddock, but if they know next year that they will be able to catch the same amount of cod they can work out their plans for next year. As I said, it is all down to business plans and it would certainly give more stability. Whether it is a two- or a three-year quota it remains the same, obviously, subject to huge changes within the scientific advice. From my perspective it makes it a lot easier as well because we know what kind of quota we have to play with and then we can make arrangements for next year for adding or taking away quota with anybody we want to.

Q551 Lord Cameron of Dillington: You work with effort limitations or things of that nature?
Mr Dougal: The ironic thing is that each vessel gets a similar amount of days to catch, so they could put two vessels, yours and your neighbour's, fishing beside each other and you both get allowed 150 days at sea, but one of the vessels maybe will have three times the amount of quota than the vessel fishing next to him. In my opinion it has to be linked, the effort and the TAC. We have already spoken to the Government about this when I started five years ago, but it is too complicated. There are going to be a lot of winners and losers with doing this. You think of the conservation side of it as well. Do you really want vessels to go to sea for 300 days but they have quota for 300 days? Do you want them to go and fish for 300 days? As long as the UK does not exceed the TAC that has been set then personally I would not have a problem with it. The same example as we have at the moment is that there is multi-rig. This is vessels fishing with more than two nets. It is now about to be banned because they say that it is too efficient, but if

you can catch your quota quicker and more economically then why hinder progress?

Q552 Lord Plumb: "They say"—who is "they"? Is it the Government?
Mr Dougal: The Government, yes.

Q553 Lord Cameron of Dillington: We were hearing this morning from the fishermen that it is kind of dog eat dog out there and they compete. Is there any sense that they have a vision of sustainable fishing?
Mr Dougal: Oh, definitely. That is definitely the case because when that last decommissioning scheme took effect and 160-odd vessels left the industry the vessels that were left within the industry were the ones that were very sustainably minded, responsible, and that goes down with, for instance, the black fish figures. I was just speaking to the SFPA that was in here earlier on. Five years ago there was lots of black fish but now there is nothing at all because the fishermen themselves did not really want to land black fish but they had no alternative through the quotas. At the moment I think we are at a perfect level with the amount of vessels we have for supplying the market on a daily, monthly, yearly basis and that keeps the processors happy in tandem with the supplies that they are getting.

Q554 Baroness Sharp of Guildford: To some extent you have already covered the question that I was going to ask you. We have heard conflicting views about whether the goals should be conservation goals implemented through controls on output, namely, the catch limits, or through controls over inputs and the time limits, and I take it the answer you are going to give us is that it should be a bit of both.
Mr Dougal: Definitely, but if you are doing it on catch limits then a fisherman is going to maximise the time he can get for the quota that he has. An example at the moment is that what is happening with the cod in the North Sea is that if anybody catches cod they discard three sizes of cod because the quotas are so tight that they keep the biggest cod, so, of course, the biggest cod in the fish market obviously realises the best prices. Is that doing anything for conservation? No. Effort limitation is a better way to conserve the stocks because, obviously, if you are allowed to land what you catch in the space of time that you have then that is a lot better than discarding great quality fish. In the world that we are in with people starving it does not make sense to throw food back into the water.

Q555 Baroness Sharp of Guildford: We were hearing this morning from the conservation officer about the time-limited quota where you have an area where the fish are spawning and so forth and where you keep them away completely for a certain amount of time.

As you say, it requires voluntary co-operation but people are co-operating with that quite well.

Mr Dougal: Yes, that is right. This started last year but with regard to the spawning it is something that we did have in the past two or three years ago to encourage vessels to keep away from spawning areas. It was closed areas, but you are right: this year it is voluntary and most of the fishermen know themselves that they do not want to kill all the cod that is spawning because it is the future that they are thinking about. It is just what I say. The vast majority of them are sustainable and they want a future. Another thing with regard to this spawning area for the cod is that, just as it happens, the cod are at their poorest quality after they have spawned. They are very thin and therefore they get a very poor price on the fish market for them, so it is to the fishermen's benefit not to catch them. The problem is that it displaces effort into something else and this is what has probably happened this year with regard to the whiting. Everybody has listened to what is happening with the closed areas of cod. They went to catch something else, they have got too much whiting and now the whiting is closed. That is one of the problems, that it displaces effort. Then you tie the vessels up. That is probably the best way. If you tie the vessels up you do not have processors. They do not have any fish.

Q556 *Baroness Sharp of Guildford:* Another suggestion that we have heard is that the quota should run from April to April rather than in the calendar year from January to January so that the end of quota period would be the spring spawning period.

Mr Dougal: I am certainly in favour of that because the majority of the POs, because we work a calendar year at the moment, including myself, would run out of fish at the latter part of the year. If that is going to happen it makes sense to keep the vessels in when the fish are spawning. Why it has never been introduced I do not know. When Mr Borg as Fisheries Commissioner first got in that was one of the things he was going to look at but years on we are still in the same state in that we are still working a calendar year. Yes, I am all in favour of that.

Q557 *Viscount Ullswater:* If you are in favour of real-time closures on a voluntary basis, and that probably makes sense, especially if you are looking after spawning fish, is there an alternative that can be done which would be real-time increments when the fishermen report that there is a much bigger supply of cod in the sea this year, which I think is what we are talking about, so that you can increase the quota?

Mr Dougal: What do you mean by "increments"?

Viscount Ullswater: To increase the size of the quota.

Chairman: In-year increases.

Q558 *Viscount Ullswater:* If you can agree to stop fishing, I am just wondering whether there could be agreement which would be accepted in the RAC, in particular that if everybody could agree there are reasonable cod could we have an in-year review.

Mr Dougal: For a fisherman that would be the best way. As I said to you, I am a great believer in nature taking its course, but if you find now that there is more cod in the sea than the scientists thought and what was agreed at the December council, then of course it makes sense to have an in-year review.

Q559 *Viscount Ullswater:* Rather than discarded?

Mr Dougal: Yes, of course. Nobody wants to discard fish. Contrary to what some people may think, fishermen do not want to discard cod or any kind of fish. It is against their nature. They are in it to catch fish, not discard it.

Q560 *Viscount Brookeborough:* Something you said I may have misunderstood. At one stage when you talked about two boats and one having a small quota and another having a larger quota but being restricted by days, I think you said that it would be easier not to restrict them by days but merely let them go on until they caught their quota, and then I think a few minutes ago when talking about cod in particular you said that they should be effort restricted by days. Did I misunderstand you?

Mr Dougal: No. I said that the best way to conserve the stocks is effort control.

Q561 *Chairman:* But then you did say earlier that in order to fulfil the quota—

Mr Dougal: Yes, that is correct. That is what I am saying. With fishermen you have got one fisherman saying one thing with regard to the fact that he has a large quota and he should be allowed the days to catch it, and then another fisherman sitting next to him will say, "No. The best way to conserve the stocks—". I am not here to make judgments. As I said to you, if you have ten different fishermen in the room there are 11 different responses to a question.

Q562 *Viscount Brookeborough:* Now we will get on to enforcement. To what extent do disparities in the control and enforcement of the CAP by different national authorities across the EU continue to undermine confidence in and compliance with CFP rules? Has the adoption of a common catalogue of sanctions for serious infringements, and the establishment of the Community Fisheries Control Agency helped to mitigate the problem?

Mr Dougal: I read this question and my note that I wrote down was that I feel as though I am not really in a position to respond to that because it is more from the fishermen's side with regard to the penalties. We are just in the process of introducing admin penalties for the industry. Years ago there were a lot of misdemeanours within the industry but now there are in my opinion no deliberate misdemeanours. If a fisherman makes a mistake through paperwork it is a genuine mistake because, as I have said to you, the guys that are left in the industry want a future. They are not blatantly going out to break the law. Years ago, yes, there was a lot of illegal activity and you have to look at the Scottish Fisheries Protection Agency, the amount of prosecutions they took in a year, but they still set targets. In my opinion they are now nit-picking with tiny little things, for instance, that a boarding ladder for boarding a vessel is inadequate. It is a lot of things like that.

Q563 *Baroness Jones of Whitchurch:* But that is deliberate though, is it not, not having a boarding ladder? That is not an accident.
Mr Dougal: We have just had a vessel taken into Norway about three weeks ago for an inadequate boarding ladder. He did not do it deliberately because the boarding officer, who was Norwegian, actually fell back into the sea. He was fined £5,000. He did not want to get fined £5,000. It was just an accident, but the guy is okay just in case you are curious. He is just a wee bit wet. I am sorry; I am not really in a position to answer that question.

Q564 *Viscount Ullswater:* You were saying that in the working of your own PO you have really got a tradable quota system working, an internal tradable quota system. Do you think that is something that ought to be adopted by the UK nationally?
Mr Dougal: Do you want my opinion or do you want NESFO's opinion?

Q565 *Viscount Ullswater:* I would like your opinion.
Mr Dougal: My opinion is yes, I think we should go down an ITQ route. We had a board meeting on Friday and there were only five of them there, and it would have been worth you sitting there to listen to them arguing round the table about who wants an ITQ system and who does not. Personally, with the work that I do within the organisation at the moment I have already said we work an internal ITQ system. With all the dealings that we do within the UK and internationally with other Member States we are operating an ITQ system as it is, so personally I would not have a problem with it.

Q566 *Viscount Ullswater:* If it was adopted would you see a danger of it being bought out or small ITQ owners being bought out by larger concerns and maybe not based in the area of the locality, like Peterhead, for instance?
Mr Dougal: That is a possibility but there are two points here. I certainly do not think it would go down the route that Iceland went down, just because we are

such a mixed fishery. That is one of the main things about Scotland. We catch about six or seven of the major stocks, not just one stock. If somebody from another country wanted to come in and buy up cod, haddock, whiting, whatever quota it may be, there is nothing to stop them in the past five or six years of doing it.

Q567 *Lord Cameron of Dillington:* Yes, but what they are doing is buying in a year's lease of a year's catch that then reverts back to the original owner, whereas an ITQ is transferred for good.
Mr Dougal: Where, in Iceland?

Q568 *Lord Cameron of Dillington:* No, in this country. You are saying that what you are doing is tantamount to being an ITQ. It is not actually, is it, because the quota does not leave the producer organisation?
Mr Dougal: No, you are right. The example I gave was doing a swap with Holland with regard to North Sea plaice because they need to access North Sea plaice. They came in ten years ago and bought up the amount of plaice that they required, and it is just swapped annually to Holland to get fish back, so it has to work in an ITQ system. Everybody thinks that the fish that is in the UK belongs mostly to the UK vessels. It does, but the difference with the Netherlands is that it was a single fishery, it was a plaice fishery, and it is a lot easier on a single fishery, but, as I have just said, the Scottish industry operates on a mixed fishery. It makes it a lot more complicated. There is nothing to stop them coming in, but with regard to your point about organisations possibly buying it up, it is happening already with regard to major processors or major players within the UK buying up little bits and pieces. They are keeping their business going because what is happening is that you have larger organisations within Scotland buying up quota but they also have the vessels and they have got the factory, so they are buying the vessels going to sea to catch the quota that they own to supply the factory that they own to give to the consumer, because that fish is going to Marks and Spencer or Sainsburys or whoever it may be. Is there anything wrong with that? Probably not because they are just covering the whole spectrum of the industry.

Q569 *Viscount Ullswater:* That sounds like business to me.
Mr Dougal: That is all it is, yes.

Q570 *Viscount Ullswater:* What about people who decommission their boats and then reclaim the quota? Is that sensible? Is that fair? They could lease it, of course.

Mr Dougal: In an ideal world what would have happened is that when we had the decommissioning the Government took the quota back, but I was at the meeting with the Scottish Fisheries Minister, who was Ross Finnie at the time, and he said, "We cannot buy back quota that does not belong to the fishermen", which I can fully understand, but it is happening in Belgium because the Belgians are introducing a decommissioning scheme and the owners have to give up the quota so it benefits the vessels that are left, or the owners that are left, but it did not happen in Scotland. Whether it is right or wrong, ideally they would have taken the quota back and split it up amongst everybody who was left, but it did not happen that way. The last decommissioning scheme was in 2003. There is only a handful of guys left that decommissioned and kept their quotas because most of them sold out.

Q571 *Lord Plumb:* Do you want the quotas to continue after 2013?
Mr Dougal: I do not know if I will still be here in 2013. I do not know. I am not sure quotas work if you set TACs, to be perfectly honest.

Q572 *Lord Plumb:* It is an important question though. This is the way it is going to be.
Mr Dougal: Yes. I do not know if quotas work at the moment. As I have just said, there are 20 vessels that work out of Peterhead that are now going to discard fish for the rest of the year because of the quota system, whiting, so does it work? No.

Q573 *Lord Plumb:* I am more familiar with quotas in other commodities.
Mr Dougal: I believe so.

Q574 *Chairman:* Can I just put one very quick question? The opposite point of view has half been expressed, which is that the fishing industry is associated to some extent with small, vulnerable coastal communities that have limited economic opportunities, and if you have transferable quotas that can be bought out for ever then you nasty big east coast boys are going to make offers that these people in these small communities cannot refuse. You will take their quota and Fred Macdonald will be all right but Jimmy McBride and whatever will not

because they will not have anything going on in their community.
Mr Dougal: Do you not think that is happening already? Can I give you an example? As I say, I come from the Scottish Borders, Eyemouth. My brother has a fish business in Eyemouth and it is 220 miles away. He used to travel up to Peterhead every week to get his fish supplies because there is no fish landed at all between Eyemouth and Peterhead. Are there any communities left? I do not think so. Yes, there is a very small community in the Firth of Forth catching bream and nephrops, but, reading the *Fishing News* last week, that is probably not going to be viable now because they catch so little and there are escalating fuel costs, so even that is in jeopardy. When I was a fisherman for the two years with my father there were about 20 vessels catching fish from Eyemouth. There is not one left now. The nearest port for my brother to get fish is Peterhead from Eyemouth, 220 miles away, and the nearest port going further south is Grimsby about the same distance. I think it would be great to leave the community aspect within Scotland but I think it is a fallacy because I do not think there are any communities left. If you go from Fraserburgh north you finish up at Scrabster. That is another 200 miles away so there are only three ports within about 400 miles.

Q575 *Viscount Brookeborough:* Have these people got other jobs? They are not all on the dole today?
Mr Dougal: No; they are probably still involved with the industry.

Q576 *Viscount Brookeborough:* They have merely diversified?
Mr Dougal: Yes.

Q577 *Chairman:* Management by effort limitation or ITQs or both?
Mr Dougal: You never had that on the list of questions.

Q578 *Chairman:* No. You see, you make us think.
Mr Dougal: Personally, ITQs.

Q579 *Chairman:* Okay. Well done. Thank you very much. I hope you enjoyed it.
Mr Dougal: And I hope you have a safe flight home.

WEDNESDAY 7 MAY 2008

Present:	Arran, E	Palmer, L
	Brookeborough, V	Plumb, L
	Cameron of Dillington, L	Sewel, L (Chairman)
	Dundee, E	Ullswater, V
	Jones of Whitchurch, B	

Examination of Witnesses

Witnesses: MR POUL DEGNBOL, Scientific Adviser, MR ERNESTO PEÑAS, Head of Unit, Fisheries Conservation and Environmental Questions, and MS LISA BORGES, DG Mare, European Commission, examined.

Q580 Chairman: Good morning. We perfectly appreciate that Mr Fotiadis is not able to be with us today but thank you all for coming. We are a Sub-Committee of the House of Lords Select Committee on the European Union. We are doing an inquiry into the future of the Common Fisheries Policy. We have been taking evidence in the United Kingdom and, as in the case of all our inquiries, we have now come to Brussels to see the Commission and Members of the Parliament and some of the Member State representatives as well. At the moment we are still enormously confused—I am not going to say "impressed"—by the complexity of the Common Fisheries Policy.
Mr Degnbol: Welcome to the club.

Q581 Chairman: That is an awful relief. Technically this is a formal evidence-taking session so a note will be taken, a transcript will be made available to you as soon as possible and you can do any corrections that are necessary if errors have come into it. Would you like to start by making an initial statement or would you prefer to go straight on to the questions that we have identified?
Mr Degnbol: We would just like to say thank you for inviting us here and again we apologise on behalf of Mr Fotiadis that he was not able to make it to this meeting. We are, as I am sure you have appreciated, in the process of an internal reflection on the CFP and the future of it. We look forward to the product of this Committee because it is very important work which is being done here and it will certainly be a very important input into our process as well as for your own purposes.

Q582 Chairman: Could you give us an explanation for the reorganisation of what was "DG Fish" into DG Mare and what the structural changes have been and the reasons behind that change?
Mr Peñas: In short, there are two main motivations for this change of structure. First, there is the need to integrate the former task force for maritime policy. Once the task force had accomplished its work it had to be integrated into the whole structure as maritime policy is going to be integrated as part of the policy

of the Commission. The second motivation was that it was felt by the Commissioner and the Director-General that there were not sufficient symmetries among the different pillars of the policy, particularly between structural policy and conservation policy, and in order to improve the synergies it was preferred to take a regional approach to this. It was felt that it was much better to look into the synergies among the different pillars of the policy at a national level and also at a regional level, and that obviously required a change in the structure to turn a structure based on the vertical pillars of the policy—conservation on the one hand and structures, markets and extra navigations on the other hand—into a regionally based structure. We now have three regional directorates covering three broad geographical areas—the Western Atlantic, the North Sea plus the Baltic and Mediterranean/Black Sea. Within these three general directorates of a regional nature there are units responsible for the different pillars of the policy. Therefore, in a single directorate we will be able to handle all the policy elements and issues of a given region and a given Member State. Of course, this regional approach includes on a regional basis the maritime policy into which the Common Fisheries Policy will be integrated. Those are the two motivations for this change.

Q583 Viscount Brookeborough: The introduction of recovery and management plans was the main plank of the 2002 reform of the CFP. Why have so few recovery and management plans been adopted so far? What can be done to speed up the process and improve the results delivered? We understand that you have recently published a revised cod recovery plan.
Mr Peñas: Yes, it is true that the number of recovery and management plans is limited. They have focused on the main species but they are still admittedly rather limited. The reasons are that the capacity of the Commission to produce these plans, the capacity of stakeholders within RACs to examine Commission proposals and the capacity of Member States to try to discuss and digest these plans are very limited. If we try to produce more plans RACs

immediately react by saying, "We cannot handle so many things at a time. We need more time for this", and then the system does not absorb so much initiative. A similar problem happens with Member States. We do have a committee in the Council, the Technical Committee, that examines at technical level all Commission proposals, and if we speed up dramatically the number of Commission initiatives this group immediately reacts by saying, "We cannot handle so many proposals at the same time. You have to space them over time", and therefore the whole system in the Commission, in Member States and among stakeholders within RACs is not capable of absorbing and handling so many plans at a time, particularly taking into account that these recovery plans inevitably have to have an impact assessment. That impact assessment is sometimes a complex exercise in which we have to evaluate economic consequences and data for these evaluations are not necessarily at our disposal immediately, and therefore it requires time to get the data to do the impact assessment, so the whole process is complicated. It was always complicated but it has been made more complicated by a relatively newly introduced element, the stakeholders' consultation, which is, of course, a major step forward in the CFP but is a step that does require time, not only from us but also from stakeholders to absorb, discuss and handle these proposals.

Q584 *Viscount Brookeborough:* Is part of the problem with this lack of data going back far enough and/or lack of funds being put into scientific research either in the past or currently, and are there sufficient methods whereby you can get accurate reporting from the stakeholders real-time as opposed to meeting them two or three times a year? Could there not be a more streamlined mechanism for reporting what is going on?
Mr Peñas: As I see it, there are two questions within your question. First of all, there is the question of data availability. Data availability is a problem in terms of quality for the biological part of it, and this is nothing new, but it is also a problem of the absolute lack of data in historical terms on the economic side. It is a well-known fact that, while biological information for the main fisheries has existed for decades (it may of imperfect quality but it does exist), the economic data to carry out the economic evaluation are often missing. The Commission is now making a big effort to try and collect this data, primarily through the Data Collection Regulation and funding to Member States in this regard, and the problem is that it has been helpful to try to provide recent data but it is much more difficult to build a historical series of data and therefore the economic data are still missing from a certain lack of tradition of collecting and studying these data. We are making

a big effort, but money is part of the problem and money is being spent by the Commission through the Data Collection Regulation to fill this gap. The gap that cannot be filled so easily is this lack of tradition and also a certain shortage of well-trained people on the economic side of fishery to carry out all the necessary work.
Mr Degnbol: There is an issue regarding scientific advice in general.

Q585 *Chairman:* You mentioned the problem being one really of time, just how long things take. Surely one of the new complexities is the move to co-decision. Is that going to add even further to the time problem?
Mr Peñas: Yes.
Chairman: Nice and crisp!

Q586 *Lord Plumb:* I spent 20 years in the European Parliament and co-decision has been on the go for a long time. There has been an element (not compulsory) of co-decision taking place, so why should it take any longer once it becomes established?
Mr Peñas: It is for the simple reason that we should compare co-decision in the fisheries sector to the current way of doing things. Perhaps in other sectors they are used to using this method but you have to remember that the Common Fisheries Policy is a common policy which is worked out through Council regulations. There are many of them every year. This is a typical example of a very heavy production of regulations every year. This is not a policy where you do a directive every five years that you can do through co-decision without a major problem. This is a sector where we produce several or even dozens of regulations per year and if all those have to be done through co-decision then you can certainly expect a prolonged procedure to adopt them. Basically, co-decision in the Common Fisheries Policy only adds an extra layer to the current administrative burden.
Mr Degnbol: It is seen as more cumbersome, and you will discuss this with Mr Borg this afternoon, but there may be a beneficial outcome in that first of all there is more democratic scrutiny to the process, but the second issue is that it may help in terms of making a clear hierarchy between decisions which are on a longer term principle, ie, the real policy level, and more the implementation level. The TACs and quota decisions are exempted from co-decision but that in our view means that they should follow more mechanically from the principle which has been established, such as long term management plans through co-decision, and that may contribute to a more sustainable fisheries in the longer term. It is a possibility.
Mr Peñas: It is clear that one of the challenges that we have ahead of us is whether we can succeed in changing the relative weight of the Council of

Ministers vis-à-vis other institutions, indeed, the Commission, and also why not in certain instances Member States in terms of who does what. For example, it is simply unthinkable that you will require Parliament and Council decisions to just adapt on technical grounds a regulation on technical conservation measures. The introduction of co-decision really will force every one of us in Member States to re-think who does what and particularly who does technical regulations. I think we all know that parliaments do laws, not regulations. The Common Fisheries Policy is done through a series of regulations, some of which can be considered as being laws in the sense that they basically state principles, but many others—and this is our daily job—are very technical and detailed regulations and then the question is, should Parliament with the Council still do these kinds of technical regulations or should that be done by the Commission through comitology or in some cases can this be devolved to Member States?.

Q587 *Viscount Brookeborough:* We are aware that the new cod recovery plan allows Member States to develop specific mechanisms to encourage the reduction of discards and the application of cod-avoidance programmes. You are presumably aware of the Scottish Executive's real-time closures and conservation credits scheme. What is your view of those schemes and what other types of initiative might you expect Member States to adopt?
Mr Peñas: The acceptance of this principle comes from the fact that the regulation applicable to the effort limitation system within Community law was considered by everyone as overly complex. I think this is nobody's or everybody's fault and it is the December negotiation in which basically Member States, under pressure from the industry, request more special conditions, derogations and things like that, and that results inevitably in a regulation that tends to be overly complex. In order to resolve this we undertook last year to try to devolve some of the technical details of what you can do to avoid by-catches of cod to the industry itself or the Member State concerned. That was the philosophy and under this philosophy Commissioner Borg, who I am sure will explain it to you this afternoon, considered that it was worth giving this a try and therefore he was very happy to give the opportunity to Member States to set up plans at national level where, on the basis of initiatives from fishermen, we will be testing other ways of reducing cod discards, so yes, the Commission considered that we should try new ways of handling this, and if the centralised, very complex regulations do not seem to be working to everyone's satisfaction let us try another approach. This is what is happening this year and the Commission is very interested to see what is happening with this

development. What is important also to note is that the position of the Commission in this case is that this is an opportunity for Member States to make this work but at the same time it is a big responsibility because now you can no longer blame Brussels if this goes wrong. You have only yourself to blame if this does not work. This is the philosophy under which this was done.

Q588 *Viscount Brookeborough:* And has each nation come up with a similar type of operation as Scotland or are some of them very different? Could you give us an example of one or two?
Mr Peñas: There are other projects going on, for example, a project presented by Germany to try to use industry-based initiatives to reduce by-catches of cod and discards, and in Denmark there have been some attempts to do this. You are probably aware that Scotland has been able to agree on certain measures with Denmark, but by and large the kind of complexity and sophistication, dare I say, of the Scottish initiative I have not seen from other Member States.

Q589 *Lord Plumb:* Can I follow up that point because we got the impression last week, when meeting with some of the people in Aberdeen, that they are also trying to get some agreements with Norway?
Mr Peñas: Yes, I think there have been informal contacts with Norway but, as you know, whether these agreements are formalised will have to be decided through the annual negotiation with Norway.

Q590 *Lord Plumb:* That is what I hoped you would say.
Ms Borges: I would like to add a little bit more on the discards just to say that, although some of the Member States took the initiative to do some of the projects to reduce or at least to study discards, we felt it was not enough to deal with the issue of discarding, and therefore we have just released a consultation paper for stakeholders on ideas for how we can progress in the future with discarding. We still maintain the attitude that it should be for Member States to resolve the issue specifically on fisheries, but we want to put a bit more incentive into that and so we have established targets for discarding which are specific to fisheries and give a specific time limit which Member States should follow. In a way we were saying, "Yes, please give us initiatives. We would very much welcome that, but you do need to follow those targets". We are now in the process of negotiating with stakeholders and we will have a legislative proposal at the end of the year.

Q591 Viscount Ullswater: The Commission currently manages fisheries very much through TACs and effort control—quotas, days at sea, however it is interpreted. How satisfied are you that these are the correct management tools? Should more emphasis be put on effort control and do you see that there are problems with the implementation of effort control? I think you mentioned a moment ago that it might be too overwhelming.

Mr Peñas: It is fair to say that we are not particularly satisfied with the way TACs are working. It is a well-known fact that TACs have basically two problems. First of all, there is a general problem of lack of compliance with TACs. The quota overshoot by national fleets is a phenomenon that exists all round the Community, so from the Baltic to the Iberian Peninsula it is a widespread problem. It is a system that has not been strictly respected, to say the least. Another problem is that it is still a system based on individual species, so it is a system that sets individual TACs, individual catch limitations from individual species, when we know very well that fishermen do not catch individual species; they catch assemblies of species that are found together in the same fishery, and therefore that almost inevitably carries the risk of making the TACs for individual species not match each other, so that what you have at the end of the day are different catch limitations for species that are caught together but do not necessarily match and this can produce discards, it can produce shortages of certain quotas while fishing for other species that are fully available and so on, so they have at least these two major problems. In fact, the scientific community for a number of years has been telling us very clearly that the TACs are not really controlling fishing mortality (which is the basic parameter we need in order to manage fisheries) and that direct effort control is necessary. This is the reason why we introduced effort control. Effort control existed in certain schemes before but only as of 2003, in the context of 2002, in the context of the cod recovery plan, has it started to be used as a real management tool. Now it has been extended to other areas. We have effort control now in the Baltic, in the Iberian Peninsula, in other places, and the experience of this is mixed. In principle you may expect that effort control should resolve some of the problems that I have mentioned in terms of the multi-species nature of the fishery. Effort control is a good solution for that, and the other potential benefit of effort management is that it should in principle be easier to enforce and simpler to control. We are not there yet and the reason is that, because of the political negotiation in the December Council, the effort management system that we have in place today has grown so complex that it has become just as difficult to control as the TACs, if not more. This is an instrument that still carries tremendous potential for being very easy to control but the way it is applied now within the famous Annex 2 of the TAC and Quota Regulation certainly this complexity does not lend itself very much to good control. An added problem is that it is easier at Community level to add a new instrument like effort control than it is to get rid of another one like TACs and quotas, and TACs and quotas are extremely difficult to get rid of for a very simple reason, which is that they are the carriers of relative stability and relative stability is a principle that for most Member States has been a sacred principle of the Common Fisheries Policy and it is politically extremely sensitive and extremely difficult to do away with it in the way that we believe we should do away with it. What this has meant as a result is that we have introduced a new instrument, effort management, as recommended by the scientific community but we have not done away with the existing one and the problem is then that we have a kind of double system of management of catch limitation through TACs and quotas and effort limitation at the same time, so we have a system which is growing very complex because we can develop one instrument but it is not easy to do away with the other one.

Q592 Viscount Ullswater: Are you suggesting with effort control that you should land all the fish that are caught?

Mr Peñas: At present that is not possible.

Q593 Viscount Ullswater: Would that not be the purpose of effort control?

Mr Peñas: Yes, that would be the idea.

Q594 Viscount Ullswater: So why are you saying it is not possible?

Mr Peñas: Because of relative stability. For example, if a vessel from a Member State that has no quota for cod goes out and respects effort limitation but inevitably catches some amount of cod, even if that vessel from that Member State has fully complied with the effort limitation that vessel is not entitled to catch any cod and therefore it will have to discard it immediately because relative stability in terms of catch quotas does not allow that Member State to keep that cod on board. Therefore, while the TAC and quota system with relative stability survives, it will not necessarily be possible to keep all the fish on board.

Q595 Viscount Ullswater: Would it not be a good idea to do so in order to measure the by-catch, the discards, because at the moment you talk about relative stability but that is purely a figure on a piece of paper? It does not measure the fish mortality of the species, so do you still feel that that is irreconcilable with the present structure of management?

Mr Degnbol: Yes. In the framework in which we have the discard policy, and I do not know whether you have looked into the complications we made on that last year, there is the concept of trying in the longer term to move to a system where it is mandatory to keep fish on board. Of course, within relative stability, within that TAC-based system, you would not be allowed to sell this fish above your basic quota on the market so you would be required to land it but it would basically be confiscated, but it is part of that perspective and that would be a strong driver to avoid catching it because there are costs involved in keeping fish on board which you are not paid for.

Ms Borges: Some of this discussion has also been included in the latest released consultation paper. There are issues with a discard ban about how good is the data. One of the issues is that there are good data available already now with observer programmes and scientific programmes, although, of course, you would increase those data if you had access to what is discarded. There is also the issue that some of the species that are discarded can survive. If you have a discard ban you are forcing fish mortality in species that could otherwise survive, such as shark. It is complicated. There are a lot of issues related to the discard ban that might not be initially seen, so although we still discuss it we are going for a reduction of discards and in the longer term we might consider a discard ban.

Q596 *Viscount Brookeborough:* Would there not be an issue sometimes in the boats if there was a discard ban about the amount of room that these discards were taking up in that it may not be beneficial financially to dump them but the quantities would be a problem?

Mr Degnbol: Exactly. This is a strong economic incentive not to catch them. The whole concept of this initiative is to leave it to the industry to find solutions and not make all kinds of detailed technical measures. You say, "Okay: you have a problem keeping it on board. Don't catch it in the first place. That solves your problem."

Chairman: This is fascinating. It is obviously a very important issue but we have spent quite a lot of time on it and we are going to have to miss some of the questions, but let us press on.

Q597 *Baroness Jones of Whitchurch:* We have touched on this a little bit already, the issue of scientific advice. We have received, as I am sure you already know, a lot of evidence about the frustration of fishermen who are telling us that their experience out at sea is very different from the scientific advice that you are receiving, and we know that part of that problem is the retrospective way that the information is provided to you. It seems to me that one of the advantages of the current system, as you were saying,

is that we have quite long records going back because the scientific evidence has been collected in the same way for a very long time, but it is equally very frustrating because you would think that science would have moved on and that people would be slightly more sophisticated than they were 20 years ago. First, I think you have already acknowledged that there is a problem, but do you see a way round that and a way of improving the scientific advice, which I think is key to a lot of the things we are talking about?

Mr Degnbol: I think we have first of all to identify what is the real problem here, and when it is said that there is large uncertainty, there is uncertainty when it comes to prediction of the catch next year, but for nearly all our stocks there is not large uncertainty about the state of the stock or in which direction to move in management. It is very clear that for most of our stocks they are over-fished and we need to reduce the fishing pressure. There is no uncertainty about that. When it comes to making a catch prediction next year there is an uncertainty issue and there are several contributors to that, some of which we can do something about. The first problem is that when you have over-fished stocks the catch prediction for next year is based on the incoming year class, which is the one which is the most poorly known of everything. It is a paradox that when we have most need of good data, which is mainly when we have serious over-fishing, we have the largest concerns about the forecasts because we live from the new-borns and we do not have a good number on those, so just by reducing the fishing pressure, which is our aim in the MSY policy, we would increase certainty in the forecasts; that is part of that. I hope it is not too technical now but basically we are creating uncertainty by over-fishing. The second problem is non-compliance, that we have a problem with black landings, non-legal landings, and we can see this in the data, that there are fish disappearing from the system to unknown places and this adds to the uncertainty in a lot of cases, so better enforcement is a key also to repairing that. But then, of course, there remains an uncertainty, which is the assembling of the data and not actually making a census on the fish in the sea. Biological parameters are not always precise, and that is an irreducible uncertainty and that has to be addressed by the way we set the management system up. You may ask what is the problem if there is some uncertainty in a catch forecast, a residual uncertainty. To some extent you can say that it does not matter that much because basically the fish we leave in the sea this year are available for you to catch next year. The system will regulate itself in that if there is a bit of under-fishing this year you will get a higher catch forecast next year and you will catch up with it. The way we are proposing TACs these days, we are proposing a kind of window so you can only move within a window to give stability to the industry, and that contains this uncertainty, so that you are able to keep up with the uncertainty next year. We are a little bit concerned about this focus on having the most precise and up-to-date prediction because it is based on this illusion that you have to be there now and get it. If I could be a little bit provocative, we have as an example presently a proposal from France, supported by the UK and Ireland, to increase the quota on Celtic sea cod next year, and this is based on an observation from a survey that there is no more from the incoming year class than we saw when the advice was coming out. We do not need to increase the quota because these are two-kilo fish. If you leave them one year more in the sea they will be 4.5 kilos. By fishing them this year you are burning up future catch options and if you look for more than one year you are having a negative result of this. You do not need to be that up to date because they are in the sea still and you will have better options next year for catching them, so uncertainty may not need to be such a big problem because the system is a kind of cybernetic. It will adjust along the way.

Q598 *Chairman:* Does that not argue against single-year TACs? Does it not argue in favour of multi-year TACs?

Mr Degnbol: Not necessarily. It argues against setting a single-year TAC by focusing on the catch in that year only. You should always look at this in a medium-term perspective, that you can go the whole line down and set a multi-year TAC where you would then need monitoring mechanisms to warn you if there was a really serious problem going on, but you could have a system of multi-year TACs with mechanisms for warning and fast decisions if an issue arose.

Q599 *Viscount Ullswater:* It is interesting to see that you have reorganised your DG to coincide with the RACs.

Mr Degnbol: It is no coincidence.

Q600 *Viscount Ullswater:* We have heard from a lot of stakeholders that perhaps they see the future for the CFP being more organised down RACs, and I think the general tone has been positive as regards Commission engagement with the RACs but some disappointment was expressed at the Commission's apparent rejection of the North Western Waters RAC's proposal with regard to the future management of hake. It was put to us that where the scientists and the stakeholders agreed it was surprising that the Commission then wanted a rather more demanding management plan and I wondered if you had any comment to make about that. Also, I would like to hear what your feelings are about the

establishment of RACs and how they are getting on in terms of the consensus that they bring.

Mr Peñas: On the first one, I wonder whether there is perhaps some kind of misunderstanding. On the northern hake we do have a management plan that has achieved its objectives. That management plan requires that when we have achieved those objectives for two years in a row we should go to the next step, which is to make a proposal on a long-term management plan that will focus on the maximum sustainable yield for this fishery. Now what has happened is that we have presented our papers. The objectives of the first recovery plan have been achieved. We have now a fishery which is at the level of the precautionary biomass, so that was achieved, but now it is built into that recovery plan that we should move automatically to the second phase, so what we have done so far in that respect is to present our ideas in a consultation paper to the RACs on what this second phase will consist of. Basically, the reaction has been that now we are being overly ambitious over this. Actually what we are doing with this second phase is not only fulfilling the obligations of the Commission in the context of the previous phase, so first of all to respond to a legal obligation, but, more importantly, this new approach that we are suggesting for the northern hake is simply the kind of approach that all Member States and the Community signed up to in the 2002 World Summit on Sustainable Development in Johannesburg, which had the objective to bring all fisheries to maximum sustainable yield levels by 2050. We take this commitment seriously and this certainly inspires all our proposals so this is exactly what we are doing. The problem from a number of meetings we had with the North Western RAC is that they are relatively satisfied because the fishery now is not over-fished; it is on precautionary levels, but they consider perhaps that it is too ambitious to go further than this. On the question of our experience in RACs, generally speaking the experience is very good, particularly because for those of us in this house who have a certain number of years' experience perhaps the most important thing we have achieved so far is to dramatically improve the quality of our dialogue with the stakeholders. Only a few years back I remember some meetings with the stakeholders here in Brussels in which they were basically shouting at us and telling us such sophisticated arguments as, "You only look at the fish but not at the fishermen", and some meetings did not go much beyond that. Since then I think things have improved quite dramatically and now the fishermen's representatives, put it this way, speak our language and they try to convince us of their suggestions by telling us, "This will contribute to reducing discards, which is your objective, Commission", so I think we are increasingly talking the same kind of language. In terms of the follow-up of their suggestions, I think that the picture is mixed so far. We have followed a great many of their suggestions and proposals but others we have not followed so far. I think the biggest challenge we have is to establish a system where our reaction to their proposals can be perhaps more predictable. We have tried to do this by telling them that we will be accepting their proposals insofar as they go in the direction of achieving the objectives of the Common Fisheries Policy, but, of course, this is easier said than done and there is ample room for manoeuvre to interpret this. Both parts, the Commission and the stakeholders in RACs, are in this learning curve in which we know much better what are the criteria for us to accept their ideas, and our ultimate goal is for them to be the measure of their own success, in other words that they should know before they tell us whether a certain proposal is acceptable or not. If it goes against sustainability of the stocks then they should take for granted that we cannot follow that, but if it goes in that direction they should be sufficiently reassured that they have a fair chance that the Commission will support it.

Q601 *Viscount Ullswater:* Is that not saying, "As long as you agree with us we will agree with you"?
Mr Peñas: No, not exactly.

Q602 *Viscount Ullswater:* They are looking for a little bit more flexibility, are they not?
Mr Peñas: Not exactly. I will try to explain the point a little bit better. The question is that the Common Fisheries Policy has objectives that have been established by the Council of Ministers and that are certainly an obligation for the Commission services and for national governments and for stakeholders as well. The Commission is the guardian of the treaty, so it is our obligation to make sure that those objectives are respected. We can have flexibility as to how we get there but we cannot have flexibility as to whether those objectives should be ignored or achieved. We have to be guardians of this and we have to say, "If the objective of the Common Fisheries Policy is to achieve fish stocks and fisheries that are sustainable then everything that goes towards sustainability we have to support. Everything that goes against it we cannot support". We can have flexibility as to the means, the modalities and the methods to get there but we cannot compromise on the objectives.

Q603 *Earl of Arran:* Just continuing with the RACs, which I think is extremely interesting, of course, last year their financial position was made much more secure. We understand that they still have several problems, one of which is the need to find a guarantor and the second is from accounting rules preventing transfers between budget lines within their budgets.

There is obviously a lot of goodwill among Member States concerning the future of the RACs and their finances but it would seem also that there is not so much goodwill from other Member States about their future and their financing. Would you like to enlarge upon the financial situation in the future?
Mr Peñas: The Commission has shown recently, as you mention, that we are prepared to provide the funding that is necessary for the RACs to carry out their work. It is clearly essential that RACs are given the financial means to do this, and providing some level of public funds is also important because among stakeholders you find some people who represent strong fishing companies, and I could mention some well-known companies such as the pelagic fishing companies that are strong enterprises and that are capable of doing this and following up all the necessary work in the RACs perhaps without public funding, but many other sectors represent more traditional fishing where, unless there is public funding, they will have trouble to be represented, to attend the meetings, to make a significant contribution, so from that point of view we tend to think that in order to ensure equal opportunities for everyone within RACs for different segments and different levels of income and organisation it is essential to ensure adequate public funding. On the other hand, I think that this has to be done in the perspective of gradually empowering RACs to run their own business and be responsible for the work, so we have to find a combination which provides them with sufficient boost at the beginning so that they get their organisation running, but in the long run tells them, "Gradually you should learn to walk on your own". What is the reason why some Member States are more forthcoming than others in this? Probably the Member States who are a bit more reluctant can tell you better than we can, but my personal impression is that perhaps there is a slightly different perception of the role of RACs in some different Member States. In some Member States perhaps RACs are still seen as an open door to re-nationalisation of the Common Fisheries Policy and that may explain the reason why some of them are a bit more reticent, but this is a personal opinion.

Q604 *Earl of Arran:* For instance, the Spanish do not believe in the decentralisation of power that much, the power involved from the centre, so to speak, and therefore they might be rather reluctant to part with future financing within RACs, but we shall come to that when we see the Spanish gentleman later on.
Mr Peñas: I think so, yes.

Q605 *Chairman:* Can I move on to control and enforcement? You mentioned the persistent problem of black fish. The evidence we have would seem to suggest that the registration of buyers and sellers has had a significant impact on decreasing the level of black fish. Is that your view and one of the difficulties the uneven implementation of the registration?

Mr Peñas: On the registration issue, certainly we are convinced that this question of the registration of buyers and sellers has provided much better control of quotas in the UK. Our control services basically control the controllers, as you know. They are quite clear on this, and so we believe this has been a substantial success. Then what is the problem? Not only in the UK but in many Member States the problem is not so much what goes through the normal channels, which in some cases works relatively well, but what goes outside the normal channels and is basically fish sold to certain factories that does not necessarily go through official channels. Another difficulty is the fact that there is an increasing number of vessels that are landing abroad and therefore the control of those catches in some cases is realised by the coastal state but the data on this is not necessarily transferred back to the country of origin of the vessel and in some cases then some of these catches may go unregistered for that Member State, so this is another problem. There is a variety of problems. I am not a specialist in control but what I can say is that our control colleagues have confirmed that the registration of buyers and sellers has provided a big improvement in the UK. I would not say that in the UK this is today a big problem but certainly marketing of fish outside the legal channels is still one of the biggest problems overall in Europe.

Q606 *Earl of Dundee:* In enforcing the Common Fisheries Policy what do you consider to be the respective roles of the Commission and the Member States authorities and the Community Fisheries Control Agency?

Mr Peñas: As you know, the control is primarily and fundamentally a Member State responsibility. There have been attempts, particularly on the occasion of the last reform, to try to enhance the role of the Commission but this was not considered acceptable from Member States and therefore we stay where we were a few years back, that is, that Member States have full responsibility for control. There the role of the Commission is, as I said before, to control the controllers. It is just to evaluate how Member States are doing the job in controlling their own fleets. As to the Control Agency, the Control Agency does not have any large powers as compared to the Commission. Basically, the Control Agency was created to try to make economies of scale in control. In many fisheries in Europe you will find an assembly of vessels from different Member States being deployed in one fishing area. If those vessels

were all controlled independently by the control systems of different Member States you would find a number of duplications in the effort and therefore it was very strongly felt that there was a lot to be gained from trying to pull together the national control means of Member States through joint deployment plans, to find economies of scale in order to make much better and more efficient use of the very expensive and very limited control means, and that is exactly the role of the Agency. The Agency does not have universal powers. The Agency still cannot set fines to individual fishermen. The Commission, incidentally, cannot set fines to individual fishermen either. That is the role of the control systems of the Member States. The role of the Commission, as I said, is to check how Member States are doing the job and the role of the Agency is to try to develop joint control deployment plans so as to pull together and increase the efficiency of the national means of control.

Q607 *Earl of Dundee:* Nevertheless, what new enforcement tools at the disposal of the Commission or the other bodies are proving to be useful?

Mr Peñas: I think perhaps the biggest powers of the Commission are those when it has evidence that a Member State is not doing its job; then it can take different actions. It can take a Member State to the court or it can even take direct action and I will mention two examples. Recently it was felt in Poland that the level of control of the catches of cod in the Baltic and other species (but particularly cod) were so bad that they were fishing easily twice their national quota. On the basis of the evidence gathered by the Commission inspectors the Commission made a case for establishing a penalty to Poland to the effect of withdrawing from the Polish quota all the estimated catches above and beyond the Polish national quota. This ended up in a procedure recently adopted by the Commission whereby Poland for the next four years will have its own national quota cut back in order to pay back what they fished in excess in previous years. This has been, I think, a system whereby the Commission has exerted its powers to try to discipline a Member State. Another example is that we also have clear evidence that some of the national quotas for blue fin tuna in the Mediterranean have been so clearly overshot that the Commission is using its powers to close the fishery before Member States recognise that the quota has been fished because the statistics cannot be trusted. We have gathered with our inspectors sufficient evidence showing that the quotas for blue fin tuna are not being respected and therefore in order to preserve this highly endangered species we needed to close the fishery even before the Member States recognised that they had exhausted their quotas. Those are two examples of the Commission using its powers.

Q608 *Earl of Dundee:* What you have described may be existing constraints but if some of them prove reluctant to apply existing rules might it be helpful to place additional enforcement obligations on Member States themselves?
Mr Peñas: Yes indeed, that will be our intention, but the problem is that this question of control touches upon a question of national sovereignty and every time we discuss with Member States controlling their fishermen they say that is a question of national

sovereignty and they are not prepared to give away powers to Brussels, to be blunt. This is the difficulty we have always had and whether this is going to change I do not know.

Q609 *Chairman:* We have been just over an hour. It has been an excellent session. Thank you very much. I am afraid we have not covered many important topics that we would have liked to cover. Would it be possible for us to follow some of those topics up through writing to you?
Mr Peñas: Yes, no problem.
Chairman: Thank you very much indeed.

Memorandum by the Spanish Government

CONSERVATION MANAGEMENT

The Common Fisheries Policy (CFP) has not made much use of the fisheries management methods. In fact, recovery and management measures have only been adopted for a limited number of stocks, and emergency measures only in those instances when the conditions set out by Community legislation have been met. One criticism with regard to the adoption of these measures is that, often, the proposals have lent more weight to biological criteria than to socioeconomic issues, putting forward, therefore, measures which are adequate for the conservation of fishing stocks, but lacking in information with regard to the socioeconomic repercussions of their implementation.

Given that the CFP makes provisions for criteria on sustainability and contemplates socioeconomic aspects, these should not be forgotten or relegated to the background when adopting management measures for the various fisheries.

With regard to management tools, it must be noted that Total Allowable Catches (TACs) are set up in accordance with scientific advice which, in turn, is based on precautionary criteria. The establishment of TACs and their distribution into fishing quotas among Member States are key elements in fisheries management and in the profitability of the various fisheries.

The establishment of TACs has often been criticized for being too empirical and for not taking into account the reality of the various fleets. It has also been pointed out that international organizations tend to announce their assessments too late in the year, almost coinciding with the dates when the Commission presents its proposals to the Council. Consequently, there is not sufficient time for these proposals to be studied by the scientific organizations and the fisheries managers of the Administrations of the Member States, nor between the Commission and the fishing sector through the Regional Advisory Councils (RACs). Some improvements have, however, been introduced in recent years like the publication of some scientific reports earlier in the year, something that facilitates their study and allows for the better planning of the fisheries.

Further improvements have been made by achieving a greater rapprochement between scientists and the industry. In this regard and for some years now, the International Council for the Exploration of the Sea (ICES) has favoured meetings with fisheries representatives from the RACs, in order to seek a rapprochement of viewpoints as well as a greater understanding.

Although the methods used for the establishment of TACs has improved, their transformation into quotas for the various Member States does not always match reality. In fact, the assignation of quotas has been based for many years now on the principle of relative stability which, with the passing of time, no longer reflects the fisheries reality or the depedence of the various coastal regions on this industry.

Another point to be made with regard to the management system based on TACs and quotas is that the current system of distribution based on relative stability grants quotas above the needs of the fleets of some Member States, whilst assigning inadequate quotas to others. This situation is sometimes remedied by resorting to exchange mechanisms among the fisheries Administrations of the Member States. These mechanisms, however, always require a compensation in the form of fishing quotas. Therefore, Member States have to resort to swaps of certain amounts of a certain stock in return for another or others, based on a principle of equivalence so that the exchange is proportional. Therefore, this mechanism does not involve a free cession, but merely an exchange.

However, for certain stocks, some of high commercial value, this mechanism is not sufficient to meet the needs of the fleet of a Member State which is forced to close a fishery before the end of the year, while other Member States may have available quotas of the species in question but are unable to consume them. Therefore, these quotas remain in the sea uncaught at the end of the year. This situation is not occasional for, in effect, it occurs on a yearly basis.

In order to solve this problem, the CFP should adopt agile and efficient mechanisms which, practically in real time, would identify the quotas that are not going to be used by a Member State so that they could be assigned to another Member State in need of them and which, otherwise and through lack of quota, would be forced to close the fishery before the end of the year.

With regard to the current management regime based on the fishing effort, the last change took place in 2003, and it involved the fisheries of demersal and deep-sea species in the Atlantic Ocean. This change established effort limitations for each Member State in relation to that developed during a period of reference (1998–2002).

This fishing-effort plan has been completed in the case of species subjected to recovery plans (cod, south hake, amongst others) with a maximum assignation of "days at sea" for those vessels with the largest catches of the species under recovery, effecting progressive reductions of the "days at sea" in the years following the implementation of the recovery plan. In addition to the extreme complexity that the management of the fishing days for each individual vessel involves for each Member State, in practice the accumulated reduction of the fishing days are rendering the fleets unviable from an economic standpoint.

It is noteworthy that in certain areas and on an experimental basis consideration is being given to the management of the fisheries based on a plan of limitation of only the effort and not the quotas. The results of this new experience should be considered carefully because in the future and in order to solve many of the problems that the CFP will face it may prove interesting to study a management system based on the fishing effort, instead of the current double system of effort and quotas.

With regard to marine conservation areas, it must be pointed out that the last years have witnessed the creation of numerous protected areas of significant consequences for the development of the fishing activity which is either limited or prevented in the interest of the protection and conservation of the marine habitat.

In this regard, it can only be said that this measure is correct, and that when the necessary conditions are in place new protection measures should be adopted. However, several facts will need to be specified.

Consequently, the proposals made should be based on solid scientific evidence confirmed by internationally recognized organizations. These proposals should also be coupled with clear control mechanisms to guarantee compliance in the designated areas. This will be particularly important in those areas where only certain fisheries are permitted, thus ensuring that this particular aspect is adhered to.

Finally, both the limits of the areas and the fishing activity that might be undertaken inside them should be continuously assessed by means of the necessary reports, as well as being subjected to revisions. Coinciding with the closure of an area or the limitation of its activity, assessment mechanisms should be in place to confirm whether the measures adopted are having the expected results. In this regard, the assessment campaigns undertaken should be carried out by the coastal State, but leaving an option open for the participation of other Member States.

Real-time closures are being used by some third countries in the management of certain fisheries, and some scientists regard them as effective for avoiding catching juvenile fish during the fishing activity. At a Community level there is no clear experience in the operation of this management system. However, its introduction is envisaged within the future management plan for the Atlantic cod fishery.

What is certain and agreed upon by scientists and the industry alike, is the existence of areas and times of the year when there is a greater presence of juvenile fish in the sea, and when real-time closures during a specified period would be highly beneficial for the fishing stock. This option should therefore be further explored, so that there could be areas which would be closed or the fishing activity within them limited at certain times of the year. This would allow a better planning of the activity, with much less serious socioeconomic consequences resulting from the implementation of the above-mentioned closures.

In brief, Spain supports the advancement of scientific studies so that, when deemed necessary, spatial and time closures may be implemented in a clear and precise manner and in specific areas and times of the year, instead of adopting real-time closures.

With regard to rights-based management tools, it should be remembered that, firstly, fishing is a common resource of exploitation for the fishermen of a certain Member State and is only its exploitation and in order to manage it in accordance with the principles of rationality and to distribute it among the vessels, the reason why it could be advisable to resort to rights-based management tools.

The use of fishing rights is necessary particularly for those fisheries that cannot guarantee of availability of the fishing resource for all vessel throughout the year. Right-based management tools have been accused of having some flaws such as, for instance, to encourage discards so that only the best fish, and therefore the most valuable, arrives at ports. However, in practice the number of Member States and the fisheries that are being regulated in accordance with fishing rights are on the increase.

Spain has a long tradition of fisheries regulation based on fishing rights and possibilities. In effect, some fisheries adopted this operating system in the 1980s which has been continued and to which some new fisheries have been incorporated, given that is regarded as advantageous from a biological and economic standpoint. It follows that this management system compels Members States to regulate the mechanisms that govern the transfer of rights among vessels, so that these operations can be totally transparent.

Nevertheless, in order that this system was more effective, the transfer or rights should not be confined to the Member State itself, but there should be the possibility that the transfer of fishing rights could be done between different Member States.

With regard to the technical conservation measures, the legal basis is found in a Council Regulation, which the Commission plans to amend. To this end the Commission prepared a proposal in 2004, which for several reasons has been delayed and has not yet been put forward to the Council.

In relation to this new proposal, our position is that it must be of an horizontal nature and should, therefore, refer to all sea areas and fishing zones, as well as to the different fishing gears. In any case, the regional approaches should be avoided and only be considered in the cases where are really necessary, that is to say, the regional approach should be used as an exception.

On the other hand, we are of the opinion that the responsibility for the establishment of technical measures should fall within the scope of the Ministers Council, including any possible regional approach that may be intended to be tackled in the future, so that the current balance of responsibilities between the Council and the Commission in this subject is not changed.

Finally, we also understand that, in the interest of simplification, all rules referring to technical measures should be found in a single legal text, in order to facilitate its implementation.

Regarding the discards, we must firstly indicate that this problem has been linked, almost exclusively, to the selection of fishing gears that are used in the different fisheries. Although this might be true in some cases, the insufficiency or lack of quotas favour likewise the discards.

Modifying the current concept of fisheries and compelling to unload all the catches, will undoubtedly have a positive impact on the assessment of resources, since better and further information on its situation will be made available. Nevertheless, from the point of view of fisheries management, that will force to apply important changes to the current management systems, specially with regard to fishing quotas. The lack of quotas for one species, the closure of some fisheries due to the depletion of one fishing quota will not be able to continue operating in the same way that it is at present.

In this sense, it seems absolutely essential not to introduce any changes in the current management systems while a response to these new situations that will present in practice is available. A possible solution to this problem could be given by switching the current fisheries management system based on a double system of fishing quotas and fishing effort to a system based only in the fishing effort.

Climate change is a definite fact that also has an impact on the marine environment since it is observed that global warming is affecting oceans and this will have a great impact on the development of the fishing activity in the medium and long term. There have been some attempts to make the fishing industry responsible for the climate change due to its high consumption of fuel, especially by certain fisheries that require a high level of consumption to operate. However, in fact, the fishing industry is also suffering the consequences of this effect, especially regarding the changes in the behaviour of fishing species or even changes in zones where those fisheries were usually operating. This is the reason why scientists must pay attention to this fact and include it in their assessment in order that the management measures in the fishing industry take into account the consequences that can be derived from these possible changes.

It is true that throughout the years some changes linked to climate changes of an isolated nature have been produced in the different fisheries, but now is safe to think that new changes will take place, or are already taking place, which will have an impact on the ecosystem as a whole. This is caused by an unprecedented combination of climate change and other alterations, such as acidification and other changes derived from pollution and overexploitation of certain resources. The impact on fisheries is expected to be complex and affect some aspects other than the mere change in the distribution of stocks.

In this respect, instead of falling to drama or adopting measures without making any check, we consider necessary to have further information on the impact of climate change on fisheries and coordinate the efforts of the scientific community at an international level, since this impact is felt beyond the EU fisheries and fisheries zones. It would serve to no purpose to oblige to make efforts in EU waters, if similar principles are not kept in adjacent zones.

We should also bear in mind the possible impact of climate change on the current management system of the fisheries activity. Given that the stocks are managed on the basis of TAC and quotas, referred to certain management areas, any change produced in the fishing grounds will oblige to introduce changes in the current management systems, including the allocation keys, and this aspect should be studied with great care and all that without forgetting the likely social and economic consequences, which will also have to be previously assessed.

Control and Enforcement

With regard to the aspects related to the control of the fisheries activity, and if we take into consideration the conclusions of the Court of Auditors Report in this subject, it can be noted that this document shows the important deficiencies affecting the fisheries Administrations of both the Member States and the Community.

It is a fact that the aspects linked to control could improve, but it is also true that it is necessary to analyze the real reasons for which the quality of control is not considered satisfactory.

In this respect, it must be pointed out that the aspects mentioned in said Court of Auditors Report refer to the existing situation in 2005 and, at present, that is to say, three years after the verification mentioned in the report was made, some improvements have been made in the control systems, at least as far as the Spanish Administration is concerned, which are not reflected by said report. These improvements refer to both human and material resources, as well as the technological field, all of which are intended for enhancing the number and quality of the control activity.

The problems experienced in control can also be put down to the high number of disperse pieces of legislation that regulate the obligations in the subject of control, to the duplicity and reiteration that oblige Member States in the aspect of notifications and communications, as well as to the ambiguity and vagueness with which other many control obligations are presented. All this is translated into a huge bureaucratic charge for the Member States' fisheries administrations and the own fishermen. In this sense, it is necessary to unify, to codify and simplify all the control legislation currently in force and study carefully the new obligations that may be introduced in this subject so as to lighten the workload and be able to pay more attention to the quality, rather than the quantity, of the data.

On the other hand, the Control Agency has just started to operate and, therefore, we will have to observe how it tackles the tasks that it is undertaking before thinking of assigning it further tasks and duties. In the case that the situation requires other duties, it will have to be done in a coordinated way so that the above-mentioned duplicities are not produced.

The experience of working with the Commission during the preparation of these documents was highly positive, having achieved full support from them, which allowed us to finish both documents on time. In this sense, the Operative Programme was approved on 13 December 2007.

Regarding the implementation of the EFF, given that it was recently passed, it is not possible to share our experience, only point out that the prolonged period of negotiations delayed its introduction.

Structural Policy

Ever since Spain joined the European Union in 1986, the Spanish Government has made a significant effort to adjust the capacity of its fleet to the available fishing opportunities, a fact that is reflected in the figures related to the latest years.

One of the most important measures implemented within this structural adjustment was the compulsory withdrawal of fleet capacity to allow the incorporation of a new one, measure that the European Union adopted with the Reform of the Common Fisheries Policy—CFP through Regulation (EC) 2371/2002 of 22 December 2002 on the conservation and sustainable exploitation of fisheries resources.

Indeed, within the strict observance required for the mentioned Regulation, Spain has maintained and doubled its efforts to adjust their fleet to the conservation and management of the fisheries resources and reduce to the minimum the fishing effects on the conservation of the stocks of marine species.

The decommissioning policy to allow the building of new vessels was aimed to avoid the increase of the capacity and the withdrawal of the fishing activity has been encouraged with the support provided in the structural programmes co-funded with the Institute for the Promotion of Fisheries (Instituto de Fomento Pesquero—IFOP), in order to adjust the capacity of the fleet to the existing stocks.

The data to 31 December 2007 reveals the effort made in this regard by the Spanish fleet, which was reduced by 1,871 vessels, that imply a decrease of the tonnage by 51,438 GT and of the power by 199,716 KW during the scope of five years of the new CFP.

According to the Spanish Government, this reduction and that which will probably occur in the future under the provisions of Regulation (EC) 1198/2006 of 27 July on the European Fisheries Fund, fulfils the aim of sustainable exploitation of fisheries resources.

Related to the European Fisheries Fund (EFF), it was established at the Council of Fisheries Ministers on 19 June 2006 and published in the Official Journal of the European Union through Regulation (EC) 1198/2006 of 27 July.

The EFF sets the framework for Community support for the sustainable development of the fisheries sector. It came into force on 1 January 2007.

Spain, being the first receptor of funds for the period 2007–13, received 1,131,890,912 euros of which, 186,198,467 euros relate to the Regions not included in the Convergence Aim and 945,692,445 euros relates to the Convergence Aim.

The drafting process of the mentioned Regulation was long and complicated. The dossier has been at the Council's office for two years and was debated more than six times at the Council of Ministers. Also 25 working groups' meetings have taken place, as well as more than 17 informal meetings and a hundred bilateral meetings of Spain both with the Commission and with the rest of the State Members in order to gain support from the majority in pursuit of the creation of the EFF.

In this sense, the work carried out during the drafting process of this Regulation has been arduous, aiming to the fullest improvement of the proposals that initially were so restrictive, in benefit of the Spanish fisheries sector interests.

On the other hand and according to the provisions of the Regulation in question, the Spanish Ministry of Agriculture, Fisheries and Food (MAPA), through its Fisheries General Secretariat, started in 2006 the drafting of the documents for the Programme, which must be coherent with each other and are:

— the National Strategic Plan,
— the Operative Programme,
— the Advance Assessment, and
— the Environmental Assessment.

The Spanish Government committed to carry out this task aiming at the greatest participation and agreement, both from the Autonomous Communities and other Public Bodies, as well as from the fisheries sector, from the social representatives and NGOs and other associations and stakeholders.

Regarding the subsidies in the fishing sector, in paragraph 28 of Doha's Ministerial Statement, the Ministers agreed to start negotiations to clarify and improve the disciplines of the "Agreement on Subsidies and Countervailing Measures", preserving its basic concepts and principles, and taking into account the needs of the developing countries. They specifically mentioned the subsidies in the fishing sector as an important one for these countries. These negotiations take place at the WTO Negotiating Group on Rules.

After several meetings, the Chair of the WTO Negotiating Group on Rules circulated a draft text on rules (Doc. TN/RL/W/213 of 30 November 2007).

Observations given by the Under Secretary for Fisheries Commercialisation:

— the document is too complex;
— inexistence of a first article setting out the scope and the definition of subsidy;
— aquaculture is not included;
— practically all the subsidies for developed countries are banned. There is no exception for artisanal fisheries and fishing for shellfish;

— the bans affect the tax for diesel, special social security regime, temporary unemployment subsidies, reduction in port taxes. . .;

— we wonder how the WTO is going to evaluate the degree of exploitation of stocks, when it does not have a mandate to that effect;

— with regard to the external assessment of the management systems applied, any interpretation could clash with the competences of the countries and regional and international fisheries organizations that have their own mechanisms for solving disputes and which should prevail;

— there are very reasonable doubts about the competence of the WTO in the evaluation of management systems and the will of FAO to participate.

Subsequently, a meeting of the Negotiating Group on Rules took place on 30 and 31 January 2008, where Spain, besides stressing the imbalance of the text, requested in Community coordination the defence of the preservation of the CFP.

The Commission reminded that they already showed their disappointment in December 2007 and expressed the following:

— The text lacks balance.

— The support to the prices or income in poor areas should not affect the fishing capacity.

— The text does not take the pro-environmental measures into account, which have a positive effect and now they are prohibited.

— The transfer of rights is not regarded as subsidy.

— Infrastructures should be excluded.

There will be a new meeting of the Negotiating Group on Rules on 18 and 19 February at WTO, where the same document of 30 November will continue to be debated (TN/RL/213).

This Office reiterates the opinion previously given and trust that in the short term a new revised document will be available in accordance with the conclusions resulting from the debates and gathered by the President of the Group, in order to provide a new point of view.

Governance

Further to the governance of the CFP and the operation of RACs, it must be noted that, with the exception of the Mediterranean RAC, which has not yet been established, the rest of RACs created within the framework of the CFP, have been operating for several years and, therefore, some assessment on their work can be provided.

RACs have to be given a clearly positive effect in the sense that they are favouring the approximation of the fishing industry of the different Member States involved in each RAC on a nearly permanent basis, which facilitates a better understanding of the problems of each of them and better systems to find the best solutions in each case.

Nevertheless, opposite to these advantages which are very important, there are certain flaws that have to be considered. Failure to pay the required attention to these flaws, which are detailed below, will make question the beneficial effect of RACs.

The first difficulties are derived from the own operational framework which is defined in the Council Regulation establishing RACs. In this sense, the geographical ascription of one of them, and the species ascription in other cases, causes lack of coordination and duplicities in their work subjects. Apart from this, there is also a difficulty regarding the definition of the fishing industry, since it groups different activities, from the catching sector to commercialization passing through aquaculture and certain fisheries, that clearly have opposing interests. There is, finally, another difficulty regarding the composition of the RACs structures of governance, since their limited number of members, without taking into account the number of the composing Member States or the singularities of its members in each case, makes of RACs an structure where the interests of the different associations and organisations that constitute them are not clearly reflected. Making the number of members flexible according to the needs would facilitate the operation of some RACs.

With regard to the operation itself of RACs, some deficiencies which make them less efficient should be noted. In this sense, a high number of meetings are held: focus groups, working groups, which are in many cases subdivided in fishing areas or zones, apart from the executive committees and general assemblies that all of them have. All these meetings cause repetition and reiteration of the same matter, with the subsequent danger of examining the problem in a too fractional and local way and, therefore, slowing the presentation of proposals. If we add to this the fact that the Commission very often is not present in the debates, the conclusions tendered are too theoretical.

Another problem posed is the lack of clear objectives with regard to which matters must be examined in the framework of RACs and which ones within the framework the Fisheries Consultative Committee (ACFA). The same documents are examined sometimes in the same forum, which amounts to a duplication of the works.

It must also be noted that in certain cases, perhaps due to lack of time, and less and less frequently, the Commission submit its consultation to RACs after its proposal is put forward to the Council, thus the statements the fishing industry may make are given after the Commission has made its proposal, which adds complexity to the position of the own Commission and even the Member States.

Coordination between RACs should likewise be assured. Although some approximation has been made at the initiative of RACs and some meetings have been held with the participation of members of some RACs, these meetings do not take place as often as it should be desirable given the subjects that are dealt with, which makes it necessary to duplicate the number of meetings.

Finally, it must be pointed out that we must keep an eye on the RACs' proposals since we could end up having a too decentralized and regionalist fisheries policy which opposes the principles of the common fisheries policy.

In view of the above, it seems clear that the CFP, although has achieved important accomplishments, has not yet provided itself with the necessary management and control systems to assure its objectives of biological sustainability and economic profitability, thus we must continue reflecting on this subject in order to find the most appropriate systems to meet these objectives. It is true that the specific circumstances of each region and coastal areas on which the CFP is applied must be taken into consideration, but that does not mean that we will have to resort to a regional approach. A regional management model could endanger the CFP's foundations and principles and, therefore, it will be necessary to search for general and universal implementation models, leaving the regional approach and management for specific cases for which it is justified in a transparent way. That is to say, the regional model is an exception and not the general rule.

25 February 2008

Examination of Witness

Witness: MR CARLOS LARRAÑAGA, Fisheries Counsellor, Spanish Government, examined.

Q610 Chairman: Thank you very much indeed for finding the time to come and help us with this inquiry. This is a formal evidence-taking session of our Sub-Committee, so a record will be taken. The transcript will be made available to you as soon as possible and you can modify it if any errors have come in. I wonder if we could start by me asking you a general question. Where do you see the Common Fisheries Policy going? What changes would you like to see in the CFP?

Mr Larrañaga: First of all, it is a pleasure for me to be here and respond to your request. The second thing is that I ask your patience because, I am sorry, I will make mistakes with my English.

Q611 Chairman: So do we!

Mr Larrañaga: It is a pleasure for me to be here and it is an honour to respond to your request. We are following the questions that I have received?

Q612 Chairman: Yes. I think the difficulty is that there are more questions than we have time to cover because we only have half an hour, so, rather than asking question number one, how would you like to see the Common Fisheries Policy developing, the future of the Common Fisheries Policy?

Mr Larrañaga: I would like to put on the table the Spanish position about that. In general it is difficult to explain this but, as you know, the targets of the Common Fisheries Policy are the same as those of the Common Agricultural Policy and take into account that for us it is necessary to continue working to support the stakeholders, the fishermen, and to try to give them more possibilities to develop economic and social solutions to their problems, but at the same time it is necessary to take into account the new situation with research and so on. The problem for us is that there is a balance to be struck between continuous fishing at a sustainable level and at the same time maintaining our fishermen and our jobs. We have a lot of problems right now because the WTO is putting on the table a liberalisation of fisheries products. It is so difficult to defend or prioritise European products with respect to the problems for Third Countries, and at the same time the European Union is the best market in the world for fisheries products. This is the reality right now. Everybody outside, Third Countries, wants to put their fisheries products into our market. We are importing right now in Spain over one million tonnes of fisheries products. In the United Kingdom I think the quantity is similar. In the European Union there is a need for fisheries products but at the same time

Spain thinks it is impossible to continue asking for priority for European fisheries products. As you know, one of the targets of the Common Fisheries Policy is to maintain the presence of European product supplies against the others. It is difficult to maintain this today but we are interested in continuing to offer solutions to our fisheries sector so that they can change their way of life if it is necessary to abandon the fishery sector, but also to offer fishermen other possibilities to continue working near the fisheries, not only directly but also with the producers of the fishery activity.

Q613 Lord Cameron of Dillington: You seem to want more flexible arrangements with possibly individual transferable quotas, and I was wondering how far you would like to go with that, whether quotas could be transferred between producer organisations and between countries and what the long-term result of this might be for your communities.
Mr Larrañaga: Spain supports totally this possibility but we are taking into account as well that there could be in the future the possibility of problems if there are several associations with all the rights for fisheries products, and to avoid that it will be necessary to include several conditions, but we think the best way to deal with this is to offer the possibility of changing the situation and doing business with the fisheries rights. We have in Spain several examples of that. We had a problem about 15 years ago with the swordfish fisheries. Spain decided to agree the quotas with the fishermen and after two or three years the fishermen decided to change the rights between them and we have right now a fishing fleet only with swordfish. It is at a good economic level. It has good performance and continuous fishing and we can control the catches and the markets as well. We have a problem right now with imports of swordfish from Third Countries but in general the problem has been solved and we are happy with this. I think it is possible to continue working in this way with the other Member States.

Q614 Lord Cameron of Dillington: So would you help your fishermen to buy quota?
Mr Larrañaga: No. Quota is another big problem in Spain. We are saying "rights" but they are not rights in general because the state of Spain has got the rights and agrees these rights between the fishermen, but in general, taking into account the history of the families and other people working in the fisheries sector, Spain agrees these rights between the fishermen but Spain does not give the fishermen money to buy these rights. We only use the money from the European Union in bilateral fisheries agreements.

Q615 Lord Cameron of Dillington: What would happen if you could transfer rights from, say, Poland to Spain? Would you want to do that?
Mr Larrañaga: Yes. If fishermen from Poland decided to divide between the stakeholders the rights, in this case Spain would accept that but all we are saying is that the last control, the last power, is the Spanish Government's, but it is possible between the fishermen. Right now I do not have the answer to that. Yes, it is an important question. What would happen in the future if another fisherman of another Member State had got all the rights of our fishermen? I do not know right now but in general we are open to discussion about that. We are open to working in this way and trying to find solutions to that.

Q616 Viscount Ullswater: I note from what you have said that you would like to control a lot of the fishing by controlling effort, although I think you explain that it is a very complex way of deciding between individual vessels what the effort should be. Would you see effort being more important than quotas in the future? How would you think that should be controlled?
Mr Larrañaga: That is an important question because, as you know, right now we have a Commission proposal, the modification of the Cod Recovery Plan. The Commission is trying to establish a new system with effort only. It is with the TAC at the same time but the most important point of view of the Commission is to try to deal with the problem with fishery effort limitation. Spain totally supports this point of view but we have several problems which it is necessary to solve first. For example, right now there is a problem about knowing how many cod are one kilowatt. It is difficult to establish but it is better to decide it. In general it is better to deal with effort limitation because it will be cheaper and it will be easy to control, and at the same time the fishermen at the beginning of the year could try the campaign the whole year, "I have 100 fishing days. I will try to establish my business, taking this into account. I will make contracts with other fishermen, using the best moment of the market to sell my fish". Taking into account all these questions will it be better for the fishermen to work with fishing days and at the same time for the Government will it be cheaper and easier to control the activity? There are several technical and political questions to solve before we can effect this proposal.

Q617 Viscount Ullswater: Do you think the fishermen, the stakeholders, are in favour of this because they must be worried about the viability of their boats if they are only allowed to fish a certain number of days? Are they worried?

Mr Larrañaga: Yes. For example, in the United Kingdom the problem was difficult about the fishing days for the cod fisheries. In the end, if I only have 12 or 15 days it is impossible to maintain my company because I will need money and I will need to obtain a balance in this company. With the new Cod Recovery Plan the Commission is trying to avoid this problem by offering more days to continue fishing but the Commission is aware that if I put only a few days the sector will immediately reject that because it is impossible with ten or 12 days per month, and fortunately the Commission is trying to put effort limitation in a package with the Member States. The Member States will have a whole package with this effort limitation and the Member States will agree this effort limitation, taking into account the necessities of the sector and avoiding giving just a few days, impossibly few days.

Q618 *Viscount Brookeborough:* Would you see trading in fishing effort, in kilowatts or days at sea, as a natural progression? How would it work?
Mr Larrañaga: This is another problem because if the Commission decided to change totally and work only with fishing days, the first question to establish is the period, taking into account my level of fishing effort. The Commission has figures taking into account the fishing effort in 2002, but there are now fewer fishing boats than in 2002 and the Commission will discuss with Member States reducing the top level of fishing effort. In this case there will be a political problem and it will be necessary to solve this question in the Council because again I will have fewer days than I have right now, and it is a problem because immediately I will need to decommission fishing boats and I will have not only an internal political problem but a social problem as well, and I will need to put more money on the table to solve the internal political problems of Member States. Right now we have the European Fisheries Fund. I think it is enough to support the target of the Member States right now but if you put on the table a new scenario the European Fisheries Fund will not be enough to solve this problem. It will be necessary to put on the table a new proposal to support the fishermen in order to reduce the capacity.

Q619 *Chairman:* Would Spain want to have a decommissioning policy now to reduce capacity further?
Mr Larrañaga: We are in favour of that. We are happy with the European Fisheries Fund. We are making proposals to our fishing sector to decide to take this opportunity to reduce capacity because we have problems of balance. It is necessary to reduce capacity in order to continue sustainable activity. We are offering these possibilities. I do not know right now but I think our fishing sector would continue

using the new possibilities with the new European Fisheries Fund, and at the same time they are asking us for solutions to reduce the fuel price. We are offering them possibilities to change the engine power of the fishing boats and to find more practical ways to continue fishing but reduce the price of the activity.

Q620 *Earl of Dundee:* We learn that the Commission is now consulting on a review of the Control Regulation. What are Spain's priorities for the new Regulation?
Mr Larrañaga: If the Commission continues putting on the table more control measures then we will have a policy closed to the fishermen and we are saying it would be better to find other ways of solving the problem. It is necessary to improve our co-ordination system to deal with the dates and the figures in a better way because there are differences between the figures from the catches and the figures of the landings. It is necessary to resolve the lack of information about that. We need more co-ordination and we need to request the new European Control Agency to work with all the Member States to establish a system of managing the co-ordination system. At the same time it is necessary to harmonise in all the European Union the system of sanctions in order to avoid argument if the sanctions are penal. We need to establish co-ordination and harmonise all the sanctions so that if I catch fish under the biological measures I will have similar sanctions in the United Kingdom, in Spain, in Italy and so on to avoid. Right now there is a huge difference.

Q621 *Earl of Dundee:* In that connection how do you see the role of the Community Fisheries Control Agency evolving as part of your overall enforcement strategy?
Mr Larrañaga: There are several Member States that do not want to give more power to the Agency but Spain is supporting that. It is necessary to give more power to the Agency and the first role will be to establish the co-ordination between the Member States. For example, right now we have a problem with blue fin tuna in the Mediterranean and the Atlantic, and I think it will be very useful this year if the Agency can bring about co-ordination between the Member States. We have a deployment plan, including the Agency. The Agency controls co-ordination with Member States and at the same time with the patrol system. That will be very hard this year because there will be more blue fin tuna caught in the Member States than in previous years because if you have the Agency making the co-ordination, having the information and dealing with the figures there will immediately be more quantity of blue fin tuna. It will be a catastrophe for some Member States but that will be good for everybody.

Q622 Earl of Dundee: We seem to be talking all the time about these enforcement problems. Why do you think they persist?

Mr Larrañaga: I think it is a problem because it is difficult to put the fishing sector in our rules, in our policy. We have a fishing sector in several Member States. The problem is not with the huge fishing sector fishing over long distances. The most important problem is with the fishing sector which fishes day after day in a family fishing boat. They go out to fish and sometimes they try to take the fish and sell them without controls. For that reason we are supporting a fisheries organisation. I think that will be a good solution. I do not know why right now in the European Union this possibility is not acceptable to all Member States. In Spain we are offering this possibility to make a fisheries organisation and to agree quotas with them.

Q623 Viscount Ullswater: Governance is our last question. Many of the stakeholders we have heard from wanted a more decentralised model of fisheries management but what we have read is that the Spanish Government are concerned about decentralisation, perhaps even to a regional management model, because it would undermine the principles of the CFP. What do you see would be the proper role of the Regional Advisory Councils and whether they should or could make decisions on the technical conservation matters?

Mr Larrañaga: We agree with the RACs but we think right now that several RACs have got a lot of people working inside them and it is difficult to focus. The first intention of the RACs is to study and discuss closely with the Commission the rules and the Common Fisheries Policy. Sometimes it is so difficult to reach an agreement inside the RACs about that. Spain wants to do things in the correct way, to reduce the discussion inside the RACs and focus on the real problems. This is the first thing. The second thing is that we are afraid of discrimination. I will explain. In a juridical mentality, if you have a problem in the United Kingdom with a fisherman and the same problem in Spain do you have the same solution or a similar solution? With regionalisation we are afraid that in future it could be possible to have different treatment of the same problem in different regions of Europe. With our Common Fisheries Policy there will not be a problem because there will be a policy in the North Sea, in the Mediterranean Sea and so on. We are aware that the problems in the Baltic are different from the problems in the Mediterranean Sea. Their idiosyncrasies are different but we must not forget that our first duty is to maintain the common policy. We support the RACs. We think there will be a good solution at the same time. We are pushing the Commission to take into account the opinion of the RACs about that, but with regionalisation we are thinking it will be better to establish several contracts to avoid these problems in the future.

Chairman: Thank you very much indeed. Thank you for your time.

Examination of Witness

Witness: MR MARCIN RUCINSKI, Fisheries Counsellor, Polish Government, examined.

Q624 Chairman: Thank you very much indeed for finding the time to come and help us with this inquiry. We are a Sub-Committee of the House of Lords Select Committee on the European Union. This is a formal evidence session, so a note will be taken. You will be given a transcript as soon as possible and you can have a look through it and make corrections if any errors have slipped in. Can I start the questions and ask what has been, do you think, the experience of the more recent accession countries, the accessions that took place in 2004 and 2007? Do you get the feeling that that has changed the coalition of interests on fishing within the EU? What is your experience of being part of it?

Mr Rucinski: Thank you very much, Chairman. First of all I would like to thank you very warmly for the invitation to come here. It is a great honour and distinction for me. Personally also I am sure it will be a very interesting and precious experience for me. In response to your question, it is difficult to say whether something has changed or not because if there has been a change then—

Q625 Chairman: You did not know what it was before?

Mr Rucinski: Precisely. The change would have been a natural situation for me anyway, so it is difficult to judge whether there has been a change. What I can say is that in the specific area of fisheries what I have noticed is that many interests are strongly region-based. In terms of TACs and quota, for example, there are many regional issues of high sensitivity for different Member States and I think their coalitions have remained rigid. This is the case for the Baltic. When we discuss matters pertaining to the Baltic we rarely see colleagues from other regions intervening save for some who like to see coherence here and there but regionalisation elsewhere. Other than that I would say that in general matters such as financing the EFF I think we have brought in a change. I would imagine we have. In the discussion of the EFF that I had the opportunity to take part in in the year 2005/06 I saw a shift of interests and more attention given to areas of cohesion and Objective 1, the areas with less GDP, as it were, so certainly there has been a shift. The other shift I can see, which is dear to us because we have a fairly well developed sector of inland agriculture and inland fisheries, is that this has been given considerable attention in the context of the EFF and also in such dossiers as eels regulation. Other than that I would say that we are expecting to have a great change from what will certainly be a co-decision, that is, if the Irish referendum goes well. That is going to be a reality for us as of next year. It certainly will be a great change but I would not endeavour to go into more detail as of yet. It is still ahead of us. The most interesting time is yet to come, I think. Perhaps one other remark is that we have a new area within the CFP, which is the Black Sea with the accession of Romania and Bulgaria. That is quite interesting if you look at quantities. It is not on a very big scale but interesting nevertheless and a new area for EU policy.

Q626 *Baroness Jones of Whitchurch:* Before I ask my question on the objectives of the CFP, it would be really helpful if you could say what proportion of the people who live in Poland are involved in the fishing industry. I have not got a sense of it.

Mr Rucinski: The proportion is very small. If I remember correctly, according to our estimates made during the preparation of our operational programme for the last programming period, it was 0.07 per cent which was directly concerned with fisheries. Our coastline is not that long. It is just 500-odd kilometres. In terms of people directly concerned with fisheries, it is several thousands perhaps, but if you add processing, if you add the local context, then it becomes different. It is the case everywhere in Europe, I think. The three voivodships[1] that are interested in fisheries quite a lot are basically Pomorskie-Lakonie, Pomorskie and WarmiAsko-Mazurskia—I am sorry for that! Other than that there are also certain regions on the mainland, such as Silesia or Wiekopolska around Poznan that have meaningful exposure to inland agriculture and inland fishing, also places where you have large numbers of lakes. That is how I would characterise it.

Q627 *Baroness Jones of Whitchurch:* That is very helpful. We have received some evidence that not enough emphasis is put on the socio-economic impact of the Common Fisheries Policy and too much is put on marine conservation, and I just wondered, in the context of your experience in Poland and the people who directly work in the sector, whether they feel that.

Mr Rucinski: I am certain that if you asked any fisherman in any given EU country he would accept that we need more social emphasis. In my adventure in fisheries, lasting something like seven years now, one of the first lessons I learned is that the task for us,

so to speak, managers of this profession is sometimes to guard fishermen against themselves. It depends whether you want to see it in the very short term year-to-year or whether you want to see it long term. When you look at it long term there is no big contradiction between a sensible conservation policy and the socio-economic policy. There is no huge contradiction. This is what we see and this is also the point of departure of my Government.

Q628 *Viscount Brookeborough:* Since you joined the EU in 2004 have you found it a very difficult journey being involved with the EU legislation in an area which is so close, like the Baltic, and to what extent do you think it could be simplified, considering that you have come into it at a very late stage compared with others?

Mr Rucinski: I will start at the end. I would say it certainly could be simplified. It is one of the most complicated and over-bureaucratised areas in EU policy as a whole, if I can be so bold as to judge as a humble fisheries and maritime attaché. Certainly this is a place where we can find ways to simplify it and where we can find ways to explain to people better what we mean by the regulation. One of the ideas we have been advocating (not yet realised by the DG) is, for example, to give leaflets to fishermen so that they understand the regulations better because it is a certain language that they are written in. Outside Brussels you can get difficulties understanding this. In our experience since 2002 when, as I said, my adventure in fishing began, the pre-accession process has been quite a task. It has been difficult in some places but I think overall we have managed. I think there are some regional aspects to this. In comparison to the North Sea in the Baltic some things are less complicated, as yet, at least. Overall it has been a success though many fishermen would not agree with me, but in terms of implementing the provisions, in terms of transposing the *acquis* to our own legal system, I think overall it has been right.

Q629 *Viscount Brookeborough:* So do you think, joining the EU, that fishing in the Baltic has become more stabilised and is more sustainable in the future?

Mr Rucinski: I saw in the following questions you are going to ask that you have seen that sustainability is still a goal for us, and we are heading towards it, though perhaps not in a very straight way all the time.

Q630 *Chairman:* You did have a recent problem.

Mr Rucinski: We will come to that later on, I am sure. I think that for fishermen it has been a lesson. Some issues have been difficult for us. There are certain provisions I could name that have been difficult for and have been poorly understood, if at all, by the sector, such as the drift-net ban, which from our point of view, for example, is the only way we can

---

[1] Polish Administrative Districts

fish. We can seriously fish for salmon for now, but this means that our second most valuable and fairly important socio-economic fishery has been essentially brought to an end, so you can imagine that, though we have had some success in prolonging the phasing out of certain gears, such as drift nets, which are a taboo almost in the Council context, especially for Mediterranean Member States, it has been difficult and it is still difficult, but we will have to find ways around that. I think it is very important that we have substantial financing to overcome the problems and, as it were, sweeten the pills that are sometimes very bitter. This may be an important thing also for the newcomers, and I think we have used that quite a lot in the last programming period.

Q631 *Lord Palmer:* Following a highly critical report by the Court of Auditors, as you are aware, the Commission is currently consulting on a new Control Regulation. What are your priorities for this new regulation and how does your Government intend to tackle the enforcement problems which you after all have had to inherit, and do you think you will be able to carry your own stakeholders with you?
Mr Rucinski: I have before me my minister's speaking note from the informal ministerial council in February. To answer I could return to what I said in reply to question 2, that in the long term there should be no real contradiction between conservation goals and socio-economic goals. For us the point of departure is that we need the fishermen to understand that it is not against them that we are doing this. We are catering for the long-term future. They have to understand this even if sometimes the short-term pills may be quite bitter. Otherwise, if they do not understand, this is a fight; this is a policeman and thief game. In the policeman and thief game any law-maker in my personal view is one step behind reality and he has to be a good law-maker. I would not dare say that in my country we are just one step backwards.

Q632 *Lord Palmer:* But you have quite a good rapport with them at the moment?
Mr Rucinski: You mean with the fishermen?

Q633 *Lord Palmer:* Yes.
Mr Rucinski: It is difficult to say. Fishermen are not a homogeneous group. In our own back yard there are many groups with many different views which are wildly diverging, I would say. There are situations where we have to find a middle ground. We have to find ways between the hard-liners and those who want real measures because they feel that confidence is important. Speaking of confidence, confidence is becoming more and more important because of the interests of consumers in the legality of the fish. I think in the UK you have more of this than in our

back yard but it is getting to our back yard too. Coming back to the control reform targets, it is very important that we ensure the legality of the products that are on the market because consumers are getting more and more aware of this. One of the measures which we see here as important is the broadening of responsibility beyond just fishermen because they do not function in a world of their own. They have certain demands from processors, traders, and so I think you have to broaden responsibility to the whole market place and not just concentrate on those fishermen at the end because they are driven by certain processes, by certain companies even, I could say, here and there. Other than that, for control targets what we support—and this is something that the Court of Auditors have called for—is a methodology for control activities. It should be streamlined, certainly, and we should develop common methodologies at the Community level by way of guidelines. This is something that we would like and something that I spoke of today with respect to the IUU Regulation drafts that we are now hammering out, so to speak, in the Council working party. We could also see the mandate of the Control Agency broadened. Simplification is the way forward because it will ensure better understanding of goals, and, of course, we have to bear in mind the question of costs, so this is also something that we have to address in the new reform. Also, of course, the question of sanctions must be dealt with with respect to national systems and traditions.

Q634 *Lord Plumb:* In the proposals that will come forward for the next reform of the Common Fisheries Policy you and the new Member countries may be in a unique position because you do not have baggage to bring with you; you are looking at the whole policy afresh. One of the major issues, and it has become more obvious for me as we meet with people involved in the fishing industry, is the business of the challenge between the change from quota possibly to what is called effort management. At the moment we seem to have a combination of the two which adds to the complication, and I think everyone we see would say let us work towards simplification rather than further complication. Therefore, would you perhaps join with others in saying, "Let us get rid of one", which might be the quota, "and let us concentrate on effort management", or where does your Government stand on this at the moment?
Mr Rucinski: At this stage, having been strongly reminded lately of the importance of quotas and attaining them rightly, I think there is understanding that we should, at least in our Baltic situation, in our regional situation, which is the most important politically to us, base ourselves on catch and landing controls to ensure that we exert the right fishing effort. We have, of course, the effort management

system within the Baltic based on days at sea, but it is far simpler in our version, let us say, than in the North Sea version. I can only say that it is just one page that suffices to regulate it in the Baltic whereas you have at least 50 pages in the North Sea, so there are ways to deal with days at sea in a simple manner and this is dependent on gears, technically speaking. We are lucky to have one net rule in the Baltic in this context for demersal fishing and for the controls, so perhaps this is where it comes from. The real problem I have with effort management is that it is a fairly difficult concept to define. If you think of kilowatt days, for example, it might be a good way forward but kilowatts in terms of fishing vessels technically are a concept that might well be escaping control. Of course, it would have been nice to get rid of quotas, fine and good; maybe we could then get rid of some of our payback until 2011, but, joking aside, it is difficult for me personally to imagine that the Commission will live with this. I know that some Member States have this as a priority but in the Baltic context, for now at least, the way I see it personally is that the quotas still matter more than the fishing effort. That is not to say that it will not change, that it will stay set in stone for years and years. It might evolve in the years to come, but for now catch and landing control is key in the Baltic context.

Q635 Lord Plumb: Let us suppose that the quota will stay after 2013. How would you simplify that system then, because there is going to be a lot of change?
Mr Rucinski: Yes, I know we are going to have a new CFP. Our Presidency will be deeply involved in this, although it is quite far off. The second half of 2011 will be a nice moment to be involved in the discussions. If I look at the example of the Baltic Sea, I would not say I understand the specifics of North Sea fishing but you have so many fishing gears that sometimes I get lost in this, and then you have all those special conditions. We have just one net rule in the Baltic. I myself, in my humble lack of understanding of the North Sea, have to accept that we are all western waters. I have been always asking myself the question, "Why do you have so many gears?", because with the gears you get those days multiplied and then the system becomes for me practically almost impossible to apply. I salute your administrations for coming to terms with it. That is my feeling. It is just a personal feeling. I have to be very clear: it is not a government position. As far as the Government's position is concerned, it is that predominantly we are in the TACs and quota reality and we will certainly look with interest look at replacing it with fishing effort, but the fishing effort would have to be a really sure measure to restrict real efforts down there and, as I say, fishing effort is a concept that is not immediately easy to grasp.

Q636 Lord Cameron of Dillington: How is your Baltic RAC doing now? Are the Polish Government supporting it enough, both in terms of finance and also in terms of encouraging responsibility?
Mr Rucinski: We always encourage responsibility. This is again a concept that is not so easily spread in these circles, especially some, but it is not just our phenomenon. On the financing, we have never had a problem with that. Whether we finance it enough is a good question. Financing something enough is always a good question.

Q637 Lord Cameron of Dillington: But is it working well together?
Mr Rucinski: The feeling we have in terms of administration, at least as far as I can tell from my administration, is that it is working fine, yes. They provide us with valuable advice. They provide us also with what I would call valuable policy stimulus for different important issues here and there. Let me just recall the conference on control and enforcement that we had last year in March, and I think this approach has also been emulated by the North Sea RAC this year. This conference certainly was an important support. It was attended by many important figures, our minister included. I think there have been important outcomes from this policy stimulus that we are now realising, both in terms of quota issues and broader control issues that we will plunge into as of next autumn under the French Presidency.

Q638 Lord Cameron of Dillington: It is helping make the fishermen be more responsible, is it?
Mr Rucinski: It should, but whether the knowledge or experience of becoming more responsible comes down to where it should be is another question and, of course, this is something fishermen have to work out for themselves. It is not for us as a government administration to deal with this. In the written form of your question you have asked about management responsibility. That will be required in the preparation for the RACs. I would say that from our point of view their advisory policy stimulus role is very important, but that should remain enough for now.

Q639 Viscount Ullswater: We have heard from quite a lot of people we have seen that they feel that the CFP is currently very over-centralised and they have suggested that the EU institutions might in future just dictate principles and set objectives but devolve a lot of the implementation of the regulation to the Member States or even to the regional organisations, including the RACs. Would you support that movement and what sort of governance structure would you like to see?

Mr Rucinski: I would say that not everything can be done from Brussels, so total regulation from here in one place is not good and perhaps a move into the direction of regionalisation is a good one. I think that also the Commission have realised with the new structure that it is more regional now. Another question arises of coherence, so we have to balance regionalisation, or respect for regional differences, particularly specificities, whatever we call them, and coherence because we are after all in a Community context where you have to have uniform application, or at least uniform in general terms, so the balance of these two should guide any devolving of responsibilities. Essentially some regionalisation is needed, but we have to maintain coherence. There is a balance between the two that has to be kept; otherwise we end up with three, four, five different practices in different seas and then we will lose sight of the level playing field. I think the move that the Commission has made with regionalisation is a good one, provided they manage to maintain coherence, of course—good luck to Mr Borg and his colleagues. I would also say that perhaps institution-wise the question arises, whether from Brussels, or indeed in the future from Vigo, whether you can maintain coherence from there. One of the ideas I personally would support, and I emphasise "personally"; this is not a view of Government, is perhaps some kind of regional offices that oversee what is happening because you cannot see everything from Brussels, less still, I would say, from Vigo, because you would have to catch the planes for free in some instances to get there in the first place, so I think the idea of some regional offices for the main regions, maybe not necessarily from the Commission but in the agency, could be considered. Personally, again personally, I would not rule that out.

Chairman: That is excellent. Thank you very much indeed.

Memorandum by the Directorate-General for Fisheries and Maritime Affairs, European Commission

In response to your call for evidence of 18 January 2008 the Commission can offer the following comments:

CONSERVATION/MANAGEMENT

1. *Chapter 11 of Regulation 237 1/2002 on the conservation and sustainable exploitation of fisheries resources under the Common Fisheries Policy introduced new methods of ensuring conservation and sustainability, including recovery plans, management plans and emergency measures. To what extent have these been effective?*

Recovery plans were introduced in 2002 with the main objective to reduce fishing mortality on stocks that were in very poor state. A reduction in fishing mortality decreases the pressure on a weak stock, thus allowing for the recovery of the stock, regardless if the recovery was caused by nature and not a direct product of lower fishing pressure. These programmes were set up for several stocks of cod, hake and sole in European waters.

After a few years of implementation the results are mixed. For most of the cod stock fishing mortality did not decrease as expected and the stocks have yet to recover. For northern hake, there was a reduction of fishing pressure that allied to good recruitment. This has allowed for the stock to recover. Nevertheless, the southern hake stock still remains subjected to high fishing mortality.

Recovery and management plans are a very useful "tool" to progressively bring stocks, and associated fisheries, to sustainable levels, and they will continue to be used in the management of European fisheries. However, the plans are been reviewed and improved (particularly the cod plan) with the introduction of measures, such as for example changes in target objectives or specific control measures, to make them more effective in reducing fishing mortality.

2. *A wide range of management tools are available to fisheries managers. What are your views on the following tools:*

— *Total Allowable Catches*
— *Effort limitation, including "days at sea", marine conservation areas and real-time Closures*
— *Rights-Based Management tools*
— *Technical Conservation Measures*

Management tools should not be seen in isolation but can only be analysed within an overall management framework. Fisheries management should apply a mixture of tools which should be adequate to the specific situation. The efficacy of various management instruments is very different for different fisheries. While effort management may be a useful tool for demersal mixed fisheries, it may not achieve its objectives in relation to pelagic fisheries.

TACs will remain a basic management instrument as long as relative stability exists. TACs have however proven insufficient to ensure sustainable fisheries for several commercially important stocks. The reasons are many but include that the control of landings has been insufficient as indicated in the recent report of the Court of Auditors[1], that under the present management regime discards will occur in mixed fisheries when the quota of one species is exhausted while there is still quota for others. The Court also stated that TACs create incentives to high-grade in order to maximize the value of the quota. This is especially a problem when stocks which are outside safe biological limits and therefore subject to recovery plans are taken in mixed fisheries. In these cases the intended effects of recovery plans fail to materialise because the amount of fish killed remains constant, because what was formerly landed now becomes discarded. The Community has therefore supplemented TACs in these cases with measures to keep the effort at a level which should be equivalent to the effort needed to take the quota of the recovery stock.

Rights based management instruments can be an important supplement to management measures if they are coupled with responsibilities to harvest responsibly. The Commission has presently no competence on this issue as the allocation of fishing rights are a Member State competence. A Communication has however been published in order to inspire a debate about this instrument in the Community[2].

Technical conservation measures are very useful to effect the exploitation pattern reduce by-catches of juvenile fish or non-targeted species. Technical measures thus has a completely different role than other measures such as TACs or effort control, which aim to reduce the overall fishing pressure, and technical measures can therefore not replace such measures. Many years of experience have proven that technical measures in most cases result in very modest outcomes relative to what was expected. The reason is simple, technical measures, which not only result in reduced by-catches but also in some loss of the targeted fish, will be seen as an economic loss by the industry and ingenious (legal and in some case illegal) ways which neutralise the economic loss are therefore found in response to such measures. The countermeasure has been to make ever more detailed technical regulations resulting in a negative spiral of micro-legislation and industry adaptation. More selective fishing gear and fishing practices are better promoted through results-based management whereby standards for the outcome of the fishery (such as maximum acceptable by-catch) are established and it is left to the industry to find the technical means to fish within these standards. This is the basic thinking in the new policy to reduce discards as explained in the Communication on discards[3].

3. *To what extent have current management tools increased the levels of discards and bycatch? What is your view on how these problems can best be tackled?*

Discards of species of commercial interest are caused both by specific management tools and by economic drivers. As for management instruments, the emphasis on landing quotas as the main instrument to distribute access to fisheries between countries and within countries leads to discards when above-quota quantities of some species are taken while there is still quota left over for others. The use of minimum landing sizes also leads to discards, especially in mixed fisheries where species of different adult size are caught together. By-catches and subsequent discarding of species without commercial interest is entirely driven by economic considerations. The relative importance of economic and management drivers vary between fisheries and is difficult to measure. In some fisheries discarding due to market considerations (high grading) dominates. There will be unwanted by-catches in mixed fisheries even in the absence of TACs for economic reasons and it is therefore important to work on means to reduce these by-catches independently on whether TACs are used or not.

One should note however, that the large amount of discarding of under size fish is due to the fact that most fish stocks are overexploited. Overexploitation results in few large fish left in the sea and the fish stocks are dominated by small fish. Landings are for many stocks dominated by fish which have just grown above the minimum size and in order to catch that, large amounts of smaller fish have been caught and discarded in the process. The main measure to reduce discards is thus to reduce exploitation as the Commission intends with the MSY policy linked to long term management plans.

Beyond that the Commission considers that a combination of tools is required including temporary closures, requirements to move when unacceptable by-catch rates are encountered and eventually a discard ban. The most effective approach is considered to be results-based management rather than detailed technical

[1] Special Report No 7/2007 on the control, inspection and sanction systems relating to the rules on conservation of Community fisheries resources. European Court of Auditors 2007.

[2] Communication from the Commission on rights-based management tools in fisheries. COM(2007) 73 final

[3] Communication from the Commission To The Council And The European Parliament. A policy to reduce unwanted by-catches and eliminate discards in European fisheries. COM(2007) 136 final

regulations because that approach will leave it to the industry to find the most feasible technical solutions and will best support bottom-up initiatives. The discard policy was described in a recent communication[4] and implementation regulations will now be prepared for specific fisheries.

4. *Do you consider that fisheries management policies may need to adapt to climate change? If so, how might this be achieved?*

The impact of climate change on marine ecosystems and the fish populations will have implications for fisheries management.

Fisheries management will, also without climate change concerns, need to integrate closely with environmental management in order to get to an ecosystem approach, and this will be even more pertinent when climate change impacts are considered as adaptations will only be meaningful if seen in an ecosystem context. The Commission is preparing a Communication on the ecosystem approach to fisheries management and integration of environmental concerns to be adopted in March 2008.

The main expected impacts are that distributions of fish stocks change, that the productivity and vulnerability of fish stocks and marine ecosystems will change and more generally, that it must be accepted that predictability may be low and management (and industry) therefore must be robust to insufficient knowledge about the future.

This means that new allocation mechanisms may need to be established as fish stocks change their distribution, that reference points will need to be adapted to changed productivity and that management plans must be increasingly adaptive rather than predictive.

Knowledge will be important to guide policies and the Commission is developing a comprehensive research effort regarding climate change and adaptations, including marine and fisheries, under the 7th Framework Programme.

One should not forget that fisheries should also be expected to contribute to mitigation. Some fishing practices are very energy hungry spending 3–5 kg of fuel for each kg of fish landed. The Commission is facilitating interchange of information and experiences on energy saving but does not presently foresee specific measures regarding the energy use in fisheries beyond the general policy to reduce emissions of greenhouse gases.

CONTROL AND ENFORCEMENT

5. *Chapter V of Regulation 237 1/2002 lays down the responsibilities of the Member States and the Commission as regards the control and enforcement of the rules of the Common Fisheries Policy. The recent Court of Auditors Report on the control, inspection and sanctions systems relating to the rules on conservation of Community fisheries resources was very sceptical of the systems currently in place. What is your view of the efficacy of the systems in place? To what extent has the Community Fisheries Control Agency already assisted in improving matters?*

Despite certain progress illustrated by the strengthening of cooperation between the Member States, the introduction of a satellite monitoring system for the European fleet and the adoption of electronic reporting, it must be noted that not all objectives have been achieved. Numerous weak points were identified in the various reports published by the Commission on control of the CFP as well as in the report of the Court of Auditors. It can be concluded that the control system is inefficient, expensive, complex, and that it does not produce the desired results. The major efforts undertaken over the last years to achieve sustainable exploitation and long-term management of stocks simply cannot bear fruit in the absence of an effective control system.

There is an absence of a European culture of control. National systems are largely ineffective and there are limited means at the disposal of the Commission to put pressure on Member States to take their control obligations seriously.

Due to the aforementioned weaknesses a review of the whole control and enforcement system is undertaken and a revised system is foreseen to be in place during 2009. The review concerns development of a new strategy as regards fisheries control, rationalisation of the rules, strengthening the capacity of the Commission, harmonisation of sanctions, strengthening of cooperation and of assistance, development of a culture of compliance, use of modern technologies, increase in cost effectiveness and adaptation of the mandate of the Community Fisheries Control Agency.

---

[4] Communication from the Commission To The Council And The European Parliament. A policy to reduce unwanted by-catches and eliminate discards in European fisheries. COM(2007) 136 final

The community fisheries control agency (CFCA) is currently establishing itself and the recruitment of staff is ongoing. However, it has started its operations but it is not possible to make an evaluation yet on its impact on coordination and improvements of control as only a few joint missions organised by the CFCA are undertaken so far.

6. *The European Commission has regularly highlighted how serious infringements of the CFP are penalised differently across the Community. This was a matter that was also raised by the Court of Auditors and sanctions were included in the recent Commission Proposal in IIJU fishing. What is your view on the issue?*

The Commission set up common regulations for control at Community level, but their implementation and enforcement are the responsibility of the Member States. This leads to differences in the way regulations are applied. Both implementation rules and sanctions vary greatly from one Member State to another. In order to reduce the disparity in the way the regulations are applied the Commission has proposed in October 2007 a first harmonisation of sanctions in the context of the fight against IUU fishing. In parallel, the possibilities for revising the list of serious infringements as well as establishing a catalogue of all sanctions will be explored in the context of the revision of the Control Regulation.

STRUCTURAL POLICY

7. *Chapter 111 of Regulation 2371/2002 obliged Member States to put in place measures to adjust the capacity of their fleets in order to achieve a stable and enduring balance between such fishing capacity and their fishing opportunities. To what extent has this been successful?*

First it should be underlined that, although Member States are obliged to adapt the size of their fleet to the available resources (Article 11 of Regulation 2371/2002), no mandatory capacity reductions are established under Community law. Having said so, it is clear that globally the capacity of the Community fleet has not been sufficiently reduced.

During the past five years, after the reform of the CFP which entered into force on 1 January 2003, the total fishing capacity of the Community Fleet has been reduced by approximately 2% per year in terms of tonnage and power. This reduction is for the most part the result of public aid for decommissioning. The reduction trend is similar to the one observed during the previous 10 years, under the MAGP programmes when capacity reduction targets were in force. Capacity reduction rates in the order of 2% are insufficient, given the magnitude of the effort reductions required to achieve a sustainable exploitation in many community fisheries. In addition to that, this reduction may not compensate for the technical progress, which is estimated to increase the catching power at similar or higher rates. This result is no real decrease in effective fishing power.

The assessment of overcapacity from a biological point of view is difficult to carry out because fishing capacity cannot be completely isolated from economic considerations. Vessels often target different fisheries, making overcapacity assessment more complex. Reductions in activity complement the reductions in capacity so as to adjust fishing effort and reduce fishing mortality. However, a significant and permanent capacity underutilisation and economic underperformance are commonly seen in most Community fleets, and these are clear signs of overcapacity.

With or without a fleet management programme it remains an economic decision of a vessel owner to stay or to leave the sector and decommission his vessel. It is therefore important that Member States within any fleet policy framework make it attractive for fishermen to leave the industry by putting in place attractive and recurrent decommissioning schemes. With the present overcapacity Member States should therefore increase their efforts, including financial efforts, to reduce the capacity of the fleet.

8. *The new fisheries structural fund, the European Fisheries Fund (EFF), has now come into force. What has been your experience thus far with the new instrument?*

The experience gained to date with Council Regulation (EC) No 1198/2006 on the European Fisheries Fund is limited in terms of practical implementation. Most Member States submitted their National Strategic Plans and their proposals for Operational Programmes (OPs) (covering the period between 1 January 2007 and 31 December 2013) to the Commission in the course of 2007, and it has been possible to adopt 19 OPs by the end of 2007. The UK has not yet formally submitted its OP.

The Commission expects all OPs to be adopted by mid-2008.

All OPs will cover the period 2007–13 and according to the regulation and expenditure incurred after 1.1.2007 will be eligible for aid under the EFF, under certain conditions, even if the OP is adopted after this date.

The total EFF budget committed for the 19 adopted OPs amounts to 3,299,636,833 euros.

This sum is shared between five Priority axes defined by the regulation as follows:

— Priority axis 1, measures for the adaptation of the Community fishing fleet: 888 M€ (26.9 %).

— Priority axis 2: aquaculture, inland fishing, processing and marketing of fishery and aquaculture products: 1056 M€ (32 %).

— Priority axis 3: measures of common interest: 929 M€ (28.2 %).

— Priority axis 4: sustainable development of fisheries areas: 314 M€ (9.5 %).

— Priority axis 5: technical assistance: 112 M€ (3.4 %).

In its guidance to Member States on OPs, the Commission has invited Member States to put more emphasis on the decommissioning of vessels.

For the OPs adopted, the Managing authorities are preparing the first meetings of the Monitoring committees, and a clearer picture concerning their implementation will be available in the near future.

9. *What are your views on the possible impact on EU fisheries structural policy of WTO level discussions as regards subsidies in the fishing sector?*

On 30 November 2007 the Chair of the WTO Negotiating Group on "Rules", Ambassador Valle (Uruguay), circulated a draft consolidated text to Members on the subjects covered by the "Rules" chapters, ie anti-dumping and countervailing measure and subsidies, including fisheries subsidies.

The Commission notes that a number of elements included in the aforementioned text reflect the two key principles guiding the EU's policies for aid to the fisheries sector, namely to prohibit subsidies that encourage overcapacity, leading to overfishing, while allowing subsidies that help to remove capacity in excess of available fish resources. These elements of the draft negotiating text are incorporated in the so called "red" (prohibited) and "green" (allowed) box types of subsidies.

Nevertheless the Commission is concerned that the proposals by the Chair, as they now stand, could prevent public authorities from granting support to the fishing sector to ensure the transition to a sustainable state. Examples of this are the case of aid programmes intended for a smooth and efficient restructuring of parts of the fishing industry. Furthermore the proposed exceptions ("green" box) seem insufficient to allow for the implementation of cleaner technologies, including the replacement of engines, in order to limit emissions harmful for the environment.

Besides the proposals to prohibit or to allow certain types of subsidies, the Chair's text includes certain provisions to reinforce the notification of subsidies. In this respect, the Commission would like to see a very ambitious result of the negotiations, one which would bring WTO Members at least to the same level of transparency as the one shown by the EU internally, when implementing structural funds, and externally, when notifying aid to the WTO. Increased transparency will not only generate knowledge about the types of subsidies given but will also provide a much needed insight into the impact of such subsidies both on trade and on the sustainable use of fishery resources.

In sum, the Commission's assessment is that the current negotiating proposals, as set out in the Chair's text, should be more balanced. In other words, the WTO should be given the tools to tackle the problem of overcapacity and overfishing while allowing for the provision of aid that positively contributes to the sustainable exploitation of available fishery resources and that mitigates the negative impacts of adjustment measures on fishing communities. This assessment is shared by other WTO Members in the developing world as well as developed countries.

More details on the positions of the European Union in the fisheries negotiations are available in the three submissions made to the WTO Negotiating Group on Rules on 23 April 2003 (WTO document TN/RL/W/82), on 11 April 2005 (WTO document TN/RL/W/178 and on 26 April 2006 (WTO document TN/RL/GEN/134). These documents are public and can be downloaded from the WTO's website.

GOVERNANCE

10. *As a result of Regulation 2371/2002, Regional Advisory Councils (RACs) were established to advise the Commission on matters of fisheries management in respect of certain sea areas or fishing zones. What is your assessment of the success thus far of the RACs? What is your view on their future evolution?*

In terms of process, six out of the seven RACs foreseen in the relevant Community framework, have been established since 2004. The Mediterranean RAC should also be established in the course of 2008.

Recognizing the important contribution of RACs in the development of the CFP, the Commission proposed and the Council decided in 2007 to provide RACs with permanent and increased Community co-financing.

As foreseen by Council Decision 2004/S8SIEC, the Commission is preparing a review on the functioning of Races, which will be discussed at the April Council of Ministers. The review will evaluate the input of RACs to the development of the CFP, highlight good practices and put forward suggestions to improve the functioning of RACs.

In parallel, the Commission is also evaluating the performance of ACFA (Advisory Committee on Fisheries and Aquaculture) which is the second pillar of the CFP governance. One of the issues under evaluation is the co-operation between ACFA and the RACs. The evaluation study will be available in June 2008.

The on-going evaluations of both RACs and ACFA will offer a good opportunity to start a discussion about the performance of CFP governance. The discussion will involve Member States, European Institutions and stakeholders. The Commission is not in a position to prejudge the outcome of this debate.

11. *How do you consider EU fisheries should ideally be governed? How appropriate and feasible do you consider a regional management model to be?*

The Commission is presently considering options for future governance in EU fisheries; at this stage some considerations can be made on the qualities of a good management system. There are three components to an effective management system: that the institutional setup for decision making is adequate, that industry incentives promote a responsible and productive production chain for fisheries products and that all players are willing to utilise the instruments available effectively.

The institutional setup for decision making should be such that there are clear objectives which support accountability by enabling outcomes to be measured against objectives, that there is a clear hierarchy in responsibilities for decision making between decisions on principles, community standards emerging from these principles and technical implementation decisions. A regional management model may contribute to this if it is a part of a setup whereby there are clear objectives and principles decided in co-decision, community standards for implementation by the Commission and technical implementation decisions are delegated to member states which will need to organise themselves on regional level, subject to community control of outcomes against standards and objectives.

It needs to be considered how the industry can best be motivated to support the objectives of the policy. Industry incentives need to be turned around from the present setup where it pays to be irresponsible. An option is to link longer term access rights closely to responsibilities where access is contingent on a demonstration from the industry that exploitation of public resources takes place within the standards set by society. This implies a reversal of the burden of proof within a results based management and a sharing of management costs. Other options may include parts of this but should always be based on the principle that rights and responsibilities should be coupled.

Any setup, including the present, will only work if it is used effectively and supported by all parties concerned. Creating a supportive environment is crucial. Good communication with the public and close interactions between policy makers and stakeholders is therefore a key to the success of any management system.

28 February 2008

Examination of Witnesses

Witnesses: COMMISSIONER JOE BORG, European Commissioner for Maritime Affairs and Fisheries, MR POUL
DEGNBOL, Scientific Adviser, and MS KIRCHNER, DG Fisheries and Maritime Affairs, European Commission,
examined.

Q640 Chairman: Good afternoon, Commissioner.
Commissioner Borg: First of all I would like to
welcome you, not exactly to my office, but today has
been one of those hectic days. We start off on a
Wednesday with the usual college meeting. Today we
had two somewhat sensitive issues, one relating to
GMOs, and we therefore had quite an intense
discussion in the college with regard to this subject,
and the other relating to the increase in food prices,
so that occupied more than most of our time and I
apologise if I am running just a little late. I
understand that you would like to discuss a number
of topics which relate to the Common Fisheries
Policy. We have received 11 questions to which I have
drawn up written responses which we will be
circulating to you, so rather than repeating what
there is written I could respond to any other
questions that you would like to put and maybe also
just give comments on the different questions over
and above what there is in the written responses if
that is okay by you.

Q641 Chairman: That is very helpful,
Commissioner, thank you. In that case, thinking as
radically as possible, can I put to you the proposition
that really the Common Fisheries Policy, if it has not
outlived its usefulness, has got to the stage where it is
in need of some fairly radical reform in that it does
not sit very easily with current approaches, it is
centralist, it is excessively top-down, there is little
buy-in from those who are the biggest stakeholders
and TACs and quotas are seen as being an inefficient
way of managing the industry? Do you share the view
that it is a matter of looking forward to a major
reform of the Common Fisheries Policy, or is it a
matter as far as you are concerned of perhaps making
relatively modest adjustments to what is already
there?
Commissioner Borg: When.

Q642 Chairman: Yes, when.
Commissioner Borg: I share your view, subject to one
qualification, which is that I like to draw a distinction
between, so to speak, attacking the Common
Fisheries Policy and attacking the way it is
implemented. I firmly believe, and over these four
years my conviction has become stronger rather than
weaker, that we need a common policy with regard to
fisheries. We are dealing with a stock which does not
conveniently reside in a particular area. Some do, on
which we normally do not regulate. Others stride
across Community waters and therefore, unless you
have a common policy, you are going to have a
situation whereby one reaps benefits at the expense of

the other by all who are fishing in one spot. We have
experience of this in other areas. Where you have
waters which are subject to exploitation by different
operators you have to have certain common rules,
even insofar as they might have an impact on areas
which belong to other countries. We have
agreements, therefore, with regard to fisheries with
Norway, Iceland, Canada and the Faroe Islands,
where we have TACs and quotas, where we have a
regulatory regime, because at the end of the day if we
carry out fishing activities, even if it is exclusively in
waters other than Community waters, over-fishing
there will have an impact on the stocks which straddle
Norwegian waters as well, and over-fishing there
would have an impact on stocks that straddle our
waters. If we are speaking of certain categories of fish
it makes even more sense to have a common policy.
Having said that, the way that the common policy is
implemented in practice can be subject to criticism. In
2002 the Common Fisheries Policy went through a
radical reform. The problem is that most of the
objectives which were agreed to in 2002 are only now
being effectively implemented. To mention a couple
of examples, with the changes in 2002 the result was
an agreement that there should be more stakeholder
consultation and that brought about the formulation
of a regulation to form Regional Advisory Councils.
This regulation took some time to be adopted and
then the formation of these Regional Advisory
Councils took some time to be agreed to, and in fact
of the seven there is one that has not yet been set up,
which is the Mediterranean Regional Advisory
Council. The first one to be set up was the North Sea
Regional Advisory Council and that took till 2005, so
we are still in the initial stages of the operation of
these Regional Advisory Councils. To take another
example, with the reform of 2002 there was also the
decision that there should be much more multi-
annual planning, but the multi-annual management
plans or recovery plans where, according to scientific
advice, the stock was in very bad shape are very
complex, very difficult and very sensitive processes
which involve the Council with the new Lisbon
Treaty. It will also involve the European Parliament
by co-decision and therefore the actual drawing up of
these multi-annual plans takes quite some time. In
reality, therefore, we underwent a reform in 2002
which was quite radical, but in a way the impact of
that reform is only now starting to be realised.
Having said that, we have also identified a number of
problems with the operation of the Common
Fisheries Policy, the question concerning technical
measures, for example. We have quite a large number
of technical provisions which are drawn up centrally,

as you said, and which are complex and sometimes difficult to understand and implement, and therefore they themselves create some complaints, to say the least, by those who are required to operate under those rules. We have started thinking of moving from this sort of management regime to one which is more results oriented and therefore you set the parameters under which it should be achieved, which would be what would be the optimum sustainable fishery, and then let the Member States and the operators themselves determine to a large extent the optimum regulations that should be in place in order to achieve that. One pilot project which is moving in that direction was agreed to in the December Council with regard to the Scottish fishery concerning cod in the North Sea, and we are hopeful that that will give good results. In this way there would be a shift from a lot of detailed central management to setting the policy parameters centrally and then leaving it up to the operators almost to see how those parameters are to be achieved but then monitoring that what has been done waś done in the direction of achieving those and intervening only if your value judgement (based on science) is that the objectives are not going to be achieved or you are moving in the opposite direction. We are starting to look at this. Another issue concerns the discarding of fish. We have started to take action to tackle the very big problem of discarding fish. I hope that later on this year we will be proposing two measures which will be very much discard-oriented, one which relates to flat fish in the south of the North Sea and the Channel and the other which relates to nephrops in the Irish Sea. One is relatively simple, which is that of nephrops. The other is much more complex because with regard to flat fish we are speaking of discard levels of 60–70%. We took two cases, one which would be relatively simple and one which would be much more complex, in order to learn from these how to try to plan for the future. We are addressing issues at the moment which are somewhat radical in nature. A third is illegal fishing. We have drawn up a proposal which is very far-reaching. The criticism, when one looks at the proposal, is that it is perhaps too tough but we feel that it has to be tough if we really want to effectively correct illegal fishing activities. We do not want it to be discriminatory, so we are having some arguments with Member States on the basis that you should not distinguish between illegal operators on the basis that they are Community operators or non-Community operators; it does not make sense, and that we should find a solution whereby we do not have a weak link in the chain, either by virtue of the fact that you allow processed products to come in without really ensuring that the original raw material was legally caught, because otherwise you might end up having a plant for illegal fish somewhere abroad and then importing it into the Community, no questions

asked, and that would be a disaster just the same and would not solve the problem, or by having the situation whereby the sanctions that are imposed cover a spectrum which goes from taking it on board as a very small part of operational costs to being something very prohibitive. Those where it is very prohibitive will not have their ports used to land illegal fish and the others will continue landing illegal fish because the sanctions are not sufficiently deterrent. These are issues which are very sensitive for Member States.

Q643 Lord Plumb: If the radical proposals go through, first, to what extent are you talking to WTO about your proposals at the moment and to what extent do you think they will want to see the final proposals, and will that not affect the changes which you have in mind?
Commissioner Borg: The WTO would come into it very much with proposals, for example, with regard to IUU, illegal fishing, because my proposing that we will not allow illegal products to be served, so to speak, upon any Community plate means that if imports coming from third countries are not properly certified as being the provenance of legally caught fish they will not be allowed in and therefore certain third countries in particular, unless they are developed countries, might have problems with the provision of certification. What we are doing in the proposal is seeing to it that a transitional period is allowed so that we would be able to work out with these third countries (with many of which we have also standing arrangements, for example, concerning health and sanitary provisions from these countries) in order to extend the set-up they have to cover legal or illegal fish so that they would not suffer any further consequence further, and also use funds coming from our own funds or from development funds in order to help these countries build their infrastructure, because at the end of the day it would also be in their interests if their waters were not used by illegal operators, by pirates too, to catch fish at minimal expense and then dump it into our own market. It would be in their interests if we strengthened their set-up so that operators in their waters were lawful operators and paid the proper price for the catches.

Q644 Chairman: Total traceability of fish; is that the idea?
Commissioner Borg: Yes, the objective is to have total traceability of fish. As long as we are not discriminatory and as long as we show that the measures we are introducing are genuine measures to guarantee lawful operators and are not artificial barriers to trade coming from third countries, we should not have any problems WTO-wise, and obviously these go through our own internal arrangements, what we call inter-service

consultations, and DG Trade is very keen to see to it that whatever is proposed would not be WTO incompatible. On this we have had the support of the whole college, including trade, and in Council the decision was unanimous that we come up with a strong proposal. Now we are facing the reality that the devil is in the detail. There are three aspects to it, and perhaps I can briefly say something on this. One is scope. As I said before, some Member States tend to argue that the measures should only affect third country operators or operators in third country waters. We are of the view that the measure should cover everyone, and on the basis of the latest information I have Member States are getting round to accepting this and have introduced some minor changes to the proposal in order to have a situation in which blacklisting Community vessels should only happen if a Member State does not take action under our existing control regulations. It would be a second step and it seems that on the basis of that we should be home and dry and therefore the proposal would remain covering all operators and all illegally caught fish irrespective of where it is caught. The second point, and again I have already alluded to it, is the question concerning certification both with regard to fish that is landed in Community ports and with regard to fish products processed and what-have-you that come into the Community market. There has to be certification and this is a tough nut to crack because you need to do it in a way whereby you do not add exorbitant costs to the operators, who are importers, et cetera. There the thinking is that we would have what a general requirement but with exceptions, and therefore products that are imported into the Community which are not debarred, which represent a small percentage, would be exempted so that you do not create unnecessary bureaucracy, so to speak, but the main products would require certification because there one needs to attack where it really hurts if we leave it unregulated and therefore you leave an easy way out to illegal fish ending up in the Community market. There, because you are speaking of large quantities, the cost element would be fairly evenly spread out. We are thinking along these lines and I think that we will be able to convince the Member States to move in this direction. Again, I repeat: the problem is not so much with regard to fish that are caught and landed in port. The problem is much more with regard to processed fish products. With regard to those which are exempted, one would have the possibility of reviewing it so that if there are fish products that are exempted but which then start being imported heavily into the Community then certification would need to be included there. That is one option. The other option is to have a list of the products that need certification and all the rest would not. I do not prefer this because that means that whenever you want to work to the list you have to go

through hell in order to have that product included in the list because it would mean that now with co-decision it would have to go to Council and the European Parliament to try to find a solution to it. The third option with regard to legal fish is the question of sanctions. Again, I referred to this before. It is also important to have a situation where the playing field is level, where you therefore do not have the situation that in some Member States the level of sanctions is, let us say, on average €100 per fine whereas in others it is €7,000 or €8,000 per fine. It does not make sense for the same type of offence or the same type of breach. Therefore we need to level out the difference as much as possible because if you do not do so you are stuck with the situation where those which are lenient would be at a perverse advantage with regard to illegal operations. In essence, if we want to regain sustainable fishing, which has always been the objective of the 2002 reform and which is the objective with regard to fisheries worldwide, there is no doubt about that, but we have to attack, first, over-capacity. We have ourselves in the past encouraged construction of vessels and therefore indirectly encouraged over-capacity. Now we need to undo that. We gave, for example, European assistance for construction of vessels. Member States were encouraged to do this. Now we have realised that this has given rise to a situation where there is significant over-capacity and therefore we need to undo that and now we are looking at it from the opposite end in that we encourage Member States to enter into restructuring programmes for their fleets in order to reduce capacity, to have capacity match what the fishing possibilities are, and therefore to encourage decommissioning of vessels and using Community assistance for the purpose of decommissioning of vessels. That is one area which it is essential that we deliver on. The other is illegal fishing. Illegal fishing represents revenue of about €8 billion per annum, so it is big business. If we manage to make the Community market inaccessible to these operators, whether they are Community or non-Community, and most of them would be non-Community, then it makes this business less lucrative and therefore indirectly, if this is adopted also by third countries (and we are working also with a number of Third Countries), the end result would be that there would be less pressure on fish if you weeded out of the market the illegal operators or at least reduced them considerably. Then there is the question of discarding. In certain fisheries we are speaking of discarding which runs into figures of 50, 60, 70% of the catch, which means a lot of added pressure on the stock because most of the discarded fish do not survive. There are certain species which can survive if they are thrown back into the sea. Most of them, especially the more valuable ones, do not survive, so it is just dumping that fish back into the sea. We would like to find solutions in the direction of more selectivity and encourage more research into selective methods of fishing, for example where—and this is the experimentation going on with the Scottish fishers—if you have an area which in a particular period of the year tends to have aggregations of spawning fish of a particular species, cod, for example, you close that area for that period and move elsewhere. These are experiments which have been tried and tested by our neighbours and others, for example, Norway, Iceland, Canada, New Zealand, Australia. We are learning also from their experiences how to move forward. Basically, these are the three major objectives which I think, if we implement them, or at least start effectively implementing them, will mean significant, and I would say radical, changes to the way we manage the Common Fisheries Policy today without attacking its commonality.

Q645 *Chairman*: You said that you saw the future being that centrally the policy parameters would be set and go down to regional level for implementation at Member State level. Could you give me an idea of what sort of policy parameters would be set?
Commissioner Borg: Yes. Basically, one would establish the right level of the mortality rate of fish and say that the mortality rate has to be, let us say, 40%. That is the objective. That is the result that has to be achieved, so if the mortality rate was 60 then it needs to go to 40. Then you allow the operators to discuss with Member States how that is to be achieved, and with the use of Regional Advisory Councils, for example, if a plan is presented which is very much the plan of the Member States, very much the plan worked out by the stakeholders, and you see that that plan will deliver those objectives, then that is okay, but then you have to monitor, one, that there is conformity with the plan because it is useless saying, "Okay, this is our plan", and then doing what the hell you like, and, two, the plan itself, because it might well be, with all the knowledge the stakeholders and we have, that at the end of the day, in spite of the plan, the results do not move in the direction that we want them to move in, so then you would have to revise again. Very broadly speaking, this is how we envisage that would work. I mention this because, for example, in discussions with Norway we agreed on the 40% mortality rate.
Mr Degnbol: It is around 40. It is very close.
Commissioner Borg: Therefore we set that as the objective and then, obviously, one has to work within those in order to attain those objectives. It can be tough but it does in itself encourage the operators themselves to find ways and means of doing it because the range of instruments can vary, and if they want to avoid a lot of measures that are relatively simple to operate in the form of significant reductions in TACs and quotas or in the form of significant reductions in fishing days, et cetera, then you encourage them to come up with alternatives, and the alternatives could be closures, more selective gear or other measures, whether they are closed areas or temporary closures, which would deliver those results. As I said, with Scotland I was given a presentation a couple of weeks ago and it is very interesting how the Scottish Executive, together with the operators, identify the areas which are to be closed for three weeks, if I am not mistaken, during specific periods of time, and they are also co-operating with Denmark and with the Netherlands and Belgium, if I am not mistaken, because during that closed period it is not just the Scottish fishers that do not go there but also the others, and therefore it becomes much more effective. I think that this is the way forward.

Q646 *Viscount Ullswater*: Commissioner, you seem to be describing a pretty brave new world because what we see at the moment in the December Council is intense political negotiation and the unfolding of a myriad of regulations and paperwork that thick, all decided on a political level at that particular Council. How are you going to get rid of that and now you are going to have co-decision with the European Parliament so you obviously want to bring down just the policy at that sort of level, but are you thinking of using the RACs as the regulatory bodies or the areas where the regulations will be able to be made?
Commissioner Borg: In a way it is true that what happens in the December Council is very political, but it is also true that we come up with a proposal which is not a perfect reproduction of science but which is very closely based on the scientific advice that we receive, and then in Council we have to give up on certain aspects but by and large the final outcome is still something which is less than what we would have wished for but which still moves in the direction of regaining sustainability. To give just a couple of examples, having seasonal closures in the Baltic Sea for cod is something which is of recent origin. As a result of Council decisions, obviously, the closures are less than we hoped for. Having situations where then a particular fleet of one of the Member States considerably over-fished cod in the Baltic Sea, and then having a decision taken by Council to remedy that, and now monitoring closely with that particular Member State to see to it that that does not recur is a significant development in the way the Council operates. With regard to blue fin tuna, using the Community position in order to attain certain decisions with regard to blue fin tuna in the Mediterranean and the East Atlantic and a recovery plan for blue fin tuna was quite a significant achievement, ending up in a situation in the first year

where a couple of our own Member States over-fished considerably but are coming up now with a position which has been accepted by Member States whereby the controls are something which is unknown by Community standards. We are speaking of a whole fleet of vessels controlling the blue fin tuna fishery in the Mediterranean in this particular period, round about 50 vessels and 18 aircraft that we are speaking of that are monitoring Community plus Member State vessels and the blue fin tuna operations. We are speaking of significant measures. Yes, it is political but I think there is a willingness on the part of Member States to work together in order to try to achieve results in the direction of sustainability, one, because, yes, the RACs and therefore stakeholder involvement I think has started to give positive results, that they feel now that they are involved in the process leading to decisions, maybe not enough but at least they feel that they are being consulted and that their voice is heard, but sometimes obviously not necessarily acted on, but at least that they form part of the process, and, secondly, there is also a realisation that the picture with regard to fishing in Community waters is not exactly a rosy picture and that we have big problems, and therefore there is a realisation by the sector itself that something needs to be done and a realisation by the Member States, notwithstanding the political realities, that something needs to be done, which is significant. Over the last month we have been in intense discussions with France with regard to restructuring of the fleet, and the drive for that was the realisation that operations could not continue with the numbers that there are by way of the French fleet fishing in various waters and that there has to be a significant reduction in capacity to bring about a reduction of effort to levels which would be moving in the direction of sustainability. We have in the last week virtually agreed internally with the French administration on a restructuring package. Now we have to go through the mechanisms here of inter-service consultations to see whether that package will fly, and if it does we will be making it public so that first of all these should be transparent, and secondly because we believe that it could serve also as a model for others to look into in order to see what is and what is not acceptable even by way of state aid and what-have-you in order to restructure your fleet. As I said before, unless we deliver on the problem of over-capacity, unless we deliver on IUU and unless we deliver on discards, we will remain with the problem for the long term. At least if we deliver on those then there are very good prospects that more and more fisheries will start being carried out sustainably. With regard to multi-annual planning, an increase in multi-annual planning would give more stability to the sector, and also, rather than having decisions taken just in the December Council we have started having decisions taken, for example, with regard to the Baltic, in October, with regard to deepwater fish in November, and with the agreement that we have reached with ICES that as from 2009 scientific advice will be given to us for all stocks before summer rather than in October, it opens up the gap so that you can have more front-loading, more stakeholder consultation, more consultations with Member States and also some flexibility with regard to when decisions are taken, and yes, I do see that if we move in the direction of more results-oriented management the pressure of decisions taken almost exclusively on the basis of TACs and quotas can become less, but this takes time and also takes some culture changes.

Q647 *Lord Cameron of Dillington:* Are you saying that if you do get the capacity down to exactly where you would like it over many years and you stop maybe the non-EU landing of black fish you think that in the long run you will be able to dispense with quotas and effort restrictions? If you get the capacity right would that be the final solution?

Commissioner Borg: Maybe this would be a little simplistic, but yes, if you get the capacity right, if you get the virtual elimination of illegal landings, if you have a system whereby discards will be at a very low level, in other words at what would be sustainable levels, and if you have the scientific data available, which is another problem which we need to invest more time and effort in, and to have the scientific data available you have to have the facts available and to have the facts available you have to have the co-operation of the operators first and foremost so all these work together, then you can work on the basis of what is the optimum fishing or maximum sustainable yield, although that is criticised in different quarters because of what one exactly understands because it can land you in a straitjacket unless you leave measures of manoeuvrability within it, and how to manage fisheries on the basis of maximum sustainable yield need not necessarily be TACs and quotas or mainly TACs and quotas. Maybe I am looking too far ahead and people are looking at what my point of view is, but yes, I do not exclude the situation where, if you have a situation where you establish what the objective is, what the result is, then how you do it, whether it is TACs, whether it is quotas, whether it is technical measures, whether it is closures, whether it is this, that or the other or a combination of everything is relative because at the end of the day what you need to see to is that the objective is there and that the objective is based on science as to what is sustainable and that you have a plan which very much moves you in that direction, and that once you attain it you remain at that level.

Q648 *Baroness Jones of Whitchurch:* I wanted to follow up what you were saying about the ultimate aim being sustainable fishing because it is a nice aspiration and there are lots of warm words about the need to balance the interests of the environment and the interests of the fishing industry but it seems that at every step and every call the interests of the fishing industry win and the interests of the environment do not really get a balanced consideration, and a lot of that is structural things about the way the negotiations are organised, the way the committees are organised. How can you make sure that there is a real balance, that the environmental interests really are taken into account, because it always seems that they get squeezed out at the end of the day when the negotiations are over?

Commissioner Borg: On the one hand when we speak of sustainability we speak of environmental sustainability but we are also speaking of economic and social sustainability. Having said that, if, because of social or economic considerations, short-term considerations, you over-fish to the extent that you deplete the stock, then the long term effect is going to be that you are creating more social harm because the communities will suffer for it, operators will suffer for it and also there will be economic problems.

Q649 *Baroness Jones of Whitchurch:* We see that. Other people do not necessarily see it.

Commissioner Borg: No, but it is to try to strike the right balance, and that is easier said than done. On the one hand we, it is true, move at a slower pace than science would prefer. Scientific advice very often tells us that there should be no cod fishing in various waters. We do not ignore that advice because it is very tough advice, but we cannot really implement it and close all the cod fisheries if there is a possibility of recovering the stock by measures which impact less and this is what we try to do. However, if we get indicators that the stock is depleting to such an extent that there is a significant risk that it cannot recover, then the only solution would be complete closure. It happened in Canada where they ended up with a complete closure. We are not at that stage—or at least I hope we are not at that stage—and on the basis of the measures we have taken we have had first signs of the recovery of the stock in the North Sea and therefore at the last Council we were a little more open-handed, so to speak. It is very complex because, if you just take cod, for example, since we are mentioning cod, is it just over-fishing that is causing less cod in certain Community waters? Are there impacts with regard to pollution, for example? Are there impacts with regard to climate change and therefore cod stocks are moving further north, because at the same time Norway and Iceland are finding more cod? Is it because they are more efficient in managing? It may be that they are. Is it also

because the climate helps and more cod are moving in that direction? It is not easy to point the finger of blame at one particular cause. This is why we try to work with the aid of the scientific data that we have. Yes, we need to try to balance out all the different factors and then what is important at the end of the day is that the decision that is ultimately taken will lead to regaining sustainable fishing in a way which is maybe at a slower pace but still at a pace whereby we can attain that so that in that way you cause the least possible harm to the operators themselves as long as you can do it. As I said, where we had to take tough measures we did, for example, with anchovy in the Bay of Biscay. We closed the fishery, notwithstanding almost a French revolution, and notwithstanding also having to intervene between the French and the Basques, which is not very easy, but we did for two years. We are hoping that now in May we will have the first advice which will allow us to reopen.

Q650 *Baroness Jones of Whitchurch:* Those are emergency situations where the stock is virtually depleted anyway. What we are looking for is more of a genuine eco-system.

Commissioner Borg: Yes, but this is why we have been working in the direction of more multi-annual management and more management on the basis of achieving results and working hard in order to reduce capacity. I think this is the first European Fisheries Fund which has just now come into effect that can start making use of the funds. This is a guesstimate but I would say that on average 20–25% of the funds available are going to be used on the basis of the operational programmes submitted by the different Member States for perhaps the decommissioning of vessels, and it took some convincing. During last year when we were in the process of approving the operational programmes under the European Fisheries Fund where we saw certain Member States dedicating less to the axes which relates to decommissioning we contacted those Member States in order to convince them to beef up the part of the programme or the part of the funds that they wanted to dedicate for this purpose. If one looks at the experience over the last few years, I would say that, yes, there are specific instances where the state of the stock has gone down further. I do not want to hide that, but I think there have been more instances where the state of the stock has improved over the last years. It is still in bad shape; I am not saying that the situation has changed from bad to good, but on the basis of the scientific advice that we are receiving there is an improvement in the state of a number of stocks, but we and the operators are seeing this and we are obviously telling them not to hurry because if we say, "Okay, the state of the stock is improving; therefore we can open up" almost indiscriminately, then you end up going downhill again, so yes, we are starting to see signs that a number of stocks have improved through a combination of factors. If we see that we need to take drastic action in exceptional cases, as we did with anchovy, as we did with cod, as we did with blue fin tuna, we will take it, but if we can avoid it so as not to create in the short term enormous problems with regard to the operators, we will do so as long as we see that over a time frame things can improve.

Ms Kirchner: There is also a significant difference between the anchovy fishery and the cod fishery. Anchovy is a single stock fishery, so you only fish anchovy if you put the net in the water, but if you put a white fish net in the water you catch haddock, whiting, saithe, nephrops, so closing the cod fishery is not an option. It would be closing the white fishery, the whole fleet, and it would mean basically the end of the Scottish white fish fleet for a decade. It is something we would wish for but it needs to also be operational in practice.

Commissioner Borg: This is a very good point because at the end of the day if we have a clean fishery you can close it and you affect only those with anchovy and to a large extent blue fin tuna, but if you have a fishery which is essentially mixed, even though you have a targeted fishery you catch others with it, so immediately you close that you are going to affect all those others as well, so there you have to be somewhat more cautious if you can afford to be, sustainability-wise. With anchovy you also have the problem that they are very short-lived. Because they are very short-lived you can have significant fluctuations and therefore you need to be somewhat more precautionary in the decision you take, whereas with others which are less short-lived you can have indicators over a time which are clearer on the basis of science.

Q651 *Viscount Brookeborough:* Could I ask you about quotas and fishing effort? To what extent do you think that currently this should be tradable within nations or between nations, and should there be a price on it, and do you agree with the Spanish proposition that it should be freely tradable and that in their view it is almost a crime for any quota surplus to exist anywhere? I took that from one of their papers, that no quota should be left anywhere that is not taken up.

Commissioner Borg: Individual transferable quotas are very hotly debated. There are examples of countries that operate individual transferable quotas. At a Community level it is not regulated so individual Member States have the system which they feel is the best in the circumstances. Although you can have transferable quotas within one Member State there is not at Community level regulation of transferable quotas across the Community. Spain might be

interested in this because they feel that their operators are strong and therefore they would acquire through transfers the lion's share, but it raises a number of very sensitive points, one of which is sacred to Member States, and that is the question of relative stability because with ITQs you can affect relative stability between Member States and that is something which every particular Member State fights tooth and nail for, including Spain. Maybe the calculations of certain Member States are that they will win out of it because their operators are strong and therefore they will have a stronger relative stability but immediately you try to touch on relative stability because the allocation is not fully exhausted, that Member State, and it could be Spain as well, will be up in arms, so, although we do encourage discussion and I do not exclude that maybe something will happen in the future, I do not see it happening in the very short term because it is extremely sensitive and unless we have a change of mentality with regard to relative stability it will be extremely difficult. We have introduced a measure of flexibility with regard to relative stability when it comes to fisheries partnership agreements that will happen with third countries. If we are in a way buying fishing possibilities from third countries it will be a waste if those fishing possibilities are not utilised to the full because we are paying good money and now with the new philosophy behind fishing partnership agreements we are not just paying proper value for the fishing possibilities; we are also paying over and above the value to help those countries modernise their set-up. It is quite a significant amount that we end up paying. If you end up with the situation where you allocate those fishing possibilities and some Member State does not use its share to the full, it makes sense that the unutilised parts could go to others who have utilised theirs to the full and may want to utilise more, but that means that you could be affecting the relative stability in that particular agreement, so the only way we can manage to do this is, for example, the way we managed it in the Greenland Agreement, which was to have an in-year review, let us say, in August, in order to see what has been utilised, and if the allocation of a particular Member State is low then you re-allocate that to other Member States who have utilised their allocation fully or almost fully. That is on a one-year basis so it does not set a precedent, so the year after you go back to square one and then you repeat it every time because otherwise Member States would not accept it.

Q652 *Viscount Brookeborough:* But internationally we have longer than one-year agreements, do we not, with some African countries, so we are happy to do it in other places but not within our own Community?

Commissioner Borg: With other places we have, for example, with Mauritania, with Morocco, et cetera, where we have started also to impinge on the absolute meaning of relative stability, and therefore introduce some measure of flexibility in order to try to maximise the full potential of the fishing possibilities, as long as this does not create precedents. That is always spelt out because Member States would only accept it if it is spelt out that this does not set a precedent with regard to what are the traditional fishing rights in those third country waters.

Q653 *Earl of Dundee:* Commissioner, for the system of common fisheries control why do so many problems still remain and, apart from occasional examples of closures and other pragmatic measures to which you have referred, do you believe that within Member States in general there is insufficient political will to achieve proper controls and enforcement?

Commissioner Borg: Yes. I think that Member States find it difficult to be tough where they need to be tough because of day-to-day political realities. They are on the front line, it is the ministers that have to face the fishers every so often, so it makes it more difficult to take a tough position. However, increasingly, as I said before, because there is more stakeholder involvement what we are doing here centrally Member States are doing hopefully more of when it comes to regular meetings, dialogue meetings, discussions with stakeholders, and there is realisation that we have big problems with regard to certain stocks, so because of that there is, I would say, more of a willingness to introduce measures which are tough and to see that they are properly enforced. You mentioned the question concerning control and enforcement. I made reference to it indirectly when I was referring to IUU, illegal fishing. First of all the Court of Auditors came out very strongly with regard to lack of proper controls, with regard to inadequate enforcement, and we agree with the Court of Auditors findings 100%. In fact, we ourselves have been saying this for the last few years, that the controls left a lot to be desired and that enforcement was the exception rather than the rule. We will be coming up with a new control regulation proposal, hopefully in October, which will incorporate all the different control measures that we have in place, and having it all in one piece of legislation will make it simpler to operate because, rather than having to look around 100 different regulations, we will have one piece of legislation, but it will also strengthen it. Obviously the strengthening part is going to be the tough nut to crack because what we are proposing in the IUU, for example, concerning the harmonisation of the sanctions will then have to feature in the control regulation and there are other measures which will have to feature in the new control

regulation which will strengthen the control and therefore will create the obligation, for example, to have inspectors on board vessels. At the moment in a way Community inspectors are an option, so having an obligation to have inspectors trying to set percentages (but those depend on the type of fishery as well), including land-based controls, port controls, more direct controls at sea because controls at sea are much more difficult to operate, are the aspects which we are going to address in the new control regulation. We are hoping that in spite of the co-decision requirement—and I am not saying this in a negative way but it is a fact that with co-decision, because there is the involvement of the European Parliament we will need more time—the European Parliament will be an added force in favour of more sustainability, so although you need more time the results will hopefully be better if one looks at the final objectives that need to be attained. We are targeting that this control regulation will be in place by the end of next year and that will substitute for the existing control mechanism. We will also be harmonising the sanctions regime in the sense of setting a maximum and then also trying to set parameters for different serious infringements with regard to the level of sanction that should apply with regard to different serious infringements, because in that way, if Member States agree to these parameters—and that is not easy because this is a sensitive subject—you would avoid having the problems that you have today where you have significant loopholes because certain Member States operate a system where the sanctions are very low and therefore you cannot really have an effective system which operates against over-fishing, et cetera.

Q654 *Earl of Dundee:* How do you see the role of the Community Fisheries Control Agency evolving as part of your overall control?

Commissioner Borg: Before going to the Fisheries Control Agency, I would just like to say with regard to the Regional Advisory Councils that we are in the process of now assessing how they have operated over these last few years, and come next year we will be coming up with some proposals to change how they have been operating where we feel that we can improve on how they have operated. I say "we". However, it is very much what they themselves are telling us as to what the teething problems have been, so where we can improve on that we will. I do not envisage that in the short term we will be moving in the direction of the RACs themselves being the ones who will be taking the decisions with regard to certain management issues, so in the short term it will still be a question of them providing advice which hopefully will be more solid and which hopefully will mean that to a very large extent we will follow that advice, but I do not exclude either that if the RACs continue evolving in the direction of providing strong, solid advice which is based on sustainable fisheries they will also acquire the right to manage, at least in part, the fishing operators. That is as regards RACs. With regard to the Control Agency, the Control Agency is still very new. It does not have the direct right of control but it co-ordinates the control activities of the different Member States, so the primary responsibility is in the hands of the Member States to effect controls. This is why I was saying before that we need to have measures in place which will make it more difficult for Member States not to implement controls properly, but we do hope that the Fisheries

Control Agency will be able to deliver effectively when it comes to co-ordinating control between the different Member States and even though it is still very early we will be doing a new Control Regulation in October with some amendments to it in order to strengthen the Control Agency when it comes to monitoring the control activities carried out by Member States, and therefore, as I said, having more possibility of seeing to it that Community inspectors have the right to board in certain situations.

Chairman: Thank you very much indeed. You have given us well over an hour. It has been very helpful and interesting. Thank you.

Supplementary Memorandum by the Directorate-General for Fisheries and Maritime Affairs, European Commission

THE POLITICAL CONTEXT

1. *The adoption of decisions affecting Community fisheries is dominated by the Member States working through the Council. To what extent do you consider there has been any change in the basic constellation of interests in the Council since the last CFP reform in 2002? What impact, for example, have the 2004 and 2007 accessions had on policy outcomes?*

It is difficult to give a straight answer to such a question. At first sight it would seem that the last accessions have consolidated the more conservative tendencies in conservation policy. The new Member States seem to share the same approach to fisheries management, based on short term socio economic considerations. Adopting a longer term approach remains difficult for both old and new Member States. The new Member States also justifiably went through a period of adjustment but now have come to realize the objectives set by the Commission and whilst clearly still fighting their corner tend to join in the forming of consensuses in the Council much more easily.

2. *Looking to the future, the European Parliament will gain co-decision powers upon entry into force of the Lisbon Treaty (assuming ratification by all 27 Member States). To what extent is that likely to alter fisheries policy outcomes at EU level?*

Co-decision may introduce a longer term perspective in the fishery policy outcomes (in contrast to the present focus on short term perspectives dominating in Council) because in practice it will be impossible to continue to make decisions on technical details in a co-decision procedure. The annual TACs are specifically exempted from co-decision but the annual TAC decisions may be bound by longer term principles if such principles have been established through co-decision. Long term management plans (to be decided in co-decision) are examples of such longer term principles which may guide the annual decisions on TACs so that the combined result will be the development of sustainable fisheries.

At present some Members of the Fisheries Committee of the EP tend to defend the short term socioeconomic interests of their fishing constituencies. In the future decision making in the EP in general terms will have to take broader considerations and other general concerns into account, either because other Committees take an interest in the matter or because voting in plenary will involve broader interests.

3. *How has the relationship between fisheries policy and environmental policy changed since the last CFP reform, and how do you see it developing in future?*

The last reform introduced the ecosystem approach as a basic element of the CFP. We think this entails important developments. We have tried to explain in the recent communication on the ecosystem approach how this has been implemented and how we see it develop.

An ecosystem approach cannot be implemented through one sector alone—an approach involving all relevant sectors must be established. In the EU this is done through the Marine Strategy, and the Communication therefore does not deal with an ecosystem approach to fisheries management as such but how CFP measures can contribute to this cross-sectoral ecosystem approach.

The key elements in this approach are to minimise the impacts of fishing on the wider marine environment by reducing the overall level of fishing pressure, and to ensure that fisheries measures are used fully to support the cross-sectoral approach defined by the EU's Marine Strategy and Habitats Directives.

The eco-system approach is already being enacted through the introduction of multi-annual plans which set target rates for fishing mortality in line with the EU's commitment to manage for maximum sustainable yield, and with the Commission's new policy to reduce by-catches and reduce discarding in European fisheries. In the longer term these measures will not only lead to lower fisheries impacts on ecosystems but also to a more profitable fishing sector as fish stocks recover their productivity. Beyond this, specific supplementary measures are taken under the CFP to diminish impacts of fisheries on sensitive species or sensitive habitats. A number of specific measures have been implemented since 2002 specifically to address particular environmental issues for example, to protect specific vulnerable habitats, to reduce incidental by-catch of sea mammals, to protect specific stocks on which sea bird colonies depend, or to ban destructive fishing practices.

CONTROL AND ENFORCEMENT

4. *The Court of Auditors issued a scathing report on the Community system of CFP control and enforcement last October. Could you please comment on why serious problems remain? To what extent do you consider that there is political will in all Member States to make use of the available control and enforcement tools, let alone of potential new ones?*

As you rightly point out, numerous weak points were identified in the report of the Court of Auditors but also in various reports published by the Commission on the control of the CFP.
The major underlying problem is overcapacity and the fact that the harvest capacity is much larger than legal catch opportunities. There are in that situation very strong economic drivers for illegal behaviour. Better compliance must therefore be achieved by simultaneously removing the strong drivers for non-compliance (ie ensuring that the harvest capacity does not exceed legal catch opportunities) and strengthening control and enforcement.

Despite successive reforms aimed at solving the deficiencies in the implementation and enforcement of the CFP, the control system remains inefficient, expensive, complex, and it does not produce the desired results. The reasons for that are the following:

1. The regulatory framework is fragmented and obsolete.

2. There is an absence of a European culture of control.

3. National systems of control are ineffective.

The means at the disposal of the Commission to put pressure on the Member States are limited.

In fact, the control system is so inefficient that it undermines the system of TAC and quotas and fishing effort management. The major efforts undertaken over the last years to achieve sustainable exploitation and long-term management of stocks simply cannot bear fruit in the absence of an effective control system.

As to the second part of your question, Member States generally share the analysis of the Court of Auditors and of the Commission. Without waiting for new enforcement tools to be in place, the Commission, in agreement with the Member States, has launched a series of initiatives to ensure that current control provisions are respected. For instance:

— Member States have committed to implement fully the VMS system in conformity with Community rules by the end of 2008.

— Also, Memorandums of Understanding have been signed with several Member States regarding Community financial contribution towards expenditure incurred by Member States in implementing the monitoring and control systems applicable to the CFP. These memorandums represent a change of approach, as they contain clearly defined benchmarks for improvements in the fisheries control systems in the MS concerned.

5. *In response to the Court of Auditors Report the Commission issued a consultation paper in February with a view to revising the Control Regulation in late 2008. Could you explain to us what your priorities are? How do you see the role of the Community Fisheries Control Agency evolving as part of your overall Control strategy?*

Against the background identified above, it has become necessary to envisage a reform of the current control system of the CFP. The main objective of the reform will be to ensure the respect of the CFP by building a new standard framework which will enable the Member States and the Commission to fully assume their responsibilities. To this end, in the context of the new legislative framework the priorities will be to:

— Develop a harmonised approach as regards inspection and control covering all aspects from the capture right through to the consumer.

— Increase compliance with the CFP rules, and contribute to the development of a common culture of control, through harmonised proportionate sanctions, a systematic cooperation and exchange of information and a simplified system ensuring a uniform implementation of the control measures.

— Increase the overall cost-efficiency of the control policy with a view to reducing administrative costs both at the level of operators and at the level of administrations, while at the same time ensuring that the CFP rules are effectively applied.

— Regarding the role of the Community Fisheries Control Agency, let me first of all recall that the Agency is still very young. It has been operational since 2007 only. The competencies of the Agency remain limited: it can only coordinate Member States' control and inspection activities at sea and not at land.

— However, in order to address some of the shortcomings identified by the Court of Auditors, the reform will envisage an extended mandate for the Agency, in order to cover the development of cooperation between Member States and with the Commission, to include extended responsibilities for the coordination of inspection at land, and cross checking of data.

We intend to present this legislative proposal for a new control regulation to the European Parliament and to Member States in October 2008 and we hope that this proposal can be adopted in Council by summer 2009.

REDUCING CAPACITY

6. *It seems that capacity continues to exceed available resources. To what extent is there real political will among Member States to address excess capacity where it persists? What can the Commission do to promote capacity reduction in the absence of such political will? What is the possible role of the European Fisheries Fund in this regard?*

The Commission considers that the size of the Community fishing fleet is well in excess of the available fishing opportunities. Although the capacity of its fleet has steadily decreased during the past 15 years, at an average yearly rate between 2 and 3%, the Commission considers that this reduction is not enough to bring capacity in line with fishing opportunities. This is even less so considering that technological progress allows an increase in the efficiency of a capacity unit in the order of 3–4% per annum. The harvest capacity of the fleet has therefore been stable at best, in spite of nominal capacity reductions. This fact is not reflected by the trend in nominal capacity and has never been taken into account in fleet capacity management under the CFP.

The result of continued overcapacity is excessive pressure on the resource base and strong economic incentives for non-compliance. Overcapacity is therefore a key problem to be addressed. This was also the conclusion of the Court of Auditors which identifies fleet overcapacity as a major risk factor for the CFP in its special report on the control, inspection and sanction systems.

The new regime after the 2002 reform handed back to Member States the responsibility to find a balance between capacity and resources. Under the current legal framework, the Council cannot impose fishing capacity reductions on Member States. They are nevertheless obliged (Article 11 of the basic regulation) to seek a sustainable balance between fleet and fishing opportunities, established by the Council in the form of quotas or fishing effort allocations.

This system is a considerable simplification relative to the former system. It ensures that nominal capacity cannot increase but real reductions depend on the will of MSs to establish the balance between capacity and resources. We do however not see real political will among most Member States. This is indicated by the annual reports from MSs which in nearly all cases fail to analyse the relation between harvest capacity and resources and which therefore demonstrate that MS do not seriously consider this balance. It is also difficult to see that capacity reduction is an important objective for MSs when they submit their programmes for the European Fisheries Fund. There are however some exceptions. Since 2002 an important number of vessels have been decommissioned for example in the Scottish whitefish fleet. While this has been a painful exercise for those fishermen that decided to leave the industry and take the decommissioning premium, it has been proven a successful move overall. The profitability of the industry has increased and it has taken off pressure from stocks such as cod in the North Sea.

The increasing fuel prices have led to a situation where for the first time we find ourselves in a situation where the industry is asking for adaptation and for decommissioning plans to be offered and the governments hesitate to take action.

In the short term the Commission can take action to better monitor and enforce compliance with limitations on fishing opportunities, especially quota and fishing effort consumption. Effective enforcement is one way to make overcapacity visible and reduce the economic incentives to maintain overcapacity. The Commission can also closely watch that rules on fuel subsidies are respected in order to avoid maintenance of fleet capacity, which would no longer be able to operate economically.

The Commission is also working with Member States and the STECF to better assess fleet capacity, which is a technically controversial issue. It is necessary to establish methodologies to objectively determine what the adequate fleet size is so that MS has a common guidance for their analysis and reporting and to enable the Commission to argue in favour of concrete capacity reductions. If fleet overcapacity is clearly and openly displayed, Member States will be better motivated to take action.

It may in the longer term be necessary to make some modifications to the present regulation to address some of the weaknesses which have been identified.

The EFF provides for funds to reduce the size of the fleet. Additional funding may be available in some cases if Member States are willing to re-programme the initial allocations from fleet modernisation or other axis to fleet decommissioning. But again this would only be possible if MS had the political will to do so. Member States may provide additional funding by the way of state aid for decommissioning although the current economic context makes it difficult.

REGIONAL ADVISORY COUNCILS

7. *We have taken a range of evidence regarding the Regional Advisory Councils, the advent of which was a key development arising from the 2002 CFP Reform. What is your view on the development of the RACs? To what extent does the Commission take on board the opinions produced by the RACs? What sort of relationship does the Commission have with the RACs and how does that vary across the different RACs?*

RACs have become active players in the CFP. The number of recommendations addressed to the Commission is increasing, as well as the number of meetings/seminars with participation from both sides. Whereas many recommendations have been in response to requests from the Commission, the RACs also often take the initiative and organise events and workshops on various issues such as rights-based management and control and enforcement.

Overall, RACs have contributed to softening hostile attitudes towards the CFP, allowing for further direct contacts between stakeholders, EU officials, Member States and scientists. The quality and timeliness of RAC advice has increased over time. Some RACs submitted particularly well grounded advice on long-term management plans, and the Commission took these recommendations into account. When consulting the RACs, the Commission is looking for concrete comments to factor in more effectively the regional and local realities or those linked to specific types of fisheries.

The quality and hence the Commission's follow-up of RAC advice depends on whether that advice is compatible with the CFP objectives and sustainable fisheries. There have been cases where the Commission could not follow RAC advice. A difficult case in RACs input on TAC and quota proposals. Due to the nature of the exercise (annual decision) and the resulting short-term interests of the catching sector, it has proven difficult in some cases to reach consensus. In fact, several environmental organisations withdrew from discussions and refused to endorse RAC proposals.

The Commission has repeatedly explained that it cannot follow RAC recommendations when they are widely at variance from scientific advice, or in contradiction of international obligations or Community long-term management plans.

There are some differences between RACs which partly are due to differences in previous experience (the North Sea RAC had for instance benefited from former regional initiatives in place), partly to different industry structures as fewer and larger enterprises are in a better position to utilise the RACs.

The reorganisation of DG Mare will allow for a closer follow up of RACs work and closer relations with the stakeholders through the work of our new Regional Units.

8. *An important question that we have been considering in the course of our inquiry is how RACs might most usefully develop in the future. Looking forward, how do you see the RACs evolving? Do you see any possibility that a level of management responsibility might be transferred to them?*

In the longer term the RACs should continue to play a key role as advisory bodies and their focus on longer term issues should be strengthened. The balance between different societal interests may need to be redressed to correspond better with changing markets and more public focus on marine management. The RACs can also play an important role as a forum for exchange of experiences from initiatives by the industry and as a forum for communication between stakeholders and scientists.

Initiatives from the industry will also become increasingly important to an extent that there is a change towards results based management where legislation specifies outcomes but leaves it to industry to develop a more management responsibility within such a framework in the sense that results based management will leave more implementation decisions and initiatives to be with stakeholders. It is however, difficult to envisage at this early stage of their operation that the RACs should be transformed from being advisory bodies into bodies having some level of wider management responsibility outside a results-based management framework.

DISCARDS

9. *In the Commission's written evidence (Q2) it is suggested that more selective gear and fishing practices are better promoted through results-based management whereby standards for outcomes in a particular fishery are established and it is left to the industry to find the technical means to fish within these standards. Could you explain how this might work in practice, including its monitoring and enforcement?*

In the past more selective fishing gear and fishing practices were promoted through direct regulation of the legal design of fishing gear. This has lead to increasingly detailed and unenforceable regulation similar to what one would have if speed in traffic were regulated by specification of legal car designs and not by speed limits. This is why the Commission in its new policy on discards is suggesting a reversal to results-based management.

A change to results-based management is a challenge to everybody including the industry and public authorities. We consider it a necessary step as it engages the industry in taking responsibility and gets us out of the very detailed management we have had regarding technical measures so far.

We have initiated a debate with stakeholders about the options for some specific fisheries, based on the comments we have received to the Communication on a new discards policy published last year and analysis made by STECF. The idea is then to issue regulations regarding these fisheries and then proceed with regulations on other fisheries until the policy is generally implemented.

It is suggested that maximum allowed by-catch limits (MABL) are established for each fishery accompanied with a plan for annual reductions until these limits are achieved. An MABL would apply to the total by-catches for a national fleets and it is left to the member state to decide how it would allocate this. Member States are invited to utilise the options of the EFF to support adaptations to the necessary changes in respect of more selective fishing gear etc.

Monitoring and control will require both some observer coverage and comparisons of landings across vessels with and without observer coverage. Minimum requirements for observer coverage may be set out and there may be provisions to encourage voluntary schemes for reporting including reference fleets.

The Commission intends to come forward with an initial legislative proposal to decrease discards in two fisheries by October 2008.

RIGHTS-BASED MANAGEMENT

10. *The Commission published a Communication on rights-based management tools in fisheries last year. How have stakeholders responded to your Communication? What further steps do you plan to take as regards this agenda?*

There has been considerable interest in discussing this sensitive subject. The European Commission has received 25 written contributions from stakeholders and held several meetings with industry, other stakeholder and authorities in several Member States. The European Economic and Social Committee adopted a constructive own initiative opinion on the Communication in mid-February 2008.

The European Parliament also adopted recently a resolution on the Communication. The EP resolution strikes a delicate balance between the need for caution regarding the use of RBM, as they can have significant impacts on small scale fisheries, coastal communities, and the recognition of the positive aspects thereof such as reduction of capacity, and simpler monitoring. Questions raised most frequently in contributions received pertain to the competence of MS vs. EC (currently RBM are responsibility of positive/negative effects of different types of RBM—particularly of Individual Transferable Quotas (ITQs), to which nearly all contributors refer—the impact of RBM on relative stability, the degree of transferability of rights, the likely concentration of quota in fewer hands (and its social impacts), the legal ownership of a public resource—in particular the question whether private property rights can be envisaged for common fisheries resources-, the related issues of allocation of rights and access by new entrants and the likely effects on discards. There have also been negative opinions based on two main sources of concern: the privatization of a public resource and the protection of coastal fisheries and communities.

Some contributors see ITQs as unavoidable in order to redress the poor economic performance of many fleets. Some others see RBM as an opportunity to crack relative stability. The European Economic and Social Committee has gone as far as envisaging the setting up of Community-wide management system based on tradable fishing rights, managed at Community level. Other contributors have held, more moderately, that the European Commission should investigate about quota imbalances following the yearly TAC and quota negotiations and propose ways to reallocate unused quotas to other MS which could use them, within the framework of relative stability.

The European Commission will continue working on RBM over the coming months. A study to provide a knowledge basis of all RBM tools currently applied in the EU is on-going with results expected by the last quarter of 2008. The most likely follow up in the short term could be information documents or guidelines on RBM (including good/best practices) addressed to Member States. In the medium to long term, the European Commission will consider RBM in the context of the forthcoming CFP reform.

LOOKING FORWARD

11. *The Commission's written evidence gives an indication (Q11) that the Commission would be willing to move towards a scenario whereby principles are adopted at the Council/EP level, standards emerging from those principles are adopted by the Commission and technical implementation decisions are delegated to Member States. Could you comment further please on how the governance of the CFP might evolve in the medium to long term? To what extent might any of the possible future governance models exacerbate control and enforcement problems?*

The Lisbon Treaty introduces co-decision for most issues relating to the CFP. This change will broaden the political scrutiny to which the CFP is subject and it will also make it impossible in practice to continue with a set-up where both strategic decisions and decisions regarding very detailed implementation issues are taken at the political level. It may be necessary to move towards a set-up where more technical implementation decisions are left to lower levels, within principles established in co-decision. There are furthermore limits to how far the services of the Commission can continue to be involved in implementation on as detailed a level as has been the case in the past. Member States will have a better basis for addressing very specific implementation issues. Clearer division of labour could help to keep the policy better on track in the long term because lower level decisions will be accountable to decisions about principles taken at higher level. In the present setup, where the competence for strategy and tactics are at the same level, it is possible for the Council to decide on a management plan in one Council meeting and then deviate fro it in another Council meeting where the fishing opportunities for next year are decided.

This division of labour already exists today as regards control and enforcement: it is the responsibility of Member States to deliver control and enforcement, subject to Community control. A clearer hierarchy in decisions may even be the basis for more effective control and enforcement because it will be required that there are very specific standards on Community level against which performance can be measured. However, the main challenge with regard to control and enforcement is obviously to develop the "culture of compliance" that was referred to above and to put an end to the present situation of relative neglect by several Member States of their control responsibilities. It may also be considered to give the Control Agency more power to ensure compliance.

In agreement with the forthcoming French Presidency, the Commission intends to launch a debate on the future of the Common Fisheries Policy six and a half years after the last reform in 2002. An informal discussion between the Ministers will take place in September. My services have already started the work on a mid-term evaluation of the reformed CFP. Given the serious challenges that our policy is facing and in the light of the Court of Auditors report, we need to start working immediately on a reform of the CFP framework.

May 2008

Examination of Witness

Witness: MR HARM KOSTER, Executive Director, Community Fisheries Control Agency, examined.

Q655 *Chairman:* Thank you very much for finding the time to spend with us, particularly on a day like this, but we have our duty to perform. We are a Sub-Committee of our House of Lords EU Scrutiny Committee. We are carrying out an inquiry into the future of the Common Fisheries Policy and where it should be going. This is a formal evidence session so a note will be taken and you will get a transcript as soon as possible. You can look through it and do any corrections that are necessary. Would it be useful if we started with the questions and answers?
Mr Koster: That is fine.

Q656 *Chairman:* Could I start by saying that the Control Agency is a very recent animal, so could you give us some idea of how it came about, why was it thought necessary, and then if you could give us a brief description of its responsibilities and how it goes about its job that would be very helpful?
Mr Koster: Thank you very much. I am delighted to share my experience in the Common Fisheries Policy with you. The Community Fisheries Control Agency was established in 2005 as a product of the 2002 reform. I will say a few words about the history. Fishing used to take place in international waters which started beyond territorial waters, so most of the seas in the past were international waters, and the need to conserve fish stocks was already recognised long ago. To that end the country states in the world today have established regional fisheries organisations which we still have. They are now less important because international waters are now beyond 200 miles and 80–90% of the fish are now inside economic zones, but there was already a tradition in international organisations to agree on conservation and then subsequently to implement more or less what was internationally agreed, and that more or less was not always to the letter. There was already a certain experience of this, so when we started with the Common Fisheries Policy in 1983 it was basically in the Act of Accession for the UK and then Norway negotiated as well at the time and Denmark and Ireland, and then it was certain in that that in ten years' time there would be a Common Fisheries Policy. That was in 1983 so in 1983 this policy was started for a period of 20 years, which brings us to 2002. There was a mid-term review after ten years. At the start the Member States agreed to give the Commission a team of Commission inspectors. That was not for nothing because there was already a certain tradition that you could agree on conservation, you could agree to catch restrictions but to implement them was another question and so there was already a certain—maybe I should not say "mistrust", but there was—

Q657 *Chairman:* I think you should.
Mr Koster:— already in 1983 the Commission a team of inspectors to control Member States because that was felt necessary. In the mid-term review in 1992 it was recognised that control was a poor element of the Common Fisheries Policy, it was not properly implemented, so when we came to 2002, the reform after 20 years, in the Green Paper the Commission was very open in noting the shortcomings on the implementation of the policy side. Basically, in 2002 there were two big problems. The first problem was that there was too much capacity. Too many vessels were chasing too few fish—" Mr Fishery" you will remember was the slogan of Mr Fischler—and the second problem was control. Subsequently, in all the discussions on the control side there was a certain consensus among stakeholders in the fishing industry. Basically, the fishing industry was frustrated about the way the Common Fisheries Policy was implemented, the way control was carried out. It was very fragmented. There were lots of holes in the system. They felt that it was an uneven playing field, there was not equal treatment and even some fishermen said that they felt discriminated against when they were fishing in waters of other Member States; they felt that they were discriminated against in relation to fishermen from the other Member States, so the fishing industry came with a consensus position which requested the Community for a much bigger and more direct involvement in control, in the process of implementing the policy. Whether this was all serious is another question because we always said at the time that probably half of the fishing industry was really frustrated and they wanted to have better

control and enforcement but for the other half supporting the idea that at Community level there was more direct involvement in control would be the best guarantee to continue with very poor enforcement because the Community would never be able to do this job properly and therefore it would continue in a situation where there was poor enforcement. Anyway, they were politically correct and they said that there was unanimity that there should be more direct involvement at Community level in control of the rules of the Common Fisheries Policy. We were reflecting with Mr Fischler at the time on what kind of reply we should give to this and that was not so easy because there were some ideas already before—a European coastguard, a common inspection authority at Community level, but these ideas were institutionally not correct. Because we have independent sovereign Member States, in Community policies decisions are taken in Brussels by the Community institutions but the implementation is always a question of the sovereignty of Member States. They have to implement. Of course, if you are a member of the club you have to respect the rules of these competent authorities to make sure that an inspector has the right to inspect an economical person. These kinds of matters really belong to the sovereignty of Member States and they are matters for Member States to settle. It is not a matter for the Community to establish a European coastguard because this is a matter for Member States, and in the UK you have the Scottish Fisheries Protection Agency in Scotland and in England it is the Ministry, and now there is an independent agency as well which is in charge of implementing control and enforcement of the rules of the Common Fisheries Policy. These are really national matters. If you establish a European coastguard you also need inspectors which have to do the job and these inspectors must have a mandate and it is not institutionally correct in accordance with the current rules to give them a European mandate. They need still to have a national mandate, so we have these institutional problems. There has been quite some discussion about this and Mr Fischler did not want to make a revolution. He wanted to stick to the construction of the Community as it was but he was then prepared to be pragmatic and to do a feasibility study on a European Community Control Agency to see how such an agency could operate, and then the idea was not to take away the responsibility of Member States for the implementation of the Common Fisheries Policy. On the contrary, in the reform of 2002 it was emphasised what were the responsibilities of Member States. Member States are responsible for controlling enforcement, nobody else. The feasibility study on the Agency was just to study how an agency could help Member States to implement the rules of the Common Fisheries Policy

in such a way that we would have at Community level a level playing field, so this agency should assist Member States in co-operating between them in order to make sure that there was at European level a level playing field. If you have a common policy, a European policy, I think the industry, the stakeholders, would see this as a common policy and they would wish that there was a level playing field in the Community. If you have 27 Member States and the implementation of a common policy is done by 27 different Member States at the end if everybody does it in their own way it is very difficult to keep a common policy because every Member State has its own priorities, every Member State has its own organisation and every Member State applies things in its own way. Therefore, the idea was to create an agency to help Member States to do the job, to co-operate between them and do the job together. The feasibility study, and that is in the best traditions of Community decision, was contracted but at the same time the heads of state in the last meeting before the accession of new Member States from eastern Europe wanted to decide on the place of the agencies, and in the first drafts they did not include an agency for which the Commission had not yet made a proposal, but after the negotiation it appeared that in the last draft there was a kind of recital in which the Commission was invited to come forward urgently with a proposal on a Community Control Agency which should be located in Vigo in Spain. At that moment it was only Spain, but the Spanish Government at that stage had already said that this would be Vigo in Galicia, so we had not even started the feasibility study at that time but—

Q658 *Chairman:* But we know where it is going to go!

Mr Koster: But these are the good traditions, I would say, of decision-making at Community level. That is a little bit of history of the Agency.

Q659 *Viscount Brookeborough:* Looking at your experience to date, what would you identify as the strengths and weaknesses of your performance thus far, being self-critical, and what indicators do you rely on in making this assessment?

Mr Koster: It is a little bit early to have a full assessment of the operation of the Agency. The Agency was created in 2005 and the Commission formed an administrative board which met for the first time in February 2006. They nominated the Director in June and I started my function in September 2006, so we have been operationally active as from January 2007 but with very few people. We have tried to make the best out of it and now we are in 2008 so we are expanding our activities but I cannot say today that we are fully implementing the regulation constituting the Agency. It was a political priority that we would deliver very fast on our core activities. It was felt that after the reform in 2002 the process to establish the Agency had taken quite some years and, given the fact that there was not a proper level playing field, it was a priority to deliver as fast as we could on the operational co-ordination. We started in 2007 taking over the NAFO vessel that was in international waters outside Canadian waters. The Commission have traditionally had an inspection vessel and Commission inspectors carried out inspections under the NAFO scheme. That was not really a Commission task and the Commission has been criticised by its own audit services that this was not really a task for the Commission because control and enforcement is a primary task of Member States and the Member States concerned—Spain, Portugal and other Member States—should do this by themselves, so we had also as a first urgent duty to take over this vessel as from January. The Commission still financed that in 2007 and we had to take over and operate the vessel, which we have done, with national inspectors on board of the Member States concerned and with one co-ordinator of the Agency on board, and so we have run the scheme and this has caused very little disruption from the activity which was carried out beforehand by the Commission. During 2007 we brokered a deal between Member States concerned on burden-sharing because all Member States have to share the burden, Spain 50%, Portugal about 30%, and then other Baltic Member States—Poland, Germany—all share smaller quantities. We have brokered burden-sharing on the basis of the fishing activities in the reference period. That was all agreed and so we have chartered on behalf of the Baltic States and Poland an EU inspection vessel and other Member States decided to deploy their own inspection vessels in the NAFO area. Meanwhile, also, Portugal had difficulties with their own navy vessel and so we had to charter very urgently an inspection vessel for Portugal as well but that operation is running and we have extended this year as well with port inspections to having exchange of inspectors between Member States and to carry out also a number of port inspections mixed in. In the North Sea we have started discussions with all those Member States surrounding the North Sea. I want to say here that I am very grateful for all the co-operation which we got from all the Member States around the North Sea. We adopted our first joint deployment plan in July. We did eight campaigns last year. We had about 130 days of operation during the campaigns in the second half of last year, which was quite good, so the experience in the North Sea was good, I think, because we followed the model that inspection patrol vessels and aeroplanes are pooled and then they are jointly deployed. There can be only one captain on a vessel so there must be one who is in charge of the co-ordination, and since we have not the means to do it

by the Agency we have asked Member States to volunteer that the co-ordination centres of Member States are in charge of the co-ordination, not only of their own means but also of the means of other Member States. The Scottish Fisheries Protection Agency has guided several campaigns in France and Denmark have guided campaigns. Not all Member States have the same resources. There are Member States which have much better resources than others. You have in the North Sea Belgium which has a very small part of the North Sea. They have not the same means as, for example, Scotland or England or Denmark, so there is quite some difference in the number of means. We have seen that by pooling all these patrol vessels and then we deploy the patrol vessels just across the borders so we ignore national borders. We have asked all Member States also for access to territorial waters. That is still an authorisation to be done by the coastal Member States. Not all Member States have granted access but most of them have. Especially in the southern North Sea and the Eastern Channel it is important because territorial waters take an important proportion of the areas where fishing activities are taking place and in that area in the northern North Sea the territorial waters are not important at all so there we do not need to have access to territorial waters. If you take an example, Germany has a tiny part of the North Sea, which is the German part. They have two very good inspection vessels. If we want to make sure that the Cod Recovery Plan is properly implemented there is not a lot of cod fishing going on in the German part of the North Sea so if we can use these two inspection vessels at a Community level in the northern North Sea where most activities of cod fishing are taking place these means are used in a much more rational way and they are only used in two national waters. In the beginning, when we had the discussions with Member States, there was the comment, "Yes, but that means that you are creating holes in our own system". I think Member States now understand that it is not a competition between the Agency and a Member State. They now understand that they have two options: either they do it themselves in their own waters or we do it together, and if we do it together it is the Agency which can co-ordinate the whole operation. That has political advantages because we are also exchanging inspectors. The inspection vessels operate across the borders. That gives the industry much more a feeling of a level playing field. We are trying to operate as uniformly as we can. We exchange best practices and in this way for an individual Member State this will have a political advantage because they will not have their own fishermen on their back who say, "Yes, but you are much more strict than your neighbour", because this is a joint operation. We have had quite positive reactions from the fishing industry even where we found very serious infringements. It allows us also to discuss with the RAC. Fishermen often complain about complexity of rules. I think they are right in many cases; the rules are very complex. Even inspectors sometimes have difficulty understanding the rules, but on the other hand, if you find infringements, if they have blinders in their nets, that is not complicated. If you have a blinder in your net that is pretty deliberate and it is not very complicated: you put a net inside the other one to restrict the mesh size. They also have other operations when they put a chafer around the content and they pull it together and they fix it with little cords which snap if the net comes to the surface, which are very deliberate attempts to reduce the selectivity of the trawl. On the one hand they say yes, the rules are complicated, which is true, but there are also very deliberate infringements, so I think if we discover this in a joint operation that has a political advantage because this is not only one Member State; it is all the Member States together. It is an advantage also if there are fundamental problems, because in some cases this relates to compromises which have been made in December in the middle of the night. If you take the sole fishery, at a certain moment the mesh size needed to be increased and the Commission had proposed 80 millimetres for the mesh size, but in a night compromise they made a compromise not to adjust the minimum size of the fish, and so the minimum size of the fish, the small sole, remained the same, but if you then apply 80 millimetres you are losing legal fish and there are not many fishermen who want to lose legal fish because sole is very expensive, so there is an incentive to use blinders or other restrictions because they can get a bigger return from legal fish which they take out of the sea. If we discover these things together the Commission will have to deal with them because it is not Member State which turns to the Commission. I think we can turn to the Commission as a group of Member States around the North Sea and say, "In this particular case we think that the legislation should be changed". These are all advantages. We are also more effective if we work together because the inspection activities become much more coherent and they therefore become more effective. We can use in the southern North Sea and the Eastern Channel, because we regularly use four inspection vessels at the same time and they change areas. The fishermen have a tendency to follow where the inspection vessel is and sometimes if it is far away they feel themselves quite safe, but if you have four inspection vessels which are manoeuvring just from one area to another they are every time surprised again. Maybe that is only an effect which we have at the beginning and later on if they are used to it they adapt, but I think it was an important experience and Member States felt that doing things together added to the value. If you ask me which indicators we need

for proper regulation, we are not yet so far, so for the moment we do not have indicators yet. There was some initial experience. There was a very good mood among control authorities to do things together. They felt happy that if they did things together they could easily accommodate criticism from the fishing industry, so therefore I think this experience was felt to be more positive, but we will have to see how it develops further. In terms of how it develops further, we also should reflect that at sea maybe it is not the most efficient way to control fisheries. It is very expensive and we need to think of the landing controls. We did also quite a number of landing controls with a mixed team of inspectors but there I think we have to realise that the inspectors who are working in other Member States are only observers. I think in the future therefore we have to reflect on whether they should not have the right to draw up an inspection form. At sea they have the right because in international waters each inspector, because we have created Community inspectors with our national inspectors who are trained in Community and common fisheries legislation, has the right to draw up an inspection report to ensure security and continuity of evidence, but if there is an infringement then again it is the coastal state which has the first right to follow up the infringement, but the coastal state could also decide to transfer an infringement to the flag state of the vessel, for example. There a Community inspector, who is a national inspector from another Member State, can draw up an inspection report, but if the same inspector comes into a port and is inspecting in the port of another Member State he is not mandated to draw up an inspection report; also not in territorial waters because Member States are then afraid that this is prejudicing the third pillar but I think we could live with it if they have no police powers. That is not necessary but the only right which an inspector should have is that he is allowed to draw up an inspection report and then only as a fisheries inspector. There are still many things which we have to consider. In the Baltic we get a number of complaints and also in the Baltic we have a lot of experience already. The Baltic is again a different situation and we have survived in spite of all the difficulties which we had last year with one Member State which did not want to comply with Community law, but we still managed to keep co-operation among all the services, including the Polish inspection service, and we had some good experience with that. I think that is the basis of it this year. We are in discussions with the Member States because the sea campaigns which we do are not good enough. The main problem is the landing inspections, and so there also we have already had several meetings with Member States wherein the Agency is asking Member States to exchange more inspectors to reinforce the landing inspections, notably in Poland because there are weaknesses in the system. This year we also are involved in blue fin tuna. We have set up a control scheme which is a little bit different because that is co-ordinated from the Agency and we have these national officials from France, Spain and Italy who are seconded by their governments and are working in the Agency. These are national co-ordinators so every day we share all the information. We get satellite information, we get information from inspections and surveillance and we then guide inspection vessels to the areas which at Community level are the most important for the blue fin tuna fishing activities. For the moment the fishing has not really started on a large scale and we also have a lot of co-operation from the Mediterranean Member States. We have got a lot of means but we have to see how that continues when it is gets really sensitive in the main part of the season which starts perhaps in a week's time, and then the catches will explode, and I think we may reach Community quota in early June and then it should be stopped very quickly because if we are one day too late the catches in one day are then huge.

Chairman: Thank you very much. I think what we are going to have to do, because we have so many questions and relatively little time, is prioritise the questions and I will start with Baroness Jones on the culture of compliance.

Q660 *Baroness Jones of Whitchurch:* We went to Scotland last week and one of the interesting things there when we were talking to the Scottish Fisheries Protection Agency was that they talked about the fact that increasingly their evidence came from other fishermen, that other fishermen were telling them when illegal fishing was going on. I cannot remember if they gave a proportion but they certainly said that that was very helpful. I wondered if that was symptomatic of the changing culture of compliance. I wondered how widespread you thought that was and what else needs to be done to create that atmosphere where people do recognise the need for enforcement and also, dare I say it, shop their colleagues if they think they are not living up to the same standards that individuals are.

Mr Koster: Every industry should have a culture of compliance. You cannot have an industry which consists of anarchists, to put it a little strongly. I think in the past in fisheries the fishermen were really individuals and they acted sometimes a little bit anarchistic and did not really follow a culture of compliance. I think that is essential. We have to establish a culture of compliance because that is for the fishing industry the only way to survive. If we want to achieve sustainable exploitation of resources the only way to do it is to create a culture of compliance. The example in Scotland is not the only example in the Community. We have other areas

where we have the same problems. In some areas they have come to grips with the situation. In other areas they have not really come to grips with it yet, and I have already pointed to Poland. There are other situations in the Community where the fishing industry and the Member States have not come to grips with the situation.

Q661 *Baroness Jones of Whitchurch:* When you say "with the situation" do you mean with the need to comply?

Mr Koster: To explain what was black fish in Scotland, black fish in Scotland is less black than you think. It is rather grey, I would say. In Scotland one of the issues was the quantity which they had in the boxes.

Q662 *Chairman:* Packing the boxes?

Mr Koster: Yes. Now in the boxes there are about 45 kilos and you can see if you are in Peterhead that all the boxes are filled to the same level. If you had come into Peterhead about ten years ago you would have seen that the boxes were packed even with the top on the boxes.

Q663 *Baroness Jones of Whitchurch:* So that is counted as one box?

Mr Koster: That was counted as one box and that was also counted as a weight of about 45 kilos. I can tell you, I have taken the figures for 1996 because the situation at that time—and it is still the same situation—was that the boxes were not weighed in Peterhead. They are still not weighed today but each fishermen has to put 45 kilos in the box and I want to believe that today there are 45 kilos in a box and they are filled to the same level and I think that is about 45 kilos. In the past they were filled far more but then the Scottish Fisheries Protection Agency had a duty to weigh a number of boxes to see what was the actual weight in the boxes. In 1996 in Peterhead there were more than 1.2 million boxes landed. A little bit more than 7,000 were controlled. Only for the 7,000 was the weight adjusted because for the others there was no proof that there was too much weight in the boxes. Everybody could see that there was a big pile of fish but if Commission inspectors then said, "Why do you not weigh more?", they would say, "We do not have enough resources", so every day there was somebody paid by the Scottish Fisheries Protection Agency to weigh a number of boxes but that was maybe one per cent of the total number of boxes.

Q664 *Earl of Arran:* Was the ice included in the weight?

Mr Koster: I think the Commission inspectors weighed certain boxes where there were 70 kilos of fish, which was almost double the quantity which should have been in the boxes, and only the ones which were weighed had the weight corrected because they had established that there was a different weight in the box, but for all the rest there was no proof. It is a pretty grey situation.

Q665 Baroness Jones of Whitchurch: What has happened to change that, or has it changed?
Mr Koster: That is a good question. It has changed; it has absolutely changed. I was so lucky because I had to go to Scotland in about 2001. We were then doing the preparation of the 2002 reform of the Common Fisheries Policy and I had found letters in the files from, I think, 1988 where the Commission discussed average box weight with the Scottish authorities and where the Scottish authorities accepted that they should establish an average box weight, and then during the next ten years I found that on regular occasions the matter of average box weights was discussed and they always said yes and it was never done, and so I was the one who went then, during the preparation of the Green Paper. I had to go to Scotland and say, "Now enough", and that the Commission would start infringement procedures, and I went also to London to announce that now it was enough. They explained how difficult it was for them to control with all these landing ports in Scotland, and also in England they said, "Yes, but we have improved", but then Mr Fischler said, "If I am going to have a reform of the Common Fisheries Policy the Commission has also a responsibility". The Commission can start infringement procedures. If you say in France, because they have not respected the minimum size of hake for 20 years, that that is symbolic of the non-application of the Common Fisheries Policy and there are black fish", the French say, "Yes, but there is black fish in Scotland, so also black fish in Scotland is symbolic of the non-application of the Common Fisheries Policy". Everybody points to Spain. Then I started infringement proceedings for the cases which are symbolic of the non-application of the Common Fisheries Policy. This then had to go back to the court for France for insufficient enforcement of over-sized hake landings, for the UK and for Spain. For France the difference was that there had already been a ruling in 1992. France was condemned for not complying with Community obligations, so for France it was the second time. When the Commission is doing this for the second time it can ask the Court to impose a penalty. The Commission then proposed to the Court that it impose a penalty. The Court imposed first a penalty for not complying during ten years with these Community obligations, plus an amount of money which France had to pay for each six months that they did not comply with this obligation, and France paid about €80 million which was deducted from the Community contributions to France for the agricultural policy. For the UK and

Spain this was not possible because this was the first infringement procedure. Mr Fischler wanted to make a press release, so when we did the press release we put in it that we estimated that about 50% of the cod landed in the UK was black. When Tesco and Marks and Spencer saw these press releases they asked their Scottish providers, "We want you to sign that we get only legal cod in our shops", and then, as I understood later, there was a big panic in Scotland because no supplier wanted to sign that he was only selling legal fish. Afterwards I think they did a very good job in Scotland and also the industry made their buyers and sellers scheme and they now have a culture of compliance. I do not say that there is nothing going wrong any more, but I think broadly speaking things are correct and there is now a culture of compliance, which must be really difficult this year because there is much more cod than expected and it must be difficult for fishermen not to take on some additional cod, which is quite expensive, or even to have to discard it. It must give them a lot of pain.

Q666 Lord Palmer: Last October the Court of Auditors issued a damning report on control and enforcement, and I would be interested to know what you thought of it, and do you consider that there is the political will on the part of Member State governments to address the problems identified and to make full use of the available enforcement tools?
Mr Koster: That is a difficult question to reply to. First of all the Court of Auditors did a very good job because they made a very good report. Of course, many of the findings are already in Commission reports. The Commission have already produced reports in the past about the control and many findings are based on these reports, but I think they did quite a balanced report which shows that in the Common Fisheries Policy we have not managed to implement it properly. There were very good intentions on capacity but since the 2002 reform there has not really been a reduction in capacity. In certain areas yes, there was. For example, in Scotland there is a culture of compliance, but if there had not been the decommissioning of an important number of vessels it would have been impossible to create a culture of compliance because one of the elements of it is that a fishermen should have a viable living and must have the legal quantities to support a viable living. In general, however, I think the 2002 reform has not brought about an important reduction in capacity, which is the most fundamental issue which we have to bring about. I think we have been lucky lately because of the high fuel prices and the economy in fisheries, especially trawl fisheries, is turning worse and there have been many vessels which have been offered for decommissioning in several Member States. I think the changes in the policy itself which were made in the 2002 reform have not really brought

about the reduction in capacity which is necessary to re-establish a balance. We have got improvements in control but not really on the capacity side. We have since implemented fishing effort reductions as a scheme and we have also reduced fishing effort, which was good, but this is not sufficient by itself. It is much more important that we reduce the number of vessels and then reduce only the time that each vessel can be at sea. In that sense the 2002 reform did not bring about a reduction in capacity. Now the Court of Auditors has written this report which has come at a good time. The Commission will now propose again a reinforcement of control but we also need to work on other issues, such as capacity, and I think that will be essential for re-establishing that balance. Since the issue of fishing is politically much more sensitive, I think it is also fairly important to work on the market side. If the big buyers insist on selling only legal fish I think also that will be very important for reducing the outtake and reducing the quantities of fish on the market. We need also to work more on the market side to make sure that there are limitations. There is the political will in Member States to enforce this. We have all democratic Member States and a fishing minister will always listen to its fishing industry. If there is no culture of compliance or if there is still an industry which thinks it can grasp advantages from non-compliance there will always be pressure on the Member State concerned to look a little bit less strictly at what is happening and that will be a problem in ensuring proper implementation of the Common Fisheries Policy.

Q667 Lord Cameron of Dillington: I want to talk to you about decentralisation. It is the future not only of the RACs but also of the whole policy. The policy has been decided centrally but implemented according to Member States' own ways and technical solutions. How would you cope with that in a future world?
Mr Koster: Decentralisation for me has also to do with regionalisation. When I became Director of the Agency one of the first things which the board members insisted on was that if we were undertaking the work of the Agency this must be on a regional basis. I had to organise the Agency on a regional basis. It is now also the Commission, this DG Mare, which is organised with regional directions. I think Mr Borg has emphasised very often that we cannot continue with a one-size-fits-all approach if we have a Community with 27 Member States. We cannot continue to say that we need to respect all kinds of requirements, that in the Black Sea it should be respected in the same way as in the Baltic, so I think that is the kind of policy which does not work. It is technocratic. Also, the Community must be based on a political approach and I think the approach must be on a regional basis. If we have the North Sea then

we need to bring together the stakeholders from all Member States, and they can consider together how they want to go about this conservation and exploitation of resources in the North Sea. They can make sensible proposals to the Commission and I think they could agree what for them means sustainable exploitation.

Q668 Lord Cameron of Dillington: Do you have the resources to deal with the different solutions they are going to come up with?
Mr Koster: For the moment we have set up our activities on a regional basis. We do not have a lot of resources. I do not think I need a lot of resources because I am relying mostly on the resources of Member States and I am organising co-operation between Member States, so there are Member States' competent authorities which have quite a number of resources. Others have less, but I think if we are organising co-operation on the level of the North Sea the big services will take on the smaller ones and I think we can use that together. The Agency is independent and I have a desk with co-ordinators. If I have one desk manager and three or four co-ordinators for the North sea then for the rest I am relying on the national authorities and on the staff of national authorities. Of course, the most expensive part is still in the Member State. For me, if I spend Community money, I spend maybe a few per cent. If you calculate the total costs—patrol vessels and aeroplanes—they are very expensive.

Q669 Lord Cameron of Dillington: But you have to police the Member States.
Mr Koster: I do not police myself. I use Community inspectors which are designated by Member States and they can work across borders, so it is the national inspectors who are doing the job. I have to train them. That is costing money for me. I need to have some resources for training these inspectors and I need to have resources for co-ordinating the national means, but I do not need to have a hell of a lot. If you come to Edinburgh with the Scottish Fisheries Protection Agency you will see the co-ordination centre for them. If they co-ordinate their own means in the Scottish part of the North Sea with the same number of people they can also co-ordinate the whole North Sea because they have all the facilities, they have skilled people, and so we are also giving them some co-ordinators from the Agency in the co-ordination centre. We are putting liaison officers in from other Member States and so I do not need to. If there is this operational co-operation in the North Sea the fishing industry which operates in the North Sea will feel this is much more of a level playing field. In the Baltic we can adopt maybe different solutions which are more appropriate for the Baltic because there are smaller vessels operating in that area. In the

Mediterranean we have adopted again a somewhat different approach with which Member States are happy.

Lord Cameron of Dillington: Is it effective in the Mediterranean? One gets the impression that—

Q670 Chairman: Hang on. Yes or no to that and then we have to go.

Mr Koster: It is too early.

Chairman: Even better! Thank you very much indeed for your time. It has been very helpful.

Memorandum by Elspeth Attwool MEP

What follows is an expression of my own personal views and should not be attributed to the Fisheries Committee of the European Parliament or to my political group

CONSERVATION/MANAGEMENT

1. The recovery plans, management plans and emergency measures introduced following Regulation 2371/2002 have brought improvements in general but the success of each has depended on its individual features. For example, the Cod Recovery Plan was initially regarded as having failed, despite evidence of an increase in stocks. Arguably, this was because the targets set were unrealistic in terms of the speed expected.

Long term management plans are clearly preferable to year on year decision taking as they provide for a better balance between the sustainability of fish stocks and the sustainability of the fishing industry. The main issues here are the degree of flexibility that should be built into them and the method of measurement used. Much depends on the accuracy of scientific evidence and assessment and the models used for computation. Maximum sustainable yield is favoured by many but there are some doubts as to whether the concept is adequately refined and. in particular, whether it is applicable to mixed fisheries. See the Report of the European Parliament Fisheries Committee at http://www.europarl.europa.eu/oeil/file.jsp?id = 5386052

Also, some plans and measures have been less beneficial than they might because of a delay in putting them in place. Plans for the Mediterranean and measures relating to ghost fishing of the north-west of Scotland might be cited as cases in point.

2. On my understanding, Total Allowable Catches and Quotas were initially introduced as market measures. They have, however, effectively become converted to tools for conservation. There must at least be a question over whether they are really fit for this purpose. It has to be accepted that, if conservation is to be taken seriously, management measures must relate to sustainability criteria, so that something akin to TACs must be in place. Quotas, however, can be counterproductive to conservation, particularly where mixed fisheries are concerned.

Effort limitation, including "days at sea", marine conservation areas and real time closures all have rote to play. "Days at sea" have the advantage of simplifying control but can bear heavily on fishermen in respect of fuel prices and bad weather, particularly where found in combination with a quota system. Marine conservation areas and real time closures are both of considerable value but are much more likely to have the desired effect if established in close consultation with stakeholders. The recent voluntary agreement by Scots fishermen to close areas where there is an abundance of undersized cod deserves to be copied elsewhere.

Rights based management tools effectively operate already at all levels of the Common Fisheries Policy but they are varied in form and sometimes inchoate. At times transfer of the rights for economic value is encompassed and sometimes it is not. Rights based management is sometimes equated with Individual Transferable Quotas (ITQs) but this is only one possible form of such management. See further the Report of the European Parliament Fisheries Committee (scheduled for the April Mini Plenary Session) at http://www.europarl.europa.eu/oeil/file.jsp?id = 5484612

Technical conservation measures contribute considerably to conservation but more support for research is needed and it would be helpful, too, if fishermen could be brought to adopt them through incentives rather than imposition.

3. Discarding is not solely the result of the quota system, since high grading is also a possibility, but there cannot be any doubt that quotas are a major cause, particularly where mixed fisheries are concerned. On how best to tackle the issue, see the Report of the European Parliament Fisheries Committee at http://www.europarl.europa.eu/oeil/file.jsp?id = 5484622

CONTROL/ENFORCEMENT

4. I feel that it is early days to comment on the efficacy of the Community Fisheries Control Agency but the systems that have been in place are clearly in need of improvement. One of the problems within Community waters is the lack of adequate resources being deployed at member state level. Here the planned reduction south of the Border in monitoring by the Royal Navy is a cause for concern. The plans that the Control Agency is establishing for the pooling of resources between member states could undoubtedly assist overall but there is a danger that these could simply turn into cost cutting exercises rather than bringing increased surveillance. I would argue that more resources also need to be deployed outside Community waters, too, if IUU fishing is to be tackled effectively, and that there is a special responsibility, too, for adequate monitoring and control in the areas where fisheries partnership agreements have been established.

5. There is a clear case for establishing a uniform level of minimum sanctions for serious infringements across the EU. That said, this should be understood as meaning a minimum, as there is clearly room for a measure of upwards discretion relating to the extent of the infringement, how far it seems to have been deliberate/inadvertent and whether it is repeat offence or not.

STRUCTURAL POLICY

6. The extent of capacity reduction across the member states has been rather varied. Where it has been extensive, this has not always been adequately recognised in relation to quota allocation. A sufficient distinction is not always made between artisanal and distance fishing fleets.

7. Because of the time it has taken to put operational programmes in place, it is too soon to comment on the actual operation of the EFF. There are concerns, however, that the amounts allocated to it are inadequate, particularly in the light of the increase in the number of member states with fishing fleets consequent upon enlargement.

8. My only comment concerning subsidies is that ways need to be found of assisting fishermen with and compensating them for necessary adjustments that are WTO compatible, at least until such time as the proper balance between the sustainability of stocks and the sustainability of the industry has been struck.

GOVERNANCE

10. There is no doubt in my mind that Regional Advisory Councils have made a major contribution to fisheries management, with the North Sea and Western Waters RACs important pioneers in this regard. I believe that they should be given increased responsibility for management of the areas that they covet, becoming capable of taking actual management decisions subject to this fitting within policy guidelines established at EU level. Some concerns have been expressed as to whether this approach is compatible with conservation of marine biological resources being an exclusive EU competence, particularly since this is incorporated into the Lisbon Treaty. As RACs can be seen as "arms" of the EU itself, however, this exclusivity should not, in my view, operate as a barrier to their acquiring decision making powers.

11. One of the major problems with EU fisheries policy has been micro management at BU level and a tendency to treat what may actually be quite discrete fisheries as if they were all on a par. A regional management model would be both appropriate and feasible, allowing greater communication between scientists and those engaged in the fishing industry.

On a more general level, I would add that there are difficulties at any level in operating a management model that involves both the regulation of output (such as quotas) and input (such as "days at sea"). In my own personal view, consideration at least should be given to the advantages and disadvantages of moving to a system of input regulation, involving different types of effort limitation, provided a way could be devised of ensuring that this remained compatible with the principle of relative stability—for example, by limiting the right to harvest to certain geographical areas, found in the tom of rights based management that concentrates on territorial use (TURFs).

February 2008

Examination of Witnesses

Witnesses: MR IAN HUDGHTON MEP (SNP), MS ELSPETH ATTWOOLL MEP (Lib Dem), MR STRUAN STEVENSON MEP (Conservative), and MS CATHERINE STIHLER MEP (Labour), European Parliament, examined.

Q671 Chairman: Good afternoon, and thank you for coming to assist us in our inquiry. Could our MEPs introduce themselves please for the sake of the record, then I think the best way of starting is to ask you to say how you would like the Common Fisheries Policy to progress and what would be the main elements of any reform.

Ms Stihler: I am Catherine Stihler, one of the Labour MEPs, and I represent Scotland.

Mr Hudghton: I am Ian Hudghton, one of the SNP Members of the European Parliament and a long-term member of the Fisheries Committee.

Mr Stevenson: I am Struan Stevenson, a Conservative Member of the European Parliament, a member of the Fisheries Committee. I was Chairman of the Fisheries Committee for two and a half years.

Ms Attwooll: I am Elspeth Attwooll, Liberal Democrat Member of the European Parliament, a member of the Fisheries Committee since I was elected in 1999 and currently one of its Vice Chairs.

Ms Stihler: We were given the list of questions and I thank you for inviting us to have the opportunity to speak with you. Just in summary, Elspeth, Struan, Ian and myself worked hard on the 2002 reform of the Common Fisheries Policy where we saw the introduction of Regional Advisory Councils, the end to EU money for subsidising boat-building, which is a great success for us, and the protection of relative stability which we wanted to see there and in terms of the preservation of historic fishing rights. For this next reform, how do we go forward with the review on the work of the Regional Advisory Councils? We know that Joe Borg will come forward in the next few weeks with his own analysis of what is happening with RACs, which is of great interest to us. Again, the issue of relative stability and historic fishing rights and the preservation of those for the United Kingdom and in particular for Scotland are also very important. In the recent report, which I had to withdraw my name from, we saw the very real threat that the issue of relative stability was being undermined and that we needed to do our utmost to protect that very basic principle of the Common Fisheries Policy, but then on discards, conservation, and finally again on the retention of relative stability, those are the ways I see in terms of the health check that is going to happen on the Common Fisheries Policy in the next few months. We were told that the next Fisheries Council meeting in September will include this debate about the health check and the Common Fisheries Policy, so we wait with interest to see the results from that, but we are very conscious that the reform in 2012 of the Common Fisheries Policy is only four years away and we really need to get our act together now to see what we would like to see come out of that reform.

Mr Hudghton: Thank you for this opportunity. I think it is fair to say that, in the run-up to the 2002 reform, in Scotland politically, as well as Scotland in terms of its diverse range of fisheries business interests, were united in proposing something that did not happen at the end of the day, and that was zonal management as opposed to regional advisory input. I was certainly extremely disappointed that Scotland had put so much work over a two-year period or more into a well argued case for a more local element to have real control over the management of the resource, which is fisheries. Since then we have seen substantial scrapping of vessels in Scotland and a very substantial reduction in the number of people involved in the industry, but as a result, I suppose it could be said, an element of stability for those who are still active in the fish catching sector. Already, as Catherine has said, the 2012 review which was part of that 2002 agreement is not just being spoken about but actively considered in the Commission, in terms of interests in Scotland, the Government and the industry, and the Commission last July received a report from a couple of scientists which it had commissioned. It has not been published although it has been leaked all over the place and it is pretty damning in its introduction to the conclusions that have been provided to the Commission as a result of this request, that it is a "top-down, command and control fisheries management instrument, its objectives are broad and do not provide much guidance on how to manage fisheries", and then it goes on to list a substantial number of areas where the CFP has basically failed, including the status of stocks. We would not have a crisis and the need for recovery plans if the CFP had been successful over its life. We had another exchange of views with Commissioner Borg on Monday afternoon here in our committee and it was about the priorities of 2009 and the implications of the Lisbon Treaty, but amongst all of that he said that he was of the view that a "root and branch" reform—those were his words—of the CFP was what he had in mind and he hopes that the present Commission will make some progress on that before handing over to the new Commission in 2009. I would agree that we are in need of a root and branch reform of the CFP, but, of course, there may be different ideas about the nature of "root and branch". Mine would be pretty straightforward, namely, that we do indeed build upon the tentative steps towards stakeholder involvement through Regional Advisory Councils and I would certainly be looking for a root and branch reform of the CFP to mean absolute devolution of management, the return of real management control of the whole business of fisheries management and conservation to sensible areas like the North Sea. I was interested to note at the same committee meeting that we had here on Monday when we had Mr Fotiadis, the new Director of DG Mare, that he was talking about maritime policy being devised, constructed and managed in logical maritime basins. If that is logical and sensible for maritime policy in general I hope that that kind of thinking finds its way into the Commission to begin with and indeed into Member States' thinking in terms of reform of the CFP.

Mr Stevenson: Again, can I echo my thanks to the House of Lords for inviting us to come and say something about this. Like Ian, I believe that the CFP has been something of a disaster for the UK which has seen roughly 60% of our white fish fleet scrapped and decommissioned over the last five years, and, of course, with far fewer vessels now chasing white fish there is a better living to be had; it is inevitable. The fishermen are doing better. We have seen new white fish boats being built without any subsidy. One of the things that we have achieved in the last five years has been doing away with subsidy for new build, which was ludicrous, while at the same time Member States were subsidising the decommissioning of vessels, so we were subsidising vessels being broken up in Britain while the Spanish were subsidising new vessels being built, all to catch our white fish. We have done away with that and the Spanish are still nibbling at the edges trying to reintroduce it by the back door. They are asking for subsidies for safety measures, for refurbishment, for improving fuel efficiency, for hygiene and welfare of the crew and all the rest of it, so we have to beware that we do not allow this subsidy to creep in by the back door. Our opinion here really has been that the CFP has been driven, as far as the North Sea is concerned, by the Cod Recovery Plan. Everything has been focused on cod recovery. We have seen again and again ICES making their annual recommendation that the cod fishery should be reduced to zero because the cod stocks were not recovering but they have then gone on to say that because it is a mixed fishery we should also reduce the haddock catch despite the fact that we have seen three really excellent years of haddock stocks with an abundance of haddock on the grounds. They have been talking about cutting the nephrops fishery because, again, the occasional cod gets caught. The cod is hardly even any longer a targeted species by the fishermen in the North Sea. It is not an important fishery. Haddock and nephrops are highly important fisheries and for the fishermen to be told to cut those species to save cod is not going down terribly well, as you can imagine. The fishermen also deny that they are entirely responsible, although they admit that there has been heavy over-exploitation of cod in years gone by. They say that

that is not the only reason the cod stocks have diminished and that it is necessary for ICES and the scientists to look at the other reasons. For instance, we have taken evidence from and visited Plymouth University where they have studied over 60 years the movement of calanus, the phyto-plankton on which cod larvae feed, and they have noted that the calanus has moved several hundred miles north in search of colder waters. This may be climate change, it may be cyclical. In fact, there is some evidence that many hundreds of years ago the cod moved out of the North Sea at that time as well and it could be a cyclical thing; they could start coming back. The cod, the scientists tell us, are a very slow evolving creature and continue to spawn in the same grounds that they have always spawned in and, of course, the young cod larvae find that there are no phyto-plankton for them to feed on. The calanus has all moved up to waters around Iceland and Norway and there is huge mortality as a result amongst the cod larvae. That is part of the reason that cod stocks have diminished. In addition, there is the seal problem, the problem that dare not mention its name. You cannot speak about it. In all of the studies that you hear from the Commission you never see a mention of seals but we know for a fact that there are now about 160,000 grey seals in the North Sea. They eat on average a couple of tonnes of fish each a year. That is a hell of a lot of fish. It is a lot more than our fishermen are allowed to catch, and at least some of that will be cod. We have studies that prove that. We are not allowed to take account of that in any of the studies that we do in the Commission and that is ludicrous; that is political correctness gone mad. We should be allowed to take into account the deprivation of the cod population, or indeed fish stocks in general, by seals. After all these years of the ICES telling us that we should stop catching cod and close the fishery it was remarkable that this past year we were suddenly told by ICES, "Actually the cod stocks are recovering and you can start catching them". Having ignored them for the last ten years and having been blamed by the WWF and Greenpeace for ignoring the scientific advice, we now find that the scientific advice could not have been entirely correct because suddenly the cod stocks, despite our having ignored their advice, have begun to recover and they have agreed that there should be a certain cod TAC set this year. Against all of that background I am not a fan of the Common Fisheries Policy and I agree with Ian that what we should see is devolved management down to involving the Regional Advisory Councils, involving scientists at that level with the fishermen and getting them working together. When we come on to discuss discards later we can talk about the more intrusive management that I think is going to be necessary and which has been tried and tested elsewhere. Finally, I have to say that when Mr Fotiadis was telling us about the new set-up for DG Mare, and Elspeth Attwooll raised this very salient point, he was talking about six new units and we will see that there will be a directorate for the Baltic Sea, the North Sea and landlocked Member States with a Director-General, John Richardson, and that will include under its jurisdiction Belgium, Denmark, Germany, Estonia, Latvia, Lithuania, the Netherlands, Poland, Finland, Sweden and the landlocked Member States, but the UK will be under Directorate C, which is the Arctic, Atlantic and Outermost Regions; presumably that is because of our attitude to the CFP, and that will include Ireland, Spain, France, Portugal and the UK and that will be under Director-General Richard Priebe. Separately, in Directorate A under Mr Deben Alfonso, we see the Common Fisheries Policy and Aquaculture. He will have jurisdiction over that. It seems to me that this is not a terribly clever reorganisation of the new DG Mare and that the position that the UK finds itself in is such that the company we are keeping there with Spain, France and Portugal may not be to our long term wellbeing, particularly when the North Sea is in a different directorate. That does not make sense.

Ms Attwooll: My thanks too for the invitation to speak to you. Since 2002 we have had limited but nonetheless very positive steps towards improving the Common Fisheries Policy in the sense of trying for much longer term planning, more stakeholder involvement and moves towards, if not decentralised management, at least greater sensitivity to local conditions and I think this is reflected in the most recent proposal for cod recovery, which seems to me to reflect a lot of the concerns that were put forward by a stakeholder symposium in Edinburgh. I would agree with my colleagues that we need to move towards a much greater role for Regional Advisory Councils and towards decentralised management. I was not, because of problems with flights, at the part of the meeting where it was suggested that there might be a root and branch reform of the Common Fisheries Policy There are two comments that I would like to make, however, in relation to the possibilities that might involve. For a long time I have had a purely personal concern about the compatibility of a system which manages fisheries at one and the same time through quotas and through effort management. It seemed to me that quotas were initially introduced as a market mechanism in order to make sure that prices were reasonably sustained and they have now been converted into a conservation mechanism, and marrying them with effort management as well I think creates a large number of complications. As your questions also ask about rights-based management, I think perhaps I should touch on this and in particular comment on

the nature of the European Parliament debate on the issue. In my original report I tried to make it clear that there were various different types of rights-based management and that in fact individual transferable quotas, which are basically tradable quotas, should not be confused with rights-based management. They are simply one form of it. However, it was quite clear that the impetus to discuss this coming from the Commission was from the economists in the Commission, and I think various issues came out in the course of the discussion, which I have to say in a sense was polarised in the European Parliament, and because there were differing imperatives somehow in the course of the amendments we came out with a relatively balanced report which did admit that there are advantages in having transferable, indeed tradable, quotas in terms of reduction of capacity, but these can at the same time bring certain disadvantages as well. One thing that has become clear in the course of the discussions, and certainly is clear if you look at the way that what I want to call tradable quotas were introduced in Iceland, is that unless you have a limit on the amount that individuals can acquire you can have a large shrinkage in the number of people engaged in the fishing industry. You can have effectively perhaps not a monopoly but a kind of oligopoly and the problem with that is that it can have adverse effects on fisheries-dependent communities when the fishing rights pass into a limited number of hands. We do in the UK at the moment have, as I understand it, a somewhat inchoate system of individual transferable or tradable quotas and I can see both the advantages and the disadvantages of those. I think we have not actually yet paid enough attention to the system operating in the Shetland Islands, which is community transferable quotas, and I think this is something that should be investigated more closely. I do have concerns because I think there is an impetus from certain quarters of the European Union to move from a system where some Member States at least allow quotas to be traded between their own fishers towards a European-wide system of individual transferable quotas, and I think the effects of that on relative stability could give very great cause for concern indeed. I think that is all I want to say on the initial questions.

Q672 *Earl of Dundee:* On the prospect of the management of the Common Fisheries Policy, a nice Pavlovian objective from which none of us would wish to dissent, does the panel agree that the RACs should graduate from being an advisory body to a hands-on management one? How much political will within the EU and Member States is there for that to happen, and, if it did happen, which particular benefits would then ensue?

Mr Stevenson: There is no political will for that, except from us perhaps, from our Irish colleagues, maybe from some of the Scandinavians, but the southern Mediterranean Member States see great benefits from the way the CFP has been run. They are inexorably moving towards a rights-based management system of ITQs which would destroy relative stability and they see huge advantages for themselves in that, so they are totally opposed, I would say, to seeing RACs becoming anything other than advisory at any time and they will vote against it all the time. You have heard from all of us that we would see great benefits in devolving management down to that level. Perhaps you could allow the overall supervision to remain in Brussels under the Common Fisheries Policy and devolve the actual hands-on management to that level. Maybe that would be the way of dealing with it but I do not see the political will for it and if the Lisbon Treaty is implemented from 1 January next year the Fisheries Committee will have full co-decision powers, equal powers with the Council, and I would not hold my breath that you would see a majority on our committee in favour of it.

Mr Hudghton: I would not necessarily say that the Regional Advisory Councils as currently constituted would continue to be management bodies but management in logical zones by countries which have fishing entitlements in certain fishing areas like the North Sea. One of the reasons I was less than enthused about the 2002 reform was that it established Regional Advisory Councils but it allowed any Member State to volunteer to sit on any Regional Advisory Council. That has not caused any great difficulty at the moment because they are only advisory, but I most certainly would not envisage having devolved management other than to countries and representatives of countries who have fishing entitlements in particular areas. The big political problem with that scenario is that the CFP as reformed in 2002 states that "there shall be equal access to waters and resources" and there are people around who are looking forward to the day when that might be translated into reality. One of the few protections that we still have, or at least Scotland still has, is relative stability, which was seen as a temporary variation from this principle of equal access to waters and resources, and that is, I think, big political difficulty that surrounds real devolution and real change or "root and branch" change, as the Commissioner described it. That is certainly what I would do.

Ms Attwooll: Could I say that I am not quite as pessimistic as Struan because I have, I think, in recent months, particularly because of problems with blue fin tuna and also because of differing fishing interests in the Mediterranean, detected something of a move towards a more conservation-minded attitude and a recognition that stakeholders do actually need to talk together in order to resolve some of the problems. Certainly there has been pressure from some of my colleagues for a separate Regional Advisory Council for the outermost regions, so those colleagues will obviously have come from the more Mediterranean-type countries. I also detected when we were discussing the funding of Regional Advisory Councils that there was not perhaps quite so much resistance on the part of some of our colleagues to this, so I feel there is a slight softening. I agree that perhaps there is not the same level of enthusiasm yet in all parts of the European Union for this method of doing things but, as I said, I am not quite so pessimistic on this one as perhaps Struan is.

Ms Stihler: As I said previously, we are waiting to see what the evaluation is of the functions of the RACs and we should get that in the next few weeks. The Commissioner told us that when he was in our committee. There is an issue which has just come to mind, that with the new DG and the new structures within the new DG we need to look at how RACs are monitored and supported. I think there are a number of issues that we need to look into but on the whole I think the RACs have worked well, certainly the one that we have been involved with, the North Sea RAC, has worked well, and they have enthusiastic people working within it who all wanted to contribute, which makes a difference when people are wanting to work together. I think this evaluation will be very interesting and I hope that you will get a copy of it when it is published in the next few weeks.

Q673 *Lord Plumb:* You have all been fairly critical to a different level or degree. I assume you still want a Common Fisheries Policy at the end of the day if it can be a policy that is more acceptable and you do not want to get rid of it and you do not necessarily want to go down the regional route, or you may want to go down the regional route but you want a common policy at the end of the day. In terms of the Lisbon Treaty, first we have got the referendum in Ireland and secondly it is being debated in the House of Lords at the moment, not today but it was being debated yesterday; we have got six days of debate on the Lisbon Treaty, one of the proposals is, of course, that we have a referendum in the United Kingdom. We shall see. Subject to it going through, it does mean that you will be involved in a totally different way because of the co-decision procedure. I am disappointed to hear from one or two today that we have been taking evidence from that there are those who say that if the European Parliament is going to be involved that means considerable delays. That disturbs me a bit because, and I have not told my colleagues this as yet, I proposed the co-decision procedure in 1988 and I thought it was time that the Parliament grew up and co-decision has been going for a considerable amount of time. Therefore, in the say that the Parliament has, which is means that they do have a say, you have now a better chance, I would have thought, of reforming the Common Fisheries Policy; in fact, I know you have, but I do not think it is right to wait for debate. You say you want to delay until you hear what is going to be said by the Commission. I think you want to be in there now and say what should happen. I am sure you have to the Commission in your own way, but if you are going to be involved then I do hope that that does not mean a delay, and I would like your views on it, because it should not if you are all party to it and it could be surely that the Parliament itself is ahead of the game and pushing as part of the team rather than hanging about and saying, "We do not like what we see and therefore we will refuse to go along with it", on the decision principally.

Ms Stihler: It has not been the Parliament that been doing it; it is the Council that has been doing it. If you look at the issue of fishing authorisations and the IUU, the Parliament has produced the reports, kept to the timetable, produced our opinions, so in fact it is quite the opposite situation. I thought you might be interested in that. The reason I was talking about waiting to hear about the evaluation of RACs is that it is important before we give RACs more powers to have the evaluation in front of us so that we know that what has been happening has been effective. With regard to the Lisbon Treaty, what is coming out is that the Commissioner said that by the end of the year we would be clear about how we would work within the competences and all this but there is still a lack of clarity in the legal advice we get about the different things that we are going to be involved with. For example, there is a big controversy about the fishing agreements because of what is happening in the developing world and some people say that there is real exploitation of fish and that we are not getting value for money and that the poorest in the world are suffering because we are taking their fish, and so we have the assent procedure now under which we will be able to say yes or no, as far as I can understand, to these fishing agreements. On other issues in terms of conservation and how we work with other committees, one of the debates that is happening is about what will happen with the new structures, such as DG Mare. Should we have maritime as well as fisheries? Should that be how we are structured as a committee? We are also more a neutralised committee which means that we are not as supported in terms of secretariat and also we are considered one of the lesser committees in the Parliament. Many people believe that we should now be considered a full committee rather than a neutralised committee.

These things have to be agreed upon and so I thought I would just share some of those issues with you that have been happening in the committee.

Q674 *Lord Plumb:* Can I just clarify what I really meant? We cannot wait. We are a committee that has to come out with a report, hopefully in July, so therefore we are out in the field to listen and to learn and therefore to try to represent the views of those who are involved in the business. We need your views. It is the future we are concerned about, not the past. We know a lot about the past and some of the difficulties. Our Chairman was minister at the time so it is a long time ago.
Mr Stevenson: We have not forgotten.
Chairman: It is all my fault!

Q675 *Lord Plumb:* I just wanted to say that. That is what we are after. We want to get to grips with this and we want to be helpful and we want to produce a positive report, but we do not want to be giving a history lesson. We want to be saying, "This is where we should be going". I just wanted you to understand what I was saying.
Mr Stevenson: Can I throw something back then in response to what you were asking? You were talking about whether we would favour reform of the CFP in some shape or form. There is a problem at the Member State level just now and it is a problem unique to the UK, and that is co-financing. You will know well how it did not work to our advantage, to our farmers' advantage, and still does not, and it is exactly the same with fishermen. We came up against it this week with the issue of the fuel subsidies that the French and Spanish are giving to their fishermen. If you fill a 4,500-litre, average-sized trawler tank with subsidised red diesel it is costing our fishermen £765 more because of the £230 million subsidy that the French have agreed to give their fishermen. We asked Commissioner Borg on Monday, and he said that they are looking at a sectoral restructuring which will enable this to take place provided it is part of a package of restructuring, and he said, "It is not up to us in the Commission to force a Member State to involve itself in that restructuring, but if they do then there will be money available from Brussels, from the fisheries fund, but on a co-financed basis". Britain will never access that money. We came across this at the time of the decommissioning when major parts of our fleet were being scrapped, and at that time Fischler was the Commissioner. At our request he even held a press conference to plead with the British Government. He said, "The money is here in Brussels. It is ready. Come and access it to help the socio-economic costs of your fishing communities who are going to suffer from the

scrapping of these vessels, but you have to co-finance it." It is on a 50-50 basis. You put one euro on the table, you get one out of Brussels. With us, because of the rebate, it is 71-29. You have to put 71p on the table to get 29p out of Brussels because the rest of the money has already been paid back to the Treasury by way of the clawback, and they have it in their war chest. I am not pointing the finger at this Government or the previous Government. It is any Government in Britain that will not give this kind of aid to fishermen or farmers. They would rather hold on to that money and use it for some other purpose, usually as tax sweeteners before a general election. What a cynical thing to say! It is a unique British problem and until we start accessing the funds that are available in Brussels to help our fishing communities and our fishermen for all sorts of things --- we are talking now, with the discards issue, about perhaps insisting on CCTV being fitted on the decks of all fishing boats. They have just implemented this in Denmark and it is working successfully in Alaska and in New Zealand and it will eventually come, but again you will see every Member State co-financing it, Brussels putting a share in and the Member States putting their share in, and Britain will say, "It is up to the fishermen. They can pay for it themselves", and it will cost them thousands. This is deeply unfair and it puts us at a competitive disadvantage all the time. If you take any message back, and I am sure my colleagues will agree with me on this, this is something that we have to overcome. It is not that the rebate has been a bad thing. It has netted Britain a lot of money back from Brussels, but we have to overcome this problem of a level playing field.

Mr Hudghton: On the substantive question, do I envisage a CFP in some form, not really, not one that could be compared in any way to what we have had anyway, because when I say that I favour the devolution of management to countries, I mean totally and there would be very little that I would envisage the European Union assisting with in terms of the management, which is really the nub of the whole series of problems and bad experiences that we have had. In short, what we need to get to is somewhere where we have never been with the CFP and that is to a position where those who have most to gain from conserving the resource, the fishing communities, have the incentive to conserve for the long term, knowing that they and their families in the future will benefit from the sacrifices that will be required from time to time under management rules, whoever is setting them. That has not been the position and it is not the position if you take the current CFP. Literally, the much talked-about scary Spanish Armada is not that much of a figment of imagination when you look at that one-liner about

"equal access to waters and resources". We have to get rid of that. We have to get real management returned to the countries around the North Sea, the countries in other fishing zones who have fishing entitlement in these areas, so that they themselves can make the rules and benefit from the results.

Ms Attwooll: Could I just say that I agree with Ian on that insofar as we are talking about management by the countries having fishing entitlement in a region. I think it is difficult to imagine having relative stability and historic fishing rights and holding those dear and saying that that is consonant with re-nationalisation because if you look at the pure geography of the United Kingdom and the waters which we effectively share with other people and where, if the line were drawn, our fisheries would then be fishing in other people's waters, I cannot see that as the way forward, but proper regional management by countries with the fishing entitlement in clearly defined zones I think is very much the way forward.

Mr Hudghton: I forgot to mention co-decision. Generally I have welcomed co-decision to the European Parliament. It was a great thing to get started and the more areas that we have it in the better for the whole working of the European Union in general. Fisheries is the one potential example where I am less enthusiastic because it brings in MEPs from half a dozen countries, just as we have ministers from half a dozen countries, who have no interest directly and therefore their input is tradable, buyable, and that brings all of that into the European Parliament. Things may well take longer because in areas where we have co-decision we take it very seriously and we want to do it properly. In an area like fisheries, if we, or whoever is representing Scotland or Britain in the future, actually make some headway in here on fisheries matters then it is possible that we will find ourselves at loggerheads with the Council and therefore we may end up with lots of negotiation, hopefully. That is just the way it works.

Q676 *Chairman:* The discussion that we had with the Commissioner was along the lines of him envisaging, not tomorrow but further down the track, a situation where the EU would "set the policy parameters", was the phrase he used, and that turned out to be setting basically stock mortality rates and then leaving it to some regional management body, undefined but he did not look totally unfavourably upon the gradual emergence of the RACs as playing that role, although it was not absolutely clear, to choose how to get to those policy parameters. Would that approach appeal to you?

Mr Hudghton: Yes.

Mr Stevenson: Very much.

Ms Attwooll: Yes, definitely.

Q677 *Chairman:* Is everybody nodding at that?

Ms Attwooll: Yes.

Mr Hudghton: Yes.

Mr Stevenson: There may be varying degrees of enthusiasm, but yes.

Ms Stihler: I think most of it we will accept. One of the things that keeps coming back in terms of the CFP is the fact that the CFP is part of your membership, part of being part of the European Union.

Q678 *Chairman:* Exactly.

Ms Stihler: And much as there are things that we detest about it, I believe that you reform from within and that is why I think having Commissioner Borg as the Commissioner responsible for fisheries has been very helpful.

Mr Hudghton: Yes.

Q679 *Viscount Brookeborough:* I thought we almost had a male/female split on support for the CFP but if everybody thinks that we can reform it perhaps it is okay. I was interested in what you said about communities and funds for communities. We have just come back from Peterhead and what definitely surprised me, who had only read a lot about that side of the fishing community in the newspapers, was that even after decommissioning and a number of people had left the industry Peterhead is thriving with an unemployment rate of only one per cent, and the people who do remain in fishing are also doing oil rig work, so I am not quite sure where you needed the money from. Perhaps you would like to say something about the other fishing communities who may not be lucky enough to have oil as a fallback position. Secondly, whatever we end up with in the CFP, it will need policing and I wondered if you would like to say something about the Community Fisheries Control Agency and how you might perceive it in the future giving an overview to the management side of the policing of it in the future.

Ms Attwooll: We had a report on the developments in the Community Fisheries Control Agency from the Director this week. It does look as if the joint deployment plans are moving forward and there is good co-operation between the Member States in relation to these. I still have some anxieties as to whether enough resources are being put into that. One particular concern I have relates to the fisheries partnership agreements and how well those are being monitored. That side of things does seem to be developing slowly, but I think until the Agency has completed its move to Vigo it will not really get under

way. Where I have a continuing concern, and there seems to be a reluctance on the part of the Commission to move forward, I think because there is a reluctance on the part of Member States, is in terms of the variety of sanctions that there are for serious infringements of the Common Fisheries Policy. There is divergence between Member States as to the extent to which they use administrative and penal sanctions and there is an enormous variety in the kinds of fines that are imposed. I think if we want our own stakeholders to accept that there is a level playing field this is something we have to press towards trying to get a degree of uniformity in. Obviously you have to have some variety because people can make honest mistakes as opposed to doing something with deliberate intent. Sometimes it is the first offence, sometimes it is a repeat offence, so you have to have some flexibility but we do really need to achieve a greater degree of equivalence if we are to have effective control.

Mr Stevenson: On the question of where the socio-economic help is needed, I said earlier on that the north east has come out of all this really rather healthily and new boats are being built up there and the white fish sector seems to have recovered because there are so many fewer fishermen now involved in the sector. When you look at some of the smaller ports, for instance, only last week Anstruther said goodbye to its last white fish boat when the fisherman whose boat it was retired, and yet recently I was in Asda having a fight with the directors of Asda over their pricing policy and where they source some of their foodstuffs. They had Spinks Seafood Cocktail and they had a lovely picture on the box of Anstruther harbour in Victorian times with happy fishermen pulling full nets onto their boats in Anstruther harbour. When you read the small print the seafood cocktail contained squid from Vietnam and mussels from Chile. There is nothing now of any significance being landed at Anstruther. Similarly, if you go round the north west coast, places like Lochinver have suffered terribly.

Q680 *Viscount Brookeborough:* Really it is about hardship to these communities. Have they got vast unemployment there or have these people found other employment, because after all in other industries there have been large redundancies, whether it is farming or various other things, and the question is, have those people found suitable employment, not necessarily whether they are still farming sheep or shipbuilding?

Mr Stevenson: I would hope that they have been able to find suitable employment but it is always difficult in remote peripheral areas where fishing and farming are the mainstay. We have tried to develop aquaculture as a way of taking some of the displaced employment from the sea fishery but aquaculture itself is befuddled with problems in Europe, mostly of our own making. We had a conference the other day where the leading fish farmer from Ireland was telling us that before they land their fish his fish farmers have to deal with 400 different regulations, emanating not only from DG Mare but also from DG ENVI, DG Sanco, DG Trade. I repeated this information in a speech I made in Denmark last week to fish farmers, and one of them in the question and answer session said to me, "400 bits of red tape? We have 400 regulations to deal with just from our Environment Directorate, never mind all the others you mentioned". He said, "There are over 1,000 regulations". We are only 50% self-sufficient in fisheries products in Europe. We still import 50% of what we eat from outside the EU and yet we have the perfect environment, the perfect coastal environment, the perfect technology, leading the world, for aquaculture, but we are hamstringing our aquaculture industry with regulations. It is not necessarily the case that we are finding employment but after these problems occur it becomes then a matter for the Member State to deal with the consequent unemployment. They say that six people are displaced on shore for every fishermen that loses his job at sea, and the consequences can be quite significant, but who deals with that and where you can find this information I do not know.

Ms Attwooll: There is definite hardship in some of the remoter communities. I am not just talking about Scotland but I was recently on a Fisheries Committee visit to Ireland, and in those communities there is a particular problem. In some ways people in the fishing industry are almost being forced to become like Scottish crofters. Crofting is not the full-time occupation but you have to do something else as well to survive, but people do want to carry on in the fishing industry. Although I am a person who is inclined to effort limitation rather than quotas as the better system of management, I do have to say that it is understandable that if you have effort limitation in terms of days at sea, if you have a rise in fuel prices and then you get bad weather you are put in a situation where you are really struggling to make ends meet.

Ms Stihler: I would just like to mention the Court of Auditors report. I do not think anybody has mentioned that. That is why we have got great concern about the serious weaknesses of control and enforcement.

Mr Hudghton: Just on that subject, since the European Fisheries Control Agency issue was raised, I think it should, for as long as we are muddling along with the CFP, be an institution which polices the policemen and does not try to do it all itself from Vigo, which would be impossible. We already have,

as has been highlighted, some differences not just in methods but also in penalties and so on for enforcement and there is, as indeed the Court of Auditors report has indicated, a case for looking at how control and enforcement is (or rather is not) working. The Court of Auditors report has resulted in the Commission agreeing to bring forward a proposal on improving control and enforcement and that is one of the things that the Commissioner was referring to when he used the "root and branch" quote the other day. The Commission sees this as a significant part of reform of the CFP and I am not quite so sure that that is tackling the real problem. It is tackling a problem that exists and for the time being is the responsibility of the Commission to tackle, but the real fundamental problem of the CFP is the structure of decision-making, the cumbersome nature of it, the centralisation, the lack of incentive and the lack of local input. One small improvement last December which gives encouragement is that largely the argument by the Scottish Government and industry persuaded the UK minister and the Commission to support an element of a return to hands-on management, allocation of days at sea, within Scotland in this current year and also for the first time enabling Scotland to use an element of carrot rather than just stick, which has been one of the issues about enforcement to date. If you say to people who think the law of the CFP is a complete failure then it follows that they are not necessarily going to be terribly enthused about compliance. We have done a lot in Scotland on a voluntary basis to ensure compliance and to deal with many of the problems and it is only right that that should be recognised in this way and that we should not just be saying, "If you do bad things you will be stopped from doing bad things"; we should also be saying, "If you do good things then you should get some recognition for that". One point for the record about this famous Court of Auditors report is that it is based upon data which were gathered in, it says, the six most important fishing Member States, including the UK, but in the UK part it has in brackets "England and Wales", so the data that were used by the Court of Auditors in that report as far as the UK is concerned were only from England and Wales. Who knows what would have happened if Scotland had been included, but in Scotland, as I have said, because of registration of buyers and sellers and other things, there is a particular set of circumstances there and the fact that some 70% of the UK's industry is in Scotland makes me want to raise that point every time I have the opportunity, and I am doing it again now. England and Wales are not the UK and particularly they are not the UK as far as the fishing industry is concerned, and if we are going to have from the Commission proposals to improve control and enforcement in Scotland then they ought to be based on the situation in Scotland and not on a general perception or analysis EU-wide. That, just like management control and enforcement, has to be directed to the situation that exists in particular areas.

Chairman: Before I hand over to Lord Palmer, one little observation is that there are, of course, those who claim that the north west communities suffer dreadfully because of the rapacious nature of the north east boats, but I would not dream of making that claim.

Q681 *Lord Palmer:* I was really rather shocked, Mr Stevenson, to hear you mention the seal destruction. I was not aware of this until you mentioned it. Did you say that it was ICES who said that seal destruction could not be taken into consideration?

Mr Stevenson: No. ICES do not consider it. They consider all sorts of other fish mortality levels—over-exploitation and all the rest of it. They reluctantly even looked at the climate change issue when we raised it in the committee but they will not look at seals. It is the Commission themselves who give the lead on this. The Commission are being somewhat disingenuous because I recently was in Denmark and was shown by some fishermen leaflets that the European Commission had printed where they were paying for Norwegian seal hunters to train Swedish people how to hunt seals, and this was being done at the Commission's expense but being kept very quiet, and certainly it has never been trumpeted over here. There would be a hell of a row. The Commission are being somewhat two-faced on this issue, but when it comes to us discussing seals as part of the depredation of the fish stocks it is a no-go area. We are not allowed to do it.

Ms Stihler: Thanks for giving me a good written question to put down to the Commission. I totally disagree with Struan's perspective about how seals are the cause of our lack of fish, and many of us in the committee find Struan's perspective on this quite disagreeable, so I want that put on the record. Struan is very interesting because he does a lot of animal welfare stuff, so I do not know what the difference is between cats and dogs and seals. Anyway, I think I would like that on the record.

Q682 *Lord Cameron of Dillington:* I wondered what you felt about the idea of having a ban on discards or, if there was not going to be a total ban, how we minimise the discards because it is one of the more disgraceful aspects of the Common Fisheries Policy?

Mr Stevenson: I am entirely in favour of a ban. In fact, we were pressing with a series of amendments in the recent Commission proposal for a total ban, because we are talking now about a million tonnes of good,

healthy fish being dumped into the water every year, which is an improvement; it used to be two million tonnes estimated a year. It is hard to tell because, of course, the fishermen do not log what they are dumping. That in itself is having a huge impact on the fish stocks, but also at this time when we have a shortage of fish meal, which is a vital ingredient for feeding salmon and trout and all the other fish being reared in the aquaculture industry, and the price of fish meal internationally has rocketed although it has slightly eased recently from places like Chile and Peru, the fish processors are saying, "We would be delighted to pay for any discards that you insist on your fishermen bringing back to port. We are prepared to pay at a level that does not encourage targeting of these immature or over-quota species but a level that you could set which might be not enough to encourage targeting but would be too much to encourage continual dumping", say £50 a tonne for fish that otherwise would have been discarded, so there is a potential way for dealing with these discards. The industry are desperate to get their hands on them. It is healthy fish, and we need not think that they are going to be brought back and landed, which itself would be useful because the scientists then would get a clear picture of what is being caught, the real state of the fish stocks, but they will not necessarily then have to be dumped in landfill; there is an outlet for them. The one thing that we were insisting upon was that if you are going to insist on an end to discarding you will have to fit a CCTV to monitor it, to make sure that the fishermen are complying, and this is what the Danish Government have now implemented on a trial basis. They are also putting observers on board the boats that they are trying this out on, so it is a belt and braces approach in Denmark with CCTV and observers on board. It seems to me that you would have to go to that length to ensure compliance.

Ms Attwooll: One of the reasons that I tend towards effort limitation rather than quotas is that I do not quite see how you can get rid of discards as long as you have the quota system. Even if you land them they are essentially discards. There is just a different way of discarding them and perhaps getting some kind of economic value out of them. If you had an effort limitation system you might still have some discarding because of high grading, although if you get your effort limitation right, and particularly with high fuel costs, I think this is going to be less and less of a problem because fishers just will not be able to afford to go through a high grading process. In addition to that, whether you stick with the quota system or have effort limitation, there is a lot that can be done by way of technical measures. I was slightly shocked at a presentation that we had on technical measures at the Fisheries Committee this week, where they talked about the different types of nets and ways in which discards could be prevented but there did not seem to be that much agreement and perhaps not enough research yet on what the best technical measures were. We had thought in Scotland that the development of the square mesh panel was a step forward, and I am sure it is, but we were told that there were other configurations which were better than the square mesh panels. So much more needs to be done by way of research into the best ways of preventing fish being caught in the first place, and this applies not just to fish but indeed to by-catches of various kinds as well, porpoises and sea birds and so on. I really think that we need a great deal of impetus in that direction. Also, I think the voluntary closure of areas, as has been happening in Scotland, is a big step forward and that ought to be emulated in other parts of the EU.

Ms Stihler: We now have the Schlitter report, which is our report on discards, which was an own initiative report we voted upon at the end of January. In an ideal world we would love to move to an instant ban but the reality is much more complicated and we started to investigate the subject. Struan's approach about CCTV on every fishing vessel is a bit of a big brother approach in my opinion and many in the committee did not support Struan's approach to that. With regard to the practical aspects in terms of the cost of dealing with landed discards, Struan has one opinion about that. Other people have other things that they would like to discuss on that, such as the cost of introducing more selective gear, which we have talked about—I think there are something like 11 different sets of gear that are used in the EU—and the implications for total allowable catches and the quota regime if discarding is banned, and the need to give fishermen an incentive to fish in a more sustainable way. In the Schlitter report there is also a clear indication that there is a difference in the causes of discards from fishery to fishery. One approach is not enough. You have to look at the individual fisheries. Perhaps having an amnesty in discards is not going to be a solution because you may create a market in discards instead of encouraging fishermen to fish in a more sustainable way. Karl Schlitter is a Swedish Green, so for a Swedish Green not to come out and say, "Have a complete ban now", but, "Let us look at ways that we can try and gradually get to that ban" was very interesting. It was quite a shock that a Swedish Green came forward with that approach, and I think he came forward with it because he wanted to have as much consensus within the committee as possible. He also suggested a range of pilot discard projects with a geographical range, and I definitely supported that approach, to look at what worked where and how effective those projects would be, so we now have to make sure that what we try to get through the Schlitter report is implemented in practice.

Chairman: Thank you all very much indeed.

THURSDAY 8 MAY 2008

Present: Arran, E

Brookeborough, V

Cameron of Dillington, L

Dundee, E

Jones of Whitchurch, B

Palmer, L

Plumb, L

Sewel, L (Chairman)

Ullswater, V

Examination of Witness

Witness: MR JÜRGEN WEIS, Fisheries Counsellor, Germany, examined.

Q683 Chairman: Good morning. Thank you very much for coming and meeting us and helping us with our inquiry. I will explain who we are. We are a Sub-Committee of the House of Lords Select Committee on the European Union and we are conducting an inquiry into the future of the Common Fisheries Policy. This is a formal evidence-taking session, so a note will be kept of the proceedings and you will get a transcript as soon as possible, so you can have a look at it and see if any errors have slipped in. Would you like to say anything by way of introduction or would you prefer that we go straight to the questions?

Mr Weis: I will introduce myself. My name is Jürgen Weis. I work in the German representation to the EU. I am the Fisheries Attaché and as such I am the fisheries expert, but you know how you become an expert. You take a seat and then you see that it is labelled as "Fisheries Expert". That is why I am grateful that you provided some of the questions in advance so I could co-ordinate with my Government at home which made it easier.

Q684 Chairman: If I could start, the first question is how things have changed since the 2002 reforms and two waves of accession, 2002 and 2004. Has that changed the dynamics of fisheries policy in the EU or not?

Mr Weis: Yes, in our view the enlargement has had a significant impact on the performance of the CAP—sorry, the CFP.

Q685 Chairman: It has on the CAP as well!

Mr Weis: Yes. I also work in the agriculture sector, so I will try not to confuse them. The accession of the new Member States in 2004 and 2007 has in our view strengthened the position of the Commission and weakened the decision processes in the Council. As to whether this is good or bad for the fisheries policy as such, there are different opinions on that.

Q686 Chairman: Why do you think that has happened, that move to strengthen the Commission and weaken the Council?

Mr Weis: As in other areas, it has become more difficult to have a decision of the Council against proposals of the Commission. It has become very difficult to have coalitions against the Commission. That is an institutional fact that we see in other policies too.

Q687 Viscount Ullswater: Obviously, what was done in 2002 was to introduce more the recovery and management plans but it seems to us that only one or two of them have got started and I would be interested to hear what your views are as to why more have not been introduced, if there is an organisational reason why they have not been and whether they could be speeded up, because obviously the science would like it to move in that direction.

Mr Weis: We agree that the introduction of recovery and management plans was expected to accelerate the processes and enhance the international reputation of the CFP, and there are many reasons why only a few plans have been adopted so far and why the overall success of these plans is so limited. To name a few, one reason is that a number of fish stocks are straddling or are migratory, so there is a need to agree and co-ordinate with different coastal states, such as Norway or Iceland, and this process is cumbersome and time-consuming and it also leads to results which are more or less an agreement at the lowest common denominator. That is one reason as regards the organisation. Another reason is that due to data sufficiencies or lack of scientific advice it is difficult to determine the biological reference points which are always requested in these plans, and this scientific uncertainty gives rise to controversial views among the stakeholders and among Member States about the distribution of the biomass or the measures to be taken. As to the question of how to speed up the process and how to improve the results; for us one decisive factor would be whether the plans are accepted by the industry. Acceptance can only be increased in our view by an early involvement of all stakeholders and transparent processes. In this regard we would welcome the involvement of the Regional Advisory Councils and we would encourage them to develop their own initiatives on the elaboration of management plans.

Q688 *Viscount Brookeborough:* In response to the scathing report produced by the Court of Auditors last October the Commission is consulting on a review of the Control Regulation. What are Germany's priorities for the new regulation and would you support any form of harmonisation of penalties? How do you see the role of the Community Fisheries Control Agency evolving as part of your overall control strategy?
Mr Weis: We support the main objectives of the new Control Regulation. We are in particular favourable to a consultation on the regulation and a widening of the scope to other activities, such as transport or marketing activities. Since many of the stakeholders in the industry are operating internationally this would seem a logical step to us and that is also why we support the new approach of the Commission as regards the IUU Regulation on illegal fishing. We do in principle also support the Commission's aim to harmonise sanctions within the Community. We know and acknowledge that this is difficult for many Member States and that traditions and legal systems have to be respected and taken into account when we develop harmonised sanctions. But we are convinced that sanctions for the same category of infringements need to be comparable and equally deterrent across the Community. As to the role of the Fisheries Control Agency, we believe that this organisation should play an important role in improving the European culture of controls. Beyond its main task of ensuring efficient co-ordination between Member States we think that other areas of activity could include the development of methods for inspection and auditing and the development of training programmes. The European Fisheries Control Agency could also play an important role in facilitating cross-checks of data or risk analysis.

Q689 *Viscount Brookeborough:* Could you please tell us something about what the German control set-up is, for instance, whether you have ships and aircraft, and to what extent you have a problem in your own nation as far as illegal fishing, net size and that sort of thing is concerned?
Mr Weis: We know that our fishermen are not holy.

Q690 *Viscount Brookeborough:* Neither are ours.
Mr Weis: Our control problems are not as difficult as those of other Member States in the Baltic or in the Mediterranean, for example, but—**that's my personal view** – there are problems. Our control set-up is that the port controls are done by our Bundesländer, our federal states. Our coastal federal states perform the coastal and port controls. Furthermore we have a federal agency of agriculture and fisheries, and they

have control vessels. I think they have four or five of them. Some of them also are appropriate for the high seas.

Q691 *Viscount Brookeborough:* How far away do your trawlers go? How far north do German fishermen travel to fish?
Mr Weis: Most of them fish in coastal waters but we also have a long-distance fleet which goes as far as the South Pacific, for example.

Q692 *Chairman:* You mentioned that you favour harmonisation of sanctions. Do you think that is a view that is shared across the EU or are there some Member States who find that particularly difficult?
Mr Weis: We are having this debate at the moment in the context of the IUU Regulation where the Commission proposed minimum sanctions for the most dangerous infringements, and these are quite high amounts of money, €300,000 for individuals or €500,000 for juridical entities. We support, like some other Member States, a harmonisation of sanctions at a high level because we think that it must be a deterrent. We see the problem that there are quite different levels of sanctions in the Member States at the moment. Many of the Member States which object to the proposal of the Commission do not, as far as I understand it, really object to high sanctions but they have problems with their own legal systems. I understand that the UK is one of these Member States which have a system without administrative sanctions and which have a problem if the Commission forces them to apply administrative sanctions which they do not have in their system. The Council Legal Service says that it is not a problem because the Commission has the right to define that this or that sanction is administrative and that if a Member States applies its own system which is a criminal sanction system these sanctions remain virtually administrative. Whether that is right or wrong, I am not a lawyer.

Q693 *Earl of Dundee:* To conserve fish stocks does the German Government prefer controls on catches or controls on effort?
Mr Weis: We think that here we have to differentiate between fisheries. It seems possible that there are advantages in managing pelagic fisheries mainly through controls on catches, but that is not possible for all fisheries. Effort controls seem to be working for certain fisheries on demersal species like cod, but a large number of practical problems still have to be solved. As concerns the effort measurement, we are, for instance, concerned about the lack of uniform and reliable methods for measuring and verifying engine power. That is what the Commission now proposes, a switch to an engine power system.

Q694 *Earl of Dundee:* How confident are you that we can make systematic progress with that problem with the measuring and allocating of effort? Are you confident that that is an exercise which will work systematically or are you a bit despondent?

Mr Weis: We are hesitant. If we moved to a simple allocation of fishing effort instead of quotas this would possibly have an effect on relative stability and that we would not like. There are also other problems that have to be solved, for example, a proper definition of the vessels actively involved in fishing and the treatment of fisheries that have only a minor impact on the endangered and regulated resources. We would also have to make sure that a new effort management system would not discriminate against Member States which have recently reduced their fishing capacity. Those are our concerns and that is why we actively participate in the debate on the new Cod Recovery Plan where the Commission has proposed moving to a kilowatt-based system.

Q695 *Baroness Jones of Whitchurch:* From what you are saying it sounds like you would prefer the *status quo* to some of the changes that are being proposed, that stability is really important to you. With the big debate that is going on at the moment it seems that you are on the side of no change rather than change. Is that a fair assumption?

Mr Weis: We are not against any changes but in a way relative stability is a holy cow—for many Member States; that is for sure.

Q696 *Chairman:* When you said that quota for pelagic works for pelagic and effort more for demersal, is that really a reflection of the fact that pelagic is not a mixed fishery whereas demersal does tend to be a mixed fishery and that you can use quotas where you have got one species but if you have a mixed fishery then effort is a better way than quotas?

Mr Weis: I have to admit that our position is not really clear at the moment on this point because there are many developments going on. We have the rights-based management discussion, we have discussions on a discard ban and the question of whether we maintain quotas or not is dependent on this. If you have a complete discard ban and you have an obligation to land anything that is fished then it is very difficult to work with quotas.

Q697 *Earl of Arran:* You have already said that you think the RACs are a good thing. Let me press you a little bit further. To what extent would your Government think that they should be more executive than advisory, which they are at the moment, for instance, and also would you be prepared to give them more funding? What do you think the future of the RACs is from the German point of view?

Mr Weis: The German Government participates as an active observer in those Regional Advisory Councils to which the German fishing industry holds membership. These are the North Sea RAC, the Baltic Sea RAC, the Pelagic RAC and the Long-Distance Fleet RAC. Support for these RACs is given by annual contributions and technical assistance to the executive committee and to the meetings and general assemblies taking place in Germany. We welcome the work of the RACs, as I told you, and their contribution to the policy-making processes in the CFP. But as to the question of whether they should have more responsibility, we are a bit hesitant. According to the Council decision establishing these councils, the role of the RACs is defined by offering advice and we appreciate their advice to the Commission and to the Member States. But we are not in favour of giving them real management responsibilities.

Q698 *Earl of Arran:* Why not?

Mr Weis: This is also institutional. We feel that this regionalisation, which may be good for some examples touches upon the primacy of the CFP. If we give more competence to the RACs then there is the question where this regionalisation ends.

Q699 *Earl of Arran:* Have you set your mind against it for ever?

Mr Weis: No. Nothing is for ever.

Q700 *Chairman:* Can we put it the other way? At the moment the Common Fisheries Policy is a very top-down policy and I would have thought that to get a culture of compliance you need to have quite a bit of bottom-up as well so that those involved in the industry, the stakeholders, feel directly involved, having some say in the future of the industry. You get a little bit of that through the advisory role of the RACs but one of the potential future models that we have heard about is really the Commission setting what are called the policy parameters and saying, "Reduce mortality rates to, say, 50%", or something like that, and then saying to the RACs in different areas, "Look: that is what the policy parameter is. It is up to you to advise on how to get there, and if you come up with something that is credible then we will almost automatically take that advice". Would you be comfortable with that sort of model?

Mr Weis: The way you describe it, it seems okay. But on the other hand the challenge is not to define nice objectives and to ask the Member States or the RACs or whatever organisation to reach them. The problem in my eyes is the implementation of the policy and that is where we have the problems, in particular the implemention of controls. That is why we would not like to give too many responsibilities to the RACs or to the Member States or to regions too soon. You mentioned the Court of Auditors report on the

problems of controls that we have, and I think it would not be any good to ignore that and do nothing about it.
Chairman: If you go down that route you clearly need to have some big sanctions behind you to make sure they do it.

Q701 *Viscount Brookeborough:* Are you worried that because you are a relatively small fishing nation in terms of, for instance, the UK you will not get enough say and you will have to abide by another Member State's rules rather than the CFP, and therefore you would like protection by the CFP from other the other Member States? Are you an example of a smaller fishing Member's attitude to RACs?
Mr Weis: Okay, but it would mean that we were under-represented in a given RAC. On the other hand we have the problem that now we are one Member State with 29 votes but there are 26 others and we are not amongst the biggest fisheries Member States. My feeling is that in the fishing sector and the Common Fisheries Policy the interests of the main concerned Member States are in most cases considered in the decisions.

Q702 *Viscount Brookeborough:* Who else shares your views? Do you know?
Mr Weis: In the fisheries policy normally we are of the same view as the United Kingdom as regards relative stability and other questions.

Q703 *Baroness Jones of Whitchurch:* We have been talking about governance, but the point I put to you is that we have heard some very powerful arguments from the industry itself and from other representatives who have come to see us about the need for reform, that the CFP and the way it is currently organised needs reform, and one of the ways that people have felt it is not functioning is that it is over-centralised. How can you make a decision for one region or one nation if you make very generalised policies? It seems to me again that you are just saying you almost do not accept that powerful need for reform, which decentralisation would be one way of tackling.
Mr Weis: We support the reform processes that are going on and, as I have told you, we support the primacy of the Common Fisheries Policy. We are not completely against decentralisation of certain responsibilities in order to better adapt the implementation of the CFP to regional or sectoral particularities. But we can only accept this if it does not undermine the principles of the CFP and if cost efficiency is ensured.

Q704 *Viscount Ullswater:* I would like to go back a little bit. One of the problems has always been that the fishermen and the scientists and those controlling them have never really got on very well, whereas now in the RACs there is an opportunity for all the

stakeholders to get together and agree certain policies or methods. Is that the form of decentralisation that you think would be effective? You talk about decentralisation and yet I have not quite worked out the formation that you are considering as an alternative to a RAC or where this decentralisation can happen or where the discussion can happen that would have the agreement of all the stakeholders.
Mr Weis: We support that the RACs discuss the objectives for their areas and we would certainly like the Commission to take on board more of these recommendations. Another question is if they should have their own management responsibilities. We do not know where this would look lead to. How would integrate a control system? Would they have powers to sanction?

Q705 *Viscount Ullswater:* It is really just that they have not been around for a very long time and they need to mature a bit before you are prepared to give them more trust?
Mr Weis: Yes, maybe.

Q706 *Chairman:* I am beginning to think there is not all that much difference between the two positions now. It seems to me that in a way you are saying you would be quite happy if they were giving advice and the Commission then endorsed it; they are keeping the Common Fisheries Policy. What you do not want to do is to give the Commission power. The power exercised by the Commission at the moment you do not want to go down formally to the RACs?
Mr Weis: By the Commission and the Council. We still decide in the Council.
Lord Plumb: And yet doing that would surely be adding to the complications if we are not careful. At the moment you have two methods—a quota and the effort scheme, which seem to complicate things. Last night we were hearing about the hundreds of forms that fishermen and others involved in the fishing industry have to fill in. Surely decentralisation ought to simplify that but it does mean that you have to give more responsibility to those who are in the field doing the job, involved in the industry, involved in the business, rather than leave it to the politicians. Politicians are fine, but you are going to have yet a further layer of politicians if the Lisbon Treaty goes through and that means, of course, that you have a joint operation between the Council and the Commission and with the European Parliament. Is that going to delay things? Is it going to make it more complicated? Should we not be saying in the beginning that if further reform of the CFP is on the cards, as a fisherman would tell you it has to be, then the priority should be how can we cut the red tape and how can we simplify the whole scheme to make it more adaptable and more acceptable to those who are fishing? May I just add to that a very practical point? When the

skipper of a trawler comes in after ten days, as we saw at Peterhead in Aberdeen last week, and tells you that his bill for oil alone for his ten-day trip is €36,000 or whatever, you begin to think that this is going into a range of business that is a killer. You have to sell fish at an enormous price to cover the costs that these trawlers are facing. The whole thing is changing. We are going to be dealing with capacity and opportunity in a moment. I think we need a fresh look at the whole thing rather than maybe that we keep that and maybe these would combine better and maybe we should decentralise. I would just like to see it set down on one side of a piece of paper so that we could have the points that we think matter. That is my philosophy.

Q707 Chairman: Prices up, taxes down!
Mr Weis: We support the reduction of red tape.

Q708 Lord Plumb: But how are we going to do it?
Mr Weis: It is really difficult, especially in fisheries, because it is a control issue. We have so many problems with illegal catches, with the implementation of and with compliance with the rules. You could easily reduce red tape by saying, "I do not control any more and I trust that the fishermen will do the right thing", but that will not solve the problems. The European Parliament is very fond of having stricter rules as regards IUU fisheries and as regards control. But whenever you call for official action, whenever you call for the state then it comes with rules and controls and bureaucracy. We are in a dilemma there. It is very difficult to reduce red tape. We are trying to improve the proposals of the Commission in order to make them more pragmatic. On the other hand, there are many other Member States trying to improve and change the proposal and the outcome is unpredictable in many ways. The other point you mentioned was energy prices. This will give a big incentive for a reduction of capacity. This will maybe change the conditions so much that it will become much easier to have a fundamental change of the European policy in the end.
Chairman: You have already, I suppose, pinned your colours to the mast on relative stability.

Q709 Lord Cameron of Dillington: As the Chairman says, you have already indicated that you support the principle of relative stability. What is the political mood within the Member States in your view for supporting this principle?
Mr Weis: My impression is that most of the Member States support the principle, like we do.

Q710 Lord Cameron of Dillington: Apart from Spain, perhaps.
Mr Weis: Well. Perhaps more and more Member States will open up to other ideas and I also think that this principle is perhaps not carved in stone forever.

But it is very important for us that our fishing industry has a long-term perspective to plan its activities. That is what relative stability is good for. We can discuss amendments to our position if these long-term planning possibilities are provided to our industry by other means. But on the other hand we would not support any amendments if the background were only that some Member States are not to adapt to the changed conditions, the changed fishing opportunities. But if we have to change our policy because they have missed that train then it is not okay.

Q711 Lord Cameron of Dillington: I am slightly going back to the whole question of fuel. What is the general view of the support that France and Spain are giving to their fishermen by subsidising them for the increase in fuel costs?
Mr Weis: We do not support it. We are against it.

Q712 Lord Plumb: Can I follow that because I think this is important? "We are against it", you say, the UK are against it and yet it is happening. How can we talk about a level playing field and fair play? You cannot just say, "We are against it". What can you do about it?
Mr Weis: You can make it clear in all the Council discussions what our position is and try to influence decisions on that.
Lord Plumb: And you can therefore block it?
Chairman: No, you cannot.
Lord Plumb: Exactly. I am asking the question.
Lord Cameron of Dillington: You should be able to.
Lord Plumb: Exactly.
Lord Cameron of Dillington: You cannot at the moment.
Chairman: Part of the relative stability argument goes on to rights-based management, so shall we go on to that?

Q713 Lord Palmer: What is your Government's position on the tradability of fishing rights and are you worried that an ITQ system might lead to an undesirable concentration of fishing rights either in particular waters or indeed among certain types of fishing vessel?
Mr Weis: Our Government has not yet determined its position on that. We are debating and co-ordinating the position. We think that these marine biological resources are a public property. Therefore their use should only be based on rights to harvest them under special conditions and limitations and not be considered a property right. If you are considering such an ITQ system then we have to differentiate again between the fisheries.

Q714 *Lord Palmer:* But how can you do that?

Mr Weis: One could make some quotas and rights transferable for some species or fisheries and for others not. I think it would be possible. You mentioned in your question some concerns and I think we share these concerns. Such a system could lead to an undesirable degree of concentration and could have consequences for local communities which depend on fisheries or artisanal fisheries. Another risk is the concentration of the rights in the hands of individuals or companies that are not actively involved in fishing. It is easy to predict that it will be very difficult to come to an initial allocation of these rights. On the other hand, we see the advantages that it might have in terms of rationalisation of fisheries policy and enabling simpler monitoring of fisheries. It would also have positive effects on the reduction of fleet capacity in many Member States. So we have not yet determined our position.

Q715 *Chairman:* It has the potential, has it not, to lead to more efficient, more profitable proponents of the industry? The agricultural equivalent is not a direct one but it is farm amalgamation, is it not? You concentrate the industry.

Mr Weis: Yes.

Chairman: And you get the benefits of scale.

Q716 *Viscount Ullswater:* What about temporary adjustments so that the opportunities, even between Member States, if quotas were not going to be filled, could be temporarily transferred or temporarily purchased—and I know we are going to be talking about capacity—so that an individual's vessel which only has so many days at sea or has maybe run out of its own quota could become more economic by either leasing or buying quota for that particular season and the quota then goes back either to the Member State or to that particular fishery the next year?

Mr Weis: We have procedures in place in most of the Member States to distribute and to exchange fishing opportunities between the fishermen, and it works. As regards the Cod Recovery Plan, where the Commission is now proposing the kilowatt-based system, the objective is to enhance the possibilities for redistribution amongst the fishermen in the Member States. Between the Member States we have exchange of quotas and that is no problem either, so the flexibility is already there. But it will create problems, if we create property rights. We have examples in the agricultural policy where we have done that with quotas.

Q717 *Viscount Ullswater:* With milk quotas particularly.

Mr Weis: It is very difficult.

Q718 *Lord Plumb:* It is a question of balance, is it not, between capacity and opportunities? Are we capacity building and are we missing opportunities? You have already said that economic forces could well affect capacity, and I am sure that is true, but how do you see the situation in Germany between big capacity and opportunities? That is really what it is about, is it not, in the present-day circumstances?

Mr Weis: We do not have a real problem with over-capacity at the moment. At the end of 2006 we had about 2,000 vessels with 61,500 registered tonnes and about 155,000 kilowatts, we are amongst the ten smallest fishing fleets of the Community. Today our capacity is hardly sufficient to make use of our fishing opportunities. Therefore our Parliament, the German Bündestag, has explicitly declared the aim not to further dismantle our fleet capacity. At the moment there is also no intention and no reason of limiting or restricting our fishing effort on a national basis. But that does not mean that we would generally oppose a national management of effort or capacities. At the moment there is simply no need to do that. Nevertheless, we feel obliged to consider any measure to adjust the fishing effort in the context of sound conservation of endangered stocks. That is European policy and, as regards the EFF, we think that the tools which are provided there are appropriate and sufficient.

Q719 *Chairman:* The 2006 report by the Commission said that across the EU as a whole not enough had been done to reduce capacity. You have stated what the German position is. If you look at other Member States which Member States are taking the lead in reducing capacity and which are saying, "No, no, we are not doing that"?

Mr Weis: I do not think that there is any Member State really taking the lead in reducing capacity because over the last years we have seen that every year we have agreed on reductions of fishing opportunities by ten per cent or 20% in certain fisheries and it is impossible to reduce the capacity at the same speed. So I think more or less all Member States have enough capacity or too much capacity. We have Member States which definitely have big problems, for example in the Baltic. We support that those Member States receive funding from the EFF to reduce their capacity. A problem arises if we then move to a kilowatt-based system with the vast possibilities for manipulating engine power where you could have a reduction of power on the paper but not in reality. Therefore we have problems with a move to a kilowatt-based system.

Q720 *Lord Plumb:* Would you agree that this is dependent to a large extent on technology for development, in other words, two vessels might have been hoovering more fish than intended not long ago? What effect has this had in Germany and what effect do you see it having generally on employment?

Mr Weis: We have a coastal fishery where we have not seen too much progress either in capacity reduction or in modernisation of the fleet. The influence should be there but it is not really measurable in my eyes. As regards our very small high seas fleet, these are modern ships, only a few, and there is no over-capacity and they behave in a sound and reasonable manner in my eyes.

Chairman: It seems as though the German industry is small but perfectly formed. I think that is it. Thank you very much indeed.

Examination of Witness

Witness: MR SUJIRO SEAM, Fisheries Counsellor, France, examined.

Q721 *Chairman:* Thank you very much indeed for coming and finding the time to meet us. We very much appreciate it. I will explain who we are. We are a Sub-Committee of the House of Lords Select Committee on the European Union. We are carrying out an inquiry into the future of the Common Fisheries Policy. We are coming towards the end of collecting evidence for the inquiry. This is a formal evidence session so a note will be taken. You will be sent a transcript of it. You can look through it and make any corrections that are necessary. Would you prefer to start by making an initial statement about the French position on reform of the Common Fisheries Policy or would you prefer that we go to the questions that we have sent you?

Mr Seam: Whatever is best for you. I am prepared to do both. I have to say that I have covered myself with formal instructions from my Government on the questions you raised and therefore I will be in a position today to express the official views of the French Government. There is absolutely no problem with that. What I say could be perfectly attributed to the French authorities and I am prepared to both respond to the questions I received last week and give you the general views of the French Government on the reform or the mid-term review of the Common Fisheries Policy.

Q722 *Chairman:* I think we will just go through the questions that we have. The first one is, of course, the one on the objectives of the Common Fisheries Policy. We have heard argument during our visit to Brussels that perhaps for too long the Common Fisheries Policy concentrated, not unsurprisingly, on fish, on the biological side, rather than the socio-economic objectives of the Common Fisheries Policy. Do you think that is the case or do you think that in a way from year to year the December Fisheries Council has been guided much more by employment considerations than it has by stock considerations?

Mr Seam: On this first question I think within the European Union all the institutions agree that the general objective of the Common Fisheries Policy should be sustainable development of the fisheries industry and sector, which means we have to strike a balance from the biological point of view and from the socio-economic point of view. In this debate our standpoint is that we consider that the socio-economic aspects are not taken into account sufficiently in the current way the Common Fisheries Policy is decided. In all the circumstances where we intervene we always intervene so that the socio-economic aspects are more taken into account. Indeed, we could say that we believe that right now the emphasis is much more on the biological aspects than on the socio-economic aspects, at least when it comes to the proposals from the Commission, and our role and our behaviour afterwards in the negotiation process is to try to put the balance right, which is moving it more towards a socio-economic approach than a biological approach. I can illustrate that with some examples. This was our position when we discussed the European Fisheries Fund where we believe that this instrument should give more priority to the socio-economic development of the sector. This is also true when we discuss specific plans like recovery plans or management plans where we consider that the objectives should be set at a level which allows recovery of the stock or management of the stock but at the same time allows our fishermen to conduct their business in a profitable manner.

Q723 *Chairman:* It is a difficult one to know where the balance is, though, is it not, because if you get the biology wrong ultimately the socio-economic side is going to go wrong as well?

Mr Seam: Indeed, but, as we all know here, we have to balance long term and short term. The common line which is very often explained to us is that we have to make efforts right now to try and preserve the stocks to allow long-term gains. That is the approach which is proposed by the Commission in particular when it comes to the maximum sustainable yield, but at the same time we consider that even though the long-term objectives are important we should not forget and just give up the short term profitability of the sector. Of course, we have to strike a balance. We all agree that it should be sustainable from the biology point of view. Our position right now is to consider that the proposals we receive very often, if not in all cases, are not enough in the direction of the socio-economic balance and lean more towards biological preservation or conservation of the resource. That does not mean that we are not willing to ensure the sustainability from a biological point of view but every single time it is feasible we defend an approach which takes account of both, which means that maybe we have to go for a more progressive approach. For example, when it comes to reaching the MSY, decreasing the fishing effort at the rate of ten per cent annually means it could be achieved in a longer period without endangering the stock. That is something we have defended with the UK, I believe, because the United Kingdom was the other Member State directly interested in the Western Channel stock, for example, where there the reduction in fishing mortality is not ten per cent annually; it is 20 per cent spread over a longer period.

Q724 Chairman: Within socio-economic considerations can I raise the issue of fuel subsidies? What is the argument for fuel subsidies at the moment?
Mr Seam: We do not have fuel subsidies. We have a whole package which is designed to address the general situation of the sector. We are aware, and this is the diagnosis we have, that the sector faces right now serious difficulties because of the high prices of fuel but also because of other causes, such as the constant reduction of fishing possibilities. Therefore, my Government has tried to develop and implement a global plan for the fishery sector to address all the issues on the table. This plan comprises basically three main elements. There is a biological aspect where we try to reinforce the quality of the scientific advice to have a better knowledge of what is going on. There is the economic aspect where we try to put in place measures which would bring the sector back to a reasonably profitable situation, and there we have a whole package of subsidies (and I will come back to that later) and we also have this training and safety aspect because that is also a very important issue for us. The *Plan Barnier*, which is named after our Minister, Michel Barnier, who is trying to implement this plan tries to address all these different issues, so this is not fuel-specific. As far as bringing back the sector to a profitable situation is concerned, what we decided to do was implement what the Commission proposed I think two or three years ago in a communication on the rescue and restructuring of the sector. This comprises two phases. One phase is dedicated to the rescue of firms which are facing bankruptcy and there we are allowed under Community law and competition rules to provide subsidies for the running costs of the enterprises. This is, of course, of a limited and temporary nature, and this phase, which is dedicated to the rescue of companies, has to be followed up by a restructuring phase. In the restructuring phase we have a huge decommissioning plan in France and also

modernisation subsidies focused mainly on energy saving, like research on more efficient engines in terms of fuel consumption and fishing techniques which are less fuel consuming. We also encourage a change of gears and a change of engine or a change of fisheries if possible within the limits which are available, so there is no fuel-dedicated subsidy here. It is a global subsidy scheme within the plan which does not only cover subsidies, because we have many other issues to address, and this is the way we try to help our fishermen to face the situation arising from the high cost of fuel.

Q725 Baroness Jones of Whitchurch: I guess from what you are saying that the fishing industry is quite an important sector in France but can you give me some idea of what proportion of industry it is?
Mr Seam: In terms of absolute value it is not important at all. We used to compare the annual turnover of the fishing industry in France for the first landings to the turnover of the annual sales of tomatoes, half a billion euros a year. It has the same value. We sell, in terms of value, as much tomato as fish in France.

Q726 Lord Cameron of Dillington: How many people are involved?
Mr Seam: I do not know the specifics but beyond the absolute value of the sector it is true that politically it has always been considered important to support that sector.

Q727 Viscount Ullswater: When we look at the science and the control of the fishing stocks it is very important that all the fishermen should obey rules but they do not always and therefore control and enforcement is a key factor. Of course, there was a rather a damning report from the Court of Auditors last October which indicated that some of the control measures were not being put in place. Could you tell us what France's reaction to that report was and perhaps you could also consider where you think the Community's Fisheries Control Agency fits in with the new control strategy.
Mr Seam: The report from the Court of Auditors indeed depicts quite a gloomy image of the way controls are performed throughout the Community. We do not dispute this diagnosis. We agree that the situation is not rosy. We consider that, at least in France, we have taken steps to address the shortcomings identified in the report from the Court of Auditors and those are the ideas which we are promoting for the forthcoming revision of the control framework for the Common Fisheries Policy. I would say that we have four general ideas. The first one is to take advantage of the new technologies, for example, to develop a centralised database of control reports which is accessible to other controllers.

Second, we put the emphasis on the quality of the control when it comes to the design of the control strategy, and we try to elaborate a control strategy which is based on risk analysis with cross-references between different instruments to know exactly where we have to target the controls because, like many other Member States, we are on a limited budget, so the idea is not really to increase the means of control because we have to work within limited budgets but to make it more efficient, so make more with what we have. One way to do that is to increase the quality of the control, so we have this control strategy which is much more sophisticated than it used to be, I believe, and secondly we have a system whereby we control the quality of the controls when they are performed, which we call the second level control, so we have controllers in charge of controlling what controllers do. The third element is that we are in favour of more deterrent sanctions, even though we are very much aware of the difficulties of harmonising sanctions throughout the Union. As far as we are concerned, we have a system which is two-pronged. We have, like in most Member States, I believe, a criminal sanction system and also we developed two years ago a system of administrative sanctions, which is deemed to be, by the Commission at least, more efficient because it produces sanctions more quickly. You do not have to wait for the whole criminal process to take place. The fourth element, and that is where the Agency has a role to play, is that we are in favour of more a Community approach, more a common approach, because we are very much aware of the complaints by all our fishermen that there is no level playing field. The simple fact that all the fishermen have the same complaints is certainly an indication that the system does not function so badly because we all know that, for example, French fishermen consider that the UK authorities control them very strictly and it is not the same for the control performed by the UK control authorities on UK vessels, but it is also true the other way round, so altogether we should achieve some sort of common understanding on that. Nevertheless, beyond the anecdotal aspect of the situation we very much believe that a more common approach should develop. We are very much in favour of exchanging inspectors, putting inspection vessels in the waters of other Member States (of course, with reciprocal access) even though we must, for example, put on board an inspector from the coastal state for legal purposes, but we are very much in favour of developing these cross-Member States approaches to have a more common view of and a more common approach to how controls are performed throughout the Union. Those are four ideas that we will try to promote in the forthcoming revision of the Community control framework for the Common Fisheries Policy.

Q728 *Viscount Ullswater:* Control obviously will remain with the Member State. I cannot see that

moving or it being agreed to by Member States to have a common control agency running around the whole seas effecting control. It will still need to be done by the Member States, but do you see having the Agency as a useful co-ordinator between the control operations in Member States?
Mr Seam: That adequately depicts the French position. We indeed believe that, first, control should remain a competence for the Member States to perform; second, that the role of the Agency should develop in a way that it co-ordinates, "co-ordinating" meaning acting only as a go-between for the Member States, sharing best practices, but also with the Agency in developing common standards and common methods so that things are applied equally.

Q729 *Viscount Ullswater:* So you are really giving it quite a welcome?
Mr Seam: Yes.

Q730 *Chairman:* You talk about administrative sanctions. Can you give us an idea of what they consist of?
Mr Seam: In the system of administrative sanctions, contrary to the system of criminal sanction where the judges pronounce the sanction, the administrative authority pronounces the sanction and then the recipient of the sanction is free to take that to court. The sanction is applied, there is due process and a possible judicial review afterwards but the sanction is applied, whereas in the criminal sanction normally there is no sanction until the final judgment is decided. That is the reason why I believe the Commission considers that this system is more reactive and addresses infringements more adequately. We developed that, and this is in the public domain so there is nothing to hide, in response to the fine we received in the undersized fish case.

Q731 *Chairman:* That is a direct product of that case?
Mr Seam: Yes. This is one of the elements that convinced the Commission that we had reformed our control and sanction because the two of course go together in a way which adequately addresses infringements now.
Chairman: That is very interesting.

Q732 *Viscount Brookeborough:* We have heard conflicting views as to whether conservation goals should primarily be implemented through controls on catches (or, in practice, landings) or through controls on effort. The German representative that we have just had said that it may even be a combination of the two. The former allows you to target outcomes directly and precisely, but the latter may be easier and cheaper to enforce. Where does the French Government stand in this debate?

Mr Seam: We believe that the primary tool for management and conservation of fisheries resources lies in the TACs and quotas regime, so we are more in favour of TACs and quotas than effort management. That is the longstanding position we have taken.

Q733 Chairman: Can I come in here? The evidence we have taken seems to be moving in the other direction, that people seem to be moving away from TACs and quotas and looking more at effort.

Mr Seam: Indeed. I was not there at the time of the reform of the CFP in 2002 but I believe at that time the Commission, and now the Member States, considered that the TACs and quotas combined with control measures on TACs and quotas was not a tight enough system to ensure conservation and management of fisheries resources, and that is the reason why the effort management theme was introduced in the 2002 reform with days at sea, kilowatt days, but this is a system which is extremely difficult to administer, as you say, because we have to re-design every single year following the TACs and Quota Council the way we allocate those fishing days or kilowatt days, depending on the outcome of the Council. Because it is extremely difficult to manage our position already at the time of the reform in 2002 was that the combination of TACs and quotas and control should be the main driver for the management and conservation of the stocks.

Q734 Viscount Brookeborough: There is an argument that TACs and quotas encourage discards. What is your view on discards?

Mr Seam: It is true that discards are a problem. We are aware of the need to reduce discards. We have some doubts with the main option put on the table by the Commission, which is a ban on discards, because we have underlined on several occasions the difficulties associated with that in terms of control management and allocation of the quotas, how you count your catches with the understanding that no discard is available against your quota, and the impact this could have on relative stability, which is a topic, I understand, that we will touch on later. It is extremely difficult to envisage a total ban on discards, so we would favour more a technical approach encouraging development of more selective gears, which is what we already do in some fisheries with quite successful outcomes, for example in the nephrops and hake fisheries, where the nephrops fishery has developed adaptations to the fishing gear which allow them to minimise the by-catch of hake. Of course, we are waiting for the proposals from the Commission on that one because the Commission is planning, to table a proposal to that effect before the end of the year.

Q735 Viscount Brookeborough: But would you not agree that the advances on these technical measures like net sizes and so on have been very slow because, even when we did a previous inquiry some years ago, people were talking about exactly what they are talking about now in the types of windows in the nets and so on? Why has this not progressed, not necessarily in your nation, but throughout? Is it because there is not enough money being put into it or will we still be talking about this in five or ten years' time?

Mr Seam: I cannot predict the future, but I am afraid you are right.

Q736 Viscount Brookeborough: It has not happened.

Mr Seam: Progress is slow. Nevertheless we have some progress, maybe not to the extent that zero by-catch is achieved. I am not sure we can ever achieve a zero by-catch target. Of course, I am a layman in this business, but if you put the gear at sea and it is designed to catch fish you cannot just prohibit some types of fish from entering the gear, even though you have the technical means to design escape windows, a special form or shape or mesh and other tools to minimise by-catch. Of course, when it comes to multi-specific fisheries where you target one specific species because it is of high commercial value but in the area where you fish you have a mixed basket of fish, it is difficult to design a gear which would allow under the same ratio a minimisation of discards for all the other species which are associated with the target species, so it is a technical debate that I leave to the technicians. The official position I am able to defend here is that we will be extremely cautious with the intended implementation of a total discard ban within Community fleets.

Q737 Chairman: It is very difficult, is it not, in a mixed fishery like the demersal white fish fishery? If you have quota for one species and know that you have run out of quota for the rest, you inevitably end up with high discards.

Mr Seam: Yes, indeed.

Q738 Earl of Dundee: How does the French Government assess the performance to date of Regional Advisory Councils?

Mr Seam: We are very satisfied with the way the scheme is implemented in the areas where it is implemented, because, as you know, it is not implemented everywhere yet. Progress is slower in the Mediterranean Sea than in the cold waters maybe, I do not know why, but we are happy with this tool which provides in our view a useful place for the sector and other stakeholders to meet and discuss and exchange views either between different Member States or between different types of stakeholders, so we are very much in favour of Regional Advisory

Councils in terms of their advisory function, but we are not prepared to go for a further step whereby those Regional Advisory Councils would be given a decision-making or management power at this stage.

Q739 Earl of Dundee: If you do not like that idea and do not want them to go for a management role what other thoughts and plans do you have to achieve some proper measure of decentralisation?
Mr Seam: Decentralisation is the next question, is it not?

Q740 Chairman: You are trespassing! You have not got quota for that!
Mr Seam: I am sorry. I read the whole set of questions before coming.

Q741 Lord Cameron of Dillington: Perhaps I could ask a further question on RACs. The Mediterranean RAC has so far failed to get off the ground. Can you explain the problems and how you see that developing?
Mr Seam: The problems I cannot explain. I can only, just as you do, realise that it is slower, it is more difficult. Maybe it is the climate, maybe it is the weather, maybe it is the culture of the countries, I do not know, but certainly the Mediterranean RAC is not the one which was created at first. Nevertheless, we are right now in the process of deciding on the last elements which would allow formal establishment of that Regional Advisory Council. We have to decide on budget, composition, headquarters, but we are making fairly good progress right now.

Q742 Chairman: I can understand your concern to make sure that the RACs remain formally advisory bodies, but the alternative is not just to go from advisory to executive decision-making. A model that we have been presented with in the evidence we have received would take the form of something like the Commission or Council setting the policy parameters by saying mortality rates were to be reduced by X per cent, then going to the RACs and saying, "How do you think it is appropriate in your area to achieve that policy objective? What is necessary to achieve that policy objective?", and then, if the Commission is satisfied that the RAC is coming up with something that is credible, accepting that advice? Is that a model that you would be comfortable with?
Mr Seam: That is as far as we can go in terms of advisory function. We can even discuss with the RACs or ask the RACs to advise us on the validity or the opportunity of the targets you mention, so we can request advice from RACs on any parameter of the management and conservation of the fisheries resources or the fisheries sector, but even if in the context of a RAC (or several RACs for that matter) a common view is achieved, this common view will

have to be factored into the Commission proposal if the Commission so wishes, or afterwards within the negotiation process if the concerned Member States are willing to defend that view. This is a way for the functioning of the system which we can accept but this remains an advisory function. It is not for the RAC to decide on legally constraining instruments, legally binding tools and implement them. The decision-making, the enforcement, the control and the sanction will rest with the public authorities in the Commission and the other institutions here in Brussels and the Member States concerned.
Chairman: I do not think there is that degree of conflict in the two positions that initially might appear. Having slapped the Earl of Dundee down for mentioning the word "decentralisation", perhaps the Earl of Arran would cover that.

Q743 Earl of Arran: There is the criticism, as you well know, that the CFP is too centralized and the suggestion is that some EU institutions might agree on principles and set objectives but that they would devolve technical decisions on implementation to Member States or even to individual regions, so it is a question of balance. What is the French Government's view on this and if that were to happen what do they see as the problems thereby if that were to be suggested?
Mr Seam: I am not sure you will be satisfied with the answer.

Q744 Earl of Arran: I have a feeling you are right.
Mr Seam: I will read it or maybe translate it because it is written in French anyway: "France is favourable to subsidiarity where it is possible but we are cautious with the coherence and the equity of the system".

Q745 Chairman: Magnificent!
Mr Seam: Having said that, I may go beyond my formal instructions which rest in these two lines. We are very much in favour of a regional approach or even a fisheries approach where it is relevant, meaning that we have to take account of the specificities of the regions or the fisheries. This is a position which we have always advocated, most recently—and this is an ongoing process—for the revision of the Cod Recovery Plan where we consider that, contrary to other Member States, the Commission has not gone far enough in the direction of a fishery-specific approach or a regional approach. For example, we dispute the fact that a common target in terms of fishing mortality is equally relevant for all the areas involved. We dispute the fact that the same pace of reduction of fishing mortality or fishing effort is relevant for all the areas involved. Those are elements where we consider differentiations should occur to take account of the specificities of the stocks and the fisheries involved in the different areas. I

think this shows that we are very much in favour of regionalisation. On the other hand, on some issues of principle we consider that the common approach should be preserved at the Community level, for example, for controls. Of course, we have to take account of the specificities of the regions but we cannot go so far as to consider that because of the hot climate in the south the ten per cent control rate is sufficient whereas in the north it should be 50%. It depends on the very specific issues we address and the general statement I gave can be refined according to the very specific elements which we are discussing. For some issues we will defend a regional approach such as fixing targets, fixing the relevant period of reference for assessing the situation of the stock, or the relevant period of reference for assessing the fishing effort because of different trends and different evolutions in the development of the fleet, for example, but for some other elements we are very much in favour of consistency across the board. I cannot give you off the top of my head, beyond those two examples that I have tried to give you to illustrate my position, a general line on those issues which would fall into the square "Common approach" and those issues which would fall into the square "Take account of the specificities".

Q746 *Earl of Arran:* Do you find that general line is in line with the thinking of other Member States?
Mr Seam: Within the limits of my experience so far it seems to me that the southern Member States put very much emphasis on regionalisation which could be labelled otherwise as "the Mediterranean is a different issue".
Baroness Jones of Whitchurch: We have touched on relative stability a little bit already. We have had conflicting opinions in the discussions that we have been having about the importance of relative stability. For example, your colleague from Germany who was here this morning said that this was absolutely crucial to them in terms of future discussions and we wondered what the French position was on this issue.

Q747 *Chairman:* Spain said they would like to do away with it tomorrow.
Mr Seam: Our official position is that we consider that relative stability is a crucial element of the Common Fisheries Policy. I believe we should be quite comfortable with this statement—and this is not in my instructions—because we were not badly treated, I would say, when we decided first the allocation of quotas between Member States, so we are fairly happy with the way it is. Nevertheless, we consider that some elements which are considered as relative stability by some other Member States are not relevant for relative stability in our view. I guess you understand what I refer to. We have a joint

statement from a lot of Member States every year in the Council to express the view that the Hague Preferences undermine relative stability. The Hague Preferences is a system whereby, if the UK or Ireland claim an entitlement to the application of the Hague Preference, the allocation between the Member States concerned is revised to leave a larger share of the quotas to the UK and Ireland to the detriment, of course, of the other Member States concerned because the general TAC remains the same. This is a mechanism which allows a modification of the allocation *acquis* between the Member States concerned in an area concerned with a specific stock, which we consider runs counter to the principle of relative stability because it indeed modifies the allocation *acquis* between Member States, but of course the UK and Ireland do not share that view. They consider that it is an integral part of the relative stability.

Q748 *Chairman:* So is France a signatory to that?
Mr Seam: Yes. We are not only a signatory but I think we were the original drafters of that statement. I should underline that this system does not only exist for Ireland and the UK, even though it does not have the same name. We also have specific preferences for mackerel for Denmark. The system operates in a different manner. It is not upon request from Denmark that the allocation *acquis* is modified between Member States. If the TAC reaches a certain level then the mechanism automatically kicks in and the allocation *acquis* is modified to the advantage of Denmark and to the detriment, of course, of other Member States involved.

Q749 *Baroness Jones of Whitchurch:* So what you are saying is that there is no agreement on the precise application of relative stability? In a sense it could be a meaningless phrase that everybody signs up to but they all have a different interpretation.
Mr Seam: The principle itself is subscribed to by all the Member States which consider that it is a very important element of the Common Fisheries Policy.

Q750 *Lord Cameron of Dillington:* Apart from Spain.
Mr Seam: Even Spain where it suits their needs. The problem for Spain is, of course, that they were not allocated specific quotas in the North Sea and they would like to revise the relative stability in the North Sea. It is not for me to tell you but if you talk to Spain and the way they view relative stability, for example, in the context of fisheries partnership agreements and the way licences are allocated to Member States, for example under those agreements, they would consider that the licences allocated to them are an entitlement for the future, but, of course, in the world in which we live all the Member States will just defend

relative stability where it is convenient. It is the name of the game.

Chairman: Let us go on from relative stability at that level to rights-based management which impacts on relative stability.

Q751 *Lord Cameron of Dillington:* Do you favour the transferable ability of quotas now individually or between Member States or within producer organisations? How far would you take any quota transfer as an individual right, or is the existing system whereby you can change various quotas in various fisheries (which seems to happen even internationally already) sufficient although it is not necessarily fully recognised?

Mr Seam: There are several elements in your question. Are we in favour of individual transferable quotas? The answer is no. We do not want tradable quotas. We do not want to have a private market for quotas. The position is very clear. One of the underlying reasons is that we all realised the way the allocation of fishing rights evolved in some countries where this system applies and the main conclusion we draw from that is that the final result is a concentration of fishing rights within a minority, which is something we do not want to happen in France. When it comes to exchange of quotas between Member States we believe this is an important element to allow flexibility in the system and this is something we are very much in favour of, so it is totally different, of course, because we do not buy the quota. We have to swap quotas, so the quota swapping system is something we are very much in favour of, but beyond that, when it comes to the allocation of quotas within one Member State, we believe subsidiarity has to apply. If in some Member States there is a tradition of allocating within that Member State quota on an administrative basis, which is that the central government or the central authority decides how things are allocated to different areas, different fisheries, different boats maybe, it is fine. If it is a more decentralised system because of other arrangements, it is also fine. It is up to each of the Member States to decide without interfering with the general functioning of the system or within the functioning of the system of another Member State to decide what is best suited for its specific situation.

Q752 *Lord Cameron of Dillington:* But always based on annual TACs rather than long-term quota rights?

Mr Seam: So far, yes, but, talking about individual quotas, we developed in the blue fin tuna quota management an individual quota system with an allocation of a specific annual quota in France to specific boats, the larger boats, but this system of individual quota is not a transferable system. When the quota is exhausted we close the fisheries for the

specific boat concerned. There is no possibility of exchanging quotas from one boat to another, so we retain the competence within the central authority to close the fisheries for those specific boats.

Q753 *Lord Cameron of Dillington:* And that competence should remain with the Member State or the producer organisation or the Community?

Mr Seam: We are flexible on the first two elements you quoted, not the third one. We do not think it is for the Community or for the Commission acting on behalf of the Community to decide on the quota for individual boats. This is a competence which rests within the Member State concerned, but afterwards, whether the Member State wants to have that done by a director of the central administration or the sector itself is up to that Member State.

Q754 *Lord Palmer:* In its annual report for 2006 on Member States' efforts to achieve a sustainable balance between fishing capacity and fishing opportunities, the Commission concluded that insufficient action had been taken by the Member States. Your country, for example, cut its gross tonnage by just over eight per cent over the three-year period 2003-2006. Do you consider this to have been sufficient? How is France using the EFF to assist in making further capacity reductions? Do you plan to allow the EFF to be used to purchase, for example, new engines for certain types of fishing vessels?

Mr Seam: I think to some extent, sir, I have answered that in response to your inquiry on the so-called fuel subsidies.

Q755 *Lord Palmer:* But you said there were not fuel subsidies.

Mr Seam: Indeed. That is the reason why I called them the "so-called fuel subsidies". To complement my first answer and in response to the specific questions you have here, I can say that within this *Plan Barnier* we envisage huge decommissioning budgets because we are very much aware that with the currently high costs of the operation of fishing vessels and the limited stocks to fish we have too many boats.

Q756 *Chairman:* And that is a permanent reduction of capacity, is it?

Mr Seam: And we would address that through a reduction of capacity.

Q757 *Lord Cameron of Dillington:* Have you any percentage?

Mr Seam: I do not have any percentage because we do not decide that alone. We have to tell the sector we have a budget available, but afterwards it will be for the sector itself to figure out whether they want to stay in the business or whether they would be better off quitting the business and scrapping or decommissioning the boat. I cannot just tell you out of 30 purse seiners for blue fin tuna we want to scrap half. This is a voluntary scheme at the end of the day. It is up to the sector. We provide the incentive to do so and we provide sufficient budget to cover all the requests if they arise, but I can tell you that it is a very significant budget we have put in place. Having said that, this should not be a dogma. Decommissioning should not be the only way to address fisheries management and conservation. This is an important tool but we have to design that to make sure that it is targeted either on the segments of the fleets which are the least profitable or, because the costs are too high, for example, of course, bottom trawling would qualify more than gill nets, or because of the specific state of specific stocks. Of course, there is a willingness right now to encourage blue fin tuna vessels to quit the business.

Q758 Chairman: It seems to be subject to some slight contradictory tensions within the Plan Barnier in that at one level you are providing support to enable people to continue in the industry and at the other level you are wanting to decommission.
Mr Seam: We have to do both. It is also through decommissioning that, of course, the size of the fleet will be reduced and that the quotas allocated to those remaining in the business will increase.

Q759 Chairman: But if you did not provide direct support then decommissioning would be a lot more attractive to people.
Mr Seam: It might be.

Q760 Viscount Brookeborough: And you are subsidising an increase in efficiency which is an increase in fishing effort by those that will remain.
Mr Seam: I am not sure because we do not encourage them to adopt more efficient fishing techniques.

Q761 Viscount Brookeborough: But I thought you said earlier that you did, that you were running a plan for making the engines more efficient and for investigating more efficient net techniques.
Mr Seam: I specified more efficient in terms of fuel consumption, not in terms of capacity to catch fish. We are not encouraging more powerful engines, for example, but maybe the same engine or an engine with the same power with a lower consumption of fuel.

Q762 Viscount Brookeborough: Biofuels.
Mr Seam: Maybe, even though we have some doubts on this issue and even though it does not touch on fishery specific concerns.

Q763 Lord Cameron of Dillington: So do we.
Mr Seam: It is out of my portfolio.
Chairman: Thank you very much. That was a superb performance.

THURSDAY 8 MAY 2008

Present
Arran, E.	Palmer, L.
Brookeborough, V.	Plumb, L.
Cameron of Dillington, L.	Sewel, L. (Chairman)
Dundee, E.	Ullswater, V.
Jones of Whitchurch, B.	

Examination of Witness

Witness: MR ROBIN ROSENKRANZ, Fisheries Counsellor, Sweden, examined.

Q764 Chairman: Welcome and thank you very much for coming. Can I explain who we are and what we are? We are a Sub-Committee of our House of Lords European Select Committee and we are carrying out an inquiry into the future of the Common Fisheries Policy. We are coming to the end of our evidence-gathering process and hope to report by the end of July. This session is a formal evidence-taking session so a note will be taken so you will get a transcript as soon as one can be produced and if any slips or errors have come in you can correct them. How would you like to proceed? Would you like to make an opening comment on how Sweden sees the future of the Common Fisheries Policy or just go straight onto individual questions?
Mr Rosenkranz: I could start with a short introduction. In general the debate in Sweden for the past few years has been quite critical of the CFP. We have not come as far as you have but we are starting the procedure of what will be our position in the future CFP and it is very clear already that we find the CFP has failed in many different aspects and needs to be changed fundamentally in its goals and objectives in order to have, as we see it, one of the most important tasks of the CFP, sustainable fisheries.

Q765 Chairman: You are based here and when you look round at your colleagues from other Member States do you see that as a general perspective or is it limited to a relatively small number of Member States, this degree of criticism of what is already in existence?
Mr Rosenkranz: Both, I would say. Speaking to my colleagues on a personal basis, I think there is quite high awareness of the difficulties with the CFP. There is quite a high knowledge of what is wrong. However, when you raise it to ministerial level things become a bit different and more complex. The question is whether we have the courage and the political will to change it, but that is a completely different issue.

Q766 Chairman: Let us try and expose some of those issues as we go through the questions. My opening question is based on the objectives of the Common Fisheries Policy. Certainly the Spanish Government

in their written evidence and also your Spanish colleague when he spoke to us earlier put very strong emphasis on the fact that the Common Fisheries Policy has been too concerned with fish stocks, the biology, and has not recognised the socio-economic dimension. At one level there is not a contradiction there because if you get the fish stocks wrong you do not have any socio-economic dimension.
Mr Rosenkranz: I am glad you said it and not me.

Q767 Chairman: Where do you think the balance has been? Is it right? Is it wrong? What needs to be emphasised?
Mr Rosenkranz: Our position is the opposite of that of the Spanish. I would say we are giving too much concern to the short-term socio-economic aspects. That is our very firm belief, and we think that we have enough evidence to prove it because, looking at the stock situation, in particular the demersal stocks which are the human consumption stocks, it has been going down for quite a while. Looking at the profitability of the fisheries policy, it has also been down. I do not know if you have read David Symes and Michael Sissenwine's report[1]. It is quite illustrative when it comes to the deficiencies of the Common Fisheries Policy. We have very low net profit in the Common Fisheries Policy. It is on average less than 7% of landed value, whereas New Zealand has almost 40% of landed value and the performance is also better in for instance Australia and the United States. Our conclusion is that we have taken too little concern when it comes to the long term gains of not fishing too hard. To come back to your question about the objectives, when we decided on the CFP in 2002 we had some objectives. We had social, economic, biological, cultural and consumer objectives; they were all there in Article 2 in the framework regulation. So by having all these priorities, we in fact have no priority. I do not think it was a mistake because we knew what would happen but we did not have the political strength to do it, so what we have been doing since 2002 is negotiating on

---

[1] "Reflections on the Common Fisheries Policy"—Report to the General Directorate for fisheries and maritime affairs of the European Commission. Prepared by Michael Sissenwine and David Symes, July 2007

a year-by-year basis, never being able to set the priorities between these competing objectives, and that is one of the flaws we have in the CFP. We have not asked what is the first and foremost objective of the CFP. We will, of course, have different opinions on that, but from our point of view the highest priority is conservation, because if we do not have biologically sound stocks it is difficult, as you said yourself, to speak of socio-economic concerns. From our point of view we would like to see in the new CFP much clearer divisions of the priorities between these different objectives. We have to be able to say that the important thing is to have a stock in balance, and to achieve that we have to do certain things. And furthermore, we need to have measurable goals. One issue which is quite interesting is the debate on the MSY, the maximum sustainable yield. Could this be a way of making the policy-makers and politicians understand that we have to find a level of fishing pressure in order for the stock to remain the same or even increase to next year? If we find the optimum level of fishing pressure then we do have a surplus we can fish on and hopefully build up the stock as well. As it is now, in taking these short-term socio-economic concerns what we are doing is fishing harder on stocks which are declining year by year, so from our point of view we see that we have to have conservation as the first and foremost objective. This is the basis and the ground for everything we do afterwards.

Q768 Viscount Brookeborough: Just on that point, if we look at the longer term it becomes really based on scientific knowledge and one of the major problems is between real time (which is the fishermen and what they want to do) and the scientists and whether or not the science is good enough.
Mr Rosenkranz: I would pose the question a bit differently. We have had the knowledge of declining stocks for many years. In Sweden biologists say, "Why do you not listen to our advice? It is obvious", and since we don't listen to them, what they do is shout even louder. But the problem is not the politicians not being able to read what the biologists say. Because the advice is quite obvious; it says, "No fishing in the North Sea for cod". It is not difficult to read that, but we still do not do it, so the question is why? I find the problem in the inherent difficulties in the CFP and what we have created. I am not saying we have created a monster but we have created something which is very difficult to change.

Q769 Viscount Ullswater: A lot of my question you have already answered because fisheries management has traditionally been dominated by the Member States working through the Council and I think you have indicated that there are various pressures that the Member States feel under when addressing the

management tools at their disposal. Can you indicate anything that might have occurred since 2002 with the accession of the other Member States in 2004 and 2007 that might have altered the balance in the CFP Council?
Mr Rosenkranz: This is a very good question. We had both fears and hopes with the accession of the new Member States. I would say that neither of them has been fulfilled. It is different but still the same. If you look at it from the Swedish point of view, we were, of course, hoping that we would have more Member States on the conservationist side. We might not have got that many on that side, but on the other hand there have not been many Member States on the other side either, maybe with the exception of—

Q770 Chairman: Poland.
Mr Rosenkranz: Thank you for saying it. But, looking at the major bulk of Member States, they more or less follow the majority, so there has not been that much change. One thing that we have been trying to see if there has been a difference in in whether it is easier for Member States to gather blocking minorities. That could be one thing that has happened and we have seen a few examples of it already, for instance, on the Eel Recovery Plan which we decided on about a year ago. There was a minority there but it was not blocking. It was France, Spain and a few more. Then, for some reason, Romania came into that blocking minority, and they had no interest whatsoever in eel but they kept on until the bitter end to form a blocking minority. It was very obvious that a new Member State helped an old Member State to form a blocking minority on an issue which couldn't have been of major importance for them.

Q771 Viscount Ullswater: So this was effectively horse-trading on another issue, was it?
Mr Rosenkranz: Yes, that could be one explanation.

Q772 Chairman: That is fascinating because your German colleague said exactly the opposite. He said that the effect of the new states coming in was that the Commission was getting its own way.
Mr Rosenkranz: I just gave you one example. Then we have all the other examples where I cannot clearly see where this has been a disadvantage. We were a bit afraid of this but, as I said, neither my fears nor my hopes have been fulfilled so it is quite difficult to give a clear answer on that. It is different but still the same.

Q773 Lord Plumb: Can I ask whether it will improve or delay after the co-decision procedure starts when we look at the Parliament itself? There is a greater responsibility, I put it that way, rather than an involvement. If they have responsibility surely they have to get their act together a bit and not just complain all the time.

Mr Rosenkranz: That is one of the things that we are trying to analyse at the moment very thoroughly because we all want to know what will happen when the Parliament has co-decision on most issues of fisheries. They will not have that on TACs and quotas but they will have on recovery plans and on many other issues. It will delay things, of course, and in some aspects it might get worse from our point of view because it is the Fisheries Committee that will deal with the issues and traditionally there are more people there from Member States with clear fishing interests rather than conservationist interests. However, looking at the Parliament as a whole, the situation is a bit different, so we would try to raise the fisheries issues to the whole Parliament and not just the Fisheries Committee. This is an issue that we will look through very clearly and thoroughly for the coming years.

Lord Plumb: I share your view, having been there.

Q774 *Viscount Brookeborough:* The introduction of recovery and management plans was the main plank of the 2002 reform of the CFP. What is your explanation of why so few recovery and management plans have been adopted and what can be done to speed up the process and improve the results delivered by those plans that are in place?

Mr Rosenkranz: Now you come to the core of the problem, I would say. We have had some plans that have been adopted. We have had the Eel Recovery Plan, which I mentioned, we have the North Sea cod stock and the Baltic Sea cod stock management plans, and we have the Plaice and Flat Fish Recovery Plan, so we have had some management plans. The problems is that they have not worked. We are now revising the North Sea Cod Recovery Plan.

Q775 *Viscount Brookeborough:* But your plan is no fishing?

Mr Rosenkranz: No. The recovery plans are for fishing but why do they not work? I think it has a little bit to do with the inherent problems that we have when we come to these recovery plans, and one of these problems is that the European fishing fleet is way too big. It is huge compared to the fishing resource we have. As long as it is like that it will be difficult to come with any recovery plan, any technical measures, any closed areas, et cetera, as long as we do not deal with the major and inherent problem of having way too big a fleet in balance to the available resource. With the fleet we have the pressure is strong from the Member States' fishing industries that they have to make a living. They pay rents on these boats, they keep their families, we have the concerns from the regions, et cetera, and these boats are extremely expensive and they have to pay for them, so with this huge over-capacity (and I would think it is most Member States), in spite of all the recovery plans, all the measures taken, it will be very difficult to make them work because we will have this pressure. We will always have the exceptions, we will always have these socio-economic concerns, so I think that is one of the reasons why most things we do and most things we have done since 2002 have not worked sufficiently.

Q776 *Viscount Brookeborough:* So where in your view is the over-capacity? Looking at the UK, we found that probably there was not over-capacity there. The French representative who was here just previously said, "Yes, we have over-capacity and we want to reduce it". Where else is this over-capacity?

Mr Rosenkranz: We have it.

Q777 *Viscount Brookeborough:* And Spain?

Mr Rosenkranz: Yes, Spain, but I would say most Member States. I know very little of the UK capacity or over-capacity but I would say that there is some there as well.

Q778 *Viscount Brookeborough:* Yes; there might be some in England rather than Scotland.

Mr Rosenkranz: Possibly. The Commission's assessment is that we are speaking in general about 40 or 50% over-capacity. Also, looking at the profitability of the European Community Fisheries Policy, as I mentioned earlier, we have maybe 8% profitability, and in some species we pay more money through our funds than we gain from the fishing resource. Why could we not have a much higher profitability like they have in New Zealand or Canada or Australia? There is a relation between too many vessels and too little resource, so I would think most Member States have over-capacity.

Q779 *Viscount Brookeborough:* Approximately what size is your fleet?

Mr Rosenkranz: We have around 2,000 fishermen and I would say we have an over-capacity in the pelagic sector, which is a bit better, with about 30% and in the demersal stocks like cod maybe 50% over-capacity, and still we have already cut down a lot. There are extreme benefits from having a fleet in balance with the resource, and having over-capacity is very detrimental for all the decisions we take on technical measures and activities.

Chairman: What you have been saying so far leads to the conclusion that the politicians are not up to managing the problem, and the question then is why is that?

Lord Plumb: Because they are politicians.

Q780 *Chairman:* They seem to be up to managing coal mines and things like that much more easily than they do fishing.

Mr Rosenkranz: I fully agree. We cannot blame the politicians completely. We also have to look at the history. We started building up the European fleet after the Second World War and we have done it up until now. In the eighties and nineties we realised that the stock could collapse, which was news to us then. We could not understand that the stocks could collapse, so after building up the fleet with taxpayers' money for 30, 40, 50 years, suddenly we had to change the policy and cut it down to what it was 20, 30, 40 years before. It is quite difficult for politicians if they come from coastal regions which have large fishing interests. Nevertheless, I think this will happen in one way or another, either with bankruptcies or more fish stock collapsing, but then it will be more of a market issue where a lot of fishing vessels will be available to market because the fishermen has gone bankrupt, or we can do it by helping partly with funds but also partly with the market.

Q781 *Earl of Arran:* As you are aware, the Court of Auditors were scathing in the report they produced last October in relation to control and enforcement. What is your view about this, about the new regulation? Do you support some form of harmonisation and minimum penalties? Do you give added strength to the Fisheries Protection Control Agency? What do you think about this?

Mr Rosenkranz: In spite of us being very conservationist and finding ways to improve fishing control and so on, we do have a problem on having harmonised rules and having penalty rules decided by the European Community. It is a constitutional difficulty for Sweden as well. What we have tried to do is at a national level increase the penalty levels and increase also the administrative sanctions, because we have a penal system an administrative sanction system. It has to be painful to commit a crime in fishery but we have not come to the stage where we can allow the Community to regulate on penal levels; we are not there yet in Sweden. I wish we were but we are not. When it comes to the new control reform, yes we are for simplification. We are also for what you might call risk-based assessment. Control is expensive and with the amount of money we have we have to make sure that we get the best result from it. That means that we are not in favour of having all these forms. I am perhaps being a bit negative but, just to make my point, we do not want the control agencies having to spend hours and hours filling in forms. We want them to find the ones who are breaking the law and do that as efficiently as possible, so we do not want a huge administrative system. We want them to be able to say, "There is the problem; let us go for it", so we want simplification and flexibility in order to make control as inexpensive and as efficient as possible.

Q782 *Earl of Arran:* Having said that, would you be confident that within three, four or five years' time the Court of Auditors would not bring in the same critical and scathing report?

Mr Rosenkranz: No. We still need a couple more parameters to get that working, and that is a social contract with the fishermen. We can speak of all the control policies we want, we can have all the controllers we want on the boats, but this has no effect compared to if we get social control by the fishermen themselves. This is what we see in Sweden now in cod fishing because we have had a lot of difficulty with illegal fishing in the Baltic Sea. Now, speaking with fishermen, they check each other, they control each other, and that is so much more efficient. If we can create regulations and rules that are accepted by the fishermen and used by them because they feel they should abide by the rules this would be worth so much more than all the control regulations we can come up with, but we need this in combination so you cannot look at it separately.

Q783 *Viscount Ullswater:* Can I just ask about illegal fishing? What form does it take with your fleet, for instance? Is it landing in unauthorised places?

Mr Rosenkranz: I think it is mainly misreporting. Let us say they catch 200 kilos; they only report 170 or 180. As far as I know we do not have black markets where they have landings at night and they do not have trucks at night transporting to Holland or Germany or wherever[2]. That is what we saw up until recently in Poland, where they had organised black fishing. They were fishing at night where they knew there were not control agents out and they landed at night. It was very organised. So far we have not seen this going on in Sweden. I hope we won't in either and I think it has diminished in Poland as well.

Q784 *Viscount Ullswater:* It is as important then to exercise control on the land, to inspect the markets, to see the fish landed, to weigh it or whatever, as it is on the sea?

Mr Rosenkranz: It is less expensive to do it on land and it is also less expensive using what the Commission calls cross-checking, so not only at landing but they go to the next level, to the distributor, so by using sales notes, et cetera, this can be done in an office from nine to five, seeing, "There are 500 kilos here but there is only registered 100 kilos there. What happened?". That is a very efficient way of doing it and I think the Commission is working on that and we are open to using that method as well because controlling at sea is very expensive and sometimes quite difficult.

---

[2] This is of course difficult to know for sure, since illegal fishery tends to be very unofficial.

Q785 Chairman: You mentioned what I suppose is a culture of compliance now in the industry. What brought that about, do you think?

Mr Rosenkranz: One of the reasons was that last year—and I am speaking mainly of Sweden now; I cannot extrapolate to other Member States—we had this statistical measurement where we registered the fishermen, what they landed when they knew there was a controller at the port and how much they landed when they knew that there was no controller. There was a difference. When having a controller waiting at harbour they always reported much more than when they knew there was no controller at harbour, so there was a difference there and, taking all the landings together, you had quite a large statistical number showing that the difference between controlled landings and uncontrolled landings was about 20%. Extrapolating this to the whole fleet, we assumed that the unreported landings were about 20%. In the end it turned out to be 9 or 10%, using the whole fleet and the whole cod stock. What we did, based on these statistical results, was that when we had 90% left of a quota we stopped it and said, "We have exhausted our annual quota, because we have also included illegal landings". The message to the fishermen was, "You cannot get away. We will do this", so they knew that reporting when there was no controller at landing and recording less, which is what they did, did not help because if you have 1,000 or 2,000 landings you get a statistical trend. Stopping our fishery gave the very clear message, "Do not fish illegally because we will catch you anyway", and so far they have not tried suing us in court because we think we have enough statistical evidence showing it. We cannot prosecute anyone, but we are collectively penalising them by diminishing the quota.

Q786 Viscount Brookeborough: And has it now evened out?

Mr Rosenkranz: We will soon find out because we are taking new measurements, but this has made very good results in Poland, for instance, because they did the same thing. What they did, which is very important to say, is that they included the overfishing in their statistics, so instead of fishing 30% of the quota, they claimed, "We have fished 60% because we have also included illegal landings", and these are signals which I think are extremely powerful and important for fishermen. There is, of course, a risk that they will stop reporting altogether and use the black landings at night because those do not exist in the statistics and then we have to find other means of approaching that, but we are trying to reach the fishermen that are in the grey zone. With the ones in the black zone it is much more difficult but with the ones in the grey zone it is a bit easier to get them into the white zone if they know that it is difficult to cheat.

Q787 Earl of Arran: Are they criminal prosecutions or civil prosecutions?

Mr Rosenkranz: I am not sure about the difference.

Q788 Earl of Arran: When you do prosecute a fishermen for breaking the law, is it a criminal offence or a civil offence?

Mr Rosenkranz: It could be two kinds. We have criminasl prosecutions and administrative sanctions which could be applied.

Q789 Earl of Arran: It depends what he has done?

Mr Rosenkranz: Yes, for serious infringements we apply criminal prosecutions, for less serious we have an administrative system. But in some cases both could be applied.

Q790 Baroness Jones of Whitchurch: We have heard all sorts of different views on which is best, quotas or effort management, and I wondered where Sweden stood in this debate.

Mr Rosenkranz: Quota management is not very good but it is the best we have so far. Effort management is, of course, in many ways much better. We tried to launch an experiment in the Kattegat, which is a small region between Sweden and Denmark. If you have the map in front of you you can see that there is water between Sweden and Denmark. It is a very limited area. It is mainly two Member States, or three with Germany but they have opted out of this project. We are trying to see if we can have a pure effort management system where the fishermen have much fewer fishing days but they are allowed to land everything they catch. This has become very difficult to agree on because they want to land everything but on the other hand we are still bound to the quota system through the European Community, so we are trying to find a level where we can have enough effort for the fishermen to be able to survive on a pure effort system but low enough that we do not reach too high quota levels. The benefits of an effort system where you can land everything you catch is that you have much fewer discards, for instance. The disadvantage is a bit of what I spoke earlier about, which is that we have a huge fleet and they can, if they want to, fish very efficiently with very few fishing days.

Q791 Chairman: Long holidays!

Mr Rosenkranz: Yes, but it becomes a bit awkward if they can catch their annual quota in maybe 20 days, which is the case with the low quotas we have at the moment. I think that would go also for the North Sea, maybe not 20 days but very few days, so we are getting to the same problem again with a very big fleet which is not in balance with the resource.

Q792 Baroness Jones of Whitchurch: But you are defining effort management as days at sea, are you not? There are other ways of controlling it.

Mr Rosenkranz: Yes. We have no clear stand on which would be the best. You have the kilowatt system, you have the tonnage system, you have the days at sea system. We have tried a little bit of all of these systems. I am afraid I am not expert enough to say which is the best but we do want the effort system to expand because with the quota system we see, at least in Sweden and the Kattegat but I think particularly in the North Sea as well, a lot of discards and for fishermen that is completely unacceptable and they cannot understand, it and I understand that.

Q793 Earl of Dundee: How does the Swedish Government assess the performance to date of Regional Advisory Councils in general and those in the Baltic and North Sea areas in particular?

Mr Rosenkranz: I have to be very careful here because we find them extremely important and they need to be in the centre of the decision-making process because, as I said earlier, having a social contract with the fishermen is one of the most efficient ways of controlling them, so having acceptance by the fishermen when we make decisions is one of the vital keys to having a system that works. In saying that, I do not think the RACs have produced much so far, a bit but not much. We need to give them time and we need to give them the resources to do it. I think that we will find them a key player in having a scheme that works but for that they need time and they need to develop.

Q794 Earl of Dundee: In due course would you like these bodies to develop a management role?

Mr Rosenkranz: I think we need to give them the chance and I think we need to find ways of giving them that power[3]. It is very difficult because politicians want to keep the power, of course, but at the same time in certain cases, and I would say on a case-by-case basis, we will need to try to see if we can give them those powers because we also need to make the RACs feel that they have an importance. If they do not feel they have an importance then we will lose them.

Q795 Chairman: Some of your colleagues have expressed real concerns about RACs, seeing them as a threat to the commonality of the Common Fisheries Policy and as the introduction of regionalisation and even renationalisation of the fisheries.

Mr Rosenkranz: I would not agree, and that is not because we have a Swedish Chairman in the North Sea RAC and a Swedish Chairman in the Baltic Sea RAC.

[3] This, however, is my personal point of view.

Q796 Chairman: We have met your North Sea Chairman.

Mr Rosenkranz: I think that in analysing the difficulties with the scheme before the one in 2002 we saw that there was too big a distance between politicians and fishermen. The construction and the creation of the RACs was a way to remedy that problem. I think it would be the wrong way to go to stop that process. We need to integrate them even more in the decision process but it is tricky and difficult and there will be a lot of reluctance but we need that.

Q797 Baroness Jones of Whitchurch: Many of our witnesses have taken the view that the CFP is currently over-centralised. They have suggested that the EU institutions might in future decide on principles and a set of objectives but devolve technical decisions on implementation to the Member States or even to individual regions. Would Sweden support moves towards decentralisation along these lines, and to what extent might this type of governance structure exacerbate control and enforcement problems?

Mr Rosenkranz: To the first question, yes and no. It is a bit like the RAC issue. There are certain issues that need to be centralised. There are certain issues that do not. Looking at the new North Sea Cod Recovery Plan, for instance, the Commission has proposed that effort management and the division of effort between fleets could be managed by the Member States themselves. The proposal sets the level of the effort and then it is up to the Member State to divide this between fleets and segments. That is, I think, an obvious way of decentralising and letting it be at a lower level. This could be decentralised even more. The Member States could leave it to regions to divide on this, so we have ways in which we could decentralise. On the other hand, taking, for instance, gear definitions and restrictions, it is extremely tricky. I do not know if any of you have read these regulations on gears—ten millimetres mesh with a square mesh panel, et cetera. I never understand them. I always look at them but I always leave it to my experts because I have never been able to understand these regulations. Looking at the selectivity and how this can be used, misused, abused, et cetera, I think we will create even more problems if we decentralise this because then we will have one type of gear in one Member State, another type of gear in another Member State. They both claim that these are very selective but then we need an independent scientist to compare these measurements, and, speaking of the control, this poor control agent who will have to look 20 or 30 different gear fishing for the same kind of fish, it will be impossible for him to do this. I would say yes to decentralising but looking at it on a case-by-case basis, because if not we will have a lot of difficulties.

Q798 Viscount Ullswater: Do you think it is helpful then that DG Fish, now DG Mare, has split itself into various sectors? Do you think that is helpful in encouraging decentralisation?

Mr Rosenkranz: I think that is one of the reasons they have done it. I do not want to comment on the reorganisation but if they can find benefits from doing that I will, of course, support it, and if there is a possibility that it will work, because the Mediterranean is not the Baltic Sea and the Baltic Sea is not the North Sea and we have to look it that way, that these are completely different fishing methods, fishing times, fishing fleets, segments, et cetera. They are not the same.

Q799 Viscount Ullswater: One size does not fit all?

Mr Rosenkranz: No, it does not.

Viscount Ullswater: I think they have learned that.

Q800 Baroness Jones of Whitchurch: Do I gather from what you were saying that you do not approve of the way they have grouped some of their responsibilities, because we have heard some other comments along those liens?

Mr Rosenkranz: I try not to. Let us say we might have some fears as well but we will definitely give the Commission the benefit of the doubt. We will not be able to influence this anyway, at least not Sweden, so—how do you put it?—if you cannot beat them, join them.

Chairman: We will move on to Lord Plumb's question on rights-based management. In responding to Lord Plumb could you also touch on your view of relative stability and the centrality or otherwise of it?

Q801 Lord Plumb: This refers to the debate that has been launched by the Commission on rights-based management. If you could tell us what your Government's position is on the tradability of fishing rights, which is something that has come up in the whole of our discussions, and whether you share the concerns that an ITQ system might lead to an undesirable concentration of fishing rights either in particular geographical regions or among certain types of vessel, we would be very interested to hear your views on that.

Mr Rosenkranz: This is a pertinent and very important issue. I might start by saying that in Sweden many years ago we were not in favour of ITQ systems or rights-based management systems. The reasons were various but one of them was, is it right to have a public resource like a fishing resource turned into a commercial interest? This is a common heritage for the citizens and the states. Why should this be handed over to private interests? Now we

might look at it a bit differently. As I said before, one of the major problems with the CFP is that the fleet is too big in balance to the resource and that puts pressure on the politicians to decide on quotas which are unsustainable, which means that the next year we have to decrease the quotas or keep them at an unsustainable level. It is a vicious circle and one of those vicious circles is, of course, that the fishing fleet is too big. However, using the fisheries funds and the public money we have in the community is not enough to decrease the fishing fleet to a sustainable level. It would cost us so much money to decrease the fishing fleet to a sustainable level. Therefore, now we are beginning to think differently and we see that some of this could be also financed by the market by introducing rights-based management systems. What we as an example could do is turn over the resource to the fishermen and allow them to decide whether they want to try to stay in the market or sell it for a reasonable price. Of course, coming to your second question, this will mean fewer vessels and for every vessel leaving the fishery it will be more profitable for the ones that remain, but this will be regulated partly by the Government's fund, by the scrapping and decommissioning, but also partly by the market. This might be a way of speeding up the necessary decrease of the fishing fleet. How do we do it to avoid disadvantages? In Sweden, as in the UK, we have a big coast. So we have coastal regions which we think should in some way benefit and we think that there should be ways of introducing ITQs or rights-based management systems and still taking regional concerns. We could for instance set aside part of the quota for regions—and we ccould say that everything within the 12-mile zone should be fished by the regions and everything outside can be distributed with ITQs. You can go even further than that. Why should it just be in Sweden? It could be a market between Sweden and Denmark and the Netherlands. Looking at the Netherlands pelagic fleet, they own a lot of the UK quota already as well as the Swedish quota, so we have that already in some aspects, but this is for the future to see how we can construct a system which can help us decrease the fleet faster, but we think that we can, in constructing the system, also take regional concerns into account because as long as we have these regional concerns we will have to take care of them as well.

Q802 Lord Plumb: Is this an area where the RACs would have a role?

Mr Rosenkranz: Yes, absolutely.

Q803 Lord Plumb: This is regional, as you say, very much a hands-on operation, I think.

Mr Rosenkranz: Yes indeed. It is very difficult for me to foresee exactly what role they would have, but they could very much be involved in this.

Q804 *Lord Cameron of Dillington:* Just carrying on from that, as you rightly say, over-capacity is the big problem and you have 30% over-capacity in your pelagic fleet and 50% in the rest. Even if you transfer the quotas you need somehow to reduce the capacity in a more effective way than just in the marketplace. Have you got a big decommissioning programme?
Mr Rosenkranz: We have a decommissioning programme but there is not enough money in it to decommission all that we need to. I spoke to the Commission the other day about it. There has been a huge change within the fishing fleets around Europe. Before they said, "We do not want to decommission. We want to stay in our business. My father did this, my grandfather did this; I am not leaving". Today it is very different. With the present fuel prices and lack of resources there are probably more fishermen asking for decommissioning money than before. We are in a different situation now.

Q805 *Lord Cameron of Dillington:* If there were to be encouragement from the European Fisheries Fund, for instance, for major European-wide decommissioning, should it be left to Member States or do you think there would be Member States trying to hold their fishing fleet together and not utilising it?
Mr Rosenkranz: That is a very good question because, of course, the one who remains in the end is the winner. It will have to be managed in some way. It has to be managed by the Member States but maybe you could find incentives from regulations like the new CFP or from the Commission to make sure that all Member States do what they need to do. You can have some kind of coercive diplomacy. I am not sure what we are looking for here but it has to be divided so that all Member States make an effort. We have failed when it comes to decommissioning because we have not reached the level that we have aimed for, but the Commission could propose much higher levels of decomissions so that all Member States have to make a large effort and then they would have to take a clearer stand on ITQs, et cetera. Trying to find stronger incentives could be a way forward.

Q806 *Chairman:* Just to finish off, what do you think of so-called fuel subsidies?
Mr Rosenkranz: I think they are horrible[4].

Q807 *Chairman:* That is why I asked. It seems to be a particularly perverse policy.
Mr Rosenkranz: Yes.
Chairman: Thank you very much indeed.

---

[4] The fundamental problem in the fisheries sector is the poor stock situation and the over capacity. The net profit of the European Fisheries is very poor (less than 7% of landed value). Furthermore, the stock situation in EC waters on average, is poor; European fish stocks are overfished by 81% to be compared to a worldwide average of "only" 25%. By subsidizing fuel we continue to lower the net profit, we continue to make it less expensive for fishermen on declining and weak stocks. The result will no doubt make the trend of declining stock continue. What we should do is rather adjust the fleet capacity with decommissioning and scrapping vessels so that there is a balance between fleet and stock.

THURSDAY 8 MAY 2008

Present   Arran, E.   Palmer, L.
                          Brookeborough, V.   Plumb, L.
                          Cameron of Dillington, L.   Sewel, L. (Chairman)
                          Dundee, E.   Ullswater, V.
                          Jones of Whitchurch, B.

Examination of Witnesses

Witnesses: Mr Geir Evensen and Mr Paul Oma, Fisheries Cousnellors, Norwegian Government, examined.

Q808 Chairman: Good afternoon. Thank you very much for coming to help us. Let me briefly explain what we are about and who we are. We are a Sub-Committee of the House of Lords Select Committee on the European Union. We are carrying out an inquiry into the Common Fisheries Policy and we have had one and a half days solid of the Common Fisheries Policy. You are our last witnesses. I am glad to say that the words "Common Fisheries Policy" are banned for this session. It is a great opportunity for us to hear from you. We are very grateful to you for coming along so that we can hear about a totally different system, something to reflect on and think about. This is a formal evidence session so a note will be taken and you will get a transcript of it and be able to correct it in the light of any errors that may happen. Would you like to start by making an introductory statement and then go on to questions and answers?

Mr Evensen: Yes. Let me first say that we are pleased to come here and have the opportunity to talk a little about the Norwegian policy. I have prepared some numbers for you which give a little overview of the Norwegian fisheries. Let me introduce my colleague, Paul Oma. He works here at the Mission as a Fisheries Counsellor. He is responsible for the resource management. I am also a Fisheries Counsellor. I am more into trade and exports and agriculture. The total production in 2007 was somewhere between 3.5 million and 3.6 million tonnes. We do not have the exact numbers yet, but it is a bit too early but it is a little more than 3.5 million tonnes. That includes fish and fishery products from both Norwegian vessels and foreign vessels. The wild fish was 2.8 million tonnes approximately. 300,000 tonnes of that was from foreign vessels and it leaves 2.5 million tonnes from Norwegian vessels landed in Norway. We have about 7,300 vessels. That was in 2006 according to the register. We have about 14,000 fishermen. If you look at the aquaculture sector the production in 2006 was 708,000 tonnes. We do not have the exact numbers for 2007 but it will be a lot more, probably more than 800,000 tonnes. We have about 2,900 licences in the aquaculture sector. The important ones are 929 licences for salmon and rainbow trout. That is the commercial end, big industry. In addition we have a lot of licences for shellfish, cod, halibut and other species which are very small in quantity. Our industry is certainly an export industry. About 95% of the production is exported and seafood exports are about 5% of the total exports from Norway. Of course, oil and gas are the big articles here. I think they were 68% of total exports in 2006. Seafood will be the third biggest article when it comes to export value but it is important to remember that the seafood industry is something which takes place along the entire coast. It is very important to all the small societies we have in Norway. We are proud of our exports. Last year the amount was 37 billion Norwegian kroner, which is about £3.7 billion. That was a new record. The biggest articles are salmon, of course, with more than 17 billion Norwegian kroner, and cod and herring are second and third on that list. Every day 27 million meals of Norwegian seafood are served around the world. When it comes to land-based industry, we have about 700 plants which are approved to process fish in one way or another. In addition we have vessels which are approved for processing fish, like factory vessels. Those are some figures for you. I do not know exactly what you are planning but you have a note from the Ministry of Fisheries which explains a little about the politics of the fishery arena but if you want to hear about aquaculture or the organisation of the market in Norway we can explain that.

Chairman: So far we have tended to put aquaculture on one side and I think we will continue with that. We are interested in how you organise, regulate and control your sea fishing industry.

Q809 Viscount Ullswater: In your paper you emphasise that restrictions on access to fisheries are critical to conservation as well as to the economy of the fleet. How do you ensure that the capacity of the fleet is in line with the available fishing opportunities?

Mr Oma: First of all I have to say that we do not have a balance yet between resources and fishing capacity. There is still to a large extent over-capacity in the fishing fleet. However, we are trying to get there and we have over the last 10 years seen a significant reduction in the number of vessels. My colleague mentioned that in 2006 we had 7,300 vessels approximately and 10 years ago we had 13,600, so it is a 46% reduction in the number of vessels. We have also been looking at engine power. There was an increase in engine power even though the number of vessels was reduced. For many decades we have had a reduction in the number of vessels but the total engine power went up for the fishing fleet, so not until 2001 were we able to turn that capacity in engine power around. Since 2001 we have had approximately an 8% reduction in engine power for the fishing fleet. We have several measures in place for trying to get a better balance. For the smallest coastal fishing fleet vessels below 11 metres we have a scrapping programme in place. We have had that for many years. That has been very successful and now there is not much over-capacity in that segment of the fleet. I believe that perhaps this year will be the last year of this scrapping programme. When you are building a new vessel or trying to upgrade your vessel we have limitations on stowage capacity. For instance, in the purse seiner fleet you are not allowed to have stowage capacity beyond 2,000 cubic metres and in the coastal fleet the limit is 300 cubic metres. It sets a limit on how big the vessels can be. Some years ago we introduced a fee to be registered as a fishing vessel and that simple measure actually removed a huge number of small, inactive vessels which constituted a potential fishing capacity if we introduced tradable quotas.

Q810 *Viscount Ullswater:* Is it an annual licence fee?
Mr Oma: It is an annual licence fee now, yes. In the first years it was quite high and now it is at a lower level. Also, we have what we call structural measures. This means that we have divided the fleet into different segments or groups, so within your group, for instance, if you are in ocean-going vessels, you are not allowed to buy or transfer quotas from coastal vessels; there are fences between the different groups, but within your group you are allowed to transfer quotas. The general rule is that you can fish three times your original quota with one vessel. The vessel that transfers its quota is not allowed to fish in that fishery, of course. If I have a vessel with 100 tonnes of cod, let us say, and my colleague here has another vessel with 100 tonnes of cod and we are in the same group, I can offer him an economic compensation and then I will be able to fish his quota but only 80 tonnes of his quota. The 20 remaining tonnes go back to the group so it means that everybody benefits from these structural measures, including those not participating in it. Everybody buying quota will, of course, have more to fish but also the ones not buying extra quotas will have some extra bigger quotas to share among themselves.

Q811 *Baroness Jones of Whitchurch:* Is there a set price for the quota?
Mr Oma: No. The market takes care of the price.

Q812 *Viscount Brookeborough:* And is the quota redistributed every year to the boats or do they own it individually?
Mr Oma: In the most important fisheries we have divided up the quota into factors, so every vessel with a licence has a certain percentage of the Norwegian quota.

Q813 *Viscount Brookeborough:* But the size may vary from year to year?
Mr Oma: Yes, but you have this factor that is stable, and then it will vary according to the level of their total allowable catch, of course. If I just can mention a few things about the profitability of the industry on the fleet levels, we have seen that we have increased profitability according to this. We believe that structural measures have increased the profitability in the industry.

Q814 *Earl of Arran:* You mentioned technical regulations but how do you go about them? Do you impose measures such as mesh sizes or gear types, et cetera, to be used on your vessels or do you incentivise and reward them for using the best technology available? How does it work?
Mr Oma: The simple answer is yes, we impose regulations. We have no incentive-based regulations. When it comes to technical regulations they are fixed and have to be followed.

Q815 *Earl of Arran:* Do you use mesh sizes?
Mr Oma: Yes. We have a very sophisticated system of technical regulations and they range from twine thickness to mesh size to minimum sizes of fish and everything. We have also very specific regulations when it comes to what kind of gear technology you have to apply.

Q816 *Earl of Arran:* Are they similar mesh sizes for catching similar types of fish as used by Member States in the EU?
Mr Oma: Yes. We have the same mesh size. When it comes to demersal fisheries in the North Sea, for instance, we have 120 millimetres. I know that in the Community waters you are allowed to use 110 millimetres fishing for saithe but in the Norwegian economic zone it is 120 millimetres. Other than that we have the same mesh sizes in the demersal fisheries, but we do not allow for what you call nephrops fisheries in your waters with 70 or 90 millimetres. That is not allowed in Norwegian waters.

Q817 *Chairman:* Can I go back to quotas for a moment? How is the Norwegian quota calculated or decided upon and to what extent are fishermen's organisations involved in that discussion?

Mr Oma: First and foremost it is based upon scientific advice. We enter into negotiations with the EU or Russia and we have our share of these quotas which we agree with you. Then we have internal discussions in Norway on how to distribute them between the Norwegian fleet groups and the Directorate of Fisheries makes a proposal for how we should regulate the fishery for the coming year and he invites then the full spectrum of interested parties, the NGOs in environmental organisations and all the fishing industry from fishermen's organisations to processing organisations, and they exchange views on the Director-General's fisheries proposal. Based upon these discussions, the Director-General of Fisheries will send his proposal to the Ministry of Fisheries and the final decision will be taken by the Minister of Fisheries. Normally in these meetings we will try to get a compromise solution and it is very rare that the Minister does not follow the recommendation. In certain cases, of course, the Director-General of Fisheries has only to reflect the discussions and say, "My recommendation is this and the industry needs this", and the Ministry has to take the decision on how they want to do it.

Q818 *Lord Cameron of Dillington:* When it comes to trading quota does the Government act as the broker?

Mr Oma: No.

Q819 *Lord Cameron of Dillington:* But there are independent brokers, are there?

Mr Oma: Yes, sure, there are independent brokers.

Chairman: Let us go on now to an area which has fascinated us, which is your discard policy.

Q820 *Baroness Jones of Whitchurch:* We have seen what you have written about the discard ban and, as the Chairman says, we are very interested to know a little bit more about it. Can you explain how it fits with the quota system, because if you have an operating quota system you must be catching fish that are outside the quota, so how do you designate those, and how do you enforce it to make sure that it works well?

Mr Oma: It is a complex system and it is difficult to explain in very few words but I will try. First of all, you are quite right that there are fish caught in Norway outside the quotas, but all landings of fish, for instance, of cod, will be deducted from the Norwegian quota even if it is illegal catch from a vessel without a quota accidentally getting by-catch. When he lands this, for which he has no quota, it will be deducted from the Norwegian quota. However,

the fisherman will not receive any money or payment for this. He will only get a small compensation to cover the cost of landing it. The general rule is that if you land illegal fish or fish outside the quota you will receive 20% of the minimum price in Norway. It is just an incentive for them to land it, so they can legally land it but they will not have any profitability from such activities. The basic principle is that everything is counted against the Norwegian quota. There are no free fish for Norway, so to speak. Also, before we divide the quota to all the vessels in some fisheries, we take out what we expect to be landed outside the quotas. That is one mechanism we use. How do we enforce this? It is, of course, very difficult to monitor everything that goes on at sea because the discard ban has to be enforced at sea, of course, and we have traditionally spent most of our effort on control at sea. The reason is obvious, because we have this discard ban in place. We spend huge resources on control at sea and the coastguard and the Norwegian Directorate of Fisheries have approximately 20–25 vessels monitoring the sea, but, of course, it is a huge area to cover from Svalbard in the north to Denmark in the south, so it is a difficult task but we have flanking measures in addition to the discard ban that help us to monitor the discard ban. For instance, we have temporary and permanent closed areas, which is a tool we use in order to enforce this discard ban. If we have a certain area where it is highly likely to get illegal fish which they have an incentive to discard then we close the area, if you understand what I mean.

Q821 *Baroness Jones of Whitchurch:* Have you noticed that people's behaviour has changed? In other words, if they put their mind to it, can they realistically limit the by-catch?

Mr Oma: With our system of closure of areas and also the gear technology and technical regulations we believe that we have changed the fishing pattern into a more sustainable fishing pattern where we have improved the exploitation pattern of the fishing fleet, fishing larger fish, leaving the juveniles in the sea to grow. One of the benefits of this system is that over the years since we introduced this system in 1987 it has been widely accepted by the fishermen so everybody knows that it is illegal to discard fish but they feel that perhaps it is a bit wrong as well, so it becomes a moral issue for them. This is a maturing process, of course. It has not always been that way, and, of course, discarding happens in Norwegian fisheries. We are not so silly that we believe that it has disappeared just because we have introduced a ban. We believe that there has been a change of mentality among fishermen as well.

Q822 *Lord Plumb:* Should the European Union be following suit?

Mr Oma: Definitely we believe that it would be beneficial to the European Union's fishing industry and we also believe that it would be beneficial for the Norwegian fishing industry for our shared stocks because in the North Sea the situation is not good, to say the least. For certain stocks it is quite bad and we believe that a discard ban would improve the situation significantly.

Q823 *Lord Cameron of Dillington:* Just so that I am clear, when there is fish caught that is over quota, is it just that fisherman who has to leave the fishing grounds or is the fishing ground then closed to everyone?
Mr Oma: That may vary. We have this surveillance programme. A vessel hired by the Directorate of Fisheries sails around in the Barents Sea and takes trial hauls, and wherever their percentage of juveniles is too high or if the mixture of illegal fish, for instance, red fish, Greenland halibut, is too high then we will close the area for everybody, but in certain cases, perhaps one vessel has quota and another one has not, only the one without a quota has to leave the area. It is the fisherman's own responsibility because the fisherman knows exactly what the limits for by-catch and undersized fish are, so if he goes into an area that is not closed and he discovers in his last haul that the level is too high of illegal fish then he has an obligation to change fishing grounds.

Q824 *Viscount Ullswater:* Can he purchase quota on the high seas? If he finds his vessel is full of illegal fish can he then buy the quota? Can he trade the quota at that stage or does he have to buy the quota before he sets out, is effectively what I am asking?
Mr Oma: You are talking about trans-shipment at sea?

Q825 *Viscount Ullswater:* No. I am talking about the fact that he goes out to fish legally and when he hauls in his net he finds he has got fish for which he has no quota or no further quota. Can he get on the radio and purchase quota for that ship before he lands it?
Mr Oma: That is not known. I do not think that is a realistic scenario.
Mr Evensen: I think he should bring it to land and we will see if he gets compensation.

Q826 *Viscount Ullswater:* I was just trying to think of a way of making money.
Mr Oma: No. The quota transfer system is not that efficient.
Viscount Ullswater: It just would save on the discards and save on the temptation to discard.

Q827 *Viscount Brookeborough:* As I understand it, you run a survey ship which goes around the different areas doing trials?

Mr Oma: Yes.

Q828 *Viscount Brookeborough:* If and when it gets what it believes is the wrong size of fish it then closes the fishery, just like that?
Mr Oma: Yes.

Q829 *Viscount Brookeborough:* Are the fishermen relatively happy with the performance of that?
Mr Oma: They are happy with the service because they have seen good results.

Q830 *Viscount Brookeborough:* It helps them avoid problems?
Mr Oma: Yes, and it helps to preserve young fish which then they can fish at a later stage. However, we have been criticised quite heavily that we wait too long to open the areas. There is no automatic system for reopening these fishing grounds. They are closed until we have taken new tests in that area.

Q831 *Viscount Brookeborough:* Do you also rely on fishermen reports? If you have not got a survey vessel there do the fishermen call in and say, "We are hitting too many juveniles", and you then say, "Okay. We will close it", on fishermen information?
Mr Oma: No. We will not close it based only upon fishermen information.

Q832 *Chairman:* The Scottish Executive have introduced this voluntary real-time closures scheme which seems to be meeting with some success and is certainly being observed by the majority of boats. Do Norwegian boats fishing in those areas observe the real-time closures in Scottish waters?
Mr Oma: We were informed that these measures had been introduced. However, to my knowledge channels of communication about these closures have not been established between Norway and Scotland, so I do not know. Of course, Norwegian vessels fishing in Scottish waters should follow EU regulations but I am not informed about how they observe these recommendations from the Scottish Executive. If such communication channels were established I am certain that Norwegian authorities would distribute this information to the fishing fleet and we would, of course, highly recommend them to observe these regulations.

Q833 *Chairman:* Can I ask a technical point? It is to do with prosecution. We were talking to our own people in Scotland last week and one of the problems that that they have with prosecution is that although they have an aeroplane, for example, going ahead and seeing that discarding is taking place, they cannot prosecute unless they board the boat. Do you have to board the boat and whom do you prosecute? The owner? Is there a difference between ownership and the person in charge, the skipper? How does the prosecution system work?

Mr Oma: We have zero tolerance for discard. We do not have any limit, so if it is disclosed that there has been discard it will be prosecuted and there will be fines and administrative sanctions will apply to that vessel. We can, of course, board.

Q834 *Chairman:* You have to board?

Mr Oma: No. We can discover that in different ways. Also, video evidence taken by aeroplanes or helicopters has been used.

Q835 *Lord Palmer:* We have been very impressed by nearly all the witnesses we have had since doing this inquiry. However, Norway comes out with your flag-flying very high, particularly with regard to your control and enforcement. Why do you think the Norwegian control system has been so successful? We are all green with envy. Everybody has been so complimentary about your method of control. Also, how effectively do you work with your counterparts in other jurisdictions?

Mr Oma: I will try to start to answer that and then my colleague, Mr Evensen, will say a few words on how we co-operate with sales organisations in this matter. We really appreciate it if other evidence that you have heard has suggested that the Norwegian system is a success, but we believe that there is room for improvement in the Norwegian system and we are continuously trying to do that. As I mentioned earlier, we have focused mainly on control at sea in previous years. However, since we got clear indication of a large-scale IUU fishery in the Barents Sea we have focused more and more, in addition to control at sea, on control at landings, document control. We try now to investigate the whole value chain from sea to the consumer, but we have not increased our control effort on landings on the coast over control at sea because that will always be the cornerstone of Norwegian control. When it comes to co-operation, we have a fairly good system for document control in Norway now and perhaps my colleague can elaborate on that.

Lord Cameron of Dillington: Just before you come to that, you have a huge number of rules, including your by-catch limits, your trawler-free zones, your no discards, you called it earlier "sophisticated technical measures", a very good phrase. You must have an enormous police force doing all this. Do you have any idea how many vessels, how many aeroplanes, how many people are involved?

Q836 *Lord Palmer:* You mentioned 25.

Mr Oma: The coastguard and the Director of Fisheries together have approximately 20–25 big vessels and maybe some smaller ones for fisheries in

the fjords, and we have a force of maybe 50 or 60 inspectors.

Mr Evensen: Yes, I think so. What is working very well in Norway is the system with sales organisations. It is based on the old Raw fish Act, which is a trade act. Originally it was (and still is) an effort to police the fisherman and to ensure that the fisherman receives reasonable value for the fish. We have a system with sales organisations. They are allowed to set minimum prices. They try to look at the market to see what is the situation now and they set minimum prices which the buyers have to respect, but every time fish is landed in Norway, or, if you take Norwegian vessels, wherever they go in the world they are obliged to fill in a landing note which is sent to the sales organisation they belong to. We have six sales organisations. By doing this the sales organisations know all the time what they have been fishing, where they have been fishing, when they did it, and they send this information to the Directorate of Fisheries which then uses it to manage the quota. This is not something you can choose; this is an obligation. That is the secret. In the EU it is voluntary membership of the producers' organisations. That is not the fact in Norway. You do not have to be a member. Also, foreign vessels have to respect the sales organisations. They have to issue this landing note, so it means we have a very good overview of what has been caught. We have the necessary data. The sales organisations have been around for 60 years. They know very well how things work. It is not that easy to try to go around them. It might happen but it is a very transparent system and so we believe this is one of the most important factors in our control. This Act is, as I said, an Act according to how we organise the market but the consequence is that it is very useful for finding out where the resource comes from.

Mr Oma: Just to answer the last part of Lord Palmer's question, when it comes to international co-operation we should be very humble from the Norwegian side because we would not have seen the resource we have seen in the Barents Sea without international co-operation, and in particular we have had very fruitful co-operation with the European Union which we have worked with also on a Member State level, exchanging landing information, and we are working with the European Union within the North East Atlantic Fisheries Commission to get this Port-State control scheme in place which is the main reason why the IUU fishing in the Barents Sea has been reduced by more than 50% over the last year. This Port-State control scheme is very important and very useful in combating in IUU.

Q837 *Viscount Brookeborough:* These landing notes which you say are very good, who verifies them? Do they have to be signed by the port at which they have landed?

Mr Evensen: They have to be signed by both the buyer and the fisherman.

Q838 *Viscount Brookeborough:* This landing note is a Norwegian note. Do they then have to hand a note to the port authorities where they have landed, and is it just between the buyer and the fisherman?

Mr Evensen: Yes. They are submitted to the sales organisation and they will collect them and then send them to the Directorate of Fisheries. I should also mention that the sanctions are serious if you fail to do that. Imprisonment is an option.

Chairman: Let us finish of with the liaison with the North Sea RAC and the possible regionalisation of fisheries policy.

Q839 *Lord Plumb:* We have taken evidence from some of the representatives of the Regional Development Councils which, as you well know, were set up after 2002, and we have questioned everybody on the advisability of using the RACs, their role and their responsibilities. What level of co-operation do you have, particularly with the North Sea Regional Advisory Council, and do you see this as an important part of the possibility of further development in the ref of the Common Fisheries Policy?

Mr Oma: We promised you that we would not talk about the Common Fisheries Policy, but since you ask, this is a question that Norway has no formal position on. However, we do participate in the North Sea Regional Advisory Council as an observer. We are also an observer in the Pelagic RAC. We attend meetings and executive committees and general assemblies but we are not active in the working groups in these two councils. I have discussed this issue with some of my colleagues and our reflections are that we believe that since there are such big differences between regions within the EU when it comes to the fishing fleets, the species that are being caught, the fishing gear, tradition and not least the traditions for regulations, it would be difficult, looking from outside, to create a system that fitted all. I believe that from the Norwegian side we share perhaps more the traditions for fisheries management with the countries around the North Sea, such as the UK, Denmark, Germany, the Netherlands and maybe Sweden. If the CFP were to be regionalised I think it would perhaps become easier to find a common position between Norway and the EU in negotiations on technical regulations, quotas, what-have-you, but, of course, this is speculation. I do not know where or how this processes in the EU will go. It has just started, I have learned. Regionalisation will certainly affect the relationship with Norway and I think it may have some positive impact on the relationship. I have to stress that relations on the management side are quite good at the moment. We have not many outstanding issues on negotiations when it comes to the division and allocation of quotas. We have for many years have been working to find agreement on these two important issues and we co-operate quite well with the European Union.

Q840 *Earl of Arran:* To speculate even further, what would your view be if the CFP were scrapped altogether and it was a free-for-all?

Mr Oma: Certainly from the Norwegian perspective our concern is that we have to come to agreements with the European Union on management in the North Sea and we have to agree upon exchange of quotas from the Barents Sea to the areas west of the UK and Ireland. This is a very difficult question. I cannot comment. My imagination is not good enough.

Chairman: Thank you very much for coming and spending time with us. It has been very interesting.

WEDNESDAY 11 JUNE 2008

Present	Arran, E of	Palmer, L
	Brooke of Alverthorpe, L	Plumb, L
	Brookeborough, V	Sewel, L (Chairman)
	Cameron of Dillington, L	Ullswater, V
	Dundee, E of	Wallace of Tankerness, L

Memorandum by The Fishermen's Association Limited

INTRODUCTION

"I cannot recall another example in history of a free country without compulsion from outside entering on an arrangement so damaging to itself." *Peter Shore 22 February 1972 Col 1164 Hansard.*

Equal access to the common resource . . . a non discriminatory principle . . . is the real Common Fisheries Policy.

The decisions made at the December 2002 Council meeting were not designed to change that fundamental priniciple.

There is a very great misunderstanding of what the Common Fisheries Policy really is. The European Court of Justice has made it absolutely clear that the community system of national quotas and the regulations governing these quotas at the end of each year is a derogation from the principle of equal access to fishery resources and non-discrimination laid down in Article 40, clause 3 of the Treaty of Rome. Article 40, clause 3 is a very simple Article which says there must be no discrimination between producers or consumers within the Community.

It is entirely misleading to refer to reform of the CFP. The CFP is equal access to the common resource not the management regime (the transitional derogation) introduced in 1983 under which the discriminatory principle of Relative Stability was introduced in the allocation of fish quotas to Member States. However it is naïve to believe that other Member States are going to be content for all time to allow a discriminatory principle to over ride EU law of equal access to the common resource.

The CFP has been a social and environmental disaster. For the sake of European Union integration, the environmental and social price which has been paid throughout Europe and beyond has been enormous. That policy—the real CFP—can not be reformed.

The real CFP of equal access to the common resource has caused a Sea Clearances for Scotland and other parts of the UK. This was not unexpected. The Commission had warned the industry on 11 June 1992 that the way forward, as envisaged by the Commission for the re-structure of the industry, would involve thousands of fishermen losing their jobs.

— 196 vessels over 10 metres in length left the Scottish fleet between 2001 and 2004.

— 165 were unnecessarily scrapped as a result of the 2001-02 and 2003 decommissioning schemes.

— Almost 1100 boats have left the fleet in the 20 years since the UK joined the then Common Market.

The political end game for the EU is an integrated EU fleet, operating in EU waters under the central control of the EU Commission being told where, when and with what to fish.

THE ECONOMIC LOSS TO SCOTLAND AND THE UK

Scotland

The effects of the CFP on the Scottish fishing industry:

— The annual loss of direct income to the catching sector of a minimum of £334 million. Of this, £110 million would have been crew wages, with the remaining £224 million lost to the vessel services like fuel, repairs, gear, insurance, banks, groceries, harbours, etc.

— Added value, fish processing and marketing, etc., raise the economic value of the annual loss considerably. The recognised GDP impact ratio for fisheries is 2.35 times the landed value. So, the direct economic impact of the reduction of the Scottish fishing fleet in 1975-2003 is now a current annual loss to the Scottish economy of a staggering £785 million.

— The costs to public funds of unemployment and other social benefits as well as broader economic consequences, including loss of tax income, probably bring the total loss nearer to £900 million every year.

— This exceeds by a huge margin any economic benefits Scotland receives from the European Union and funds like the European Fisheries Fund

DEFRA stated that the UK catching industry lands over £540 million pounds in catches each year, resulting in between £800—£1200 million of economic activity in the UK.

However the value of fisheries products, at landing values, extracted annually from the British Exclusive Fishing Zone, amounts to £2.5 to £3 billion pounds, of which a mere £540 million goes to the British Industry.

That represents a loss of between £ 2.0 billion and £ 2.5 billion to the UK economy.

SPECIFIC ISSUES

FAL has had the opportunity to see the excellent submission of David Thomson and endorses his comments. We have however the following additional points

CONSERVATION AND MANAGEMENT

FAL assumes that the Committee would agree with the following statement:

> A sustainable and profitable sea fisheries industry must be well-managed, with effective communication and understanding between fisheries managers and regulators, catchers and processors. This will lead to policies and rules which are better understood and better reflect day to day reality. This in turn leads to high levels of compliance, to everyone's benefit

FAL fully supports responsible well managed fishing. But the CFP (equal access to the common resource) is not a system designed to ensure responsible fisheries management but one that has been the antithesis of conservation and it is the CFP that drives the UK and Scottish Marine Directorate's future fisheries strategy.

Conservation and sustainable exploitation of fisheries resources requires compliance.

It appears that compliance is a one way street. The rules are there and you must comply even if they are illogical. The aim of simplifying the current morass of rules and regulations does not mean a weakening of controls.

Disproportionate action will not convince fishermen that compliance is in their best interests and that they should take responsibility for their actions and the consequences thereof.

Full compliance needs full viability. Fleet viability is imperative to a sustainable and viable fishery. Full compliance can only come at a price if there is not full viability in the existing sectors of the fleet.

If vessel operators are being forced to bankruptcy due to inadequate quota allocations or limited days at sea or the inability to access the resource due to marine closed areas what recourse do they have?

How are the vessels to be treated that are currently viable but then find they are unviable due to a cut in certain species in the future and so unable to realise sufficient turnover due to inadequate quota allocations? The deep water fleet that operated to the West of Scotland is a graphic example of what can happen.

TACS: They have not worked. It is an immoral practice to dump perfectly mature fish dead back into the sea on a science which is 60% accurate at best.

Current management tools: They are not working as science is disproportionate to what skippers are finding on the grounds.

RIGHTS BASED MANAGEMENT TOOLS AND MARINE PROTECTED AREAS (MPAs)

Fishermen have for many years supported temporary closed fishing seasons and areas to allow fish populations to grow to optimum size provided there is scientific advice that supports such closures unlike the so called west of Scotland "windsock area" that was closed without any scientific justification to appease the EU Commission's cod recovery ambitions.

However there is a growing concern within the fishing community that advocates of MPAs as a management tool actually wish to close vast portions of the sea to all forms of fishing on a permanent basis. They want these areas declared off-limits to fishing without scientific proof that permanent no-fishing zones would actually produce more fish. Bio-diversity and sustainability are only two of the arguments used to support such proposals and Marine Nature Reserves.

Fishermen are easy targets and if MPAs/Marine Nature Reserves are to be introduced then the customary rights of fishermen have to be given priority. They are not just stakeholders and they must not be denied access to the resources that have supported them and their communities for centuries. They must be protected from pollution, marine transport threats, pipelines, gravel extraction, telephone networks, and eco-tourism if it displaces the fishermen's access to local grounds.

The key principles, at least in the opinion of the EU Commission, for setting up MPAs were spelled out by John Farnell Director Conservation Policy in the European Commission at a Conference organised by The Sustainable Development Intergroup of the European Parliament in November 2005 and chaired by Struan Stevenson MEP. These are:

(a) Such areas should not include a complete ban on fishing.

(b) MPAs must be built on a solid scientific basis, although the precautionary approach may be necessary.

(c) MPAs must demonstrate economic and social equity, particularly where fishing communities rely on the areas in question.

(d) The governing authorities must ensure careful monitoring to measure the impact on bio-diversity.

(e) There must be full consultation with stakeholders at all stages, including the design, operation and review of MPAs.

To each of the above principles, we would comment:

(a) Neither should they include a partial ban, unless there is clear scientific proof that it is absolutely needed to protect the stocks.

(b) The scientific basis must be sound long-term research with the onus of proof on the proposer. The fishing community should be entitled to present alternative scientific opinion if such exists.

(c) We fully agree with this principle.

(d) The monitoring should be initiated before the MPA is set up.

(e) The consultation must be genuine and meaningful, and not as often occurs, a mere sampling of fishermen's views which are then ignored

CONTROL AND ENFORCEMENT

COMMUNITY FISHERIES CONTROL AGENCY

FAL understands that the CFCA was established *to ensure a level playing field of enforcement across the EU.*

A level playing field is a much misused phrase. Whose ball will we be playing with? If the Commission achieves its objective then an EU fleet operating in EU waters on a non discriminatory basis and run by a centralised agency will be the outcome.

The Commission has little regard for the UKs criminal justice system as being too ineffective in securing compliance with its targets and wishes to see severe administrative penalties as the norm.

FAL cannot support such an Agency particularly as we know so little about it at present.

As for the Commission being sceptical about the systems currently in place the introduction in the UK of the Registration of Sellers and Buyers legislation has eliminated the trade in over quota in this country.

Structural Policy: Has removed 165 whitefish vessels from the Scottish fleet.

European Fisheries Fund (EFF)

The Scottish Government has secured 40%—£38.83 million—of the UK budget for a new European grants scheme for Scotland's fishing and aquaculture industries.

The new European Fisheries Fund is designed to help modernise and secure the sustainability and international competitiveness of the fishing industry.

The £38.83 million will be split between the Scottish Highlands and Islands Convergence area (£12.41 million) and the Lowland Scotland Non-Convergence area (£26.42 million).

Details of the timetable and how to apply for grants will be announced by the Scottish Government Marine Directorate, following a UK wide consultation on priorities for the funds early next year.

The European Fisheries Fund replaces the Financial Instrument for Fisheries Guidance (FIFG) grant programme which ran between 2000 and 2006.

EFF is programmed to run until 2013.

The UK money has been allocated as follows:

—	England	£26.42 million
—	Scotland	£26.42 million
—	Northern Ireland	£12.76 million
—	Wales	£1.07 million

Separate funds will be available for Cornwall (£7.3 million), West Wales (£10.68 million, and the Scottish Highlands and Islands (£12.41 million).

We still await advice on the timetable and information on the priorities that have been agreed.

Governance

Regional Advisory Councils (RACs)

RACs were established ostensibly on the basis that they would provide for a more devolved fisheries management However subsidiarity does not exist under the CFP. Competence for fisheries was transferred to Brussels. It would be contrary to the legal and institutional framework of the Treaty to grant RACs increased responsibilities in the decision making process. They are purely advisory bodies and do nothing to transfer decision-making power away from Brussels. In fact the Amsterdam Treaty explicitly rules this out.

The real nature of RACs is a different matter

- RACs can not provide for a more devolved fisheries management.
- Subsidiarity does not exist in the CFP
- They will remain advisory
- They will not have a role in management.
- They will not become management organisations.
- Competence for fisheries has been transferred to Brussels.
- They do nothing to transfer decision-making power away from Brussels. In fact the Amsterdam Treaty explicitly rules this out.
- They are designed to promote the development of the CFP equal access to all Member States to the common resource

However, if there was national control, a repatriation, then the principle of an Advisory Council, in fact a management council, would not only be welcomed but should be implemented.

Conclusion

The fishing industry provides tens of thousands of jobs and generates hundreds of millions of pounds for the UK economy. It also provides the heart of many of our coastal communities who depend on the success of that industry.

FAL suggests to the Committee that in taking evidence it considers the views of the fishing communities throughout the UK perhaps even visit a cross section of ports.

It is important that the Committee understand that it is not only an industry which is a provider of employment but also a historic part of Scottish and UK heritage and culture.

Communities through out the UK that are dependant on this unique industry can not tolerate any further decline. They are still suffering the aftermath of decommissioning in 2003 /4.

Although fish prices have high for most of the last 18 months any profit made has been spent on leasing more quota and days in order to catch the fish. So there has been no real improvement to the industry and its communities. As long as the UK remains in the CFP that will continue.

21 February 2008

Examination of Witness

Witness: MR RODDY McCOLL, Director, The Fishermen's Association Ltd, examined.

Q841 *Chairman:* Good morning. Thank you very much for coming. I suppose it would have been easier all round, if we had had the time and the opportunity, to see you when we were in the north-east of Scotland, and I regret that we did not have that time but it is very good of you to come down and meet us in London. Thank you very much indeed. Would you prefer to start off by making a brief opening statement and then go on to the question and answer session, or would you prefer to go straight into questions?
Mr McColl: Thank you, Lord Chairman. I will make a few brief comments and explain what the association represents and then take it into the question session after that.

Q842 *Chairman:* Okay.
Mr McColl: Good morning, Lord Chairman and members of the committee. The Fishermen's Association Ltd was incorporated as a company limited by guarantee in September 1995. It is a UK fishing industry trade protection association with members representing both off-shore and on-shore interests. It has some 250 members in Scotland, England and Northern Ireland. Northern Ireland is represented on the Association by the Northern Ireland Fish Producers' Organisation, in England we have the South Devon and Channel Shell Fishermen's Association and the on-shore interests are represented by the Scottish Ship Chandlers' Association, which represents some 14 member firms from Shetland to East Lothian. I am the secretary/manager of the association. I am a Scottish solicitor. I have been involved in representing fishing industry organisations for some 36 years. The objectives of The Fishermen's Association (FAL) as far as UK and EU fisheries policies are concerned, are to manage, through the restoration of national control, those fisheries falling within the UK exclusive economic zone (the EEZ) in an effective, sustainable, equitable and transparent manner with the full co-operation of all stakeholders to maximise the socio-economic and food production benefits for the nation. Those are my opening remarks, Lord Chairman.

Q843 *Chairman:* Thank you very much. Could you give us an outline? Are individual fishermen members of your association?
Mr McColl: Yes, there are individual members in the north-east of Scotland. The other members are represented through the affiliates, the Northern Ireland Fish Producers' organisation, the Ship Chandlers and the South Devon and Channel Shell Fishermen.

Q844 *Chairman:* How many, say, in the north-east of Scotland, individual members would there be?
Mr McColl: Including affiliated members, probably in the region of 100, but I am not counting---. There are also, of course, the levy payers, the fishermen, the fishing vessels, and we have about 35 to 40 of these.

Q845 *Chairman:* Your written evidence did not mince words, did it? It was fairly "in your face". Clearly you are not the greatest fan of the Common Fisheries Policy; not that there are many great fans of the Common Fisheries Policy.
Mr McColl: As I am sure you have probably realised in taking evidence.

Q846 *Chairman:* There is an interesting point that you make in about the fourth paragraph. It says, "It is entirely misleading to refer to the reform of the CFP. The CFP is equal access to the common resource not the management regime", and you point out that the management regime has been a derogation since 1983. You conclude, "It is naive to believe that other Member States are going to be content for all time to allow a discriminatory principle to override EU law of equal access to the common resource." I suppose the argument is that it has been there since 1983. In all the conversations that we have had with representatives of the Member States, the first thing they bang on about is the importance they give to relative stability. I do not see how the perspective that we are getting from Member States indicates that they are going to want to move to open access to a common resource.
Mr McColl: May I also ask if that applies to Spain, because over the years, since Spain has become a member of the European Union, it has attempted on

a number of occasions to seek to change that distributory policy and they have been very vocal and they have not succeeded so far in their attempts through the European Court of Justice. I think that they will continue to seek to ensure that their fishermen obtain what they were properly promised when Spain acceded to the European Union, i.e. equal access to the resource.

Q847 *Chairman:* When we spoke to the Spanish representative in Brussels, you are absolutely right in saying that they clearly want at least an adjustment to the present outcome of the application of the principle of relative stability. They were not clamouring to throw it overboard altogether. Of course, Spain is one Member State, and the overwhelming weight of opinion from other Member States that we talked to was that actually relative stability was the primary policy objective that they sought, that they wished to defend.
Mr McColl: I accept what you are saying, of course, that that is the evidence that you have taken. I continue to remain sceptical, given the fact that this is the most discriminatory and principled policy within the EU, and I cannot see how the Commission will allow that to continue to operate for ever and a day.

Q848 *Chairman:* It has been there for 25 years?
Mr McColl: It has been there for 25 years. That does not mean to say that it will continue for another 25 years. It will be interesting to see what happens in 2012 as to whether or not there might be changes in the regime which might even impact on the in-shore fisheries around the UK and other Member States which are currently protected.

Q849 *Chairman:* You also say that "the political end game for the EU is an integrated EU fleet, operating in EU waters under the central control of the EU Commission being told where, when and with what to fish". What is the evidence for that?
Mr McColl: I think that the centrist policy of the EU has shown that it has been unresponsive to the needs of local communities, local fishing interests. The evidence is the statements, the actions of the Commission and the EU over the last 30 years. It is the evidence of huge decommissionings in Member States, particularly in the UK, it is the whole gamut of regulations that have demonstrated this.

Q850 *Chairman:* That adds up, do you think, to an integrated EU fleet operating in EU waters under central control?
Mr McColl: I sincerely believe it does. I have seen the demolition of fleets, supposedly for the purpose of matching resource to the effort. I am extremely sceptical as to whether or not that was anything other

than a determined socio-economic policy decision to manage people in a way that has caused so much distress to fishing industries throughout the EU, to their families, to their communities.

Q851 *Viscount Brookeborough:* You have told us who you represent. Who do you not represent in the fishing industry, what proportion of fishery industry producers?
Mr McColl: I cannot say I have ever done a calculation to determine what the percentage is of the industry represented by The Fishermen's Association. The industry must be in the region of 12,000 people, perhaps, when you look at the on-shore jobs. It is said that there are five on-shore jobs for every off-shore. We represent a proportion, but just how significant is that.

Q852 *Viscount Brookeborough:* I am interested because presumably you tried to increase your membership, and so why might some people not wish to join, and when you talk about managing things, and so on, to the extent that you do, and your views are quite extreme, maybe there are those who might not agree.
Mr McColl: Whether they are extreme or not is for others to judge. I think they are measured in many respects as a result of the experience that has been gained, suffered some might say. We have many sympathisers who might not join for a variety of reasons. For example, some people might not join because we are unable to provide work off-shore in the guard-ship industry, where vessels are contracted to guard oil installations. There is a monopoly almost of that work and it is something that we have not been able to break into, so people might not join us for an economic reason.

Q853 *Viscount Brookeborough:* In your opening remarks I think you said that your aim was to manage resources in the fishing industry. To what extent do you have any management powers?
Mr McColl: No, that would be for the UK to manage, not for this association to manage. I am sorry if I misled you on that.

Q854 *Lord Wallace of Tankerness:* Mr McColl, you indicated in your remarks that your association's view is that the United Kingdom should exclusively manage I think it is fisheries falling within the United Kingdom's exclusive economic zone, which would be contrary, but could sit hand in glove with the Common Fisheries Policy as we know it. Is it fair to say that your association would like the United Kingdom to leave the Common Fisheries Policy? Is that a fair characterisation of your association's policy?

Mr McColl: No, it is not, Lord Wallace. The association has a rich variety of opinions about the European Union, but it has never stated that it supports withdrawal of the UK from the European Union.

Q855 Lord Wallace of Tankerness: I did not say the European Union, I said the Common Fisheries Policy.

Mr McColl: I misunderstood. Yes, absolutely. To withdraw from the European Union fisheries policy, the CFP, and to have repatriation of sovereign rights over the marine resources to the UK.

Q856 Lord Wallace of Tankerness: If we were to follow you down that line, but even outwith the Common Fisheries Policy we saw international obligations under the international law for the sea where states are required to co-operate regarding the sustainable harvesting of fisheries resources, can I ask what mechanisms your association would envisage of the way in which we could actually discharge that international obligation given that, as it were, a haddock does not recognise when it is entering into the United Kingdom's exclusive economic zone?

Mr McColl: Yes, that is right. We have many examples throughout the world of co-operative management. You have it in the North Sea, of course, because the EU, representing the Member States, is required to enter into third-party agreements with other sovereign nations—Norway, Faroe, Iceland. The position there, of course, would be that if the UK has managed to secure the repatriation of the right to manage the marine resources within the EEZ on the median line, then it would be a player in that co-operative management regime. The EU would still be there, but the UK would be there as well.

Q857 Lord Wallace of Tankerness: You think the UK would get a better deal arguing from without than arguing from within, given it is bound to be the same people you would have to negotiate with?

Mr McColl: I believe that it would. There have been soundings taken over many years by people within the industry which have indicated that would be the case. Whether or not that is a mirage, is another matter.

Q858 Chairman: Can I probe a little bit. The position of the Association is for the United Kingdom to leave the Common Fisheries Policy, and you have no views as an association on the United Kingdom's membership of the European Union. Is that a summary of your position?

Mr McColl: The association has taken no view on the EU membership by the UK.

Q859 Chairman: But is that being absolutely frank, because the Common Fisheries Policy is embedded in the Treaty and it is not possible to be a member of the EU without accepting the Common Fisheries Policy? So if the ultimate policy objective is to get free from the Common Fisheries Policy, it inevitably means leaving the EU. The one follows the other.

Mr McColl: It may or may not follow the other. The Association has certainly not taken a decision on the EU membership by the UK. There are people within the Association who probably wish to see the UK come out of the EU completely.

Q860 Chairman: I am not saying whether people wish or wish not. You described yourself as a solicitor and you know, in terms of European law, that a Common Fisheries Policy is part of the Treaty.

Mr McColl: I am aware of that, yes.

Q861 Chairman: So how is it possible legally to be a member of the EU and not accept the Common Fisheries Policy?

Mr McColl: I think that the consequences of the UK withdrawing from the EU fisheries policy might result in what you have described. That is not for The Fishermen's Association to concern itself with. They are purely concerned with this objective of repatriation of the fisheries policy to the UK.

Q862 Chairman: Do you accept that in terms of European law and the way in which the whole EU is legally constructed that it is actually not possible to be a member of the EU and not to accept the Common Fisheries Policy; that that is an automatic relationship?

Mr McColl: There is a relationship. Whether it is automatic or not, I am not entirely sure. Although I am a Scottish solicitor and have some knowledge of EU law, I am not an expert in it, so I will have to not answer that. I am not trying not to be frank, I have come here to be as frank as possible and to answer your questions as honestly as possible.

Chairman: Sure. Thank you.

Q863 Lord Plumb: Could I probe one little bit further on that point? Supposing, in the light of what the Lord Chairman has said, but it may be a hypothetical, you were able to withdraw from the fisheries policy, have the fishermen considered what their situation might be if they were out and the other 26 countries were in?

Mr McColl: I think many of them would relish the thought of being able to have a more participatory involvement in managing their affairs at national and local level and entering into arrangements with other states, which would benefit them as well as giving the other Member States access to UK waters, provided, in terms of NPOs, there is sufficient available to allow that to be done.

Q864 *Lord Plumb:* In other words, you would have to be in the same situation as Norway?

Mr McColl: Norway, Iceland, Faroe; all countries who have control over their own waters.

Q865 *Lord Palmer:* The role of the RACs is prominently featured in all the evidence sessions we have had. What has been your experience of them and how do you think they should evolve in the future, and what would, in your view, be the best way to realistically fund them?

Mr McColl: As you will probably have realised from the written submission, we are not particularly a fan of RACs. To some they represent a sensible move towards regionalisation of the European Union fisheries policy by ensuring that there is greater stakeholder involvement at the regional and local level, but, in our view, RACs are what they say they are, regional advisory committees, and as such they do not have any management role. Some have proved to be weak, others perhaps, like the North Sea RAC, have proved to be a bit more robust, but at the end of the day it is the Commission which will determine whether or not they will take into account the advice that is given by the RACs. Competence for fisheries has been transferred to the Commission. I believe it would be illegal for the Commission to devolve proper management to these bodies. I am aware that the Scottish Government has supported them and continues to recognise them as being a useful intermediary and no doubt will be helping to fund them in the future.

Q866 *Lord Palmer:* Does your organisation think perhaps they ought to be disbanded altogether in that they only came in in 2002?

Mr McColl: I think the concept of an advisory committee is an excellent concept, bringing into the fold the relevant stakeholders. Going back to what you hear again and again, if we have national control, such a concept should, and must, be introduced into the management regime for the UK.

Q867 *Earl of Dundee:* One view has been that a strategic decision should be made at the centre and those of technical management devolved. Do you share that opinion or not share it, or do you half share it and wish to qualify it?

Mr McColl: If I may refer to the written submission that was made to the committee by David Thompson, he dealt with this centrist policy of the EU very, very ably. Looking at the range of fishing resources, fishing methods, areas to be fished, the local consumption patterns, local fisheries culture, he concluded, and quite rightly so, that a central model

is insensitive to local needs and is not one that has proved, in the shape of the EU fisheries policy, to be anything other than a disaster for fishing communities. So I do not believe that a central model is the right way forward, I believe it should be a devolved method, and the appropriate technical conservation method, measures, effort control, could still be introduced for the effective management of the resources.

Q868 *Earl of Dundee:* But could there be evolution in this direction? We know that there is going to be change anyway in the next year or so. At present it might seem unsatisfactory to seek an accommodation between centrist strategy and local devolution for the reasons which you give, but if that is going to alter anyway, could it evolve? Could a new relationship, perhaps, constructively evolve between a sensitive strategic management and a pragmatic local devolution?

Mr McColl: It might be possible to achieve that. I understand that the Scottish Government is trying to look at alternatives to the Common Fisheries Policy and, as a result of the debate on that, which of course will involve the Commission, that might result in that evolution. That evolution is not, of course, what my association would like to see. They would prefer revolution.

Q869 *Chairman:* Counter-revolution as well.

Mr McColl: Lord Chairman, I was hesitating to use that expression in this House, but I did pass the statue of Oliver Cromwell on the way in! I hope that has answered your question, Earl of Dundee.

Q870 *Chairman:* When we talked to the Commissioner in Brussels a few weeks ago, he was working towards a view of a more devolved management system because, basically, most observers of the Common Fisheries Policy say that it is centralist, it is regulation driven, it is top-down and all the things that are really pretty hopeless, but he was working towards a model that was saying really that the EU role would be to set macro policy at a level perhaps expressed in terms of mortality rates for particular stocks and then go down to a regional body, maybe or maybe not building upon the Regional Advisory Committees, and say to that body, "Come up with your own management plan to make sure that these stock figures are achieved and, if that management plan is sensible, go ahead and deliver it." Would that not give a degree of ownership and this degree of basically stakeholder involvement that is missing at the moment? Would that not be better than what we have got?

Mr McColl: It would be better than what we have got, I agree with that, but it would only be a step in the ultimate objective.

Q871 *Chairman:* You are a hard-liner, are you not?
Mr McColl: I have had experience, Lord Sewell, of being involved in the fishing industry, lobbying on their behalf, for a long time and have seen many arguments put forward which are very genuine, very reasoned, not being accepted and the resultant consequences for many people—quite a lot of heartbreak over the years—and that helps to shape and influence you. I am sure, as a former fisheries minister, you will have taken some very difficult decisions knowing that consequences were going to be quite difficult. So that is where the hard line comes from, Sir.

Q872 *Chairman:* Do you think it would be possible to get this sort of buy-in through a form of regional management?
Mr McColl: It may be possible, but it would not be one that would be favoured by my association. The trouble with Mr Borg, or the Fisheries Commissioner, and I have read this as well, but at the same time he is stating that the fleet requires even more reduction, and it must now be a fuel-efficient fleet, but we seem to have beneficial crises that come along that help to drive the Commission's objectives. Cod recovery is, in my view, a beneficial crisis, and now we have got this major problem with the world-wide increase in fuel, and that has also again helped to drive the Commission's objective of reducing the size of the EU fleet. We do not have one yet, but that is the objective.

Q873 *Viscount Brookeborough:* Taking what you have just said, do you therefore believe that the fleet should stay at the size it is when, quite clearly, the resources are not there to maintain it at that size?
Mr McColl: No, I do not actually.

Q874 *Viscount Brookeborough:* So what are you going to do about it?
Mr McColl: What I would like to say is that the UK's EEZ is probably one of the richest in marine resource and fish resource terms, and if we had the opportunity to manage that ourselves, there would probably not be a necessity to reduce even further the number of boats in the UK fleet.

Q875 *Viscount Brookeborough:* But you were talking about EU-wide. You said the EU policy, I think, is that there should be further decommissioning, if you like?
Mr McColl: Yes.

Q876 *Viscount Brookeborough:* But you said you disagreed with that. How do you then envisage that the fishing effort will remain the same, but, quite clearly, regardless of specifying different stocks in particular, the fishing effort far exceeds the capacity of the sea to produce?
Mr McColl: But does it? Where is the evidence for that? Is that evidence tainted in some way by political persuasion? There is a lot of scepticism about what is relied upon. There are decisions taken on the basis of information that is less than robust.

Q877 *Viscount Brookeborough:* So you believe that if there was a free-for-all, without quotas, without anything, because, quite clearly, if those could fish to their capacity then—
Mr McColl: No, perhaps you misunderstand me. I do not believe it should be a free-for-all. I believe that there will be have to be restrictions. Whether these restrictions are by way of effort control only, which some other countries have in place, or by individual transfer of quotas which other countries have in place but which would not suit the Scottish fleet for example, in fact I do not think it would suit the UK fleet, there would have to be restrictions. There could not be a free-for-all.

Q878 *Viscount Ullswater:* Perhaps we could therefore turn to control and compliance, because whether it is under EEC rules or UK rules, compliance is obviously very important. You state in your evidence that conservation and sustainable exploitation of fisheries resources requires compliance. I think there is no doubt about that. You also state that full compliance needs full viability. I would like to know how you square that particular circle and how can compliance best be achieved?
Mr McColl: I agree that, unless something is owned, it is not going to be looked after properly; so we come back to the need for ownership to be with the nation state. When that is in place we will have a simpler and a more relevant set of legislation which would, I believe, help to achieve compliance with fishermen buying into the need for compliance: because if they are being targeted with rules and regulations that they feel are designed to put them out of business, they are going to find ways and means to continue their business, unless they decide just to hand in the keys, walk away and let the bank take their business. I think that if we had appropriate control within the nation state, we would be able to licence the boats, to permit them to fish in our waters, fishing under our laws, rules, regulations and enforcement policy that is in place.

Q879 *Viscount Ullswater:* I am sorry to interrupt you, Mr McColl, but what we are looking at is the Common Fisheries Policy as it exists at the moment, and my question was directed to: how do you see compliance being done by your association members with the existing regime rather than the regime that you would like to see in place?

Mr McColl: Clearly they have to comply with the laws of the UK. If they do not, they will face very severe penalties, and in many respects it has taken them some time to realise that compliance with the buyers and sellers registration legislation has been for their benefit. They have taken that time, but now they realise it has been essential for their future well-being. I think that the compliance is proving to be much more robust than it used to be, and there is very little fish that can be called over-quota or black fish now. I would imagine that there will be further legislation to ensure that the rules and regulations of the fisheries policy are applied, I think that you might find that administrative penalties will become stricter than they are at present, and they have just been introduced, but all of that, including the fact that if that is not handled sensitively, could result in fishermen rebelling against what they see to be over-zealous rules and regulations. So there has to be this balance between trying to ensure that there is a management regime to protect the stocks but also a regime that looks at the economic factors of the fishing industry and the communities that they support.

Q880 *Lord Plumb:* You speak of the morass of rules and regulations and call for simplification, and that is a point that has been shared by many of the witnesses we have received, and many of us, I think, would readily agree with you, but how do you do it? You have got the existing policy. The French takeover the Presidency of the council on 1 July. Each country now has its points and even the ambassador yesterday who was speaking to us spoke of the importance of simplification, which is good news, but how do we set about it in the fisheries policy?
Mr McColl: With the current fisheries policy.

Q881 *Lord Plumb:* Yes.
Mr McColl: I would find it very difficult to do, but to start with, given the amount of rules and regulations, how do you strip away the ones which are less relevant to ensure that you have a more effective and a simpler set of rules? In my view, though, simplification in the Commission's eyes does not actually mean less rigid rules. It may make it easier to understand. Although a lawyer, I find it quite difficult to get to grips with some of the rules and regulations that I have got to read to try to explain them to members. I have no view on how to make it simpler. I hope that Defra and the Scottish Government officials might be able to come up with some ideas that we can have a consultation about. I am sorry, I cannot answer it any better than that.

Q882 *Lord Plumb:* Representing the Federation of Fishermen, would it not be to your advantage and the advantage of the organisation to start thinking about ideas of simplification? Your chances of withdrawing, which is what you recommend, are nil, and so would it not be better if you came up with a general view on what you think could be done. That surely is what we are looking for, are we not?
Mr McColl: We try to take a pragmatic view of how we deal with the EU fisheries issues. There are some that we have to prioritise more than others. This particular one we do not think will get us very far, and to devote time and energy to something like that when there are more important issues to be dealt with is something that we are not taking part in just now.

Q883 *Lord Cameron of Dillington:* To some extent my question has already been asked, but virtually everyone we have met has said the basic problem with the Common Fisheries Policy is that there are too many modern, technically advanced, increasingly efficient fishing boats, fishermen, chasing, because of its efficiency, reducing resource and, therefore, some form of decommissioning, form of reduction in capacity, is what is required. I might also add that we got the impression that, having gone through the pain, the current remaining Scottish fisheries industry seems to be doing rather better that in has done in the past partly as a result of the pain it has gone through. How do you bring about a better alignment of capacity and resources without the decommissioning that you are very much against in your written submission?
Mr McColl: I think that, because of the pain that has been suffered as a result of the 2001, 2003 decommissioning schemes when some 165 vessels were scrapped, and I think the Scottish Government's paper suggested that 360 odd vessels have come out of the Scottish fleet since 1993, given the current economic circumstances of the fleet, there will be many more people now willing to look at decommissioning than when I put this paper together in February of this year. The impact of the fuel crisis has been quite horrific in certain areas of the UK, and I think there probably will be a willingness now to go down a route that they would prefer not to.

Q884 *Lord Wallace of Tankerness:* You said you have been campaigning for the fishing industry for 30 years and I think we have encountered each other a number of times?
Mr McColl: We have indeed.

Q885 *Lord Wallace of Tankerness:* I think you would agree that over that period there have been number of occasions when, in fact, the pressure for decommissioning has come from the industry itself and, indeed, was often resisted by government.

Mr McColl: Yes.

Q886 Lord Wallace of Tankerness: Is it not fair to say that these things are cyclical and that decommissioning is a relevant management tool, if the circumstances require it, in order to get the resource and the catching capacity into alignment?
Mr McColl: It has been a management tool, and that has been used effectively in some areas, as a blunt instrument in other areas, but I think that the current set of circumstances facing the industry will see a growing clamour for decommissioning to be used.

Q887 Lord Brooke of Alverthorpe: You responded to Lord Plumb on simplification, saying that you had not done any work on that, it did not figure very high in your order of priorities in the Association. Leave aside the "let us get us out of the fisheries policy completely" and the problems that might arise with Europe on that, but what would you identify as being your principal priorities and what other priorities are there that you think we could address that perhaps might help your members?
Mr McColl: That is a question I had not anticipated.

Q888 Lord Brooke of Alverthorpe: Neither had I until I heard your response to Lord Plumb!
Mr McColl: I think that there is a need for funding to be made available for continued training in the fishing industry, both on shore and off shore, to ensure that we have a work force that has relevant skills for the industry just now. There are many immigrant workers in the fishing industry, both on-shore and off-shore. There were Latvians and Lithuanians and Poles, and it is now Philippines who are crewing many boats. I even heard there were Egyptians crewing some vessels. They are taking away the berths from the local indigenous fisher people. I am not quite sure how that can be addressed by this committee, but there needs to be a system put in place that helps new entrants into the industry from the local communities rather than having to employ non-indigenous fishery people.

Q889 Lord Brooke of Alverthorpe: Anything else?
Mr McColl: No, I think that would be a priority. It is training. I am a manager of a training association in Scotland representing the highlands and islands. That tends to be a particular pet subject of mine.

Q890 Viscount Brookeborough: Quite clearly one of the major issues is people, apart from whether there are fish there to catch, and so on. When we were in Peterhead we learnt that unemployment was less than 1%, and admittedly it was because of the oil industry nearby. Can you give us any idea as to the effect of the decline of the fishing industry in other areas throughout the UK? For instance, if you take Devon and Cornwall, or wherever, what is the unemployment rate? Have people been able to find alternative jobs and, therefore, moved away from the area or, in fact, is there depopulation in certain areas as a result of the reduction in fishing? Is there misery out there?
Mr McColl: There is misery out there. I was reading a letter to the Cabinet Secretary, Richard Lochhead, from Ship Chandler, the other day pointing out the misery in Fraserburgh where young people cannot get a job. They have the skills but they cannot get a job in the fishing industry because of immigrant labour; the fisherman who has had to give up his vessel because he cannot afford the fuel prices. So there is misery out there.

Q891 Viscount Brookeborough: But there are people, for instance, who come out of university with certain skills in education who subsequently cannot find a job there but do find a job elsewhere. What is the unemployment rate in Fraserburgh?
Mr McColl: The unemployment rate is probably quite low, below 5%, because of what you have already said about the availability of oil work still being very high. There are people willing, of course, to move away to get that work.

Q892 Viscount Brookeborough: What about other parts of the United Kingdom?
Mr McColl: I do not have the actual statistics. If it would help, I can easily get them and provide them to the committee.

Q893 Chairman: Do you have to hand statistics on fishermen's incomes, the average Peterhead share fishermen?
Mr McColl: I personally do not have that to hand, but, again, that is information that could be easily obtained and provided to the committee from the Sea Fishing Industry Authority.

Q894 Lord Plumb: Could we also then have some information on costs?
Mr McColl: Yes.

Q895 Lord Plumb: It was interesting talking to some of the skippers when we went to Peterhead, in fact, the cost of a 10-day fishing trip for instance. I think with the rising costs at the moment, it must be a very worrying feature.
Mr McColl: Yes, the Sea Fishing Industry Authority, again, would provide economic analysis and the impact of the rising fuel prices. A paper was done for the Scottish Fisheries Council, of which I am a member, about a month ago, showing the impact on the various types of fishing vessel if the oil price went up from 50p to 60p to 70p a litre, or whatever it may

be. That information, again, could be provided quite readily.

Q896 Lord Wallace of Tankerness: You also mentioned the oil and gas industry. I am certainly aware that a number of fishermen actually use their vessels for some of the services to the oil and gas industry. Can you give the committee an indication from your knowledge of the extent to which that has developed over the years, and is it seen as a diversification of activity and helping to fill in the gaps if they are not allowed to be at sea for fishing purposes?
Mr McColl: It most certainly has filled in the gaps. It is a diversification. Unfortunately, members of the Sea Fishing Association Ltd are unable to secure these jobs. It is work that is basically a monopoly, controlled by a fishing organisation, the largest in Scotland, and they have not found it appropriate to provide any jobs to members of the Fishermen's Association, a matter that is of deep regret and which we have raised with our local MP. However, I understand that these jobs are becoming less

available and that instead of, say, 30 or 40 contracts being on the go at any one time, they are down to about 10 now. So that will have a knock-on effect as well because people will then come back into the fishery which were not there with more effort being put onto the stocks.

Q897 Chairman: Thank you very much, Mr McColl. We have come to the end of our questions. Is there anything that you feel that you want to say to us that you have not had the opportunity of saying to us yet?
Mr McColl: No, Lord Chairman. I think that I have said, perhaps not as eloquently as I would have liked—

Q898 Chairman: We all have that problem!
Mr McColl: However, with the combination of the written evidence and this oral session, hopefully I have covered everything that the Fishermen's Association would like to say, and thank you very much for the opportunity you have given me to do so.
Chairman: Thank you very much indeed and thank you very much for coming all the way down from Aberdeen.

WEDNESDAY 11 JUNE 2008

Present	Arran, E of	Palmer, L
	Brooke of Alverthorpe, L	Plumb, L
	Brookeborough, V	Sewel, L (Chairman)
	Cameron of Dillington, L	Ullswater, V
	Dundee, E of	Wallace of Tankerness, L

Examination of Witness

Witness: MR ANDREW CHARLES, Director, Scottish Seafood Processors Federation, examined.

Q899 *Chairman:* Good morning. Where have you come from today?
Mr Charles: Aberdeen.

Q900 *Chairman:* Thank you very much for finding the time to come today.
Mr Charles: Thank you for inviting us.

Q901 *Chairman:* It would have been more convenient, I think, if we had been able to see people when we were up in the north-east of Scotland, but it was a couple of days and, in terms of time-tabling, it just disappeared, but we are indebted to you for coming down.
Mr Charles: Not at all. I am glad to be here.

Q902 *Chairman:* Would you like to start by, if you wish, making an opening statement, and then we can get on to questions and answers?
Mr Charles: Yes; certainly.

Q903 *Chairman:* The other thing I ought to say, and I forgot to say this last time, is that this is a formal evidence session, and so a transcript will be taken. That will be sent to you to revise and it is also technically being webcast. There is a million to one chance that someone is listening! We have never had any evidence that there is, but at least there is the possibility. There you are; go ahead.
Mr Charles: I am Andrew Charles; I represent the Scottish Seafood Processors Federation. To give you a little bit of background on myself, I am involved in three businesses: one is processing farmed salmon, one is processing white fish, another one is processing crustaceans. So that gives you an idea that I have a fairly broad view of how the processing industry works.

Q904 *Chairman:* You do not process any black fish then.
Mr Charles: I do not believe there has ever been any black fish, Sir, but we will come on to that point later. Anyway, that is my processing background. I started out processing fish, joining a business that my grandfather started some 70-odd years ago. I came

into that industry and it was a thriving industry that delivered top quality fish, reliably, consistently. We had fantastic customer bases, we had customers lining up at our door to buy this product, and we did an extremely good job for many, many years. I would say the last 10 years have probably been the most difficult of my life in the business. Every aspect of our business has been undermined by the Common Fisheries Policy. It has been a total disaster to fish processing in Scotland, and I believe it has actually been a disaster to many processors in Britain. There are some that thrive on our fishing industry in Britain being reduced in size, the importers of fish prosper, but I truly believe, in the needless destruction of our valued fishing fleet, we have lost an incredible amount of talent that we will never get back, we have lost an incredible amount of really good processors, quality processors, skilful processors—we have lost them, and we will never get them back—and I think we are at the point now where we are at end of a cliff. We cannot go any further, because once you actually get to that point the whole thing collapses in a heap. You look at transport links and the whole efficiencies of the business. At the present moment probably our industry thrives on the back of farmed salmon. If it was not for the volumes that were going up and down the country of farmed product I think we would have lost an awful lot more processors that we have done. When I started in business there were roughly 200 processors in our area. There are now about 50. It is a dreadful situation that need not have happened. I truly believe the Common Fisheries Policy is responsible for that demise, and I would like you to fire questions at me and I will give you my opinion as to why I think that is the case. Thank you.

Q905 *Chairman:* I am sure that will come out during the course of the next little while. Can we clarify the nature of the organisations, the range of companies, that your federation represents and speaks for?
Mr Charles: Yes. We represent many companies from the small one-man, two-man band operation up to companies that employ maybe 100, 150 people. So it is a wide variety of companies. The white fish companies, the shellfish companies and a little bit of

farmed product. It is important to stress "farmed" product. To say that if you starve a fish processor, a skilful white fish processor, of white fish, he can just move and become a farmed processor, he cannot, or he can, but it is really difficult. It is a bit like saying somebody who produces timber could overnight become a metal merchant. It is two completely different industries and is not a solution to the way forward for the processing industry in Scotland.

Q906 Chairman: It was pointed out to us when we were in Peterhead a few weeks ago that, as a rule of thumb, what we catch we export and what we eat we import. Is that a rough rule of thumb in terms of fishing?
Mr Charles: No.

Q907 Chairman: It is not.
Mr Charles: No, I do not believe so. I think that problem has been magnified by the point of fact for the last five years, I believe, we have had a fishing minister, prior to Jonathan Shaw, who discredited our Scottish fishing industry. By blackening its name by bad management of it and keeping harping on about black fish, illegal landings, he did it no favours whatsoever. As a result of this customers do turn their back on that product, and I think the Scottish fishery industry has got a huge task ahead of it to get that credibility back into our product and get it back on to the shelves of our supermarkets; and, believe me, our supermarkets wanted it. It is a fantastic product, and we still provide a lot of product on to the shelves of the supermarkets but less than 10 years ago. A lot of the supermarkets said, "We are no longer running with this product because there is far too much bad publicity about it."

Q908 Chairman: Is your industry affected by what seemed to us to be the movement of processing to places like China?
Mr Charles: I do not believe so. I think it was a horrible thing to see shellfish processing going outside the country and jobs being lost, that is not a nice thing to see, but as far the white fish processing business is concerned, Scottish caught fish still gets processed in the UK. Very, very little white fish, if any, is exported to places like China. I think that was very much a snowball that the media picked up on.

Q909 Chairman: Surely you are encouraged by that, because what we heard was that, okay, there will be some very preliminary processing done on the boat and in Scotland, and then the product would be exported to China, was the example we are given, to be blocked and then re-imported.
Mr Charles: I think a lot of the product that would go into China would probably come from Russian block-frozen factory ships and containers would go over to China for reprocessing, but I know of no company in

our scope of companies that freezes Scottish white fish and sends it over to China for reprocessing. I do not know of any.

Q910 Lord Palmer: Can you remember who it was who gave us that evidence, because it was very, very strong?
Mr Charles: As I said, you could find that there is fish but it is not Scottish fish. You could get a container in from Russia, you could get a container of haddock in from Norway, so it may come in and then be shipped out to be reprocessed and then shipped back, but certainly, to my knowledge, practically all Scottish landed fish is processed within the UK, or Europe, whole fish certainly. A lot of whole fish now is processed in Boulogne, in France, and a lot of whole Scottish fish is processed in Spain. Some of that is caught by the Scottish fleet but, unfortunately, the majority of it now is caught by Spanish and French vessels fishing in Scottish waters. When I first started in the business I used to buy my fish in Aberdeen. Come lunchtime I would jump into my car and I would drive up to Lochinver or Kinlochbervie or Mallaig, I would buy fish until nine ten o'clock at night and be back in the fish market for half past six the following morning buying fish again. Those markets have been devastated—Lochinver: never a market there; Mallaig: part-time market; Kinlochbervie: part-time market; Scrabster: part-time market; Wick: part-time market; Aberdeen, one of the finest white fish ports in Scotland, faces, I believe, closure. That was 37 miles away from Peterhead. Yes, things are going well in Peterhead, but 37 miles away there is a port with a fish market, one of the finest fish markets that we were ever to have, on the verge of possible closure, and that is an absolute disgrace.

Q911 Lord Palmer: How many companies does the Federation represent?
Mr Charles: The Federation has 50 members.

Q912 Lord Cameron of Dillington: To some extent you have already dipped into this area, but I wanted to clarify or expand a bit on the connection between the fishing industry and the processing industry. The reduction from 200 processors to 50 processors which you spoke of a moment ago is clearly as a result of some of the decommissioning that has been going on in the early part of this century, shall we say. When the quota gets revised on an annual basis does that also affect the processing industry? How do the links work? Then, as a subsequent question to that, you mentioned aquaculture. What percentage of the processing industry deals with the products of aquaculture at the moment?
Mr Charles: Out of the 50 companies we represent, the amount of farmed product that would go through there would be very small. As I have tried to explain

earlier, it is a separate business. Your farmed salmon companies, your marine harvest, the big players, produce their own product, and it is very much a highly automated, different skills, different business.

Q913 *Lord Cameron of Dillington:* Okay, ignore that question and go back to the links?

Mr Charles: The links between the quotas being set and the processing industry is incredibly important. If we do not have the right quota to go through and keep the processing companies going, they go bust. It is as simple as that. This has been a complete failure, in my opinion, of the way that the Common Fisheries Policy has worked. If I go back, if I am allowed to, to the eighties when the Common Fisheries Policy was working, what seemed to happen was we had this Common Fisheries Policy, the ministers had their yearly bun fight and the industry got on with it. If there was a lot of cod or a lot of haddock, it was taken in and the industry got on and the next year there would be another bun fight, and there was never any serious penalisation of over-quota fish, it was just considered part of the negotiation. What happened over the last eight years and during your time was that those parameters were suddenly, over night, fixed in stone. If you were granted 400 tonnes of cod, you took 400 tonnes, and if you go a kilo over 400 tonnes you are facing legal action. That is okay if you are working in a common fisheries policy that is working with good science. I truly believe the science in our industry is under-funded, unreliable and very often so far out it is not funny. I think a very good example of that was last year when we were told that there was no cod in the sea any more and the Shetland fishermen were walking over cod. The scientists said, "Yes, you are walking over cod, but they are very small cod." They were not, they were a mixed bag of cod, some large cod, some medium cod and some small cod. In discussions with one fishery scientist, I was told the possibility for this is that they have completely missed out a year-class in their calculation. It is not the scientists' fault. We have got good scientists. I believe there are 300 marine scientists looking after our industry, but if the parameters of where those scientists can go is so tied in by European legislation and they are not allowed to explore the whole nature of the industry, we are always going to get poor science. Can I give you an example of that? I am not a scientist, but this is what we are hearing; when we are speaking to Defra and speaking to people this is what we are told. One of the ways science is brought forward to count fish is that the boat goes out, it goes out with the scientists and it tows in a straight line for 50 miles. They count the fish and this acts as a percentage for biomass. Those boats were going into areas where the fishermen knew there were no fish. These boats were going into areas; the fish had moved on. The experiment that they were trying to perform had changed. There was absolutely no consideration given to global warming. Our seas had warmed and possibly the cod had moved further away; they were in colder waters. Is that why the scientists suddenly believed there was no cod in the sea? There were many different areas. The scientists were not allowed to go and change the way that they did this experiment, and we ended up getting information that would lead to our industry being destroyed and, also, beautiful mature cod being thrown back to into the sea dead. As long as we have a management in place that allows that to happen, we are in deep trouble. We have got to change it.

Q914 *Lord Brooke of Alverthorpe:* Let me go back to illegal landings, which we had some figures from a statement from a former fisheries minister earlier on. We have heard that the problem of black landings has largely been eradicated in Scotland. In stating that, we are making an assumption that it did, in fact, exist previously. Do you agree with that analysis, and, if so, what has been the impact that has had on your members' operations and what do you think really has happened in the past?

Mr Charles: I think in the past, as I spoke about earlier on, the way that the fishery was managed and the way that the Government allowed the fishery to be managed, there was this political bun fight, parameters were set and the industry got on with it. There was then this change to say, "No, you are not taking it out. Okay." You are told haddock are on the verge of extinction. Our fishermen are walking over haddock. What do we do? We take out only the big ones because that will maximise our catch so that our weekly trip will pay; so we will discard hundreds of boxes of small haddock over the side in order to achieve getting a larger, more expensive fish to meet the expenses of the trip. There is also the situation where you have the choice: do you take the fish out or do you destroy it? For years they took the fish out and got on with it. As I said, they then changed. When there was what I call mismanaged fish being landed, it had a devastating effect on the processing industry. Like anything, if you suddenly put volumes of fish onto a market that is not on the radar, it devalues it. So suddenly processors who were legitimately buying their product were maybe competing against a processor who had got a lorry load of the product and they are told, "Please can you do your best price on it." So the processor who was legitimately trading was being very badly undermined, his business was being undermined, and it was an awful time, a terrible time the industry went through during those times. Some processors took advantage of it and others did not, but our federation did not support illegal fish landings. The fact that they are now completely eradicated and we have a new way of thinking has been welcomed by our federation, and I think we do have a completely different attitude in that industry to five, six years ago.

Conservation is playing a huge role in our industry now. We are having fishermen working with conservation groups, processors working with conservation groups, rebuilding the image of our industry so our customers will regain trust in our industry. It has been a rollercoaster, but the fact it has gone has been welcomed by our members.

Q915 *Lord Brooke of Alverthorpe:* Is that partly due to the introduction of the registration of buyers and sellers?
Mr Charles: A small part, I would suggest. I think most of the credit for eradicating mismanaged fish must lie with the fishermen themselves. They got their act together. I think they knew the writing was on the wall if they continued down the same vein that they were continuing down—it was not in anybody's interests—and also the fact that a lot of boats were decommissioned, so it was far easier to manage.

Q916 *Viscount Brookeborough:* It was the effort that equates to that?
Mr Charles: Yes.

Q917 *Earl of Arran:* A brief moment before we get on to discards. Am I not right in thinking that on the scientists' advice they did actually get it right recently, the scientists, when they predicted the quantities of haddock around the coast in the last year or so? I think their prediction was that there would be more than the fishermen believed. I think I am right in saying that, and it did turn out to be correct.
Mr Charles: I do not know is the honest answer to that one. What I can tell you is that the fishermen I speak to are saying there is a very, very good stock of fish out there of all species and it is not surprising considering there really is not much fishing effort going on out there compared to years past. If they have got it right I think they have been lucky because, quite honestly, I do believe we need to spend much more on science and we need to open our minds to how that science is put into practice working with the fishermen at the coal face. With the voluntary closures that the Scottish fishermen adopted, to their great credit, the scientific work that could be done off the back of that, by having scientists out there seeing what is happening and then managing it allows the scientists to say, "Gosh, there's a lot of small cod" or "There's a lot of large cod. How could we manage that today?".

Q918 *Earl of Arran:* Of course, giving more scientists more money does not necessarily make them any better at their job.
Mr Charles: Correct. That is why you need to give thought to how they go about that job. I am sure you could pour a lot of money into science and they would manage to burn it up, but if you give clear parameters as to how we can manage this fishery better we could

get a very practical scientific function going on there to tie in with our management.

Q919 *Earl of Arran:* Does your industry have any influence at the moment upon the reduction of discards? Do you think it should have the responsibility anyway? What happens at the moment?
Mr Charles: We have no responsibility over discards. What I would say is define discards. Do you define a large, mature cod as a discard, because I do not? I would describe that as a complete and utter waste of money and asset that our nation has. If we are talking about the discarding of small fish, I think the fishermen have a huge responsibility to discard nothing. Seafish must be credited for doing a huge amount of work into technical measures, mesh sizes and improvements in gear. There are all kinds of things going on there that have contributed to a massive reduction in discards by the Scottish fleet. Can it be improved? I am sure it can. The processing sector unfortunately has no input in that area.

Q920 *Earl of Arran:* Do you not talk to them? Do you not try and influence it? Do you not try to bring out moral indignation or bear some influence towards them?
Mr Charles: Yes. The fishermen and the processing sector talk a lot. They know our feelings about discards, ie we do not approve of them. Discards were not the fishermen's fault; they were the fault of a failed Common Fisheries Policy. They caused the discards. If you are going to force a boat with a very limited quota to go into a huge stock of haddock, he is going to pick the most valuable haddock to land and the rest of it is going to go back into the seabed. That is what Europe watched the Scottish fishing industry doing year in, year out and they did nothing about it.

Q921 *Lord Brooke of Alverthorpe:* Mr Charles, do you have a view as to how the fish processors could help if there was a ban on discards, such as in Norway, where you would pay a minimum price for the small fish that might have been discarded? Would you be able to manage that do you think?
Mr Charles: That already happens. Small fish generally make small money, although what you must understand is that the Scottish industry is based around a fairly small haddock, the block haddock. That is a huge industry in Scotland. Underneath that size of haddock, if the boat is caught landing it, it would be fined and it would never enter into our food chain.

Q922 *Lord Brooke of Alverthorpe:* But you can manage it now.
Mr Charles: We would not receive it. It would not be allowed to be landed.

Q923 *Lord Brooke of Alverthorpe:* Let us say there was a ban on discards and the boats had to bring back those fish, would you be able to market such fish in a comparable way to what they do in Norway where they only give the fisherman a small amount of money?

Mr Charles: Yes, we could absolutely use every bone of fish the fishermen landed. There is absolutely no reason to discard any fish. What I would say is let us not go there. Let us have the right technical measures so the fish are released back into the sea alive. There has been huge progress made in those areas over the last few years.

Q924 *Lord Plumb:* You spoke earlier of the decline in numbers both of processors and of fishermen. I could say, "What's new?". Whereas there were almost 150 farmers not so long ago, there are now less than 50. You could say the same with car manufactures and every other business. We would be interested to hear how you see the various organisations working together, the processors and the people who are catching the fish and the retailers, of whom there are only now a few. Is there a degree of vertical integration which is taking place with the fishermen related to the processors, cutting out the middleman to some extent or at least cutting costs?

Mr Charles: I think the industry is as efficient as it gets. You have got to process your fish somewhere. You have got to catch your fish. They are two different industries. Although we do have companies now, if you look at the pelagic sector, which actually owns its boats and they own their factories and they produce the whole thing under one umbrella, I would suggest that they are separate businesses in the unit of that picture. The pelagic model cannot be put aside the whitefish model because they are two completely different fisheries. The whitefish industry is so diverse. What we need is a lot of small boats, medium size boats and large boats. We need them spread geographically over many areas in Scotland for two reasons. The first is the weather. If the weather is bad in one area the boats will fish in another. That is something we have paid a huge price for with the contraction of the fleet. We are integrating with fishermen and we integrate with our customers. That is nothing new and it will always happen. The retailer, the processor and the catcher have always worked reasonably closely together. You might not think it.

Q925 *Lord Plumb:* Come on, pull the other one!

Mr Charles: Over the years the fishermen and the processor have had many bun fights, but if you actually go under the current of what the leaders of that industry are saying and you actually go under the current where the trade is going on, that is where the real talk happens between the skipper and the processor, the people who are trading are talking about what they are catching, and there is a lot of talk goes on between the retailer and the processor and they do work closely together. They work together more so now on the conservation side and the presentation side, which we were forced to do because of the way that our fishing industry has been handled over the last five or six years.

Q926 *Lord Plumb:* I think we witnessed that at Peterhead to some extent. To what extent are contracts used between the fishermen and the processor or direct to the retailer?

Mr Charles: It is quite common. Like in any business, fishermen will land fish directly into a processing unit for a specific retailer. It is a way of trading and there is nothing wrong with it. I do not think you will ever stop a true fisherman from presenting his fish on a fish market to see exactly how much money he gets. Peterhead is a thriving fish market. They get extremely good money for the fish in Peterhead. When Aberdeen lands fish it still gets very, very good money for its fish because we have a nucleus of buyers down there. The fishermen are hunters and they like a gamble. I do not think you will ever take away that spirit from our industry. I hope that spirit never leaves the industry. There is nothing finer than when a fisherman has been out in a gale force ten and he lands fish when there is very little fish on it and he gets a fantastic price for it. He deserves it. They really are some of the bravest people in industry in this country.

Q927 *Viscount Ullswater:* When we want to Peterhead we did not see any shellfish. Is that something which is more under contract?

Mr Charles: Yes, very much so. The nephrop industry is practically all under contract. Had you gone to Fraserborough you would have seen a lot of shellfish on the market there. One processor, the SFO, which is a cooperative of boats, a tremendous amount of that shellfish now goes into there and three or four other companies. You do not see so much of it on the market.

Q928 *Lord Wallace of Tankerness:* Mr Charles, one of the more recent innovations in the fishing industry is the advent of the Regional Advisory Committees. Could you give us some indication of your Federation's engagement with the RACs for the North Sea and what your experience has been as to its effectiveness or otherwise?

Mr Charles: We have not had huge engagement with it. We have been to meetings. We fully support regional management. We believe that regional management is a way forward for the industry. If we could get rid of the Common Fisheries Policy completely and give every European country control of their fishing area, I believe we would have an extremely prosperous fishing industry and we could revitalise the fishing communities around not just Scotland but Britain because we could tackle the issues there and then and we would not be doing destruction to our fishery. We would be able to manage that extremely well. I think it is a fantastic way forward. I cannot emphasise enough the fact that politicians need to support regional management. It is a great idea. It is the only way forward in our opinion for the industry.

Q929 *Lord Wallace of Tankerness:* Is the processing industry represented on the RAC at the moment?
Mr Charles: Yes, I believe so.

Q930 *Lord Wallace of Tankerness:* But it is not your Federation specifically?
Mr Charles: No. It is just not my department!

Q931 *Lord Wallace of Tankerness:* Would you know what opportunities you have to shape agendas?
Mr Charles: If we had an opinion on the fishery, we would have a very good opportunity to have input there on that Committee, there is no question of doubt about it. I do not see that as a problem and far less so than trying to deal within our Common Fisheries Policy.

Q932 *Lord Wallace of Tankerness:* One of the issues you raised earlier was your frustration with the way the science was limited. Do you see the RACs as having an opportunity, because it brings people together from the science and the catching sectors, for more fine tuning of where the science takes place?
Mr Charles: Regional management in our fishery is like a breath of fresh air blowing through it. There is so much we can do. The real-time closures is a fantastic example of how you can spring that idea forward, implement it, act on it and then, instead of fishermen being penalised, they get a reward for conservation efforts. It is a fantastic opportunity. I cannot say enough about it.

Q933 *Lord Wallace of Tankerness:* At the moment what we have got are advisory councils. You have used the word management many times. Would it be fair to say you would like to see advisory councils evolve into management?
Mr Charles: I think we have got to take the hot air out of managing the industry. There are so many committees and so many people talking about the industry, but what we need is action. Clearly we know what we need to do to revitalise the Scottish fishing industry. Lord Plumb suggested the only way is down, our farmers are getting less and our fishermen are getting less and less. I have never heard a European committee of any description suggest that our fishing industry should increase in size and we should prosper and that is the thinking that we need to get through.

We need to ask how we can revitalise our fishing communities. I will give you one example. Probably one of the most conservation-friendly methods of fishing is hook and line by little boats throughout the fishing areas in Scotland, in Fraserborough and Peterhead in particular where wonderful little boats are fished by local people. They are tied to the harbour wall most of the time because they do not have any quota to go out and fish for those mackerel. That product is a hugely valuable product. Those boats could fish from now until the end of time and they would not damage the stocks. All it needs is a very simple agreement by Europe which said, "Take away the red tape. Go out and fish and catch your line cod and mackerel and let's have a thriving harbour of small boats and of young skippers." That is where your blood comes from. That is the next generation. We face a massive problem in the fishing industry and that is that we have an ageing filleting workforce and we have an ageing skipper. We are seeing very little young blood coming into the industry, which is not surprising with the bad publicity. If you were to invest in a whitefish processing plant, dare I say it, somebody may take you along to the doctor because, after what we have had to go through over the last five or six years, you just would not invest in it. What we have got to do is change that. We have got to create an environment where we attract entrepreneurs into the industry. We can expand this industry. There were 30,000 people employed in the industry in 1980 and there are 10,000 employed now. If you manage your fishery and get it back to the kinds of stocks there were back in the 1980s potentially Scotland may have not 20,000 new jobs but possibly 10,000 and that is at a time when oil might be running out. That might be something Scotland might need and, dare I say, Britain as well and the fishing communities down there. It is not something that we need to be thinking negatively about all the time, we have got to be positive about it.

Q934 *Chairman:* We still get lots of young boys leaving Peterhead Academy at the earliest opportunity to go to sea.
Mr Charles: You get one or two. I am not saying there is nobody going out there. If you look at the average age of our processing and filleting capacity, it is very old. There is very little young blood coming in. There needs to be big training work done there. The knowledge and experience of many skippers whose boats were chopped up by the Common Fisheries Policy have left the industry. What you used to find is that most skippers would hand their boat down to their son, but the families of the ones that were chopped up and destroyed have left the industry and that experience we lose forever. That was hugely valuable fishing experience of where the fish were, of fishing in the blood, which was lost and we will pay a

massive price for that in the future. I hope I never see that happen again.

Q935 *Chairman:* Can I just tease out your view on the Common Fisheries Policy because when you were answering Lord Wallace you were saying that regional management was a breath of fresh air and that real-time closures are absolutely excellent. That is all within the framework of the Common Fisheries Policy.

Mr Charles: Yes, it is and I suppose it has been fought for very hard, but it does not take away what the Common Fisheries Policy has done to our industry, it has destroyed it. It is a huge tanker that was too slow, it cannot react. The processors believe the best way forward to manage our fishery is outwith the Common Fisheries Policy. If you are going in to negotiate about what and where the Common Fisheries goes then give your minister a gun full of bullets. Do not let him go into the negotiation with no bullets in his gun.

Q936 *Chairman:* The fundamental difficulty with the position you have outlined is that the Common Fisheries Policy is an integral part of the legal structure of the European Union. The Common Fisheries Policy is grounded in the Treaty. It is not legally possible to come out of the Common Fisheries Policy while remaining a member of the European Union.

Mr Charles: That is what we are told.

Q937 *Chairman:* It is true.

Mr Charles: I will have to take you up on this point. I was very interested to hear Commissioner Borg say that if Scotland went independent it would have to reapply for membership of the European Union and if it suggested coming out of the Common Fisheries Policy it would have to be thrown out of the European Union. I think that is total nonsense. I think it is up to ministers to negotiate a position that is fair and good for the Scottish fishery. All laws can be changed, all management structures can be changed and if there is a strong will from Westminster and from Scotland to change something then I believe we can do it. I think Scotland deserves a chance to manage its own fishery after the destruction that the Common Fisheries Policy has put on Scotland. I can think of no other nation in Europe that has been penalised with so much taken away from it over something as unnecessary as destroying communities and destroying businesses. I

think we must have a strong case for saying, "We've had 30 years of you making a mess of it. Give it to us to manage. We can do it better." It is not anti-European saying that because if we have a stronger fishing stock more European boats will be able to come in and enjoy the fruits of our fishery.

Q938 *Chairman:* Let me put to you the alternative, which is not to go down the route of saying, "Let's come out of the Common Fisheries Policy because we do not like the Common Fisheries Policy" because really that position is not legally compatible with continued membership of the European Union. The only way to get a change like that would be to get a treaty change and to remove the Common Fisheries Policy from the treaty and the chances of that happening are minuscule. The other way is to say, "Yes, let's change the Common Fisheries Policy. Let us move away from it being a top-down regulation driven policy. Let us have some much more bottom-up, much more regional involvement, much more regional management. Let the role of the EU be at a very broad, very high level, setting overall objectives and targets and the delivery of the successful fishery being managed at a much more regional level." The signs that that is possible are through the way in which, as you said, the RACs are going with the real-time closures and things like that. Can we not build on that, which is much more likely to deliver success in a shorter term rather than chase this chimera of coming out of the Common Fisheries Policy?

Mr Charles: My Lord Chairman, in a perfect world you may be right. Europe has made so many promises to our industry and broken them. They have gone a long way to destroying the Scottish fishing industry. I do not think they deserve to manage our industry. The best way forward is to remove it from their management. I think that is something Britain should feel is worth fighting for. Why do they want to manage an industry that they are making a mess of? Allow somebody else to manage that industry for the good not only of Britain but of Europe.

Q939 *Chairman:* That is a clarion call on which to end! Thank you very much. Is there anything else that you feel you want to say that you have not had the opportunity of saying?

Mr Charles: No. I think we have managed to cover all the areas. Thank you for allowing me to come down and give our views.

Chairman: Thank you very much for coming.

WEDNESDAY 11 JUNE 2008

Present	Arran, E	Plumb, L
	Brooke of Alverthorpe, L	Sewel, L (Chairman)
	Brookeborough, V	Sharp of Guildford, B
	Cameron of Dillington, L	Ullswater, V
	Dundee, E	Wallace of Tankerness, L
	Palmer, L	

Memorandum by the Department for Environment, Food and Rural Affairs

CONSERVATION AND MANAGEMENT

Q1. *Chapter II of Regulation 2371/2002 and the conservation and sustainable exploitation of fisheries resources under the Common Fisheries Policy introduced new methods of ensuring conservation and sustainability, including recovery plans, management plans and emergency measures. To what extent have these been effective?*

Background

1. The introduction of mechanisms that are designed to ensure the viability of fish stocks in the long term is a principle that we continue to support and is consistent with Defra's Fisheries 2027 Vision and the fisheries target from the World Summit on Sustainable Development (WSSD).

2. Since 2002 recovery plans have been adopted for cod in the North Sea, Eastern Channel, Irish Sea and West of Scotland, northern hake, and hake and Nephrops in the Bay of Biscay. Long term management plans have been adopted for Western Channel sole, Bay of Biscay sole, North Sea flatfish, and one is being developed for West of Scotland herring. There are also joint management arrangements with Norway for North Sea herring, saithe and haddock, and with Norway and other north eastern Atlantic states for the widely distributed stocks of mackerel and blue whiting.

3. The UK has used the emergency measures to protect the Darwin Mounds, but were unsuccessful in invoking them to protect dolphins vulnerable to the pair trawl fishery in the Western Channel. The Commission also introduced an emergency measure to ban deep water gill netting which has since been modified to allow monkfish and hake fisheries to continue (on the basis that they do not catch the deep water sharks and other species the measure is designed to protect).

Strengths

— The plans are agreed by all countries.

— The plans contain harvest control rules that limit fishing effort if the spawning stock biomass (number of individuals capable of reproducing) of the target stock falls below a precautionary level or if the fishing mortality (proportion of the stock removed by fishing) is above a precautionary level.

— The recovery plans have delivered some results: the northern hake spawning stock biomass has increased to the point where a recovery plan is no longer necessary and a management plan is being discussed. There have been large scale cuts in effort on cod in all areas of the cod recovery zone, and there is now the first indication of a recovery in the state of the North Sea cod stock.

— The concept of long term management of fish stocks is one that is supported by most stakeholders. A number of Regional Advisory Councils have been involved in developing management plans, and RAC advice has been accepted by the Commission in some cases.

Weaknesses

— Long term management plans exist for a relatively small number of species and most are still managed on an annual basis.

— There is no clear monitoring of success, which may make it unclear as to which policies are effective and which options are most likely to succeed in the future. For example, the effort management regime (days at sea) under the cod recovery plan has been amended significantly almost every year since it was introduced in 2003, in each case with no or minimal evaluation of the effects of the previous year's changes.

— In some cases unrealistic targets may have been set when plans were adopted. This seems to be the case with the target of a 30% annual increase in spawning stock biomass which is the basis of the cod recovery plan. This has not been achieved in any year since its adoption but the Council of Ministers has demonstrated that it is not prepared to make automatic annual 15% cuts in days at sea. It is notable that the more recently adopted plans such as that for Western Channel sole are based on a fishing mortality rather than a biomass target. There is broad support for adopting this approach in the cod recovery plan too when it is reviewed this year.

— Impact assessments have been absent or of poor quality.

— The management plans are based almost solely on the biological parameters and have taken little account of social and economic factors. The concern here is not to water down necessary conservation measures simply because they will have an impact on the fleets in question, but rather that those impacts need to be properly understood to be sure that policies are not giving rise to unintended consequences. Where measures are restrictive on fishing businesses in relation to one aspect of their activity they will try and make good losses by intensifying other activities or moving into different areas, and policy makers need to be aware of these types of impact.

— Measures are adopted to apply in a number of sea areas, where the local circumstances are not taken into consideration, making the plans less effective in some areas than others.

— There are some issues of transparency of the data on which plans are based. For example making accurate estimates of the level of fishing mortality on cod has been complicated by poor or absent discard monitoring data in some member states.

— The system of TACs and quotas and technical and control measures are running in parallel with management plans and recovery plans, sometimes with elements of overlap between them.

Possible areas for further work

4. The North Sea and North Western Waters Regional Advisory Councils have set up groups to develop long term management plans for key species and areas. These include setting social and economic as well as biological objectives which many consider to be crucial to the success of the management plans. The extent to which this has already been done has been extremely limited and ways in which this can be achieved through existing or new procedures needs further development.

Q2. *A wide range of management tools are available to fishing managers. What are your views on the following tools?*

— *Total Allowable Catches*
— *Effort Limitation, including days at sea, marine conservation areas and real time closures*
— *Right- based management tools*
— *Technical conservation measures*

5. It is important that fisheries managers have a wide range of tools available to manage fisheries (reflecting their individual circumstances) and these are deployed in a manner that best fits the objective of the management measure. The Commission tend to propose measures that are relatively simple, can apply to many sea areas and are easy to enforce, but which are prescriptive and leave little scope for flexibility to adapt to local conditions or to offer incentives for good practice. Because of the diversity of fishing activity, the complexity of the ecosystems and the extensive human use of the marine environment, there is unlikely to be a perfect, one size fits all management solution.

6. Total allowable catches are used to set limits on stocks which are more vulnerable to fishing activities. Without TACs, an alternative system would be needed to limit targeting of the most valuable stocks at the expense of their long term viability. Originally, TACs were set on the basis of the estimated composition of the stock based on a single stock assessment. ICES subsequently introduced mixed fishery advice to ensure that the most vulnerable fish stocks were protected for fish stocks that swim together.

7. In recent years TAC changes have generally been limited to a 15% change to allow some stability for fishermen, although larger cuts and increases have been made where particular exceptional circumstances suggest the need for these. The general limitation on TAC changes means that if there is a rapid change in the composition of fish species it may not be reflected in the TACs and discarding can result. This is partly a consequence of the time lags built into the international scientific advice: strong new year classes can start to be caught in fishermen's nets before their size is confirmed in scientific advice (this was the situation experienced with North Sea cod in 2006–07, subsequently confirmed in the October 2007 ICES advice, and we seem to be seeing a similar phenomenon in the Channel cod stock at the moment). In addition, those TACs whose management areas are not closely aligned to the biological distribution of the stock may lead to discrepancies between the availability of the stock and the quota.

8. The principle of relative stability in which the TACs are allocated is a simple method to allow Member States who have a track record for fishing to continue to receive an "equitable" share of the stock, without the need for frequent decisions about allocations. There are issues at the margin where as a result of the changing nature of fisheries some national quotas are persistently over-subscribed or not taken up, but on the whole the principle of relative stability has worked well.

9. Effective setting of TACs is dependent on accurate assessments which are data intensive and costly. When the data is not representative of the true picture (for example when there are high levels of discarding or large volumes of illegally caught fish that are not recorded as part of the landings) the basis for assessing the stock and predicting changes is weakened. However, the same or very similar data would be needed to operate any alternative system not based on TACs, for example in an effort-only management system it would still be necessary to estimate fishing mortality rates and stock sizes in order to set a responsible level of fishing effort.

10. Limiting the time the vessel is allowed at sea is one of the most direct and easily enforceable measures available to fisheries managers to limit the capacity of vessels to fish. It can be highly effective when stocks are at high risk of collapse and removes the requirement to regulate activities at sea. However, it is generally unpopular with the fishing community because although it can achieve the protection of a vulnerable stock, it limits the scope to fish for more abundant or resilient stocks. For example fishermen subject to limits on days at sea under the cod recovery plan may have quota for haddock or prawns that they are unable to fully exploit because their days are limited. Many fishermen take non-quota species which are an essential part of their income. There is some evidence also that limits on fishing effort have been less effective than originally expected in reducing cod mortality as fishermen have responded to the days at sea restrictions by using their time at sea more efficiently, so that fishing mortality has not always reduced as much as the reductions in fishing effort.

11. The TAC and quota Regulation for 2008 recently set a precedent that allowed increased flexibility for Member States to control the number of days allocated to vessels operating under effort management. This allows Member States to provide incentives to those who sign up to measures that help to reduce cod mortality, such as observing real time closures, taking part in trials for more selective fishing gear and fishing plans that reduce discards. Defra and other UK Fisheries Administrations are currently developing such schemes, which allow fishermen to be rewarded with extra days if they take additional steps to reduce discards of cod in consultation with the fishing industry.

12. Marine conservation areas are likely to be effective in protecting species of a sedentary nature. They may also in some circumstances help to protect highly aggregated fish such as spawning concentrations, although there have been examples where closures of this type have had unintended adverse impacts. Such closures will generally be less effective for fish species that have a wide distribution or migrate. Many closures have been put in place to protect fish stocks, but they have often had no procedure to monitor their effectiveness or provide a mechanism for their removal. This has meant that many restrictions have remained even when their effectiveness has been questionable.

13. Real time closures have recently been put in place in the North Sea by the UK industry and Fisheries Administrations to help avoid high concentrations of juvenile plaice and cod as part of the effort management scheme for 2008 referred to in paragraph 11 above. This follows a trial of real time closures on a voluntary basis in Scottish waters in the autumn of 2007, and previous voluntary trials by the Dutch beam trawl sector and the Dutch administration in the southern North Sea. Although it is difficult to quantify the contribution of such closures to reducing fishing mortality, there is evidence from their use in Norwegian waters that these are an effective fisheries management tool, and they are responsive and flexible systems supported by fishermen.

14. Rights-based management tools in the UK take the form of the quota management system. This is carried out collaboratively by DARD, the SE and Defra/MFA. Under the present quota management arrangements, the UK's quotas are allocated to (i) fish producer organisations (POs), who manage quota for the vessels in their membership; (ii) the "non-sector", a group comprising vessels over 10 metres not in POs; and (iii) the

under 10 metre fleet not in POs. Quota allocations to these groups are based on the "Fixed Quota Allocation units" (FQAs) held by the individual vessels in membership of each group, or by a group collectively. These FQAs were originally based on vessels' historic landings (track record) during a fixed reference period (1994–96 for most stocks). Each group's share of the total UK quota for a particular stock is based primarily on that group's share of the total FQA units for that stock which are held by the UK fleet as a whole.

15. Quota allocations are issued by Fisheries Administrations to the groups listed above. FQA units are not therefore allocations of quota from Departments to the vessels in question, but are merely a mechanism for Fisheries Administrations to share quota annually to POs and the other groups. POs are allocated quota in line with the number of FQAs attached to licences on the boats in the membership. The quota allocations for the non-sector and the under 10 metre fleet are managed by Fisheries Administrations in consultation with industry. Monthly catch limits are set for all non-sector fisheries, and for most under 10 metre fisheries.

16. During the course of the year compliance with quotas is measured through recorded landings. Skippers of vessels over 10 metres long must record the quantity of any quota species landed in a "landing declaration". Fisheries Administrations aggregate information from landing declarations to show total quota uptake, and if necessary close a fishery when the total quantity landed approaches the quota ceiling.

17. Vessels under 10 metres are exempt from the requirement to submit landing declarations. Data on landings by these vessels is obtained on the basis of data collected under the arrangements for the registration of buyers and sellers of first-sale fish. Once the under 10 metre fleet's allocation for a particular stock has been taken in full, vessels are prohibited from further fishing for that stock.

18. To maximise their fishing opportunities and to try to avoid the need to close fisheries, fishermen in the UK arrange quota exchanges, and lease quota from each another. This happens within POs and between POs. In addition, Defra organises international quota swaps with other Member States, which result in exchanges of quota for different species to meet the in-year needs of the catching sector in different countries.

19. Technical conservation measures allow improvements in efficiency and selectivity which can make a real difference to improving the quality of catch or reducing unwanted parts of the catch. Changes to gear regulations that are not supported by the fishing industry can be difficult to enforce and it can be difficult to isolate and identify the effects of some technical changes (such as mesh size increases) from the effects of other management measures taken at the same time. Technical conservation legislation has become highly complex, particularly where rules on catch composition (intended to restrict targeting of species with a gear designed for another species) inter-act with rules in recovery and management plans, eg on days at sea limits for different categories of gear type. However, where gear modifications have been trialled in commercial conditions with industry involvement and are generally accepted, they can deliver useful improvements.

Q3. *To what extent have the current management tools increased levels of discarding and by catch? What is your view on how these problems can best be tackled?*

20. Fishermen discard fish for many reasons, and the extent to which discarding takes place is dependent on the market for different species, the local abundance of the fish stocks available, the legal framework which applies, the level of enforcement and business decisions made by individual fishermen. The following examples explain some of the reasons for discarding:

— Some species of fish have no market value in the local area where they are landed and would be discarded regardless of the regulations in place. For example a study of patterns of discarding in waters to the west of England and Wales published in Fisheries Research[1] showed that the 10 most discarded species by otter trawlers registered in England and Wales included boar fish, great silver smelt, poor cod and dragonets, 100% of which were discarded.

— For some species there are market outlets, but at low price levels, and particularly for smaller individuals the price available does not justify the handling costs involved in landing the fish. This is the case with species like dab, gurnard and whiting in some but not all parts of the country. (NB: 40 years ago monkfish was generally regarded as unmarketable and discarded but is now the UK's third most valuable marine fishery.)

— For most but not all commercial species there are regulatory minimum landing sizes (MLSs) set (designed to discourage targeting of immature fish) which automatically requires discarding of fish below this size. Larger bodies species such as plaice are particularly likely to be caught while still below the minimum landing size.

---

[1] R. Enever et al., Fisheries Research 86 (2007) 143–152

— In some cases there is poor selectivity of the mesh sizes used. CFP legislation sets minimum mesh sizes for most of the main fisheries in EU waters, which are designed to try and avoid catches of fish below MLSs. But the highly mixed nature of many European fisheries makes it impossible to get this right for all species simultaneously. For example, the minimum mesh size generally used in fisheries targeting sole is 80mm, which is effective for catching sole above the MLS of 23cm, but which also tends to catch immature plaice and cod below the MLSs of 27cm and 35cm respectively for these species.

— In some circumstances, catch composition rules (designed to discourage targeting of relatively depleted stocks such as cod and sole with gears designed for other purposes) set maximum percentages of certain species in the catch, which can on occasions lead to discarding. For example, in the North Sea otter trawlers using 80–99mm mesh nets have to have at least 30% of prawns in their catch or have at least 70% of their catch composed of a long list of species which excludes cod, haddock and saithe. In either case they may have no more than 20% cod.

— Fishermen will sometimes discard otherwise marketable fish because they have reached their quota limit for that species. This is a consequence of mixed fisheries where fish of the species for which quota is exhausted will probably continue to be caught while fishing for other species for which quota is still available or which are not subject to quotas. There have been cases where this has resulted in high levels of discarding when a successful recruitment results in big increases in "catchability" of the species without a corresponding increase in the quota (eg North Sea haddock in 2001 and monkfish in the south west in 2003–04).

— In any quota system where there is effective enforcement discarding will tend to be higher than where enforcement is ineffective. The significant tightening up of enforcement which has taken place in the UK over recent years, which of itself has been highly desirable, may have had the side effect of increasing levels of discarding.

— So-called "highgrading" occurs when fishermen discard marketable fish which is both above MLS and within quota, a practice which results from a combination of market reasons and quota limits. This arises with species such as cod for which quota limits are highly restrictive and for which there is a price premium for larger fish, creating an incentive for fishermen to discard marketable but lower price bracket fish in order to use their limited quota to land fish commanding the highest price.

21. Fishermen continually make business decisions based on the opportunities available to them. These decisions can lead to high levels of discarding depending on the circumstances. The Defra-funded research study cited in paragraph 20 above suggests that market reasons are responsible for the majority of discarding, rather than the TAC and quota system, but in individual instances where a strong recruitment of a particular species has not been reflected in the relevant TAC (eg North Sea haddock in 2001, North Sea cod in 2007), this can be reversed.

22. Although there is no solution that will address all the causes of discarding, there are improvements which could be considered to help fishermen reduce discard levels:

— Increase focus on helping fishermen maximise the value of their catch by increasing quality and developing new markets for currently low value species.

— Encourage uptake of gear modifications proven to reduce levels of unwanted by-catch, eg the "benthic release panel" developed by Cefas in collaboration with beam trawlers in south west England (see pages 13–14 of the attached booklet).

— Consider options for simplifying technical legislation (the European Commission will be proposing a revision of the Technical Conservation Regulation (Council Regulation 850/98) this year which offers an opportunity to take a fundamental look at rules in areas such as minimum landing sizes and mesh sizes and catch composition rules.

— Consider moving to a more outcome-based approach to regulation which sets targets for levels of discarding but leaves it to individual member states and fishing vessels how to meet those targets, rather than specifying technical gear configuration in detail in European legislation.

— Establish incentives to promote more sustainable fishing practices.

— Increase participation by fishermen, for example in trialling new gear solutions to increase understanding of the options available and willingness to buy into them.

More general ideas for consideration

— The way in which the legislation is structured means that regulations for a certain fishery are complicated and multi-layered, making the practical operation of the fishery complicated for fishermen, enforcement officers and administrators. The result is that there are unintended consequences such as high levels of discarding. There may be a case to restructure the regulations to allow high level objectives to be set by the Council of Ministers and a system of more detailed regulations to be set at more regional or local levels.

— Improvements in participation from stakeholders have taken place, particularly through the introduction of Regional Advisory Councils. However there may be a case to further develop the role of stakeholders in developing and implementing fisheries policy.

— Improvements in the system to set TACs and quotas could be considered, such as developing a more transparent use of information, a system which takes into consideration new information quickly and is flexible to new market and stock information.

Q4. Do you consider that fisheries management policies may need to adapt to climate change? If so, how might this be achieved?

23. Climate change already seems to be having quite marked impacts on fish stocks. For example, we are seeing increased abundance of stocks such as red mullet and squid in the North Sea and increased abundance of stocks such as sardine and anchovy in the waters around the south west of England. Bass also seems to be being found in greater numbers further north than previously. At the same time, scientific research on temperature and changes in plankton suggests that conditions for species like cod are becoming less favourable in the North Sea. This does not mean that cod cannot recover, but rather that conditions are less favourable so recovery may be more difficult.

24. However, there is much that we do not know about the impact of climate change on marine ecosystems and hence on fish stocks. The inherent natural variability in the marine environment and in fish stocks makes it difficult to isolate unambiguously climate effects from the range of other impacts and a naturally fluctuating baseline. Similar comments can be made about the effects of increased acidification, which is sometimes termed a "climate change" effect, and impacts may be direct, for example on the formation of shells in shellfish, or indirect through ecosystem changes.

25. In the short term current management systems can probably cope with these changes up to a point. For example, all of the stocks quoted above as increasing in abundance in our waters are "non-pressure" stocks, ie not subject to catch limitations under the CFP. In recent years these stocks have in some cases provided useful alternative fisheries for fishermen whose traditional target stocks have been declining. Equally for stocks where conditions have become less favourable, this does not mean that current management measures cannot cope, for example if a big recruitment of cod has become less likely that may only mean the need for a cautious approach to levels of fishing and/or accepting that recovery may require a longer timescale.

26. However, if these effects become more marked we can expect current management measures to come under increasing strain. For example key "reference points" used by the scientists in assessing the North Sea cod stock are the precautionary and limit levels for the spawning stock biomass (set at 150,000 tonnes and 70,000 tonnes respectively). These levels were set based on long time series of stock data which include the years of the so-called "gadoid outburst" in the 1970s when all North Sea whitefish stocks were at high levels. If conditions have changed it may be that these reference points are now set at unrealistically high levels. However, it will probably take a number of years before the scientists can be confident of this and recommend new reference points, and in the meantime fisheries managers may be working towards targets which are no longer appropriate.

27. In the longer term if the species mix changes dramatically this would imply the need for a more fundamental adaptation of current CFP mechanisms. Specifically, this could lead to a situation where the current division of catching opportunities for particular stocks between member states (based on track record in the years prior to 1983 when it was established) would become manifestly inappropriate. Arguably there are already cases where the current "relative stability" shares are out of line with reality, but it was so difficult to agree in the first place that there is little appetite for re-opening it as long as the current division does not cause acute problems.

28. There is also a need to be increasingly sensitive to indirect effects on the fishing industries. For example, fishing exerts a pressure on the habitats and biodiversity of our seas. Climate change may alter the status of non commercial species, bringing them into vulnerable or threatened categories, which in turn may need protection from the additional pressures of fishing.

29. It is clear that we are moving ahead under significant uncertainties of even the direction of change in abundance of species. We need to maintain our fisheries and marine monitoring systems to detect these changes and so respond appropriately. We are also investing in a range of underpinning research (see pages 14–18 of the attached booklet).

CONTROL AND ENFORCEMENT

Q5. *Chapter V of Regulation 2371/2002 lays down the responsibilities of the Member States and the Commission as regards the control and enforcement of the rules of the Common Fisheries Policy. The recent Court of Auditors Report on the control, inspection and sanctions systems relating to the rules on conservation of Community fisheries resources was very sceptical of the systems currently in place. What is your view of the efficacy of the systems in place? To what extent has the Community Fisheries Control Agency already assisted in improving matters?*

30. The current EU control regime has been in place since 1993 (Regulation 2847/1993, as amended). Since then it has been amended on a number of occasions but has not been subject to a comprehensive review. In that time the regime has become cumbersome and difficult to implement effectively and implementation varies across the Community. A review of the Control Regulation has for some time been planned for 2008 as part of the Commission's simplification initiative. That review has clearly been given added impetus and focus by the findings of the European Court of Auditors report.

31. The Community Fisheries Control Agency is still in its infancy. It has a very strictly defined remit, which in terms of operational coordination is to establish joint deployment plans for the coordinated use of Member States' control resources to fulfil the Community's international control obligations (eg in NEAFC and NAFO) and to implement specific monitoring programmes for recovery stocks. To date, only one joint deployment plan has been agreed and implemented, that for North Sea cod. Results of the first exercises in the latter half of 2007 have been encouraging, but it is too early to assess the impact of those exercises on control systems generally.

32. More generally it is clearly important that there is consistency in the effectiveness of control and enforcement across the Community. This is primarily a responsibility of individual member states and for the Commission in pursuing vigorously instances of member states failing to exercise proper controls. There are indications that the Commission have been performing this role increasingly effectively in recent years. The importance of consistency in control standard is one UK Ministers have raised formally with the Fisheries Commissioner on a number of occasions over recent years.

Q6. *The European Commission has regularly highlighted how serious infringements of the CFP are penalised differently across the Community. This was a matter that was also raised by the Court of Auditors[2] and sanctions were included in the recent Commission Proposal in IUU fishing. What is your view on the issue?*

33. It is certainly true that the level of financial penalties applied across the Community can vary widely and indeed within individual countries, including the UK. This is a reflection of the fact that decisions about the level of criminal penalties are a matter for the Courts and not one of Commission competence. For this reason Commission attempts to include severe financial penalties in the proposed IUU regulation have run into difficulties. There is however a place for the use of dissuasive administrative sanctions, including financial sanctions, within the control system. That is one of the areas that will be looked at as part of the review of the Control Regulation.

34. In October 2007, the European Commission has proposed a European Council Regulation to establish a Community system to prevent, deter and eliminate illegal, unreported and unregulated (IUU) fishing. This draft regulation is still in consideration at Council working groups.

35. The proposed regulation and associated Communication represent a major initiative by the European Commission to address the incentives and governance gaps which drive IUU fishing. The regulation effectively states that instances of IUU fishing may be found in all fisheries, whether inside or outside Community waters.

36. The regulation acknowledges the existing mechanisms within the Community to address illegal and unreported activity and therefore concentrates on 3rd country imports of fish to the Community. The proposals under the regulation include:

— only allowing imports of fish and fish products if certified as legal by Flag States;

— blacklisting of non-compliant vessels and Flag States;

---

[2] European Court of Auditors, Special Report 7/2007 on the control inspection and sanctions systems relating to the rules on conservation of Community fisheries resources.

—   the designation of ports within Member States for landing and restrictions on transhipments; and

—   measures on compliance and sanctions, including in relation to third countries and nationals of EU Member States involved in IUU fisheries anywhere in the food chain.

37. In addition, the Commission's communication on the IUU regulation highlights the need for tough and effective enforcement and sanctions regimes within Member States, establishing a level playing field. Within the regulation certain articles propose to establish sanctions regimes with an aim to ensure the regulation is WTO compliant, in that measures against 3rd countries and EU Member States are equivalent.

38. The regulation would introduce measures that allow individual EU vessels to be added to an IUU blacklist. The blacklist in effect limits the ability of an EU vessel to continue fishing. The Commission indicates that this sanction could be used in individual cases should infringements have occurred, but the relevant Member State had not taken any action against its vessel. This would be distinct from the normal infraction proceedings the Commission takes for systematic failures in Member States' enforcement systems.

39. The regulation also aims to introduce maximum penalties for fisheries offences set at a minimum of 300,000 Euro for natural persons and 500,000 Euro for Legal Persons. However, such maximum levels of fines in the UK Government view, would fall within the definition of criminal rather than administrative sanctions and are outwith Community competence. EU Council Legal Services and other Member States share our views on competency.

STRUCTURAL POLICY

Q7. *Chapter III of Regulation 2371/2002 obliged Member States to put in place measures to adjust the capacity of their fleets in order to achieve a stable and enduring balance between such fishing capacity and their fishing opportunities. To what extent has this been successful?*

40. The latest annual report from the Commission under Article 14 of Council Regulation (EC) No. 2371/2002, assessing the degree to which Member States have succeeded in bringing fleet capacity and fishing opportunities into more effective balance, concludes that Member States have not achieved the necessary balance.

41. The Commission's overall view is that the general quality of the reports from Member States is insufficient to allow it to draw any reasonable conclusion on the level of overcapacity of the EU fishing fleets compared to its fishing responsibilities. For example, under the rules in place to control fleet capacity, all but two Member States operated within the overall fleet capacity limits set for them. The Commission accepts this and the fact that there has been a decline in fleet capacity in recent years, but suggests that this is at a rate much smaller than that required for the sustainable management of key commercial fish stocks.

42. In addition, much of the reduction seen is more than compensated by technological improvements, which make it possible to catch more fish per unit of effort. As such the Commission's overall view is that there is an excess of fishing capacity, but they are unable to state the extent of the reduction in capacity that might be needed, and that more work is needed to ensure that the correct incentives to control and limit fishing effort are in place at national level.

43. This conclusion is somewhat simplistic, because it looks at the position in the round and does not reflect the variety of results. The UK has for example, delivered a more than 60% reduction in effort in its whitefish trawling fleet, and has reduced overall capacity by 11% in tonnage terms and 8% in engine power from 1 January 2003 to 1 January 2007.

44. One problem is that the Commission have yet to state how exactly Member States are to judge the balance between fishing opportunity and fishing capacity. The latest report is the fourth such report and this comment over the quality of the information included in reports from Member States has been made each time.

45. The lack of guidance was a contributing factor to the UK report being submitted late in 2007, as a format for reporting the appropriate information had to be developed without sufficient guidance from the Commission on what the report should include. The Commission are looking to provide more guidance to Member States in future to ensure that a coherent and consistent assessment can be made across the EU.

GOVERNANCE

Q10. *As a result of Regulation 2371/2002, Regional Advisory Councils (RACs) were established to advise the Commission on matters of fisheries management in respect of certain sea areas or fishing zones. What is your assessment of the success thus far of the RACs? What is your view on their future evolution?*

46. The UK Government strongly supports the RACs and believes they have a vital role in producing a better quality of decision-making under the CFP. Defra and the other UK Fisheries Administrations have provided significant practical and logistical help to the four RACs in which the UK has an interest (the North Sea, North West Waters, Pelagic and Long Distance RACs) in order to help them fulfil their role as effectively as possible, for example by funding scientific support to help them develop long term management plans for stocks in their areas (see pages 31–32 of the attached booklet).

47. It is still relatively early in the life of the RACs. The North Sea, Pelagic and North West Waters RACs were in the first wave of RACs to be established in 2004–05 and so have only been operating for about three years. However they have already demonstrated significant successes. The cod symposium organized jointly by the NSRAC and NWWRAC at North Queensferry in March 2007 was a key event which has influenced thinking on cod recovery at European level and all three RACs have demonstrated that they can produce thorough and well-researched opinions on major current issues.

48. However there are a number of problems in relation to RACs' role which have not been resolved:

— the RACs do not have funding to commission their own research or new analysis/evidence gathering (the budget they have from the European Commission and member states covers administration such as meeting costs, interpretation and translation, and the cost of a small secretariat, but not externally commissioned work). The UK has sought to help fill this gap in the short term, either by providing Government scientists to assist at RAC working group meetings or by funding new research in support of the RACs' work through Defra's Fisheries Challenge Fund, but this is not a long term solution. This is an issue the UK has raised formally with the Fisheries Commissioner.

— For the North West Waters RAC in particular, the fact that it covers such a huge and diverse area has made managing the issues it addresses and arriving at consensus views particularly challenging. It has sought to deal with this by doing most of its work through four regional working groups covering respectively the West of Scotland, the Irish Sea, the Celtic Sea and the Channel. This seems to be working, but it is much more difficult for the RAC as a whole to develop a shared view of the fisheries in its area than it has been for the North Sea and Pelagic RACs.

— The RACs have generally been able to offer high quality advice on longer term management issues such as cod recovery, other long term plans and CFP simplification. They have found it more difficult to develop coherent and reasoned responses to the Commission's annual TAC & quota proposals because of the timescales involved. The timetable up to now, which has generally allowed only about three weeks from publication of the Commission's proposals to the December Fisheries Council, has simply been too rapid for the RAC meeting and coordination mechanisms to operate as effectively as would be desirable. The change in the timetable planned for this year should help address this.

49. Overall it is probably therefore too early to say confidently that the RACs have been an unqualified success, but it would be fair to say that those in which the UK has the closest interest have made a good start and are growing in influence, so the signs are positive for potential development of their role in the future.

50. For these reasons it is probably too early to give a clear view of the RAC's potential future role. It flows from the analysis above that there is much that could be done to enable them to be more effective within their current remit. For example, addressing the funding issue referred to in paragraph 46 above to allow them to commission their own analysis to help inform their advice would contribute significantly to improving the quality of their work and hence their influence. Changing the timetable for the annual proposals for fishing opportunities for the following year to allow the RACs and others more time for analysis and comment would also help them contribute more fully to this key part of current CFP processes.

51. In general terms we see scope for RACs to take on a greater role in the future (eg in drawing up long term management plans and in relation to some of those issues involving technical measures and discarding where we identify above a need for less prescriptive legislation at EU level and more scope for regional variation).

Q11. *How do you consider EU fisheries should ideally be governed? How appropriate and feasible do you consider a regional management model to be?*

52. On this question too, it is too early to give a clear view. There is early thinking going on at the moment in preparation for arriving at an agreed UK view on this sort of question in preparation for the 2012 review of the CFP, but this is still at a relatively early stage. However, it is possible to set out in very broad terms the sort of principles we would want to see govern future management of EU fisheries:

— A more stable regulatory framework with more regulation by long term management plans and fewer annual changes.

— A more regional approach to decision making with less micro-management from Brussels and more discretion to manage at regional level within an overall EU framework.

— Better stakeholder involvement.

A more regional management model could and should be appropriate and feasible, but it is essential that this remains within an overall EU framework to ensure things like consistency of control and enforcement standards and consistency of monitoring and data gathering.

February 2008

Examination of Witnesses

Witnesses: Jonathan Shaw, a Member of the House of Commons, Minister for Marine, Landscape and Rural Affairs, and Mr Lindsay Harris, Head of Sea Fisheries Conservation Division, Department for Environment, Food and Rural Affairs, examined.

Q940 Chairman: Hello, welcome and thank you very much for coming along. I know it has been a bit difficult to arrange diaries, but we are very obliged to you for coming along. It is also actually, between you and me and nobody else, quite refreshing to have a Minister other than Jeff Rooker!
Jonathan Shaw: I can hear his response to that!

Q941 Chairman: So can I! The formalities: this is a formal session, a transcript will be taken; obviously there will be an opportunity to look through it and correct it, if necessary; and also I think we are being webcast so there is about a one in six million possibility that somebody may be listening to what we say.
Jonathan Shaw: You never know when they are listening.

Q942 Chairman: Would you like to start with an opening statement or would you like to go straight into Q and A?
Jonathan Shaw: I want, my Lord Chairman, to say a few opening remarks. To begin with, can I bring the Committee's attention to the gentleman on my right who is Lindsay Harris, one of the senior fisheries officials in the Department, who will make a contribution as and when I am searching for various details perhaps that your Lordships wish to know of. First of all, can I say that I very much welcome this inquiry and the opportunity to give evidence to you. Looking forward, we are seeing that we will have Common Fisheries Policy reform in 2012 and so your inquiry will help us with that process that we are at the beginning stages of. Officials are discussing within the UK between the various administrations as to how we formulate our UK position on CFP reform.

We want to see a more long-term management approach to fisheries; we want to see more of a regional approach; and also we want to see a greater stakeholder involvement, all underpinned by a good compliance system that provides that level playing field for all Member States. Those are some opening remarks and I hope that I am able to answer the questions that you have provided for us.

Q943 Chairman: We could just say "snap" to everything you have said and we could go home basically, but I think the difficulty of course is knowing how to get to the end point that I think is critical there is agreement on. Can we start by looking at the individual bits of the Common Fisheries Policy and can you identify specific reforms that you would like to see?
Jonathan Shaw: We are at the beginnings of that discussion with our colleagues in the devolved administrations and it is important that we have those discussions and, indeed with industry as well, but, as I said, broadly we favour more long-term management plans for different stocks, recognising that sometimes a management plan for one species can interfere with the management of other species. It is not easy within the mixed fishery that we have around the UK shores, but we want to see more of that and we want to see less micro-management from Brussels and we want to see, as I say, a better involvement with the industry. I think from last December we are at the beginnings of improving on that. The Fisheries Science Partnerships, which I think you have heard evidence for, have brought together the industry and science in a way that has not happened in the past to agree areas of work and things particularly to look at, so that then informs us

as we take forward our proposals for reform. We are seeing the cod-avoidance programmes that came out of last year's negotiations. We want to see more involvement with industry working up proposals for long-term management and that is underpinned by the science partnership approach. We believe that it is more desirable to have a more regionalised approach, particularly when it comes to certain stocks rather than a one-size-fits-all approach.

Q944 *Chairman:* Could we have a look at recovery and management plans. What do you see as the strengths and weaknesses that can be identified and how do you think they might be improved?
Jonathan Shaw: In terms of the recovery and management plans, we have got a number of plans in place. We are seeing some good examples of where it is working well—cod in the North Sea— but part of that recovery plan has been alongside a large decommissioning process, so some of the recovery is getting the number of vessels in relation to the amount of quota available right. We think that for the over 10 metre fleet we have got that right. We do want to see more plans in place but I think that they need to be long term. They need to take account, as I say, of factors of particular species. We want to see it based on species and understanding how one set of plans can actually have an impact upon others. For example, if you have a sole recovery plan and you put in a certain mesh size, that may then impact upon small codling. It is that type of arrangement plus also in terms of the recovery and management plans we want to be able to respond to much quicker if there are on-the-ground changes apparent. At the moment it does take a very long time. In the present situation we are seeing a higher level of Channel cod reported but the TAC was reduced considerably at the last December Council hearing, and we, along with the French, have asked for that to be reviewed, and I think that it will be reviewed but it takes many months.

Q945 *Chairman:* I suppose one of the emerging debates that we have picked up is the need to perhaps more explicitly identify social and economic as well as biological objectives. First of all, one of the things to say is they should not be in conflict because if you do not get the biology right you will not have anything to have social and economic consequences for, but do you see that it is possible to have the RACs developing social and economic objectives? I should have thought there are quite a number of difficulties.
Jonathan Shaw: There are difficulties and competing demands there as you have highlighted. Internally when we are taking decisions on new legislation or changes, we do have a socio-economic impact

assessment that the Chief Economist of the Department provides. A recent example would be where I made the decision not to increase the bass minimum landing size. Part of that assessment is looking at the scientific and biological aspects as well as the social and economic impact on the inshore fleet, which was a factor in my decision.

Q946 *Chairman:* It is difficult to get objectives though, is it not?
Jonathan Shaw: Yes it is.
Chairman: Okay let us move on. Viscount Ullswater?

Q947 *Viscount Ullswater:* Minister, the principle of relative stability is fundamental to the Common Fisheries Policy, although some Members are perhaps less keen on it than others. How sustainable do you think that principle is in the long term considering that it effectively amounts to a derogation from the free movement principles of the European Union? You recognise in your very full briefing to us that the principle is sometimes out of line with reality and that climate change might exaggerate it. Do you therefore expect pressure on it from other Member States for its reconsideration?
Jonathan Shaw: I think that if we were starting now we may want to divvy up things in a different way, but in considering when coming before you this afternoon, it is a can of European worms, or sand eels maybe, and if one did open that it would be a negotiation. Of course, if you just look at the economics of it, then you can have an economic conclusion, but of course life is not quite like that, and each Member State will want to negotiate, and so what you might have going in might be something different coming out. Given the demands upon the Commission, and our desire to get some good reforms and ambitious reforms for the Common Fisheries Policy in the way that I have just described, I think that that is where we need to concentrate efforts. That is our position. Re-opening the allowances to each Member State would require a very, very long negotiation. There would be winners and losers, there are swings and roundabouts, but we do not detect a huge enthusiasm for the re-negotiation of the allowances.

Q948 *Viscount Ullswater:* Can I just have a supplementary on that. I can see from your point of view that there is a convenience in having the status quo, but do you think you are in line with the British fishing fleet and British fishermen as to whether we have got the best divvy that we can out of the CFP?
Jonathan Shaw: In the meetings and discussions that I have with both the NFFO and the SFF neither of those organisations have said to me what we need

to concentrate and spend our time on is re-negotiations. I think it would be my former point in terms of the long-term management plans, tackling discards, having a more regionalised approach, less of the micro-management, with a compliance system that is the same across Europe.

Q949 Lord Plumb: On the question of quotas there is reference in paragraph 18 to the international quota swaps. How common are these swaps and how are they organised? When we were in Peterhead, we visited there and talked to a lot of fishermen and it seemed there was growing interest in international trading quotas. I just wonder whether you are encouraged by this and whether you see this as an extension?

Jonathan Shaw: I think there are between 100 and 120 international quota swaps every year and that is, as you will be aware, arranged through the MFA, and that seems to work reasonably well. The industry do those themselves as well but we do have the right to veto if we think that it is not in the best interests of the UK. In terms of the Quota Management Change programme, you will be aware that the Scottish Executive have recently published a consultation on separation of the UK quota. Up until the elections in Scotland, officials from all of the administrations have been working on a Quota Management Change programme, but obviously that has now been stopped and we have not finished our conclusions as to the consultation paper. We are going to look at that because it has implications for all parts of the UK. The interesting point is that the consultation is only on the operational side and how it will be implemented, rather than the principle, and I signalled some months ago that I would issue a consultation on the principle. Where we are at the moment is we need to consider that, and so we are not any further forward in terms of the Quota Management Change programme, I regret, but these are issues that we need to manage.

Q950 Lord Plumb: Just if I may Chairman on a supplementary, on the principle one hears it said that fishermen sell their quotas to the Spaniards and then complain bitterly that the Spaniards are pinching their fish. You get mixed reports, particularly through the press, of whether this is good, bad or indifferent—usually it is bad for the British fishermen as seen by them.

Jonathan Shaw: I am sure we can provide you with examples where UK fishermen have bought quota as well, and we can intervene if we do not feel that that is in the UK interest in terms of the swaps, but people do sell quota. As I say, we want to have a look at the Change programme and we have not been able to do that, but we have not had

opposition and we are not opposed to international swaps.

Q951 Viscount Brookeborough: Before asking question three you mentioned earlier, Minister, the socio-economic impact assessments of various regulations that you might put in force. When we went to Peterhead we found that obviously over the last 10 years there have been great changes in the fishing but they have unemployment down to below 1% and they are flourishing because of the oil industry and diversification and whatever. Can you give us some examples of where those assessments become really important in other places around the country where areas are suffering where there may be a large amount of unemployment from ex-fishermen or their population may have moved away because there is no longer employment?

Jonathan Shaw: In the two largest ports in the south-west of England, Brixham and Newlyn, which I have visited, fishing is very much central to the economies there, not just the fishing itself but a lot of related industries, not least of all one of the largest industries, particularly for Cornwall and Devon, that of tourism. People enjoy going to Brixham Harbour and they want to go to the fish market and they want to see boats and they want to see fishing vessels. I think we do take account of that and I know that the regional development agencies take account of that and they have invested considerable sums in supporting both the industry and related industries. I think the quayside for example in Brixham is getting considerable investment. The regional development agencies in England certainly take account of that and see how they can maximise the economic benefits of the industry.

Q952 Viscount Brookeborough: Thank you very much. TACs and fishing effort are obviously very important management tools. Would you like to tell us a little bit more about the advantages and disadvantages and whether we have got the appropriate balance of management tools in order to control our fishing?

Jonathan Shaw: Yes, they need to work in harmony. We would not want to just have effort control on its own because that would then mean that we would see targeting of particular species and further discards, so it is about getting all three of those tools working in harmony. I think that we need to take those a stage further in terms of where we look at things such as using selective nets. I think that you have heard from the Chief Executive of the NFFO Barry Deas about the eliminator net which is proving to be very effective in separating cod, haddock and whiting, so I think it is about using those tools in relation to selectivity of new gear and also, as I briefly referred to, the real-time closures and getting fishermen to sign up to these new ways of working and, indeed, working with them to come up with the ideas in the first place. We have got some agreements with real-time closures for cod avoidance and obviously we are very keen for those to work because we were able to make some progress this year at Brussels based on plans. What we want to do this year is go back based on actual facts of what has happened in practice to be able to take us to further stages of being able to have more of our own management in place.

Q953 *Viscount Brookeborough:* In your evidence in paragraph 7 you talk about TACs and scientific evidence and you in fact say that "this is a consequence of the time lags built in". They probably occur without being built in because of the slowness of the scientists in working things out. Do you feel that more resources or that some other help could be given to bring the science a little bit more up-to-date quicker because it does lag so far behind that we do get problems with that?
Jonathan Shaw: It does lag behind and I think Joe Horwood from CEFAS talked about that in his evidence to you and also the accuracy of that science is variable, and whiting particularly this year has proved very difficult. But I think that the ICES advice is coming quicker to the Commission and then obviously we are able to make judgments on that.

Q954 *Viscount Brookeborough:* Are we resourcing it enough?
Jonathan Shaw: We are resourcing it. We have CEFAS and we are funding that. We have funding arrangements in place for a 10-year period so that they can plan and ensure that they have got scientists in place, so I have no reason to believe that we are not putting in sufficient resources into fisheries science.

Q955 *Chairman:* Real-time closures are obviously a big step, almost a change of mentality—
Jonathan Shaw: Yes.

Q956 *Chairman:* But they hang by a very delicate thread, do they not, and certainly for other Member States' boats, it is voluntary observance of them and one wonders if it breaks down what the consequences would be.
Jonathan Shaw: You are absolutely right to say a thin thread. If it breaks down then what are the alternatives? It is to continue with the system that we have; a very crude, centralised approach that is not satisfactory and does not really engender a partnership approach between those who have to enforce and those who want to make a living, and so it is "put up" time, is it not?. There are monitors on the vessels that are taking part in the cod-avoidance programme and so the proof of the pudding will be in the eating, my Lord Chairman, because there is

everything to gain and everything to lose, so it is high stakes in many ways.

Q957 *Chairman:* But you can get to the position where you can have all the British fleet signed up to it and then just a rogue other Member State steaming through and that is it.
Jonathan Shaw: We are wanting to be at the reforming end of the Common Fisheries Policy in the same way that we want to be at the reforming end of the Common Agricultural Policy so it does require us to take a lead. Clearly other Member States will be watching and we will have gained some benefits from this. If they are allowing their vessels to simply ignore the arrangements that we have made with the Commission, because you quite rightly say we cannot legally stop a vessel, but again we have not heard any reports that I am aware of to say that other Member States are not co-operating. I guess the Commission will take a pretty dim view, the Commissioner wants to reform, he wants to see us going in this direction, and if other Member States' vessels were going into closed areas then that would not do them any good.

Q958 *Earl of Dundee:* Minister, you have touched on this but could you please tell us a bit more about how we might reduce discard levels?
Jonathan Shaw: One of the recent announcements from the Commission, which is very welcome, is that rather than having a ban on discards, which is a very blunt instrument, he has said that we can have targets for discards, and that brings in much more flexibility and it allows us to work with the industry to work up ways on what I have referred to in terms of whether it is avoidance plans, selectivity or providing incentives in terms of additional days at sea. It has to be in the long term. A last-resort crude ban will create all sorts of implications as to what we do with all of that fish that there is not a market for, for example. It is problematic within our mixed fishery area and we do not want to see markets created for undersized fish obviously either, so we welcome what he has said about targets rather than a blunt instrument. We do want to see additional markets for other fish and that has happened in recent years. The red gurnard is the fish that is often referred to and many of my Lords here will be aware that monkfish now is the third most popular fish. Who would have thought that 10 or 20 years ago? It is a very important fish. I think Mr Harris might be able to tell the Committee a little bit about some of the partnerships we are doing on discards with whiting with the French, which is encouraging.
Mr Harris: Yes, whiting is one of the species that is most heavily discarded and in the North Sea in the English fleet it tends to be boats targeting prawns that have high amounts of discarded whiting. The French fleet are targeting different species so it is a slightly

different problem. We have each been doing trials of different selective gear to try and find ways with the scientists and the fishermen working together both releasing more of the unwanted, smaller whiting while not losing the valuable prawn catch. There have been experiments done for decades on more selective gear, but it is getting the balance right that there is enough in it for the fishermen that they actually want to use it so that it is taken up. It looks potentially as if there are some quite encouraging things coming out of that.

Q959 *Earl of Dundee:* Do you think there may be further ways in which government can promote the consumption of alternative products?
Jonathan Shaw: I think that a number of the celebrity chefs influence things to eat and would probably be a little more influential than the Fisheries Minister. It crushes me to think that but I have to face up to the reality; my culinary skills are not the same as Rick Stein's! Hugh Fearnley-Whittingsall has done that and I think celebrity chefs have certainly raised the profile of alternatives, and pollock is another species that is often seen as an alternative to cod. I think that doing that helps and obviously that then creates new markets for fishermen. People did not eat sea bass in the way that they do today and that is a sustainable stock and that has provided an additional opportunity particularly for the under 10 metre fleet.

Q960 *Chairman:* You mentioned that a discard ban itself would be pretty much of a blunt instrument and clearly one of the problems is requiring fishermen to land fish which have zero economic value. It would be an extraordinarily difficult thing to achieve.
Jonathan Shaw: And monitor.

Q961 *Chairman:* A halfway house would be a requirement to land all species that were subject to quota.
Jonathan Shaw: Yes.

Q962 *Chairman:* Is that something that has been considered?
Jonathan Shaw: We are beginning a Fisheries Science partnership with the under 10 metre fleet and we will allow them to keep everything that they catch. This will be 30 vessels around the English coastline. They will be investing around £280 million—I mean £280,000—that would be a lot of money, would it not, most of the Defra budget!

Q963 *Chairman:* I think there might be some black fish amongst that!
Jonathan Shaw: Yes, thank you, I stand corrected, £280,000, and because we are using a Science Fisheries Partnership that will allow the under 10 metre fleet to keep all quota fish that it catches. We

are doing that over one year initially and then a possible following year. What we will do with that is it will then assist us with our negotiations with the Commission because the under 10 metre fleet—and I know there are questions in this area—will say they do not have the demands on fuel such as a beam trawler does and they will complain that they have not got enough quota and they will say that it is a sustainable fleet. We want to get some evidence on that so that is why we have instigated this new Fisheries Science Partnership with the under 10 metre fleet. I am grateful for Lindsay pointing that out. We are doing that with this particular part of the fleet.

Q964 *Viscount Ullswater:* Is that not moving towards relying on effort rather than anything else with that particular fleet?
Jonathan Shaw: The under 10 metre fleet is very much governed by the weather so that will often govern this.

Q965 *Viscount Ullswater:* But that is effort, is it not, they would not go out if they cannot?
Jonathan Shaw: That is right and they are not able to go out in the way that the larger vessels are. We are getting the fishermen signed up to this agreement and we are putting in this resource. Obviously we have to ensure there is a proper compliance regime in place so we will be investing in kit, spending that money on kit for the vessels, so then we have got a good and accurate picture. I know we are going to come on to talk about the under 10 metre fleet but that is one of the projects that we are doing to try to assist them and perhaps it goes some way to answering your point.

Q966 *Lord Brooke of Alverthorpe:* Since this inquiry commenced there has been a dramatic change in the cost of fuel. I just was wondering in the light of that going back to the question on discards whether there may not start to be, if the price of fuel continues to rocket, some different approaches to discards and to the possibilities of marketing when one considers just how much it does cost to discard in the light of increased fuel costs. I was wondering whether generally on policy the way in which price has been moving on fuel that is also starting to bring some fresh thinking in a number of areas?
Jonathan Shaw: As has been reported, I have met with the industry from across the UK to discuss fuel and there are going to be further meetings with ministerial colleagues on this, but the industry certainly acknowledge that we are going to have to make some considerable changes, and it is not just the fishing industry, if we are going to be living with fuel prices, they are 139 now, we do not know.

Q967 *Lord Brooke of Alverthorpe:* It could be 200.
Jonathan Shaw: We do not know what they are going to be, my Lord, do we, but we do know they are not going to plummet; I think that is for certain. We do have to make adjustments and that will require us to have a discussion/debate both in the UK and at a European level as well and the industry know that; indeed they have said that to me when asking for some short-term finance that I was not able to help them with.

Q968 *Chairman:* The problem with increasing fuel costs is that the pressure on discards increases because you will get discarding for highgrading.
Jonathan Shaw: That is right.

Q969 *Viscount Brookeborough:* What is the evidence that the Spaniards are compensating for fuel?
Jonathan Shaw: They are on strike, Sir! Shall I talk about fuel now if we are here?
Lord Palmer: Your last question was going to be on fuel.
Chairman: As long as you are not going to give way, that is all right, on fuel.

Q970 *Lord Palmer:* I accept the Spaniards are on strike but have the French not given their fishermen a subsidy and it is certainly rumoured in the Scottish press—and I live in Scotland—that the Scottish Executive are going to give the Scottish fleet various compensations for these very high fuel costs. I absolutely accept your point that this does go across every industry, not just the fishing fleet.
Jonathan Shaw: The fishing industry is a very important integral part of our coastal communities and we want to see it continue and we want to see it flourish. Up until the big hikes in fuel, particularly for the over 10 metre fleet, we reckon that we got the quota and the number of vessels about right. In the over 10 metre industry, fish prices have been high. An example of how it has changed, in 1987, 170,000 tonnes of cod out of the North Sea; last year 20,000, and about the same price. So huge pain in terms of the decommissioning but getting it about right in terms of fishermen versus how many fish we can catch. If we were to go down the road of applying the full maximum that we are legally able to do, that would provide one month's relief, so it would give the UK fleet one month at last year's prices, and then we would not have any more money to spend to help because once you have gone up to the maximum then it is three years. Now that is not to my mind even short term, but of course there will then be many other industries and businesses, and so we are not in a position to be able to make that type of contribution. I think that for the English figures that is around £35 million . It is per business of course, Chairman, not per vessel.

Q971 *Chairman:* Ultimately and in the relatively short term cost increases lead to market adjustments that actually involve price increases as well?
Jonathan Shaw: I think that the industry will say that it takes quite a while for the prices to come through and so their argument would be that they needed this assistance in the short term and, as I say, we are not convinced that that is the right way. We are putting in place a number of other measures to assist the industry, for example, the European Fisheries Fund, which is around £100 million over the next seven-year period, and we will work with the industry to see how we can best utilise that. There are other measures as well that we are going to assist them with but those type of sums for such a short period of time is not something that we can contemplate.
Chairman: Let's go on to control and enforcement with Lord Cameron.

Q972 *Lord Cameron of Dillington:* Yes, dealing with a specific first before we go to the general, in your written submission you talk about the importance of consistency in control standards, which is an incredibly diplomatic way of saying that you are concerned about the lack of vigour with which certain Member States pursue infringements of the Common Fisheries Policy. I realise there are sensitivities about Europe itself enforcing law and order as it were rather than Member States doing it, but how do you achieve harmonisation of administrative penalties?
Jonathan Shaw: We have in place a range of tools. At sea we have in England and Wales three naval vessels and in Scotland I think there are four vessels and the VMS system.

Q973 *Lord Cameron of Dillington:* I am not too concerned about our enforcement; I am slightly more concerned about how we get harmonisation of enforcement across other Member States.
Jonathan Shaw: I think we would want again to lead by example. As I was referring to the cod-avoidance programme, we want to lead by example. It has not always been the case around the UK and we certainly cannot be complacent, but reading the evidence from the fishermen's leaders, I think we concur that the amount of black fish in the UK now is probably at an all-time low. It is for the Commission and they have tools at their disposal to ensure compliance. I think that as we go forward with the Common Fisheries Policy reform that is the time in which we can produce evidence of what is effective and have that discussion, because in order for the public to have and the industry to have confidence, you are right, we have to ensure that there is a level playing field. We have to counter that by saying we have not always been perfect ourselves, but we have learnt from our

mistakes and we need to find ways of encouraging others to do the same.

Q974 *Lord Cameron of Dillington:* For instance I gather the EU is proposing to put forward proposals later this year to amend the EU's control regime. What input are you having into that process and what changes are you looking for?
Jonathan Shaw: We will have an input and we think in terms of some of the changes they are proposing we are ahead of the game. You are familiar with the regime that we have in place. I think the other thing is—and I am not sure if you are aware—that as well as VMS and aeroplanes we have also, within the MFA, officers who are trained in forensic accounting as well so we can use the TACs system as well. I think that it is a raft of instruments and we would want to have the discussions saying, "This is what we are doing," and ensuring that all Member States are meeting the same standard. It is, as you rightly say, difficult and there are sensitivities, but it is not one that we are going to shy away from. As I said in my opening remarks, compliance is absolutely key for all of this to work. Whether it is illegal landings, whether it is discards, or whether it is the cod-avoidance programmes, you have to have a good compliance system across the board.

Q975 *Lord Cameron of Dillington:* Yes, calling a spade a spade, how are the Commission going to get Spain to enforce the Common Fisheries Policy? Basically that is the question. Us leading by example is all very well but—
Jonathan Shaw: A number of states have received considerable fines.

Q976 *Chairman:* Poland has been fined.
Jonathan Shaw: Indeed, yes, Poland has been fined.

Q977 *Lord Palmer:* Will they pay the fine?
Jonathan Shaw: There is a regime in place where they will lose quota. They will have to pay back.
Chairman: The regional advisory councils, Lord Arran?

Q978 *Earl of Arran:* I think the school report will show so far that they show great promise but just a couple of problems. The first I would like to highlight is the funding arrangements and some seem keener than others to help with the funding. How do you view not so much the funding problems but the different attitudes of different states about funding in the future?
Jonathan Shaw: I agree with your point. The UK supports the development of the regional advisory councils. They are still to some extent in their infancy and some more than others. One of the more mature is the North Sea RAC. They get some

administrative costs from the Commission but they do rely on handouts and have to go round with the begging bowl. The North Sea RAC gets accommodation and support from Aberdeenshire Council—and good on Aberdeenshire Council. The UK administrations have all given funding, particularly for research. This is the key thing; if the regional advisory councils are going to mature and have the credibility so that those sceptical Member States actually see the benefit of regional advisory councils, then they have got to have the funding. I have written and I have met with the Commissioner Joe Borg and made this point to him. We will continue to support the RACs financially but they need to be able to call upon their own resources and determine their own projects with some confidence that they have got some funding. They have not got that at the moment but I think that this is part of our discussion and argument for reform of the Common Fisheries Policy that these bodies need to have that funding. One might assess them to be able to have funding in different stages as to where they are in terms of their maturity and how well they are functioning because obviously some are functioning more than others. The one in the Mediterranean is not functioning at all because it does not exist.

Q979 *Earl of Arran:* Some Member States are wary about giving them too much management responsibility/executive responsibility rather than an advisory role. What is your view on this? Do you think they should, by and large, have more of a management role?
Jonathan Shaw: At this stage we have not considered that carefully but we would not rule it out. I think it would depend upon the point that I have just made, it depends on the capability of the particular RACs. As I say, some are at a more capable stage than others. One could envisage a RAC that has a number of different Member States on it with a range of different stakeholders that they have to have—30% have to be outside of the catching industry—and manage it, in real time, with avoidance programmes, with management programmes. One could see that happening and with buy-in from everyone that would be highly desirable. We will see whether we can get there.

Q980 *Earl of Arran:* Many Member States are of the view that they represent the future of a better, bottom-up rather than top-down, management system which they are very keen on by and large.
Jonathan Shaw: Yes, but I think the bottom-up needs to be underpinned by a good compliance system.
Chairman: Exactly.

Q981 Earl of Arran: Thank you.
Jonathan Shaw: So that is something that we need to impose centrally.

Q982 Chairman: Can I dip back to compliance; what is your view on harmonising administrative sanctions, accepting that we cannot do harmonisation of criminal sanctions?
Jonathan Shaw: I would not get out alive! I think I might get a call from someone if I did advocate that!

Q983 Chairman: It is a problem, is it not, making sure that there is something approaching a degree of harmonisation when it comes to sanctions and perhaps the only route is through administrative sanctions?
Jonathan Shaw: We are having that discussion now about how we implement that. In the pursuit of a level playing field that our fishermen want to see, we are going to have to have some form of harmonisation. Can I ask Mr Harris if he has got any more detail on that.
Mr Harris: Just to say that it is something that the Commission have at times pushed for but have never really made an issue of because different Member States have been at different stages in their use of administrative sanctions in fisheries. As the Committee probably knows, we are moving towards greater use of them in the UK, and I think that is an issue that the Commission will come back to and it may be something that will be in the revision of the control regime that was referred to earlier. I do not think it has gone away as an issue and it is probably the right way to go.

Q984 Chairman: It has not gone away and it may be coming in. Are you for it or against it?
Mr Harris: I would think for.
Chairman: Okay. Let us continue with regional management and Lord Wallace.

Q985 Lord Wallace of Tankerness: I think you have already touched on the principles which you would like to see when the review comes in in 2012 and it is well set out in the final paragraph of the Department's submission to us concluding that: "A more regional management model could and should be appropriate and feasible, but it is essential that this remains within an overall EU framework . . . " The Earl of Arran indicated perhaps the desirability of more management that is going to work but what about its feasibility? How likely do you think it is that Brussels is going to let go of the micro-management?
Jonathan Shaw: I think the Commissioner wants to but of course he has got to have the confidence that there will be compliance, so taking us back again to the cod-avoidance programme, the proof of the pudding will be this December when we are able to

present to him what we have managed to achieve, and I think, as I say, other Member States will be looking carefully at this. I think it is about how the RACs provide their advice as they do at the moment, their ability to be able to mature, their ability to be able to get the resources to do the job of work that they are so keen and I am keen for them to do independently rather than relying on handouts. I think the picture that I have painted, just answering the Earl of Arran's question in terms of one day you will have this regional advisory council that does manage and there are a number of Member States sitting round, so there is ourselves and Denmark and maybe Norway as an observer role looking at cod management in the North Sea with NGOs and fishermen. We have travelled a long way in recent years since the publication of *Net Benefits* from the Prime Minister's Strategy Unit that advocated far more working with scientists and fishermen, and the proposals that came from Scotland in terms of the kilowatt hours which I know you will be familiar with, and a buy-in from the fleet and also the stuff that came from the English fleet as well. That points the way. This is where we want to be in terms of reform; that is where we want to go. Will it be feasible? That is the course that we are charting as it were, so we will see. Certainly within the UK I think there is the ambition to be in that type of position.

Q986 Lord Wallace of Tankerness: On the other side of the coin, which you refer to in that final paragraph, is the overall EU framework. Could you please put on the record why you think there should be an overall EU framework and perhaps expand on what you see as being the components of an overall EU framework.
Jonathan Shaw: In terms of compliance?

Q987 Lord Wallace of Tankerness: Generally in terms of the future of the CFP. What do you see as the central role?
Jonathan Shaw: I think that it is very, very important that we manage our fisheries collectively and that we have an agreed set of management tools in place. Without that I think the consequences upon stocks could be very, very serious indeed, and will prevent us from reaching the key goal which is to meet the 2015 target so that stocks are in a recovering state. Have I answered your question?

Q988 Lord Wallace of Tankerness: You say in your paragraph things like consistency of control and enforcement standards and consistent monitoring and data gathering. Is there anything beyond that that you see as being essential about the European role?

Jonathan Shaw: No, I cannot think off the top of my head, other than getting that consistency across all Member States which is a task in itself. Are there other areas, Lindsay, we would be looking at?

Mr Harris: Presumably if you moved to that more regional approach you would still want to set some sort of principles/parameters within which the regional bodies would work, simply to provide assurance that one body was not going off in an irresponsible direction. It seems to me that is the trick we have got to get right to make this feasible; getting the right balance between having a framework which gives a level playing field but still leaves sufficient flexibility. It comes back to the question that the Chairman asked about the real-time closures because it is the same issue there. You need to have a framework that allows those sorts of things to be done flexibly without it having to go through a Commission proposal and go to the Council, which is very cumbersome and is not a responsive way of doing things, but still gives reassurance that an individual Member State is not going off and doing something wacky on its own initiative.

Jonathan Shaw: I am sure no Member State would do anything wacky!

Q989 *Viscount Ullswater:* Just before we leave this concept of regional management, are the regional advisory councils a bit strapped at the moment because they do not really have funds to commission any work, their funds are very limited to just a small amount to pay for a secretariat and a small amount for travel and Aberdeenshire Council manage to put most of the people up in hotels.

Jonathan Shaw: We should applaud Aberdeenshire Council.

Q990 *Viscount Ullswater:* If they are going to give real advice which may lead the Commission to thinking they have got sensible plans, they will need to come up with commissioning new work rather than relying on old studies or other academic studies or whatever it is. Where do you think that money will come from?

Jonathan Shaw: I wholeheartedly agree with you and that is why I have written and met with the Commissioner to discuss this very point. Defra have funded a number of projects as have the Scottish administration as well and we would want to continue to do so.

Viscount Ullswater: Excellent.

Chairman: Lord Palmer?

Q991 *Lord Palmer:* I do apologise most sincerely for not being here for your opening remarks. I did warn the Chairman that I was going to be late, and I was not quite as late as I thought I was going to be. My main question was going to be on the desperate plight because of the high cost of fuel. You have largely touched on that but six of us around the table are involved in what I like to call "rural activities" and, as we all know, the price of red diesel has quadrupled in the last two years, and I think basically you have touched on that. If I can go back to paragraph 44, the Commission have yet to state how exactly Member States are to judge the balance between the fishing opportunities and fishing capacity. How does our Government consider this judgment should be made and what further measures might the UK take to bring fishing capacity into line with fishing opportunities, including the under 10 metre fleet? I would be particularly interested to know how closely you consult with the Scottish Executive on this particular point.

Jonathan Shaw: Lord Palmer, just to illustrate the jump, three years ago the industry was spending around £90 million on fuel; now it is over £200 million. That puts it in pounds, shillings and pence; it is colossal. In terms of the structural policy, we think that putting aside for the moment fuel prices for the over 10 metre fleet, in relation to its quota and the number of vessels, we have got it broadly right and the industry have enjoyed a good income because fish prices are high and more people are wanting to eat different types of fish, and so it has been a good news story compared to how it was for many years, and that is underpinned, as I say, by scientists and fishermen working together with funded projects from government. As I say, that happens in Scotland and that happens in England. We have put in £3 million up to 2008 following the *Net Benefits* report and we have put in a further £3 million over the next three years as well, so we have continued to do that. What has not happened in the same way as in the over 10 metre fleet for England is the decommissioning of the under 10 metre fleet and so for the number of vessels, which is around 4,000 many of which are not active, the amount of quota that they have available is not sustainable, it does not add up, and so what are we doing about that? I am issuing a consultation with the industry and part of that is something that I have referred to which is the Fisheries Science Partnership where we have got about 30 vessels and a number of those are signing up, in addition to which we want to get some of the vessels out of the pool because 9% of the vessels in the under 10 metre pool take up 70% of the quota. Many of you may have been to Hastings and seen the largest beach fleet anywhere in England, and what I am sure is all in your mind's eye is those little wooden boats and that is part of the culture and that is part of the heritage of that part of East Sussex and Hastings.

Q992 *Chairman:* I see another visit coming up.

Jonathan Shaw: Also when I went there—and I live in Kent so going to Hastings is something that I have done over the years on many occasions—on my first visit as Fisheries Minister, coming up the beach was a huge (comparatively) catamaran and, as I say, these are some of the vessels that take 70% of the quota. That is not what we have in mind so we need to rebalance the fleet. Some of that will be about moving some of these larger vessels. Although they might be under 10 metre, it is not the size, it is the capacity. We will also put in between £3 million and £5 million to decommission and take out some of these vessels. There are also monthly catch limits. Also part of the consultation will be about licences and whether we restrict the number of licences and that would be based upon track record since our records came in in 2005. We are consulting on that and the initial responses have not been entirely positive, but we do have to do something if my grandchildren, as yet unborn, are going to be able to go to Hastings beach and see the little boats that I love to see so much. It does feed into the point that Viscount Brookeborough was asking me about the wider economic benefits. So we are doing that and it is not easy but it is something that has been an on-going argument about the amount of quota that has been distributed between the over 10 metre and under 10 metre fleet in England for a long time. Another point that I wanted to make in terms of the number of vessels and the reasons why we want licences and a new track record is because we have closed North Sea cod to the under 10 metre fleet, the allocation and we have not had to do that before because in some ways we have been able to swap in the past but because it was known it was there fishermen who perhaps are not fishermen all the time but have got a licence think, "Jolly good, let's go and get some of this lovely cod." and those vessels that are fishing as the main part of their livelihood now find themselves with that fishery closed. If you look back over the course of history bringing about restructuring within the industry is difficult, it is painful, but in terms of getting the balance between the number of fishermen and the number of fish you can catch, these are nettles that we have to grasp.

Q993 *Lord Palmer:* And how closely do you liaise with the Scottish Executive because a lot of us are from north of the border around the table?
Jonathan Shaw: Our officials liaise very closely and of course when we are presenting the UK position that is something we need to reach agreement on. We did that effectively last year when I was appointed. I met with the NFFO and explained to them that there was an SNP Fisheries Minister in Scotland, there was a Plaid Cymru Fisheries Minister in Wales and in Northern Ireland there was a Sinn Fein Fisheries Minister and they said, "How do you cope?" I said, "There would probably be a lot more arguments if we were all Labour." But it went very well last December and we are determined to ensure that that continues.

In politics you have different relationships with the same people so we will have differences, but, importantly, where we need to work together we do, and I certainly meet with the Scottish Fisheries Federation led by Bertie Armstrong. I meet him on a regular basis and I will see him and Barry Deas together regularly. So consultation with the established industry representatives is there and is frequent and on-going and what I am setting up in England is a joint working group where it will make decisions that will inform me and that will have an independent chair. We have these type of arrangements with the agriculture industry making decisions on Bluetongue and the vaccine was something that the industry and Government did together. That is why we want to pursue the responsibility in cost sharing, which I am sure Lord Rooker has spoken to you about. That it seems to me is how you need to do business and, as I say, coming afresh to this—and I have been in the position for a year now—much of the industry has settled down, there are good relations and things work well; other parts of it do not, and I need to find a way of managing those relationships so that we can more effectively pursue good fisheries management policy.
Viscount Brookeborough: This morning, Minister, the representative from the Scottish seafood processors mentioned in passing that, yes, there are a lot of small boats tied up and there were in some cases unnecessary quotas, for instance in mackerel, and he made a comment that you can go out and catch as many mackerel as you like, number one we could process them and number two we would not damage the stocks. Is that a realistic point or is it not really so?

Q994 *Chairman:* We are talking about line fishing for mackerel.
Jonathan Shaw: Yes.

Q995 *Viscount Brookeborough:* He seemed to say there was a quota.
Jonathan Shaw: There is a quota.

Q996 *Viscount Brookeborough:* But is this quota really totally unnecessary?
Jonathan Shaw: I think there are some discussions about whether we can help out with that quota at the moment.
Mr Harris: Yes, I believe there are.
Jonathan Shaw: There are some discussions on-going about whether we can help with a swap from England into Scotland.

Q997 *Viscount Brookeborough:* Is there not an argument where if what he said is true then it is not necessary to have a quota on such fish?

Jonathan Shaw: The quotas are in place at a European level and obviously we have to take account of the ICES advice and the advice from scientists from Scotland and England. I thought you were going to say he could walk on the mackerel.

Q998 *Viscount Brookeborough:* Well he did almost.
Jonathan Shaw: I have heard that a few times.

Q999 *Chairman:* We have also heard from Scottish Officials that Scotland want to go it alone with a Scottish Fisheries Policy outside the Common Fisheries Policy. I was wondering whether you have any views about this or what advice you have given them?
Jonathan Shaw: I have gone into some remarks in detail about the Scottish administration's consultation on quota separation. In terms of the policy of the SNP to leave the Common Fisheries Policy and remain within the European Union, that is quite a challenging equation.

Q1000 *Chairman:* But the problem that we have come across, and it has been a frustration, quite honestly, in much of this inquiry, given the hostility of certain sections of the fishing industry to the Common Fisheries Policy, is that there is this assertion that it is perfectly possible to leave the Common Fisheries Policy and yet remain in the EU, and that misunderstanding actually prevents a proper discussion of the reform of the Common Fisheries Policy.

Jonathan Shaw: I think it was Conservative Party policy at one stage and when that was challenged I think that people then understood that and, as I understand it, now it is no longer a Conservative Party policy, so it is not just the SNP who have got form on this.

Q1001 *Chairman:* That is true but, with enormous respect to the Conservative Party, it is actually more important that the SNP are saying it than the Conservative Party were saying it because of that band of SNP representation in the North East of Scotland where the fishing industry is and where it is a deeply held view that it is possible to come out of the Common Fisheries Policy and remain in the EU, and until that is broken we cannot have a debate.
Jonathan Shaw: I think that it is easier to pedal a line in opposition than continue it when you are in administration. That is the policy that the Fishermen's Association Ltd (FAL) advocate and the SNP have echoed that. I think the chickens will come home to roost and then the policy will be exposed for what it is, as the Conservative Party found out.

Q1002 *Chairman:* Minister, thank you very much indeed. Can I also thank you for the help that we have received from your officials during the course of this inquiry; it has been absolutely invaluable.
Jonathan Shaw: They will appreciate those remarks. As I said at the beginning, I look forward very much to receiving your report; it is very timely.

Written Evidence

Memorandum by the Sir Alistair Hardy Foundation for Ocean Science

1. The Sir Alister Hardy Foundation for Ocean Science (SAHFOS) welcomes the opportunity to contribute to the House of Lords Call for Evidence on the above policy. Our Foundation is a charity that operates the Continuous Plankton Recorder (CPR) survey so that the comments below will focus more on environmental rather than technical issues.

CONSERVATION/MANAGEMENT

2. I do not have the latest information available to advise on the effectiveness of the new regulations and can only respond on the basis of a general background view that the measures in general, in general have not been as successful as might be hoped, but that there are some positive signs eg for cod. This is an issue that I wish to draw to your attention. In researching the background to my reply I found it difficult to locate a good summary of the current status of the stocks in relation to improvements from the new measures. I draw your attention to the SAHFOS Ecological Status Report http://www.sahfos.ac.uk/annual_reports/ecological%20status%20report%20(ebook)%202006.pdf. This document is produced each year by a small charity and I am sure that it would not be impossible for the EU to produce a similar document for each RAC outlining progress in relation to the new measures and the current status of stocks.

3. To improve the management of coastal stocks and in particular in relation to proposed protected areas, an extension of the 12 mile national limit to further offshore with similar restrictions as for the present coastal zone would be a positive step forward. It would likely improve the livelihood and sustainability of small coastal fishing communities as well as the state of the coastal stocks.

4. There is a need for a more rapid establishment of marine conservation areas where fishing is not allowed. Some of these should be seasonal and some should be permanent. There has been a considerable scientific debate on this issue both nationally and within the EU, it is now time to act and implement without delay.

5. Research based on the results of the CPR survey has shown highly significant correlations between stock biomass, landings and recruitment of commercial fish species, including salmon, and long-term changes in the plankton and hydrographic variables eg sea surface temperature of the North Sea and Northeast Atlantic. Large changes have occurred, at times step-wise in the environment and appear to be ongoing. Other research indicates that the changes appear to be linked to climate change. An important part of the changes has been a northerly movement of subtropical species and retreat towards the pole of boreal species of plankton. This pattern is seen also in fish species with new fisheries starting up in the North Sea on warmer water species. Evidence that this pattern is continuing and possibly accelerating is seen in the now regular occurrence of new fish species off Portugal that have migrated to the north from off the coast of Africa. These changes must be having a large impact on the multispecies interactions of current stocks.

6. As a consequence of global warming future predicted changes in NW European seas are likely to be substantial and will have a big impact on fisheries and the biodiversity of fish and other biota. The information from the CPR and other environmental data is currently not taken into account in the modelling used to assess stock size and allowable catches. Because of the speed of expected change the management systems for stocks will need to adapt more rapidly than has occurred in the past and environmental factors need to be included in the models. The potential for the incorporation of environmental data was shown in the REGNS project that is now no longer operational. A follow on to this research should be put in place asap.

7. The need to link assessments to environmental factors and take into account potential changes due to climate change also applies to distant water fisheries especially in developing countries. Unfortunately, there is often very little environmental data available in these areas to link to the fisheries. The EU should encourage the development of appropriate monitoring systems in these areas.

8. The same situation arises outside the 200 nm area that applies to the EU. We are fortunate to have information on changes in the plankton over large areas of the northern North Atlantic from the CPR survey. Equivalent information is not available for most other oceanic areas of the world.

9. SAHFOS would be pleased to provide further advice to the inquiry should we be requested.

22 February 2008

Memorandum by John & Rosalind Brooks, Angling School

We are recreational sea anglers, who hold Level 2 Certificates in Coaching Sea Angling from 1st4 sport, and regularly coach youngsters and adults. As well as shore angling, we own a 26' boat which we use for recreational sea angling based in Falmouth. We are both teachers and trained as Biologists. We are both members of a local club which is affiliated to the Cornish Federation of Sea Anglers and also members of the National Federation of Sea Anglers. I am also a member of the Conservation Group of the NFSA.

1. Throwing back dead fish is not an option. The immoral practice of throwing back dead fish because a boat does not have quota or sufficient quota must stop.

All fish should be given a chance to breed before they are considered to be above minimum landing size. Anglers are already suggesting voluntary codes of practice along these lines, see "Give Fish A Chance".

No fish should be targeted whilst they are shoaling in readiness for or during spawning. Closed areas and seasons should be introduced and more importantly enforced so that both anglers and commercial fishermen observe these laws.

An aspect of the present management of fisheries, seems to be that scientific advice is ignored if the lobbying by commercial interests is loud enough. If there is scientific evidence of a decline in fish stocks, then it is pointless to try and justify increasing quota on other grounds, such as preserving coastal communities. The iron and steel industries, the car factories, and more locally to Cornwall the loss of tin mining and china clay extraction have had a far greater effect on communities. The economic importance of commercial fishing seems to be greatly exaggerated. Similarly, the economic importance of recreational sea angling, both directly through tackle manufacture and sales, and indirectly through tourism seems to be underplayed.

2. Marine Conservation Areas should be introduced based on scientific evidence. Reading reports from around the world, and closer to home from Lundy, would seem to indicate that areas around MCAs have a richer and more abundant mix of fish.

3. Total Allowable Catches should include species caught as by catch. More North Sea cod have been reported as discards during fishing for sole than there is official quota. This just does make sense.

4. Climate change is affecting the mix of fish caught. Here in Cornwall we are seeing new species and more examples of species which were until recently rarities. Anglers need to be involved in recording of these fish as they often target these rarities far more keenly than commercial fishermen in the process of setting new records.

5. It would seem that the general public's scepticism of the slack enforcement of EU rules and regulations is backed up by the Auditors Report. There seems to be a lack of honour and honesty and responsibility, whether it is elected politicians, civil servants or NGOs.

6. We all need to sing from the same hymn sheet. People are fed up of different sanctions being applied by different countries and the fact that when the UK makes rules for British fishermen, they do not apply to continental fishermen.

7. Looking at the figures for landings at Newlyn, this is now about 55% of what it was 10 years ago. More and more public money is being pumped into this industry. But then we have the fraud case at Newlyn and therefore all figures must be suspect. It does leave one wondering what the MFA and CSFF were doing during those years.

8. No experience of this.

9. Fisheries belong to us all, they are not the provenance and only for commercial fishermen. Anglers, divers and wild life devotees as well as other fauna and flora all have a right to be considered in the sustainable management of this public resource and good.

10. Regional Advisory Councils seem to have had little impact so far.

11. Scientific advice should be obtained. All evidence needs to stand rigorous examination, but all too often it is overruled for political reasons. Sea Fisheries Committees and Defra departments seem to have an undue bias towards the commercial sector. Other stakeholders and their views need to be considered. I must admit that I was impressed with Rodney Anderson of Defra at a meeting in Newlyn last year and his approach to the 25 year vision. However, his political masters come and go and the follow through of political will does not always run consistently.

4 February 2008

Memorandum by Álvaro Fernández, Biologist Oceanographer, Fisheries Scientific Adviser, Spanish Institute of Oceanography

I. POLICY ON THE MANAGEMENT OF FISHERY RESOURCES IN EC WATERS

1. The EC's fishery resource policy is based on two regulations that were not approved until 1983, due to the major difficulties planted in the way of approval by the member countries.

2. These two basic regulations are Regulation 170/83 and Regulation 171/83. The former is the framework by which all policy on the management of fishery resources in waters of Member State sovereignty and jurisdiction has since been guided. It is based on, for a start, the establishment of technical measures, such as the mesh size of fishing gear, the minimum landing sizes of fish (and crustaceans and molluscs), the proportions of catches of certain species when small mesh is used, areas and/or seasons closed to fishing, etc.

3. Regulation (EC) No 170/83 moreover bases its policy for the management of fishery resources in Blue Europe on the supervision of total effort by means of the introduction of the TAC system ("TAC" stands for "total allowable catch") and the establishment, after arduous discussions among the member countries, of the distribution of these TACs into catch quotas or shares for each country, using the oft-invoked principle of relative stability as the reference point. In order to arrive at the formula for distributing TACs, the Commission and the then-member countries took the catch statistics of the previous years as the basis for their discussion, using said statistics as the "relative needs" of the different States' fishing fleets. In the successive revisions of the UE management fisheries policy, this TACs and quotas system was maintained (Reg. 3769/92 and 2371/2002).

4. The application of this system thus calls for a number of phases of study and discussion. The first, to determine the annual overall catch for each stock of each species of fishery importance. In the objectives of the science of fishery management, finding a TAC is simply an indirect method of supervising the fishing effort, and this parameter, along with mesh size (fundamentally in trawl fishing), is basic in regulating a fishery.

5. The priority objective of these ICES scientific working groups is to evaluate the stock or stocks in question in order to ascertain their fishing exploitation rate. The mathematical models of population dynamics in use in these groups indicate the demographic structure of the marine population and its development over the years, the biomass of the population and its spawning stock, as well as the development of annual recruitments, or waves of juveniles joining the stock each year. Lastly, they indicate the population's mortality rate due to fishing (by age class and total), which is a direct consequence of the fishing effort targeting that particular population and the selectivity of the fishing gear used. Ultimately, these evaluation results indicate the fishing exploitation rate. A mortality rate due to fishing that is higher than that needed in order to achieve the maximum sustained yield (or that corresponding to precautionary biological reference points) leads to yearly catches that are lower than the possible catches, and the stock is overfished. To correct the situation necessitates lowering the mortality rate due to fishing by reducing the fishing effort, which is the direct instigator of the fishing mortality rate.

6. From what has been said, it may be gathered that, in order for these working groups to be able to meet their objectives, there is a series of conditioning factors that must be met, and yet those very conditioning factors often render the working groups' objectives unfeasible. For example, there must be catch statistics that accurately reflect the real situation; a size-sampling programme at ports so that the annual catch can be estimated in terms of the number of fish caught per size class; teams to research the growth of species, who can in addition make it possible to ascertain the annual catch in terms of the number of specimens per age class and moreover make headway in our knowledge of aspects of these species' biology such as sexual maturation, fertility, feeding, geographical distribution, selectivity, effort and areas of recruitment or spawning.

7. On the quality and quantity of this information will the reliability of the results of the attempted evaluation models depend. In the best of cases the current mortality rate due to fishing is found analytically, and according to this result further endeavours are made to draw nearer to the optimum rate, or to the level of precautionary approach. If that cannot be done, the development of catches, output figures, recruitment figures, etc, is analysed and an attempt is made to provide some guidance concerning fishing exploitation.

8. The procedure ends when ICES recommends a TAC to the EU Commission.

II. A Critique

9. Let us analyse what we consider this system's defects to be, based on the following points:

    1) The basis of what are termed "precautionary TACs".

    2) The possible statistical distortions caused by the quota system.

    3) The concept of quota ownership by Member States.

    4) The problem of TACs and quotas in mixed or polyspecific fisheries: demersal fisheries.

10. 1. As stated in the first chapter, precautionary TACs are set for those species or stocks for which either the statistical data are not good or research has not reached a sufficient level of development ("sufficient" meaning that research has been conducted over enough years to form a minimum historical series) so that evaluations can yield valid results.

11. In our opinion this system is flawed at its foundations. The objective of this type of fishery management, according to the precautionary approach principle, is to keep the fishing effort stable so that no increases will adversely affect the condition of fishing stocks (a condition not yet determined, by the way). The stocks at issue, then, are stocks for which there is no evidence whatsoever of overfishing, and nevertheless the system of TACs distributed into quotas, by using the system established by the relative stability principle, means that countries that comply with the objective of not increasing their effort, or even reduce their effort, consume their share before the year is out and have to stop fishing or else return to the sea all catches of the species whose quota has been filled.

12. We conclude this point by stating that there appears to us to be no easy justification for forcing a fleet to give up fishing a species that is not overfished and has not been the target of increased effort. At least with the objective of optimising catches in hand.

13. 2. The TAC and quota system itself can lead to statistical distortions, which have an effect on evaluations. When we described the system for conducting scientific evaluations of stocks, we emphasized the need for the base data to be reliable, since research institutes' fish size- and age-sampling programmes have got to be applied to catches by species, area, month and fishing-gear type. In this sense, potential temptations to declare underestimated figures when the quotas are low (eg, cod, haddock, mackerel), or overestimated figures when the quotas are too high, or to shift figures by areas or even by species (eg, mackerel/horse mackerel) would lead to erroneous total catches and biased evaluations whose results would not reflect reality, thus leading to incorrect management recommendations (TACs). Such supervisory defects really do occur, as already shown, more that 20 years ago, by the Commission's communication to the Council (17-6-86) on the execution of common fishery policy, and more recently, the strong 2007 report from the EU Court of Auditors. This can lead to a dynamic process that is quite undesirable in terms of meeting the objectives of rational management of fishery resources. In this sense, the ICES complains frequently of national statistics' reliability for scientific use.

14. 3. Thirdly, the established principle of "relative stability" poses another disadvantage for compliance with the theoretical objective of TACs. Indeed, the purpose the oft-invoked principle pursues is to keep the relative fishing capacity of the Member States steady from year to year, so that any possible reductions or increases in TAC are passed on to the Member States in the pre-established proportions. As years go by, some countries develop such that their quotas become too large for their real needs, and others, such that their quotas lag behind their capacities. The Commission's communication to the Council of 3 November 1986 makes this clear. The solution envisaged in EC regulations is confined to the terms addressing this point in article 5 of Regulation 170/83, which reads, "Member States may exchange all or part of the quotas in respect of a species or group of species". The practical application of the system leads to a concept of "quota ownership" by countries. If countries that need supplementary quantities have nothing to offer in exchange that the countries with a quota surplus want, the countries with shortfall must stop fishing, and the end-of-the-year TAC is not entirely consumed. The system of management by total catch does not, then, in this sense either, meet the objective of keeping the fishing effort stable or even reduced to a certain level. It is even a contradiction of the very definition of TAC (total allowable catch), because the concept of quota ownership may prevent the total potential catches of a stock from ever actually being made.

15. This concept of ownership, too, is a very peculiar sort of ownership. It appears that a country can own, say, a thousand tons of cod that are swimming freely through the ocean depths, and can fish them or swap them to another country for another species. But if the year reaches its end and the country in question has not caught all its quota (for lack of capacity or lack of interest) and has not exchanged its leftover quota (for lack of agreement in bilateral negotiations), on 31 December it loses its property and the fish remain in the sea as an unconsumed portion of the TAC, available for re-allocation the following year.

16. Again we must say that the system, which is supposedly designed to optimise catches, prevents the catches that at the start of the year were originally found possible (one might say "economically recommendable") from ever being made. The stumbling block is the fishery management procedure itself.

17. 4. But the most irrational point in our view is the application of the system of TACs and quotas by species to mixed or polyspecific fisheries. We refer to bottom-trawled fisheries, where the very fishing system used means that the species caught together are several and the commercial species making the fishery profitable are several. Therefore the fishing method cannot be said to seek a single target or objective species, as the seine, longline or gillnet does, or as occurs in tuna fisheries. When a bottom-trawled fishery contains no component species whose fishing condition is especially sensitive, when the appropriate mesh size for the fishery has been determined, and when the fishing effort is supervised, the system of TACs and quotas should not prevent the normal exercise of the fleet's fishing activity.

18. This is not what actually happens, though. Sometimes due to defects in the area and species statistics used as the basis for finding TACs, and sometimes due to the allocation of TACs in quotas for the Member States as a result of political negotiations (eg, EEC-Spain Treaty) or in response to commercial undertones (meanly States that have entered EU after 1985), the quantities assigned to each country in each area bear no relationship to the reality of fishery biocenosis nor to the authorised fishing effort of the fleets involved.

19. Nowadays, and since many years before, the fishery management system leads to the absurdity of having to return to the sea tons of specimens, even large-sized ones, of species of great commercial interest that are not overfished but whose catching cannot be avoided because they live alongside other species. Thus, the country does not exceed its quota, but the scientific objective of preventing a certain level of stock mortality due to fishing is not reached, because the country can continue to fish the other species that live alongside the filled-quota species. The filled-quota species thus would be caught and dead but could not be landed.

20. To wind up this chapter we will say that the current system of fishery resource management in the EC does not seem very often to meet the objective expected of it for rational resource use. At least sometimes the system more closely resembles a method designed to create added hindrances for the exercise of fishing activities and to uphold certain economic interests of countries, thus leading to bilateral negotiations where national positions are unyieldingly defended.

III. An Alternative

21. The type of model to be employed in fishery management should actually depend on the objectives that are to be pursued. In this sense, we believe that the objectives expressed in the recitals of Regulations (EC) No 170/834, 3760/92 and 2371/2002 are perfectly valid. Let us recall, inter alia, the end of the first recital:

> ". . . it is therefore desirable that the provisions of Council Regulation (EEC) No 101/76. . . be supplemented by the establishment of a Community system for the conservation and management of fishery resources that will ensure balanced exploitation".

And article one, which reads:

> "In order to ensure the protection of fishing grounds, the conservation of the biological resources of the sea and their balanced exploitation on a lasting basis and in appropriate economic and social conditions, a Community system for the conservation and management of fishery resources is hereby established. For these purposes, the system will consist, in particular, of conservation measures, rules for the use and distribution of resources, special provisions for coastal fishing and supervisory measures."

22. The alternative that we propose is based more on rationalising resource management and avoiding what we have called "added hindrances to the exercise of fishing activities" than on defending national catch-rate rights. In this sense, we believe that, although the relative activity of fleets must be respected, the system must be flexible enough, one, to permit it to absorb differential evolution among the fleets of the different countries (the countries' percentages would not have to be unchanging over many years), and two, to make it possible also for the annual catches of each country, with a certain fishing effort, to oscillate from one year to another according to variable factors such as fishable biomass, species catchability, variation in target species, etc.

23. In this sense, we ought to recall the reflections in our first chapter, where we described the fishery evaluation methodology. One of the final results was to find the mortality rate due to current fishing and its relationship with either the optimum mortality rate or the precautionary approach mortality rate for rational resource exploitation. In practice scientific recommendations (ICES, ICCAT) tend to consist in finding the percentage by which the mortality rate due to current fishing ought to be modified, which actually means changes in fishing effort.

24. The fishery administrator (DG Fish) can meet this objective by supervising the fishing effort, which is, furthermore, the factor that directly causes fish mortality. When the effort aimed at a stock or at a fishery is known, that effort can be adapted according to recommendations; and where reductions are necessary, those reductions can be distributed proportionally among the countries that have been fishing in the fishery in question, according to their approved fleets' capacities or their fishing efforts authorised in recent years. A system of temporary fishing licenses related to fishing days allowed could ensure compliance with the level set for total fishing effort, for supervisory purposes. Log-books, VMS control and electronic log-books would help to attain this objective.

25. In mixed fisheries, such as demersal fisheries, where several species of commercial interest are fished together, finding the total fishing effort and distributing it by countries, plus regulating mesh size and minimum fish size, should be enough to permit the Member States' fleets to engage in their fishing activity. Scientific working groups and advisory committees for fishing management are perfectly able to consider the exploitation condition of the species that make up the fishery, or base themselves on the species that displays the highest mortality. But once the fishing-effort level has been determined, regulations should not lead to the absurd extreme of having to return to the sea adult fish whose stock is not overfished, as happens now.

26. The idea, then, would be to replace the current type of supervision (based on TACs and their distribution in the form of quotas) with supervision of the fishing effort itself, shared by countries, by means of a generalised system of fishing licenses by stock or by fishery (indicating fishing days allowed), and fleet census permanently updated:

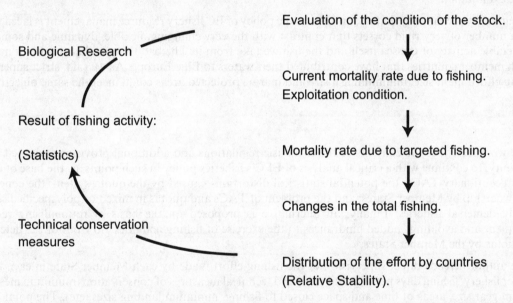

Recommended Model to Fisheries Assessment and Management

27. When the mortality rate due to current fishing cannot be found, a "precautionary" total fishing effort could be set, based on fleet activity in recent years.

28. The system would have the great additional advantage of not prompting possible biases in statistics, since the fleets would not have catch ceilings. Instead, with a given authorised fishing effort, fleets could land all the captures made throughout the year in compliance with technical measures on mesh size, fish size and percentages.

29. That would certainly have a favourable repercussion on the reliability of evaluations of the condition of the population and of the scientific management recommendations, and the process outlined above would form part of a more realistic scheme.

30. Furthermore, ships authorised to fish could distribute their effort throughout the entire year instead of stopping all fishing when their quota is reached, as they do now. Suffice it to recall that the fishing effort depends on two factors. The first is "fishing power", which depends on the fleet and its characteristics; the second is "fishing time". Reductions of the latter per ship lead to reductions in the rate of mortality due to fishing, which –together with the requirement of minimum mesh sizes and minimum landing sizes, as well as marine protected areas– would be our objective in order to recover over-exploited fisheries.

31. At all events, even if the TAC and quota system is maintained, there are still issues of the current regulation that in our opinion ought to be changed, for the sake making management measures more easily understandable to fishermen too.

32. We mean to say, when a TAC is found, it is recognised that a total capture of that size can be made. But if, in the distribution of quotas according to the principle of relative stability, the resulting quota for a country is too low for its catch capacity, and the quota for another country or countries is too high for any reason (evolution of fishing capacity, change of fisheries or target species, changes in market demands, etc), the imbalance arising from the situation can only be offset through the quota exchange system. One result could be that the country with the shortfall has nothing of interest to offer the country with the surplus quota, with the final result that the former has to stop fishing and the TAC is never reached. Another community policy in resource management, one that would be more rational in the optimum exploitation of resources, could certainly be to look for a formula to indicate that, when the evolution of catches throughout the year predicts a situation such as that described, the countries that have a shortfall can continue fishing until the TAC is exhausted.

33. In layman's terms, it would go something like, "Tell me where, when and what mesh size I can fish with, but let me land my whole catch of fish as long as they're bigger than the permitted minimum size".

34. The current system, under which fleets must throw overboard commercially important specimens legally fished in combination with other species for which there is a quota, does not seem to meet objectives of rational resource exploitation.

35. In summary, we may say that in our opinion the policy of EC fishery resource management is laced tightly within a number of very rigid corsets that contrast with the very changing, flexible, dynamic and sometimes unpredictable activity of the sea itself and the fish we take from it. The bad thing is that this has a negative affect on member countries that have contributed their waters to Blue Europe. As we said, strict supervision of fishing effort, mesh size, minimum fish size and marine protected areas could meet the same objectives.

Abstract

36. The work describes the contents of the two basic regulations and additional provisions adopted by the Community, to continue with a critical analysis of EEC's fisheries policy in such points as: the base of the so-called precautionary TACs; the potential statistical distortions caused by the quota system; the concept of quota ownership by Member States; and the problem of TACs and quotas in mixed or polyspecific fisheries, especially demersal fisheries. Finally, an alternative is proposed on the basis of rationalising resource management and avoiding "added hindrances to the exercise of fishing activities" in front of the defence of catch quotas by the Member States.

37. The author defends direct supervision of the fishing effort made by each Member State in each fishery (ships per fishery, fishing days per ship and year) and technical measures of conservation (minimum mesh size, minimum gear size, areas of time and space closed to fishing, minimum landing sizes, etc). The point would be to tell ships' masters where (in what areas), how many days and with what means (meshes, gear sizes, etc) they can fish, and to permit them to land everything they catch under those conditions (except for illegal sizes). The mortality rate due to fishing would be supervised by delimiting the fishing effort directly (ships and days per country and fishery). As a consequence of the system, statistics (the reliability of ships' logs), scientific evaluations of stocks and fishery management recommendations would be improved. It would certainly be a much wiser fishery resource management policy for the fishing sector in general, and supervision of stocks would also be much closer to reality.

End note

38. This article is based on another article by the same author, published in 1988 (1). We congratulate ourselves upon the fact that since then other, more authoritative pens have questioned the TAC and quota system as the cornerstone of the European Union's fishery resource management policy. Mike Holden, who applied the policy for many years at the Commission's DG XIV, criticized it harshly after his retirement (2). The Green Paper on the Future of the Common Fisheries Policy does likewise in point 3.1.2, "The Causes of Current Management Deficiencies" (3). Michel Sissenwine and David Symes (4) also analysed this problem in 2007 in points 4.2. Scientific Information, 4.6. Impediments to Fisheries Management Under the CFP and 6.3. Move Toward Effort Management. Lastly, the devastating report of the European Court of Auditors in late 2007 (5) denounces very clearly that the TAC and quota system is not working effectively in the policy on management of the EU's fishery resources and generates major statistical defects.

39. Nevertheless, in the above-cited Green Paper the Commission sees no possibility of a alternative to the TAC and quota system (point 5.1.4.1.) and consequently no alternative to the principle of relative stability. Despite this, Council Regulation 2371/2002, the basis for the current PPC (6), clearly states the alternative of management by catches or by direct fishing effort: Recitals 7 and 9, Article 4.2 f, g and especially Article 20.1, which reads, "The Council, acting by qualified majority on a proposal from the Commission, shall decide on catch and/or fishing effort limits and on the allocation of fishing opportunities among Member States as well as the conditions associated with those limits. Fishing opportunities shall be distributed among Member States in such a way as to assure each Member State relative stability of fishing activities for each stock or fishery."

40. But it seems clear that in this issue the economic and commercial interests of the Member States prevail above the rationality of fishery management and exploitation. Consequently, the answer to the question formulated in the title of this article, is, in our opinion, "No".

References

(1) Fernández, A. Valoración crítica y alternativas a la Política Comunitaria de Gestión de Recursos Pesqueros. Revista de Estudios Agro-Sociales. Ministerio de Agricultura Pesca y Alimentación. N 144. 1988.

(2) Holden, M. The Common Fisheries Policy: Origin, Evaluation and Future. Blackwell Scientific Publications, Oxford. 1994.

(3) Green Paper on the future of the CFP. European Commission Com (2001) 135

(4) Sissenwine, M. and D. Symes. Reflections on the Common Fisheries Policy. Report to the General Directorate for Fisheries and Maritime Affairs of the European Commission. July 2007.

(5) European Court of Auditors. Special Report No 7/2007 on the control, inspection and sanction systems relating to the rules on conservation of Community fisheries resources. (and Press Release ECA/07/35). 2007.

(6) Council Regulation (EC) 2371/2002 of 20 December 2002 on the conservation and sustainable exploitation of fisheries resources under the Common Fisheries Policy.

22 February 2008

Memorandum by Fisheries Research Services (FRS)

Introduction

1. Fisheries Research Services (FRS) is an Agency of the Scottish Government providing scientific advice on a range of marine resource and environmental issues. In relation to fisheries FRS' main activities include monitoring and assessment of stocks of key importance to Scotland. The agency's remit does not include fisheries control and enforcement responsibilities or development of structural policy. As a consequence, the evidence provided here mainly focuses on conservation and management aspects. In recent years, FRS has played an important part in initiatives to increase stakeholder involvement (for example the North Sea Commission Fisheries partnership and Regional Advisory Councils). A few comments are also offered on governance issues.

General

2. The consultation mainly raises questions framed against a background of existing European management experiences. Much of this has evolved in response to developing circumstances in fisheries. For thousands of years, there has been a basic assumption of freedom to operate and innovate until a constraint is deemed necessary. Frequently, the introduction of new management measures and changing economics elicit a mitigating response from those exploiting stocks so that subsequent management processes (including enforcement and monitoring) are always involved in a process of catching up. In some fishery models elsewhere in the world such freedoms are constrained and new developments are only introduced when they will i) not lead to increased mortality on the stocks concerned ii) are accompanied by compensatory measures to constrain mortality. While a completely restrictive process may be unattainable in multifaceted European fisheries, it is perhaps nevertheless time to give consideration to a process requiring constructive and collective discussion in advance of introducing technological advancements.

SPECIFIC ISSUES

Conservation/Management

3. The new methods for promoting conservation (recovery plans, management plans and emergency measures) have been introduced to varying degrees and their effect has been mixed so far. It is helpful to make a distinction between emergency measures and recovery plans on the one hand and management plans on the other.

4. Evaluating the effects of *emergency plans*, introduced for a few stocks in very poor condition, is difficult. These have tended to be established quickly, are often based on limited prior analysis and are sometimes disruptive in the short term. The emergency measures for North Sea cod in 2001, including a large scale spawning closure, did not lead to a detectable stock improvement. Furthermore, unintended consequences arose from effort transfer onto juvenile haddock. On the other hand one of the most dramatic emergency measures, the closure of fishing for North Sea herring in the 1970's was followed by stock recovery. This action also coincided with reasonably good recruitment but there is little doubt that the resultant industry restructuring and closer attention to controlling fishing mortality rate (F) has been beneficial.

5. *Recovery plans*, again directed at stocks outside safe biological limits and where reproductive capacity is impaired, define a more structured approach and are frequently underpinned by predictive modelling. One of their advantages is that focus is maintained on a problem situation until this resolved. There have been recent improvements in some European stocks subject to recovery plans, notably Northern hake and Bay of Biscay *Nephrops*. The biomass of cod in the North Sea is also predicted to increase. In each case, recruitment to these stocks has increased but the extent to which recovery plans have contributed to this is not known. Encouragingly, fishing mortality on North Sea cod has come down by about 20% since 1999. Unfortunately, other stocks, for example Irish Sea cod, have not shown such improvement despite this being subject to the longest standing recovery plan.

6. There are several general difficulties with the current recovery plan approach. Firstly, the plans are linked to biological reference points defined by ICES. The achievement of some of the biomass targets set is often dependent on environmentally driven processes (such as recruitment success) and an assumption that the reference points are fixed through time. Secondly, attainment of the reference point value (by no matter how small a margin) relaxes the requirement for a recovery plan but unless the overall population structure has improved and fishing mortality has dropped to a more sustainable rate, the stock can quickly deteriorate. This leads to an unsatisfactory 'on/off' situation. Finally, the annual December EU Council of Ministers can (and sometimes does) establish TACs inconsistent with the analyses of what is required to deliver recovery. This disrupts the expected recovery process.

7. *Management plans* ideally operate under circumstances where a stock is not overexploited and does not have impaired reproductive capacity. The general objective is to establish a fishing regime and mortality rate which leads to long term sustainability where the stock stays well away from trigger points requiring more serious action. Management plans are therefore more strategic, take a longer term view and are generally based on more thorough analysis incorporating estimates of risk associated with actions taken. In recent times, European commitments to international agreements requiring stocks to be fished at maximum sustainable yield (MSY) have influenced the development of plans. A number of key stocks fished by Scottish vessels are subject to management plans particularly stocks shared with Norway. In these cases, ICES provides advice consistent with the management plan and comparison of the agreed TAC with this advice suggests that it is closer than for stocks not subject to plans. The inclusion of annual TAC change constraint rules (eg no more than +/- 15%) helps to stabilise year to year fluctuations. Management of North Sea haddock, herring and also mackerel has benefited from tailored plans although the existence of a management plan does not of itself guarantee the stock will remain in good condition. At present, declines in herring associated with poor recruitment are causing concern. Significantly, the management plan provides for these circumstances and defines fishing mortality rates to try to reduce the risk to the stock. It remains to be seen how successful this is.

Management tools

8. *Total Allowable Catches*—TACs—From the point of view of establishing a basis for the share-out of resources between member states, TACs have arguably been successful in the European context. As a tool to control fishing mortality they have generally had low success rates, particularly in mixed species fisheries. This scientific view has remained for a number of years. In fact, the term 'total allowable catch' is something of a misnomer—'total allowable landings' is a more accurate description. If it was possible to limit catches the tool might perform rather better. Unfortunately, in a mixed fishery the exhaustion of a TAC for one species does not automatically lead to the stopping of its capture and it continues to be taken as bycatch in the pursuit of

other species. Furthermore, there is frequently an assumption that the scientific predictions underpinning a TAC are made with high precision. In practice, the precision of forecasts is generally too low to support small reductions in fishing mortality sought by managers. The uncertainties in the predictions and changes in fishing pattern and behaviour from one year to the next can lead to an imbalance between the TAC and the out-take. Political decisions out of line with advice further disrupt the process. Evidence for continuing difficulties with TACs as currently implemented can be seen in the continued high discard rates of marketable sized fish in some fisheries.

9. *Effort limitations*—Considering first the controls on fishing vessel time at sea, there have been two main initiatives. Some Member States including UK and in particular Scotland, undertook significant decommissioning in recent years. The removal of a large number of fishing units led to a major reduction in effort that could be deployed and this is most evident in the haddock stocks where serious over-fishing has been reduced to levels close to maximum sustainable yield. This played an important part in sustaining the fishery through a period of low recruitment. Days at sea limits set out to control the activity of active vessels. Assessments by the EU Scientific Technical and Economic Committee on Fisheries (STECF) suggest there has been some reduction of effort arising from days at sea although not enough to reduce cod mortality sufficiently (cod remaining a key driver for this action) and not as much as implied by the percentage reductions in days legislated for. This is in part because many vessels have rarely fished up to their maximum capacity. Fishing mortality on cod in the North Sea has reduced recently, nevertheless. It is tempting to assume that further effort cuts will deliver bigger mortality reductions but the relationship is unclear and at a point where reductions in effort become especially restrictive, a likely response from fishermen is to use their available time to target areas delivering greatest economic return. These could well contain cod and so mortality may not reduce further.

10. *Conservation Credits.* Scotland (and possibly other parts of the UK) has now taken advantage of a Council provision which allows the allocation of a total KWdays effort package to the Member States to manage how it chooses. This has been linked to a 'Conservation Credits' scheme intended to deliver further reductions in cod mortality and reduce discards.

11. *Marine conservation* areas come in many shapes and forms. As a tool for conserving particularly vulnerable habitats, features or critical life stages they are potentially very useful—especially when policed with the assistance of satellite vessel monitoring or observers. As a more general tool in the management of fish stocks, their effectiveness is less clear. Most analysis suggests that large areas need to be closed to have any effect and that without accompanying reductions in effort, the transfer of activity into other, unprotected, areas can have undesirable and unpredictable effects. A common experience with closed areas is that once established they are difficult to remove, even if no benefit to the feature or stock being protected is demonstrable.

12. *Real time closures* (RTCs) offer a more reactive approach which responds to variations in local abundance and therefore triggers closures when they are needed. The approach has been used in Norway for many years for the avoidance of young fish. Within the EU legislative framework, such short term tools have not hitherto been possible. Under national schemes however, the required responsiveness is available and Scotland has recently been trialling a scheme. Its effectiveness is as yet unknown but it seems likely that to deliver significant direct benefit to the stock in avoiding cod (or other species requiring protection) numerous closures would be required to make a difference. The value of RTCs is probably increased by focussing them at times and areas associated with fish aggregating to spawn. Like permanent closures their value is determined by the impact of displaced effort in other areas. They are often weakened by compromises leading to inappropriately high thresholds for closure etc. Taking a broader view, as much value may be attached to the changes in behaviour prompted by RTCs encouraging fishermen to move away from areas of abundance. RTC effectiveness will be monitored under the Conservation Credits scheme.

13. *Rights based management*—It is difficult to comment from first hand experience but rights based management appears to have some benefits where it operates (Western Australia etc). Where rights are conferred and players consider they have a 'fair-share', this seems to engender greater stewardship to look after the resource for the long term. From a biological point of view, if this translates to lower, sustainable fishing mortality, this is good for stocks and potentially the wider environment. This contrasts with the condition of 'tragedy of the commons' prevailing for many years throughout many European fisheries. Under these circumstances the 'better fish it now before someone else does' approach leads to higher fishing mortality rates. It is probably fair to say that economics tends to drive rights based management systems towards smaller, efficient fleets with rather few highly committed operators. This may not match social policy for vulnerable rural communities.

14. Technical Conservation Measures- These have great potential to contribute but a long history of industry response which appears to lead to mitigation of the effectiveness of the original measure. For example, benefits from mesh increases in the early 1990's designed to reduce discards and lower mortality on young fish were offset by the development of multi-twine gears (double-twine etc) which tend to restrict the lumen of the net. Out turn fishing mortality showed no improvement. Given the ease with which 'adjustments nullify the effectiveness, fishermen have to want the measures to work in order for them to do so. Developments in the area of square mesh panels, grids and separators offer potential for the release of, particularly, juvenile fish. Under the latest Scottish initiative (Conservation credits scheme), incentives for implementing more selective gears or ones reducing cod and discards are being considered. Considerable research continues in this area and it is likely that in circumstances of more sophisticated consumer demand and better pricing, the role of technical measures will increase.

Discards

15. Management measures in place over several decades have contributed to the discard problem (see TACs above) and in general, the most recent measures have not increased the problem. In some fisheries where mesh has increased substantially or square mesh panels are effectively used, discards have reduced. The issue is complex and there were numerous contributory factors— a reducing TAC at the time of stock increase did not help matters.

16. It is worth noting that discarding is often blamed on TAC regulation implying that catch restrictions create the problem. In fact most discarding in mixed demersal fisheries is symptom of over-exploitation where the average size of fish in the stock has reduced to close to the minimum landing size because fish never live long enough to grow large. In trying to catch fish of marketable size, vessels take a large bycatch of undersized fish.

17. There is no single, simple solution to the problem and a range of measures tailored to the characteristics of different fleets is required. Avoidance plans (RTCs etc) to avoid aggregations of unwanted fish coupled with relevant technical measures will continue to play a major role. The pressure for fisheries to be accredited and 'clean' is also likely to be a key driver as well as a focus on quality rather than quantity.

Climate change

18. Fisheries management policies need to reflect fish productivity in the marine system. During periods of altered stock productivity as a result of environmental forcing, the expectations for the fishery need to be adjusted downwards (or upwards) accordingly. The precise linkage between the population dynamics and environment is complex but environmental drivers do play a significant part. At present it is clear that the distributions of many fish stocks have changed in response to changing climate and will continue to do so. These changes can be related to wider changes to the ecosystem in terms of oceanographic conditions and plankton communities. Climate change is currently probably one of the greatest sources of uncertainty in evaluating the sustainability of fish stocks and hence the management regimes that should be applied.

Structural policy

19. Recent UK policy on the reduction of the mixed whitefish fleets has been successful in reducing fishing on haddock to close to maximum sustainable yield and has contributed to a reduction in the exploitation rate on some cod stocks.

Governance

20. *RACs*—These have had successes in some areas and their extended funding from the Commission ensures their persistence for some years. The forums are encouraging better engagement between EU managers and other stakeholders and better cooperation between stakeholders. The nature of each RAC is rather different and some such at the North Sea RAC are more advanced than others. This is reflected in the kinds of submission and comment offered to the Commission with some RACs more willing to make difficult decisions than others.

21. For the scientific community, the emergence of RACs places additional demands on a limited pool of expertise. Experts that assist the RACs are very often the same experts that contribute to ICES and the STECF. This can lead to duplication of effort in analysing the same problem. Consideration needs to be given

to rationalising the advisory landscape into a more integrated system so that the scientific resource can be made better use of and advice to managers can be made more coherent. At present the Commission receives advice from ICES, STECF and RACs, often on the same issues using the same scientists, yet the advice is uncoordinated and as a result can provide mangers with a potentially confusing array of information. This is not desirable for good decision making.

February 2008

Memorandum by Greenpeace UK

1. INTRODUCTION

1.1 *Greenpeace*

Greenpeace UK is the autonomous regional office of Greenpeace, one of the world's leading environmental campaigning organizations. Greenpeace has regional offices in 40 countries, 2.8 million supporters worldwide and around 150,000 in the UK. It is independent of governments and businesses, being funded entirely by individual subscriptions.

The World's oceans have reached a state of crisis. They are woefully unprotected, hugely overexploited, polluted, and face the uncertain impacts of global climate change. Supported by the weight of credible scientific findings, Greenpeace believes that a crucial part of achieving environmentally balanced and sustainable oceans is a representative network of large-scale Marine Reserves covering 40% of our oceans, with environmentally responsible fishing practiced in the other 60%

1.2 The evidence of overexploitation of global fisheries is startling:

(i) Large predatory fish species such as cod, tuna, sharks and swordfish have declined by 90% in the past 50 years. 65% of all fisheries exploited since 1950 have collapsed. *(Myers RA, Worm B (2003). Rapid worldwide depletion of predatory fish communities. Nature 423: 280–3)*

(ii) The European Commission's latest advice states that 80% of European fish stocks are outside known safe biological limits

http://eur-lex.europa.eu/LexUriServ/LexUriServ.do?uri=COM:2007:0295:FIN:EN:PDF

(iii) The UN FAO estimated that in 2003, 76% of the world's assessed fisheries stocks were either fully exploited, over exploited or depleted.

http://www.fao.org/docrep/007/y5600e/y5600e00.htm

1.3 Moreover, there is widespread and consistent criticism of the failure of Fisheries management and nowhere is this more acute than in European waters. In addition to the Court of Auditors Report, the recent report to the European Commission by Sissenwine and Symes is a damning critique of the failure of the CFP:

http://www.greenpeace.org/raw/content/denmark/press/rapporter-og-dokumenter/reflections-on-the-common-fish.pdf

1.4 Greenpeace believes that the solutions that are needed to address the crisis facing our oceans are well-known, supported by credible scientific evidence and enjoy popular support. Only by setting aside large areas off limits to all destructive activity, including fishing, as Marine Reserves, can we hope to rebuild the resilience our oceans and our ocean species need, so that we may exploit them sustainably outside these areas. We would welcome the opportunity to present evidence to this inquiry.

2. CONSERVATION/MANAGEMENT

Chapter II of Regulation 2371/2002 on the conservation and sustainable exploitation of fisheries resources under the CFP introduced new methods of ensuring conservation and sustainability, including recovery plans, management plans, and emergency measures. To what extent have these been effective?

2.1.1 The implementation and application of conservation measures under the CFP are extremely disappointing. Firstly, a significant number of stocks that are outside safe biological limits have no recovery plans, and management plans also remain underutilised. Secondly, many of the plans that have been adopted are both weak in content and restrictive in the conservation measures they outline. For instance, little use is being made of closed areas, fishing bans and specific gear restrictions.

2.1.2 Most, if not all, plans fail to apply the precautionary principle. In the case of the cod recovery plan, for example, ICES has recently concluded that since it does not allow for a complete closure of the cod fishery, it is not consistent with the precautionary approach (ICES Advisory Committee on Fisheries Management, North Sea cod 2007).

2.1.3 In particular, the rules aimed at maintaining relative stability in the annual fishing opportunity by limiting TAC changes to no more than 15% (up or down) between any two years, restrain the management of depleted stocks in unsustainable patterns of overfishing. Given that many stocks are in such a severe state of depletion that much more drastic cuts in fishing quotas would be necessary, the 15% rule seems just another misguided management ploy that favours the short-term interests of the fishing industry and politicians over the long-term benefits of stock recovery and sustainable management.

2.1.4 Moreover, many management and recovery plans have only very recently been adopted and therefore have not been in place for long enough to show results. No stock has yet recovered as a result of an EU recovery plan. There is also considerable pressure both politically and from the fishing industry to increase levels of fishing at the earliest possible opportunities, meaning that any apparent recoveries in stocks are seemingly viewed as short-term bonuses with little long-term consideration.

2.1.5 It makes no coherent sense for marine conservation to be the (sole) preserve of the CFP, when clearly protection should be given under Environmental auspices.

2.1.6 Overall, we would respectfully adopt the following expert conclusions:

"[T]he track record of fisheries management in Europe has been disastrous." Prof Callum Roberts, *The Unnatural History of the Sea: The Past and Future of Humanity and Fishing,* Octopus Publishing Group, London, 2007, p. 346–7

"Over the past 25 years (1982-2007), EU institutions have presided over an unparalleled period of decline for Europe's fishing industries. In denial of the basic principle of Sustainable Development, they have apparently allowed the satisfaction of demands by the present generation to compromise the ability of future generations to meet their needs from the living resources of Europe's seas. : David Symes 'Institutional Issues' in Michael Sissenwine and David Symes, *Reflections on the Common Fisheries Policy,* Report to the General Directorate for Fisheries and Maritime Affairs of the European Commission, July 2007 at http://www.fishsec.org/downloads/1193925814_63294.pdf

". . . EU national-level and European Commission fisheries advisory groups are often dominated by interests from the fishing industry through powerful lobbying and this has often led to scientific advice being ignored or compromised . . ." *Turning the Tide—Addressing the impact of Fisheries on the Marine Environment,* Twenty-fifth Report of the United Kingdom Royal Commission on Environmental Pollution, December 2004 at http://www.rcep.org.uk/fishreport.htm

"In summary, the overall performance of the CFP has been poor. In terms of conservation of fish stocks, it is doing worse than the US and the rest of the world." Michael Sissenwine, "Challenges, Peformance and the Future" in Michael Sissenwine and David Symes, *Reflections on the Common Fisheries Policy*, Report to the General Directorate for Fisheries and Maritime Affairs of the European Commission, July 2007 at http://www.fishsec.org/downloads/1193925814_63294.pdf

A wide range of management tools are available to fisheries managers. What are your views on the following tools:

Total Allowable Catches

2.2.1 Setting a TAC for an individual stock is meant to help keep catch levels at or below sustainable levels. However, as the European Commission itself reports (COM(2007)295), the Council of Fisheries Ministers has consistently set EU TACs 50% above the scientifically recommended catch levels. This renders them useless as a tool for sustainable fisheries management, is entirely unprecautionary, and instead makes them part of the problem rather than a solution to overfishing. To the contrary, the US has passed fisheries legislation that stipulates that TAC must be set at, or below scientifically recommended levels.

2.2.2 TACs also lose their value when i) they are set for individual species, which are then caught in a mixed fishery, and/or ii) fishermen get away with high-grading their catch by throwing small or undersized fish overboard, so as to replace them by larger, more valuable, fish.

2.2.3 Clearly TACs must be set at, or below, scientifically recommended levels, and not simply at levels that are the result of political bargaining. If there are socio-economic repercussions associated with setting a recommended low level of TAC, they should be addressed accordingly, but bending or ignoring the science to cause as little socio-economic disruption as possible ultimately helps no one.

Effort limitation, including "days at sea", marine conservation areas and real-time closures

2.3.1 Days at sea limitations only work if there is i) consideration taken of the effect that the advancement of technological improvements have in increasing catching ability (eg through sonar fish finders), and ii) steps taken that less time doesn't mean increased effort in a shorter period, but actually results in a reduction in fishing effort.

2.3.2 Closed areas are a huge part of the solution, crucially the provision of a network of large-scale Marine Reserves that crucially prohibit fishing and allow stocks to recover, thrive, and offer resilience. The current attitude by the fishing industry is that protected areas should be as small and unrestricted as possible—and that long term protected areas are only acceptable in areas they don't want to fish in. The science says that for any real gain an area must be closed to all fishing—resulting in bigger animals, bigger stocks, and greater biodiversity; the essential bedrock of a long-term future for a sustainable fishing industry.

Technical Conservation Measures

2.4.1 Technical Conservation Measures must accompany measures aimed at effort and capacity reduction, better enforcement, and measures aimed to protect particularly sensitive habitats and species (such as the creation of fully-protected Marine Reserves), including fish. Fisheries must move towards selective, non-destructive and sustainable methods of catching fish. The most destructive methods, such as beam trawling, should be stopped as soon as possible, and more progressive and selective measures should be encouraged and promoted.

2.4.2 However, there have been numerous examples where the conservation objectives of technical measures have not been achieved (for example acoustic "pingers" on static nets to deter porpoises, mesh sizes etc.). In such instances it is imperative that the original conservation objective is addressed—and if no "technological fix" is forthcoming, action should be taken in other ways to halt the detrimental impact of these fisheries, up to and including stopping the fishery.

To what extent have current management tools increased the levels of discards and bycatch?

2.5.1 Greenpeace has seen first hand the discarding of perfectly marketable but 'non target' fish as part of the North Sea whitefish fleet, the wholesale destruction ravaged by bottom-trawling vessels in the North East Atlantic, and the bycatch of threatened species in the Mediterranean. Similarly the UK's coasts are still littered with the corpses of dolphins and porpoises that die in fishing nets in our waters.

2.5.2 Recent debates on the problem of discarding appear to have spectacularly missed the point in terms of addressing the main cause of high discarding and bycatch rates: ie destructive and indiscriminate fishing practices. The solution to discarding and high by-catch rates is thus neither in the lowering of conservation standards, nor in the raising of fishing quotas.

2.5.3 Greenpeace agrees that certain policies—in particular provisions that prohibit the landing of undersized and over-quota fish but fail to prevent their capture—have aggravated the problem of fish being wasted as a result of discarding.

What is your view on how these problems can be best tackled?

2.6.1 Greenpeace supports a discard ban, so long as it is used to complement other management and conservation measures, in particular those that lead to more selective and sustainable fishing practices. A discard ban would move the focus of management measures from landings to catches and from fish production to fish mortality. In conformity with the precautionary approach, by regarding "no discards" as the norm, any discarding then requires adequate justification (eg high survival potential). Experience shows that discard bans may be effective where control of shore-based infrastructure is efficient, and where other complementary measures, such as introduction of selective gears and real-time closures, reduce discards to a minimum.

2.6.2 The following considerations should be noted:

— Any policy on bycatch and discards must be complementary to, and not replace, other necessary management measures, such as capacity and effort reduction, technical conservation measures and area closures, including the establishment of a network of fully protected large-scale marine reserves that allow species, stocks, and ecosystems to recover and thrive. Overall, present stock levels dictate that we need to fish less.

— The key issue is to avoid unwanted catches in the first place, by prohibiting the most destructive and indiscriminate forms of fishing and by requiring, for example, the best available technology for all other gears, as well as by introducing real-time closures etc.

— An EU policy needs to effectively tackle all the different types of bycatch (mature [over-quota] specimen, juveniles, endangered and protected species) and the two reasons for discarding (high-grading and getting rid of [general] unwanted catch).

— Greenpeace agrees with the Commission's proposed approach to tackle the issue on a fishery by fishery basis, and considers that a range of measures tailored to specific types of fisheries will be required, but only after the establishment of a general EU-wide framework within which certain standards are set—including rules on storage, documentation and landing. A fishery-by-fishery approach must prioritise the worst offenders, ie the fisheries with the highest bycatch and discards rates, for example beam trawls, *Nephrops* trawls and whitefish trawls.

— More selective fishing gears and practices should be promoted, including by providing appropriate incentives (tax-breaks, financial assistance, preferential licensing conditions etc), and non-selective gears prohibited or their use discouraged by introducing licensing and impact assessment requirements and/or financial disincentives.

— The general framework to reduce bycatch and eliminate discards should apply to all vessels, although small-scale vessels may need special consideration, as some will be too small to carry onboard observers and/or be fitted with VMS.

— Much of the Commission's proposal relies on industry initiative to, for example, improve the selectivity of gears, but it should be noted that the sector is not generally organised in a way suitable to collectively deal with such issues, and consideration should be given to support development of structures and processes that can facilitate, for example, the exchange of best practice, sector-based real-time-reporting on spawning aggregations and high by-catch rates etc.

Do you consider that fisheries management policies may need to adapt to climate change?

2.7.1 Yes.

If so, how might this be achieved?

2.7.2 Building in resilience means adaptable measures, a precautionary approach, and moving towards an ecosystem-based management. A representative network of large-scale marine reserves is essential in allowing all marine species (including commercially important fish stocks) space to survive and thrive, as well as room to move as and when temperatures and food distribution change.

2.7.3 While every effort is made to reduce greenhouse gas emissions, it is vital that we build up the resilience of ocean ecosystems and improve our understanding of the impacts of climate change on marine ecosystems.

2.7.4 The experts warn that we have depleted marine biodiversity, and with that have eroded the ocean's ability to cope with and mitigate the consequences of global warming. They recommend that we reduce our exploitation levels of marine fish and other maritime activities in order to improve the resilience of our seas and oceans and ultimately safeguard their role in stabilising the climate. Simply aiming at the sustainable use of sea-life is no longer a sufficient management strategy; marine protection has become an insurance policy for an unpredictable future, which will be on average hotter, with more intense extreme events and more hostile.

2.7.5 Marine Reserves, areas set aside from all extractive and destructive activities, offer the highest level of protection for marine life, superior to areas with a limited number of restrictions. Through protecting the diversity of marine life, Marine Reserves boost the oceans' capacity to rally its own defences against a changing climate. In addition, ocean sanctuaries act as valuable reference areas that can guide complementary management measures and recovery targets in areas beyond the reserves' boundaries, so underpinning the ecosystem approach.

2.7.6 In 2001, the United Nations Intergovernmental Panel on Climate Change (IPCC) warned that climate change in turn will "affect the physical, biological, and biochemical characteristics of the oceans and coasts", and warned of "significant feedback on the climate system" of such changes. In light of these findings, the

Secretariat of the Convention on Biological Diversity (CBD) has advised that "genetically-diverse populations and species-rich ecosystems have a greater potential to adapt to climate change".

2.7.7 Subsequently, the European Commission's own Research Centre (JRC) advised that "protected areas contribute to the good health of the ecosystem which then could become relatively more resilient to environmental changes in comparison with those affected by additional anthropogenic pressure", and called for the creation of new conservation areas in Europe's Seas, including fully protected no-take zones.

3. CONTROL AND ENFORCEMENT

Chapter V of Regulation 2371/2002 lays down the responsibilities of the Member States and the Commission as regards the control and enforcement of the rules of the CFP. The recent Court of Auditors Report on the control, inspection and sanctions systems relating to the rules on conservation of Community fisheries resources was very sceptical of the systems currently in place. What is your view of the efficacy of the systems in place?

3.1.1 The UN Convention on the Law of the Sea and the UN Fish Stocks Agreement are clear in so far as the right of a state to fish is not an absolute right, but is conditional upon that state meeting its obligation to protect the marine environment and fish stocks. One of the fundamental failings of the Common Fisheries Policy is that it separates the exercising of the rights to fish (rights are allocated exclusively at EU level, largely through the TACs and quotas system) from the responsibilities of conserving the marine environment and enforcing fisheries management rules, which are almost exclusively the responsibility of the Member States.

3.1.2 Greenpeace has documented first hand the multiple and varied ways in which illegal, unreported and unregulated (IUU) fishing are conducted by the nationals of EU Member States, vessels flagged to EU Member States, vessels fishing in EU waters and/or operating and landing fish and fish products in EU ports. In addition, the products of IUU fishing enter the EU market by road and by air.

3.1.3 Greenpeace agrees fully with the Court of Auditors Report and is alarmed at the scale of mismanagement that it has brought to light. Greenpeace would like to underscore the conclusion that an apparent lack of will amongst the Member States is to blame for weak EU fisheries management rules and an even weaker implementation of in particular those rules that are designed to provide the mechanisms for control and enforcement at national level (including the use of reporting and accounting system, statistical analyses, licensing schemes etc).

3.1.4 Not only is there an urgent need to rectify weaknesses in the rules and application of fisheries legislation, it appears ludicrous that this level of non-compliance is being allowed to continue without serious consequences in terms of infringement procedures, fines, cuts in the allocation of public subsidies and restrictions on the way operators and Member States continue to benefit from other EU policies and services. The concept of "cross-compliance" (which in the EU's agricultural policy stipulates that farmers must comply with all legislation affecting their businesses, if they are to receive direct financial aid from the EU) should be applied to fisheries. It should also be considered a principle that should be adhered to by the Member States themselves. For instance, it simply is incomprehensible that Member States can continue to benefit from subsidies and the allocation of fishing rights, if they are so evidently in breach of the most basic EU conservation and fisheries management rules.

3.1.5 Greenpeace believes that the Commission should encourage a mandate for EUROPOL to investigate organised transboundary crime relating to IUU fishing, including but not limited to the laundering of money earned in IUU fishing. http://ec.europa.eu/fisheries/cfp/governance/consultations/contributions150107/greenpeace.pdf

3.1.6 The issue of the link between organised crime and fishing has been highlighted by Ben Bradshaw, the then UK Fisheries Minister,

> "Illegal, unreported and unregulated fishing is a huge problem. It destroys fish stocks and marine biodiversity, it depresses the market in legally caught fish, and drives legitimate fishermen out of business.
>
> "It's driven by sophisticated criminal gangs who don't care what or who they damage in the pursuit of easy cash. It's a crime that should concern the world, because it plunders a world resource.
>
> "We all have a responsibility and a duty to make sure there is adequate governance and enforcement in place to stop illegal fishing and to block illegal produce entering the food chain. New laws will target not only fishermen but processors and importers who trade in illegal fish." http://www.dfid.gov.uk/News/files/illegal-fishing-tracking-system.asp

To what extent has the Community Fisheries Control Agency already assisted in improving matters?

3.2.1 Given the fact that the CFCA has only just started to operate, it is too early to judge its contribution. However, given its weak mandate, we have fairly low expectations as regards its effectiveness in tackling the problem of IUU fishing and improving the state of compliance with fisheries rules in the EU.

The European Commission has regularly highlighted how serious infringements of the CFP are penalised differently across the Community. This was a matter that was also raised by the Court of Auditors and sanctions were included in the recent Commission Proposal in IUU fishing. What is your view on the issue?

3.3.1 Greenpeace agrees that the EU should adopt a common approach to sanctions and penalties, including the introduction of criminal sanctions in severe cases of non-compliance. In fact, Article 25 (4) of Basic Regulation 2371/2002 already requires the Council to come forward with a "catalogue of measures to be applied by Member States relating to serious infringements". This has not yet been developed.

3.3.2 As well as the problems that inconsistent application and enforcement bring, this also has an effect on the perception of European Fisheries management. The pervasive view of the CFP is that it benefits other countries' fishing industries and not ours, which may well be reflected in every EU fishing industry. Lack of clarity, simplicity, and transparency do not help. Nor does the apparent lack of common sense and action on things like discards and bycatch – which industry, politicians, public, NGOs all find unacceptable and scandalous.

4. STRUCTURAL POLICY

Chapter III of Regulation 2371/2002 obliged Member States to put in place measures to adjust the capacity of their fleets in order to achieve a stable and enduring balance between such fishing capacity and their fishing opportunities. To what extent has this been successful?

4.1.1 The policy has been entirely unsuccessful. The EU is still maintaining a fleet that is roughly twice as large as it should be.

4.1.2 That said, it is clear that effort reduction measures have had greater impacts on some fishing communities than on others. Some communities feel that they have suffered unfairly to the benefit of others. This in part is the result of crises management, which requires drastic cuts in fishing effort on those stocks that suffer a severe state of depletion. A more strategic approach to cutting the EU's fleet size should discourage unsustainable means of fishing and encourage selective, sustainable and labour intensive fisheries.

4.1.3 The overall reduction in effort has not been adequate, and is a result of political timidity against a vociferous and well-supported industry lobby.

What are your views on the possible impact on EU fisheries structural policy of WTO-level discussions as regards subsidies in the fishing sector?

4.2.1 We would refer you to the 2007 Greenpeace report 'Trading Away Our Oceans'; http://oceans.greenpeace.org/raw/content/en/documents-reports/tradingaway.pdf

5. GOVERNANCE

As a result of Regulation 2371/2002, regional Advisory Councils (RACs) were established to advise the Commission on matters of fisheries management in respect of certain sea areas or fishing zones.

How do you consider EU fisheries should ideally be governed?

5.1.1 The Court of Auditor's Report and the Sissenwine and Symes study call into question the very framework and principles on which the CFP is built. A much more substantial reform of fisheries management in the EU is urgently needed:

5.1.2 Faced with unprecedented crises in fisheries management, the Community must switch from a focus on managing the commercialisation of fish to a policy that protects fish as a principal component of marine biodiversity. Greenpeace is of the opinion that the conservation of fish stocks should be managed on the basis of Article 175 of the EC Treaty, that is as part the EU's environment policy.

5.1.3 Moreover, given the importance of fully protected marine reserves for the renewal and recovery of ocean resources, and considering that Member States are over eight years behind in implementing relating commitments under the Habitats and Birds Directives, the EU ought to ensure that payment of money from the EU structural and fisheries funds are made conditional upon complying fully with the aforementioned Directives (in the spirit of cross-compliance and the precautionary principle). Likewise, Member States and ultimately the fishing operators at national level should be required to verify that they are complying with fisheries and conservation rules before they are granted fishing rights.

5.1.4 In addition to ensuring an accelerated implementation of the above Directives and strict enforcement of the CFP, the European Commission must provide for a system that can ensure the prohibition of fishing where it is in conflict with the conservation needs of a protected area. Greenpeace maintains that the currently proposed procedure, by which a Member State that has identified the need to regulate fisheries activities in order to achieve compliance with Community provisions under the Habitats and Birds Directives, must first apply for measures with the European Commission and then with the Council of Fisheries Ministers, and in addition consult fisheries bodies, such as ICES and the Regional (Fisheries) Advisory Councils (RACs), contradicts existing law and is out of line with the EU's commitment to (progressively) implement the ecosystem approach to fisheries management. It further is an obstacle to integrated decision making, as it promotes a scenario in which the Council of Fisheries Ministers may veto a management decision that has been taken on grounds of conservation needs. Even if it agrees with the measures, it will have been an overly-bureaucratic process, wasting time, effort and resources, and been to the unnecessary detriment of the area designated for protection.

5.1.5 The current system hinders Member States in effectively discharging their duties under the Community's environmental policy. Greenpeace is of the opinion that the European Commission has failed to consider a number of more constructive mechanisms for the protection of Natura 2000 sites from fishing, including:

(i) Amend, if necessary, the Basic Regulation (Reg. 2371/2002) to place all measures that are aimed at the conservation of fish stocks firmly in the field of environmental policy, with Article 175 as the legal basis. In accordance with the Treaty, measures to ensure a common and stable market, availability of supplies, etc. would remain under the Common Fisheries Policy, but measures dealing with fish before they are taken out of the sea would fall under Article 175 of the EC Treaty. Greenpeace acknowledges that this would present a change of magnitude and go beyond the task of ensuring compatibility of conservation and fisheries policies in Natura 2000 sites.

(ii) Amend the Basic Regulation (Reg. 2371/2002) to introduce a complete or partial derogation of powers to the Member States to regulate all or certain aspects of fishing in all Special Protection Areas (SPAs) (Birds Directive), Sites of Community Interest (SCIs) and Special Areas of Conservation (SACs) (Habitats Directive), in recognition of the fact that these sites are of special conservation interest and therefore require as a matter of priority a conservation regime that provides immediate protection. The Common Fisheries Policy already includes a precedent for the derogation of powers to the Member States in the case of the "inshore derogation" (Article 9 and 17 of Regulation 2371/2002). This can act as an example for drafting relevant provisions; or

(iii) Regulate fisheries in Natura 2000 sites by means of Commission Regulations, in recognition of the fact that the need to restrict fisheries in certain Natura 2000 sites (on the basis of a request from a Member State) results from provisions under the Community's environmental aquis and is necessary to ensure consistency and compatibility between Community laws. It should therefore be considered as a 'mundane' implementing measure that falls under the Commission's implementing powers under Article 26 of the Basic Regulation, amended if necessary.

How appropriate and feasible do you consider a regional management model to be?

5.2.1 Greenpeace is of the opinion that the Court of Auditor's report and the Sissenwine and Symes study have shown in stark terms that a lack of political will and a breakdown of the administrative structures that are meant to ensure compliance with existing rules are at the heart of the mis-management of EU fisheries. These issues are hardly rectified by the establishment of RACs.

5.2.2 RACs are unaccountable to the issues of broader stakeholders, being very biased towards the interest of the fishing industry. In effect they strengthen the stranglehold that the fishing industry lobby has on the marine sector, to the detriment of conservation issues. We need to move instead towards a different system, with a different set of constituents, and manage our seas at an ecosystem level.

February 2008

Memorandum by The Institute for European Environmental Policy

INTRODUCTION

The Institute for European Environmental Policy (IEEP) has established itself as an independent and effective centre of new thinking and, increasingly, a key player in the area of fisheries and the environment in the UK and Europe. IEEP has a long track record of working on a coherent set of initiatives on detailed areas such as subsidies, indicators and inshore fisheries management and made significant contributions to the major review of the Common Fisheries Policy (CFP) in 2002.

IEEP policy researchers includes economists, political scientists, lawyers and natural scientists and, by consistently focusing on the core policies actually or likely to affect UK and EU fisheries, IEEP has plugged a major gap in the policy debate, strongly complementing the work of other actors. IEEP has also played a key role in guiding the European Commission, NGOs and national policy-makers on various aspects of fisheries policy during the 2002 Reform. We thank you for this opportunity to provide evidence for this critical inquiry on the performance of the CFP over the last five years.

GENERAL COMMENTS

The Common Fisheries Policy (CFP) provides the framework for fisheries management in the EU. Indeed, Member States can only act to conserve fish stocks if they are given express powers to do so under the CFP. Securing sustainable fisheries at national or local level in any of the Member States therefore depends on getting the EU policy framework right, as well as ensuring its correct implementation on the ground or at sea.

Prior to 2002, the CFP was criticised for mismanaging the fisheries sector and *forcing* fishermen to overfish, leading to irreversible damage to stocks of major economic importance, as well as to invaluable marine ecosystems. During the reform of the CFP in 2002, policy actors were forced to contemplate the changes required to address the alarming state of EU fish stocks and new measures to change fisheries management. A new approach to management of EU fisheries was reflected in the 2002 CFP reform and the new Basic Regulation adopted by the European Commission in December 2002.

At the end of December 2002, the Council agreed to an important package of reforms to the CFP. These were primarily legislative changes to the conservation and structural policies. They reflected:

1. a move towards a more long-term approach to fisheries management. The revised CFP should lead to a shift away from annual decision-making on Total Allowable Catches (TACs), to multi-annual planning;

2. a commitment to the progressive implementation of the ecosystem approach to management;

3. a new fleet policy to limit and gradually reduce over-capacity. Members States are given more responsibility to match capacity with fishing possibilities, while vessels' renewal and modernisation subsidies are phased out;

4. a better application of the rules. This is to be achieved through an increased co-operation between national authorities and a more uniform control and sanction system throughout the EU; and

5. improved governance. The aim is to involve stakeholders more closely into the policy making process. This is to be achieved through the setting up of Regional Advisory Councils (RACs).

The 2002 deal was significant, but in many ways just marked the beginning of a longer term reform process. The new CFP framework Regulation sets out the objectives, principles and instruments to support EU fisheries management in the 21st century. However, real change on the ground or at sea required the subsequent adoption and successful implementation of detailed "daughter" legislation.

Five years after the 2002 reform agreement, it is time to judge whether the new CFP has been transformed from paper to practice. The European Commission made some efforts to implement the reform agenda, by developing its ideas on various aspects of management, from inspection and enforcement, to scientific issues. It also came forward with a series of important legislative proposals, covering recovery plans, cetacean by catch, regional advisory councils and deep sea fisheries. A more in-depth analysis of progress is provided below under the various elements of the CFP.

SPECIFIC COMMENTS

Conservation Policy

The cornerstone of EU fisheries management fisheries management in the North East Atlantic and the Baltic Sea has traditionally been the TACs and national quotas. The TAC system has several advantages—it is relatively simple and it has built-in subsidiarity, allowing Member States to decide how quotas are distributed among their fleets. Nevertheless, it is rather a crude management tool and not sufficient to conserve European fish stocks and the system of TACs was heavily criticised during the 2002 reform. Despite its shortcomings, TACs and quotas were retained as a key management measure post 2002. In addressing some of these shortcomings, the European Commission and ICES have placed increasing emphasis on the precautionary approach in proposing TAC levels. The calendar for setting the annual TACs was brought forward, in 2006, to allow enough time for stakeholder consultations prior to the drafting of legislative proposals and decisions. Through improving the basis for TACs and increasing and transparency it is hoped that the year on year fluctuations and deviations from scientific advice, which happens on an annual basis, will be reduced. In addition to these modifications to the establishment of TACs, the Commission has also adopted a longer term approach to management which should lead to better conservation of stocks in the long term.

A longer-term approach: the use of multi-annual plans and recovery plans

The reform of the CFP in 2002 had a clear ambition to adopt a longer-term approach to fisheries management. Consequently, two types of multi-annual plans have been developed as crucial components of this approach: management plans and recovery plans. Management plans are implemented to maintain stocks at safe biological levels (above limit spawning biomass) before stocks reach a critical level. However, certain fish stocks are already in a dangerously depleted state and, in these cases, recovery plans are developed and implemented as a means to halt and ultimately reverse further decline. During the years following the CFP reform, the Council has largely acted on implementing those multi-annual plan although it has also adopted a series of management plans and species recovery plans since 2004: North Sea cod, Northern hake, Southern hake and Norway lobster stocks recovery plans, as well as Bay of Biscay sole multi-annual plan; and more recently the long awaited recovery plans for European eels and the Baltic Sea cod to enter into force this year.

The implementation of recovery plans in Europe has been a fairly new development. It is too early to evaluate the effectiveness of these plans and their associated measures although stakeholders and decision-makers have begun to comment and proceed with preliminary evaluations and there are indications that most of these plans have failed. The lack of success in these cases has been attributed to a number of factors including:

— The lack of stakeholder participation in the plan drafting, implemention or monitoring.

— The lack of progressive reduction in fishing mortality to complement other measures in the plan.

— Ill-defined recovery process (eg unclear harvest control rules); unclear references and target points, as well as the lack of precise timeframes for subsequent action.

— The lack of socio-economic data to ensure efficient management options were used for recovery planning.

— The lack of data on the social impacts of existing recovery plans.

— Ineffective Monitoring, Control and Surveillance measures (MCS) to ensure compliance with the measures in the plans.

Regardless of these shortcomings, it may be too early to draw conclusions on the success or failure of the recovery plans in Europe. Importantly, there are claims that the slow recovery of biomass (a key objective of the recovery plans) is not necessarily due to overfishing and excess of fishing capacity. Environmental conditions may also be affecting recruitments and further slowing down the recovery of some of these stocks. Further studies are needed to evaluate the impact of other environmental factors during the period of the recovery plans. A thorough evaluation of the recovery plans would therefore require more time and more accurate data in order to reach a conclusion.

Technical Measures

Fisheries in EU waters and by EU vessels in international waters are covered by different technical measures regulations, one for each of the areas of the Mediterranean (Council Regulation 1626/1994), the North Sea (including Kattegat and Skagerrak) and the Atlantic (Council Regulation 850/1998), the Baltic Sea (Council Regulation 88/1998) and the Antarctic (Regulation 600/2004). The current Regulation for the North Sea

(Council Regulation 850/1998) which came into effect in 2000 and the rules were simplified and adapted to the current needs of the industry to promote conservation of fish stocks.

In 2004, the Commission set out its plans for improving technical measures in its Communication, COM(2004) 438. In this Communication, the Commission presented a set of actions and timelines which included:

— A review of current technical measures Regulations;

— A reduction of discards;

— Research in support of environmentally fishing methods through the 6th Framework Programme of Research; and

— Proposals for new financial incentives.

By 2007, the Commission has progressed on all four proposals. In relation to technical Regulations, the North East Atlantic Regulation was revised in 2004. A further revision of this Regulation and those for the Baltic and the Mediterranean are currently underway. In relation to discards, the Commission funded a pilot project to address the problem of ghost fishing in Community waters. IEEP was involved in this project which contributed to the Commissions final decision on ghost fishing.

The need to address by-catch and discards was identified by the Commission as an important objective during the reform of the CFP in 2002. In 2003, the Fisheries Council adopted conclusions inviting the Commission to explore ways to resolve the problem. However, very few projects have materialised and demonstrated good results and by-catch and discards still remain a problem for most fisheries. On 28 March 2007, the Commission adopted a Communication to the Council and the Parliament on a policy to reduce by-catch and discards in European Fisheries (COM(2007)136). In this Communication the Commission presents issues for discussion and outlines the policy approach to reduce unwanted by-catch and progressively eliminate discard based on an internal working paper on preliminary impact assessment of three policy options. The first option—to take no specific actions but to continue fisheries management as it currently stands. The second—to take supplementary direct measures and adapt CFP instruments including real time closures and selective fishing gear and the third option—to a) implement a discard ban as a stand-alone option or b) to implement a discard ban, supplemented with additional measures. The European Commission is planning to propose a new Regulation on discards in May 2007, based on further analysis of the various options. IEEP has been assisting the Commission with the analysis. Further analysis of the options available to the Commission indicates that there may different approaches to different fisheries depending on the levels of discarding and the social, economic and environmental impacts. In addition, due to the complex nature of EU fisheries, there is no one-size-fits-all solution to the discard problem and the European Commission will need to look very closely at the environmental benefits of various options versus the social and economic costs.

The EFF Regulation[1], adopted in 2006 provides financial incentives for the promotion and use of environmentally-friendly fishing, including the development and use of more selective gears while compensating for short term losses for vessels participating in trials of more environmentally-friendly fishing methods (Axis 1 and Axis 3). The allocation of funds to these axes and activities should included in the National Operational Programmes (NOPs) currently being prepared by Member States. Not all Member States have completed this process and therefore it is too early to judge whether the new EFF will result in the use of more environmentally-friendly fishing gear (see below).

Structural Policy

Regulation 1198/2006[2] establishes the European Fisheries Fund (EFF), the structural policy for fishing activities for the period 2007–13, succeeding the 2000–06 Financial Instruments for Fisheries Guidance (FIFG). Unlike its predecessor, the EFF is no longer a structural fund. Although funding is still allocated using multi-annual programming, the EFF includes more responsibility to Member States with the development of national strategic plans and operational programmes. Also, measures available for funding fall under five priority axes clearly defining the range of actions to undertake:

— Adaptation of the Community fishing fleet.

— Aquaculture, inland fishing, processing and marketing.

— Promoting collective interest.

— Sustainable development of fishing areas.

— Technical assistance to facilitate the delivery of assistance.

---

[1] Council Regulation (EC) No 1198/2006 of 27 July 2006 on the European Fisheries Fund. *Official Journal*. 15.8.2006. L 223/1.
[2] Council Regulation (EC) No 1198/2006 of 27 July 2006 on the European Fisheries Fund, OJ L 223 of 15.8.2006

The objectives of the EFF remain slightly similar to those of the FIFG, although they are certainly "greener" and more in line with the objectives of the 2002 CFP reform. Funding for an increase in fishing capacity of any sort is strictly ruled out. The EFF also provides more room for measures contributing to more environmental integration and stakeholders' participation. The EFF is also more devolved to socioeconomic issues and the integration of the fishing economy into national economies. This is shown by the opportunities for funding retraining and alternative job opportunities. The EFF also aims at providing specific help to less favoured and remote fishing areas within the EU, by means of differential funding between "convergence" and "non-convergence" regions.

The EFF therefore marks a further step towards funding of sustainable fishing activities. However, at the beginning of 2008 the EFF is still at its early stage of implementation with the adoption of 19 of the 27 operational programmes, and some uncertainties remain about the uptake by Member States of measures consistent with the objectives defined by the European policy. The early stages of the EFF implementation process have already highlighted some dissimilarity among Member States regarding the consultation of stakeholders and the integration of environmental objectives (eg financing Natura 2000).

As the breakdown of national budgets by priority axis has been published recently, it is possible to get an overview of Member States' priorities. The EU-15 are more prone to allocate to traditional funding (ie capacity adjustment) while new Member States dedicate a large part of their budget to axis 4 "sustainable development of fishing areas" (up to 23% for Latvia and Estonia and 33% for Romania). This is likely to create more opportunities for funding new "conservation type projects" in new Member States, whereas old Member States will stick to their "business-as-usual" funding. However, it is recommended to be careful about the uptake of axis 4 funding, measures are ranging from regeneration of coastal communities to environmental protection and eco-tourism. Hence, if not correctly assessed, the important proportion given to "new" measures could be used rather for preserving social fabrics than helping the fishing economy and funding vital measures linked with safety onboard, increasing competitiveness of the fleet, developing marketing and distribution of fish and fish products, etc.

Monitoring and evaluation of the EFF is based on a close exchange between the Commission and Member States, which had to produce ex ante programme evaluations when submitting their operational programmes. Moreover, once the EFF is in operation, Member States will have to produce annual progress reports about the uptake of the EFF budget. The structural policy therefore appears to be effectively monitored and evaluated throughout the process, but efforts will be required from Member States to report correctly to the Commission and vice versa.

The CFP structural policy seems to have no long-term planning and appears to be quite unenthusiastic to review what has been achieved so far. The ex-post evaluation of the 2000–06 FIFG is still pending and is not likely to be conducted before the end of 2009 or 2010. Meanwhile, the Commission is planning a mid-term review of the EFF at the latest by mid-2011. This will be a strategic period for the Commission to assess its past, current and future structural policy. It is important that the FIFG's ex-post evaluation feed the review of the EFF and allow for a forward-thinking strategy for the upcoming fund after 2013.

The EFF surely provides a promising perspective to the CFP, but a lot still remains to achieve a well-balanced and sustainable fisheries sector and the overall CFP structural policy has to keep in line with these recent progresses by going three steps forward and two steps back. Indeed, the de minimis aid approved mid-2007, by increasing the state aid ceiling from 3,000 to 30,000 euros has opened the back door for further cost-reducing subsidies (eg fuel subsidies) while the Commission is claiming that the solution is not to give subsidies to meet part of the increased costs due to ongoing external pressure (eg rising fuel costs). The policy is bound to be radically different from 2013 onwards. Subsidies to the fishing sector will have to be phased out, according to the global context and recent WTO outcomes. This leads to further uncertainties about long-term sustainability of the European fisheries sector.

Governance

One of the most concrete actions taken by the Commission to date on implementing a new approach to EU fisheries governance under CFP since 2002 is the establishments of the RACs. There are plans for seven RACs:

—   The Baltic Sea RAC (operational in March 2006);

—   The North Sea RAC (operational in November 2004);

—   The Mediterranean Sea RAC (in the process of being established);

—   The North-western waters RAC (operational since September 2005);

—   The South-western waters RAC (operational since April 2007);

— The Pelagic Stocks RAC (operational since August 2005); and

— The Distant water fisheries RAC (operational since March 2007).

RACs were originally intended to primarily provide advice to the Commission and national fisheries managers on management issues including development and implementation of the ecosystem approach. RACs were meant to support resource management, including progressive implementation of the ecosystem-based approach. They should aim to do so, taking full consideration of existing EU legislation regarding environmental and other issues. Despite their lack of legal "teeth", RACs should be influential if their advice were allowed to drive the decision-making process. It is for this reason that industry and non-governmental groups have taken a close interest in their evolution and functioning.

It is too early to judge the influence of the RACs but their influence on decision-making is growing. In recognition of their contribution to the development of the CFP, the Council recently agreed to continue funding RACs beyond the period originally agreed. Initially, it was intended that RACs would benefit from start-up aid which would last the first five years. The Council has now agreed that TACS will receive permanent funding of €250,000 every year in order to continue their activities. The wider role of the RACs within the new European Maritime Policy is unclear but it is evident that they need to be involved and can continue to play a key role in promoting sustainable management on a regional scale.

Control and enforcement

In October 2007, the Commission made a proposal for a Council Regulation establishing a Community system to prevent, deter and eliminate illegal, unreported and unregulated (IUU) fishing. The aim of this proposal is to ban imports into the EU of fisheries products caught illegally. The proposal lays out two sets of rules. Firstly, it proposes rules to deal with illegal landings by EU vessels and secondly, it proposes actions against foreign-flagged vessels which are involved in IUU fishing activities. In the previous strategy, the EU focussed on improving monitoring, control and surveillance (MCS) at sea and identifying IUU fishing operations. However, the new proposal aims to extend the framework to the rest of the supply chain and improve its effectiveness using trade measures.

Specifically, the EU seeks to address all fishing and related activities linked to IUU practices. This includes transhipments, processing, harvesting and landing. The inclusion of the trade dimension is very important and is based on the recognition that the EU is the biggest market and lead importer of fisheries products—recent assessments have shown that the volume of illegal fisheries products imported into the EU each year amounts to approximately 500,000 tonnes to a value of €1.1 billion.

Several new developments have come up from this plan, including that the Commission proposes fines ranging from €300,000 to €500,000, though it was to be defined by Member States before. Importantly, the plan includes a catch certificate to be filled-in by vessels. One can argue that this certificate which requires an important set of data is likely to prevent developing countries fishing fleets to enter the EU market. Accordingly, this may constitute an important non-tariff barrier to the entry of developing countries fisheries goods in the EU.

On April 2005 the Council adopted the Regulation establishing a Community Fisheries Control Agency (CFCA). Its main task is to achieve the effective implementation of the CFP and to establish uniform inspections and enforcement throughout the Community. Developing and monitoring joint deployment plans, implemented by the Member States, will be central to achieving these tasks. While the Agency cannot directly strengthen enforcement measures such as penalties, it will play a key coordinating role, which is an important step in taking forward the "post-2002" CFP as it could significantly improve implementation and enforcement.

The preparation of Joint Deployment Plans (JDP) is one of the CFCA's main tools for insuring effective enforcement and equal treatment for all those involved in a particular fishery. The criteria for a JDP is that the fish stock concerned must be subject to a long-term recovery plan or a multi-annual management plan and a specific control and enforcement plan has to be adopted by the Commission. A JDP for the North Sea cod fisheries has recently been adopted by the CFCA on July 2007. This plan comes as a complement to the tightening of cod recovery plan enforcement that requires Member States to develop their national control programmes and will pool the resources from seven Member States by using inspectors, control vessels or aircrafts to ensure effective and uniform control of fishing activities. Two other JDP will be also put in place next year, focusing on cod in the Baltic Sea and bluefin tuna in the Mediterranean.

The effectiveness of the agency depends to a large extent on the details of the "control and inspection programmes" to be implemented, in which the Member States plays a central role. While the CFCA is currently moving to be based in Vigo (Spain), it is still too early to assess its effectiveness and the commitment of Member States on the enforcement of the CFP measures.

The release at the end of 2007 of a Court of Auditors report on the existing system of control applicable to the CFP[3] has highlighted some weaknesses in the functioning of the EU's control system at a national level. According to this document, shortcomings have been observed on the catch registration systems, whose data are neither complete nor reliable. Additionally, inspection activities are ineffective and inefficient, and controls of resources are too concentrated on inspections at sea rather than at the time of landing. Also, the follow-up of reported infringements does not necessarily lead to sanctions, which are in any event recognized as non-dissuasive. Importantly, these shortcomings are even more emphasized by the pervasive reduced profitability of the EU fisheries sector that prompts fishing vessels to non-compliance.

The Commission has therefore decided to begin the reform of its control process. This reform encompasses several objectives, which aims to strengthen some key elements of the EU system control: the capacity of the Commission; the mandate of the CFCA; the cooperation across national authorities and with the CFCA; the level and harmonisation of sanctions; the involvement of stakeholders into the so-called "culture of compliance"; cost effectiveness of the control process; and the use of modern technologies.

The plan to review the control regime in 2008 and propose a new improved Regulation signals the Commission's commitment to addressing the shortcomings of the current regime. However, the challenges brought by the reform of controls in the EU fisheries sector are considerable and these need to be addressed in earnest if the new control regime is to be successful.

EU's external policy

The bilateral fisheries partnership agreements (FPAs) have been developed according to a Commission Communication in 2002[4]. There have been encouraging changes in the structure and approach of FPAs compared to former fisheries access agreements (FAs). This is particularly true about developing partnerships with third countries, by means of a percentage of the financial contribution attached to the agreement to be set aside to support the sectoral fisheries policy in the third country. This percentage ranges from 18% for Micronesia to 100% to Ivory Coast.

Moreover, the general trend in FPAs away from mixed agreements and towards tuna agreements is likely to offer a more coherent exploitation of stocks and avoid conflicts between EU and small scale third-countries fleets. FPAs are likely to provide more revenue to the fishing sector, and hence better contribute to the development of the third-country fisheries sector regarding stock assessment, monitoring and control, processing and distribution, etc.

Nonetheless, FPAs show some weaknesses in the evaluation of impacts of the EU fleets. *Ex ante* evaluation of FPAs are imprecise with regard to EU fishing effort, evaluation of marine resources available for fishing and their valuation. It should also better address the benefits provided to the third-countries economies. Practically, one has to make sure that enforcement capacities from third-countries are sufficient to prevent the EU fleet from taking advantage of such weaknesses.

From a market perspective, FPAs are likely to reduce third countries' trade in fish and fish products in case of no local landings. The implementation of FPAs by the EC has voluntarily put aside the fisheries sector from the general EU trade policy, which is mostly based on the Economic Partnership Agreements (EPAs). Accordingly, this can threaten the sustainability of exports of fisheries goods to the EU.

CONCLUSIONS—ONGOING CHALLENGES

Despite the progress towards implementing the reformed CFP since 2002, there is still a need to transform the new Regulation into specific legal requirements and to ensure the successful implementation and supporting regulations. A key area which requires further actions is "bringing fishing effort in line with the fisheries resources". Despite long standing fisheries management efforts, the CFP still has not managed to balance fishing activity with fishing opportunities. Excessive fleet capacity is a major contributing factor. This is the legacy of many years of inadequate management, combining aid for building new vessels, weak fleet reduction requirements, limits on landings rather than catches and poor enforcement policies.

---

[3] Special Report No 7/2007 pursuant to Article 248(4) second paragraph, EC, on the control, inspection, and sanction systems relating to the rules on conservation of Community fisheries resources. http://eca.europa.eu/portal/pls/portal/docs/1/673627.PDF

[4] Communication from the Commission on an integrated framework for Fisheries Partnership Agreements with third countries COM/ 2002/0637 final

The challenge is still to find feasible ways to bring fishing capacity back in line with available resources. Rights based instruments—notably Individual Transferable Quotas (ITQs) for fish have been strongly promoted by economists on grounds of economic efficiency. In countries such as New Zealand, they have been instrumental in reducing fishing effort and waste and foster a general sense of legitimacy and ownership in the resource management. To date several stakeholders with vested interests in Europe have been strongly opposed to them. Within RBM systems the most controversial aspect that emerges is the transferability of rights. Introducing a resource price for fishing rights may lead to the buying of rights on a large scale, therefore concentrating ownership of quotas, geographical distribution and fleet composition while the environmental benefits may not be clear. The consultation on RBM is due to last 12 months after which the Commission will then report to the Council and the European Parliament and, if and when appropriate, make proposals or recommendations for follow-up.

EU enlargement will continue, and with it the EU waters will grow. Although the EU already includes all of the European Seas, if Turkey joins the EU will become a significant player in the Black Sea beyond what it is now with only Bulgaria and Romania as coastal Member States. This growth, together with the joining of Croatia, will increase the EU's role in the Mediterranean. Management can be expected to improve in both cases, but the extent will be limited by the fact that there will continue to be many other countries to cooperate with in the two regions.

The growing importance of the Black and Mediterranean Seas can be expected to deepen the trend towards regionalisation of the CFP. Management plans and cooperation at a regional level will become more prominent, and effective, as more countries join the EU.

The EU Maritime Policy (MP) was adopted in 2007 and the EU Marine Strategy Directive was recently adopted by the Council. The EU MP is aimed at ensuring better integration of maritime policies including the CFP towards better conservation and protection of European waters, while the MSD is reliant on Member States achieving "good environmental status" by 2020. Whilst these policies have the potential to add value, by filling some gaps that the CFP is unlikely to close, there is scepticism whether this will be the case.

The current CFP has five more years to run its course. In the next two years, it is important that evaluation of key sub-policies is undertaken to ensure that the CFP can be adapted to meet the challenges after 2012.

3 March 2008

Memorandum by the National Federation of Sea Anglers

1. INTRODUCTION

Recreational sea angling (RSA) has been recognised as a major stakeholder in the sustainable exploitation of marine resources only since the Common Fisheries Policy (CFP) was reformed in 2002.

RSA was not considered in that 2002 reform. This is a continuation of the *status quo* where RSA has historically been denied recognition in the Policy since its inception 50 years ago.

The sea angling community is, therefore, anxious to provide the Committee with the reasons why it considers RSA should be regarded under the CFP as an integral part of the EU fishing industry.

A precedent for declaring RSA to be a part of the fishing industry was set in Britain in the joint UK report Securing the Benefits, published in June 2005. This was the response to the Prime Minister's Strategy Unit report Net Benefits of 2004 which first revealed the extent of the socio-economic importance of RSA.

2. ISSUES RAISED BY THE COMMITTEE

Given that RSA is not represented in the CFP, it is only possible for the sea angling community to address two of the 11 important issues raised in the Committee's Call for Evidence, because the rest apply essentially to the commercial fishing industry.

On these two issues, numbers 10 and 11 under Governance, we wish to make the following comments:

   a) Regional Advisory Councils (RACs) are a step in the right direction (away from central decision making in Brussels). However, their composition needs some rebalancing to enable everyone with a stake in EU marine resources, including RSA, to be involved in management decisions.

   For instance, two-thirds of the members of the North Sea RAC represent the commercial catching sector and they are unlikely to willingly consider the recreational sector despite its high importance in the countries involved in this RAC— Belgium, Denmark, France, Germany, Netherlands, Poland, Spain, Sweden and the UK.

b) We believe a system of regional managements would be both feasible and appropriate. Angling differs from area to area and is not amenable to centralised regulatory decisions.

For this reason 12 sea fisheries committees regulate fishing and environmental protection within six miles of the coast of England and Wales. We would like to see their remit extended to 12 miles and their powers and composition changed to ensure RSA and commercial fishing are considered equally and the number of these committees maintained.

In this regard it may be worth noting that in its Consultation on an RSA Strategy for England published in December 2007, Defra stated that while historically RSA had been under-represented in fisheries management, it was increasingly recognised as a significant activity contributing both socially and economically to national and coastal economies.

Management adequately reflecting the needs of RSA alongside other stakeholders at national, regional and local levels was needed. We believe that the same sentiments should apply equally across the EU.

3. A Recent Development

Since originally submitting this evidence to the Committee, we have been made aware that on 24 February 2008 the EU did in fact come a step closer to recognising recreational sea angling through the publication of a Council Regulation. This, for the first time as far as we know, defined the "fisheries sector" as activities related to commercial fisheries, recreational fisheries (our emphasis) aquaculture and industries processing fisheries products, and further stated that "recreational fisheries" means non-commercial fishing activities exploiting living aquatic resources for recreation.

This document was Council Regulation (EC) No 199/2008 establishing "a Community framework for the collection management and use of data in the fisheries sector and support for scientific advice regarding the Common Fisheries Policy."

This recognition of our activities though welcome, is not the same as being recognised by the CFP or the EU Treaty and we believe that RSA needs still needs to be properly recognised at a high level as a legitimate stakeholder in the work of the CFP. In our view this needs to be both a government objective and an objective of the RSA sector itself.

4. Background to RSA and the CFP

Our purpose in offering evidence to the Committee is to provide an insight into the high value of RSA in the coastal economies of Europe, and to ask the Committee to consider expressing a view on the importance of RSA alongside the commercial industry, in the future management and/or reform of the CFP.

The CFP is intended to cover the conservation and exploitation of marine fisheries. While there are a number of stakeholders in this, the commercial fishing industry has always been seen as the primary claimant.

We argue strongly that since RSA, like commercial fishing, is an exploitation activity it should receive due and proportionate consideration in future within the CFP.

Sea angling has a minor impact on the environment and on fish stocks compared to the huge tonnages of fish regularly taken commercially from EU waters and the damage done to habitats by trawling.

RSA does not add to the alarmingly high numbers of fish and other living aquatic resources discarded dead into the sea by commercial vessels because they have no market value. We note that discards and bycatch is one of the questions the Committee will be considering.

5. The Economic Value of RSA

Recreational sea angling has an exceptionally high socio-economic value which its proponents believe strongly deserves to be preserved and encouraged to grow.

It is notoriously difficult to obtain accurate statistics on fishing activities (a recent Court of Auditors report found catch data to be unreliable). However, the latest figures available to us show that annual revenue from commercial marine fishing in the EU is about €9 billion including aquaculture or fish farming.

In contrast, the European Angling Alliance estimates there are 8–10 million sea anglers in the EU supporting a related industry worth up to €10 billion. These figures have not been challenged. The EU Commission in its Marine Policy estimated the value of salt water angling as €8–€10 billion.

We submit that knowledge of the economic value of RSA, its growth potential and low environmental impact, will assist officials managing the CFP to make informed decisions on the exploitation of marine resources.

A report in February 2008 by Fiskeriverket, the Swedish national fisheries agency, stated that RSA contributes ten times as much to that nation's economy than does commercial fishing. There are an estimated one million recreational anglers and 1,300 businesses serving angling tourism in Sweden, and about 1,000 commercial fishermen.

In England and Wales alone 19,000 jobs are supported by sea angling (Defra report into the economic impact of recreational sea angling, 2004) and in Europe (again using the figures of the European Angling Alliance) the sea angling tackle trade alone is worth €2 billion.

6. THE FUTURE: RSA AND THE CFP

It is, of course, difficult to make a strict comparison between commercial fishing (an extractive industry) and RSA (a leisure activity). However, we believe the figures we have given clearly show RSA to be an important economic activity.

Crucially it depends upon the same publicly owned resources (the fish in the seas) as the commercial industry, to maintain this economic value.

We submit, therefore, that in the future management of the CFP the EU should consider whether commercial fishing (we would say overfishing) of the seas is always the best economic use of marine resources. A fish caught by an angler is usually worth much more to the local economy than a similar fish caught commercially at the same place.

The result of the carefree regime under which the commercial industry operated for many years now threatens the survival of many species. This is impacting the legitimate leisure activities of millions of sea anglers and the sustainability of the many businesses which support sea angling.

Dr. Joe Borg, the European Commissioner for Fisheries and Maritime Affairs, said on 21 February this year: "If we don't act now all our work to bring fishing back to sustainable levels will be seriously undermined."

Recreational fishers have witnessed the decline of fish stocks and in particular have suffered from the reduction in the number of larger mature fish of many species. Many have expressed their concerns as they have noticed the deterioration in their catches over the years.

The decimation of fish stocks through commercial overfishing remains the greatest threat to the future of RSA and of commercial fishing itself.

7. CFP ACTIONS RSA WOULD WELCOME

Primarily RSA wants the CFP to recognise that its activities and the industry it supports, are legitimate stakeholders in the fishing industry and for this to lead to such changes as:

   i)   A CFP commitment to the regeneration of fish stocks to a healthy and sustainable level in a given time frame. Part of this should be a revised minimum landing size (MLS) regime under which the MLS for all species targeted by commercial and recreational fishers would be set to stop immature fish being taken. This would substantially increase the brood stock which is an essential step towards stock regeneration.

   ii) Funds being made available to improve charter angling boats, just as money is available to improve (or decommission) commercial boats.

   iii) A definition of how much environmental damage caused by commercial fishing, especially by trawling, can be tolerated. This is often referred to as "ploughing up the seabed."

   iv) More emphasis on certifying sustainable and environmentally acceptable commercial fishing practices such as line fishing for mackerel and bass.

10 March 2008

Memorandum by the New Zealand Government

SUMMARY

1. The efforts by the European Union (EU) to reform its Common Fisheries Policy (CFP) are commendable. The 2002 CFP reforms have been far reaching, not only in reshaping the overarching legal framework for fisheries management but also in initiating a process of ongoing policy and process reforms that are leading the EU in the direction of conservation and sustainable use of fisheries resources.

2. The new CFP establishes a good enabling framework for fisheries conservation, including the necessary provisions for the EU to utilise fisheries sustainably. If the EU is to meet its sustainability objectives, New Zealand considers greater policy coherence will be required within and between the strands of the CFP, key EU treaties and broader EU policies (eg trade), and Member States' own national policies.

3. As a party directly affected by the CFP (economically in EU and world markets, and in international fisheries more generally), New Zealand is vitally interested in the policy's implementation and ongoing transformation. New Zealand will also continue to engage with European Commission ("the Commission") and Member States on the implications of these changes, in particular for their trading and fishing partners.

4. The Sub-Committee will also have before it a separate submission from the New Zealand Seafood Industry Council.

INTRODUCTION

5. New Zealand welcomes the opportunity to comment on progress to date with implementation of the 2002 CFP reforms and to consider what further policy and implementation changes should be contemplated at the EU and Member State level in both the short-term and beyond 2012.

6. New Zealand's reference points in making this submission include:

— The adoption of a rights-based quota management regime in New Zealand almost three decades ago;

— New Zealand's experience as an exporter of fisheries products to the EU and the rest of the world;

— New Zealand's experience in working with the EU in international fora, including the United Nations (UN); Regional Fisheries Management Organisations (RFMOs); Organisation for Economic Co-operation and Development (OECD); and the World Trade Organisation (WTO); and

— A desire to see fisheries management strengthened to ensure fisheries are sustainably utilised in a manner consistent with the numerous international instruments on fisheries, development and sustainability to which New Zealand is party.

7. In some cases, New Zealand-flagged vessels participate in the same fisheries as EU-flagged vessels (notably in the Pacific region). New Zealand also has strong relationships with developing countries in the Pacific region. The contribution that the EU makes to utilising these fisheries sustainably through the application of the CFP is therefore of direct interest to New Zealand.

8. Fisheries production and exports of fisheries products are important to New Zealand's economic and social wellbeing. The bulk of New Zealand's production of these goods is exported and accounts for 4.4% of merchandise exports value. The EU market accounts for 18% of New Zealand's seafood exports or about €124 million. As a long-time exporter of fisheries products to the EU, and as a country which has had to compete with subsidised EU products on world markets, New Zealand has a strong interest in the evolution of the CFP.

CONSERVATION/MANAGEMENT

A wide range of management tools are available to fisheries managers. What are your views on the following tools:

Total Allowable Catches

— *Effort limitation, including "days at sea", marine conservation areas and real-time closures*
— *Rights-Based Management tools*
— *Technical Conservation Measures*

To what extent have current management tools increased the levels of discards and bycatch? What is your view on how these problems can best be tackled?

Overview

9. New Zealand adopted a rights-based management system—the Quota Management System (QMS)—in 1986, based on Individual Transferable Quota (ITQ). Since that time the system has evolved considerably to address management issues not foreseen when the QMS was introduced, and to seek improvements in the operation of the QMS. The QMS is supplemented by a range of additional tools that aim to address management issues lying beyond the scope of the QMS. New Zealand's views and experience of the management tools listed above are briefly outlined below, and should be read in the context of our experiences with implementing the QMS and seeking to address associated management challenges.

Total Allowable catches

10. Most commercial fisheries in New Zealand are now managed under the QMS. Being an "output-based" management system, the QMS centres around the setting of sustainable catch limits. 97 species are divided into administrative stocks of which there are now 629 within the QMS. Two types of catch limit are set for each stock: the total allowable catch (TAC) and the total allowable commercial catch (TACC). The Minister first sets the TAC. The TAC represents the assessment of the total amount of fish that can be sustainably removed from a stock in any one year. It encompasses all extraction from the sea by all users. Except in limited cases[5] it must be set with reference to the maximum sustainable yield (MSY) or the greatest yield that can be achieved over time while maintaining the stock's productive capacity. The stock might be fished down to MSY or rebuilt to a level that can produce MSY.

11. From the TAC, the Minister makes allowances for recreational and Maori customary non-commercial fishing interests and all other sources of fishing mortality, including the quantity required for research and an estimate of the amount taken illegally each year, before quantifying the TACC for a particular fishing year. Before setting or varying a TACC the Minister must consult with all interested parties, including representatives of customary, commercial, recreational and environmental interests. TACs and TACCs are reviewed annually.

Rights-Based Management tools

12. The QMS is a rights-based management system and was introduced in New Zealand because it was seen as the best way to:

— prevent overfishing, which had reached critical levels in some inshore fisheries, by limiting catches to levels that would result in maximum sustainable yield of each stock; and

— reduce over-capacity and improve the economic efficiency of the fishing industry in order to maximise net economic return to the nation.

13. The introduction of the QMS brought major changes to the nature of the New Zealand fishing industry. In the lead up to the introduction of the QMS part-time fishers were removed from the inshore fishery without compensation. Only full-time commercial fisheries were allocated quota. A substantial reduction in the number of fishing vessels occurred as a result. In the early 1990s the QMS provided the security for quota owners to invest in the buying of deepwater fishing vessels to fish species such as orange roughy and hoki. The fishing industry continues to be made up of a small number of large fishing companies plus many small scale companies and individual fishers.

---

[5]   The exceptions are stocks whose biological characteristics mean MSY cannot be estimated (eg squid), enhanced stocks, and
      international stocks where New Zealand's catch limit is determined as part of an international agreement)

14. Since its inception the QMS has delivered significant benefits to New Zealand. Export returns and numbers employed in the seafood industry have increased, and the QMS has been an important factor in improving the sustainability of many of our fisheries that were previously over-fished.

15. The success of the ITQ system in New Zealand has been attributed to the following four main factors:

   a.   New Zealand is isolated geographically with no major shared or straddling stocks.

   b.   Key fishing industry players were strong supporters and promoters of the ITQ system right from the start and were instrumental in getting the system introduced. The system also enjoyed widespread support from fishery managers and politicians.

   c.   The Government bought back catch histories from inshore fishers to reduce TACs in stressed inshore stocks, so fishers were compensated for catch reductions.

   d.   At the time of the catch reductions for the inshore species, the offshore, deep-water species were largely underexploited. Subsequently, catches from these latter fisheries increased, which formed a strong economic base for the development of the New Zealand fishing industry.[6]

16. That is not to say that there have not been challenges for New Zealand in implementing the QMS. While many of the basic elements of the QMS remain unchanged since its adoption over 20 years ago, New Zealand has continued to work to improve its operation and to ensure the incentives it creates produce desirable outcomes.

ITQ and Annual Catch Entitlement

17. Each QMS stock is divided into 100 million quota shares. At the start of the fishing year, the setting of the TACC for each stock determines the amount of fish (in kilograms) generated by quota holdings. The Annual Catch Entitlement (ACE) is generated by quota holdings and represents the amount of a particular stock that a fisher is allowed to catch in a particular fishing year without incurring any penalty. Each person's ACE is equal to his or her share of the TACC as determined by their quota ownership. Both ITQ and ACE can be divided, aggregated, leased, bought and sold. For all stocks in the QMS, commercial fishers must balance their catch with ACE or pay the relevant deemed value.

Deemed Values

18. Where catches of QMS species are taken in excess of a fisher's catching rights, the fisher is required to pay the Ministry of Fisheries an administrative penalty for that amount of catch. Deemed values are set for each QMS stock. Deemed values are usually set at a level to provide an incentive for every commercial fisher to acquire or maintain enough ACE to cover their catch in a particular year. Interim deemed values are payable on a monthly basis and are refundable if a fisher subsequently obtains sufficient ACE to cover the catch. Annual deemed values are payable at the end of the fishing year and are not refundable. A deemed value demand may be satisfied by acquiring ACE or by paying the amount demanded. If a person does not take one of these courses of action, his or her commercial fishing permit can be suspended. This catch-balancing regime is administrative in nature, but set within a criminal offence regime.

Effort limitation and Technical Conservation Measures

19. New Zealand's approach to managing fisheries through the QMS does not use capacity limits—relying on output controls to ensure catches are kept within sustainable limits. Under the QMS, quota holders are free to determine the appropriate level of capacity to harvest their quota. This has led to significant rationalisation of the commercial fishing industry in New Zealand as commercial fishers adjust their fishing capacity and the nature of their operations around annual catch entitlements.

20. In respect of the transfer of fishing capacity from the New Zealand fishery to other fisheries, New Zealand works within regional fisheries management organisations (RFMOs) to develop effective fisheries management measures, including capacity measures, to ensure the long term sustainability of fish stocks and ensures that New Zealand-flagged vessels fishing on the high seas or within the zones of other countries are effectively controlled. New Zealand works with other countries at the regional level to ensure that fishing capacity is kept within levels that are consistent with the long term sustainability of the fish stocks in the region.

---

[6]   Annala, John H. (1996) New Zealand's ITQ system: have the first eight years been a success or a failure?, Reviews in Fish Biology and Fisheries 6, p60.

21. While the QMS provides the overall framework for fisheries management in New Zealand, it is supported by technical conservation measures which enable more tailored management according to the characteristics of a fishery or stock.

22. The technical conservation measures commonly imposed are:

— Closed areas.

— Closed seasons.

— Size limits.

— Gear restrictions.

— Prohibited species.

23. Details of these technical conservation measures can be found in the Fisheries (Commercial Fishing) Regulations 2001 or at the following website:

http://www.fish.govt.nz/en-nz/Commercial/Management+Controls/default.htm.

Marine conservation areas and real-time closures

24. The QMS is the primary tool for managing fish stocks in New Zealand, but on its own it doesn't address wider ecosystem or environmental issues associated with fishing. New Zealand uses other tools in combination with the QMS to provide these protections. New Zealand considers marine conservation areas and real-time closures as useful tools, depending on the specific management objectives and outcomes sought, and has adopted both of these management tools in certain areas and fisheries.

25. New Zealand is a signatory to the United Nations Convention on Biological Diversity and is committed to maintaining the biodiversity on our land and in our waters. This is being achieved through the New Zealand biodiversity strategy, which has as its objective that marine habitats and ecosystems will be maintained in a healthy and functioning state and degraded areas will be allowed to recover.

Marine Protected Areas

26. Recently New Zealand released a Marine Protected Areas Policy and Implementation Plan as the key means of pulling together all the existing tools for protecting marine biodiversity. This information can be found at the following website:

http://www.biodiversity.govt.nz/seas/biodiversity/protected/mpa_policy.html

27. It seeks to achieve an integrated network of Marine Protected Areas across the territorial sea and EEZ protecting 10% of New Zealand's marine environment by 2010.

28. The country has been divided into 14 coastal regions to create a network of Marine Protected Areas (MPAs) that reflect the diversity of New Zealand's marine environment. Local groups, or forums, will be identifying which areas in each region should be protected.

29. There will be three types of marine protection in these regions:

— Marine Reserves—highest form of protection that prohibits taking anything from the water.

— Other marine protected areas—allows some activities, but prohibits anything that would significantly change the overall environment, eg bottom trawling, dredging.

— Other marine protection tools—protects certain plants or animals in the marine environment.

30. A variety of marine conservation areas will be integrated into this process:

— New Zealand has established marine reserves and management areas for customary (indigenous) fishing.

— New Zealand has closed over 1.2 Million square kilometres of its EEZ to bottom impacting fishing methods (Benthic Protected Areas closures).

Real time closures

31. New Zealand has a number of fisheries which are closely monitored throughout the season and closed when certain limits are met. For example, in the squid trawl fishery the season often ends once a pre-established limit on the number of sea-lions captured has been met. Interestingly, this limit on sealion mortality is combined with a strike rate (estimate of sealions caught per 100 tows) to determine a maximum number of tows in the fishery each season before it is to be closed. Tows are then allocated to fishers according to quota

share, allowing for flexibility in operations during the season and avoiding a race amongst industry players to use up tows early in the season. This provides a good example of how a rights-based system can be combined with other tools to achieve a range of additional management objectives beyond sustainability of target stocks.

Discarding and bycatch

32. New Zealand's primary tool for management of bycatch is the QMS based on individual ITQs. TACCs based on scientific stock assessments are set for bycatch species as well as target species. The TACC for each fishery is then apportioned to quota holders as an ACE according to the percentage of quota each company or individual holds for a fishery. At the end of the fishing year fishers are expected to balance their catch of all species, including bycatch species, with an equivalent amount of catching right (ACE). Fishers will be required to pay "deemed values", an administrative penalty, for any catch that they are unable to cover with ACE, which creates an economic disincentive for the taking of bycatch. This is known as the "catch balancing regime".

33. The catch balancing regime requires deemed values to be set at a level that ensures that fishers do not use deemed values to undermine the QMS, ie that fishers balance their catch with ACE, rather than deemed values. This is an issue that the Ministry of Fisheries has recently been working on and guidelines are now in place for the review of the deemed value of stocks when certain indicators of this behaviour are present.

34. Discarding of fish is an offence under the Fisheries Act except under specific circumstances for non-quota species where reporting requirements have been adhered to and the discarding is done under the supervision of an observer or fishery officer. While high-grading and discarding is known to occur on occasion, it is taken very seriously and prosecuted under our fisheries legislation. Severe penalties for quota/ACE infringements as well as concern about potential damage to the resource (in which quota owners have a long-term vested interest) have been cited as reasons for reductions in dumping since the early days of the QMS.

35. Other sustainability measures include controls to avoid or mitigate bycatch of protected species such as albatross or Hooker sea lions. Technical measures, such as area closures and gear restrictions, are also used.

36. In general, bycatch problems appear to have been reduced by fishers adjusting their catch mix and methods of operation, by the adoption of industry codes of practice, and by the implementation of the catch balancing regime that has evolved to take into account changing circumstances.

Further information

37. For further information please see the attached report: "New Zealand's Quota Management System: A History of the First 20 years" (2007) by K Lock and S Leslie.

STRUCTURAL POLICY

Chapter III of Regulation 2371/2002 obliged Member States to put in place measures to adjust the capacity of their fleets in order to achieve a stable and enduring balance between such fishing capacity and their fishing opportunities. To what extent has this been successful?

38. The capacity management elements of the reformed CFP will prove central to its success, both within EU waters and beyond. Over-capacity leads to over-fishing and economic waste. It also creates incentives for illegal, unregulated and unreported (IUU) fishing.

39. Commission reporting suggests that overcapacity remains an issue in EU fisheries. It has noted that decreases in EU fleet tonnage and power have been offset by a steady increase in the efficiency of its fishing vessels (CEC, 2006a). This overcapacity has negative implications not only for EU resources, but globally. Over a fifth of the EU fleet, by tonnage, operates outside of EU waters (Earle, 2006). As domestic EU management is tightened this figure is likely to increase, indicating that a global approach to capacity management is required in order to prevent displacement of effort into areas outside Commission jurisdiction.

40. Examples of this displacement effect include the growth in the number and capacity of EU-flagged vessels in Pacific region fisheries in the last decade, including since the 2002 CFP reforms. Such capacity increases have been on the high seas and under the auspices of bilateral fishing agreements with Pacific Island countries. This includes tuna fisheries falling under the Western and Central Pacific Fisheries Commission (WCPFC); and pelagic fisheries in relation to the South Pacific Regional Fisheries Management Organisation (SPRFMO), currently under negotiation.

41. While New Zealand recognises the EU's rights to exploit fisheries on the high seas and to enter into fishing agreements with coastal states, the scale of the increases and the fact that they have been accompanied by an increase in EU vessels operating in joint ventures under flags of non-EU members, is of concern. Given the environmental commitments set out in key EU treaties (including Articles 2, 6 and Title XIX of the Treaty establishing the European Community) and in the reformed CFP, New Zealand looks to the EU to provide leadership in the development of capacity and effort management regimes in the WCPFC and negotiations to establish a SPRFMO.

42. The WCPFC is currently facing the challenge of how to limit catch and effort for key target stocks that are currently subject to unsustainable levels of fishing effort—specifically bigeye and yellowfin tuna, and also swordfish. The development aspirations of Pacific Island countries are a key factor in the negotiation of conservation and management measures by the WCPFC and have inevitably led to tensions with distant water fishing nations. The increase of EU fishing capacity in the region—either under EU flags or through joint ventures under other flags—has largely been conducted in a manner consistent with the international legal framework and the measures of the WCPFC. There is no doubt, however, that it has increased pressure on key resources and made agreement on effective management measures more difficult.

43. It is in this context that New Zealand is looking to the Commission to play a strong leadership role on conservation and management measures, including limitations on the introduction of new capacity, within WCPFC. Poor data reporting with respect to fishing by EU-flagged vessels undermines the scientific processes of the WCPFC and increases the need for a more precautionary approach to fisheries management, including with respect to increases in fishing effort.

44. In April/May 2007 fishing capacity limits for pelagic fisheries were agreed in Reñaca, Chile by participants in the negotiations to establish the SPRFMO as part of voluntary interim conservation and management measures pending the adoption and entry into operation of the new Convention. The key measure for pelagic fisheries was to freeze catch capacity for two years. While the freeze did not take effect until 1 January 2008, the EC representative at the negotiations assured other participants that there would be no dramatic increase in EU-flagged vessels prior to that date. Latest information suggests, however, that over the past nine months the number and capacity of EU-flagged and EU-beneficially-owned vessels entering the pelagic fishery has increased considerably. While the increase is not contrary to the letter of the interim measures, the effect has been to test the credibility of both the interim measures and the wider SPRFMO negotiations.

45. The SPRFMO capacity increases may reflect some lack of clarity or effectiveness at the EU level over the Commission's ability to control member state fishing capacity. The entry/exit regime established under Chapter III of Regulation 2371/2002 requires Member States to simply "put in place measures to adjust capacity. . .to achieve a stable and enduring balance between fishing capacity and fishing opportunities." A "stable and enduring balance" is undefined and there is no minimum requirement for what "measures" are necessary. It would seem, therefore, that the Commission may be constrained in its ability to control Member States' fleet movements. If so, this has potentially serious consequences for the Commission's ability to give effect to agreed effort and catch limitations and for the confidence of other States in commitments made by the Commission on behalf of Member States.

46. The EU's subsidy programme was a key factor in undermining the EU's pre-2002 capacity management regime under the Multi-Annual Guidance Programmes (MAGPs). There is a risk that history could repeat itself as fuel costs and engine modernisation continue to be eligible for subsidies, which in some cases are increasing.

47. Against this backdrop of expansion and lack of clarity in fisheries/structural aid policy, New Zealand is concerned that the Commission is in the process of considering exempting the external fleet from the entry/ exit regime (CEC, 2006b). Relaxing the constraints on the size of the EU's external fleet would likely increase pressure on the Commission, which as has been noted, has had difficulty ensuring Member States manage their fishing capacity appropriately. While the fleet segment targets set under the MAGP may have had limited success in preventing overcapacity, the rules and targets for the external fleet should be tightened rather than relaxed if the CFP's sustainability objectives are to be met beyond EU waters.

The new fisheries structural fund, the European Fisheries Fund (EFF), has now come into force. What has been your experience thus far with the new instrument?

48. The adoption of the EFF in 2006 represented a useful continuation of the CFP reform process. Some of the most positive environmental elements include the codification of the phase-out of construction subsidies and the end of joint venture support agreed in 2002. There is also a reorientation of the use of funds towards sustainable development projects.

49. The level of funding available under the EFF (€3.8 billion) and direction of some spending still gives cause for concern, however. Member States rolled back the original EFF proposal made by the Commission by including engine modernisation in the final package. Furthermore, State aid rules were subsequently changed to increase the level of *de minimis* aid for fuel that Member States can provide without notifying the Commission.

50. While it is too early to evaluate the impacts of these developments and the EFF more broadly, it remains a cause for concern that subsidies persist at such levels, contributing to market/trade distortions, overcapacity and overfishing.

What are your views on the possible impact on EU fisheries structural policy of WTO-level discussions as regards subsidies in the fishing sector?

51. Subsidies exacerbate pressure on global fisheries resources and can cause related environmental impacts. Developed country support to the fisheries industry, by distorting competition in fisheries and markets, has also reduced developing country opportunities in a sector so important to their developmental aspirations.

52. The University of British Columbia recently estimated global fisheries subsidies to be between US$30–34 billion per year for the period from 1995–2005 (Sumaila *et al*, 2006). Even those more conservative estimates, such as that of the World Bank (US$14–20 billion), are significant. In contrast with other sectors, such as agriculture, accurate figures are difficult to derive because of the lack of transparency and notification to the WTO.

53. The EU is estimated to be the second largest fisheries subsidiser, as a region, after Asia, with half of its subsidies contributing directly to overcapacity and overfishing (Sumaila *et al*, 2006).

54. The EU is therefore a key player in WTO fisheries subsidies negotiations. These have the potential to deliver significant wins for trade, the environment and for development. They represent a major opportunity to establish binding global rules on the types of subsidies that are permitted, and under what circumstances.

55. New Zealand is arguing for a broad ban on most fisheries subsidies, with a narrow list of exceptions for benign or positive subsidies such as vessel decommissioning together with Special and Differential Treatment for developing countries.

56. The EU, in contrast, advocates a narrow ban. While it states that it is seeking a major environmental outcome from the Doha Round overall, in perhaps the most important area the EU has positioned itself on what New Zealand considers to be the wrong side of the debate, together with the principal defenders of subsidies such as Japan, South Korea and Chinese Taipei.

57. The EU appears to us to be seeking to use the WTO negotiations to codify the EFF, instead of raising the bar for itself and the rest of the international community. As with other areas of the negotiation, the EC and other countries must be prepared to show flexibilities beyond their existing policy settings.

58. As a progressive Member State on fisheries policy, the UK has an important role to play in pressing the Commission and other Member States to achieve comprehensive and effective disciplines on fisheries subsidies within the WTO.

59. In New Zealand's view, the WTO fisheries subsidy negotiations are an area where EU policies would benefit from greater consistency. The EU has made a number of high-level EU legal and political commitments which sit uneasily with its current negotiating position. These include the revised EU Sustainable Development Strategy (SDS) adopted in 2006, with endorsement from the EU Council, which calls for further reforms of EU subsidies "that have considerable negative effects on the environment and are incompatible with sustainable development, with a view to gradually eliminating them." Such a roadmap for fisheries subsidies has not been developed, and the position of the EU in the WTO is contrary to such calls for reform by EU Heads of States.

REFERENCES

CEC (2006a) *Communication from the Commission to the Council and the European Parliament on Improving the Economic Situation in the Fishing Industry*. COM(2006)103, Brussels, 09.03.2006.

CEC (2006b) *"Study on the European Union external fleet" Open Call for Tenders*. Reference No FISH/2006/02.

Earle M (2006) *Paying for Unsustainable Fisheries: Where the European Union Spends its Money*. pp. 227–242 in: Lavigne, D. M. (ed.). Gaining Ground: In Pursuit of Ecological Sustainability. International Fund for Animal Welfare, Guelph, Canada, and University of Limerick, Ireland. 425 pp.

Council of the European Union, *Renewed EU Sustainable Development Strategy*, Brussels, 9 June 2006. 10117/06

Sumaila, U R, Pauly, D. (eds.), (2006) *Catching more bait: a bottom-up re-estimation of global fisheries subsidies*. Fisheries Centre Research Reports 14(6), pp.2. Fisheries Centre, the University of British Columbia, Vancouver, Canada.

February 2008

Memorandum by the New Zealand Seafood Industry Council

SUMMARY

This submission is on behalf of the New Zealand seafood industry. Our interest in submitting arises from the fact that the EU is now our leading export market and the New Zealand seafood industry is encountering competition for distant water fishing resources from vessels originating from the Community fishing in the Pacific area.

The submission responds to most of the questions in the context of New Zealand fisheries and our experience of operating under a strictly enforced quota management system that manages fisheries primarily by controlling catch limits. Fishers have strong economic incentives to operate responsibly through their access rights being expressed as Individual Transferable Quota that has the legal character of being a tradeable, perpetual property right.

INTRODUCTION

1. The New Zealand Seafood Industry Council welcomes the opportunity to comment on progress of the Common Fisheries Policy since its reform in 2002.

2. The New Zealand Seafood Industry Council is a company formed by representative organisations of commercial stakeholders in the fisheries and aquaculture sectors in New Zealand to advise them and represent their common interests to government and wider publics in New Zealand. The Council supplies policy and technical advice to its shareholders and advocates on their behalf. Its governance structure as a limited liability company has been chosen as it imposes high levels of transparency; however, the Council performs functions for its stakeholders that are similar to those provided by Associations representing the fishing and aquaculture sectors in other jurisdictions.

3. The context of the evidence provided is that the countries that make up the European Union now collectively provide the leading export market for New Zealand fish and fish products—and have done so for the last decade. New Zealand is a small producer of fish and fish products. It accounts for less than 1% by volume of global production and supplies less 2% by value of the fish and fish products in global trade. But it is significant to the New Zealand economy, as it is the fifth largest export goods sector and more than 90% by value of landings and production of fish and fish products are exported.

4. In addition to the European Union being the leading export market for New Zealand companies, New Zealand fishing companies are encountering competition for access to resources from distant water fishing operations from the European Union in the Pacific Ocean and Antarctica. There is some evidence of co-operation between New Zealand fishing companies and fishing companies from the European Union. One example is cooperation between New Zealand companies and a UK company in fishing in the South Atlantic Ocean and in the Antarctic zone.

5. The New Zealand commercial fishery operates under a strictly enforced quota management system (QMS). Fishers access the fishery through individualised access rights founded on Individual Transferable Quotas (ITQs). These are proportional rights to fish stocks that have private property characteristics of being in perpetuity and being tradeable between rights owners. ITQs are expressed annually as shares of the Total

Allowable Commercial Catch called Annual Catch Entitlements (ACE). Catches of fish stocks that are included in the QMS must be accounted for with ACE or penalty payments made to the Ministry of Fisheries. There is a very active trading market for ACE, as a result. Trading of ITQ is less frequent.

6. ITQ is a property right and is recorded as an asset on the balance sheets of fishing companies. Company law in New Zealand requires that Directors act in the best long term interests of their companies and imposes a fiduciary duty to look after the assets of the company. Thus there is a legal intersection between the obligations of company law and the Fisheries Act that provides strong incentives for fishing rights owners to behave responsibly.

7. New Zealand is an isolated country surrounded by the fourth largest Exclusive Economic Zone (EEZ) in the world. The New Zealand EEZ contacts the Australian AFZ at two points only; otherwise the border of the EEZ is the high seas of the Pacific and Southern Oceans. Only a very small part of the stocks of the EEZ straddle the boundary to the high seas and due to its southerly position, the EEZ is visited by a relatively small proportion of the highly migratory fish stocks of the western Pacific Ocean. We are conscious that this is a very different resource and ocean context to that faced by the United Kingdom and the European Union at large. We do not presume that the solutions that New Zealand has chosen for fisheries management will be appropriate in all circumstances for the European Union. However we do, in large part share a cultural and institutional heritage and the mechanisms that have been employed in fisheries management in New Zealand have a strong rooting in British legal and social heritage.

CONSERVATION AND MANAGEMENT

8. The New Zealand QMS requires that Total Allowable Catches (TACs) are set for all stocks in the system. After provision is made for non-commercial catch interests in each TAC (for Customary Maori and recreational proposes) the remaining TAC is available for commercial catch and is called the Total Allowable Commercial Catch (TACC) In the last 10 years there has been a significant expansion of the number of species and stocks in the QMS and therefore stocks managed through the setting of TACs and TACCs. Currently there are 96 species or groups of species and over 600 stocks in the QMS.

9. TACCs are applied to all key target stocks and most bycatch stocks with commercial value. All catch of QMS stocks must be retained and counted against ACE. If a TACC for a stock is fully utilised and the stock is still being caught, it must be retained on board and a penalty payment (Deemed Value) made to the Crown that has the effect of removing any commercial benefit. Deliberate overcatch of a TACC is an offence. The result of this policy is that a large proportion of mainly bycatch stocks are not fully caught—and none of the key target stocks is systemically overcaught. Legalised dumping of overcatch, which is a feature of the EU management system at present, does not occur in New Zealand as it is illegal.

10. The commercial sector strongly supports the QMS, the access and property rights that it provides through ITQ and ACE, and is strongly committed to fisheries management using scientific and other evidence-based TAC setting. The industry is confident that output controls that limit fishing mortality, translated to an individual enterprise/fisher level, is the most appropriate way to manage fisheries for long term sustainability in the New Zealand context. The capacity for directly linking evidence from fishing, backed by scientific analysis, to catch limits on resources provides strong incentives for responsible individual and collective behaviour and strong incentives for stakeholders to want to take greater responsibility for fisheries management decision making. There is a growing body of evidence of commercial stakeholders calling for more conservative catch limits and actively cooperating with the government in ensuring that catch limits are set appropriately to ensure long term fish stock sustainability, even when the economic impacts of those decisions are known to be significantly negative for stakeholders.

11. Effort limitation has no industry support as a primary tool for management, although some effort based tools are deployed for a variety of secondary management purposes. One example is to limit access for larger (over 43metre) vessels to coastal fisheries, which acts a protective measure for smaller vessel operators. In general however, effort controls are not regarded as effective tools in controlling fishing mortality in the absence of TACs.

12. Spatial management tools have a place as secondary management tools to manage fishing related impacts on identified geographic or biodiversity features. They are not supported as core tools for managing sustainable utilisation of fisheries resources.

13. Fish stocks fluctuate naturally in response to variations in the ecosystem and fisheries management is an exercise in controlling human impacts on fish stocks within bounds that can deliver long term sustainable utilisation. Therefore if one of the impacts on ecosystems is climate change (or fluctuation) the fisheries management system that controls human impact must be flexible and be able to take account of exogenous

impacts on fish stock abundance. The New Zealand experience to date suggests that managing fisheries by instruments that directly control output—ie TACs and TACCs—is more effective than indirect input controls including capacity management tools.

CONTROL AND ENFORCEMENT

14. It has already been noted that ITQ is a property right under New Zealand law. It is a logical step in the New Zealand context to punish fisheries transgressions in the context of other crimes against property. The penalties that can follow even simple failure to meet statutory reporting requirements are heavy. Deliberate flouting of the Act can result in fines of hundreds of thousands of dollars, imprisonment and forfeiture to the Crown of physical property such as vessels and vehicles used in the committing of the offence.

15. Respect for property in capitalist societies thrives when it can be defended at law. The New Zealand industry experience of others lack of respect for fishing quotas and allocations has been most apparent in its experience with regional fisheries management agreements. For example under the Convention for Conservation of Southern Bluefin Tuna, New Zealand has an annual allocation of 420 tonnes that is managed in New Zealand through the QMS system with the distribution of ITQ in the fishery to individual fishers in New Zealand. The Convention has been challenged recently by instances of significant and systemic overcatch of other member states' quotas by their fishers. Such overcatch, if it had occurred in New Zealand, would have led to the individuals being investigated and criminally prosecuted and they would very likely have suffered severe penalties personally and so would their businesses. No similar penalties have been exacted on the individuals and firms that overcaught southern bluefin in the other member states and while the quota for one member has been reduced, there has been no attempt made to pursue the overcatch action to the individuals and firms that caused it.

16. The differences in treatment of illegal fishing between countries that share interests in the same resource is a significant issue. Capital is mobile and will move to the jurisdictions where the costs are least and the benefits are greatest, all other things being equal. It is of fundamental importance that illegal fishing is dealt with firmly and that fishers are provided with strong incentives—such as secure access rights—that will encourage responsible and compliant behaviour.

STRUCTURAL POLICY

17. Most of the questions the Committee asks on the impacts of structural policy are outside our experience and we are unable to comment effectively. However the Committee asks "What are your views on the possible impact . . .of WTO-level discussions as regards subsidies in the fishing sector?"

18. The New Zealand fishing industry has strongly backed the position that New Zealand has taken at the WTO to develop comprehensive rules under the Subsidies and Countervailing Measures Agreement that will reduce and eliminate subsidies to fishing industries. Our industry focus is on subsidies that have the effect of undermining the New Zealand industry's competitiveness in international markets.

19. Our competitive reality is that fishing industries that can supply markets with fish products that have been assisted to those markets with the aid of subsidies that reduce their operating costs—eg subsidised fuel, bait, vessel modernisation, subsidies to assist vessels to move to distant water fisheries, crew support etcetera—can supply fish at lower prices for longer than New Zealand.

20. The New Zealand fishing and aquaculture sectors receive no direct subsidies from Government. Rather they are levied for the full attributable costs that the Government incurs in managing fisheries—including the research costs incurred to determine advice on TAC setting. The cost recovery levies amount to more than NZ$30 million annually and represent more than 5% of the landed value of fish.

21. The fishing industry the world over is suffering high fuel costs, a weak US dollar that is the international currency that the fish business is conducted in. The New Zealand industry has also had to face up to some significant quota cuts. It has coped with these challenges by reducing costs, reducing vessel numbers and personnel and moving a significant part of the processing sector off-shore. The New Zealand fishing industry does not have any overcapacity as the ITQ system ensures that the sector is able to rationalise readily by trading to take account of resource and market changes. The harsh down-side of this is that fishing businesses are permitted to fail and the employees of failed businesses can find themselves unemployed. But the companies that remain are financially secure, conservatively managed and collectively confident of their long-term survival.

CONCLUSION

22. This submission has promoted the benefits that the New Zealand seafood industry is convinced have arisen from a property rights-based, fisheries output management system. We acknowledge that implementing such a management regime would be very much more complicated when the resources are shared among several nations with differing compliance and enforcement regimes.

February 2008

Memorandum by Oceana

INTRODUCTION

1. Founded in 2001, Oceana is an international non governmental organisation dedicated to researching, protecting and restoring the world's oceans. Teams of marine scientists, economists, policy specialists and other experts work together to campaign to tackle destructive fishing practices and marine pollution. Current fisheries campaigns include eliminating illegal driftnets from the Mediterranean Sea, advocating for a ban on discards and reduction of by-catches in the EU, developing and implementing effective measures for shark conservation and establishing global rules on subsidies at the WTO.

2. Oceana is active in many European countries and in the European institutions and has staff based in Brussels and Madrid. The organisation also works on and under the ocean with its research catamaran, the Oceana Ranger, where teams of divers and scientists record and compile extensive field research data to support its policy work.

THE 2002 REVIEW OF THE CFP

3. The so-called reviewed "CFP Framework Regulation" (2371/2002), was the result of long negotiations and compromises between the EU Member States. As a result, the Regulation did not fully match the ambitions that the European Commission set out to achieve when it launched the reform process. However, the Regulation does set out commitments for Member States, including finding a balance between fishing capacity and resources. It also provided the European Union with potential legal tools to develop a fisheries management framework capable of improving the situation of fish stocks, the marine environment and fishing communities in the European Union, such as the implementation of management and recovery plans.

4. However, the Framework Regulation was only the very beginning of a long process of making European fisheries more sustainable. Much "daughter legislation" was going to be needed to implement the good intentions agreed by the EU Ministers in December 2002. It is in the implementation phase of the reviewed CFP that the situation has floundered and where much remains to be done.

5. The recent Court of Auditors Report on the control, inspection and sanctions systems relating to the rules on conservation of Community fisheries resources corroborates what Oceana and other NGOs have been highlighting for a number of years: that the CFP is failing to find the solutions to the chronic problems in European fisheries. It is widely acknowledged that over 80% of stocks evaluated by ICES are overexploited, that the EU fleet is 40% too large for available resources, that subsidies continue to fuel overfishing; that significant quantities of unwanted or non quota fish continue to be discarded or illegally marketed; that illegal fishing is still rife in the European Union.

6. Exhaustive answers to all the questions raised by the Committee could fill many pages. Therefore the Oceana comments will focus on those areas where we have active campaigns and have conducted research and investigation work.

CONSERVATION AND MANAGEMENT

Scientific Advice

7. The most recent advice from the International Council for the Exploration of the Sea (ICES) to the European Commission pointed out that of the EU stocks it assessed only 13 are exploited in a sustainable manner while 28 are outside safe biological limits and 18 were in such a bad state that the advice was for zero catches. No reliable advice can be presented for 56 stocks because of incomplete scientific evaluation due to poor availability of data. This means that three quarters of the stocks with enough scientific coverage are at least outside safe biological limits and that scientific advice and data collection should be reinforced.

Moreover, Oceana analysis has discovered that over the last 20 years ICES has provided more than 1,500 pieces of advice to the Commission and other governments in the North East Atlantic, of which only 350 (22%) have been respected, whilst over 1200 have been ignored.

Sharks

8. Several hundreds of marine species are commercialized in the EU, but less than 50 are managed, scientifically evaluated and their exploitation limited by quotas. In the group of unmanaged species are sharks and their relatives (skates, rays and chimeras). 150 species are common in European waters and there is a large and well developed shark fishery (for valuable fins, liver, cartilage and meat) by European Union vessels both in EU waters, in the EEZs of third countries and on the high seas. But despite this large fishery, only very few shark species have any kind of catch limitation. In the few cases where scientific advice has been available, this has been disregarded. A key example is the spurdog (*Squalus acanthias*), otherwise known as the spiny dogfish, which is heavily targeted for its meat to satisfy the constant European demand, especially in the UK, Germany, Belgium, France and Italy. Years of overfishing, particularly that of aggregations of pregnant females, have made the Northeast Atlantic stock one of the most depleted in the world. The UK, France, and Ireland are the main countries targeting spurdog in the Northeast Atlantic through various bottom trawl, line and gillnet fisheries; landings are also common from the Scottish demersal trawl fleet. The IUCN Red List classifies this species as Critically Endangered in the Northeast Atlantic. Despite an ICES recommendation for a zero TAC and a reduction of by-catch to the lowest possible levels in all areas of the NE Atlantic, the recent by-catch TAC adopted for 2008 was fixed at 2635 tons. Oceana is recommending that scientific advice should be followed and a recovery plan established for this and other threatened shark species as part of the current development of an EU Plan of Action for the Conservation and Management of Sharks, which is due to be published by the Commission before the end of 2008.

9. Oceana's shark campaign is also working to strengthen the EU Shark Finning Regulation (1185/2003), which aimed to stop the process of removing sharks fins and discarding the less valuable carcasses. This Regulation is worth highlighting here as it is a good example of where an agreed legislation, following much compromise, leads to complicated Regulations that are almost impossible to control and enforce. The removal of shark fins on board vessels is allowed in some cases and a "fin to carcass" ratio is used to prevent the discarding of the carcass. The ratio implies that the amount of shark fins removed on board and landed cannot exceed 5% of the weight of the whole sharks landed. This already complicated ratio system is further complicated by another loophole which allows fishermen to land shark fins and carcasses in different ports, making the current regulation over-complicated, unenforceable and unworkable. A simple solution would be to remove the derogation allowing fins to be removed on board and requiring sharks to be landed with their fins attached.

Discards

10. Discards are the portion of the animal catch that is thrown away at sea. Although data on discards are hard to come by, it is estimated that at least 1.3 million tons of marine organisms are discarded in European waters every year, 12% of the catch. In some fisheries discards rates of up to 90% have been recorded.

11. As well as being a waste of fisheries resources, discards also hinder the implementation of effective management measures for sustainable fisheries since discards volumes are rarely reported and thus represent an unknown portion of biomass which is extracted from the sea. As scientists do not receive information about what is really being taken, the models used for evaluating the state of fishing grounds become dubious or even erroneous.

12. The reasons for discarding are various, but can be the result of legal constraints under the current Common Fisheries Policy. For example, the fish caught may be below the legal minimum size or the allocated fishing quota may have been reached. However, other discards are economic in nature: organisms may be thrown back because they have no commercial value or also because they have commercial value but less than that of other specimens caught (high grading).

13. This issue of discarding fish has been a highly criticized element of the CFP for many years. An earlier attempt to tackle the issue taken by the Commission in 2002 was not developed and now the Commission has published its plans for a radical overhaul of the system and aims to gradually implement a ban on discards in the EU, supported by other complementary measures.

14. Oceana supports the implementation of a discards ban on a fishery by fishery basis, accompanied by supplementary measures relevant to the fishery concerned such as the improvement of gear selectivity, real-time closures, and an obligation to change fishing grounds. Such a radical change of policy would have

considerable short term consequences on the sector, but it is an essential measure to achieve long term sustainability of fisheries. It should be remembered that the key aim of a ban on discards is to eventually reduce by-catches to as close to zero as possible, meaning that a vessel targeting a species would on the whole only be landing the target species.

CONTROL AND ENFORCEMENT

15. Oceana agrees with the recommendations in the Court of Auditors Report on the control, inspection and sanctions systems relating to the rules on conservation of Community fisheries resources. The lack of effective control and enforcement mechanisms means that rules can be and are often flouted and this often undermines the effectiveness of other measures taken to implement sustainable fisheries in the EU.

Illegal Use of Driftnets by EU vessels

16. Oceana has been campaigning to eliminate illegal driftnets from the European Union for a number of years. Its research and observations have highlighted a number of issues of relevance to the issues of illegal fisheries, control and enforcement.

17. Since Regulation 894/97, amended by Regulation 1239/98, came into effect in 2002 the use of driftnets of more than 2.5km length or for the capture of certain pelagic species is banned in EU waters and for any EU flagged vessel. More than five years later this destructive fishing gear is still used in the Mediterranean. During its 2007 driftnet campaign in ports and on the water Oceana found 69 French driftnet vessels using the illegal driftnets locally called thonaille and 84 Italian driftnet vessels. These vessels were targeting bluefin tuna and swordfish. Moreover, among the vessels observed in 2007 with illegal driftnets on board, 18 of them had already been denounced by Oceana to the authorities for using driftnets in 2006.

18. Apart from the fact that the observed vessels were using illegal fishing gear, further findings include: swordfish and bluefin tuna catches and landings of both the Italian and French fleets were apparently not all declared to ICCAT and the EU, although this is a legal requirement; moreover in the case of a number of Italian driftnet vessels, landings and sales take place illegally and completely outside any formal management structure. Also a large number of Italian vessels using illegal driftnets had received European fishing subsidies to assist in the reconversion away from driftnet fishing during the FIFG funding period 2000–06 and continue to fish with this gear.

19. In order to eliminate this illegal activity Oceana has recommended:

— Improving the cross checking of information between relevant administrations and Regional Fisheries Management Organisations—transparency in information between actors involved must be put in place and is an essential measure for control improvement.

— Development of an effective and deterrent sanction system.

— Implementation of a system of reimbursement of subsidies received in the event of infringement of the rules.

— Adequate control in ports is a key issue, both in terms of fishing gears and landings.

— Improved mechanisms should be put in place to oblige Member States to ensure coherence of national legislation with the EU Regulations. For example recent French decrees allowing the use of thonaille—considered an illegal gear at the EU level—highlight the lack coherence that can arise between national and European level rules.

STRUCTURAL POLICY

20. Finding a balance between fleet capacity and available resources would be a major step forward to achieving sustainable fisheries in Europe. Many of the problems that arise in our waters result from overcapacity of the European fleet. Unfortunately to date, a solution has not been found. Despite some measures in place to help Member States reduce capacity in their fleets (eg, public funding, capacity ceilings), if capacity is reducing at all, it is reducing at such a low rate that this is being "overtaken" by so-called technological creep—ie reductions are more than compensated for by the improvements in technology which make it possible to catch more fish per unit of effort.

European Fisheries Fund

21. The European Fisheries Fund (EFF) contains measures that are an improvement on the previous instrument, the Financial Instrument for Fisheries Guidance (FIFG). As well as no longer supporting subsidies for construction and export of capacity overseas, it also places more value on sustainability and environmental measures. However, the EFF contains elements that could encourage an increase in fishing capacity.

22. Fleet modernisation is still supported under the EFF, in the guise of public funding for replacing engines. At a time of chronic overcapacity in the EU fleet and considering the increased fishing potential (technological creep) associated with vessel modernization, this measure is likely to increase pressure on fish stocks and is unacceptable. Subsidies under the EFF should be targeted at adapting the EU fleet to resources, with the phasing out of unselective fishing techniques (ie certain trawling methods) as a priority.

23. It is also essential that other environmentally damaging subsidies are eliminated, such as fuel subsidies provided by Member States. These subsidies increase the fishing sectors dependence on state assistance rather than assisting in the long term restructuring of the sector.

WTO- level discussions on subsidies

24. According to a report by the University of British Columbia (Sumaila and Pauly, 2006), global fisheries subsidies amount to an estimated US$30 to US$34 billion annually. Of these they estimate that about US$2.5 billion is received by the European fisheries sector. However, it is difficult to provide more than an estimate as subsidies can take many forms such as assistance with social security, tax exemptions, grants and are also provided by many different authorities. Not all subsidies can be considered as "harmful" and fuel overfishing, but the vast majority drive increased and intensified fishing.

25. Concerns about the decline in world fish populations and the relationship of subsidies to overcapacity and overfishing led to the inclusion of fisheries subsidies in the current WTO Doha trade round. The Doha round negotiations represent a good opportunity to address the fisheries subsidies issue on a global scale. The draft text currently being negotiated contains a strong prohibition on subsidies that increase overcapacity and overfishing, including subsidies for vessel construction and operating costs.

26. A broad prohibition of fisheries subsidies is the only approach that will effectively help curtail global overfishing. To the extent that some subsidies are not prohibited, they should remain subject to WTO review and disciplines to check against risks that they might cause unforeseen increases in capacity or fishing effort. In addition, stronger provisions on notification and review of subsidies would increase transparency and help ensure that subsidies are consistent with resource sustainability objectives.

27. Since there would be a transition period for the implementation of any potential agreement once it came into effect, the current EFF would not be affected until 2011 or 2012 at the earliest. The text, as it currently stands, would affect a number of areas covered by Community legislation, notably engine modernisation, fishing infrastructure, support for the fish processing industry (including fuel, income and price subsidies) and, to a certain extent, the indirect subsidies provided to the fisheries sector via the conclusion of Fisheries Partnership Agreements with third countries. Therefore any WTO agreement would "tie in" the European Union to eliminate those subsidies that contribute to increase fishing pressure and would ensure that other capacity enhancing subsidies could not be introduced either.

GOVERNANCE

28. Over the past years, the awareness and knowledge of the crisis facing European fisheries has increased greatly. However, this increased awareness has not adequately been translated into policy changes to lead European Fisheries on the road to recovery. The momentum that surrounded the CFP reform in 2002 has somewhat diminished. The reasons are numerous and varied, but a few observations should be noted here. Vested interests in the fisheries sector continue to lobby hard for a maintenance of the status quo; Member State governments are reluctant to take decisions that will have a short term effect on fisheries dependent communities despite any long term benefits that could be achieved; the European institutional bodies and national governments continue to consider this issue of "fisheries" as not in their domain which has the effect leaving policy and decision-making in the hands of a restricted group of people.

29. Regional Advisory Councils (RACs), established by Regulation 2371/2002 are at various stages of development, with some up and running effectively and others still being developed. Although Oceana does not sit on any RACs, one clear issue does arise that would need to be resolved if any decision-making power was given to these bodies. Environmental organisations only hold very few seats on RACs, hence environmental views will always be in a minority, with the fishing sector's opinion always being in the majority. This lack of balance is inevitably reflected in opinions published by the RACs.

28 February 2008

Memorandum by Sainsbury's plc

INTRODUCTION

— We are pleased to be able to respond to the Committee's inquiry into the Common Fisheries Policy. We are one of the biggest fish retailers in the UK, selling over £400 million worth of fish in our stores last year. We have over 300 fish counters in our stores across the UK, and are the UK's largest retailer of MSC-certified fish, both in terms of range and turnover. We are committed to doubling this figure by the end of this year.

— We thought it would be helpful to the Committee if we put in context our approach to sourcing fish sustainably. We have also answered some of the questions posed by the Committee on the CFP.

OUR WORK ON SOURCING FISH SUSTAINABLY

— Our sustainability rating system: In 2006 we conducted a major review of our fish sourcing policies. We worked closely with the Marine Conservation Society and a number of other key stakeholders, including suppliers, boat skippers, aquaculture experts, government representatives and specialist campaigning organisations. This led to the development of our own sustainability rating system. Working on a traffic light basis, the system gives a sustainability rating for all the fish we sell:

Green means the fish has been scientifically verified as in plentiful supply and is fully sustainable.

Amber means there are some concerns about sustainability, but action is being taken to resolve them.

Red means there are major concerns about sustainability, so we will not sell it.

— As a result of this system, we no longer sell any red-rated fish and are working with suppliers to move any amber-rated fish to green status. We have already removed skate and huss from our shelves, and now take squid from a more sustainable source as a result of this assessment process.

— 80% of the fish we sell comes from five species—cod, haddock, salmon, tuna and prawns. This places huge pressure on the stocks of these species. Through the development of our rating system we hope to move all these species to "green" by 2010.

— Sustainable fishing practices: Alongside our rating system, we also work to develop higher standards of sustainability in fishing practices. Examples include:

(i) Wild: Line-caught wild fish: Line-caught is a less destructive, more sustainable alternative to trawling. It also ensures that fish suffer minimal stress and damage during capture. 100% of our fresh cod and haddock is now line-caught, accounting for nearly 10,000 tonnes a year. This makes us the largest retailer of line-caught cod and haddock in the UK. Furthermore, fresh line catching vessels fish for shorter periods—from one to three days maximum. Robust environmental assessments: We carry out environmental impact assessments using independent scientific data. Where data is lacking, we have commissioned further studies. Where we are aware of particular risks relating to fishing methods or species, we have commissioned independent scientists to verify the sustainability rating that we have given to the species that we sell.

(ii) Farmed: Sustainable feed: The origin of feed for our farmed fish is an important issue. We therefore apply our sustainability rating system to species used for fish feed, ensuring our processes are sustainable right the way through from egg to plate. Reducing pollutants: We avoid substances that may pollute the marine environment. For us, sustainable fisheries and protection of the marine environment go hand in hand: it is impossible to address one concern whilst neglecting the other. For example, we are working closely with our suppliers to eliminate the use of anti-foulants for cleaning fishing nets. We are encouraging our suppliers to return to traditional manual methods of cleaning their nets.

— We also stock the widest range of MSC-certified products, currently offering over 20 MSC-certified fresh and processed products. Furthermore, in January 2008, we became the first retailer to introduce MSC-certified canned tuna—Albacore tuna.

— Promoting sustainable alternatives: Offering more sustainable alternatives to our customers is an important part of our approach. We have recently reintroduced more sustainable alternatives to cod, such as pollock and hoki. We now buy more local pollock than any other UK retailer.

— We promote these alternatives to our customers through use of recipe "Try" Tip Cards, our "New In Season" promotions and the Sainsbury's Magazine. Our trained fish counter staff also offer advice on cooking and preparation.

STAKEHOLDER ENGAGEMENT

— We engaged with stakeholders throughout the development of our rating system, as well as on specific issues, and we continue to share best practice through the fishing industry. For example, our discussions with Greenpeace on beam-trawling contributed to our decision to move our cod and haddock to line caught methods.

— Seafood Retailer of the Year: In September 2007, in recognition of our positive contribution to the fishing industry, we were awarded the Seafish "Seafood Retailer of the Year" Award.

THE ISSUES

CONSERVATION/MANAGEMENT

1. *Chapter II of Regulation 2371/2002 on the conservation and sustainable exploitation of fisheries resources under the Common Fisheries Policy introduced new methods of ensuring conservation and sustainability, including recovery plans, management plans and emergency measures. To what extent have these been effective?*

These are welcome additions to the CFP and we have seen some positive effects already, such as a recovery in some fish stocks. This is a result of the increased management of fisheries and the enforcement of quotas.

We support and appreciate this range of measures within the CFP on the basis that they are supported by adequate scientific evidence in order for the International Council for the Exploration of the Seas (ICES) to accurately model the impact of such measures on fish stocks.

2. *A wide range of management tools are available to fisheries managers. What are your views on the following tools:*

a. *Total Allowable Catches*
b. *Effort limitation, including "days at sea", marine conservation areas and real-time closures*
c. *Rights-Based Management tools*
d. *Technical Conservation Measures*

Total Allowable Catches: All of these are welcome components of the CFP. TACs play a major role in most fishery management processes and, if implemented and enforced effectively, are important ways of reducing levels of discard.

We are, however, concerned that TACs are difficult to enforce in fisheries where discarding takes place at a significant level. A quota system, which allows fish that are either over-quota or under-sized to be discarded, is severely flawed. The CFP must take a fresh look at eliminating discarding through enhancements to the TAC rules.

Days at sea: These are also an effective means of effort limitation but the interaction between TACs and days at sea is a complex one and needs further consideration.

There is a clear and overwhelming body of evidence which suggests that fishery closures and Marine Protected Areas (marine reserves) play an important role in fishery productivity and the North East Atlantic fisheries need to review how these can be implemented on a wider scale to both protect sensitive marine environments and enhance fish stock recruitment.

Rights based management tools: Tools such as individual transferable quotas (ITQs) have had proven benefits in well managed fisheries outside of the CFP such as in Iceland and should be considered very seriously as a potential major reform to future CFP amendments.

Technical Conservation Measures: Some TCMs such as mesh size are made compulsory across EU fisheries yet others such as separator grid escape panels are often not. TCMs such as nets with technical adaptations, eg sorting grids and escape panels, are fundamental in reducing by-catch. The mixed fisheries for haddock, whiting and certain nephrops fisheries are of particular concern due to the high level of cod by-catch for example, and fleets in these fisheries should be required to introduce more selective gear. There is need for a review of how TCMs are implemented within the catching sector and wherever possible this should not be left on a voluntary basis with the catching sector (although assisted funding for vessels may need to be made available in order to implement this if there is a significant change to gear configuration).

3. *To what extent have current management tools increased the levels of discards and by-catch? What is your view on how these problems can best be tackled?*

This is an issue of paramount importance with a range of possible solutions—the current Minimum Landing Size must be removed and replaced with a plan that would establish a "trigger point" for capture of juveniles, which is constantly monitored and once exceeded leads to a fishery zone closure to enable depleted stocks to replenish.

4. *Do you consider that fisheries management policies may need to adapt to climate change? If so, how might this be achieved?*

In our view, ocean acidification is the biggest challenge facing fisheries and the marine environment. The increased pH levels of the world's oceans will have a significant effect on the productivity of marine eco-systems. This could lead to a worldwide decline in areas favourable to coral reef growth, as well as major changes in marine ecosystems affecting the marine food chain, and a reduced ability for oceans to absorb carbon dioxide. This must be recognised by government and the EU as a major issue.

CONTROL AND ENFORCEMENT

5. *Chapter V of Regulation 2371/2002 lays down the responsibilities of the Member States and the Commission as regards the control and enforcement of the rules of the Common Fisheries Policy. The recent Court of Auditors Report on the control, inspection and sanctions systems relating to the rules on conservation of Community fisheries resources was very sceptical of the systems currently in place. What is your view of the efficacy of the systems in place? To what extent has the Community Fisheries Control Agency already assisted in improving matters?*

We have seen some encouraging signs from the CFCA which has sought to harmonise fishing practices across the EC, but it is too early to comment yet on the efficacy of their systems. We naturally welcome the initiative to harmonise implementation and enforcement measures across the Community.

6. *The European Commission has regularly highlighted how serious infringements of the CFP are penalised differently across the Community. This was a matter that was also raised by the Court of Auditors and sanctions were included in the recent Commission Proposal in IUU fishing. What is your view on the issue?*

Punishments against fishermen who engage in Illegal, Unregulated and Undeclared (IUU) fishing should be draconian and sufficient to discourage the practice—although the economic motivations of IUU needs to be addressed by Member States.

One very important area that could affect supplies into the UK for all retailers and have a negative impact on developing countries, are the EU-proposed IUU regulations. The regulations are currently in draft form, but potentially look like a major barrier to trade for such countries if they go through in their current form.

The EU proposals to help combat IUU fishing are distinctly disadvantageous to developing countries. The introduction of a paperwork system to accompany each fish from catch to processing is concerning on two counts: (i) the chopping up of fish into separate cuts, each of which will need a certificate, will increase the level of paperwork and cost to all involved along the supply chain; (ii) this overly complex system requires heavy investment, a good level of literacy and a high level of technology on the part of all states. Developing countries lack the financial resource for many of these activities, so while EU Member States will be able to continue to fish and work in accordance with the new regulations, the UK could potentially lose out on supply from important fisheries in developing parts of the world. The working party run by the Food and Drink

Federation, in which we take part, has been working on a proposal in response to the EU's draft proposals, in which this concern will be made clear. It is important to note that while we would welcome any move to eliminate IUU, an overly simplistic, "one-size fits all nations" approach may not work.

GOVERNANCE

10. *As a result of Regulation 2371/2002, Regional Advisory Councils (RACs) were established to advise the Commission on matters of fisheries management in respect of certain sea areas or fishing zones. What is your assessment of the success thus far of the RACs? What is your view on their future evolution?*

RACs bring a local feel to fisheries management and in our view would be the ideal way to govern EU fisheries. These councils will help the Commission draft legislative proposals for the CFP, but, bearing in mind that the first RAC in the Baltic Sea is only just beginning to function, we are as yet unclear how effective such organisations will be in helping to formulate fisheries policy across the EU.

February 2008

Memorandum by Shetland Ocean's Alliance (SHOAL)

BACKGROUND

Shetland is an island community with a high level of economic and social dependence on fish catching. As such, it has a strong interest in how fisheries are managed, and in ensuring a sustainable future for the fishing industry. It also has considerable experience of the effects that the Common Fisheries Policy has had.

The Shetland Ocean's Alliance (SHOAL) is a partnership between the Shetland Islands Council and the Shetland Fishing Industry to promote the industry's sustainable long-term future.

REVIEW OF THE COMMON FISHERIES POLICY

0.1) In general terms, our view is that the 2002 review has had little substantive effect on the CFP or its implementation. Although some new initiatives have been introduced, the basic structure, mechanisms and philosophy of the CFP remain unchanged, and little has been done to address the well-known problems from which it suffers.

CONSERVATION / MANAGEMENT

1) *New methods of ensuring conservation and sustainability*

1.1) Up to a point the new (and existing) management measures may be said to have been at least partially successful. However, the new measures share many of the problems of existing ones. In general they serve as fairly blunt instruments, lack flexibility, are often draconian in nature, and may create as many problems as they are supposed to solve. Difficulties commonly arise from the fact that single management measures are often applied universally across a diverse and complex fishing industry in a "one-size-fits-all" approach.

2) *Management Tools*

2.1) A major failing of the CFP is that new management tools are added in a cumulative manner, constantly increasing the complexity of the fisheries management system. These tools may frequently have unintended consequences, which then engender further new management measures in an endless cycle of "tinkering" and increasing complexity. Fisheries managers appear unable ever to admit that a management mechanism hasn't worked, to scrap it, and to start afresh.

2.2) A general problem with the management tools used under the CFP is that their application lacks flexibility or adaptability.

Total Allowable Catches

2.3) A major problem with Total Allowable Catches (TACs) is that they are always based on out of date information (due to the time-lags involved in collecting and analysing fisheries data, producing scientific advice, and formulating and implementing management measures). This can give rise to substantial discrepancies between the amount of fish available and the amount that fishermen are allowed to catch. As well as undermining the credibility of the management system, in the minds of fishermen, this can give rise to substantial discarding of marketable fish.

2.4) A second major problem with TACs is that they are not really suitable for mixed fisheries, such as those common in UK waters. Whitefish fishermen generally catch a mix of different species, but will have a separate TAC for each. Again this can give rise to substantial discarding of marketable fish.

2.5) Overall, many fishermen view TACs as very crude management tools, which lack flexibility, are poorly suited to the fisheries many of them pursue, and often seem to cause them to have to dump marketable fish.

Effort Limitation

2.6) Effort limitation offers considerable potential, and would be favoured by many fishermen. However, although it is generally viewed as an alternative to total allowable catches, under the CFP fishermen are currently subject to both TACs and limits on effort. If TACs work then we don't need effort limits, but if TACs don't work then they should be replaced by effort limits (ie we should have one or the other).

2.7) There are substantial anomalies in the way effort limitations are currently implemented under the CFP. For example, at present North Sea demersal fishing boats that use a small mesh (80–90 mm) net get substantially more days at sea than boats that use large mesh (120 mm) nets, although the latter catch much less small and immature fish. This has encouraged a large-scale shift of fishing vessels into the small-mesh fishery.

2.8) Along with many fishermen we retain significant reservations about the value of marine conservation areas, although we accept that they may be appropriate for particular areas of high conservation value. A major risk of any sort of area closure is that it simply concentrates fishing effort in other areas. One important point we would make is that fishermen can make a considerable contribution to selecting appropriate areas and their boundaries, and should be involved in any selection process. In general we believe that marine conservation areas should not be viewed as a universal panacea.

2.9) In general, we believe that adaptable real-time closures offer substantial potential as a management tool, provided they can be applied in a manner which is sufficiently flexible, adaptable and responsive. Such closures are now being piloted in Scottish waters.

Rights-Based Management Tools

2.10) We have substantial concerns about rights-based management tools, especially over their potential to concentrate ownership of fishing rights, and over the potential loss of fishing rights to fisheries-dependent communities. We consider that the supposed benefits of rights-based management are largely based on economic theory, fail to take account of non-economic considerations, and remain unproven in the real world.

2.11) We would, however, strongly support the allocation of fishing rights to fisheries-dependent communities (ie community ownership of fishing rights).

Technical Conservation Measures

2.12) We believe that Technical Conservation Measures (TCMs) have some value, but the current system of TCMs is too complex, and characterised by too much "fiddling around".

3) *Levels of Discards and Bycatch*

3.1) In general, we believe that for the Shetland whitefish fleet current management measures have almost eliminated the discarding of under-sized fish (due to the larger mesh sizes now used in nets). However, the mismatch between low TACs and a relative abundance of fish has led to substantially increased discarding of marketable fish.

4) *Climate Change*

4.1) On this point we would note only that current management measures take no apparent account of climate or environmental changes. Instead, fishermen are generally held solely responsible for any decline in fish stocks, even where there is evidence that other factors may be involved. A key element of adapting to climate change will be for managers to accept that changes in fish stocks and the marine environment may not be entirely the fishermen's fault, and that recovery cannot be guaranteed no matter how hard the fishing industry is squeezed.

CONTROL AND ENFORCEMENT

5) *Efficacy of Systems / Community Fisheries Control Agency*

5.1) We believe that the current control systems can be effective if they are properly, effectively and equitably implemented. We would point out that the Scottish fishing industry is now subject to very tight monitoring and control, and is (we understand) viewed as an example of good practice. This appears to have been achieved entirely through improvements at domestic level; we are not aware that the Community Fisheries Control Agency has had any effect.

5.2) In general, however, we believe that there are substantial inequalities between Member States in the efficacy of their control systems, and that some states make little apparent effort to enforce fisheries regulations. As examples: in some member states large quantities of under-sized fish are openly sold; and some member states appear to export much more of particular species than they should have been able to catch under existing TACs.

6) *Equality of Penalties*

6.1) It is widely known that there are gross inequalities in penalties between Member States. A recent notorious example was the disparity between the penalties imposed on the Scottish and Irish mackerel fleets and the French tuna fleet for exceeding their quotas. While the Scottish and Irish fleets are having to "pay back" the excess fish they caught (through substantially reduced TACs over a number of years), no penalties were imposed on the French fleet.

6.2) As well as the basic injustice, such blatant inequalities play a substantial role in discrediting the CFP in the eyes of British fishermen.

STRUCTURAL POLICY

7) *Fleet Capacity Adjustment*

7.1) On this point, we would note only that this measure has been used to scrap a large proportion of the UK fishing fleet as a short-term measure. There appears to be little if any long-term planning in fleet capacity adjustment. For example, large-scale scrapping leads to a loss of not just vessels, but also knowledge, expertise and a wide range of ancillary industries. Assuming such measures are successful and fish stocks recover, where are the vessels, knowledge, etc, to exploit them to come from?

7.2) A second important consideration is that it is necessary and desirable to replace fishing vessels on a rolling basis. Older vessels are substantially less efficient (eg in terms of fuel and other operating costs) and become less safe as time goes on.

8) *European Fisheries Fund*

8.1) In fact the European Fisheries Fund is not expected to come into effect in the UK until late in 2008, at the earliest. We thus have no experience of the instrument on which to comment. It is clear, however, that the UK is well behind most other Member States in implementing this programme. This delay has resulted in a serious gap in the availability of funding following the end of the previous FIFG programme.

9) *WTO | Fisheries Subsidies*

9.1) No comments.

GOVERNANCE

10) *Regional Advisory Councils*

10.1) In our view it is still early days for Regional Advisory Councils (RACs) and their full potential remains to be demonstrated. To date, we believe that they have had some limited successes, but a major problem has been the European Commission's ongoing tendency to ignore their advice and recommendations.

10.2) A particular problem that we see with the North Sea RAC is that Norway's membership of this RAC appears to give it an unfair advantage in the EU-Norway fisheries negotiations, when management arrangements for the main North Sea fish stocks are agreed (ie as a member of the RAC, Norway gains fore-knowledge of the EU's negotiating position).

11) *How EU Fisheries Should be Managed | Regional Management*

11.1) In our view, many of the failings of the CFP have resulted from its attempts to manage fisheries throughout Europe in a centralised, "one-size-fits-all" manner that lacks flexibility and adaptability and takes little account of regional and local variations. Management under the CFP often seems to be driven by political ideology rather than practical realities, and is generally overly politicised. Above all, the CFP has proved to be an inefficient and ineffective management system, which has failed to deliver either sustainable fish stocks or sustainable fishing industries.

11.2) It follows that we would strongly favour a "regionalisation" and de-politicisation of European fisheries management. We also believe that fishermen and fishing communities need to be given a much greater role in fisheries management, both to make it more effective and to give it some credibility. We consider such a management model to be entirely practical and feasible; the only hindrance would appear to be political.

11.3) In general terms we would like to see the UK take a much more proactive leadership role in the (further) reform of the CFP than it has to date.

15 February 2008

Memorandum by David Thomson, International Fisheries Management Specialist

CONSERVATION AND MANAGEMENT

1. *To what extent have the CFP management measures, and recovery plans been effective in ensuring conservation and sustainability?*

A review of the past 30 years, or just of the period in question since 2002, reveal that the impact of CFP management on UK fisheries has been almost entirely negative. Whether we look at annual stock assessments, continuing fleet decline, or the stagnation of the economies of the coastal fishing towns and villages, there is almost no sign of recovery. Neither the fish stock, nor the harvesting fleets and shore industries, have been sustained. The decline in fish industry benefits has been especially hard on the more remote and island coastal communities. These traditional fishing villages have no comparable resource on which to base a sustainable economy. Continuing calls for further quota cuts and additional fleet reduction, are ample evidence that the whole policy and its related measures are failing, year after year.

2. *What are your views on: total allowable catches; effort limitation; marine conservation areas; rights-based management; and technical conservation measures*

Total allowable catches are based on the scientists' best estimates of stock size, plus the judgment of fishery administrators, and also the lobbying of national governments for a greater share for their respective fleets. The end result rarely satisfies any party. It should also be noted that the estimates are based on two year-old data, and in some cases on bogus statistics, as for example from the years of false reporting of monkfish east and west of the 4 degree line,—the result of scientists and administrator's failure to recognize a reality that reflected badly on their management. The colossal amount of discards—up to 600,000 tonnes a year, was never calculated accurately, by volume or species, and so not included in the estimates of production. Other governments and fishery regimes take a more flexible attitude to stock assessment, and consider estimates provided by fishers and independent observers of the marine environment. UK researchers have often complained in private about the political pressures under which their estimates are made.

Effort limitation is a much more reliable tool than TACs or quotas for managing the operations of the harvesting fleets. The Faeroe Isles for example has abandoned fishery management by quotas in favour of effort limitation, which can be achieved by limiting the number and power of vessels, the gear they may use, the seasons when they may fish, and where appropriate, the number of days they may spend at sea.

Marine conservation areas are good in principle, but suffer from hijacking by interested groups, each with their own agenda, and often motivated more by a desire for power or influence. Green and wildlife NGOs know that their involvement in and potential control of, conservation areas, will add to their public profile and increase the opportunities to draw income from the general public and from government. Some of them have no interest in the welfare of fisher-dependent communities, and a few have indicated their wish to put an end to most forms of commercial fishing. The tension between fishing communities and groups promoting MCAs is a global phenomena. Members of the Indigenous People's Forum on Bio-Diversity from South Africa, India, Latin America and Pacific states, and supporting NGOs from UK, USA and Europe, walked out of the CBD meeting in Rome Italy on 14 February 2008, protesting that they were marginalized and silenced by the Commission despite the importance of the recommendations to their lives, lands and waters, and the critical impact of protected areas on their rights.

MCAs work best when there is meaningful involvement by the communities affected who should have a right to veto extreme measures that would destroy their livelihoods. A few countries like Japan and the USA have developed useful examples of MCAs or similar reserves designed to both protect resources and sustain local economies. They give substantial fishery management authority to their coastal cooperatives. Fishermen on Scotland's west coast fear that the proposed Marine Park, if imposed on their area would simply allow the already bloated seal population to expand at the expense of the local fleet. The seals there currently consume four times as much fish as are caught by the local west coast and islands fishing vessels.

There are three fundamental principles that WWF and IUCN seek to apply abroad with considerable diligence when considering possible marine parks or sanctuaries. These principles are : 1. there must be sound scientific evidence of the need for such a measure, and also reliable indications that the measure will have the desired result; 2. there must be full and open consultation with the local fishers and their communities, whose agreement must be obtained before proceeding with the venture; 3. if some fishers or stakeholders are to lose income as a result of the intervention, then there must be adequate compensation or alternative employment provided. The UK would do well to apply these principles firmly to every Marine Park or MCA proposal.

Rights-based management is being developed in many of the world's fisheries, and can be an excellent tool to ensure some justice and equity in the allocation of resources or in ensuring continuing access for vulnerable groups. The main danger facing the UK from EC / CFP interpretation of rights-based management, lies in the assumption by some that these very rights might be bought and sold on an open market. Once that is permitted the system ceases to be rights-based and becomes market-based, with fishery sector jobs and community's economic futures being traded like any other commodity. That is exactly what will happen if ITQ arrangements are developed to their ultimate end. Several governments have allocated rights-based access to fish resources, in perpetuity, to indigenous groups that would be vulnerable if their rights were to be made a marketable entity. So community quotas and other special arrangements have been organized in the USA for native Americans, and in New Zealand for Maori peoples. Canada's Fishery Minister recently lifted the ban on cod fishing for inshore fishers using open boats, to ensure these persons and their out-ports, have a modest livelihood throughout the year.

Technical conservation measures can be good or unhelpful. Most of them have some side-effects that are unfortunate. They are most difficult to apply in mixed species fisheries such as the UK demersal or white fish sector where the size of a legitimate target fish can vary so much. The mesh size suitable for mature whiting is smaller than that for haddock, which is smaller than that for cod, and so on. But if your boat's quota allocation includes all three species, what do you do ? Fishery administrators then introduce more measures to address the side effects, such as enforced discarding, but the end result is an unsatisfactory mix of conflicting regulations that only frustrate the fishermen while doing nothing for stock conservation. It should also be borne in mind that most skilled fishers can get around technical measures. The answer must be to have the industry fully involved in all the decisions taken and to avoid any technical measure that does not have general support from the harvesters themselves.

3. *To what extent has current management increased discard and by-catch? How could these problems be tackled?*

I have seen no evidence that measures since 2002 have increased the amounts of discards or by-catch, but certainly the past three decades, the illogical fixation on single species quotas in a mixed species fishery, has been the key element that has resulted in the enforced discarding of over half a million tonnes of good fish each year, in the North Sea. By any measure of fishery management assessment, this has been a travesty for the fish stock, the markets, and the fishers, and has probably caused more damage to the resource than any degree of excess fishing pressure.

How can this problem be tackled? First and most importantly, by scrapping the whole concept of single species quotas for the demersal and mixed fish/prawn fleets. Do what many wise fishery administrations have done from Namibia to the Faeroe Isles, and instruct the fishers to land everything they catch. Second, ban discarding completely.

Namibia, which unlike Faeroes, still has a basic quota system, uses an arrangement of levies to limit targeting of non-quota species. All fish caught must be landed. On-board inspectors monitor and police that. Any fish landed excess to quota or not included in the quota, are sold. The proceeds are returned to the vessel,—minus a levy. The levy is finely balanced to achieve two purposes : one is that the fishers do not lose money by keeping, storing, and landing the fish; and the other is that they make no profit on that part of the catch. Each year when total landings are assessed and compared with the previously set TACs or species quotas in Namibia, there is little disparity, and so the system has been seen to work well.

4. *Do fishery policies need to adapt to climate change?*

None of us know yet how climate change will affect our fisheries. It would be foolish and presumptuous to adapt fishery management policies before we know what changes are definitely taking place in the marine environment. There are indications that some species are migrating northwards. We see some sub-tropical species in our southern waters, while cold water fish like cod appear to moving north from their former grounds.

CONTROL AND ENFORCEMENT

5. *To what extent has the CFCA assisted in improving matters? What are the efficacy of systems in place?*

The CFCA systems are too often self-defeating and alienating the fishers. Too many rules and penalties appear to the stakeholders to be perverse and illogical. Ill-conceived laws and regulations bring the whole law into disrepute. Many fishery officers have expressed their disgust and resentment to me, at having to punish fishers for failing to follow measures that are of no benefit to the resource. The CFP has failed to give the fishery stakeholders a meaningful say in the regulations drafted. International meetings have noted that illegal fishing and landings, wasteful discarding, rules beating, and misreporting can to some degree be a direct result of badly-conceived management rules. Some such rules may be the product of flawed science, others of political or factional preferences, and still more of disregard of advice or ignorance of fishing technology. Many skippers and observers maintain that the system has made criminals out of otherwise honest men.

6. *What is your view of different penalties for serious infringements in EU States?*

Difficult to control given the intransigence and resistance by France, Spain, etc

STRUCTURAL POLICY

7. *To what extent have Member States adjusted their fleets to balance capacity with opportunity?*

Low-impact small scale fleets have shrunk while powerful high capacity units have mostly increased in fishing power if not in number. This has been an indirect result of the CFP measures which have failed to protect the small scale fleets which have minimal impact on the resource, and have few negative effects on the marine environment.

UK has the most productive EEZ of any of the EU members, yet its fishing fleet has lost more vessels than any other state,—all in conformity to EC demands to decommission more and more boats. What is left of our fleet is faced with many more restrictions than their predecessors,—so instead of "opportunity", UK fishers are faced with a massive constraint on their operations.

8. *What is your experience of the new fisheries structural fund, EFF?*

No comment

9. *What are your views on the possible impact of WTO-level discussions as regards subsidies in the fishing sector?*

Subsidies in the fishing sector are an emotive issue which is often subject to claims that have little factual basis. While agriculture is heavily subsidized in Europe, fisheries are not (and should not) be subsidized. But we see a growing number of programmes and quangos established, each with a claim to manage part of the industry, and all wanting to be paid for by the industry, since their services are "a subsidy"! Far better to have our fishing industry manage and finance these services,—and select which ones they really need. Why should government undertake advertising on behalf of the fish merchants and processors? That is an example of something the industry can do itself. Fish product development and fishing gear development are also things the industry can do quite well.

The main work on global fisheries subsidies and fleet over-capacity, was written by Dr Francis Christie, for FAO and the World Bank. He was aware that his papers did not address the situation of the smaller scale inshore and coastal fishing fleets of the world, so he asked Dr John Kurien to investigate the subject further. Prof. Kurien's paper, which can be found on the internet, concluded that the most heavily subsidized fishing fleets were the large scale industrial fishing units. Apart from a modest fuel subsidy in some countries, most small scale fleets operate with little financial aid from their governments. Many fear that the WTO will take a sledgehammer to crack a peanut, and may fail to discriminate between the different fishing fleets, each of which has its own particular raft of taxes, facilities, and technical support programmes. WTO recommendations may also favour the large scale, high-impact commercial fleets over the small scale coastal sector.

Ref: Kurien, John; 2006, *Untangling Subsidies, Supporting Fisheries: The WTO Fisheries Subsidies Debate,* ICSF. DR F. Christy's calculations which are the basis of much of the WTO position can be found in Appendices 2, 3, 4, and 5 of the FAO *State of Food and Agriculture 1992 report, Rome 1993.* A shorter summary of Kurien's paper, *Over-capacity, Over-fishing and Subsidies,* is available from the USA secretariat in NMFS of the Pacific Fisheries Forum. The shorter version was presented at the 2006 Forum in Hanoi.

One should also take a hard look at EC fishery subsidies which are continuing and which mostly benefit Spain and France, and which have often been used to support EC fleets in their operations off West Africa and elsewhere,—usually with tragic results for the local fish stock and fishing communities. Senegal is a country whose fishing grounds and fish stocks are of great interest to European fleets. But their intervention there, while agreed to by Senegalese Ministers, and assisted by the EU, has seriously hurt the local fishing fleets and reduced some stocks to a level of concern.

GOVERNANCE

10. *What is your view on the future evolution of Regional Advisory Councils?*

No comment

11. *How do you consider EU fisheries should ideally be governed?*

How appropriate and feasible do you consider a regional model to be?

EU FISHERIES GOVERNANCE: IS A REGIONAL MODEL APPROPRIATE?

It could be, but only within strict limitations. Fisheries governance above all should be transparent, based on clearly stated objectives, and be participative, involving fully the fishing communities and the fishing industry stakeholders. Too often, consultations have been empty PR gestures with no genuine attempt to listen to those affected. (The writer has seen fishermen's leaders publicly insulted by government representatives at supposed consultation meetings). Fisheries governance should also be open to review and critique by competent, independent bodies.

There are a number of international examples. These include the SADC and ASEAN countries which have agreed regional fishery management policies. The USA has similar arrangements with Canada, Mexico, and the small states of the Caribbean and the Pacific. None of these countries have yielded their EEZs to any central management like the EU CFP. There are also the three main regional Tuna Commissions of the Indian, Pacific, and Atlantic Oceans, plus two in the Americas. (see www.tuna-org.org).

In each of those cases, the participating governments retain full control over their 200 mile EEZs and their own fleets and their national fishery management systems. But they meet annually to agree on common approaches to the management of shared stocks. That works very well, guaranteeing cooperative management but preserving sovereign rights.

In contrast the EC/EU, under the Lisbon treaty will have unlimited control over all "marine biological resources" (the part referring to joint EU/national control of fishing does not reflect the reality). Marine biological resources extend by definition from whales and basking sharks to the last frond of seaweed. This control, to be exercised from the desk of the Fisheries Commissioner in Brussels, will extend from the Baltic through the north-eastern Atlantic, North Sea, Mediterranean, Aegean and Adriatic seas to the Black Sea. It takes little account of the vast differences in regional fish species, different fishing methods, local consumption patterns, local fisheries culture and local social and employment structures. That kind of centrally-controlled regional model is a recipe for inflexible and undemocratic management from a distance that is insensitive to local needs and local situations requiring tailored responses to particular issues.

The best fishery management system by far is one that is locally based and which the local stakeholders largely operate themselves with government taking only a supervisory role and providing the overall policy. Some examples can be found in the USA and Japan, where specific fisheries form their own rules and enforce their own members. The UN Agencies and several bilateral organizations and NGOs assist a number of developing countries to adopt this model. In no part of the world that I know, has any group of fishing states considered or adopted a centrist EU type model that requires them to give up their sovereign rights over their national fisheries.

19 February 2008

Printed in the United Kingdom by The Stationery Office Limited
7/2008   400000   19585